Foundations of Food Preparation

Foundations of FOOD Preparation

FOURTH EDITION

Gladys C. Peckham

NEW YORK UNIVERSITY

Jeanne H. Freeland-Graves

UNIVERSITY OF TEXAS, AT AUSTIN

Macmillan Publishing Co., Inc.
New York

Collier Macmillan Publishers
London

Macmillan Publishing Co., Inc.
866 Third Avenue, New York, New York 10022

Collier Macmillan Canada, Ltd.

Library of Congress Cataloging in Publication Data

Peckham, Gladys C
  Foundations of food preparation.

  Includes bibliographies and index.
  1. Cookery. 2. Food. I. Freeland-Graves, Jeanne H.,
joint author. II. Title.
TX663.P32 1979   641   78-3462
ISBN 0-02-393260-0

Printing: 2 3 4 5 6 7 8   *Year:*   9 0 1 2 3 4 5

Preface

This book is designed for the first college course in food preparation. Its aim, as in the earlier editions, is to present in usable form the basic principles of food preparation and to illustrate these principles so that the student may develop high standards of food preparation.

The main task has been one of organizing existing knowledge for the reader who has had little or no formal experience in dealing with food preparation problems. An attempt has therefore been made to summarize material and to avoid citing lists of reports from various sources. Nonetheless, in the many instances where it seemed advisable, references have been made to scientific papers.

The references at the ends of the chapters are generally available to the undergraduate. They are not intended to be all-inclusive. There are several excellent advanced books in food theory and application and food chemistry that are available for students who wish to read more detailed reports of original work.

The subject matter in *Foundations of Food Preparation* has been divided into six parts. Part One is central to the understanding and acquisition of simple basic skills in food preparation, and it sets forth the scientific principles related to food.

Part Two examines the factors affecting food consumption, and Part Three deals with management in food preparation. Part Four, which discusses the preparation of foods and food products, highlights cooking principles and relates these principles to methods of preparation. It also includes discussion of factors affecting preparation, such as the composition and the storage of food, as well as the effects of cooking on palatability and nutritive values. Part Five suggests procedures for preserving food in the home and provides information about modern methods of food preservation. Part Six discusses government control of food, food additives, microwave cookery, and gives basic consumer information.

Since publication of the third edition, new food products, new methods of processing foods, and new cooking equipment have evolved. These developments are dealt with in this edition, and all material requiring updating has been rewritten. The bibliography and other related chapter references have also been brought up to date.

A large body of new information has been included in this new edition. In keeping with important trends in food science and cookery, it

v

contains new, comprehensive chapters on metric measurements in food preparation, food additives, vegetable proteins, and microwave cooking.

Chapter 10 on the economics of food preparation has been rewritten to give consideration to all aspects which affect the cost of food. The information given should provide the student with a general understanding of the factors underlying the retail cost of food.

Another important change that appears in this new edition is the reorganization of the chapters on food evaluation into one chapter. In accomplishing this, there has been no loss of pertinent material and valuable space has been made available for new information.

In the United States, conversion to the metric scale is rapidly taking place in the home, industry, transportation, and communications. The use of standard measurements and equipment is an important prerequiste to the preparation of palatable food, hence students must rapidly learn to use the new terminology and equipment that is coming into use. Accordingly, Chapter 15 on measurements has been expanded and updated to include information and conversion tables on metric units and the nomenclature and the newly designed equipment recommended for food preparation.

On the world level, there is a deepening concern among food scientists and economists that human protein needs will run out unless new protein sources are identified and used. Chapter 25 is an important new chapter that includes detailed information on the development and use of new vegetable protein foods. The subject matter contained in this chapter will give the student a basic understanding of how vegetable proteins are used to supplement and substitute for animal proteins. It alerts the student to the many new fabricated food products on the market made from vegetable protein products.

Another important development is the attention focussed, by government and consumers, on additives used in food. Chapter 43 on food additives is new and contains a vast amount of information on the role of additives in food. It also explains legislation regulating the use of additives in the country. The information in the chapter will be particularly helpful to the beginning student in food science who is learning about the components of food.

A significant development in the area of home food preparation is the increased use of the microwave oven. Since the last edition of this text, sales of microwave ovens have increased to the point where one out of every ten homes in the United States have a microwave oven in the kitchen. Thus, microwave cookery is rapidly becoming an integral part of food science and cookery. For this reason, a new chapter on microwaves, Chapter 45, has been added to help the student understand the basic principles and their application in this unique new method of cooking.

Although we have retained the very valuable step by step illustrations of some basic food techniques, many new illustrations have been added to this edition. Included are a number of color plates which add interest and beauty to the text. We are indebted to the food industry and to the United State Department of Agriculture for the use of these illustrations.

The material in this book may be more than can be comfortable considered for one semester's work. However, chapters that cannot be assigned for class work will provide much useful reference material.

For this edition it has been fortunate for Professor Peckham to have a new author, Dr. Jeanne Freeland-Graves, Assistant Professor of Nutrition and Foods at the University of Texas at Austin. The inclusion of Dr. Freeland-Graves as an author has resulted in many excellent additions to the food science content of the book, in major contributions to all chapters in the book, and in the addition of new chapters on microwaves, food additives, and vegetable proteins. Nutrient content tables in the appendix carry two new columns—zinc and copper. This edition is indebted to her and others for their permission to publish the zinc and copper content of selected foods.

A laboratory manual to accompany the text, developed by Dr. Freeland-Graves, is also available. For those students who may not have the manual in hand, a small compilation of basic recipes remains in the Appendix.

Many years of teaching beginning students in food study has directed the gathering of information for this book. The questions posed by hundreds of inquiring and enthusiastic students were the guidelines for its format. Acknowledgement with appreciation is given to the part students have played in motivating the development of this text.

Appreciation and thanks is also given to the college food teachers who critiqued the former editions. Wherever possible their excellent suggestions have been followed.

Dr. Freeland–Graves wishes to express her sincere appreciation to Drs. Robert J. Cousins and Stuart L. Feldman, the two people who, through their guidance and concern, have helped her most in her professional career. Special thanks for moral support and patience is given to Dr. Glenn R. Graves, Candy and J. J. Freeland, and her graduate students, Lavone Ebangit, Pamela Johnson, Carol Lyon and Jeanne Snowden. Acknowledgement is also given to Dr. Margaret Briley and Ms. Julie Williams for their helpful references and suggestions for the teaching of an introductory foods course.

G.C.P.
J.H.F–G.

Contents

PART THREE
Management in Food Preparation 101

PART FOUR
Preparation of Foods and Food Products 129

PART FIVE

Food Preservation 453

PART SIX

Food Controls 499

Appendix 553

Index 601

Foundations of Food Preparation

Science and Food

This section is designed to give the reader an overview of the basic scientific concepts related to the preparation of food. Students need to know how to control the changes that take place during the preparation of food so that it will be palatable, nutritious, and safe. This control can be accomplished by learning why, how, and when changes take place. A full study of food must show how its preparation affects its structure, its appearance, its composition, and its nutritive value. Knowledge of the basic principles of food preparation helps the student not only to understand the changes that occur during the cooking of a product but also to advance beyond the familiar family recipe.

Part One

Introduction

An understanding of the basic principles of food preparation must be based on a knowledge of the chemical and physical properties of foods, the environmental conditions (such as heat, cold, light, and air) to which they are subject during cooking, the nature of the reactions caused by these factors, and the effect on foods of materials that have been added during some phase of production, processing, or cooking. This information provides a foundation of theory and method on which to build a study of food preparation. The practical applications of science are well illustrated in the area of cookery. Modern methods of preparing foods are based on research.

COOKERY AS A SCIENCE

The science of cookery draws from the physiochemical and biological sciences. Scientific concepts directly related to the way foods behave during the different stages of preparation have been identified. The structure of food and food mixtures is so complex, however, that our knowledge in many areas is fragmentary. We know from observation that certain things happen in—and to—food, and we base our cooking methods and procedures on this knowledge. But we are still to learn why many of these observed reactions occur.

In order to explain food behavior in scientific terms, research has tried to rule out—as far as possible—the misleading factors of personal preference and prejudice and to depend instead on reproducible observations and measurements. Like other scientific theories, theories about the behavior of food under different environmental conditions change from time to time because they are at best only good guesses about things that cannot be proved by direct observation. But the theories are indispensable, for they are the scientist's basic working equipment and help to uncover new facts about the changes that take place in the processing and preparation of food. The growth of knowledge makes necessary the modification of existing beliefs. For example, at one time it was believed that the fermentation of sugar in wines and bread dough was the result of the direct action of the living organism (yeast) on the fermentable material. But evidence has since been accumulated to show that it results instead from the action of a certain substance known as an *enzyme* that is produced by the living organism but is not itself alive. According to the present view, in the production of carbon dioxide and alcohol from sugar the fermentation of sugar is brought about by the enzyme zymase, which is produced by and contained in the yeast cell. Zymase is associated in the yeast cell with another substance called a *coenzyme*. The presence of both enzyme and coenzyme is necessary for fermentation.

APPLICATION OF SCIENCE TO FOOD PREPARATION

The science of foods attempts to show the relation that exists between the special nature of the constituents of food and their behavior. In the manufacture of ice cream, for example, protective materials (colloids)—such as egg whites and gelatin—are added to provide smoothness. This is done because it is known that the materials in egg whites and gelatin interfere with the coagulation of the milk protein casein and with the formation of large ice particles that would give the ice cream a coarse and sandy texture.

Another excellent illustration of the way theory and method blend together is the manufacture of cheese. It is known that casein has the capacity to coagulate or to curdle under the action of rennet enzymes or acid. When these materials are added to milk and the casein coagulates, the milk forms a jellylike mass called a *curd,* which is the basis of manufacture of most types of cheeses.

ADVANCES IN FOOD TECHNOLOGY

The application of scientific principles to the production and processing of food is constantly improving our food. It is now possible to find most types of food at any time of the year. Vast improvements in agricultural methods have resulted in increased yield and better quality. Greater flexibility in food transportation and storage has been gained through such new developments as freeze drying and cryofreezing. Irradiation of food is mainly in the experimental stage but shows promise as a commercially feasible processing technique.

Packaged mixes, prepared frozen foods, partially prepared foods, and a host of other convenience foods have stimulated interest in shortcut cookery. Because these items are mass-produced, they tend to sameness in texture, taste, and flavor. Their widespread use presents a challenge to create new combinations of food in order to satisfy the need for variety in eating.

The newest food items are the imitation foods. They are manufactured so that they look like and taste like natural foods on the market. Imitation foods are generally made from agricultural products. Those on the market in greatest supply are the meatless meats, filled milk, and imitation or nondairy milk, cream, and ice cream. Flavored drinks made to taste like fresh fruit drinks are also on the market. It is predicted that the list will grow.

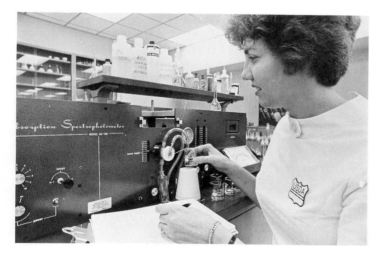

1-1 *A laboratory technician uses sophisticated equipment to run special tests on orange juice samples. (Courtesy of U.S. Department of Agriculture)*

It is significant, however, that science, in bettering our food, must still work within the framework of cookery as an art. The greatest scientific advances in food have no meaning unless it is recognized that food study is more than a science—it is part of the cultural pattern of a society.

The study of foods and how they behave is a fascinating and practical study that richly repays the interest of all who come to know its subtleties and surprises. It is important to have a clear understanding of the relation of science to food preparation, at least to the extent that the main principles are put to use. This approach rules out rule-of-thumb cookery and embraces the scientific method.

SUMMARY

The science of foods strive to explain the changes that take place in food during its preparation. Knowledge of the chemical and physical properties of foods, the effects of environmental conditions to which they are subject (including heat, cold, light, and air), and the results of the addition of other materials during some stage of preparation or production is basic to an understanding of the principles of food preparation. Continuous improvements in food and shortcuts in cookery are made possible through application of scientific principles to food production and processing, but scientific advances must be coupled with a recognition that cooking is an art, a part of the cultural pattern of society.

Composition of Food

Carbohydrates, proteins, fats, water, vitamins, and minerals are the six major classifications of nutrients. Before consideration is given to how foods react in cooking, some understanding of their nutrient composition and function is helpful. Enzymes and color pigments are substances found in food in small but effective amounts. They are involved in many of the changes that occur in food.

CARBOHYDRATES

A literal definition of the word *carbohydrate* is "hydrated carbon"—that is, carbon and water. Because the hydrogen and oxygen atoms in carbohydrates usually occur in the same proportion as they do in water—two atoms of hydrogen, one of oxygen—the general formula of most carbohydrates may be expressed as $C_x(H_2O)_y$. The values of x and y may range from 2 to many thousand. The various groups of carbohydrates, however, differ in appearance, properties, and functions.

Carbohydrates comprise 50–60% of the food that we eat. They are commonly thought of as sugars and starches. Carbohydrate foods are relatively inexpensive, produce high yields per acre, and are capable of storage without refrigeration. This makes them one of the most economical sources of calories available. They are used in the body to produce energy. Carbohydrates may be thought of as compounds that yield simple sugars (monosaccharides), sugars (disaccharides), or polysaccharides. Disaccharides and polysaccharides may be converted to monosaccharides by hydrolysis, which consists of splitting a compound into simpler units; the process involves the addition of a molecule of water. Because a monosaccharide is the simplest molecule, it is not subject to hydrolysis. A disaccharide splits into two monosaccharide molecules on hydrolysis, and a polysaccharide splits into three or more monosaccharide molecules. Hydrolysis of carbohydrates may be brought about by the action of acids or carbohydrate-splitting enzymes.

Monosaccharides and disaccharides are crystalline, water-soluble, sweet compounds. Polysaccharides, on the other hand, are noncrystalline and have little taste. Many are insoluble in water.

Table 2-1 shows some of the carbohydrates that are of importance in food.

TABLE 2-1
Classification of Carbohydrates

Carbohydrates	Food Source
Monosaccharides	
Glucose (dextrose)	Grapes, fruits, fruit juices, and honey
Fructose (levulose)	Fruits, honey
Galactose	Milk
Disaccharides	
Sucrose	Sugarcane, sugar beets
	Maple sugar
Lactose	Milk
Maltose	Cereals
Polysaccharides	
Starch	Corn, wheat, potatoes
Dextrins	Wheat products, honey
Cellulose	Fibers in stems and ribs of plants
Inulin	Jerusalem artichoke
Pectic substances	Fruits and vegetables (in the cell walls)
Gums	Seaweed, plants

Occurrence and Use. *Glucose* occurs in ripe fruits, flowers, honey, leaves, nuts, sap, urine, and blood. It is used to produce acetic acid, lactic acid, and citric acid, all of which are used as preservatives in many processed foods.

Fructose occurs as a simple sugar in honey. It is not yet used to any great extent in the food industry.

Sucrose is present in almonds, coffee, sugar beets, sugarcane, sorghum cane, and most plants. It is used mainly as a sweetening agent for all kinds of foods. The mixture of fructose and glucose resulting from the acid hydrolysis of sugar is called *invert sugar.* Invert sugar is used in candy-making processes in order to hold moisture and prevent the drying out of certain products. Honey is mostly invert sugar. (The bee converts the sucrose from flowers to monosaccharides.)

Maltose does not occur in natural foods. It is obtained by the hydrolysis of starch, induced by diastase (an enzyme present in barley). The hydrolysis of maltose can also be accomplished in an alkaline or acid solution or by the enzyme maltase. Maltose splits into two molecules of glucose. Maltose has a number of uses in the food industry. It is used in beer and malt production, in bread production, in infant foods, and in coffee substitutes.

Lactose, composed of a molecule of glucose and galactose, is found in milk. It can be converted to lactic acid, which is used to preserve many kinds of foods.

Dextrins are short fragments of starch. They are found in honey, vegetable juices, and among the hydrolytic products of starch. They are somewhat sweeter than the large starch molecules and can be created by dry heat. This is illustrated by the slightly sweet taste of toast as compared to plain bread. They are used in bakery products and confections and may be substituted for gum arabic, gum tragacanth, and other gums that are used as thickening agents in prepared foods.

Practically all plants contain *starch,* particularly in the storage cells of the seeds and tubers. Starch has many uses as a thickener in prepared and partially processed foods and is widely used in cooking to thicken the cooked food.

Pectins are classified as polysaccharides and are found in the cell walls and intercellular material in fruits and vegetables. They form a gel when mixed with sugar and acid in proper proportions and are used as thickening agents in prepared foods—especially fruit jams and jellies.

Another group of polysaccharides, known as *gums,* are used by the food industry for their emulsifying, suspending, and thickening qualities. Algin, carageenan, and agar are obtained from seaweed and gum tragacanth; locust bean gum and guar gum are exudate gums of plant origin. Carageenan is commonly used in dairy products to hold particles in suspension. It is used as an additive in chocolate milk to keep the cocoa particles from settling out.

Cellulose is the structural material of the cell walls of plants. It is the major constituent of nonnutritive fiber and is commonly referred to as *fiber* or *roughage.* It can be hydrolyzed in an acid solution to yield glucose. Cellulose is used extensively in the manufacture of nonfood materials.

The human digestive tract lacks the necessary enzymes to digest cellulose, so it cannot be considered a food. It can be used to provide bulk to

7

a diet without adding calories. This will have important implications for diet foods in the future.

Ruminants have the capacity to break down cellulose because of the presence in their stomachs of bacteria that act on this food.

PROTEINS

Proteins, along with carbohydrates and fats, are part of the solid materials of food. They are found in both plant and animal tissue and are the distinguishing constituents of such foods as meat, fish, poultry, eggs, beans, milk, and cheese. Proteins are also capable of being hydrolyzed to their unit structures, which are known as *amino acids,* but this hydrolysis does not take place under ordinary cooking conditions.

The food value of the protein is determined by the composition of the amino acids. Foods having sufficient amounts of the essential amino acids contain *complete* or good-quality proteins. Milk, meat, eggs, and other animal products have proteins of high biological value.

If a food is lacking in one or more of the essential amino acids, it is known as an *incomplete* or poor-quality protein. Proteins derived from plant sources, such as legumes, vegetables, and grains, are an example of incomplete proteins.

Proteins are classified as simple, conjugated, or derived. The *simple* and *conjugated proteins* are as they occur in nature and yield only amino acids on hydrolysis. The conjugated proteins yield an amino acid and a nonprotein moiety such as phosphorus or carbohydrate. The *derived proteins* are changed from their original form and are classified as either primary or secondary derivatives. *Secondary derivative* proteins have undergone a more extensive change than the *primary* group. Some important food proteins are listed in Table 2-2.

Occurrence and Use. The proteins found in food are responsible for many of the changes that occur when it is cooked. The coagulability of such foods as milk and eggs is dependent on the presence of certain proteins. When a protein is changed in structure from its natural form, it is *denatured.* Proteins are formed by a series of amino acids groups, called *peptides,* linked together in a chain which is coiled into a globular shape. This structure is maintained with bonds or bridges. The bonds can be broken by heat, cold, acids, alkalies, salts, or mechanical agitation. When the bonds break, the chain begins to uncoil, losing its original properties and becoming an irreversibly changed or *denatured protein,*

TABLE 2-2
Classification of Proteins

Proteins	Food Source
Simple proteins	
Albumins (soluble in water)	Egg white, milk, meat
	Plant tissue
Globulins (soluble in dilute salt solution)	Meat and plant tissue
Glutelins (soluble in weak acids)	Wheat (glutenin: endosperm cell of grain)
Prolamines (soluble in alcohol)	Wheat (gliadin)
Albuminoids	Skeletal tissue of animals (collagen)
Conjugated proteins	
Hemoglobins	Blood
Phosphoproteins	Milk and egg yolk
Derived proteins	
Proteans	Rennet-coagulated casein
Coagulated	Cooked egg white
Secondary	
Proteoses	Hydrolytic products occurring in the
Peptones	processing of foods (i.e., ripening
Peptides	of cheese)

with new properties. The action of denaturation commonly occurs during the cooking processes. Coagulation (change from a fluid to a solid) may be considered as part of the process of denaturation.[1] The rubbery texture and dryness of cooked frozen fish is also an aspect of denaturation.

Meat proteins consist of muscle, connective tissue, and blood proteins. The important muscle proteins are *actin* and *myosin*. These two proteins interact to form actin–myosin and are of considerable importance in the contractile action of the muscle.

The connective tissue proteins, collagen and elastin, have received a large amount of consideration in meat cookery. It is believed that these proteins are responsible in part for the degree of toughness of meat.

Blood proteins are dispersed throughout the muscle tissue in meat. *Myoglobin* is the protein that occurs most frequently.

Casein and the whey proteins (lactalbumin and lactoglobulin) are the proteins of milk. *Casein* is precipitated from milk by increasing the milk's acidity to a certain point. It is also precipitated by the enzyme rennin, which is found in the rennet extract taken from the calf's stomach. The casein is converted into paracasein through the action of rennin and further changed to a precipitate, calcium paracaseinate. The presence of calcium is an essential part of the precipitate action. The *whey* proteins are denatured by heat, and lactoglobulin accounts in part for the cooked flavor of milk.

The major proteins found in egg white are *ovalbumin* (the most abundant), *conalbumin,* and *ovomucoid.* The first two are readily denatured and coagulated when heated near 140°F (60°C). The egg yolk phosphoproteins, vitellin and vitellenin, are less sensitive to heat, coagulation beginning at 149°F (65°C). This is apparent in a carefully fried egg, in which the white is fully cooked while the yolk is still flowing.

FATS

Fats or *lipids* are abundant in both plant and animal materials. The adipose tissue of animals

[1] Pauline Paul and Helen Palmer, *Food Theory and Application* (New York: Wiley, 1972), p. 129.

consist mainly of fat, and many plant seeds contain fat. Cottonseed, peanut, olive, and soy are vegetable oils well known in cookery, as are butterfat and the fat of animal tissues, such as lard, tallow, and suet.

Fats are comparatively high in carbon and low in oxygen. This is in contrast to carbohydrates, which contain a high percentage of oxygen and a correspondingly low percentage of carbon. Fats, like carbohydrates and proteins, may be hydrolyzed into their constituent parts. When a natural fat is split, two separate products are obtained: *glycerol* (an alcohol) and a number of *fatty acids* (organic compounds made up of carbon, hydrogen, and oxygen).

The properties of fats are greatly influenced by their constituent fatty acids. Each molecule of fat contains one molecule of glycerol and three molecules of fatty acid. If the three fatty acids are the same, the fat is a *simple glyceride.* If the acids are unlike, it is a *mixed glyceride.* The food fats are usually mixed glycerides. All fats (oils and solid fats) are insoluble in hot or cold water.

Hydrolysis is responsible for the splitting of fat molecules into fatty acids and glycerol both in digestion and in certain food processes. (A more detailed discussion of this is given in Chapter 6.)

VITAMINS

Vitamins are organic substances found in plant and animal tissues. They are needed in small quantities to perform specific metabolic and regulatory functions in the body.

A vitamin is simply a chemical compound and can easily be synthesized. Since the body cannot distinguish between molecules of natural or synthetic origin, the synthetic forms are equal in nutritive value to natural derivatives. Synthetic vitamins are added to enrich or supplement such food products as milk, fruit drinks, margarine, breads, and cereal products. The vitamins and their most common food sources are shown in Table 2-3.

MINERALS

A mineral is the inorganic part of food that leaves an ash when burned. This method is used to determine the mineral content of both plant and animal material.

TABLE 2-3
Food Sources of Vitamins

Vitamin	Food Sources
Fat-soluble	
Vitamin A (retinol)	Dairy products, dark green and yellow vegetables
Vitamin D (cholecalciferol)	Milk and egg fat, fish-liver oils
Vitamin E (α-tocopherol)	Vegetable oils, green leafy vegetables
Vitamin K (phylloquinone)	Alfalfa, spinach, cabbage
Water-soluble	
B vitamins	
B_1 (thiamine)	Yeast, whole grains, lean pork
B_2 (riboflavin)	Milk, grain products, yeast
Niacin	Yeast, peanut butter, poultry, fish, grains
B_6 (pyridoxal phosphate)	Muscle meats, whole grains, molasses
B_{12} (cyanocobalamin)	Animal products
Folacin	Dark green leafy vegetables, nuts
Vitamin C (ascorbic acid)	Citrus fruits, tomatoes, peppers, cabbage

Certain minerals are essential for regulation of body metabolic processes and structure. Those which are required in large amounts are called *macrominerals.* Calcium, phosphorus, iron, magnesium, and sulfur are macrominerals of high nutritional significance. Sodium, chloride, and potassium are *electrolytes,* which function in metabolic water balance.

Trace minerals are elements that are essential in very small amounts. Some of the presently recognized ones are zinc, copper, iodine, manganese, chromium, cobalt, selenium, molybdenum, and fluoride. Nonnutritive heavy metals also present in small amounts, such as mercury, lead, cadmium, and arsenic, may contaminate wholesome food and create toxic symptoms.

Some foods are enriched by the addition of minerals. Calcium may be added to flour and bread, and iodine is added to salt. Agriculturists depend on minerals added to stock feed to ensure a well-balanced mineral supply for their animals.

The food sources of minerals are listed in Table 2-4.

THE BASIC FOUR FOOD GROUPS

The purpose of eating food is to supply the body with all the essential nutrients (protein, fat, carbohydrate, vitamins, and minerals) that are needed for optimal health. A wide variety of wholesome foods in the diet on a daily basis is necessary to achieve this goal.

To facilitate menu planning, the U.S. Department of Agriculture has divided foods into four basic food groups. Each of the groups is designed to supply one-fourth of at least two essential nutrients. A nutritionally adequate diet can be achieved if menus are planned according to these four food groups.

Meat Group. Foods in the meat group are eaten for their protein and iron content. Some B vitamins are also provided.

Servings per day: 2 or more.

Serving size: 2–3 oz of cooked lean meat, poultry, or fish; 2 eggs, 4 Tbs peanut butter; 1 c dried cooked beans or peas.

Milk Group. Milk products and cheese supply calcium, riboflavin, and protein in the diet.

Servings per day: 2–4 c milk, depending on age.

Serving size: Equivalent to 1 c of milk; 1½ c cottage cheese; 2 c ice cream; 1⅓ slice American cheese; 2 c cream cheese.

Bread and Cereal Group. Enriched and whole grain cereals and products are necessary to supply iron, thiamine, and niacin in the diet.

Servings per day: 4 or more.

Serving size: 1 slice bread, ½–¾ c cereal or product.

TABLE 2-4
Common Food Sources of Minerals

Mineral	Food Sources
Macrominerals	
Calcium	Milk, cheeses, and other dairy products
Phosphorus	Dairy products, meats, soft drinks
Magnesium	Vegetables, cocoa, nuts, soybeans
Iron	Liver, meats, molasses, egg yolk
Electrolytes	
Sodium	Salt, clams, kidney, egg white, shrimp
Potassium	Molasses, milk, legumes, apricots, bananas
Chorine	Salt
Trace minerals	
Iodine	Saltwater fish, iodized salt
Zinc	Meats, egg yolk, liver, seafood, legumes
Copper	Nuts, shellfish, liver, kidney, raisins
Manganese	Nuts, whole grains, vegetables
Chromium	Animal products, whole grains, yeast
Cobalt	Vitamin B_{12}-containing foods
Selenium	Fish and fish products
Molybdenum	Beef kidney, cereals, legumes
Fluoride	Fluoridated water, tea, animal products

Vegetable and Fruit Group. Vegetables and fruits contain vitamin A, vitamin C, minerals, and fiber.

Servings per day: 4 or more; including 1 serving of vitamin C every day and 1 serving of vitamin A (from dark green leafy or deep yellow vegetables and fruit) every other day.

Serving size: ½ c.

ENZYMES

Enzymes are found in plant and animal cells. They function as catalysts in chemical reactions. They are released or separated from the cells by normal physiological processes, during the decomposition of the cells after death, or by the destruction of the cell by such processes as grinding or crushing.

Enzymes may be classified into two major categories, according to the type of reaction they catalyze. One such basic reaction involves hydrolysis—the breaking up of larger compounds into simpler ones by the addition of water. These enzymes are called *hydrolytic enzymes* or *hydrolases*. The second group causes a breakdown of the molecule without the addition of water or oxygen.

A group of enzymes important in food processes are the *oxidoreductases*. These catalyze the oxidation and reduction reactions by acting as acceptors or donors of oxygen or hydrogen. An oxidase is used to remove traces of oxygen from some processed foods and thereby prevent off-flavors.

One way of naming enzymes is by adding the suffix *-ase* to the name of the substrate (material) they act on. Accordingly, the enzymes that convert amylose (starch) into simpler carbohydrates are called *amylases,* and the one that works on maltose is known as *maltase.* Enzymes that hydrolyze fat to glycerol and fatty acids are known as *lipases.*

Some enzymes are named according to their origin in the human body. Three *proteolytic (protein–splitting) enzymes,* which are capable of breaking up larger molecules into smaller constituents, are gastric protease (pepsin), pancreatic protease (trypsin), and intestinal protease.

Not all protein foods are capable of being completely broken down by enzymes. Meats, fish, and eggs are almost wholly digested (97%), but vegetables (74%), legumes (78%), and nuts (75%) are more resistant.

Enzymes can be inactivated by heat, a fact that is of great importance in food preparation.

2-1   *The basic four groups of food. (Courtesy of the National Dairy Council)*

This inactivation is brought about by a drastic change of the protein structure. For example, certain fruits—such as apples, pears, bananas, and peaches—brown easily when exposed to the air, but it is known that heating destroys the enzymes responsible for the reaction. Thus when fruit is stewed, canned, or preserved, the browning action is halted as soon as the food material is heated to temperatures high enough to bring about denaturation of the protein.

Enzymes are also inactivated by acids. For example, the cut surfaces of fresh fruits will not brown as rapidly when covered with an acid material, such as lemon juice. Fruit covered with a heavy sugar solution will not darken because it prevents the contact of oxygen with the fruit.

COLOR PIGMENTS

Both plant and animal tissue contain coloring materials. For example, cochineal is an animal coloring matter. It is a scarlet dye made from the dried bodies of the females of a certain Mexican insect. Kermes is another red coloring material, consisting of dried bodies of a female wingless insect. Vegetable coloring materials are obtained from tree bark, fruits, leaves, blossoms, roots, and mosses. For example, red beets contain betanin, a coloring material that may be used to intensify the color of such products as tomato soup and tomato sauce. Other coloring materials of plant or animal origin that have been used in coloring food products are alkanet, annatto, caramel, carotene, chlorophyll, saffron, and turmeric.[2]

FLAVORS

Flavor components in food are compounds that arise from carbohydrate, protein, fat, aldehyde, and ketone components. Esters, derivatives

[2] For fuller discussion of these, see Chapters 11 and 43. Throughout the chapters on food preparation, an attempt has been made to give some information regarding the water, fat, carbohydrate, protein, and ash present in the food. Wherever possible, information about vitamin content and color materials (pigments) is also given. Table A–12 is a valuable reference for the proximate composition of foods.

of organic acids, are colorless liquids that are soluble in alcohol and have fragrant, fruity odors.

WATER

Food contributes a considerable amount of water in the diet of man. Milk is 87% water and tomatoes are 95% water. The oxidation of fats, carbohydrates, and proteins in the body yield water, and the environmental sources of water used in the growing and processing of food are important factors in the study of food.

SUMMARY

Foods are composed of carbohydrates, proteins, fats, water, vitamins, and minerals. Enzymes and color pigments also occur in small but important amounts. Plants provide most of the carbohydrates in food, in the form of simple sugars (monosaccharides), disaccharides, or polysaccharides. Both plant and animal tissues yield proteins, the important component of such foods as meat, fish, poultry, eggs, beans, milk, and cheese. Many of the changes that occur during cooking, such as coagulation of milk or eggs, are caused by the reaction of proteins to heat and to materials such as acids and alkalies.

High in carbon and low in oxygen (in contrast to carbohydrates), fats are found in both plant and animal materials and include lard, tallow, suet, peanut oil, soybean oil, olive oil, and butterfat. Constituent fatty acids influence the characteristics of fats.

Vitamins and minerals are important factors in a food's nutritional value. Enzymes function as catalysts; color pigments contribute to a food's characteristic appearance. Carbohydrates, proteins, fats, aldehydes, and ketones give rise to flavor components.

REFERENCES

BOOKS

Adams, Catherine. "Nutritive Value of American Foods in Common Units." *Handbook 456.* Washington, D.C.: U.S. Department of Agriculture, rev. 1975.

Borgstrom, Georg. *Principles of Food Science.* New York: Macmillan, 1968, Vol. 2, Chap. 1.

Garard, Ira D. *Introductory Food Chemistry.* Westport, Conn.: Avi, 1976, Chaps. 2, 3, 4, 5, 6.

Hamilton, May, and Eleanor Whitney. *Understanding Nutrition.* New York: West, 1977.

Lee, Frank. *Basic Food Chemistry.* Westport, Conn.: Avi, 1975, Chap. 2.

Posati, Linda, and Martha Orr. "Composition of Foods: Dairy and Egg Products—Raw—Processed—Prepared." *Handbook 8-1.* Washington, D.C.: U.S. Department of Agriculture, rev. 1976.

Purposes of Cooking Food

Food fads to the contrary, experience has shown that most foods must be cooked to be acceptable to the human palate. Some foods, mainly from among the fruit and vegetable groups, are highly palatable when eaten raw—a commendable practice, for uncooked and unsoaked foods retain a good portion of their nutritive value.

Most foods are eaten cooked. The main purposes for cooking food are (1) to make its maximum nutritive value available in a palatable form; (2) to develop, enhance, or alter its flavor; (3) to improve its digestibility; (4) to increase its palatability by improving its color, texture, or flavor; and (5) to destroy pathogenic organisms and injurious substances that may be found in or on the raw food.

NUTRITIVE VALUE

The most important nutritive change that occurs in natural food through cooking is a loss of its water-soluble constituents. Hence, the retention of these nutrients in foods is directly related to the amount of water used in cooking and the duration of the cooking process. De-

struction of vitamins may also be brought about by the action of heat. According to studies,[1] the two nutrients most unfavorably affected by heat are thiamine and ascorbic acid.

Heat may also affect the biological value of protein. The browning reaction may destroy the usefulness of certain amino acids.[2] During heating of a protein with a carbohydrate, particularly one of the monosaccharides or disaccharides, the browning reaction occurs. For example, evaporated milk has a lower nutritive value than fresh whole milk when measured by rat growth (which is considered a reliable method of determining the biological value of a protein). It is thought that the reaction occurs through the amino group of the proteins. Wheat flour is low in the amino acid lysine, and baking

[1] B. Barnes, D. K. Tressler, and F. Fenton, "Thiamine Content of Fresh and Frozen Peas and Corn Before and After Cooking," *Food Res.* **8:**13, 1943; K. Causey and F. Fenton, "Effect of Four Cooking Pressures on Commercially Frozen Broccoli," *J. Home Econ.* **42:**649, 1950.

[2] C. C. Tsen, "Effects of Conventional Baking and Steaming on the Nutritive Value of Regular and Fortified Breads," *J. Food Sci.* **42:**402, 1977.

bread further diminishes its value. The significance of the effect of cookery on protein value is still questionable, however, because other growth factors in the food may well offset the effect of these small losses.

EFFECT ON FLAVOR

Another objective in cooking food is to maintain its palatability or to improve its natural flavor. When the object is to maintain the original flavor of the food, the cooking process used should be as short as possible and few, if any, flavoring materials should be added. For example, fresh young vegetables should be cooked for a short time in a small amount of boiling water or cooked for a minimum amount of time in a pressurized saucepan.

If the goal is to develop a golden-brown surface on the food, then the method of cooking should employ dry heat—that is roasting, baking, broiling, and frying in fat. Sometimes the goal in cooking is to change or to blend the flavors of food. For example, casserole dishes and puddings are enjoyed for their interesting blend of different flavors. When several foods are cooked together to bring about a new blend of flavor, the cooking process may be long, to allow time for the new flavor to develop. Long boiling of maple sap to concentrate it brings about the characteristic flavor of the sirup. Bread owes its popularity to the formation of flavor developed in the crust during baking. The flavor of meat is also developed and enhanced by heating. Roasting develops a different flavor from that resulting from long cooking in moisture. Roasting also develops the coffee flavor in the green coffee bean.

Overcooking is probably more destructive of flavor than any other mistreatment of food. Food cooked too long loses its flavor and may become soggy or stringy. One of the reasons for the loss of flavor is that the volatile substances contained in food may be changed to less desirable compounds through prolonged cooking. A dramatic example of this is the change in flavor that occurs when the members of the cabbage family are overcooked. The evolution of sulfur compounds in cabbage and cauliflower during prolonged cooking has been confirmed by studies.[3]

The effect of cooking on the color and texture of food is as important as its influence on flavor. When the goal is to maintain a certain color, the methods of cookery used must be those most conserving of the natural color of food. When the goal is to develop a new color, the methods used must be those most conducive to developing the desired color. For example, if it is necessary to develop a brown surface on a roast or on a baked product, roasting or baking must be the cooking method used. Meats and flour mixtures will not develop a browned surface if steamed. The retention of color in cooked vegetables is the most difficult of color-retention problems in cookery. (See Chapters 11 and 18 for a discussion of color in cooked vegetables.)

EFFECT ON TEXTURE

Often the goal in cookery is to maintain the natural texture of the food, but the action of heat does change texture somewhat. All fruits and vegetables undergo softening as a result of cooking. Control may be exercised, however, by the method of cooking used and the length of cooking time.

Although cooking may bring about undesirable changes, it is also responsible for beneficial changes. For example, cooking may render food more digestible. The reason for this is that some cooking processes are identical with the process involved in the breakdown of food during digestion—for example, the transformation of starch into dextrins through toasting. The hydrolysis that takes place during the moist cooking of meat breaks down the protein collagen in connective tissue, making the meat tender.

EFFECT ON ORGANISMS

Cooking food destroys organisms and materials that may cause foodborne diseases. (See Chapter 9 for a full discussion of these). It is a fact that harmful organisms in food can be de-

---

[3] J. Simpson and E. Halliday, "The Behavior of Sulphide Compounds in Cooking Vegetables," *J. Home Econ.* **20**:121, 1928.

A. J. MacLeod and G. MacLeod, "Effects of Variations in Cooking Methods on the Flavor Volatiles of Cabbage, *J. Food Sci.* **35**:744, 1970.

stroyed by heat. Most cooking methods produce an interior temperature in foods of 140–185°F (60–85°C). Some baked products may reach a temperature close to 212°F (100°C). This temperature range is one in which many harmful organisms do not grow, but it is of importance to note that all portions of food must reach—and maintain for a certain length of time—a temperature somewhere within the range.

SUMMARY

Most foods must be cooked in order to be palatable, but care in cooking must be exercised to achieve optimum palatability and to avoid adverse effects, such as undesirable color and texture changes and loss of nutritive value and flavor. Cooking may also be necessary to assure safety from foodborne diseases.

REFERENCES

BOOKS

American Meat Institute. *The Science of Meat and Meat Products.* San Francisco: Freeman, 1971, Chap. 6.

deMan, John. *Principles of Food Chemistry.* Westport, Conn.: Avi, 1976, Chap. 7.

Food for Us All: The Yearbook of Agriculture. Washington, D.C.: U.S. Department of Agriculture, 1969, pp. 94–195.

ARTICLES

Noble, Isabel. "Ascorbic Acid in Vegetables." *J. Amer. Dietet. Assoc.* **50**:304, 1967.

Water

CHAPTER 4

ROLE OF WATER IN COOKERY

Water is of prime importance in cookery. Its most commonly understood use is as a solvent for many food substances. For example, the characteristic flavors of tea and coffee depend on the ability of water to dissolve the flavoring materials in tea leaves and pulverized coffee beans. Coloring materials and water-soluble nutrients also can be dissolved in water. Hence, the ease with which certain food materials dissolve in water is a factor that strongly affects their palatability and nutritive value. Simple sugars, some salts, the vitamin B complex, and ascorbic acid are the nutrients most likely to be lost through cooking in water. This loss is increased as the area of cut surface in contact with the water increases. The length of cooking time and the temperature of the water also affect the dissolution of food substances. The strong solvency power of water is best illustrated by the fact that any odor, taste, or color in water is caused by impurities dissolved in it, for pure water is odorless, tasteless, and transparent.

Water also functions in cookery as a dispersing medium. It helps to distribute particles of materials such as proteins and starch. The proteins of milk, for example, are dispersed throughout its liquid phase. When starch is used to thicken liquids, the starch granules must be distributed throughout the liquid to achieve the proper effect.

A number of substances combine with water to form *hydrates*. A hydrate is a substance that readily decomposes to form water and is readily resynthesized. Salts, starches, and proteins form hydrates in food. Dried foods may be hydrated and restored to their original volume by soaking and cooking in water. Starch granules are hydrated when heated in water so that they swell and thicken. Gelatin and gluten are good examples of proteins that take up water. It is thought that the water-holding capacity of meat proteins has an effect on the tenderness of the animal muscle.

This action—absorption of water by certain substances in food—is also called *imbibing*. According to present thinking, this is probably brought about by hydrogen bonding.

Water promotes many chemical changes. The action of baking powder, a mixture of dry chemicals, illustrates this. As long as the baking powder is kept perfectly dry, no chemical action occurs. When water is added to the substance,

however, the chemicals in the mixture react immediately and bubbles of gas are liberated. Some substances pick up and retain water vapor from the air; this is known as a *hygroscopic* property. Solid calcium chloride, for example, will absorb moisture from the air. Pure salt does not absorb water, but common table salt contains impurities such as magnesium chloride that absorb water. Magnesium chloride is a substance that tends to form a moist environment around itself for the purpose of going into solution. This property is known as *deliquescence*. Free-running salt has the impurities removed.

WATER IN ANIMAL AND PLANT TISSUE

Water is more abundant than any other substance in most plant and animal tissues. Fruits and vegetables are more than 90% water (Table 4-1). Water is found as intracellular material, that is, within the cell itself. The water in foods may be held as bound water or as free water. The bound water in foods is held by the proteins, polysaccharides, and fats found within the living cells. The removal of bound water from living cells by pressure is most difficult; bound water is resistant to freezing and drying. In egg whites, for example, water may be so closely bound to the white that it cannot be separated by freezing except at temperatures far below the freezing point of water.

The strong opposition to release of bound water by living cells is well illustrated by the reaction of living organisms to their environment. Plants and insects that are exposed to low temperatures in winter increase their proportion of bound water to keep from freezing. Pine needles, for example, appear to lack moisture completely during the winter months. Such plants as cacti, which must live under arid conditions, hold their bound water in a bound state.

Unlike bound water, free water is not an integral part of the plant or animal tissue with which it is associated. It can be removed from the cells by pressure. The free liquid in tissue is important in that the solid materials of the cells are dissolved or dispersed in it. Examples of free water are that in the cytoplasm of the cell and that in the circulating fluids of the tissues.

TABLE 4-1
Water Content of Some Common Foods

Food	Water (%)
Lettuce, crisp head	95.5
Tomatoes	93.5
Cabbage, raw	92.9
Milk	87.4
Apple	84.4
Potatoes	79.8
Shrimp	78.2
Banana	75.7
Egg	73.7
Chicken, raw, dark meat	64.4
Ice cream	62.1
Bologna	56.2
Cornbread	50.8
Steak, porterhouse, raw	48.3
Olives, ripe, Greek	43.8
Cheese, cheddar	37.0
Bread, white	35.8
Biscuit	27.4
Apricot, dried	25.0
Fruitcake, dark	18.1
Rice, raw, white	12.0
Beans, dried, white	10.9
Oatmeal, raw	8.3
Peanuts	5.6
Vanilla wafers	2.8
Chocolate, sweet	0.9
Almonds	0.07
Lard	0.0

BONDING

Covalent bonds share electrons between two atoms. In water one oxygen atom is covalently bonded to two hydrogen atoms and also forms hydrogen bonds by which it is linked to other water molecules (Fig. 4-1). The covalent bond is

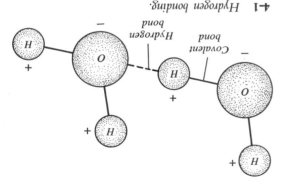

4-1 *Hydrogen bonding.*

a strong bond and involves the sharing of electrons between the hydrogen and oxygen. The hydrogen bond is a relatively weak bond and can form bridges with other water molecules or other molecules. Water molecules are *dipoles*, so called because the electrical charges are uneven on the oxygen and hydrogen sides of the molecule (Fig. 4-2). The hydrogen atoms are slightly positive and the oxygen atom slightly negative. The hydrogen bonds form between the positive hydrogen of one molecule and the negative oxygen of other molecules. A hydrogen bond can also be formed between water and other molecules. For example, water can form hydrogen bonds with carbohydrates because of their hydroxyl groups (OH). The difference between covalent bonding and hydrogen bonding is that it would take many times more energy to break the covalent bonds than would be required to disrupt the hydrogen bond. For example, it would take hundreds of degrees Celsius to change water into another chemical that would involve breaking the covalent bonds, but bringing water to the boiling point breaks the hydrogen bonds and the water changes to steam.

Hydrogen bonding can also form combinations of water and compounds having polar groups (*dipoles*). A carbohydrate that has a hydroxyl group will bind water through hydrogen binding, thus making possible the penetration of water within the molecule.

Water will form hydrates with metallic ions that tend to form complexes. The unshared electrons of the oxygen atom will fill out the shells of the ion and hold water to it. Such elements as sodium, magnesium, and calcium exist as hydrated ions in solution. The positive ions in solution—Na^+, Mg^{2+}, and Ca^{2+}—are attracted to the oxygen (negatively charged) end of the water molecule [dipole].

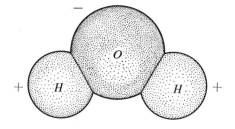

4-2 *The arrangement of atoms in a molecule of water.*

IMPURITIES IN WATER

Water is never absolutely pure in a natural state. Water that falls through the air as rain picks up dust particles and dissolves some of the gases in the air. The *impurities* present in water are of three kinds: dissolved gases, dissolved mineral salts, and organic materials. Air is the gaseous substance most frequently found dissolved in water. The milky appearance of water when it comes from the faucet is caused by air escaping from the water. Boiled water has little dissolved gas in it because the heat has driven it off. This explains the flat taste of boiled water.

Minerals in Water. A great many dissolved minerals may be found in natural water. Of these dissolved minerals, ordinary table salt is the most abundant. Sometimes it is found only in small quantities, but it can also be found in such great quantities that it can be removed in commercial amounts.

HARD WATER

Some waters contain compounds of iron, calcium, and magnesium in solution. These are called *hard waters* (Fig. 4-3). The hardness of a water is of importance in cooking processes. For instance, cooking dried legumes in hard water requires more time and may have a noticeable effect on their texture. Lowe[1] states that fresh peas cooked in soft water consistently appeared softer than those cooked in hard water. Water is spoken of as being "temporarily," or "permanently" hard, depending on whether the hardness is caused by bicarbonates or by other salts. If the hardness is temporary—that is, if it is caused by bicarbonates—heating or boiling the water will, to a large extent, precipitate the iron, calcium, or magnesium bicarbonates as insoluble carbonates. On the other hand, boiling has no effect on water that contains sulfates or other salts of iron, calcium, and magnesium. Such waters are said to be permanently hard, and the degree of hardness is recorded in ppm (parts per million). In areas where the water is so hard that

[1] Belle Lowe, *Experimental Cookery*, 4th ed. (New York: Wiley, 1955), p. 142.

must be regenerated. A strong brine, allowed to stand in contact with the exhausted zeolite, supplies it with the necessary sodium ions.

EVAPORATION

Although boiling food in water is considered a simple cooking procedure, it is a fact that water can disappear from an open cooking vessel rather quickly, which may ultimately lead to burned or badly cooked food.

The explanation for water loss is this: liquids including water, tend to disappear from open vessels even at temperatures far below their boiling points. Some liquids, such as ether and gasoline, evaporate very quickly, whereas others—glycerine, for example—evaporate much slower. The liquids, of course, do not entirely disappear; they do change, however, from liquids to gases. This is known as a *change of state*. As the liquid changes to a gas, it absorbs some heat from its surroundings, thus exerting a cooling effect.

Control of Evaporation. When water is placed in a vessel, it does not expand to fill the vessel entirely; instead, its volume is strictly limited. But there is no lack of movement among the molecules of the liquid. According to the kinetic molecular theory, the force of cohesion that exists among the molecules of a liquid is sufficient to overcome the kinetic energy (the tendency of molecules to move against each other) of the particles and force them to remain together. Nonetheless, there is movement among the molecules of a liquid (Fig. 4-4): they wander

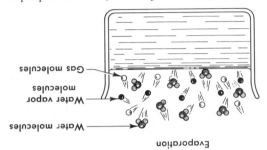

Evaporation

Water molecules

Water vapor molecules

Gas molecules

4-4 *In the process of evaporation, water molecules bounce off the surface of a liquid; some knock against molecules of water vapor or gas and fall back into the liquid.*

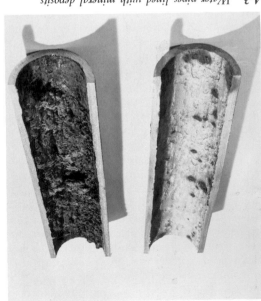

4-3 *Water pipes lined with mineral deposits indicate "hardness" in water supply. (Courtesy of Calgon Corporation)*

it interferes with home and manufacturing processes, it may be softened by the elimination of the calcium and magnesium ions that it contains. Two well-known processes for softening water on a community-wide scale are the lime–soda process and the zeolite process.

The purpose of the *lime–soda process* is to precipitate out calcium ions as calcium carbonate and magnesium ions as magnesium hydroxide. The chemicals used to do this are calcium hydroxide (lime) and sodium carbonate (soda ash). These chemicals form insoluble precipitates with the calcium and magnesium salts. The precipitates are then removed from the water by sedimentation and filtration through sand filters.

The *zeolite process* is an ionic exchange reaction that consists of replacing calcium and magnesium ions with sodium ions. Zeolite is made up of sodium and aluminum. When hard water is forced through the zeolite, the calcium and magnesium ions are removed by interaction with the zeolite and are replaced by sodium ions. The total solids content of the water is not reduced, but the nature of the salts is changed from calcium and magnesium carbonates to sodium carbonate. Because sodium carbonate is soluble, it does not form scale, scum, or sludge in the water. Zeolite material becomes used up and

about, always restrained, but not enough for all of them to be kept in place. Some of them come to the surface and break away from the liquid. These become the gaseous molecules. Thus, a continuous tendency exists for the liquid to change to a gas; in time, the liquid may disappear entirely. The rate of change depends on the nature of the liquid, its temperature, the shape of the vessel in which it is contained, the degree of pressure exerted on it, and the prevailing air currents.

The process of change from a liquid to a gas appears to stop when the container has a tight cover. In an open vessel, the gas molecules coming from the liquid are free to escape, and they seldom return to the liquid from which they originated. In a closed vessel, the gaseous molecules are held within a confined space; therefore, they frequently return to the surface of the liquid. In the closed vessel, the gaseous molecules at the surface of the liquid increase, but if the temperature remains constant, dynamic equilibrium is eventually achieved. (That is, the rate of escape of the molecules from the liquid equals the rate of their return from the gaseous state.) As a result, the molecules are trapped and held in liquid condition. When this happens, condensation—a process that is the opposite of evaporation—takes place. For this reason, the amount of liquid in the closed container may remain constant.

Ordinarily, liquids evaporate at the surface, but liquids that are boiling indicate that rapid evaporation is taking place from all parts of the mass in the vessel. Bubbles of vapor in the interior of the liquid rise to the surface. When this happens, the gas pressure inside the bubble is equal to the pressure exerted on the surface of the liquid.

Heat is required to change a liquid to a gas without raising its temperature (called *latent heat*). When water is at its boiling point, 540 calories of heat must be supplied to 1 gram of water to evaporate it (change it to steam) without changing its temperature.

WATER AND FOOD SPOILAGE

Water is closely linked to food spoilage. Many agricultural products of low moisture content, such as shelled corn and soybeans, if exposed to

an atmosphere of 75% relative humidity or higher, may take up enough moisture content to permit the growth of molds and bacteria. Even foodstuffs with moisture below the critical content required for microbial growth cannot be stored unprotected in a warm climate where high humidities may persist for rather long periods. According to Miller and Clark,[2] once microbial growth begins in food material with a minimum moisture content, the food starts to decompose and water, a product of decomposition, is formed. The release of water from one piece of decaying food can increase the rate of decay of other foods close to it.

Brines. It has been known that food can be preserved by placing it in an environment in which spoilage microorganisms are deprived of water by high osmotic pressure. Brine (a salt and water mixture) has a large amount of water, but its heavy salt concentration makes it impossible for microorganisms to draw water from the solution. Instead, water flows out of the food cell and the body of the microorganisms, thus preventing microbial activity. This principle forms the basis for the preservation of meats and vegetables by use of concentrated salt solution. From a bacterial standpoint, the preservation of meat by dehydration (removal of water, sometimes by heat) is merely another way of reducing the water activity to a level that prevents microbial growth.[3]

SUMMARY

A solvent for many food substances, water also serves in cookery as a dispersing medium and hydrating agent, and it promotes many chemical changes in foods. Water is often the most abundant substance in plant and animal tissues and occurs either bound or free. Hygroscopic substances, such as common table salt, have the capacity to pick up and retain water

[2]Paul R. Miller and Francis E. Clark, "Water and the Microorganisms," in *Water: The Yearbook of Agriculture* (Washington, D.C.: U.S. Department of Agriculture, 1955), p. 32.

[3]J. B. Evans and C. F. Niven, "Bacteriology," in *The Science of Meat and Meat Products* (San Francisco: Freeman, 1960), p. 166.

vapor from the air. Water is hard or soft, depending on the presence of such compounds as calcium and magnesium salts. Hard water lengthens the cooking time for legumes. Because many substances are soluble in water, there can be nutritive loss if cooking methods are not carefully controlled. Food spoilage is closely related to the amount of water present in the food; a damp environment is conducive to microbial growth.

QUESTIONS AND TOPICS FOR DISCUSSION AND STUDY

1. What changes take place in water when it boils?
2. How much energy does it take to change 1 gram of water to steam?
3. Explain how the shape of saucepan might affect the rate of evaporation of a liquid.
4. How would the scale that forms on the bottom of pans in which hard water is heated tend to increase the time required to cook foods in these pans?

REFERENCES

BOOKS

Borgstrom, Georg. *Principles of Food Science.* New York: Macmillan, 1968, Vol. 2, Chap. 5.

deMan, John. *Principles of Food Chemistry.* Westport, Conn.: Avi, 1975, Chap. 1.

Leopold, Luma, Kenneth S. Davis, and the Editors of *Life. Water.* New York: Time, Inc., 1966, Chaps. 1, 2.

Meyer, Lillian Hoagland. *Food Chemistry.* New York: Van Nostrand Reinhold, 1960, Chap. 1.

Weiser, Harry. *Practical Food Microbiology and Technology.* Westport, Conn.: Avi, 1971, Chap. 21.

ARTICLES

Frank, Bernard, et al. "Our Need for Water." In *Water: The Yearbook of Agriculture.* Washington, D.C.: U.S. Department of Agriculture, 1955, pp. 1–33.

Shandbhag, Sudhakor, M. P. Steinberg, and A. I. Nelson. "Bound Water Defined and Determined at Constant Temperature." *J. Food Sci.* **35:**519, 1970.

Use of Heat in Cookery

Heat is used to cook food materials that are unpalatable or unsanitary in the raw state. The following is a definition that will serve temporarily: heat is a form of energy that matter possesses as a result of the motion of its molecules. At this time, only the aspects of heat and heat transmission that apply to the changes occurring in the cooking of food will be discussed. The use of heat to destroy disease-causing organisms found in food will be discussed in Chapter 40.

CHANGES OF STATE AND HEAT

The changes of state from solid to liquid and from liquid to gas are heat-absorbing processes. For example, an evaporating or melting material takes from objects near it the heat necessary for the evaporating or melting. Conversely, a condensing or freezing material gives up heat to its surroundings. The liquefaction of 1 gram of substance at its melting point takes place when a quantity of heat (heat of fusion) is absorbed. At a higher temperature, the evaporation of a gram of substance at its boiling point takes place when another definite quantity of heat (heat of vaporization) is absorbed. Condensation of steam into water liberates heat, as does freezing of water into ice.

Freezing, melting, evaporation, and condensation are physical changes. In no case does any temperature change take place when there is a change of state. The temperatures of melting ice and of the water it forms are the same: $32°F$ ($0°C$). The heat released in freezing is equal to the heat absorbed in melting. Therefore, there is no change in the overall temperature. Similarly, boiling water and the steam that it becomes have the same temperature: normally $212°F$ ($100°C$) (Fig. 5-1).

A chemical change may either absorb or liberate energy. To bring about the decomposition of sugar, for example, heat is required, making this an energy-absorbing reaction. Chemical reactions that absorb heat as they take place are called *endothermic,* whereas those that evolve heat are described as *exothermic.*

TEMPERATURE

The temperature of a body is the measure of the average kinetic energy of the molecules that

24

Vigorous boiling   Boiling

5-1 *More vigorous boiling increases steam but not water temperature, which remains at 212° F.* (*a*) *Vigorous boiling.* (*b*) *Boiling.*

compose it. This is explained by the fact that not all molecules of a body move or vibrate with equal vigor. Some move more slowly than others, but because they are all constantly in motion, they collide with one another. These collisions frequently bring about a change in speed. It is in this manner that heat is transferred by molecules from bodies of higher temperature to those of lower temperature. Molecules that move quickly tend to transfer some of their motion to those that are moving more slowly. This is the transfer of heat. Temperature measures the tendency that a body has to transfer heat to other bodies—that is, to those of lower temperature than itself.

Measuring Temperature. The usual result of an increase in temperature is an expansion in size. Hence, a convenient way of measuring temperature is by noting the expansion of a column of mercury held in a glass tube. The mercury thermometer is a capillary glass tube with a small bulb on one end. This is filled with mercury and raised to the boiling point of mercury. Then the open end is sealed. When the thermometer is placed in a heated mixture, the mercury expands and rises in the tube. The tube is marked with a graduated scale so that the temperature can be read directly from it. In the construction of thermometers, the freezing point of water and

the boiling point of water are marked first (Fig. 5-2). Mercury is used because it expands uniformly at different temperatures and has an extensive range between its freezing point, −39°F (3.9°C), and its boiling point, 675°F (357°C).

Kinds of Thermometer Scales. The two chief kinds of scales are the Fahrenheit and the Celsius (formerly centigrade). The Fahrenheit scale, named after a German physicist, has 32° for its freezing point and 212° for its boiling point. After these points have been marked off, 180 equal divisions, or degrees, are marked off between them, and 32 divisions are marked off below the freezing point. Thus there are 212 equal divisions between 0° and the boiling point.

In the Celsius scale, the freezing point is marked 0° and the boiling point is marked 100°. The scale between these two points is then marked off into 100 equal divisions, or degrees. To convert temperatures from Celsius to Fahrenheit or vice versa, use the following formula:

$$1.8(°C) = (°F) - 32.$$

HEAT AND CHANGE OF STATE

Heat, as previously defined, is a form of energy, and the application of heat energy to a

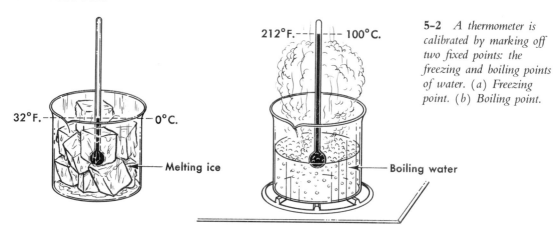

5-2 *A thermometer is calibrated by marking off two fixed points: the freezing and boiling points of water. (a) Freezing point. (b) Boiling point.*

substance results in an increased movement of its molecules. The temperature of a body or system is a measure of the vigor of motion of all the atoms and molecules in it. In a solid material, the molecules are lined up very close to each other. As its temperature rises, the molecules are energized and push against one another until there is sufficient distance among them to permit them to break away. When this happens, the solid changes into a liquid and finally—with the application of more heat—to a gas (Fig. 5-3). This change of state is accompanied by a change from the fixed molecular arrangement of the solid to the more random arrangement of molecules that is characteristic of liquids and gases. Thus, the freezing and boiling points of a substance are related to its molecular structure; substances of similar structure should freeze or boil at similar

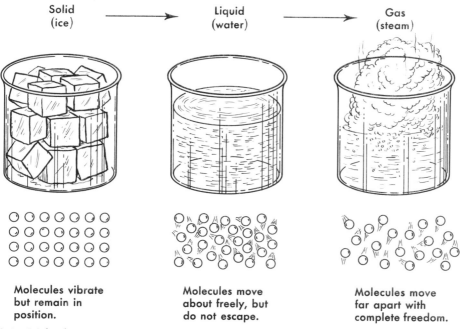

Solid (ice) → **Liquid (water)** → **Gas (steam)**

Molecules vibrate but remain in position.

Molecules move about freely, but do not escape.

Molecules move far apart with complete freedom.

5-3 *Molecular movement increases when a substance such as water changes from the solid to the liquid to the gaseous state. (a) Molecules vibrate but remain in position. (b) Molecules move about freely but do not escape. (c) Molecules move far apart with complete freedom.*

temperatures. The substance with the higher molecular weight requires a higher temperature for change of state. Hence, knowing the molecular structure and weight of a substance, one may predict the temperature at which the substance will freeze or boil.

HEAT CAPACITY OF WATER

Water can absorb a great deal of heat without itself becoming much warmer. Water's heat capacity is the standard against which the heat capacities of other substances are commonly measured. The widely used unit for heat measurement is the calorie, which is the amount of heat required to raise the temperature of 1 gram of water 1°C.[1] Another commonly used unit is the British thermal unit (Btu), which is the amount of heat required to raise the temperature of 1 pound of water 1°F.[2] The heat capacity of water is given as 1, and this is known as its *specific heat.*

The specific heat of most fruits and vegetables is about the same as that of water. The specific heat of milk is 0.9 (less than that of water) because less heat is required to bring milk to a boiling point than is required to do the same for water.

LATENT HEAT

Ice at 0°C will cool off another substance more quickly than will water of the same temperature. The reason for this is that ice absorbs more heat, the additional heat absorption being caused by the melting of the ice. This can be easily explained in the following way. If 1 gram of ice and 1 gram of water—both at 0°C—are evenly heated, it can be observed that at the moment the ice is melted the temperature of the water is 80°C. In other words, it took 80 calories to melt the gram of ice to water. These 80 calories of heat are absorbed by the water and become latent, or hidden, in the molecules of water, but there is no rise in temperature. Thus,

[1] This is used to measure the energy value of foods.
[2] Commonly used to specify the heating potential of fuels.

latent heat is the heat required to create a change in the physical state of water (e.g., from ice to liquid) without a change in temperature.

Where did the heat go and why was it used up? The answer to this question is interesting. In water in its solid state (ice), the molecules or atoms are lined up in a certain fashion because in that arrangement at that temperature they are most stable. Energy is invariably released when crystals line up to form ice. In order for the change from the solid state back to the liquid state to take place, a similar amount of energy must be supplied to break up the tendency of the particles to remain aligned. The amount of energy required to break up the crystal lattice of 1 gram of material at its melting point is the heat of fusion for that particular substance. As mentioned previously, whenever ice melts, a large quantity of heat is absorbed. In an ice refrigerator, a block of ice weighing 1 kilogram can absorb 80,000 calories of heat in the process of melting. After the absorption of that amount of heat, the temperature of the resulting ice water is still 0°C. An equal amount of water would absorb only 1000 calories of heat while increasing its temperature 1°F.

The same principle of latent heat will apply when water is being converted to steam. In order for the water vapor molecules to move far apart with complete freedom, energy must be supplied. This energy is called the *heat of vaporization.* To change 1 gram of water from liquid to steam requires 540 calories.

Figure 5-4 illustrates the principle of latent heat. Beginning at absolute zero, −273°C [or 0 Kelvin (K)], for each calorie that is added to 1 gram of water the temperature will rise 1°C. This will continue until the freezing point, 0°C (273 K), is reached. From this point on, to melt, the ice will need 80 calories for each gram of water. The extra heat required is the *heat of fusion.*

Once the ice begins to melt, the temperature will again rise 1°C for every calorie added to 1 gram of water. This will occur until 100 calories have been added and the boiling point of water is reached—100°C (373 K). Extra heat will again be needed to change the physical state from liquid into steam. The additional 540 calories needed is the heat of vaporization. The enormous amount of extra calories (540) which are required for each gram of water to boil is the

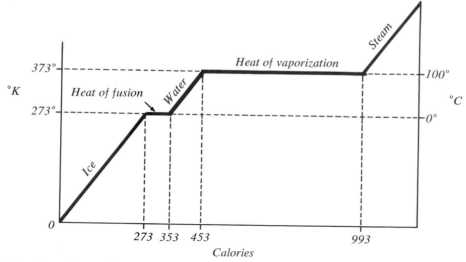

5-4 *Latent heat is shown in this graph as the heat of fusion and the heat of vaporization. They illustrate the extra calories or heat that is required to physically change the water without a change in temperature.*

reason behind the saying "a watched pot never boils."

The fact that each gram of water vapor required 540 calories to turn into vapor can be used to advantage. Spraying vegetables with water will keep them cool. As the water vaporates from the surface, it will absorb heat from the food.

RELATION OF BOILING POINT TO PRESSURE

Gas escaping as steam must push air aside. If there is less air, and consequently less pressure on the surface of the water, there is less for gas molecules to push against. This results in lower boiling temperatures. Decreased pressure may be obtained by going to a higher elevation or by creating a vacuum or partial vacuum by pumping out the air or steam from a closed vessel.

No examples of boiling at pressures below normal can be drawn from household cookery. Industry, however, employs low-pressure boiling temperatures in the processing of certain foods. Sugar, for example, is crystallized from solution in large vacuum pans. It is not possible to drive the water off at normal pressure without changing some of the sugar chemically. Con-

densed milk and evaporated milk are foods prepared by evaporating some of the water from skimmed milk and milk in a partial vacuum. Boiling milk under normal conditions would change the composition and taste of the milk much more than boiling it at a lower temperature under reduced pressure.

KINDS OF HEAT TRANSFER

Heat is transmissible by means of conduction, convection, and radiation (Fig. 5-5). All these forms of heat transfer require a difference in temperature between the source of heat and the material absorbing it, and they all transfer heat in the direction of decreasing temperature. There are, however, important differences arising from the property of the matter to which the heat is applied and the laws by which it is governed. Briefly, heat *conduction* is caused by the property of matter that allows the passage of heat energy even if a physical body is impermeable to any kind of ray and its parts are not in motion relative to one another. Heat *convection* is caused by the capability of moving matter to carry heat energy from one place to another. Heat *radiation* arises from the property of matter that allows it to emit and absorb different kinds of rays, and

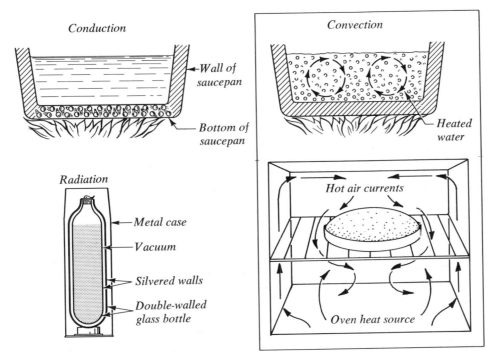

Conduction

Wall of saucepan

Bottom of saucepan

Radiation

Metal case

Vacuum

Silvered walls

Double-walled glass bottle

Convection

Heated water

Hot air currents

Oven heat source

5-5 *Heat transfer. (a) Conduction: As the bottom of the metal container absorbs heat, the molecules nearest the bottom begin to vibrate more rapidly. These rapidly moving molecules bombard adjacent molecules and set them to moving rapidly, too. (b) Convection: Convection currents are caused by the expansion of a fluid (liquid or gas). Drawing of a cake centered in oven. Arrows show circulating air. (c) Radiation: A high degree of heat insulation is attained in a thermos bottle because the bottle is double walled and the air in the space between the two walls is withdrawn. The vacuum thus created prevents loss of heat by conduction or convection. The silvered walls of the vacuum space reflect rather than absorb radiant energy just as the silvered surface of a mirror reflects rather than absorbs light. When radiant energy is reflected rather than absorbed, it does not bring about an increase in temperature.*

from the fact that an empty space is permeable to the rays and that the matter permits their passage.

Conduction. Whenever heat flows from one part of a body to another by conduction, the material of the body becomes heated so that it will vary in temperature from hot to cold, depending on the direction of the flow of heat.

A simple explanation of conduction will illustrate this point. All bodies of matter are made up of molecules that are always in vibration. The addition of heat to the material makes the molecules vibrate more rapidly. The adjacent molecules strike against each other, and molecules with greater energy give up some of this energy to those with less (Fig. 5-6). This action continues until the molecules far removed from the

source of heat receive some of the transmitted energy through conduction. Heat is conducted from the walls of the saucepan or from the cooking medium to the center portions of the food. Deep-fat frying is an example of heating food by conduction. The heat is transmitted from the hot fat to the food.

Certain materials are better conductors of heat

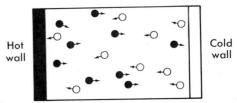

Hot wall

Cold wall

5-6 *Heat conduction in a gas. Heat lost from hot wall is absorbed by cold wall.*

than others. For this reason, it is possible through the selection of cooking utensils and cooking media partially to control the time it takes to cook food. Metals are better conductors of heat than glass, and such metals as copper and aluminum are excellent conducting materials. Wood is a poor conductor of heat and is sometimes used as a heat insulator.

Convection. Heat transference through convection currents is limited to such materials as gases and liquids, which can transmit portions of themselves from one place to another. Whether air or liquid is heated, convection currents flow in the same manner from the more dense to the less dense areas. The portions of air or liquid nearest the heat are the first to become warm and less dense; they rise and are replaced by the denser portions of the material. In the processing of canned foods, heat penetration is mainly by convection currents. This is accomplished through the free-flowing liquid in the jar or can. The general trend of the current is usually in a vertical direction. Where the progress is baffled by solid materials, the currents flow around the solid material at the nearest point at which they can pass. For this reason, the alignment of certain foods in the can is of greatest importance in regard to heat penetration. The heating of solid materials also brings about differences in density, but because movement of the solid material is impossible, convection currents cannot be put in operation.

Roasting is accomplished mainly by convection. The heat source in an oven is placed at the bottom so that the hot air will rise and continuously be replaced by colder air. These convection currents will create a uniform temperature in the center of the oven. The portion of the food coming in contact with the metal rack receives heat by conduction. Minor amounts of radiant heat are also involved in roasting.

Radiation. Heating may take place through the transfer of kinetic energy, as is the case with conduction and convection, or through the emission of waves of energy that vibrate at high frequency and travel rapidly through space. The transmission of energy by means of waves is radiation. When heat and light waves are absorbed by the matter they touch, they increase its molecular vibration and so raise its tempera-

ture. In cooking, when the waves (radiations) reach the food, only the surface is heated by them, because they cannot penetrate below it. The rest of the food is heated by conduction. Hence, conduction as well as radiation is necessary for the food to be cooked. It might well be that convection would also play a part in the heating of food.

Radiant heat is used in the broiling of foods. Toasting bread is an excellent example. Some heating by conduction takes place on all parts of the food that are in contact with the metal parts of the cooking utensil.

Radiant energy must be absorbed before it can bring about an increase in the temperature of the food material. Dull, black, rough surfaces absorb radiant heat better than smooth, white, polished surfaces. Pyrex glass is a good transmitter of radiant energy. This accounts for the need to lower oven temperatures to 325°F (163°C) from 350°F (177°C) when using glass bakeware.

ELECTRONIC HEAT TRANSFER

Electronic cookery differs from conventional cookery in its source of heat. Specially designed ovens used for electronic cookery are called *microwave* or *electronic* ranges. The microwave oven uses a magnetron to produce a form of energy that is similar to light or radio waves. This energy is directed into the oven to cook the food, which absorbs the energy as high-frequency electromagnetic waves (microwaves; see Chapter 45).

Foods contain polar water molecules which have negative and positive poles. The dipolar water molecules struggle to align themselves in the electromagnetic field generated by the magnetron. If the direction of the voltage is reversed, the electromagnetic field will also reverse its charge. A rapid reversal in charge occurs when the voltage is alternated at either 915 or 2450 million times a second. The water molecule is furiously moving back and forth along its axis in order to keep its alignment with the charge. This movement of molecules produces tremendous heat within the food.

Some foods do not depend on moisture to turn microwave energy into heat. A quantity of fat, for example, will heat up twice as fast as the same quantity of water. This has been explained by the low specific heat of fat (0.5) compared to water (1.0). Thus, fat will require only half as much heat to increase its temperature by 1 degree.

Penetration of the microwaves is about 2 inches from the outside of the food to the center. In a large solid piece of food the center would be cooked by conduction. Time control, not temperature control, is used for electronic cooking. Ovens are designed with time controls and some also have speed dials to allow for more than one speed of cooking. Defrosting is accomplished by alternating the microwaves on and off. The intermittant off periods allow for a slower transferance of heat by conduction.

Objects with essentially no moisture or fat content will not produce heat. These can be used as cooking utensils in an electronic oven. Clear glass, earthenware, plastic, and paper make excellent cookware. Metal containers or metallic finishes on glass are not suitable because metals reflect the microwaves. Aluminum foil, however, can be used to purposely reflect microwaves to reduce the amount of heat. The wings and legs of a chicken, for example, may be loosely covered with foil to prevent them from being overcooked.

Food is cooked in a much shorter time when cooked in a microwave oven than when cooked in a conventional oven, and there is much more moisture loss from electronically cooked food than there is from food cooked in the conventional oven. Covers on dishes may reduce the loss but will also increase cooking time. Waxed paper resting gently on the food is often used as a cover. Frozen and fresh vegetables retain good color when cooked in a microwave oven. According to one study,[3] the microwave oven in the home is used mainly for reheating leftovers, defrosting of convenience foods, cooking casseroles, and cooking vegetables.

SUMMARY

Without heat, foods that are unpalatable or unsanitary when raw could not be included in the daily diet. Many foods are cooked by con-

[3] F. Drew and K. S. Rhee, "Microwave Ovens," *J. Home Econ.* **69:**31, 1977.

duction, where heat flows from one material to another. Metals are good conductors of heat; thus metal pans are widely used in food preparation. Foods are also cooked by convection currents (as in food processing) and by radiation. With radiation, only the surface is cooked by the waves of energy; the interior is cooked by conduction.

The principle of heating in a microwave oven is different from the heating of a conventional oven. Electrical energy is converted into electromagnetic energy, creating microwaves in the oven. Movement of molecules within the food creates the heat.

Heat, a form of energy, increases the molecular motion of a substance. The temperature of a substance is the measure of the vigor of this motion. Freezing and boiling points are related to molecular structure: a substance with a higher molecular weight requires a higher temperature for a change of state to occur. The heat required to change substance from a frozen to a liquid state is known as the heat of fusion.

The calorie is widely used for heat measurement; it is the amount of heat required to raise the temperature of 1 gram of water 1 °C. Boiling points are affected by air pressure. The less resistance the gas encounters in escaping, the lower the boiling point.

QUESTIONS AND TOPICS FOR DISCUSSION AND STUDY

1. Explain the changes in size, state, and temperature in a food or food product that may be brought about by heat.
2. Explain why convection currents result from a change in density caused by expansion.
3. List several physical and chemical changes in materials that are caused by heat.
4. What are the important methods of heat transfer in cookery?
5. Explain why it is important that the bulb of a thermometer be completely covered with the hot food material when the temperature is being tested.
6. What happens to the temperature readings if the bulb of the thermometer touches the side or bottom of the pan?

SUGGESTED LABORATORY ACTIVITIES

1. Examine examples of all types of thermometers available for use in the laboratory. Note the differences in boiling point and freezing point of water between the Fahrenheit and the Celsius scale.
2. Practice converting from the Fahrenheit to the Celsius scale.
3. Draw up a chart and record the temperatures of water at the following stages: cold, warm, simmering, boiling, boiling rapidly. Keep the chart for reference.
4. Heat the same amount of water in saucepans of similar size and shape. Cover one saucepan with a tight-fitting lid. Boil water in both for 3 minutes. Bring back to room temperature and measure the volume of water in each utensil. Repeat using shallow pans. What conclusions can you draw about cooking time and (a) use of uncovered or covered utensils and (b) the size and shape of the pan?

REFERENCES

Books

Colborn, Robert. *Modern Science and Technology.* New York: Van Nostrand Reinhold, 1965, Chap. 3.

Handbook of Food Preparation, 7th ed. Washington, D.C.: American Home Economics Association, 1975.

Taffel, Alexander. *Physics.* Boston: Allyn and Bacon, 1969.

Van Zante, Helen. *The Microwave Oven.* Boston: Houghton Mifflin, 1973.

Report

Consumer Microwave Oven Systems Conference. Chicago: Association of Appliance Manufacturers, 1970.

Physical and Chemical Properties of Food

CHAPTER 6

Foods range from table sugar, which is pure sucrose, to complex mixtures, such as bread and meat. Milk, for example, is a very complex system made up of salts, sugar, fats, proteins, and water. The physical and chemical properties of foods are related to their component parts. For example, the action of heat on meat brings about certain physical changes that may be similar to physical changes brought about by heat in other foods containing proteins. The chemical changes, of course, depend on the proteins of the food in question and on its other constituents.

The physical properties of a material are mainly those to which the senses respond, such as odor, color, relative heaviness, and structure. The chemical properties of a material are those that make it possible for the substance to be transformed into other materials. Physical change is a transformation of matter in which only its physical properties are altered. Water may change into steam and sugar may be dissolved in water, but in each of these cases the substance remains the same regardless of the physical change it has been forced to undergo. Steam and water are chemically the same substance; sugar, although dissolved in water, is the same material as the undissolved white crystals and can be recovered by carefully evaporating water.

On the other hand, chemical changes alter the composition of matter. One or more materials cease to exist and one or more new materials come into being. Numerous examples of chemical change can be found in food preparation. The baking of bread, the conversion of solid cooking fats from vegetable oil, the curing of meat, and the reaction of baking powder in a cake batter are some of many chemical changes that take place in the preparation of food.

PHYSICAL PROPERTIES

Specific gravity is a physical property that may be used in the identification of a food material. The specific gravity of a material is its weight in reference to the weight of an equal volume of water at a given temperature. The specific gravity of water is given as 1.0. The specific gravity of food materials varies according to composition. Milk, for example, has a specific gravity from 1.027 to 1.036, with an average of 1.032. As the fat content of the milk increases, the specific gravity of the milk decreases; and as the

33

nonfat solids increase, the specific gravity increases.

The specific gravity of food may be used as a basis for the purchase of such food products as sugar, syrups, jams and jellies, milk, cream, ice cream, and alcoholic beverages. The specific gravity of a material, multiplied by the density of water, equals the density of the material. (The density of water at 4°C is 1 g/ml, or 62.4 lb/ft³). A simple way to determine specific gravity is to measure the volume of the food and then to weigh it. The specific gravity is the weight divided by the volume. The use of a *hydrometer* is another way to determine specific gravity. A hydrometer is a hollow glass tube weighted at one end with enough lead shot to make it float upright. A scale enclosed in the stem makes it possible to read specific gravity directly by noting the depth to which the hydrometer has sunk into the liquid being tested. The hydrometer sinks deeper in liquids of lower density than in liquids of higher density. Accordingly, the smaller specific gravity numbers are at the top of the scale and the larger ones are at the bottom.

Melting Point. The *melting point* of a material is commonly interpreted as the temperature at which it changes from a solid to a liquid. Pure water in the form of ice melts at 0°C. The melting point of a substance is frequently used by chemists to identify it. However, in work with foods, the *softening point* may be more helpful than the melting point. For example, fats do not have a sharp melting point. Natural fats are mixtures of glycerides and each glyceride has its own melting point.

Freezing Point. The *freezing point* of a material is the temperature at which it changes from a liquid to a solid. The freezing points of certain foods—milk, for example—may be used to determine adulteration.

It is well known that the freezing point of salt water is lower than that of fresh water. Some refrigerator systems use brines that are so concentrated they can withstand temperatures of −20°C without freezing.

Water (or aqueous) solutions of the same concentration but containing different solutes do not necessarily have the same number of dis-

solved particles. For example, the freezing point of a salt solution is lower than that of a sugar solution of the same concentration. The reason for this is that the sodium and chloride ions of each sodium chloride molecule go into solution separately. Each ion counts as a particle and has its effect on the freezing point of the solvent (Fig. 6-1). Sugar is a nonionizing solute, and the molecule units count as single particles and do not depress the freezing point as much as ionic substances do (Fig. 6-2). Hence, it is the number of dissolved particles and not their kind, size, or weight that affects the freezing point.

When 1 gram-formula weight (molecular weight) of a nonelectrolyte is dissolved in 1 liter of water, the freezing point is depressed 1.86°C. For example, sherbets and ices, in order to compensate for the extra acids, have approximately twice the amount of sugar as ice cream. Consequently, their freezing point is lower than that of ice cream. One gram-formula weight of an ionizing substance may depress the freezing point two, three, or more times as much, depending on the number of ions produced by the ionization of each molecule. This is illustrated in the making of homemade ice cream. A brine made of salt and ice surrounds the container of liquid ingredients. The heavy salt concentration of the brine lowers the freezing point to a maximum of −21°C (29 parts salt to 71 parts ice). The cold

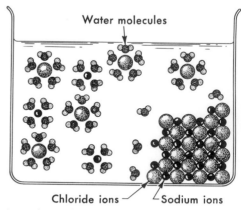

6-1 *When sodium chloride (salt) crystals are dissolved in water, the polar water molecules exert attracting forces that weaken the ion bonds. The sodium and chloride ions thus go into solution separately, doubling the number of particles and lowering the freezing point.*

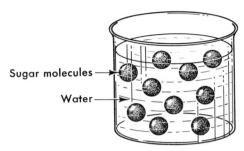

6-2 *Sugar molecules do not break down into smaller particles: ten sugar molecules dissolved in water produce only ten particles.*

brine is able to withdraw heat from the liquid ingredients to create ice cream.

Boiling Point. Every pure liquid substance has its own characteristic *boiling point*. However, the boiling points of liquids vary with the pressure to which the liquids are subjected. For most purposes, standard pressure is the average barometric pressure at sea level. This pressure is usually expressed as 14.7 lb/in.² (or psi), or as 76 cm of mercury (Hg). Another way of identifying the boiling point of a liquid is the temperature at which the vapor pressure of the liquid is equivalent to the pressure of the atmosphere or gas above it. The normal boiling point is the temperature at which the vapor pressure of a substance is equal to the standard atmospheric pressure.

The boiling point of water is lowered as the atmospheric pressure is lowered. Hence, water boils at a temperature lower than 212°F on a mountaintop, where the pressure is lower than at sea level (76 cm Hg), but it boils at a higher temperature inside a pressure cooker, where the pressure is high.

The presence of a dissolved solid not only lowers the freezing point of a liquid, it also elevates the boiling point. The boiling point of a solution is always higher than that of its solvent. An example of this is the boiling point of a syrup as compared with that of water. This explains why fruit pies boil over more freely when very little sugar is used in the filling. If ionic materials are more effective than nonionizing substances in depressing the freezing point of a solvent, they are also more effective in raising its boiling point. Dissolving 1 molecular weight of a nonionizing

substance in 1 liter of water raises the boiling point 0.52°C. Ionizing substances will cause higher elevation.

CHEMICAL PROPERTIES

The *chemical properties* of a material may be defined as those characteristics that describe its capacity for being transformed into other materials. For example, the sugar of apple juice can be transformed into alcohol and carbon dioxide by fermentation; the alcohol can be broken down into acetic acid, which imparts the sour taste to vinegar. These are chemical changes.

The following explanations of changes brought about in foods should help the reader to identify some of the important chemical changes that take place when food is processed either in the home or commercially.

Hydrolysis of Sugars and Starches. The disaccharides (sucrose, table sugar) and the polysaccharide starch are capable of being broken down to form simple sugars (glucose and fructose). The splitting of a compound into fragments by the addition of water is called *hydrolysis*. When a solution of sucrose is hydrolyzed, it is treated with a dilute acid and heated. The sucrose breaks down to form the simple sugars. The acid in this case acts as a catalyst.

Glucose and fructose are prepared commercially for the manufacture of certain foods. Glucose is particularly in demand and is used in the making of fondant, table syrups, and baked products. Neither glucose nor fructose crystallizes readily, but fructose has a strong tendency to stay in a syrup condition. Hence, if fructose and glucose are present in a syrup made from cane or beet sugar, they interfere with the crystallization of the sugar. This property is used to advantage in the preparation of cane syrup from sucrose. An enzyme is added to the sugar solution that acts to bring about hydrolysis, and the syrup may then be stored without danger of crystallizing. A similar effect is produced by the partial hydrolysis of sucrose in making jelly and fondant. If sufficient fructose and glucose are present, the unhydrolyzed sucrose is prevented from crystallizing and a smooth, even texture

35

results. Whenever sucrose crystallizes, it imparts a rough, gritty texture to the candy or jelly.

Fermentation. Chemical changes are also brought about in carbohydrates by *fermentation.* Simple sugars and disaccharides (maltose and lactose) are easily fermented by bacteria and yeasts. The spoilage of fruits and vegetables is accompanied by a destruction of glucose, and the basis for the manufacture of alcoholic beverages is the fermentation of glucose by yeast.

Maltose, a disaccharide found in germinating seeds, is capable of being fermented. Malt syrups can be made from a solution of germinating barley and water. Yeasts and bacteria ferment maltose as easily as they do glucose. Lactose (milk sugar) is not fermented by yeast to any great extent, but certain bacteria ferment it readily. An example of this is the commercial souring of milk by a lactic-acid-producing microorganism.

Starch. Chemical changes take place in starch during cooking. Starch is a very large molecule. In nature, starch molecules are built up to form a larger aggregate called a *granule.* Every plant has its own characteristic starch granules distinguishable from those of other species when observed through a microscope. Commercial starch is made from corn, wheat, or potatoes.

Starch is insoluble in cold water, but in heated water the starch granules swell and form a starch paste. On further heating the starch granules continue to swell and have difficulty in moving past one another, increasing the viscosity of the mixture. This causes the thickening of cornstarch puddings and gravies. Starch mixtures cooked with acid ingredients such as fruit juices (lemon pie filling) and vinegar (salad dressings) may become thin because of hydrolysis of the starch molecule.

Pectins. *Pectins* are carbohydrates found in the water extract of many fleshy fruits. When sugar and acid are added in the proper concentration to this extract, it forms a gel. A certain amount of pectin is necessary for making jelly. The overcooking of a water extract may bring about degradation of pectic substances and can produce harmful effects on color, flavor, and strength of gel.

Browning. The *browning reaction* in food is a complex one and the chemical changes involved in it are not completely known. There are three processes in food that can produce a brown color: (1) reaction between proteins and amino acids and sugars, sometimes called *nonenzymatic browning* or the *Maillard reaction;* (2) oxidative enzymatic changes, such as those that occur at the cut surface of an apple, which are called *enzymatic browning;* and (3) the change occurring in sugars heated to high temperatures, which is called *caramelization.*

Nonenzymatic browning results from a reaction between a carbohydrate and a protein, and it need not involve oxygen. In some food, the brown color and the flavor associated with this color are highly desirable. Many products depend on this reaction for the development of their characteristic flavor. Examples of nonenzymatic browning occur in coffee, maple syrup, potato chips, baked goods, and many other foods which have crust formation. Browning can cause deteriorative changes that are highly undesirable. The off-colors that develop in orange juice and dried fruits after long storage are thought to be caused by the browning reaction.

Enzymatic browning occurs in the presence of oxygen when fruit or vegetable tissues are cut and exposed to the air. The enzymes are effective in bringing about the change of certain chemical compounds in the food.

Caramelization is a chemical change that occurs in compounds containing sugar when they are heated to high temperatures. Like nonenzymatic browning, caramelization does not require oxygen. Browning in vegetables with a high sugar content is probably caused by caramelization.

CHEMICAL PROPERTIES OF FAT

Fat, like starch, is capable of undergoing hydrolysis. But in the case of fats, the products of hydrolysis are glycerol and fatty acids. Fat hydrolysis may be brought about by the action of acids, superheated steam, or enzymes. This chemical property of fat is the basis for making soap. When a fat unites with a base (sodium hydroxide), a soap is formed and glycerol is an important by-product. Soap is one of the by-products of the meat industry as well as of the fat industry.

When fats are heated to a sufficiently high temperature, the glycerides in the fat are partially broken down by hydrolysis, and eventually acrolein—an unpleasant chemical that may be irritating to the eyes—is formed.

Rancidity. Chemical changes occur when fat becomes *rancid*. When fats are kept for a long time, they develop objectionable odors and tastes. The presence of oxygen and certain metals (for example, copper or zinc), light, and heat accelerate these changes in fats. The principal chemical changes are partial hydrolysis of the fats and oxidation of some of the chemical compounds that form as a result of fat hydrolysis. Antioxidants are used to retard rancidity in fats. Polyunsaturated fats (oils) may contain vitamin E, which acts as a natural antioxidant.

Hydrogenation. The saturating or hardening of fats when an oil or a soft fat is exposed to the action of hydrogen in the presence of nickel (which acts as a catalyst) is known as *hydrogenation*. This is an important process in the food industry, for hydrogenated fats are used extensively in the home and in industry. For the preparation of shortening compounds, the oil is partially hydrogenated and has the consistency of lard. Great quantities of oil are converted into commercial products, such as Crisco and Spry. The oils used may be from peanuts, cottonseed, or soybeans. The quality of the final shortening product may reflect the type of oil that was used. Hydrogenated fats are more stable in heat than natural fats and are therefore better adapted to such cooking operations as deep-fat frying.

Hydrogenation is an important process in the food industry because it is the means of transforming the physical properties of a natural fat, thus making it possible for liquid fats to be used in the manufacture of plastic fats, and because it makes improvements for cooking purposes possible in certain natural fats.

The hydrogenated fats are completely bland, making them adaptable for many uses. Special hydrogenated shortenings are prepared specifically for the production of cookies and crackers, products requiring long shelf life.

Some hydrogenated fats are called *superglycerinated* or *high-ratio fats*. Chemically, a high-ratio fat differs from the hydrogenated fats in that monoglycerides and diglycerides (products of fat hydrolysis) are added to it for the purpose of increasing its emulsification properties. This change produces a fat that is ultimately capable of combining with a larger proportion of water and permits use of a high ratio of sugar to flour in cakes. High-ratio fats are generally not used for deep-fat frying, for the added glycerides tend to lower the smoke point.

Reversion. Flavor reversion can occur in refined soybean oil and soybean oil products—margarine and shortenings. On standing and prior to the development of rancidity, a beany or fishy flavor develops which may be caused by the deterioration products of linoleic acid. Reversion does not occur in products in which the amount of soybean oil is limited to about 25–35%.

CHEMICAL PROPERTIES OF PROTEINS

Each protein encountered in nature has a pH value called the *isoelectric point*. For example, the isoelectric point of gelatin is at the pH value of 4.7. At their isoelectric point, proteins are in a state of electrical neutrality and have lessened stability. The protein can combine with either acid or base and acquire a positive or negative charge. The application of this principle to food processes means that proteins in solution may be precipitated out by the addition of a material that changes the acid or basic character of the protein. Hence, milk that is slightly soured will curdle when warm or heated.

Coagulation and Denaturation. One of the well-known but least understandable changes that proteins in food undergo is their transformation from a liquid to a solid state. This process, called *coagulation,* is generally considered irreversible. Proteins as they occur in plant and animal tissue are called *native proteins*. When heat, acid, alkali, agitation, or high pressure is applied to protein foods, the structure of the protein is changed and it becomes a *denatured protein*. The denatured protein becomes insoluble in a solution in which the native protein was soluble. When this happens, precipitation occurs. It therefore is apparent that coagulation of proteins takes place in two steps: first the protein is denatured, then it is precipitated.

Denaturation of proteins in foods is commonly the result of applied heat, but it can also take place through other means. Other factors that affect denaturation are the pH value of the food, the temperature, the concentration of salts, the presence of sugar, and the process of freezing. (Lowe[1] suggests that pressure may develop to such an extent in frozen meat that it may aid denaturation.) Native proteins are unstable at their isoelectric point, and because of this they denature rapidly. The denaturation and, subsequently, the coagulation of proteins take place more rapidly at higher temperatures than at lower ones. Sugar elevates the temperature for coagulation of egg proteins. For example, sugar raises the temperature at which custard coagulates. A further illustration is seen in the beating of egg white: an egg white foam is far more difficult to form when the sugar is added at the start of the beating period; it is easier to obtain by adding the sugar shortly after the egg beating is begun. And, also important, a more stable foam is formed in this manner.

Isoelectric Point. Proteins are amphoteric, which means that they are capable of reacting with both acids and bases. The isoelectric point is the point of electrical neutrality. At this point, the proteins do not act like either acids or bases [they will not migrate to either the negative pole (cathode) or the positive pole (anode) of an electric circuit]. The isoelectric point is given in terms of the hydrogen ion concentration at which neutralization occurs. For example, the isoelectric point of casein is at pH 4.55. The number of basic and acidic groups is different for each protein, thus giving each protein a different isoelectric (point). The isoelectric points of most proteins are in the range pH 4.5–7.0.

At its neutral (*isoelectric*) point, protein tends to exhibit its maximum or minimum properties. Hence, milk sours at this point (the casein flocculates) and gelatin is at its lowest swelling

[1] Belle Lowe, *Experimental Cookery,* 4th ed. (New York: Wiley, 1955), p. 24.

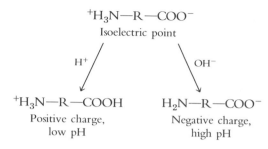

point. After a protein has reached its isoelectric point, it can be stabilized by the addition of an acid or base, giving it a negative or positive charge. It is possible to whip evaporated milk when an acid food such as lemon juice is added. It is thought that the lowering of the pH to its neutral point by the acid precipitates the casein, making it available to foam at the liquid–air interface. The addition of the acid, cream of tartar, to egg white promotes foaming. The acid neutralizes the electric charge, and at this point the surface tension is lowered and foaming is increased. The stability of the foam formation depends on the degree of acidity produced. Increasing the acid above a certain point decreases the stability of the egg white foam.

Hydration. Another chemical property of protein is its ability to form hydrates with water. This is clearly illustrated by wheat proteins. Wheat is unique among cereals in that its milled product, flour, is capable of forming a dough that will retain the gas evolved during fermentation and will, upon baking, yield a light, well-aerated bread. This characteristic is imparted to wheat by its proteins, which when combined with water form gluten. The quantity and quality of the gluten formed are what gives flour its gas-retention qualities. When flour and water are mixed into dough and kneaded, a coherent, extensible mass is obtained. This consists mainly of protein and water. Factors such as pH value and the presence of other water-attracting materials (for example, sugar and salts) affect the hydration of proteins.

ELECTROLYTIC DISSOCIATION

The theory of electrolytic dissociation has important application in food processes. According to this theory, all acids, bases, and salts when dissolved in water or suitable solvent dissociate or break up into positively and negatively charged atoms or groups of atoms called *ions*. Sodium chloride is an ionic compound; its crystals are composed of charged particles (ions) held together by electrical forces. Substances, such as sodium chloride that are capable of dissociation into ions are called *electrolytes*. An electrolyte can be defined as any substance that, when dissolved in a suitable liquid, dissociates into electrically charged ions. Electrolytes have the ability to form a conducting solution when dissolved in water. One of their properties, therefore, is electrical conductivity.

When electrolytes are dissolved in solution, the positive and negative ions of which they are composed dissociate and become free to wander about in the solution. Evidently, conductivity is dependent on the presence of these ions. The dissociation of sodium chloride ions in solution may be represented as

$$NaCl \longrightarrow Na^+ + Cl^-$$

Because the total number of charges on all the positive ions in a given solution just equals the total number of charges on all the negative ions, the solution is electrically neutral.

In contrast to the electrolytes, there is a group of compounds known as *nonelectrolytes*. When these are dissolved in water, the particles in solution are molecules. The nonelectrolytes include such organic compounds as sugars, starches, and glycerin. Solutions of organic compounds are generally poor conductors of electricity.

ACIDS AND BASES

To understand the theory of ionic dissociation, some information regarding the characteristics of acids and bases is essential.

Acids are compounds that have a sour taste, cause blue litmus to turn red, and cause carbon dioxide to be evolved when mixed with a carbonate. Most acids will react with such groups of compounds as oxides, bases, carbonates, and sulfites. The great similarity among acids, however, is that they contain as part of their composition one or more hydrogen ions per molecule. Some acids, but not all, contain oxygen.

Strong acids exhibit their acidic character to a marked degree in that they provide more hydrogen ions through their complete dissociation. Weak acids may ionize only slightly. In general, the acids in foods, such as acetic acid and citric acid, are considered weak acids; hydrochloric acid is considered a strong acid.

A *base* is any substance that accepts or acquires protons (H^+). In general, the alkaline characteristic of bases is derived from the presence of hydroxyl ions (OH^-). Strong bases are more completely ionized than weak bases.

Bases, if soluble, form water solutions that cause red litmus to turn blue. They have a bitter taste in dilute solutions and a soapy feel in a concentrated form. With few exceptions, bases are hydroxides of metals. This means that they contain metallic ions and hydroxyl ions. One of the notable exceptions is ammonium hydroxide, which contains the positive ion ammonium instead of a metal. Bases are especially reactive toward acids. When acids and bases react, the metallic ions of the base and the hydrogen ions of the acid exchange places. For example, sodium hydroxide plus hydrochloric acid yields sodium chloride plus water:

$$NaOH + HCl \longrightarrow NaCl + HOH$$

Bases also react with carbon dioxide. The very soluble bases, such as the hydroxides of sodium and potassium, are called *alkalies;* their solutions are very caustic.

The ionic dissociation of typical bases in water solution may be represented as follows (note that the negative ion is the hydroxyl ion):

$$NaOH \longrightarrow Na^+ + OH^-$$

Numerous acids of importance are found in foods. These are called *organic acids* and are composed only of hydrogen, carbon, and oxygen. Acetic acid is a typical organic acid; it gives vinegar its characteristic taste. The formula for acetic acid shows that only one of its hydrogen atoms carries the positive charge; the rest of the atoms form the acetate ion in the solution.

$$HC_2H_3O_2 \longrightarrow 2H^+ + CH_2COO^-$$

Tartaric acid is found in grapes and is used in baking powders; citric is found in citrus fruits; malic acid is found in apples, pears, and a variety of other fruits and vegetables. Oxalic acid shows up in rhubarb sauce. Succinic, lactic, and benzoic acids have also been found in fruits and vegetables. Carbonic acid (H_2CO_3) is formed by carbon dioxide dissolving in water. It is a very weak and unstable acid and its chief use is in the soft drink industry.

The only common base in foods is that supplied by the sodium bicarbonate in baking powder or baking soda.

SALTS

A salt is a compound made of any positive ions other than the hydrogen ion and any negative ions other than the hydroxide ion. Hence, a salt may be formed by the reaction of a metal and a nonmetal; or by the reaction of an acid and a base; or by the reaction of two salts, one of which supplies a positive ion and the other a negative ion.

When a salt of tartaric acid, potassium acid tartrate (cream of tartar), is mixed with sodium bicarbonate and the two compounds interact in a moist dough, carbon dioxide is produced. The reaction in full is sodium bicarbonate plus cream of tartar yields water plus carbon dioxide plus potassium sodium tartrate:

$$NAHCO_3 + KHC_4H_4O_6 \longrightarrow$$
$$H_2O + CO_2 + KNaC_4H_4O_6$$

The salt formed in this reaction, potassium sodium tartrate, is harmless.

EFFECT OF pH ON FOOD PREPARATION

The determination of pH value is important in the examination of many food products. The pH value of a material indicates its acidity or alkalinity. Acids are characterized by hydrogen ions (H^+) and bases (alkalies) by hydroxyl ions (OH^-). To test the pH value of a material, a scale of numerical values ranging from 1 (for very acid) to 14 (for very alkaline) has been developed and is in common use. Each whole pH unit is commonly divided into tenths for greater accuracy. Solutions having pH values between 1.0 and 7.0 display acid properties. Alkaline properties are associated with pH values between 7.0 and 14.0. Solutions with a pH value near 7.0 are neither strongly acid nor strongly alkaline.

A small difference in the pH value represents a large difference in degree of acidity. The pH scale has been so devised that each whole step represents a tenfold change in the degree of acidity. Thus, a solution with a pH of 5.0 is 10 times as acid as one with a pH of 6.0; a solution with a pH of 4.0 is 100 times as acid as one with a pH of 6.0.

Baked Products. Obtaining good quality is important in baked products. The color of a devil's food cake may range from light brown at a pH of 7.0 to dark mahogany red at a pH of 8.1 or 9.0. Also, the texture tends to become much finer as the pH level increases. Excessively high pH levels cause an objectionable alkaline flavor. In the case of white layer cakes, the color tends to change from white to a dull yellow and the product becomes more crumbly as the pH level rises. The pH of a white or yellow cake is affected by the type of baking powder and the character of the salts formed from the action of the baking powder. The use of phosphate and sodium aluminum sulfate baking powder will give a pH of about 7.0.

When sodium bicarbonate is used as a leavening in a baked product, it should be properly balanced with the amount of acid in the recipe. The acid content of foods such as sour milk, molasses, honey, chocolate, vinegar, and fruits varies and it is not always possible to estimate the exact amount of soda needed to neutralize the acid.

If the acid ratio is low, the baked product will have a high pH; if the acid ratio is high, even though a certain amount of the acid will vaporize, the pH of the cake will be lowered. Another important factor related to pH levels and baked products is that the lower the pH, the longer the time required for the development of staling.

Fruits and Vegetables. The pH has some bearing on the handling of fruits during preparation. In the home preparation of fruits, browning occurs very rapidly once the tissue is exposed to the air. Acid juices, effectively used, lower the pH of the fruit and delay browning (see Chapter 17.)

The pH of the cooking or canning water has a marked effect on the change in color of green vegetables. In a study on methods of preserving color in canned peas, it was found that raising the pH of the cooking medium to about 8.0 preserved their color.[2]

A high pH in cooking or canning water accelerates the breakdown of cellulose and causes food to develop a mushy texture. It also accelerates the rate of destruction of ascorbic acid and thiamine.

Jellies. It is a well-known fact that, other things being equal, fruits with a low acid content do not yield as good a jelly as fruits with a fairly high acid content. A jelly is not likely to be formed from a fruit juice until the pH is lowered to 3.6. A jelly with a pH below 3.1 will generally show some syneresis (weeping)—for example, cranberry jelly.

The pH is also significant in the sterilization of jars or cans of food. The lower the pH, the lower the degree of heat necessary for sterilization. Foods with a low pH value, such as fruits and tomatoes, require less processing than foods with higher pH values, such as meat and fish.

The pH of uncooked foods may be of importance in judging degree of freshness. The pH of a fresh egg white ranges from 7.6 to 8.0, but it will rise to 9.0 after the egg has been stored a few days. The pH of fresh meat is 7.0 or lower, but as meat decomposes its pH level rises markedly.

Table 6-1 shows the pH levels of some food products.

OXIDATION

Whenever any substance loses an electron, the process is called *oxidation*. Oxidation may convert elements into oxides, or it may convert some oxides into other oxides, representing a higher state of oxidation. A typical oxidation reaction is sulfur plus oxygen yields sulfur dioxide:

$$S + O_2 \longrightarrow SO_2$$

The substance that furnishes the oxygen to an oxidation reaction is called an *oxidizing agent*. Air, oxygen itself, and ozone are excellent oxidizing agents.

A good many other compounds can also be considered oxidizing agents because they contain

[2] J. R. Blair and T. B. Ayres, "Protection of Natural Green Pigment in Canning of Peas," *Ind. Eng. Chem.* **35**:85, 1943.

TABLE 6-1
pH of Selected Foods

Material	pH
Angel food cake	5.0–6.5
Apple juice	3.8
Asparagus	5.4–5.7
Bananas	5.6
Beans	5.0–6.0
Carrots	4.9–5.2
Chocolate (Dutch process)	6.0–7.8
Cocoa, natural	5.2–6.0
Corn	6.0–6.5
Cucumbers	5.1
Devil's food cake	7.5–8.4
Egg whites	7.6–9.7
Egg yolks	5.9–6.8
Gingerale	2.0–4.0
Grapefruit	3.0–3.3
Lemons	2.2–2.4
Limes	1.8–2.0
Milk	6.3–6.8
Oranges	3.1–4.1
Plums	2.8–3.0
Potatoes	6.1
Raspberries	3.2–3.7
Rhubarb stalks	3.1–3.2
Salmon	6.1–6.3
Shrimp	6.8–7.0
Strawberries	3.1–3.5
Stringbeans	5.2
Sweet potatoes	5.3–5.6
Tomatoes	4.1–4.4
Vinegar	2.4–3.4
White bread	5.0–6.0

Source: Adapted from "pH Values of Various Acids, Bases, and Common Substances," in *The Chemistry and Technology of Food and Food Products*, Morris B. Jacobs, ed. (New York: Interscience, 1951).

oxygen that can be released and supplied to oxidation reactions. Hence, nitrates, peroxides, and perchlorates are strong oxidizing agents. When hydrogen peroxide is used as a bleaching agent, it is the oxygen set free by its decomposition that does the bleaching or germ killing.

The speed with which oxidation takes place is influenced by the temperature, the chemical environment, the size of the particles being oxidized, and the degree of concentration of oxygen. Higher temperatures lead to more rapid oxidation. Peroxides are oxidation catalysts and will speed up oxidation if they are present in small amounts.

Oxidative changes are frequently associated with microbial activity. The compounds formed by the action of microbes may produce bad tastes and odors. But in food the products of bacterial growth may absorb the oxygen or react with it to prevent the oxidation of compounds that produce bad tastes. There is evidence that bacteria that oxidize flavors develop more easily in milk in which there has been no microbial activity.

Oxidative Changes in Food. Oxidation reactions affecting the baking quality of bread are of great importance in the milling of flour. When a freshly milled, otherwise untreated flour is processed into bread, the results are unsatisfactory. In the absence of oxidizing materials, such flours yield doughs that are called *green,* or underdeveloped. They are soft and flexible and lack elasticity. Usually, bread made from such dough is small in volume, open in cell structure, and coarse in texture. Consequently, bread flours are usually matured and treated with oxidizing agents before processing. In the bread industry, dough made from moderately matured flours is treated with small amounts of yeast foods containing oxidizing agents, such as potassium bromate. The flour is usually aged long enough to produce bread that has a good volume and a soft and velvety texture.

Some milks may have an oxidized flavor, which appears to be related to the reaction of the dissolved acid with the fat in the milk. It is thought that paper cartons have been beneficial in reducing this reaction by blocking out the accelerating effect of sunlight.

Inert Gas. Dry foods, such as dry milk and coffee, may be packed in tin containers to exclude contact with air. During packaging, the air is evacuated and replaced by an inert gas, usually nitrogen. This action retards or prevents the deterioration that results from the oxidation of milk fat and coffee oils by atmospheric oxygen. Tallowy flavors and odors in dry milk are caused by the oxidative changes of the fat caused by atmospheric oxygen.

Antioxidants. Antioxidants are used to prevent oxidation for long periods of time. The exact role of antioxidants is not yet known. It is thought that they may bind up the oxygen or

that they may interfere with the chain of reaction bringing about oxidative changes.

The process by which one substance chemically removes oxygen from another substance is known as *reduction,* and the substance acting to remove the oxygen is termed a *reducing agent.* Reduction and oxidation always occur together; one is the reverse of the other.

In the following equation, it can be clearly seen that although the copper oxide furnishes the oxygen in this reaction, the copper oxide is reduced to copper, and the substance removing the oxygen is the hydrogen. Therefore, the hydrogen is the reducing agent; hydrogen plus copper oxide yields copper plus water:

$$H_2 + CuO \longrightarrow Cu + H_2O$$

The use of nitrates in curing meat involves a reduction of compounds. The reducing conditions in the meat are made possible by the presence of many oxidized compounds formed during the slaughter of the animal. The steps can be summarized briefly. The series of reactions is not as simple as this, but these steps show reduction clearly.

Nitrate yields nitrite (reduced loss of oxygen) due to bacterial action:

$$NO_3 \longrightarrow NO_2$$

Nitrate plus hydrogen yields nitrous acid (at the pH of meat):

$$NO_2 + H \longrightarrow HNO_2$$

Nitrous acid yields nitric oxide (reduced loss of oxygen) reduction by compounds in meat:

$$HNO_2 \longrightarrow NO$$

Nitric oxide plus myoglobin yields nitric oxide myoglobin:

$$NO + myoglobin \longrightarrow NO(myoglobin)$$

SUMMARY

Like other substances, food materials have both physical and chemical properties. In physical change, as of water to ice, only the physical form of the material is changed, but in chemical change, new products or combinations are formed. Both kinds of changes are important in cookery.

Among the physical properties that have important application in cookery are specific gravity, melting point, boiling point, and freezing point.

Chemical processes or changes important in handling foods or in food preparation are the hydrolysis of disaccharides and polysaccharides to form simple sugars, fermentation of carbohydrates (such as the commercial souring of milk), starch dispersion induced by heat, formation of pectic materials to enable a fruit-water extraction to gel, caramelization, enzymatic browning, hydrogenation of fat, coagulation and denaturation of proteins, hydration, electrolytic dissociation, and oxidation.

An important identifying factor of food is its pH value, which indicates its degree of acidity of alkalinity.

QUESTIONS AND TOPICS FOR DISCUSSION AND STUDY

1. What is invert sugar? For what may it be used?
2. In what respects do starch and dextrins differ?
3. List the food-preparation processes that might bring about the denaturation of a food protein. Discuss the term *denaturation*.
4. Explain why browning, enzymatic as well as nonenzymatic, is a problem of general interest in many phases of food processing.
5. In your experience, have you noticed any examples of caramelization in food? What is the explanation for it?
6. What is the pupose of an antioxidant in fat?
7. Look at Table 6-1. Make a generalized statement about which groups of food are acid in reaction.
8. What would the addition of fruit juice or vinegar be likely to do to the pH of cake batter?
9. What accounts for the sour taste of (a) most fruits, (b) sour milk, (c) vinegar?
10. Why do baking powders produce carbon dioxide in the presence of water but not when dry?
11. Examine the labels on baking powders in the laboratory. List the acid and alkali ingredients listed for the different types.
12. What action takes place when ¼ tsp cream of tartar is mixed with ⅛ tsp baking soda and 1 tbsp cold water? Explain what kind of reaction this is.
13. Mix ¼ tsp baking soda with 1 tbsp cold water and taste it. How would you describe the taste?

REFERENCES

Books

Choppin, Gregory, Bernard Jaffe, Lee Summerlin, and Lynn Jackson. *Chemistry*. Morristown, N.J.: Silver Burdett, 1970.

Garard, Ira. *Introductory Food Chemistry*. Westport, Conn.: Avi, 1976, Chaps. 4, 12.

Keenan, Charles, Jesse Wood, and Donald Klimfetter. *General College Chemistry,* 5th ed. New York: Harper & Row, 1976, Chap. 11.

Paul, Pauline, and Helen Palmer. *Food Theory and Application.* New York: Wiley, 1972, Chap. 5.

Pottenger, Francis, III, and Edwin Bowes. *Fundamentals of Chemistry.* Glenview, Ill.: Scott, Foresman, 1976, Chap. 15.

Sienko, Michell, and Robert Plane. *Chemistry,* 5th ed. New York: McGraw-Hill, 1976, Chap. 10.

Solutions

Solutions are constantly encountered in cookery. A solution is a phase consisting of two or more substances. The substance that contains the others is called the *solvent;* the dissolved substances, distributed evenly through the solvent, are called the *solutes.* Solutions are completely homogeneous. The solute in a true solution keeps dividing until it is separated into molecules or ions and is evenly distributed throughout the solvent. The dissolved particles do not settle out even on long standing, nor can they be filtered out. Nor do the particles of a substance so dissolved reunite unless some of the solvent evaporates, or the temperature of the solution changes. Generally, the particles are no larger than molecules, but they may be in the form of ions.

The most common solutions are liquids in which gases, other liquids, or solids have been dissolved. Water is the most commonly used solvent in cookery, for it dissolves a greater variety of substances than any other. It should be noted that a mixture of oil and water is not a solution because it is not homogeneous. This is because it consists of two phases: one, the droplets of oil; the other, the body of water in which they are suspended. On the other hand, a mixture of salt and water is a solution, because the salt crystals are separated into ions distributed through the water, and the two chemically different substances form a single physical phase (liquid) of salt and water.

There are many examples of solutions in foods. Fruit syrup is a solution: the sugar is the solute and the water the solvent. After the sugar dissolves, it is impossible to see its individual particles, but the sweet taste of the fluid indicates that it is still present. A salt or sugar solution may be slightly salty or slightly sweet, or very salty or very sweet. Obviously, the composition of a solution may vary between wide limits. A solution that contains a relatively small amount of solute is said to be *dilute,* whereas a solution containing a relatively high amount of solute is said to be *concentrated.*

SOLUBILITY

Solubility is defined as the weight of solute that will dissolve in 100 grams (g) g of solvent at a specified temperature and form a *saturated solution.* A saturated solution is one that has dissolved the maximum amount of solute that it normally can under a given set of conditions. When the conditions change, the solubility changes. For example, the solubility of sodium chloride is 35.7 g at 0°C and 39.8 g at 100°C. With few exceptions, the higher the temperature, the greater the solubility of a solid in a liquid. Sugar shows a greater increase in solubility than salt: at 0°C, 179 g of glucose will dissolve in 100 g of water; at 100°C, 487 g will dissolve in the same amount.

The solubility of gases in liquids, on the other hand, decreases with a rise in temperature. More carbon dioxide is held in solution by a cold carbonated beverage than by a warm one. A chilled beverage therefore has more flavor than a warm one, which quickly becomes flat. Another principle that operates with relation to gas in liquid solutions is that the higher the pressure, the greater the solubility of the gas. For example, the cap on a bottle of carbonated beverage keeps the gas in solution. Once the cap is removed, the carbon dioxide comes out of solution and escapes with vigorous bubbling. A decrease in solubility of gases in liquids also results from agitation—shaking just before opening, pouring, or stirring.

SOLUTIONS OF LIQUIDS IN LIQUIDS

Liquids that mix completely in any ratio (alcohol and water, for example) are described as *miscible* liquids, whereas *partially immiscible* liquids are those in which there is a definite limit to the solubility of one in the other. Immiscible liquids are those that do not mix at all, such as oil and water.

WATER AS A SOLVENT FOR SALTS

Water is a good solvent for salts, because the ions of salt crystals dissociate away from the crystal far more easily in water than in air. When salt is put in water, however, it dissociates into aqueous solution. That is, the dipolar water molecules cluster about the ions (the negative ends of the molecules attaching themselves to the positive ions and the positive ends attaching themselves to the negative ions), forcing the positive and negative ions of the crystal apart. Thus, the dissolved ions may be stabilized in the

water by the formation of hydrates of the ions. Each negative ion attracts the positive ends of the adjacent water molecules and tends to attach several water molecules to itself. The positive ions, which are usually smaller than the negative ions, attract the negative ends of the water molecules and bind several molecules tightly about themselves, forming a hydrate that may have considerable stability (see Figure 6-1).

FREEZING POINT AND BOILING POINT OF SOLUTIONS

The freezing point of a solution is lower than that of the pure solvent. This is readily illustrated by the use of a salt–ice mixture in the freezing of ice cream. The salt dissolves in the water, making a solution in equilibrium with ice at a temperature below the freezing point of water. It is also true that the freezing point of a dilute solution drops in proportion to increases in the concentration of the solute. On the other hand, the boiling point of a solution rises above that of the pure solvent in proportion to the molecular-weight concentration of the solute.

A solute will dissolve more quickly not only if the temperature of the solvent is increased, but also if the solute itself is ground to a fine powder. The dissolving process takes place at the surface of the particles; therefore, an increase in surface area will increase the rate of dissolving. The rate at which a substance dissolves can also be increased by shaking or stirring the mixture, thus bringing unsaturated portions of the solvent into contact with the solute.

VAPOR PRESSURE

Liquids differ in their development of *vapor pressure*. Vapor pressure is a measure of the volatility of a liquid—its readiness to vaporize or evaporate. For example, alcohol is more volatile than water—that is, it will evaporate more readily. Highly volatile liquids have high vapor pressures; they also have low boiling points.

Dissolving a solid in a liquid reduces the liquid's vapor pressure for any given temperature; hence, its normal rate of evaporation is reduced. This is what makes it possible for the volume of syrup cooked in an open vessel to decrease at a slower rate than an equal volume of water heated in a similar vessel.

OSMOTIC ACTION

The osmotic pressure of a solution increases with increases in its concentration. When a solution of sugar and water is separated from water by a membrane (such as in plant tissue), the water molecules diffuse freely through the membrane in both directions, but the sugar molecules cannot (Fig. 7–1). The tendency, however, is for the solution to become uniform. Although the sugar cannot pass through the membrane and diffuse into the water, the water passes through and dilutes the sugar. This action continues until a pressure equilibrium is reached. It occurs in food when dried fruit is put in water: the fruit increases in size as the water flows into the fruit tissues where the sugar is concentrated (Fig. 7–2).

SEPARATION OF A SOLUTE FROM SOLVENT

A solution of a nonvolatile solvent can be separated into its components by a process known as *distillation*. When a mixture of water and alcohol is heated, the mixture will start to boil at the boiling point of alcohol, 78°C. If the distillate is collected then, it will be rich in alcohol. The boiling point gradually moves upward to that of water. The low boiling point of alcohol causing its evaporation at low temperatures is

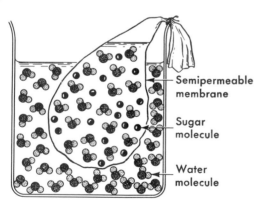

7-1 *Sugar molecules in a sugar and water solution do not pass out of a semi-permeable membrane, but water outside will pass in.*

Semipermeable membrane

Sugar molecule

Water molecule

7-2 *Soaking prunes in water causes them to increase in size. (Courtesy of California Prune Advisory Board)*

the reason why flavoring materials such as extract of vanilla are added to puddings and fillings after they have cooled (see Chapter 11).

Crystallization. Many substances form crystals when they separate from solutions. For example, crystals of rock candy may be grown in a concentrated solution of sugar by allowing the solution to evaporate slowly. Crystals are also formed when some substances change from a liquid to a solid state by freezing. Snowflake crystals are formed when water vapor changes to the solid state; ice crystals form when water freezes.

Crystals are solids with a regular geometric shape, and the crystals of a particular substance have a definite shape. Hence, the shape of sugar crystals is different from that of sodium chloride crystals. The crystals of common salt, for example, are cube-shaped. The shape of the crystal is the result of the pattern in which the molecules or ions of the substance are arranged. The rigid structure of the crystal results from the very small amount of motion of the molecules.

SUMMARY

In a true solution there is no sedimentation, even on long standing. Common solutions include fruit syrups and brines. The solvent contains the dissolved substances, the solutes. A solution may be dilute, concentrated, or saturated. Liquids are miscible or immiscible, depending on their solubility. Solutes lower the freezing point and raise the boiling point of pure solvents. Dissolving a solid in a liquid, such as sugar in water, reduces the liquid's rate of evaporation; concentration of a solution increases its osmotic pressure. Distillation may be utilized to separate a solution into its components. A dissolved solid when recovered from solution by slow evaporation may crystallize.

QUESTIONS AND TOPICS FOR DISCUSSION AND STUDY

1. How do agitation, particle size, and temperature affect the rate of solution of a solid in a liquid?
2. Why would you expect to get different boiling points for corn syrup, honey, maple syrup, and molasses?
3. Does the boiling point of a sugar solution remain constant with prolonged boiling? Why?
4. What is the effect of the proportion of salt to ice on the rate of melting of the ice and on the temperature obtained?

REFERENCES

BOOKS

Kieffer, William F. *Chemistry Today*. San Francisco: Canfield, 1976, Chap. 13.

Miller, G. Tyler, Jr. *Chemistry: Principles and Applications*. Belmont, Calif.: Wadsworth, 1976, Chap. 5.

Nebergall, William, Frederic Schmidt, and Henry Holtzclaw, Jr. *General Chemistry,* 5th ed. Lexington, Mass.: D.C. Heath 1976, Chap. 13.

Paul, Pauline, and Helen Palmer. *Food Theory and Applications*. New York: Wiley, 1972, Chap. 1.

Pottenger, Francis, III, and Edwin Bowes. *Fundamentals of Chemistry*. Glenview, Ill.: Scott, Foresman, 1976, Chap. 14.

Colloidal Systems

Many mixtures that appear to be solutions are not true solutions but near solutions. These are properly called *colloidal dispersions*. Thomas Graham, the founder of colloid chemistry, suggested that all matter could be classified into two groups: crystalloids and colloids. But since Graham's time the term *colloid* has come to mean any dispersion of particles of very small size that are larger than simple molecules (Fig. 8-1). The crystalloids, such as sugar or salt, diffuse quickly in water and form solutions that pass rapidly through filters. But materials such as starch, gelatin, proteins, and fat can be called colloids. They are without crystalline form and they diffuse slowly in water (Fig. 8-2), forming mixtures that clog the pores of most filters. Colloidal particles or *micelles* (groups of particles) form when the particles of the dispersed medium are insoluble in the dispersion medium. Hence, colloidal particles never completely dissolve and form solutions; they remain in a colloidal state. It should be kept firmly in mind that study of colloidal behavior deals with a state of matter, not a kind of matter. For example, sodium chloride may form a colloidal suspension if the sodium and chloride ions are brought together in a medium in which sodium chloride is not soluble.

One way to think of colloidal chemistry is as the science of particle size.

Some foods exist in colloidal states and exhibit colloidal behavior when cooked or manipulated. Therefore, a number of the basic concepts of colloidal systems have bearing on various food processes.

A colloidal system is a heterogeneous system. The material that forms the base of the system is called the *dispersion medium* or the *continuous phase*. The material that exists in the colloidal condition is called the *dispersed medium* or the *discontinuous phase*. All three states of matter—gaseous, solid, and liquid—may be obtained in the colloidal condition.

TYPES OF COLLOIDAL DISPERSION

Because there are three states of matter, eight classes of colloidal systems can be formed: a solid in a solid, a solid in a liquid, a solid in a gas, a liquid in a gas, a liquid in a liquid, a liquid in a solid, a gas in a solid, and a gas in a liquid.

Mixtures of gases are solutions; gases do not form colloidal mixtures.

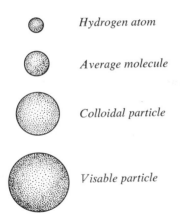

Hydrogen atom

Average molecule

Colloidal particle

Visable particle

8-1 *The colloidal range of particle size lies between that of simple molecules and that of visible particles. (a) Hydrogen atom particle. (b) Average molecule. (c) Colloidal particle. (d) Visible particle.*

8-2 *Colloidal particles are larger than the water molecules in which they are dispersed.*

PROPERTIES OF COLLOIDAL SYSTEMS

One of the best ways to distinguish a solution from a colloidal dispersion is to use a strong beam of intense light. As the beam passes through a colloidal dispersion, it leaves a bright definite path, as the result of the scattering or diffusing of light rays by their deflection from the surface of colloidal particles. This is known as the *Tyndall effect* (Fig. 8-3). The particles may not be visible, but their presence and their motion may be detected by the nature of the reflections. An important property of a colloid is this movement of the colloidal particles, brought about by the bombardment of thousands of molecules in the gas or liquid in which they are suspended (Fig. 8-4). This molecular movement is known as *Brownian movement* and it helps to explain why particles tend to remain in suspension.

Electric Charge. Colloidal particles are electrically charged. Some colloidal particles carry a positive charge ($^+$), others a negative charge ($^-$). The *ionic charge* is the same for all the charged particles in a given mass of material. This is why colloidal particles remain in suspension: particles with like charges do not clump together and form big lumps because they are repelled by one another (Fig. 8-5).

Osmotic Pressure. Unlike solutions, colloids have little or no *osmotic pressure*. Hence, there is no passage of colloidal particles through animal membranes in meat or through cellulose walls in plants.

8-3 *The Tyndall effect: When a beam of light is passed through a solution, it shows little scattering of light; when passed through a colloidal dispersion, it is reflected out.*

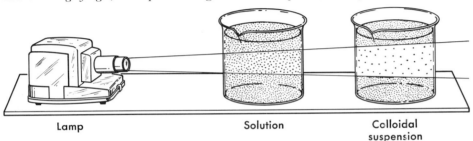

Lamp　　　　　　　　Solution　　　　　　Colloidal suspension

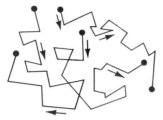

8-4 *Paths of colloidal particles.*

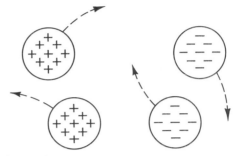

8-5 *Similarly charged colloidal particles deflect each other by electrical repulsion.*

Adsorption. One of the properties that make colloids useful is known as *adsorption.* Many kinds of materials attract, and hold to their surfaces, the molecules of various gases, vapors, and other matter with which they come in contact. The adhering materials are said to be adsorbed. The charges on colloid particles are probably caused by adsorbed ions.

Because matter in the colloidal state is very finely subdivided, the extent of surface exposed is very large in proportion to the total volume of the material. Surface forces, therefore, come into play and bring about adsorption. Charcoal, for example, is finely porous material with a large surface area. It has the property of removing noxious gases from the air and removing coloring matters from solution. This property arises from the action of surface forces, through which the undesirable gases or coloring matters are adsorbed (concentrated) on the surface of the charcoal.

Adsorption plays a very important part in the character of the colloid. By the adsorption of ions from the dispersion medium or from electrolytes present in solution, the colloid particles acquire an electric charge. In the case of the *suspensoid* ("water-repelling") colloids, the dispersed particles adsorb practically none of the dispersion medium. Their stability is due to their Brownian movement and to the electric charge they carry. (The charged particles repel one another and thereby prevent agglomeration and precipitation.) The viscosity of the mixture is no greater than that of the dispersing medium. In the case of *emulsoid* ("water-loving") colloids, the dispersion medium is adsorbed by the particles to a greater or lesser extent. The greater the adsorption of the medium, the more will the particles depend on this adsorbed medium and the less will they depend on the electirc charge.

Examples of emulsoid colloids in cookery are gelatin, egg whites, and starch (Table 8-1). The stability of the colloid arises not so much from the electric charge on the particles as from the amount of adsorbed water they are capable of holding. Such colloids, therefore, are not so sensitive to added electrolytes, and precipitation of the dispersed particles will not take place until the concentration of electrolytes is relatively high.

TABLE 8-1
Types of Dispersions

Dispersed Medium	Dispersion Medium	Example of Colloidal System in Cookery
Gas	Liquid	Foams Whipped cream Beaten egg white
Gas	Solid	Porous solids Bread[a]
Liquid	Liquid	Emulsions Milk Mayonnaise Salad dressing
Solid	Liquid	Jelly Gelatin Cheese, butter
Solid	Liquid	Suspensions Hot chocolate

[a]Unheated mixture of starch and water. This is an example of a food that exists in two different kinds of colloidal systems. When the dry ingredients of bread are mixed with water to form a dough, an elastic gel is formed in which bubbles of carbon dioxide gas are entrapped, constituting a colloidal gas-in-liquid system. In baked bread, the protein is coagulated and the product changes its form to that of a solid. Hence, the bread at this stage is a gas dispersed in a solid.

The protective action of emulsoid colloids is seen in the nature of the curd formed from milk and in the readiness with which it is precipitated on the addition of acid or rennet. Cow's milk contains a relatively large amount of casein and a relatively small amount of lactalbumin (an emulsoid colloid, called "protective"). Human milk contains a smaller proportion of casein and a larger proportion of lactalbumin. Hence, human milk is more readily digested than cow's milk. It is possible, however, to increase the protective colloid in cow's milk by the addition of gelatin, egg white, or starch to prevent precipitation out of the casein. In the manufacture of ice cream, the addition of protective colloids (such as albumin and gelatin) to milk assures a smooth product because the colloids prevent the protein from coagulating and keep ice particles small. Another illustration of this action may be seen in the use of a white sauce, rather than milk alone, in the preparation of tomato soup. The cooked starch paste helps to keep the casein particles from clumping together and thus keeps the mixture from curdling.

Sweetman[1] gives another example of the relation of adsorption to food preparation. A too-salty soup stock may be made more palatable by the addition of egg white. As a consequence of its electric charge, the cooked egg white will gather and hold the salt on the surface of its particles. The egg white will settle down to the bottom of the soup kettle.

Imbibition. The ability of colloids to pick up water and swell when they come in contact with water is called *imbibition*. Imbibition is usually accompanied by the evolution of heat, and the added materials such as acids and alkalies have a marked effect on the degree of swelling. When an acid is added to a protein gel, maximum swelling will take place at a pH of 2.5–3.00, and when an alkali is added the maximum swelling is about 10.5. Carbohydrate gels, on the other hand, show a maximum increase in imbibition in solutions at or near a pH of 7.0, and their capacity for imbibition decreases as the pH moves away from this point.

Viscosity and Plasticity. Various degrees of viscosity and plasticity are encountered in colloids. *Viscosity* may be described as resistance to flowing; *plasticity* is the property of solids that enables them to hold their shape under small pressure (although they change shape under fairly large shearing stresses). Hydrogenated vegetable shortenings, for example, can be described as plastic.

Colloidal systems range in degree of viscosity and plasticity according to environmental factors. Temperature affects the viscosity of a colloid. Generally, its viscosity decreases as the temperature increases. For example, milk becomes less viscous as it is heated; such colloidal gels as gelatin and agar are less viscous at high temperatures than at low ones. The viscosity of a colloid also increases with the concentration and aggregation of the dispersed particles. For example, cream becomes more viscous when there is an increase in the number and aggregation of fat particles in it. Increased amounts of protein solids also bring about an increase in viscosity. Thus, the viscosity of a custard is related to the amount of egg protein dispersed in the liquid. The viscosity of a liquid influences the rate of heat transfer through such mixtures as fruit juices. The rate of heat transfer through fruit juices decreases as the amount of pectin in them increases.[2]

Hydrophic and Hydrophobic Colloidal Systems. Colloidal systems may be classified as *lyophilic* (containing emulsoid, or "water-loving," colloids) or *lyophobic* (containing suspensoid, or "water-repelling," colloids). Lyophilic colloidal systems are formed by the dispersion of a material having an affinity for the dispersion medium. Gelatin dispersed in water is an example of lyophilic colloidal system. A lyophobic colloidal system is formed by the dispersion of a material that does not have an affinity for the dispersion medium. Oil dispersed in water is an example of a lyophobic colloidal system.

The viscosity of a mixture also depends on its lyophilic and lyophobic properties. Lyophilic dispersions have a large affinity for water and hold large amounts of it, resulting in a mixture of high viscosity. The cause of the viscosity is the

[1] Marion Sweetman, *Food Selection and Preparation,* 4th ed. (New York: Wiley, 1954), p. 194.

[2] Morris B. Jacobs, ed., "Physical Chemistry of Foods," in *The Chemistry and Technology of Foods and Food Products* (New York: Interscience, 1951), p. 21.

increase in friction among the particles of the dispersed phase. Conversely, lyophobic colloids show a viscosity close to that of the dispersion medium.

Electrolytes and Nonelectrolytes. The viscosity of a colloid can be changed by the kinds and degrees of concentration of salts and sugars in the mixture. An increase in the amount of sugar in certain mixtures (protein gels, such as custard, and starch gels) decreases the viscosity.

A colloidal dispersion may be precipitated by the addition of an electrolyte. If an acid material is added to a colloidal dispersion, the dispersed phase will settle because the stability of the particles is disturbed by the addition of particles with an electric charge capable of neutralizing the charges on dispersion. Hence, the precipitation of curd of milk with acid or in the curdling of tomato soup, the stability of the emulsoid colloid is disturbed by the ions released from the acid material of the tomatoes.

Effect of Colloidal Particles on Freezing and Boiling Points. As has been explained, the boiling and freezing points of solutions are altered in proportion to changes in the number of dissolved particles in them. Because the particles in colloids are far fewer than those in solutions, the freezing points or boiling points of colloids are not changed to any noticeable degree. Consequently, although the freezing point of an ice cream mix will tend to be lowered if the sugar content is increased, an increase in proteins will not change it to any degree.

Influence of Time Factor on Colloids. The age of a cooked product, such as a custard, as well as the age of the ingredients used has an effect on the viscosity of the colloid. For example, some gel structures must be kept for a certain amount of time so that all aggregates of particles may associate into larger units. Pour batters, such as are used for fritters and pancakes take on increased viscosity if they are permitted to stand for some time before use. A similar occurrence can be clearly seen when baking powder and yeast doughs are used. This may be related to the increased imbibition capacity of the colloid as it ages.

The reverse of this principle of aging is also true: older tissues in plants and animals appear to be less hydrated than younger tissues because their imbibitional capacity decreases as they grow older.

SUSPENSIONS

When the particles of a solid are separated into large aggregates of particles and dispersed in a liquid, the food system is referred to as a *suspension.* In a suspension, the particles tend to sink to the bottom of the mixture if they are heavier than the liquid (gravity is the force here) but rise to the top if they are lighter. A mixture of flour and water is an example of a mixture in which the particles are heavier than the liquid. If it is stirred and heated, a suspension of this kind will change to a gel.

SOLS

A colloidal system in which solid particles are dispersed in a liquid is referred to as a *sol,* to distinguish it from a true solution (Fig. 8-6). In a true solution, the substance separates into molecules and ions that disperse homogeneously throughout the volume of the solvent. But when a protein such as gelatin is dispersed in water, the solutionlike mixture that results is a sol. Examined under the ultramicroscope, the individual protein particles are large enough to be distinguished from the dispersion medium. Sols resemble liquids in their main physical properties—that is, they flow and they do not show rigidity of form. When a sol assumes a rigid form, it is referred to as a *gel.* Gelatin dispersed in hot water is a sol, but when cooled it becomes a rigid, transparent gel. Other examples of sols that turn to gels are fruit jellies and custards.

GELS

Gels are important in food preparation. They may be formed by the proteins of egg or flour in such products as soufflés, puddings, custards, batters, and doughs.

Gels are sometimes defined as more-or-less rigid colloidal systems. The change from sol to gel may be brought about by a change of concentration of the dispersed phase, a change in temperature, or a change in the hydrogen ion

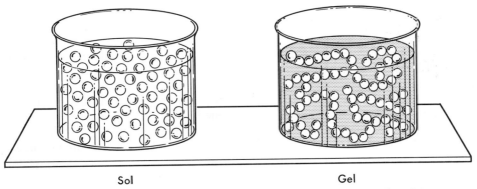

Sol   Gel

8-6 *Colloidal particles in a sol state (left) are separated from one another. The sol is a continuous liquid and flows easily. Colloidal particles in a gel state (right) cling together in interlacing strands. The gel is a spongy solid; though soft, it holds its shape.*

concentration or electrolyte content. Salts usually lessen the degree of swelling of a gel, but studies by Halliday and Bailey[3] indicate that the addition of calcium chloride has a desirable effect on jelly formation, for it decreases the requirement for pectin, acid, or sugar.

Gel Formation. It is thought that when gel formation takes place, the dispersed phase develops into a network structure that holds the liquid phase in its meshes.[4] The threads of the network "brushcap" are believed to consist of particles of the dispersed phase.

In some gels, this framework can be broken by agitation or heat. When this happens, the gel structure reverts to a sol. Examples of this reversion are seen in fruit jellies or gelatin desserts. Such gels as are formed in the baking of custards, however, are not reversible to the sol form.

When only part of the sol changes to a gel, the process is called *flocculation.* An example of this is the flocculation that occurs in heated milk when a precipitate coats the bottom of the pan.

In such products as gelatins and jellies, the concentration of the dispersed medium affects the gel formation. As the concentration of the gelatin or pectin is increased, the stiffness of the gel is increased, too. Gelatins also illustrate the effect of temperature on a gel: the rigidity of the gel increases as the temperature declines.

[3] E. Halliday and I. Bailey, "Effect of Calcium Chloride on Acid Sugar Pectin Gels," *Ind. Eng. Chem.* **16:**595, 1954.

[4] Lillian H. Meyer, *Food Chemistry* (New York: Van Nostrand Reinhold, 1960), p. 125.

Syneresis. Many gels lose liquid upon standing and the gel structure shrinks. This is called *weeping* or *syneresis.* It is considered to be essentially the reverse of what occurs when a colloid swells. The liquid that collects around a glass of fruit jelly, a mold of gelatin, or a dish of custard is an example of syneresis. Another example is the leaking of liquid from lean meat when it is heated.

EMULSIONS

A true emulsion represents a colloidal dispersion of one liquid in another when both liquids are mutually immiscible. Emulsions are of two types: oil in water and water in oil. Without agitation or the addition of an emulsifier, the two liquids tend to separate. The oil droplets coalesce to form larger droplets that rise to the surface and form a separate layer. It is possible, however, to stabilize an emulsion by adding a suitable substance termed an *emulsifier.* Emulsifiers may be in the form of proteins, gums, gels, fatty acids, and phospholipids. Materials used as emulsifiers have an electric charge opposite to that of the material to which they are added. The emulsifier reduces the interfacial tension existing between the water and the oil, thus making them less repellent to each other. This can be accomplished because one end (polar end) of the molecule of the emulsifier is soluble in water and the other end (nonpolar end) is soluble in oil. This permits a film to form around each tiny drop of oil that prevents the drops from running together.

Shortenings are prepared in the form of emulsions. Margarine is an emulsion of water in oil; mayonnaise and salad dressings are emulsions of oil in water. Gravies, sauces, cream soups, and pie fillings are also emulsions. Emulsions such as milk are stabilized by the proteins in milk. In mayonnaise, the emulsion formed is stabilized by egg yolk proteins (Fig. 8-7). Emulsions may also be stabilized by a process known as *homogenization,* in which the size of the dispersed fat globules is greatly reduced to a more or less uniform diameter by the application of considerable force.

Breaking Emulsions. The breaking of emulsions is resorted to in food processes to obtain certain products. In making butter, an emulsion is broken by agitation, with the result that another emulsion is formed by a new distribution of emulsifying agents.

The separation of water from such emulsions as mayonnaise and salad dressing is another example of the breaking of an emulsion. High temperatures and freezing may cause the separation. In the case of high temperatures, it is thought that the film around the oil droplets breaks, thus allowing them to coalesce. In freezing, the water is withdrawn to form ice, which destroys the film around the droplets and permits them to coalesce. Agitation of mayonnaise may also result in breaking the emulsion, causing the oil and water to separate. The separation that takes place in unhomogenized milk is known as "creaming."

Emulsifiers. Emulsifiers are very important in the production of such products as salad dressings, margarine, and shortenings. Lecithins (fatlike materials) are the chief emulsifiers used in margarine. They serve to delay separation of fat and water when the margarine is melted. This delay reduces spattering and helps to prevent the margarine from sticking to the bottom of the pan. (The sticking is caused by milk solids.) Monoglycerides and diglycerides are the emulsifiers used in special shortenings (see Chapter 28).

Foams are also considered colloidal dispersions. A foam is created by the agitation of a liquid, with a consequent entrapment of air in the liquid film. A foam consists of more or less stable liquid–air interfaces, the air cells being surrounded by liquid films that constitute the continuous phase. Pure liquids are unable to form a foam. The foaming properties of liquids depend on their viscosity and a low air–liquid surface tension. Usually, these conditions are accompanied by an accumulation of dispersed medium at the interface. Hence, there is a greater concentration of protein in milk foam than in the milk itself.

The foams frequently encountered in cookery are those of egg white, whipped cream, milk froth, and gelatin. Whipped cream has stability as a foam because of the cell-like structure imparted to the bubbles. These are stiffened by the denaturization of the adsorbed protein. Homogenization of cream reduces its whipping capacity.

DISPERSION OF SUBSTANCES IN FOOD PREPARATION

The changes that can be brought about in a food during preparation are caused by alterations in the dispersion of particles in the mixture. The two changes of practical importance are a decrease in the dispersion of particles, brought about by the condensation or crystallization of particles, which leads to the formation of larger particles; and an increase in the dispersion of particles, which leads to the formation of smaller particles.

Dispersion changes may be brought about by heat, mechanical subdivision of food, and certain chemical substances.

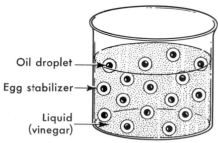

Oil droplet

Egg stabilizer

Liquid (vinegar)

8-7 Mayonnaise is an oil-in-vinegar emulsion. The egg forms a protective coat around the individual oil droplets, preventing their coalescence and holding them in suspension.

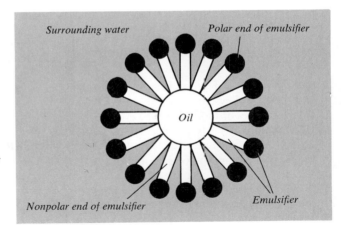

Surrounding water   *Polar end of emulsifier*

Oil

Nonpolar end of emulsifier   *Emulsifier*

8-8 *A microscopic view of an emulsion. A nonpolar oil droplet (dispersed phase) is surrounded by the nonpolar end of the emulsifier. The polar end of the emulsifier is oriented toward water (the polar continuous phase).*

Temperature. Increases in temperature may bring about increased dispersion (that is, the formation of smaller particles), as in sugar solutions, starch mixtures, and gelatin. Yet heat does not have this effect on all food materials. When proteins—for example, egg proteins—are coagulated by heat, the dispersion is decreased (that is, larger particles are formed).

Mechanical Operations. The many mechanical operations used in food preparation are responsible for changes in the dispersion of particles. Grinding, beating, stirring, and homogenization may bring about an increase in the dispersion of particles. But beating may also decrease dispersion by partially coagulating the protein. This happens when egg whites are beaten.

Chemical Agents. Acids, alkalies, and enzymes can bring about either an increase or a decrease in dispersion, depending on the other factors involved. For example, the addition of alkalies to batters and doughs in excessive amounts may bring about a dispersion of gluten, which is accompanied by stickiness and a soapy taste. The use of rennin (rennet) to clot casein is an example of the condensation of particles or decreased dispersion brought on by the action of an enzyme. The reverse of this principle is applied when an alkali is used to prevent the curdling of a food product such as cream of tomato soup. In this instance, the tendency of the particles to condense is prevented by the alkali.

SUMMARY

Colloidal systems sometimes appear to be solutions, but they are not. Eight classes of colloidal systems can be formed from the three states of matter. Gases may be combined with liquids or solids in colloidal systems, but mixtures of gases form solutions, not colloids.

Colloidal particles are in motion and are electrically charged. The colloid's property of adsorption makes it useful in cookery, giving protection against precipitation and agglomeration. Imbibition is the colloid's ability to pick up water and swell.

Colloidal systems may be hydrophilic ("water-loving") or hydrophobic ("water-repelling"). These properties affect viscosity, as does changing the concentration of salts and sugars. The addition of an electrolyte may cause precipitation.

In a suspension, particles tend to separate, rising if lighter than the liquid and sinking if heavier. In a gel, solid particles are dispersed in a liquid. Gels may be rather rigid collodial systems. On standing, liquid may seep from the gel, a condition known as syneresis. A true emulsion is a colloidal dispersion of two mutually immiscible liquids. An emulsifier aids stabilization. Homogenization, in which particle size is reduced, also stabilizes emulsions. Dispersion of particles in mixtures is influenced by temperature, mechanical operations, enzymes, acids, and alkalies.

QUESTIONS AND TOPICS FOR DISCUSSION AND STUDY

1. Summarize the differences between a solution and a colloidal system.
2. Give examples of foods that are (a) solutions, (b) emulsions, (c) gels, (d) foams, (e) suspensions.
3. Explain what happens when milk sours.
4. Would you expect salt or milk to cause a greater lowering of the freezing point of a sherbet?
5. Some colloidal gels—such as gelatin—may be reversed by heating and the original sol obtained. These are called *reversible colloids*. List any examples you can of reversible and irreversible colloids in cookery.
6. Find in a suitable reference book a diagram of a plant or animal cell. Which materials do you think are in solution and which in colloidal distribution?
7. Explain why solutions have osmotic pressure but colloidal systems do not.
8. From past observations, give examples in cookery of changes in the dispersion of particles in food brought about by (a) mechanical action, (b) heating, and (c) the addition of other substances (such as acids).

REFERENCES

BOOKS

Choppin, Gregory, Bernard Jaffe, Lee Summerlin, and Lynn Jackson. *Chemistry*. Morristown, N.J.: Silver Burdett, 1970.

Garard, Ira. *Introductory Food Chemistry*. Westport, Conn.: Avi, 1976, Chap. 8.

Jacobs, Morris B., ed. *The Chemistry and Technology of Food and Food Products*. New York: Interscience, 1951, Chap. 2.

Paul, Pauline, and Helen Palmer. *Food Theory and Applications*. New York: Wiley, 1972, Chap. 2.

Microbiological Aspects of Food Preparation

CHAPTER 9

Cooking processes not only involve the interplay of chemical and physical reactions, they also encompass biological reactions. Of these, those that are commonly observed in everyday life are the fermentation processes brought about by the life activities of yeasts and bacteria. But the activities of yeasts and bacteria are only part of the total microbial activity in food. Molds also cause changes of importance in food processes. It is important to understand how microorganisms, and the changes brought about by their action in cookery, affect the basic characteristics of the food product. It is also the purpose of this chapter to present the relationship between microbiological organisms and food sanitation. The development of good sanitary conditions in the handling and preparation of food is a sound approach to the minimization of food spoilage.

BACTERIA

The occurrence and development of bacteria in food depend on their introduction into the food at some stage of growth, handling, processing, or serving. Bacteria require nutrients, moisture, and favorable temperatures. Furthermore, the acidity or alkalinity of a substance, its oxidation–reduction potential, and the presence of inhibitory substances are factors that play a part in determining which microorganisms will grow in which food, how rapidly they will grow, and what chemical changes they will bring about.

Bacteria require moisture for growth; the amount varies with the bacterium. Each bacterium has an optimum temperature for maximum growth. Some bacteria grow well at refrigerator temperatures and some continue to thrive at temperatures as low as 15°F (−9°C). Consequently, small differences in the temperature at which a food is kept may encourage the growth of entirely different microorganisms and thereby cause different changes in the food.

The acid–alkaline balance of food, expressed as pH, is a factor that influences the kind of bacterium that will grow and the changes that will result. Some bacteria grow best in low-acid food, others in acid food, and still others in food that is neutral.

Each bacterium also has specific oxygen requirements. Some bacteria need air for growth; others thrive in its absence. Those that require air are classified as *aerobic;* those that grow better in the absence of air are known as *anaerobic.*

Some bacteria thrive under both aerobic and anaerobic conditions; these are classified as *facultative* bacteria.

Once bacteria invade food, they give off products that bring about changes. These products will, in time, slow down and perhaps even stop the growth of the organisms themselves; for example, the lactic acid produced by the lactic acid bacteria in milk inhibits their further growth.

Media containing high concentrations of sugar or salt will not support bacterial growth, although molds may grow in them satisfactorily. The high concentration of sugar in the environmental medium is in contrast to the low concentration of sugar in the cell fluids. This difference in concentration induces a movement of water from within the cell to outside the cell. Because bacteria will not reproduce with little water, the lack of moisture in the cells curtails bacterial growth. This process is, in effect, a drying of material.

The food bacteria most important in the processing of food are the acetic and lactic acid bacteria.

Acetic Acid Bacteria. Acetic acid bacteria (acetobacter) are capable of changing ethyl alcohol to acetic acid. This quality makes them useful in the manufacture of vinegar but harmful in the making of wines.

The production of vinegar from sugar materials involves first the fermentation of sugar to ethyl alcohol and then the oxidation of the alcohol to acetic acid. The first step is brought about by the action of yeast; the second step is a reaction carried out by acetic acid bacteria in the presence of oxygen.

Lactic Acid Bacteria. Such products as butter and cheese depend on bacteria, to some extent, for their flavor. These bacteria are called the lactic acid bacteria or *lactics*. The most important characteristics of the lactic acid bacteria is their ability to ferment sugars to lactic acid. Sour milk, as used for cooking purposes, contains lactic acid (less than 1%). Lactic acid is also one of the constituents of sauerkraut, formed from the sugar of the cabbage by the action of various types of bacteria. Pickles and olives are also subjected to lactic acid fermentation. Salted meats, such as ham and corned beef, undergo

pickling, which is believed to be brought about by lactic acid fermentation. Their red color results primarily from the reduction of nitrates to nitrites by the bacteria in the brine. (See Chapters 24 and 43 for a detailed explanation.) In curing meat today, it is customary to add small amounts of nitrites to the brine to supplement the reducing action of bacteria.

Lactic acid can be manufactured commercially by fermenting glucose or molasses with lactic acid bacteria. The sugars are converted into lactic acid, which is neutralized as it is produced to form lactic acid salts. Lactic acid is used commercially in such food products as soft drinks, jams, and jellies to give them a tangy flavor.

Lactic acid fermentation is the basis for the manufacture of a number of cheeses. Unripened cheeses, such as cottage and cream, have a lactic starter. The ripened cheeses also have a lactic starter, but this is then usually followed by the addition of other microorganisms during ripening.

Modern commercial methods of making rye bread involve adding considerable amounts of cultures of lactics to the dough mass as a sour to give a tangy flavor to the bread.

It is thought that fermentation of the pulp that surrounds the coffee and cocoa bean is caused partially by acetic and lactic acid bacteria.

MOLD

Mold (Fig. 9-1) may be white, gray, blue, green, or orange and it has a brushlike structure. Molds do not require as much moisture for growth as yeasts and bacteria do, and for the most part they do not require temperatures much above average room temperature. Molds have a fuzzy, cottony appearance and, generally, are unfit to eat. They are involved in the spoilage of many foods, but some are useful in the production of certain foods. Some cheeses depend on mold for their characteristic flavor. Such cheeses as blue, Roquefort, Camembert, and Brie are inoculated with a strain of mold to bring about the desired changes.

Fermented Sauces. Oriental sauces, such as soy sauce, owe their palatability to the use of molds. In the manufacture of soy sauce, a mash of

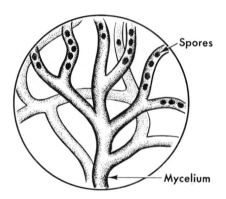

Spores

Mycelium

Microscopic view

9-1 *Mold can spoil breads, fruits, meats, and other foods. Mold spores may be white, blue, green, pink, black, or yellow.*

soaked and cooked soybeans is spread out on trays. This material is inoculated with a starter of mixed mold, yeast, and bacteria culture. Soon a heavy coating of mold appears on the surface of the mixture. This entire mixture is then added to a salt brine and fermentation is permitted to continue for 1–3 months. The soy sauce is then drained from the brine.

Soybean Cheese. Soybean Cheese is made by soaking soybeans and grinding them to a paste. The protein of the soybean is curdled by the action of a calcium salt, and the curds are pressed into blocks. The blocks are kept in a fermentation chamber for about 1 month, during which time certain white molds develop. The cheese is then placed in a salted rice wine or salted soy sauce to age for 6 months or a year.

Citric Acid. Citric acid for commercial use is

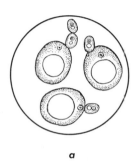

a

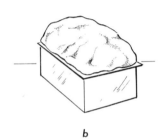

b

made by a fermentation process involving molds. The medium used most frequently is beet molasses. In the food industry, citric acid is used to flavor soft drinks and candies and as an aid in preventing the discoloration of certain foods (for example, sliced peaches) during processing. It is also used for medicinal purposes.

YEASTS

Like molds, yeasts may be useful or harmful in foods. Yeasts, unicellular plants, vary in form from spherical to cylindrical. They reproduce by budding.

Yeast is extensively used in the making of bread and certain other baked products. The most noticeable effect of yeast is the production of carbon dioxide, which expands the dough and makes the final product light and porous (Fig. 9–2). The source of the carbon dioxide is sugar, which may be added when the dough is mixed or produced from the starch hydrolysis made possible by the enzyme diastase in flour.

Fermentation not only leavens the dough but also renders the gluten of the flour more elastic when combined with a liquid. Lactic and acetic acids form during fermentation. The increased acidity changes some of the insoluble proteins into soluble forms. Because the substances fermented are monosaccharides, starch, sucrose, and maltose must be broken down into simple sugars—glucose and fructose—before they can be fermented by the action of the yeast. Yeast is capable of producing the enzymes sucrase and maltase, which bring about the splitting of sucrose and maltose into the monosaccharides.

9-2 *(a) Yeast cells produce enzymes that favor reaction with sugar to form carbon dioxide. (b) The gas expands in the air cells in the dough and makes it rise.*

Ales, Beers, Wines. Alcoholic beverages depend on the fermentation brought on by certain strains of yeast for their characteristic flavor and color. Ale and beer are made from wheat and barley malt, respectively; wines are made from different varieties of grapes.

Dry Yeast. The manufacture of yeast is a necessary industry, for the production of baked products, such as bread, depends on it. In yeast production, selected strains of yeast are added to a dilute solution of molasses, mineral salts, and ammonia and are allowed to grow. When growth ceases, the yeast is separated from the solution by either filtration or centrifugation, and is washed, compressed, and packaged.

Dry yeast may be used in place of compressed yeast. It differs from compressed yeast mainly in that it has a much lower moisture content, a feature that adds greatly to its storage life. Kept at a temperature of 70–80°F (21–26°C), dry yeast retains its baking strength and activity for many weeks. Another advantage of dry yeast is that during drying the yeast is rendered dormant and can be transported without danger of spoilage.

FOOD POISONINGS AND INFECTIONS

As has been shown, microorganisms have a useful effect on certain foods. But it is also important to understand the harmful aspects of these organisms. Microorganisms are involved in most cases of food spoilage, although spoilage may also be caused by the action of other substances, such as enzymes.

Bacteria. The bacteria that cause food poisoning include *Staphylococcus aureus, Clostridium botulinum,* and *Clostridium perfringens.* Food infection differs from food poisoning in that it is caused by species of *Salmonella* and *Streptococcus* bacteria that are able to grow in food and infect the persons eating it. The *Staphylococcus aureus* and *Clostridium botulinum* are distinguished from the *Salmonella* and *Streptococcus* groups in that their growth in food prior to its consumption produces certain toxins or poisonous substances. An example of this is the toxin formed by the *Clostridium botulinum* in inadequately processed canned foods of the low-acid variety, such as peas, stringbeans, and corn.

The food poisoning caused by *Clostridium botulinum* is fatal. Foods that have been home-canned by methods not known to the user should be boiled vigorously for 20 minutes before they are eaten (see Chapter 40). Commercial foods are usually safe from this danger, as they are fully sterilized at high temperatures under pressure. Recently, *Clostridium perfringens* has been recognized as the agent in some outbreaks of foodborne disease. The main foods associated with such outbreaks are meats, including poultry, and gravies. It is therefore recommended that meats be cooked to a temperature above 140°F (60°C), cooled quickly, and refrigerated. Both *Cl. botulinum* and *Cl. perfringens* are found in sewage, soil, and feces.

Staphylococcus food intoxication, the contamination of a food with the toxin produced by the organism, is likely to occur when the conditions of growth are favorable—a high temperature and an incubation period long enough to permit the growth of the organisms. *Staphylococcus* food intoxications are initiated by careless handling of foods. Pus from infected cuts or pimples and droplet infections from the nose spread the bacteria. Products such as cream fillings, cream soups, and egg mixtures of various kinds are highly susceptible to these bacteria.

The sickness caused by these organisms is not fatal but produces discomfort—nausea, diarrhea, and cramps. Symptoms are usually evident within 3–6 hours after ingestion of the poisoned food.

Salmonella bacteria, which can produce food infections, are able to grow in a large range of foods, including dairy products, meats and meat products, protein salads, duck eggs, poultry, and fish. Growth is accelerated if foods are kept unrefrigerated for long periods.

Salmonella bacteria that cause disease may be found in slaughtered animals, in poultry (if it is improperly cooked), and in eggs. Foods made with eggs—if they are not pasteurized or cooked long enough—may carry live organisms. The law now requires pasteurization of egg products.

Human and animal fecal material is the direct or indirect source of the contamination of foods with *salmonella*. The organisms may come from the carrier and may be spread by someone who has the disease or by a vector (flies, rodents, roaches). Poultry may be infected and transmit the organism to their eggs.[1] This is why considerable attention is given to inspection during the killing of poultry and the processing of frozen and dried eggs. The disease has some similarity to *Staphylococcus* infection in that nausea and vomiting are involved. The conditions conducive to the development of these bacteria are high temperatures and enough time for the organism to grow.

Rope bacteria may infect bread during the hot weather. Rope is caused by bacteria capable of forming a resistant spore. The interior baking temperatures of bread (rarely does the temperature reach boiling) are insufficient to kill these spores. When the bread cools, the spores revert to the growing stage and begin to multiply. The bacteria secrete enzymes that break down the proteins of the bread so that the crumb becomes soft and sticky and shows a brown discoloration. Breads are contaminated mainly under conditions of warmth and humidity.

Mycotoxins. Less familar than the bacteria toxins are the mycotoxins that are produced by molds. Recognition of mycotoxins as a health hazard is a fairly new development, initiated by British research workers when a large number of turkey flocks were wiped out in 1961. It was determined that the cause of the epidemic was a

[1]Norman McCullough, "Food in the Epidemiology of Salmonellasis," *J. Amer. Dietet. Assoc.* **34:**254, 1958.

peanut meal imported from Brazil and that the toxin involved was related to the mold *Aspergillus flavus*. The word *aflatoxin* was coined to identify the mold-produced toxin.

Presently, a number of molds other than *Aspargillus flavus* have been identified as toxin-producing. In addition to cereal grains such as corn, barley, cottonseed meal, rice, and wheat, the toxins affect a number of animals and the sensitivity range for different species varies. Rainbow trout and ducklings are quite sensitive to aflatoxins, while sheep have been found to be quite resistant. Primates are also sensitive to the aflatoxins but, as yet, their effects on man are not too well known.

In this country, through the combined efforts of the Food and Drug Administration, the peanut industry, and the United States Department of Agriculture, contaminated peanuts have been withheld from public consumption. Peanut lots not measuring up to standard are used only for the production of peanut oil, for which the processing eliminates all traces of aflatoxins. With peanuts the contamination occurs mostly during the drying period because of improper storage and drying conditions.

Shellfish Toxins. Some species of shellfish can become poisonous through the consumption of toxic marine algae, mainly the dinoflagellates. Shellfish poisoning in this country is controlled by direct sampling of shellfish beds and by examination of the water microscopically near the shellfish beds. Recommendations for the com-

9-3 *These walnut meats show a heavy contamination by* Aspergillus flavus, *the mold species which produces aflatoxin, grown under ideal conditions in the laboratory. Aflatoxin is one of a number of toxins, called mycotoxins, produced by various molds. Not all molds produce toxins, and some are useful in food processing. (Courtesy of the Food and Drug Administration)*

9-4 *Several foods are subject to contamination by aflatoxin under conditions conducive to growth of the mold* Aspergillus flavus. *Among them are peanuts, tree nuts, corn, and cottonseed. These filbert shells show growth of* A. flavus *in the laboratory. (Courtesy of the Food and Drug Administration)*

mercial collection and processing of shellfish are set up by the U.S. Public Health Service.

CONTROL OF FOOD POISONINGS AND FOOD INFECTIONS

Certain controls used by the industry and legal controls set up by federal and local governments are discussed in Chapter 42. One of the most important protections for food against harmful organisms is the application of heat, because heat is capable of destroying bacteria. But although heat is effective under certain conditions, not all cooking methods are capable of destroying all harmful bacteria in food. To be effective, heat must penetrate the entire mass of food—and herein lies the problem. It is not always possible for the interior of a food or food product to reach, within a given length of time, a temperature high enough to sterilize the food. An outstanding example of this is found in meat and poultry cookery. The low temperatures recommended for palatability and economy in the roasting of these products may fail to inhibit the growth of bacteria. Studies by Castelloni et al.[2] on frozen poultry revealed that in large stuffed frozen turkeys, heat transfer is too slow to provide a temperature high enough to destroy potentially harmful bacteria at the center of the

stuffing. Hussemann[3] found that microorganisms in ground ham mixtures were not completely destroyed by heating. In light of these findings, food products should be heated so that adequate cooking is achieved. In the case of turkeys, one that is stuffed is done when a temperature of 165°F (74°C) is registered on a thermometer inserted in the center of the stuffing.

Delayed Cooking. Modern home ranges with fully automatic ovens have increased the practice of preparing certain foods several hours in advance of cooking. The delay before cooking, however, combined with the rather high temperature at which the food is held, may afford a good opportunity for bacterial growth.

Wiedman et al.[4] found that such products as meat loaf showed a dangerous increase in bacteria when the holding time was as long as 8 hours. These same investigators found that meat loaves could not be kept at room temperature for extended periods without the rapid growth of harmful organisms.

Foods cooked in crockery cookers should be prepared as suggested in owner's manual. Overloading the cooker might allow growth of *Clostridium perfringens* and *Staphlococcus aureus*.

[3]D. L. Hussemann, "Effect of Cooking on the Bacteriologic Flora of Selected Frozen Precooked Foods," *J. Amer. Dietet. Assoc.* **27**:885, 1951.

[4]K. Wiedman et al., "Bacteria in Meat Loaf Cooked After Holding," *J. Amer. Dietet. Assoc.* **32**:935, 1956.

[2]A. G. Castelloni et al., "Roasting Time and Temperature Required to Kill Food Poisoning Organisms Introduced Experimentally into Stuffings in Turkeys," *Food Res.* **18**:131, 1953.

Thus, although cooking is one way to control the growth of microorganisms, it cannot be relied on to completely inactivate all harmful organisms.

Refrigeration. Adequate refrigeration is an important factor in preventing the growth of unfavorable organisms in foods. The danger zone favoring bacterial growth is 50–140°F (10–60°C). It is important, therefore to lower the temperatures of stored cooked food to a level that will delay the growth of bacteria. The recommended level is 32–38°F (0–4°C). Allowing food to cool at room temperature before refrigeration is not a good practice. The practice that is most acceptable for storage of cooked foods is to lower the temperature to a safe level in the shortest possible time. Studies[5,6] have shown that large masses of cooked foods should be divided into small quantities for most rapid cooling. And for most effective cooling, shallow pans (preferably not over 3 in. deep) may be used.

Proper refrigeration is almost the only measure at our disposal that will prevent the buildup of undesirable microorganisms. Whenever storage for any length of time is involved, prompt and adequate refrigeration must be provided.[7]

The U.S. Public Health Service has suggested temperature levels suitable for the storage of certain groups of food. These are shown in Table 9-1.

The length of storage time is also important in counteracting the growth of bacteria. Many of the items mentioned in Table 9-1 might be kept in good condition for as long as 48 hours. However, it is difficult to judge how long a food will remain safe in the refrigerator, because the rate of bacterial growth and deterioration depends to some extent on the condition of the food when it was placed in the refrigerator. Figure 9-5 shows the relation of temperature zones to pathogen activity.

[5]M. Lewis, H. Weiser, and A. R. Winter, "Bacterial Growth in Chicken Salad," *J. Amer. Dietet. Assoc.* **29**:1094, 1953.

[6]K. Longree and J. White, "Cooking Rates and Bacterial Growth in Food Prepared and Stored in Quantity," *J. Amer. Dietet. Assoc.* **31**:124, 1955.

[7]R. C. Bond and C. Stauffer, "Food Sanitation and the Infectious Process," *J. Amer. Dietet. Assoc.* **21**:995, 1955.

TABLE 9-1
Food Storage Temperatures

Food	Recommended Temperature Range	
	°F	°C
Frozen foods	0–20	−18 to −6
Fish and shellfish	23–30	5 to −1
Meat and poultry	33–38	1 to 4
Fruits, vegetables, and most other perishable products	44–50	7 to 10

Wherever food preparation takes place, adequate refrigeration must be provided to prevent spoilage. The growth of certain bacteria can be materially retarded at temperatures below 50°F (10°C), and a good refrigerator should maintain a temperature range of from 45°F (7°C) in its warmest part to not much higher than 32°F (0°C) in the colder sections. The lower the temperature above freezing that the refrigerator maintains, the better. Most refrigerators today provide special freezing compartments that may maintain an average temperature well below 0°F (−18°C). When this is the case, they may be used to freeze foods as well as to store frozen foods.

Special compartments may also be provided for meats, fresh fruits, vegetables, and other kinds of food. When these specialized compartments are provided, it is in the interest of efficiency to use them. The compartments are usually placed to conform with the recommended temperatures for the food to be stored in it. The meat compartment, for example, will be placed in the coldest part of the refrigerator.

To increase the efficiency of the refrigerator, the door should be opened as seldom as possible; the food should be in its proper place, and nothing should be put in the refrigerator that might interfere with the proper cooling of the other food. For example, paper bags and cartons tend to increase the amount of refrigeration needed to keep the food at a safe temperature.

Meat should be wrapped loosely in wax paper and placed in the coolest part of the refrigerator. It can be stored in its original self-service packaging for a short time. Cooked meats also require space in the coldest part of the refrigerator, but

°C	°F	
121	250	Canning temperatures for low-acid vegetables, meat, and poultry in pressure canner.
116	240	
		Canning temperatures for fruits, tomatoes, and pickles in water-bath container.
100	212	
		Cooking temperatures destroy most bacteria. Time required to kill bacteria decreases as temperature is increased.
74	165	
		Warming temperatures prevent growth but allow survival of some bacteria.
60	140	
		Some bacterial growth may occur. Many bacteria survive.
52	120	
		DANGER ZONE. Temperatures in this zone allow rapid growth of bacteria and production of toxins by some bacteria.
		(Foods in this temperature zone should not be held for more than 2 or 3 hours.)
16	60	
		Some growth of food poisoning bacteria may occur.
4	40	Cold temperatures permit slow growth of some bacteria that cause spoilage. (Raw meats should be used within 5 days,
0	32	ground meat, poultry, and fish within 2 days.)
		Freezing temperatures stop growth of bacteria, but allow bacteria to survive.
−18	0	

9-5 *Temperature of food for the control of bacteria. (Courtesy of the U.S. Department of Agriculture)*

they should be tightly covered to prevent drying of surfaces. In general, meats such as roasts, chops, and steaks can be refrigerated for longer periods of time than organ meats, and ground meats show signs of deterioration sooner than whole pieces do.

Fish should be wrapped tightly to keep in odors, but it is not desirable to keep fish longer than 24 hours in the refrigerator compartment. Fish that must be kept longer should be frozen.

If a refrigerator has a high-humidity storage compartment, fruits and vegetables should be stored in it. Otherwise, they should be stored on a low shelf for convenient removal. To prevent drying out of these foods, plastic bags may be used to wrap them.

Sanitation. Although the proper refrigeration of food is of prime importance in the control of contamination, the personal hygiene and work habits of persons handling the food are also important. The recommended sanitary practices are familiar, but they are worthy of review.

Hands must be thoroughly washed with soap and water before handling foods. Attention to this practice cuts down on the transmission of disease-carrying organisms.

The manipulation of food with fingers and hands should be kept at a minimum. Whenever possible, spoons, forks, tongs, or other appropriate tools should be used.

Dirty surfaces can contaminate food; hence, surfaces on which food is placed should be kept scrupulously clean. Grease, dust, crumbs, and other food particles collect in crevices and corners. These become excellent places for the growth of bacteria. Poor sanitation also attracts insects and rodents, which help to transmit food-spoilage organisms from one source to another.

The proper washing and sterilization of dishes is effective in preventing the spread of food-spoilage organisms. If a dishwasher is used, water temperatures should be as high as 120–140°F (49–60°C). Hand washing of dishes necessitates lower water temperatures. After the dishes have been thoroughly washed in hot water with an adequate supply of detergent, however, they should be completely rinsed with boiling water. Discard dishes with many cracks and nicks where soil and bacteria remain.

SUMMARY

Biological reactions as well as chemical and physical reactions occur in foods. Some are desirable, such as the action of yeast in leavening bread, of mold in making cheese and soybean sauce, and of acetic acid bacteria in the manufacture of vinegar. But other undesirable bacteria that invade food produce harmful, sometimes fatal, results. Adequate refrigeration, adequate cooking, quick cooling and storage, and sound and sanitary food-handling practices are all important factors in the control of food spoilage, food poisoning, and food infection.

QUESTIONS AND TOPICS FOR DISCUSSION AND STUDY

1. How are microorganisms beneficial to processes in food preparation?
2. What practices in food handling would promote the growth of microorganisms?
3. What reasons would you give for discouraging the practice of eating raw meat and raw eggs?
4. People are advised not to use their hands in the preparation of food if other means of manipulating the food are available. What is the reason for this recommendation?
5. List the ways in which food might become contaminated.
6. What environmental conditions might lead you to suspect food spoilage?
7. Foods may spoil while stored in the refrigerator. Why?

REFERENCES

BOOKS

Farmer's World: The Yearbook of Agriculture, Washington, D.C.: U.S. Department of Agriculture, 1964.

Frazier, William C. *Food Microbiology,* 2nd ed. New York: McGraw-Hill, 1967.

Nickerson, John, and Anthony Sinsky. *Microbiology of Foods and Food Processing.* New York: American Elsevier, 1974.

Osborn, Margaret, and Elizabeth Osman. *Current*

Topics in Food and Nutrition. Iowa City, Iowa: University of Iowa Press, 1968.

Protecting Our Food: The Yearbook of Agriculture. Washington, D.C.: U.S. Department of Agriculture, 1966.

Toxicants Occurring Naturally in Food. Washington, D.C.: National Academy of Sciences, 1973.

Weiser, Harry. *Practical Food Microbiology and Technology,* 2nd ed. Westport, Conn.: Avi, 1971.

ARTICLES AND BULLETINS

Bond, R. C., and C. Stouffer. "Food Sanitation and the Infectious Process." *J. Amer. Dietet. Assoc.* **21**:995, 1955.

Brackett, R. E., and E. H. Marth, "Heating Patterns of Products in Crockery Cookers." *J. of Food Protection,* **40**:664, 1977.

Campbell, A. D. "Natural Food Poisons," *FDA Papers,* Food and Drug Administration, U.S. Department of Health, Education and Welfare, 1967.

Dessel, M., E. Bowersox, and W. Jeter. "Bacteria in Electronically Cooked Food." *J. Amer. Dietet. Assoc.* **37**:230, 1960.

Gutherz, Linda, and John Fruin. "Microbial Quality of Frozen Comminuted Turkey Meat." *J. Food Sci.* **42**:1344, 1977.

Huppler, P. "Bacteriological Implications of Holding Casseroles in Automatic Ovens." *J. Home Econ.* **56**:748, 1964.

Keeping Food Safe to Eat: "A Guide for Homemakers." *Home and Garden Bulletin 162.* Washington, D.C.: U.S. Department of Agriculture, 1975.

Kramer, A., and J. Farquhar. "Fate of Microorganisms During Frozen Storage of Custard Pies." *J. Food Sci.* **42**:1138, 1977.

McCullough, Norman. "Food in the Epidemiology of Salmonellasis." *J. Amer. Dietet. Assoc.* **34**:254, 1958.

Shelton, L. R., Jr. "Frozen Precooked Foods," *J. Amer. Dietet. Assoc.* **38**:132, 1961.

Solberg, M. and B. Elkind. "Effect of Processing and Storage Conditions on the Microflora of *Clostridium perfringins*-Inoculated Frankfurters." *J. Food Sci.* **35**:126, 1970.

"Storing Perishable Foods in the Home." *Home and Garden Bulletin 78.* Washington, D.C.: U.S. Department of Agriculture, 1973.

Woodburn, Margy. "Safe Food Versus Food Borne Illness." *J. Home Econ.* **59**:448, 1967.

Factors Affecting Food Consumption

Today American families have higher living standards than they did at the beginning of the century, mainly because they earn more and spend more. Raising the food standards of the American family has been a major factor in improving living standards.

The increase in food prices in recent years has been caused by the rising cost of food production and marketing and the fact that we are buying better-quality and more expensive food than we did in the last decade or two.

Family food habits are reflected only partly in the amount of money spent on food. Other factors influencing the purchase and use of food are nutritive value, availability, seasonablity, individual preferences, and color, texture, and flavor of the foods.

Chapter 10 shows how certain changes in the food market have brought about changes in the buying and preparation of food for the home. Chapter 11 is important to an understanding of personal preferences in food, for without attention to the sensory aspects of food, there can be no true enjoyment of it.

Part Two

Economic Aspects of Food Preparation

Rising food costs in the last few years have led to a more cost-conscious consumer. (See Fig. 10–1.) The increase in the number and types of products for sale (about 1,000 in 1903 to 10,000 in 1974) have made it confusing for the consumer to evaluate which is the best product for the lowest price.

CONVENIENCE FOODS

The most significant factor influencing the consumer's cost of food has been the increasing demand for processed and convenience foods. The change in attitudes regarding a woman's place in society has led to an increasing number of women who have full-time careers. Working outside the home leaves little time for chores such as marketing and cooking. Because minutes are important, the consumer places high value on foods with "built-in" convenience. Instead of buying fresh peas that must be shelled or fresh spinach that requires several washings, today's consumer shows a preference for the canned or frozen product.

Increased consumer spending has resulted in many more food items on the grocery shelves.

The variety of food items is limitless. Today the consumer may buy apples for pie in fresh, canned, frozen, or dried form. Or she may buy the pie ready to be baked as well as completely baked.

The retailing of potatoes illustrates an important trend in consumer food-buying practices. The raw potato in the 5-, 10-, and 25-lb bag is still available in most markets, but processed potatoes are also available in at least 10 different forms. Canned, frozen, and dehydrated forms of the popular white potato are in demand for both home and commercial use, as are also dehydrated, canned and frozen sweet potatoes. French-fried potatoes probably spearheaded the trend of using the prepared product.

The constant search for convenience foods is further demonstrated by the steady growth of the instant coffee market, the increase in the number and variety of complete frozen dinners available (and not all of them in the luxury-price category), and the skyrocketing sales of frozen fruit juices.

Preprepared frozen food items are popular items, but they do not constitute the total of what is considered convenience food. Convenience foods have been defined as "any full or

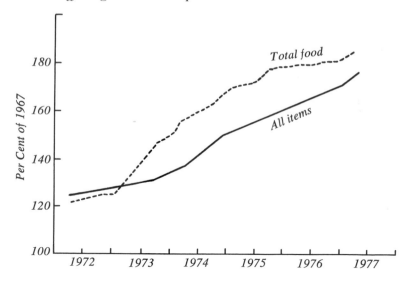

10-1 *Consumer Price Index.*

partially prepared food in which significant preparation, culinary skills, or energy imputs have been transferred from the homemaker's kitchen to the food processor and distributor."[1]

The convenience food items do not always cost more or less than the corresponding unserviced products. It is not easy to make an exact cost comparison of ready-to-serve and homemade products. To do this accurately, the amounts of the ingredients going into the prepared product must be known and their cost compared with the cost of the ingredients used in the home recipes. Also, the cost of the product varies according to the season of the year. Frozen asparagus will cost less per serving than fresh asparagus in February, but the reverse will be true in April, the peak of the asparagus season. In general, convenience foods do cost more than the unserviced products. The extra services that make the food easy to use must be paid for. Washing, combining, removing waste, standardizing, and packaging products add to the cost of the final product.

A survey of convenience foods shows that out of more than 160 convenience foods studied, about one-third cost less than the similar dishes made from scratch. The study covered June 1974 to July 1975 and was based entirely on food ingredients' costs. Cost comparisons of some selected home-prepared or fresh food items with their less expensive convenience counterparts taken from the study are shown in Table 10-1.

Not all consumers, however, place the same value on prepared or partially prepared foods. There is still a hard core of homemakers who prefer the traditional methods of preparing food. Making cakes and pies in the traditional manner often provides personal and family satisfaction. But, for the most part, consumers place a higher value on time and are willing to pay the added cost for this gain in time. In a study of the diets of preschool children, Metheny[2] reported the reasons most frequently given for use of convenience food: (1) the convenience food was less expensive than a similar one made in the traditional fashion, (2) the convenience food yielded a more acceptable product than the one made by the homemaker, and (3) the use of convenience foods resulted in a saving of time and energy. The last reason was the one most frequently given. The situation may change in the next couple of years if the price of food does not stabilize. A return to traditional cookery regardless of additional time spent in preparation may be one way to keep food costs down. This would be especially true for families having to spend a large portion of their income on food.

[1] "Convenience Foods—1975 Cost Update," Economic Research Service and Agricultural Research Service (Washington, D.C.: U.S. Department of Agriculture, 1975).

[2] N. Metheny et al., "The Diets of Preschool Children," *J. Home Econ.* **54**:297, 1962.

TABLE 10-1
Cost Comparison of Home-Prepared or Fresh Foods with Convenience
Counterparts, Four-City Average, June 1974–July 1975

| | Costs per Serving (cents) | | | |
Product	Home-Prepared or Fresh	Frozen	Canned	Other
Asparagus spears (2.10)[a]	23.07	20.35	19.52	
Corn, cut (2.90)	12.04	11.10	11.59	
Cranberry sauce (2.40)	7.29		5.88	
Green peas (2.80)	26.77	11.01	11.15	
Lemon juice (1.10)	7.96		5.75	
Lima beans (2.00)	28.67	11.24	14.40	
Orange juice (4.40)	11.90	4.29	6.60	
			6.90[b]	
Pancakes	11.15	36.40		7.11[c]
Pollock, fish sticks	34.02	22.43		
Spinach (1.40)	24.75	10.66	13.02	
Waffles	6.62	18.47		4.03[c]

[a] Weight of serving reported in ounces.
[b] Bottled.
[c] Complete mix.
Source: "Convenience Foods—1975 Cost Update," Economic Research Service Agricultural Research Service (Washington, D.C.: U.S. Department of Agriculture, 1975).

Shared cooking responsibilities in the modern home may make it easier for families to use products that are less expensive and require longer cooking times.

FACTORS AFFECTING THE COST OF FOOD

In the past government publications and agricultural experts have publicized the fact that food in this country was a bargain. However, the strong continuing increase in the cost of food has dispelled the belief that it can continue to be a bargain. Many factors combine to account for the unprecedented inflated food prices.

Wages. Strong forces to unionize farm and food industry workers and the increase in minimum working conditions, wages, and fringe benefits for these workers results in increased food costs. Organized labor groups in agriculture and the food industry are not likely to relinquish their right to bargain and strike for a greater share of the food dollar. Agricultural surpluses may well be curtailed by workers refusing to harvest at the critical time. Retailing labor costs are also very high. Fifty percent of retail store costs are labor costs[3] and here, too, organized labor has been effective in obtaining good salary contracts for their employees. Government reports do not indicate a relief from increased food costs.

New Food Products. New and improved food products are a vital part of the food retailing industry. They offer the retailer an opportunity to interest the buyer in something new and different. Increasing sales through the introduction of new and improved products is expensive. They require extensive promotional campaigns and a high proportion of new product offerings do not succeed. That is, they do not get the sales volume to pay their way and must be dropped from the market. Yet the introduction of new products in the food industry is believed to be essential to the industry. The goal of the food manufacturer and retailer in displaying new sizes, varieties, and packages of a food product is to stimulate impulse buying. The food industry is highly competitive and continually markets new and better food product items in order to

[3] Jean Mayer, *U.S. Nutrition Policies in the Seventies* (San Francisco: Freeman, 1973), p. 129.

71

keep their market position. The acceptance and rejection of new products by the retail food manager, the provision of storage and shelf space, the necessary instruction of sales personnel and product promotion all add to the final cost of food.

Consumer Movements. Consumer interest groups have been successful in spearheading programs for nutritional labeling, dating, and unit pricing on food items. Public interest has stimulated the Food and Drug Administration to propose that the drained weight of canned fruits and vegetables be declared on labels. These consumer benefits are important and necessary; however, the extra costs that result will be passed on to the buyer. The initial extra costs of improved labeling and food product pricing will over a period of time result in more economic alternatives in buying and savings of money. The recent policy of innovative food companies to employ consumer specialists will hopefully result in new food retailing policies designed to save the consumer money.

Unit Pricing. Unit pricing gives the cost of a product by the pound, quart, or standard numerical count as well as by the package. The purpose is to allow instantaneous price comparisons among similar products. This can be helpful to a consumer who is confused about which product is the most economical. Merchandising practices often make it difficult for the consumer to evaluate the difference between the various sizes and shapes of a particular product. Current practices, such as fractional quantity units, slackfill, and multiple pricing (five for 99 cents), may add further to the confusion. For example, an 8-oz can of string beans sells for 29 cents, a 14½-oz can for 48 cents, and a 16-oz can for 59 cents. Which is the best buy? In this instance the middle size is the most economical, but it was quite confusing to arrive at this conclusion. Many consumers mistakenly believe that the largest size is always the cheapest. Often consumers do not have the time or perhaps the ability to figure the price per ounce, pint, or pound. Unit pricing allows them to rapidly compare prices without the aid of a calculator. Yet unit pricing compares products strictly on quantity, disregarding quality, an important factor in food selection.

Several national chain stores have voluntarily unit-priced their products. Surveys have shown that 63 percent of the customers were unaware of its existence and that only 5 percent had changed their purchasing habits as a result. It has been estimated that unit pricing will cost one-tenth of 1% of gross sales or roughly 10% of net profit.[4] The food industry has questioned if these consumer benefits are worth the extra costs, which must eventually be passed on to the consumer.

Universal Product Code. UPC is a 10-digit numbering system designed to identify nearly all the 10,000 food items sold in a typical supermarket. The symbol is composed of closely spaced lines, bars, and numbers. The first five digits identify the manufacturer and the last five digits are the food item code. By changing bar width and the spaces between bars, a system user can accommodate the variations needed to identify the product and its size.

The UPC provides a standard labeling language that can be read by an electronic scanner (See Fig. 10–2). When a product is passed over the scanner, a laser beam reads the code, which is transmitted to the computer, which then flashes the price on the register.

The food industry believes that use of UPC code by retail food stores will increase productivity and eliminate over- and under-rings, resulting in dollar savings. By using the computerized checkout system the checker will be able to handle more customers in a given period of time. This system provides the retailer with a fast inventory method that is exact and up to the minute.

There is much consumer opposition to the UPC being used in the food industry. Food retailers claim that unless item pricing is eliminated, the computerized system would not be a cost savings to them. It is unlikely that the shopper would be willing to have item pricing eliminated, since for most consumers it is the only sure way of comparing prices. Also, it would be difficult for the consumer to keep track of the current price if the posted price was difficult to read or removed from the shelf. The consumer

---

[4] "Unit Pricing Chalks Up Some Surprises," *Business Week* **2148**:80–81, 1970.

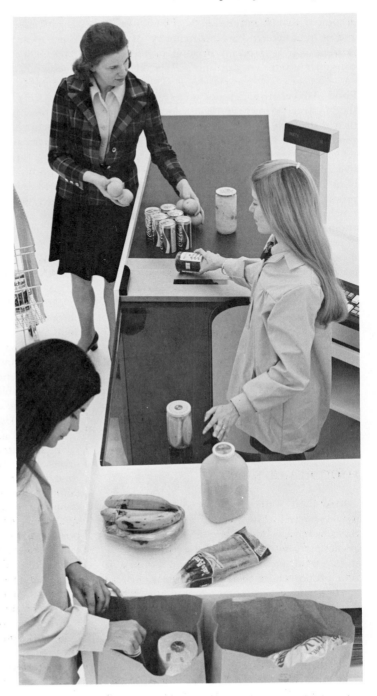

10-2 *To register an item, a checker merely places the UPC symbol face down and pulls the package across the scanning window located at the end of the checkstand. The system then automatically decodes the symbol and shows the item's name and price on the terminal's display panel. It also prints a customer receipt with the name or description and price of each item. (Courtesy International Business Machines Corp., White Plains, New York)*

argument against the use of the UPC is strong and it is unlikely that the majority of food retailers will become involved in its use until consumer groups respond more favorably.

Food Advertising. Heavy advertising in the food industry is costly (1.1% of sales), and much of it is directed toward children's food, dietary products, and health foods. These are areas in which the viewer is easily influenced by persuasive advertising. Often the homemaker's emotions are evoked by the exaggerated claim of a product's effect on family health. Although much food advertising is blatantly exaggerated and irritating to many people, constant showing of a food item reinforces its recognition and desirability, especially with children. Advertising in the form of trading stamps, games of chance, and prizes must be included in those extras that add to the cost of food. Although trading stamps have lost some of their popularity, they have been replaced with promotion sales that offer merchandise at reduced prices if the sale slip reaches a certain level. Redemption of advertised food coupons is a very real part of the food retail system today. Many consumers depend on them to stretch their food money. Once again, it is difficult to determine the real cost of the food coupon program.

FOOD RETAIL STORES

Most food in this country is sold through the *supermarket,* which is defined as a retail store, chain or independent, doing $500,000 or more in sales per year. Small retail food stores still play an important part in the retail food industry. A large proportion of these food stores are located in rural and urban ethnic communities which have a demand for unusual ethnic specialties. These stores also serve a local population that may be without transportation to the larger supermarket or without the price of purchasing more than one meal's or one day's food.

A store that stocks a large volume of mixed merchandise is classified as a supermarket. A supermarket features self-service, low prices, mass merchandising, and the policy of cash and carry. To survive in this highly competitive field, the supermarket must promote, shelve, and sell, in addition to basic food items, health and

beauty aids, garden supplies, and kitchen utensils. Since most supermarkets must stock from 8,000 to 10,000 items to keep in the race, the introduction of as many as five to eight new products each week presents a serious problem in shelf space. Since 80% of new products are unsuccessful, a new product is chosen for its ability to be profitable rather than for any nutritive value.

Supermarkets operating efficiently must assume a large responsibility for the sanitation conditions under which food is stored and shelved. Installation and maintenance of modern refrigeration and freezer storage space is a vital part of the overhead cost of the supermarket.

AGRICULTURE AND TRANSPORTATION

Americans are accustomed to a market that shows a large variety as well as an abundance of food. The excellent food productivity of the agriculture sector of the country gives the consumer the leeway to let his appetite and personal food preferences direct his food choices. Our highly desirable ability to choose does not always ensure the selection of nutritious foods but it does create less monotony in meals.

Improved agricultural methods have increased farm production so that fewer farms now feed a great many more people. A steady supply of food is assured in almost every section of the country. Foods not grown in one part of the country are transported from another section by rail, truck, or plane. Modern modes of transportation also enable the consumer to find certain seasonal food items in the local market most of the year. For example, the large supplies of oranges available in the New York area in the fall and winter are from Florida, but most of the oranges on the market during the late spring and summer are from California.

New design in transport equipment has been effective in reducing damage to food in transit. Today, trailers are built that have the refrigeration capacity to provide the proper temperatures for many kinds of fresh, frozen, and canned foods. For example, the trucks specially built to carry frozen foods now circulate air through the load to remove environmental and respiratory heat. Older designs only permitted circulation of air around the load. Air scoops have been developed that bring more outside air into piggy-back trailers, providing a good method of cooling products by ventilation instead of refrigeration.

New types of containers and better loading patterns have also reduced waste and damage for many products shipped in bags, boxes, and cartons. Boxes and crates are now packed into a trailer or van container and moved from departure point to destination as one load. The modern term for transferring a whole trailer container to a railroad car is "piggy-back." "Fishy-back" and "birdie-back" are terms used to indicate sea–land and air–land transportation of cargo.

Rapid mechanization of major food crops in the country brings added supplies to the retail market. The California tomato crop, for example, has had a changeover from hand harvesting to mechanical picking. Since the machines cut and shake the plants near the ground, plant breeders had to develop a plant of a bushy rather than a viney type and of the kind that matures at approximately the same time. The fruits are moderate in size and bruise-resistant. Elevated platforms, vacuum devices that suck the fruit from the tree, and shaking devices with catch frames positioned below to catch the loosened fruit are labor-saving devices profitable to the fruit-picking industry. Improved handling and keeping methods such as the quick cooling of cherries in cold water to minimize bruising are part of modern harvesting.

SEASONALITY

Buying food when it is in season is still practical for most people. However, seasonality in food is less pronounced now than in the past. Years ago families had to use up immediately or preserve for out-of-season use fresh foods in good supply. Hence, plentiful supplies of fruits and vegetables were canned, pickled, and made into jams, jellies, and preserves for the winter. Other food groups were processed and stored in a manner that would preserve their characteristic qualities most effectively. Poultry was canned, meats were salted and smoked or made into sausage and scrapple, and eggs were put down in water glass (sodium silicate).

Many of these practices exist today, but changes have been made as a result of improve-ments in the management of the food supply. For example, broilers are now produced in this country throughout the year, and although there is still a heavier supply in the summer and fall, the production rate does not greatly decline during the winter months. Season does affect price. Foods in season are usually less expensive than when there is a light supply. Most homemakers today are alerted to peak market supplies of food by local TV and radio programs, newspapers, and cooperative extension materials.

"ORGANIC" FOODS

Many people are showing an interest in eating only those foods considered to be organically grown or "natural" foods. Organically grown food is food that has been grown without the use of pesticides or artificial fertilizers and which has been grown in soil that has been treated only with organic matter. Organically processed food is food that has been organically grown and has not had any preservatives, hormones, antibiotics, or synthetic additives of any kind used in its processing. Organic materials used to enrich soil for organically grown food include animal manures, plant compost, and peat moss. Organically raised animals are fed on organically grown pasture and feed.

"Natural" foods are available to the consumer without any alteration to their natural state. Fresh foods are natural foods, but canned and frozen foods are not considered "natural." Natural foods may or may not be grown organically, and while there is no evidence that organically grown food is higher in nutritive value than regular food, it is considerably more expensive to the consumer. Many supermarkets carry "natural" foods to supply the growing demand for it, but marketing costs for organic foods are high and the consumer who wants only the "natural" food pays at least twice as much for it than for its regular counterpart. The trend toward eating natural foods has some positive aspects. For one, whole-grain cereals have become somewhat more popular than they have been, and these products rather than the highly milled cereals may become the preferred form of cereal products. Shoppers who choose to use only organically grown food or natural foods must be sure they are buying food that is what it is claimed to be by the seller and that the extra money spent does not prevent the purchase of a variety of foods necessary for a well-balanced diet.

SUMMARY

The desire for more and more processed and convenience foods coupled with a constant search for new convenience foods highlights the changes in consumer food demands and practices of the past two decades. Convenience foods include canned foods, frozen foods, ready-to-bake products, completely baked products, dehydrated soups and potatoes, baby food in jars and cans, complete meals, packaged cake mixes, hot bread and pudding mixes, ready-to-eat and partially cooked cereals, and many others.

Costs of convenience foods are not necessarily more—or less—than those of unserviced products, but true comparative costs sometimes are difficult to obtain. Time of preparation most often is less.

The cost of food is affected by increases in wages to workers in agriculture and food retail-

ing and to the promotion of new products and heavy advertising of all food items. Food prices are also increased by consumer benefits such as unit pricing and improved labeling. Modern transportation has widened the selection of available food (Fig. 10-3), and the many foods displayed in modern supermarkets have not only influenced buyers to comparison-shop, but have also increased the demand for high-quality foods.

QUESTIONS AND TOPICS FOR DISCUSSION AND STUDY

1. Select a supermarket for study. Revisit the store, if possible. Study and make observations that will help you answer the following questions: (a) How does the organization of the store affect the consumer's interest in purchasing food? (b) How many different kinds of cake mix are carried on the shelves? Do the numbers and kinds of mixes change?
2. Select several food items (such as a fruit, a vegetable, and milk) and compare the cost of the fresh, frozen, canned, and dried forms of

10-3 *On the packing van, the lettuce is wrapped with shrink film, boxed, and dropped off for another truck to pick up and take to the shed. (Courtesy of U.S. Department of Agriculture)*

each item on a per-ounce-of-edible-food basis.

3. Not all convenience foods "catch on." Discuss the factors you think are important in determining which convenience foods will last.
4. Why may a convenience food, such as frozen strawberries, prove to be a good buy for one consumer and a poor buy for another?

REFERENCES

BOOKS

Borden, N. *Acceptance of New Food Products by Supermarkets.* Boston: Harvard University, 1968, Chap. 1.

Consumers All: The Yearbook of Agriculture. Washington, D.C.: U.S. Department of Agriculture, 1965.

Food for Us All: The Yearbook of Agriculture. Washington, D.C.: U.S. Department of Agriculture, 1969.

Protecting Our Food: The Yearbook of Agriculture. Washington, D.C.: U.S. Department of Agriculture, 1966.

Lowenberg, M, *Food and Man.* New York: Wiley, 1968, Chap.4.

Mayer, Jean, *U.S. Nutrition Policies in the Seventies.* San Francisco: Freeman, 1973, Chaps. 9, 10.

Shopper's Guide: The Yearbook of Agriculture Washington, D.C.: U.S. Department of Agriculture, 1974.

ARTICLES AND BULLETINS

Boyd, Jacque. "Food Labeling and the Marketing of Nutrition." *J. Home Econ.* **65:**20, 1973.

Harp, H. H., and D. F. Dunhand. "Comparative Costs to Consumers of Convenience Foods and Home-Prepared Foods." *Marketing Research Report 609.* Washington, D.C.: U.S. Department of Agriculture, 1963.

Lamkin, Glenna, Mary Louise Hielscher, and Helene B. Jones. "Food Purchasing Practices of Young Families." *J. Home Econ.* **62:**598, 1970.

"Marketing and Transportation Situation." *Economic Research Service.* Washington, D.C.: U.S. Department of Agriculture, November 1967.

"Meat, Fish, Poultry and Cheese: Home Preparation Time, Yield, and Composition of Various Market Forms." *Home Economics Research Report 30.* Washington, D.C.: U.S. Department of Agriculture, 1965.

Williams, Flora, and Catherine Justice. "A Ready Reckoner of Protein Costs," *J. Home Econ.* **67:**20, 1975.

Food Evaluation

CHAPTER 11

SENSORY TESTS

The quality of food is of prime importance in determining consumer acceptance. Sensory or *organoleptic* tests have been developed by the food industry to measure the parameters of food quality. These tests can be classified into three groups: those that are designed to reflect consumer preferences; those that are intended to investigate the influence of factors in production; and those that are designed to maintain the quality of a product at a given standard. The consumer-preference test is considerably different from the other two, which are similar in that they employ the services of persons suitably trained for taste sampling the product under investigation.

Tests designed to give insight into consumer preferences help the producer to discover which qualities of the product need to be developed and emphasized. When a panel is chosen for this type of testing, an attempt is made to obtain a cross section of all potential consumers. Consumer-preference panels may consist of several hundred persons, and the products are tested under ordinary conditions of use. The results are considered to represent the tastes of a significant portion of the population and are used to predict market outlook for a product.

Another type of panel is made up of selected individuals who have demonstrated their ability to distinguish among degrees of difference in flavor (Fig. 11-1). The members of this type of panel are not required to be expert tasters of the product under investigation; their highly developed ability to identify different tastes in similar products is the key quality desired. A quality score is not given by this panel; rather its purpose is to determine whether a given variation in processing has altered the quality or the flavor of the product. It is also used to test the effects of storage and packaging on two items originally alike but subjected to different storage environments.

A third type of panel—a quality-taste panel—is made up of persons who have high ability to detect off-quality in a specific food or food product. Members of such a panel are usually trained to recognize and to evaluate the standard flavors of a food so that they can use their powers of discrimination consistently. A quality-taste panel may be used to detect incipient rancidity in fats and butter. Persons serving on the panel can be trained to increase their

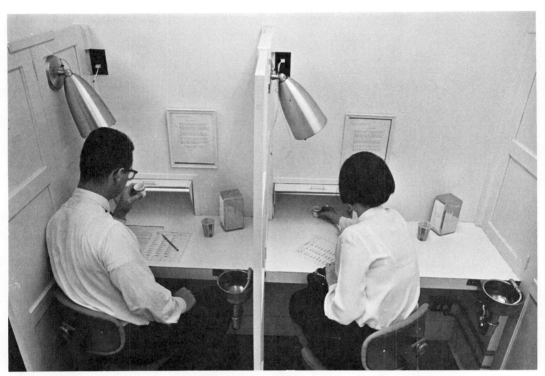

11-1 *Two employees of the U.S. Department of Agriculture demonstrate the workings of a sensory evaluation study of a new food product. Participants in such a "taste test" rate foods on a nine-point scale running from "like extremely" to "dislike extremely." (Courtesy of U.S. Department of Agriculture)*

ability to detect very slight differences among samples. Tasters usually work only when they are rested and free from colds. Also, it is believed that smoking 2 or 3 hours before tasting samples will alter the ability to identify differences.

In testing a product, a panel will make use of one or perhaps more of the standard tests used for food-testing purposes. These are classified as *direct-difference tests* and *scoring tests*. The direct-difference test is a triangular test in which three samples—two of which are identical—are presented to the subject. The taster is asked to identify the identical samples and then to express a preference for either the pair or the single sample.

The two-sample test is also used. It is the simplest of the preference tests but has a fifty-fifty chance of being wrong. In the two-sample test, the tester identifies the sample he considers to be most like the standard product.

Scoring tests also are employed by panels to

rate a given food. Two or more products may be rated for some quality by judges who assign a relative numerical score to that quality. There are a number of such scales in use, some with intervals ranging from 0 to 20 points.

The *flavor-profile method* is used to describe the intensity of the detectable qualities of taste, aroma, and texture as they occur in the food. The application of this test to a product may point up some of the desirable and undesirable features of flavor, aroma, or texture to be noted. This technique is used, for example, in the evaluation of a soluble coffee (Fig. 11-2). Using a standard brew as a reference sample, comparative evaluations of various brands of soluble coffee are made which enable a producer to set standards for quality control.

These tests, though frequently used to assist in prejudging a product's general acceptability to the consumer, cannot be considered to have a high level of reliability in reflecting the response

11-2 *One of the final steps in the processing of coffee is the taste test for quality. (Courtesy of the Pan American Coffee Bureau)*

of a large percentage of the potential consumers. It has been difficult to rule out the human factors of prejudice and preference in the individual panel members. The methods in use, however, provide valuable information about what makes a product acceptable and reveal weaknesses in the quality of a given product.

OBJECTIVE TESTS

In addition to sensory tests, objective tests have been developed for food evaluation. Most of the tests in use have been designed to measure texture and color characteristics of a food (Table 11-1). Objective methods are useful in evaluating food because they can be reproduced with precision, are less subjective than sensory evaluations, and may cost less if the instrument used is

fairly simple. Food investigators agree that the objective test used to measure a food quality should correlate with the results of the sensory panel to ensure consumer acceptance.

Chemical Tests. Specific chemical tests such as those which measure nutrient loss, products of food decomposition, and adulterants in food are standardized. (See Fig. 11-3.) These are published by professional groups such as the American Association of Cereal Chemists and the Association of Official Agricultural Chemists.

Physical Tests and Instruments. A number of instruments have been designed to measure the color and texture of food. The tenderness of meat, fish, poultry, baked products, fruits and vegetables, and jelled products is an important quality for consumer acceptability. Tenderness

11-3 *A U.S. Department of Agriculture chemist distills butter oil for separation of flavor components in the fatty part of whole milk. (Courtesy of U.S. Department of Agriculture)*

of meat is a prime concern and a number of instruments have been designed to identify this quality.

The color of food is measured to identify such qualities as freshness and maturity. A number of objective instruments are designed to measure color in food.

COLOR IN FOOD

The color of food is highly important in its appeal. For most individuals, each food has a distinctive color by which it is identified and evaluated.

Natural Colors. The color of a food may be caused by naturally occuring pigments in the plant or animal tissues. The main pigments of plants (fruits and vegetables) are classified as carotenoids, chlorophylls, anthocyanins, and anthoxanthins.

The group of pigments known as the *carotenoids* are abundantly dispersed throughout the plant world. They range from yellow to orange-red and are fat-soluble. Most of the pigments are found in the *plastids,* which are bodies occurring in the protoplasm of the cell. The carotenoids are present in green leaves, but their color is masked by the green of the chlorophyll. They may be identified in a wide variety of fruits and vegetables, such as tomatoes, sweet potatoes, carrots, squash, peaches, apricots, banana skins, peppers, and turnips. Plant carotenoids, when ingested by animals, are converted into vitamin A.

The carotenoid pigments include the lycopene of tomatoes, the carotene of carrots, the cryptox-

81

TABLE 11-1
Some Commonly Used Instruments for Tests of Tenderness and Color

Tenderness	Use
Warner–Bratzler shear	A shearing device to measure the tenderness of meat
Armour Meat Tenderometer	A probe with needles attached in two rows, which is connected to a force indicator. Measures the force used to penetrate the meat
Bailey Shortometer	An instrument that measures the force required for a bar attached to a motor to break a sample. Used for pastry, cookies, and crackers
Universal Pentrometer	A probe with a cone or needle attached. Measures the distance of penetration of food in a given period of time. Used to measure the firmness of custards, jells, cheese, fats, fruits, and vegetables
Color	Use
Spectrophotometer	Color is identified by wavelength, purity, and lightness. Used for all foods
Hunter Color and Difference Meter	Measures the value, hue, and saturation of a color. Used for all foods
Munsell Discs	Interlocking spinning color discs are connected to a motor and lamp. Hue, chroma, and value are measured. Used for all foods.
Colored chips or colored glass	Used for grading such foods as maple syrup

anthin of corn, the xanthophylls of oranges, and the capsanthin of red peppers or chilies.

Chlorophylls are widely distributed in nature. These are the green pigments of leaves and stems of plants found in the small bodies known as *chloroplasts,* located close to the cell walls of the plant tissue. The chlorophylls are of prime importance because of their key role in the process of photosynthesis. All green vegetables and some fruits contain this pigment.

Many plants contain red, blue, and violet pigments. These belong to a group of pigments known as *anthocyanins.* Most of the anthocyanins are soluble in water. Red cabbage, apple and grape skins, red plums, blueberries, sweet cherries, and raspberries are examples of vegetables and fruits containing these pigments.

The purplish-red color of beets was once thought to be due to anthocyanins, but another pigment, betaine has been isolated. Betaine acts in much the same manner as anthocyanin except that it is not as affected by acid.

Anthoxanthins are groups of pigments com-posed of flavones, flavenols, and flavonones. These are yellow-to-white pigments, usually dissolved in the cell sap of the plant tissue. They occur mainly in fruits and vegetables. Meat has only one principal color pigment, myoglobin, which imparts its red color. Hemoglobin is also present in meat tissue in lesser amounts. Myoglobin and hemoglobin are purplish but turn a bright red when the surface of cut meat is exposed to oxygen, forming oxymyoglobin and oxyhemoglobin.

COLOR CHANGES DURING COOKING OR PROCESSING

When subjected to high cooking or processing temperatures, most foods change color (Table 11-2). In some instances, such as in baking, the color changes are highly desirable and are essential for general acceptance of the product. On the other hand, a color change such as that occuring during the prolonged cooking of cabbage may be undesirable. The object in cooking food is to maximize its desirable color qualities through proper handling and treatment.

The pH of the water in which it is cooked will have some bearing on the color of the food. White foods—such as rice, potatoes, cauliflower, and onions—develop a yellow cast when cooked in alkaline waters. The addition of a small amount of cream of tartar (an acid) will prevent the occurrence of this color change.

Chlorophylls, the green pigments of leaves and stems, are unstable in the presence of heat. When green vegetables are cooked for a considerable length of time, the chlorophyll changes to olive-green and then to an unpleasant brown. The reason for this is that chlorophyll has a magnesium atom in its structure which, in the presence of mild acids, such as acetic and oxalic, is replaced with two atoms of hydrogen. The compounds formed during this change are called *pheophytins*. The chlorophyll in plant tissues are classified as chlorophyll a and chlorophyll b. *Chlorophyll a* is bright blue-green in color and is the predominate color of the two. *Chlorophyll b* is yellow-green in color. When the magnesium is lost from the chlorophyll molecule, chlorophyll a changes to pheophytin a and chlorophyll b changes to pheophytin b. The former is a grayish green and the latter a dull yellowish green.

The color changes that take place when chlorophyll converts to pheophytin are not reversible. In the presence of an alkaline medium, the original green color of the vegetable is retained. It would seem that the solution to the color problem in green vegetables could be solved by the use of an alkali in the cooking medium.[1] But the deleterious effects of the alkali on the cellulose content and on the nutritive value of the plant tissue justify not recommending its use. In a highly alkaline medium, the cellulose of the cell wall breaks down, rendering the texture soft and mushy. The nutritive value is destroyed because ascorbic acid and thiamine are unstable when subjected to heat in the presence of alkalies. When alkaline compounds such as sodium bicarbonate are added to cooking waters, the rate of destruction is increased.

[1]Evelyn Halliday and Isabel Nobel, *Hows and Whys of Cooking* (Chicago: University of Chicago Press, 1946), p. 5.

TABLE 11-2
Major Color Factors in Foods

Color Factor	Color	Effect of:				
		Acid	Base	Heat	Oxygen	Metals
Anthocyanin	Red, Blue	Red	Blue	a	a	Iron, aluminum, and tin— blue, green, purple
Anthoxanthin	Clear, white, yellow	Clear, white	Yellow	Pink if prolonged	a	Tin, aluminum, iron—bright yellow, brown
Carotenoids	Yellow, orange	a	a	Darken if prolonged	a	a
Chlorophyll	Green	Olive green	Bright green	Olive green	a	Copper, zinc— bright green
Myoglobin	Red	a	a	Brown	Bright red, purplish red if prolonged	a
Tannin	Clear, white, brown	a	a	Pink	Brown	Iron—blue, black

[a]No significant effect.

Much effort has been expended to find ways to preserve the green color in canned green vegetables without loss of their firm texture. For canned peas, it has been found that when the cooking medium is maintained at a fairly high alkaline level, softening effects may be counteracted by the addition of calcium ions added in the form of calcium hydroxide and calcium pectate. The calcium salts react with the pectic substances in the cell walls of the plant tissue to form a tough material.

The anthocyanins provide the red, blue, and violet pigments that occur in plant tissue. Fruits and vegetables that contain the anthocyanins may undergo color degradation when heated. The red pigments are very soluble in water, and because there is great leaching out of the pigments into the cooking water, the surrounding juices are always red. Canned raspberries, blueberries, and plums illustrate this. If too much of the pigment is lost in the cooking water, the cooked fruit or vegetable may lack color. The red color pigment is greatly affected by a change from an acid to an alkaline cooking medium. If the juice or the cooking medium of a fruit or vegetable becomes alkaline, a blue or a bluish-green color will form. The change is reversible to a degree, however, and with the addition of a small amount of acid the food will revert to its red color. For example, red cabbage is cooked with acids such as vinegar, lemon juice or tart apples to keep the bright red color.

In the canning of foods containing red pigments, the action of anthocyanins in forming salts with metal ions has great significance. If tin (actually tin-coated iron) cans are used for canning, they are lacquered to prevent the food from coming into contact with the sides of the can. There are also instances in home cookery when a combination of the pigment and iron salt may take place, forming discoloration. Tin pie pans that have rusted may cause colored fruit fillings, such as blueberry, raspberry, and strawberry, to discolor.

The anthoxanthins are the white-to-yellow pigments found in cauliflower, onion, turnips, salsify, and parsnips. They will also change colors according to the pH of the surrounding medium. If cooked in a slightly acid medium, the vegetable will stay a clear-to-white color. A few drops of lemon juice or vinegar toward the end of cooking will help keep cauliflower snow white. Another method to create an acid medium is to keep the lid on while cooking, which will seal in the organic acids. However, in foods of the cabbage family, such as cauliflower, this also seals in the undesirable strong flavors. If the anthoxanthins are cooked in an alkaline medium or tap water contaminated with detergent residue, the food color will change to yellow.

Anthoxanthins are structurally related to anthocyanins. For this reason, if anthoxanthin-containing foods are cooked for excessive periods of time, they will change to anthocyanin. This accounts for the pink color of overcooked cabbage.

Metals will react with the anthoxanthins. Tin and aluminum will cause the food to turn a bright yellow color. This is illustrated by the bright yellow cooking water produced when onions are cooked in an aluminum pan. Anthoxanthins will also react with iron to form a reddish color. Onions fried in an iron frying pan will have this characteristic color.

Color changes take place in meat when heat is applied. When meat is cooked, its color changes from red to pink to brown or gray. If meat is exposed to oxygen for a prolonged period of time, the oxymyoglobin will turn a purplish-red owing to the formation of metmyoglobin. This is evident in fresh hamburger, which is usually bright red on the outside but purplish-red in the middle. Cooking the meat will result in a grayish-brown color, caused by denaturization of the protein with the formation of denatured globin hemichrome. Thus, color is an index to how long the meat has cooked. A steak cooked briefly will be brown on the outside where heat has penetrated but still red in the middle.

When meat is cured, it takes on a pink or light red color that remains fixed. This color is developed when the nitrates and nitrites are added to the cure. It is believed that when the myoglobin comes in contact with the nitrite, it is changed to an unstable pink pigment, nitrosomyoglobin; but, when the meat is heated, the red color develops, which is nitrosohemochrome.

Loss of color in processed foods through prolonged storage has long been a concern of the food industry. Whittenberger and Hill[2] identi-

[2] R. T. Whittenberger and C. H. Hill, "How to Safeguard the Redness of Stored Canned Cherries," *Food Eng.* **28**:53, 1956.

fied color loss in canned red cherries with high storage temperatures. Cherries held at a 75°F (24°C) storage temperature had serious color loss after 6 months. By comparison, canned cherries stored at temperatures close to 35°F (1°C) were still attractive after 1 year of storage.

Another color change of great importance in cookery is that occurring when sugar caramelizes. Sugars will turn a dark brown when heated to relatively high temperatures. Extensive use is made of this property in the preparation of certain kinds of candy and sugar products.

Color changes in chocolate cake and gingerbread may well fit into this discussion. As the alkalinity of a chocolate cake is increased through the addition of soda or through the use of a Dutch-processed cocoa, the red color increases. There are also flavor and texture changes. Gingerbreads are darker in color when soda is used as the chief leavening agent.

BROWNING REACTIONS

Enzymatic Browning. When certain fruits and vegetables are cut or bruised, the tissue exposed to the air quickly darkens. Exactly what happens is not known. The reaction occurs in a number of steps. In general, when the exposed tissue of the bruised fruit or vegetable is exposed to oxygen, phenolic enzymes (phenolases) bring about oxidation of the phenols in the food and brown- or gray-black pigments called *melanines* are formed. Phenolases are found in many plants, with especially high amounts in potatoes, mushrooms, apples, peaches, bananas, avocados, and tea leaves. The browning that occurs in the tea leaves is beneficial, since it imparts their characteristic color.

There are several methods used to deter this browning reaction. Antioxidants such as ascorbic acid have proved to be an effective control for enzymatic browning. Citrus fruits are often added to cut food because of the citric and ascorbic acid that they contain.

Sulfur dioxide is a chemical commonly used to prevent the darkening of foods. Pineapple juice may be used due to its sulfur compounds. Dried fruits such as apricots which might turn an unappetizing brown are routinely dipped in sulfur dioxide as a processing aid to prevent color changes.

Another method for preventing color changes is to reduce contact with oxygen. This is done by coating fruits with sugar or immersing them in sugar solutions. If fruits are just soaked in water, they become very mushy. Sugar or salt solutions are necessary due to their osmotic effect.

Blanching is also an effective means of controlling browning. Rapidly heating foods by dipping briefly in boiling water will destroy or denature the phenolase enzymes responsible for the reaction with the tannins. This allows frozen foods to retain their color for a longer period of time.

Nonenzymatic Browning (The Maillard Reaction). Many cut processed foods are affected by a nonenzymatic discoloration sometimes referred to as the *Maillard reaction,* named after the man who described its occurrence. As a result of this action, foods develop a dark yellow to reddish-brown color. In some foods, such as ready-to-eat cereals, syrups, and crisp fried foods, this action leads to a golden brown color and a flavor that is highly desirable. But in other instances it presents a major problem in that it produces an off-color that may be highly objectionable, as well as off-flavors in dried eggs and dried milk.

The browning reaction occurs through an interrelationship of carbohydrates and protein. The acid–alkaline balance of the food, its moisture content, and the temperature are other factors that affect the reaction. In the case of most processed food, there is a reaction between an amino acid (protein) and a sugar (carbohydrate) when the product is exposed to high temperatures for any length of time and during the storage period. It is evident from results of studies[3] that the rate of browning is increased as the temperature goes up and, as there is an increase in the alkalinity of a food product, there is a corresponding rise in browning.

TANNINS AND COLOR

The fact that tannins give a blue-black color with ferric salts explains their use in ink and also

[3] H. M. Barnes et al., "Industrial Aspects of Browning Reaction," *Ind. Eng. Chem.* **39**:1167, 1947; A. H. Mohamed et al., "The Browning Reactions of Proteins with Glucose," *Archives Biochem.* **24**:127, 1949.

explains some of the common discolorations that occur in such canned foods as beets and certain fruits.

It is believed that tannins of food are chemical derivatives of the flavone pigments. They are present in nuts, apples, peaches, grapes, and pears, as well as in a number of other fruits and vegetables. Tea, coffee, and cocoa are also known to contain large amounts of tannins, and when these beverages are prepared with hard water, a precipitate is formed on the surface of the beverage or on the sides of the cup, giving a muddy appearance. Although the chemical reaction that occurs to form the precipitate is not yet known, it is believed to be caused by the reaction of the tannins in tea and coffee with the calcium and magnesium ions present in the water. The compounds formed, referred to as *tannates,* are responsible for the occasional cloudiness of iced tea. Adding an acid such as lemon juice or redissolving the ions by the addition of boiling water will help clear the liquid.

The grayish discolorations sometimes found in chocolate ice cream are thought to be caused by the tannins of the cocoa. Also, the dark spots on canned sweet potatoes and the green color of frosting made with coffee are attributed to the reaction of tannins with iron ions. In the latter case, the iron is believed to be introduced by the egg beater, whereas in the former the source of iron ions is the wall of tin cans.

COLOR AND QUALITY

Color is an important factor in judging the quality of food. Many foods have characteristic colors that are closely identified with certain highly acceptable qualities. For example, the desired color of a peach or apple is that color level which is present when the fruit is at its optimum maturity. Hence, if the color is faded or darkened, the chances are that the product is not at the peak of its freshness or that it has not matured. But color is not always a true evaluation of a product. For example, some mature oranges may lack the characteristic color of the ripe fruit and be rejected on the basis of color alone. Nonetheless, this fruit may be high in flavor and in nutritive value. Margarine is another example of association of color with qual-

ity in food. Before margarine was colored to look as nearly like butter as possible, it was considered an inferior food product. Increased sales of margarine during recent years are in part the result of the control of color that has been in effect.

In a preserved product, faded or darkened color may result from damage during processing or during storage. A frequent cause of color loss during processing is too-high temperature.

Color in tomatoes is a great economic significance; it is, therefore, one of the criteria for grading this food.

In the past, the color of food was graded visually. However, the human eye is subject to fatigue and is influenced by working conditions. Instruments are used that are designed to measure the surface, skin, or juice color of individual tomatoes. The most sensitive of these instruments is the Hunter meter.

Olive oil is another food largely dependent on its color, as well as its taste, for acceptance. The acceptable color range for olive oil is from pale yellow to golden yellow. But lower grades of olive oil may contain sufficient chlorophyll to impart a greenish color to the oil. Similarly, the grading of maple syrup is dependent to a large extent on its color, light amber being preferred to dark amber.

EFFECT OF STORAGE ON COLOR

A major problem in storage has to do with color changes in processed foods. Puréed food products such as apples, beets, carrots, green beans, peaches, and squash have been found to suffer color deterioration on storage. These changes are evidenced by a darkening of the contents that are exposed to the head space. Such darkening is caused by an oxidative reaction that can be prevented by reducing the content of reactive oxygen available in the head space. There is some evidence that high storage temperatures add to the initial pigment loss caused by high cooking temperatures in fruit preserves.

To prevent the color loss that occurs in preserves such as strawberry jam, the strawberry crop is frozen and batches of jam are made throughout the year rather than just when they are in season.

Trace quantities of metals such as iron, copper, and tin that find their way into fruit preserves may also cause a slight increase in the darkening of the preserves.

COLOR ADDED TO FOODS

To win complete acceptance, a food must have a uniform natural color. Because nature does not always provide the ideal color, it is quite common for the food processor to add color to bring the product up to the generally accepted standard. When color is added to food, an effort is usually made to select delicate, appropriate colors that will lend a natural appearance to the product. Unnatural colors in food may be the result of too much artificial color. The ideal color is neither too pale nor too intense. Fruit preserves, cheese, butter, margarine, ice cream, confections, oranges, and potatoes are some of the foods and food products that have added color.

Coloring matters used in food can be grouped into two classes: coal-tar dyes and natural coloring matters. Before a coal-tar dye may be used, it must be tested and certified. Artificial colors are discussed more thoroughly in Chapter 43, where we discuss food additives. In general, these must be of high quality and free from any foreign substances. Also, they must be free from such harmful ingredients as lead and arsenic. With mixtures of the certified colorings, it is possible for a food processor to create any desired shade or tint. The carbonated-beverage and fruit-preserve food industries depend to a large extent on the skillful use of combinations of coal-tar dyes to obtain the colors that closely match the flavor of their product.

The use of natural coloring matters is also well known to the food industry. The following coloring matters of natural origin are used in food products:

Annato: Vegetable dye used for dairy products and for casings for bologna and frankfurters.

Betaine: The active coloring principle in beets. Occasionally used to intensify the color of tomato products, such as tomato sauce, purée, and catsup.

Caramel: Brown product obtained by heating sugar above its melting point, at which time it changes from a white crystalline substance to a stiff brown mass. Soluble in water; gives a reddish-brown tint to a solution. Used as coloring material in carbonated beverages and confections.

Carotene: Widely distributed in nature; frequently encountered as added coloring material in such products as noodles, margarine, and dairy products.

Chlorophyll: Green vegetable dye; used to color such products as chewing gum, candy lozenges, and confections.

Saffron: Vegetable dye consisting of dried petals of a member of the crocus family. Imparts a yellow color to food; used in some meat products.

Turmeric: Yellow vegetable dye made from the rootstock of an herb.

TEXTURE

The texture of food is an important factor affecting its general acceptance.

Texture includes such qualities as toughness, elasticity, gumminess, adhesiveness, stringiness, slicing quality, and crispness. Any deviation from the generally accepted characteristic texture of a particular food may render it unacceptable. Consequently, we reject soft crackers, lumpy cereal, fibrous or stringy vegetables, and gritty butter because their texture qualities are unlike what our experience has taught us to expect them to be. And we prefer crisp french-fried potatoes, smooth candy creams, cakes of velvety grain, flaky piecrusts, and crusty hard rolls. Both objectionable and desirable texture qualities in any food depend, to a large degree, on the nature and proportions of the ingredients, the time and temperature of processing, the manipulation of the basic ingredients, and the time allowed for the setting of the product.

Perception. Little is known about the receptor processes and organs in the mouth that perceive texture. However, a general idea of how perception of the sensations of texture and other mechanical properties of food takes place can be given. Food varies in mechanical properties, from a bland liquid to the hardest nut. Some pleasant texture sensations arise at the very moment the food is ingested. Or uncertainty and revulsion may be felt when food of an indeterminate texture, such as semihard lumps of uncooked starch or uncoagulated egg yolk, is taken into the mouth unexpectedly.

When food is put into the mouth, the central nervous system uses some of the signals it receives at this stage from the taste and smell receptors and the superficial touch, pressure, and temperature organs in the soft tissue to initiate chewing or swallowing. Once biting and chewing start, an immensely complex pattern of stimulation begins. The food is rolled across and "felt" by the gums and the hard and soft palates. It is further broken up by the teeth, and the increased surface area releases taste- and smell-stimulus substances in great quantity. The total effect of these stimuli is to supply the brain with a texture perception of the food. As the food is broken up into smaller pieces, there occurs an almost automatic reduction of the chewing process and the food is swallowed as an almost unconscious act.

Evaluation. The methods used for judging the texture qualities of a food are both subjective and objective. Subjective sensory tests are set up to obtain reactions to the texture of a product. Both consumer-acceptance tests, where a panel chosen as a representative cross section of the public is asked to express an opinion on the relative merits of several samples, and laboratory tests, in which it is decided whether a difference exists among several samples, are used. The laboratory test requires a panel of expert judges, all well trained in analyzing texture.

Some texture qualities can be measured physically. Texture factors that can be satisfactorily measured with instruments are those of volume, crumb firmness, and crumb toughness. Physical measurements have an advantage over organoleptic assessments: they are not affected by factors other than the one being measured and they provide a record so that comparisons can be made over a period of time.

BAKED PRODUCTS. Texture is a factor of utmost importance in the evaluation of baked products. It affects the product's appearance and creates a mouth sensation. With the exception of hard-crust breads—such as the French or Italian varieties, in which coarseness of the crumb is a characteristic feature—the usual preference is for a smooth regular crumb in baked products. The *grain* of a baked product refers to its cell structure and distribution. A product with large specific volume and small cell size usually has thin cell walls, a characteristic generally associated with high palatability.

The visual effect of a baked product is influenced by the size and shape of the cell. Large cells with thick walls reflect less light and give a grayer color than a fine grain with thin walls. In the commercial baking of bread, texture tests are frequently made to evaluate a new formula or a new method of mixing the ingredients. For example, fine elongated cells indicate correct fermentation, whereas round, small, irregular, coarse cells may indicate incorrect fermentation.

Texture in baked products can also be measured (subjectively) by the sensations caused by moving the food over the surface of the tongue and by its resistance or lack of resistance to chewing. Tasting the product in the mouth with the tongue and rolling it around the inside of the mouth will give the feel of the crumb, often called its "silkiness." Resistance to chewing or chewability is used to measure crumb softness or doughiness.

MEAT. In eating meat, one is immediately aware of the relationship between the structure of muscle tissue and its tenderness (see Chapter 24). Meat is made up of a large number of muscle fibers held together by connective tissue. The fibers have a fairly soft texture, but the connective tissue may contribute to toughness and stringiness.

The texture of meat is quickly evaluated after the first bite or two. If the impression is one of biting down hard, it is accompanied by a need to chew the meat a number of times before swallowing it. The general reaction to these perceptions is that the meat is tough.

The texture of meat can be evaluated subjectively by using taste panels or by performing taste-difference tests. There are also a number of popular mechanical devices for objectively measuring the tenderness of meat. These machines are designed to simulate the various actions of the mouth on meat, such as shear, penetration, biting, and chewing.

The Warner–Bratzler apparatus is perhaps the most commonly used to measure the force needed to cut the meat in simple shear, usually across the fibers, and estimates the force necessary to chew the meat.

Penetration instruments are also used to measure the tenderness of meat. One, the Christal Testurometer, is designed with a series of rods $\frac{3}{16}$ in. in diameter, which are pushed into the meat sample. The maximum force or total work required to accomplish this penetration is recorded.

Another objective method used to measure resistance to chewing of meat is the process of simulating biting. Blunt wedges are used to "bite" samples of meat, and the force on the wedges is gradually increased until the wedges meet. The total force required is recorded, together with that required for penetration. Generally, the sample is cut so that the wedges bite across the fibers, as this gives the best correlation between toughness and force needed to "bite" through the sample. An instrument similar to the wedge is the bite tenderometer, which is fitted with mechanically arranged human dentures.

An electrically driven food mincer fitted with an ammeter so that the power can be measured during mincing, has been designed as an apparatus to measure the total power required to bring about a complete breakdown of meat.

Although the texture of fish muscle is tender when fresh, it becomes tough if the fish is frozen; with the passage of time, an even tougher texture will develop. Because the toughening of the fish muscle has an adverse effect on the palatability of the food, any method that is satisfactory in measuring texture changes on a quantitative basis would be highly desirable in this area of food evaluation. Taste panels have found fish texture to be extremely difficult to assess.

FRUITS AND VEGETABLES. Most investigations of the texture of plants have centered on the cell wall itself. This emphasis appears to be sound, for it is that portion of the cell that gives rigidity to the plant. In the edible portions of vegetables and fruits, the cell wall is composed mainly of polysaccharides (cellulose, xylan, araban, galactan, pectic acid, and mannan). Any change in texture occurring during ripening, maturation, or cooking of plant tissues is related to the changes in the amount and properties of the polysaccharides in the cell walls. The approach to measurement depends on the fact that polysaccharides—such as cellulose, the hemicelluloses (xylan, mannan, galactan, and araban), and the pectic substances—are built up from simple hexose and pentose sugars by glucosidic union between sugars. Total hydrolysis reveals the constituent sugars; by the determination of these, it is possible to estimate the amount of the original polysaccharide.

The firmness of some fruits, such as pears, may be measured by a penetrometer (a simple spring-loaded plunger), which is pushed into the pear until penetration occurs. The texture of many plant-tissue cell walls is affected by changes in polysaccharides, and by the part that lignin plays in firming parts of the plant tissue. Lignin combines with a variety of compounds that impart a woody texture to the vegetable. The toughening effect of lignin is evidenced in old bean pods: the fibers are highly lignified and cannot be separated by cooking in boiling water.

VISCOSITY *Viscosity* relates to the consistency of food materials. The resistance of various foods to flow (viscosity) is caused by molecular attraction, and large hydrated molecules have more attraction for each other than small molecules do. The viscosity of food is measured in a number of ways. The speed of free-flowing liquids can be compared with that of water. A Jelemeter, which measures the rate of flow of juice, can be used to measure the pectin content of fruit juice. The Stormer viscosimeter is used in determining the viscosity of foods such as cake and white sauces; it measures the rate of rotation of a cylinder with constant force through a mixture.

The changes in the viscosity of various materials that take place on stirring are regarded as evidence of a change in structure. Lecithin-free chocolate becomes extremely viscous on stirring, but chocolate treated with lecithin shows no viscosity changes. It is believed that this change is caused by the formation of fairly large particles of sugar and, possibly, cocoa.

An interesting aspect of texture that has to do with viscosity is illustrated in food emulsions. The viscosity of mayonnaise is the result of the oil and fat content of the egg yolk in the liquid phase of the emulsion. Flocculation of fat in a food affects its viscosity. For instance, the flocculation of the fat in cream gives it a somewhat plastic consistency that can be increased as the cream is whipped. The consistency of butter and margarine at any temperature is determined by the structure of the fat particles—that is, their size and distribution—but the effect of the food on the palate depends on the size and accessibility of the water droplets. If the liquid phase of the mixture is very finely divided, the water droplets may not be readily available to the surface of the palate, causing the mixture to feel greasy and dry. In butter the droplets are irregular, but in margarine the droplets are more regular and their dispersion is much more uniform.

FLAVOR

Flavor is the total sensory impression formed when food is eaten. It is probably the most important factor motivating food choices. Flavor impressions gained when food is eaten are a combination of the sensations of taste, smell, and texture. These impressions vary to a large extent among different individuals—and even in one individual, certain factors may change the flavor impressions formed by the same food. A notable example of this is the person suffering with a cold, who finds that food has a different taste than it does under normal conditions. Because his olfactory (smell) sense is not reacting, he cannot detect the true taste of food. He may find that food tastes insipid compared to how it tastes when his total taste, smell, and texture perceptions are functioning. The effect of smell on the flavor of food can be easily illustrated by holding one's nose while eating a well-known food.

Taste. Taste sensations originate when taste receptors (taste buds)—a number of cells distributed over the tongue, the soft palate, and the back portions of the epiglottis—are stimulated. A human being has approximately 9,000 to 10,000 taste buds. These die and are replaced about every 7 days. The number of tastebuds decreases with age, so young children and infants have a better ability to taste food than do adults. They do not need highly flavored foods to be acceptable. In middle age, many of the taste buds that die are not regenerated. Thus, there is a decreased sensitivity to taste, which can lead to problems in appetite of older adults. Many adults compensate for lack of sensitivity to subtle flavors by eating highly spiced, salted, or sugared foods.

Taste buds are specialized; each group detects a particular taste sensation. At present, the theory that there are four fundamental taste sensations is generally accepted. These are identified as sour, salty, bitter, and sweet. Although the areas in the mouth in which these tastes are identified overlap, generally the taste buds detecting sour are distributed along the sides of the tongue, those reacting to salt on the sides of the mouth and the tip of the tongue, those reacting to sweet at the tip of the tongue, and those responding to bitter at the back of the tongue. (see Figs. 11-4 and 11-5)

To have taste, a substance must be dissolved in liquid. This may be the liquid content of the foods or the saliva in the eater's mouth. The solution seeps into the taste buds, stimulating the nerve ending around which the taste buds are arranged in the shape of a tiny well. An impulse from the nerve ending is transmitted along the nerve fiber to a specific area of the brain, and the taste is detected. The taste sensation disappears when saliva removes the food substances from the tiny well. Tastes can be detected at a low level of concentration.

The chemical composition of a food is largely responsible for its taste. The ions of salt, such as sodium and lithium, make food taste salty. Other salts, such as potassium, may taste bitter. Sweetness may be imparted chemically to a food through the alcohol hydroxyl groupings found

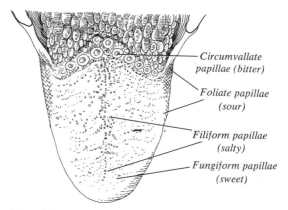

Circumvallate papillae (bitter)

Foliate papillae (sour)

Filiform papillae (salty)

Fungiform papillae (sweet)

11-4 *The upper surface of the tongue has raised elevations called papillae, which contain the four types of taste buds. (Adapted from* The Human Body: Its Structure and Physiology *by Sigmund Grollman, Macmillan, 1964)*

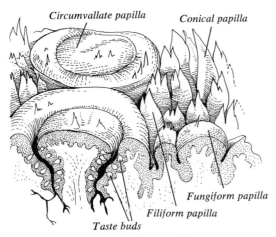

Circumvallate papilla

Conical papilla

Fungiform papilla

Filiform papilla

Taste buds

11-5 *An enlargement of the papillae on the mucous membrane of the tongue shows the location of the taste buds. (Adapted from* The Human Body: Its Structure and Physiology *by Sigmund Grollman, Macmillan, 1964)*

in the saccharides (sugars). Different sugars have varying degrees of sweetness. This is due to the number of hydroxyl groups that are exposed to elicit a sweet sensation. Fructose is the sweetest sugar, then sucrose, glucose, maltose, galactose, and lactose.

Bitterness is caused by alkaline substances, ammonia, and manganese and calcium cations. Caffeine, nicotine, quinine, strychnine, and synthetic sweeteners are also bitter substances. Sourness is caused by the hydrogen ion concentration in the organic acids found in food. Vinegar, citric acid, and tartaric acid are all sour acids. A possible artificial sweetener called "Miracle Fruit" has the ability to make sour foods taste sweet. Lemonade flavored with this substance would not need sugar. It is not understood exactly how it works, but is believed to hinder the stimulative ability of the sour taste buds.

Taste is influenced by factors other than the chemical composition of the substance. Salt and sugar may reduce the sourness of acids to varying degrees. In measuring the taste thresholds for the four primary tastes in water, gel, and foam, Mackey and Valassi[4] concluded that the funda-

mental tastes were detected most easily in liquids and with greatest difficulty in gels.

It is known that sugar can decrease saltiness and that salt can decrease the sweetness of sucrose. It is evident, too, that the eating of sour and sweet foods successively tends to alter the perception of their taste. In a study of the taste interrelationships of different concentrations of sucrose, citric acid, sodium chloride, and caffeine in aqueous solutions, all compounds tested were found to depress the intensity of the others. The most pronounced effect was the reduction of the sweetness of sucrose by citric acid and the reduction of the sourness of citric acid by sucrose.[5] Hence, any fruit eaten after a sweet tends to taste more sour than when eaten after another fruit or any nonsweet food.

It is believed that taste buds do not rapidly experience fatigue, but there is reason to believe that there is a lowering of the taste sensation as one continues to eat a particular food. Common experience verifies the impression that the first bite of food is tastier than the last.

Some people who lack the ability to taste certain compounds are called taste-blind. This is a recessive genetic trait that may affect as much as 25% of the population. The ability to taste can be tested by having individuals taste papers that have been dipped into solutions of different compounds. A common bitter compound used to test this trait is phenylthiocarbamide. People who are taste-blind for this particular substance are unable to detect any taste whatsoever. Just as people have different degrees of musical ability, people also have variations in their taste sensitivity.

Smell. Like taste, smell is a chemical sense. Odor is detected by the olfactory epithelial nerves located in the upper part of the nose. Approximately 16 million odors are detectable by man. When food is taken into the mouth, odorous materials are volatized by body heat and are carried to the olfactory epithelium by the exhaled air. In addition, the odor may reach the nose from the air even before the food is taken into the mouth. It is the size and shape of the odor molecule that stimulates receptor cites

[4] A. O. Mackey and K. Valassi, "The Discernment of Primary Tastes in the Presence of Different Food Textures," *Food Technol.* **10**:238–240, 1956.

[5] Rose Pangborn, "Taste Interrelationships," *Food Technol.* **25**:245, 1960.

in the olfactory nerve endings. When the olfactory nerve endings are stimulated by odorous materials, an odor sensation is transmitted to the brain. The sense of smell is far more acute than the sense of taste, and the olfactory receptors are much more easily fatigued than are the taste receptors. Consequently, the perception of any odor diminishes rather quickly. It is often easy to accustom oneself to an odor in a room and to take little notice of a change in intensity. But although one has become sated with a particular odor, the ability to detect another is not altered.

One frequently used classification of odors is that discussed by Crocker,[6] who gives four fundamental odors: fragrant or sweet, acid or sour, burnt, and caprylic or goaty. Each odor is a composite of these odors. The relative strength of each odor is matched with a scale ranging from 0 to 8. A food having a very strong odor of fragrance, acidity, burning, and caprytic would rate 8888. Having none of these would rate 0000. In actuality, most foods are combinations of odors, such as coffee, which is rated 7683.

Touch. The sense of touch or "mouthfeel" is another component of total flavor sensations. The tactile sense perceives the texture, astringency, and consistency of a food, as well as the accompanying temperature and pain elicited.

Pain is an irritation of the nerve fibers which is pleasurable in small amounts. Hot pepper and chiles are used for the burning or "hot" sensation they evoke. In excessive amounts they become uncomfortable.

The sense of astringency also contributes much to our enjoyment of foods. Foods that are astringent are puckery and make the mouth feel dry and drained. This is due to the percipation of the saliva proteins, which decreases the smooth feeling inside the mouth. Lemonade and apple cider are examples of pleasurable astringent sensations. Graininess, stickiness, and crispness are other qualities that are perceived by the sense of touch. We reject gravy that is lumpy, lollipops that are too sticky, and crackers that are not crisp.

The temperature of food greatly affects our ability to taste subtle flavors. Our sensitivity to

taste is most keen between 68°F (20°C) and 86°F (30°C). At low temperatures, molecules slow down and elicit less response from the receptors. It may be impossible to tell that frozen yogurt has sugar added to it until it is melted, when it tastes much sweeter. High temperatures also decrease taste sensitivity by actually destroying the taste buds, by burning them. Hot fish sticks, for example, may taste very delicate, but they often seem to develop a fishy taste when eaten at room temperature. Our varying sensitivity to taste at different temperatures is probably what governs our serving of certain foods at high temperatures (soups, stews, gravies, coffee, spaghetti sauce) and other foods at low temperatures (ice cream, salads, watermelon, sodas, coleslaw).

FLAVORING MATERIALS

Materials known as condiments, herbs, spices, and flavorings are used to modify, blend, or strengthen natural flavors. The use of these materials in the proper amount and combination may make the difference between a highly palatable food and a drab, tasteless one. A large part of the creative aspect of cookery is the skillful use of flavorings.

Salt. Salt is the material most widely used for the seasoning of food. Commercial salt is a purified product, obtained from salt beds or from underground lakes. It may have an anticaking material added to it and it may be iodized. Because very few people do not use salt, a very small amount of iodine is often added to avoid nutritional deficiencies. There are also a number of salts on the market that have had vegetable flavors, such as garlic, onion, or celery, added to them. Salt substitutes have potassium rather than sodium salts mixed half and half with sodium chloride.

Monosodium Glutamate. Monosodium glutamate has long been used as a flavor intensifier in the Orient, where fermented soybean curd is used to enhance the flavor of food. By 1934 the United States had begun to produce monosodium glutamate from wheat gluten, corn protein, and sugar-beet waste. It is generally believed that pure monosodium glutamate has little

[6] E. C. Crocker, *Flavor* (New York: McGraw-Hill, 1945).

taste or flavor and that its unique property is an ability to intensify the flavors of other foods. It is not known how this effect is brought about, but it has been suggested that it might result from the stimulation of the nerve endings in the mouth and throat. A number of authorities report that monosodium glutamate improves most foods by rounding out their flavors.[7] The foods most generally enhanced are meat, fish, vegetables, and combinations of these foods, whereas dairy products, fruits, and fruit juices are not greatly improved. Fats and oils depress the effect of monosodium glutamate. At present, monosodium glutamate is widely used as an ingredient in manufactured products. It is added to canned and dried soups, canned stews and hamburgers, spaghetti sauces, frankfurters, pork sausage, and many frozen meat, fish, and poultry dishes. Monosodium glutamate is not FDA-approved for use in baby foods. Infants derive no benefit from a flavor enhancer in their food, and too little is known about the long-term effects of the daily use of monosodium glutamate in commonly eaten foods.

It has been reported that eating Chinese food causes a reaction of numbness, weakness, and palpitation in some persons. The symptoms last about 2 hours but show no after effects. It is believed that these symptoms result from the high content of glutamate in Chinese foods and that only some persons are susceptible to the compound.[8]

Acids. Lemon juice and vinegar are the acids most commonly used to flavor foods in the home. Extracted lemon juice is available in canned or bottled form. Vinegar—the more important of the two from a cookery standpoint—is produced by the fermentation of fruit juice to the acid stage. In the United States, the term *vinegar* generally designates cider or apple vinegar. Other vinegars, however, are available and are identified by name (see Table 11-3).

Vinegars available to the consumer must contain at least 4% acid strength. A pickling vinegar must have an acid content of at least 4.5% and is often designated "45-grain" vinegar.

When apples are used to make vinegar, they are crushed and pressed. The juice is stored in large containers and fermentation is brought about rather quickly by the microorganisms normally present in the fruit juice. A beneficial type of yeast initiates the action of changing the dextrose of the fruit to alcohol and carbon dioxide. The alcohol is oxidized by *Acetobacter* bacteria to form acetic acid. After the acetic acid

[7]R. H. Walters and R. A. Isker, eds., *Monosodium Glutamate: A Second Symposium* (Chicago: Food and Container Institute, 1955).

[8]*Toxicants Occurring Naturally in Foods* (Washington, D.C.: National Academy of Sciences, 1973), p. 140.

TABLE 11-3
Vinegars: Their Description and Uses

Kind	Description	Uses
Cider or apple	The product made by the alcoholic and acetous fermentations of the juice of apples	Cooked meats, game, and salad dressings
Wine or grape	The product made by the alcoholic and acetous fermentations of the juice of grapes	Cooked meats, game, and salad dressings
Malt vinegar	The product made by the alcoholic and subsequent acetous fermentations, without distillation, of an infusion of barley malt or cereals whose starch has been converted by malt	Pickling, preserves, and salad dressings
Distilled or white	The product made by acetic acid fermentation of dilute distilled alcohol	Pickling, salad dressings

content reaches the required level, the containers are sealed to prevent air from reaching the product. Aging the vinegar in the containers for 1 year is common practice. Before distribution, the vinegar is clarified, bottled, and pasteurized.

Herbs and Spices. Herbs and spices have long been used to flavor foods (Table 11-4). The art of skillfully adding the right amount of a spice or herb to a food is basic to successful cookery. Spices and herbs come from various parts of plants (Figs. 11-6 through 11-8). The numerous spices available are obtained from roots, buds, flowers, fruits, bark, or seeds, whereas herbs are prepared from the leaves of certain plants. (Herb seeds are also available.) Some books on the subject include both spices and herbs under the term "spice." Spices and herbs are similar in that they owe their flavoring properties to small amounts of fixed and volatile oils and organic acids. Each herb or spice has its individual flavoring components; no two are of exactly the

11-7 *Nutmeg comes from the seed of an East Indian evergreen tree. (Courtesy of the American Spice Trade Association)*

same composition. Each has a characteristic flavor. The United States is a large importer of spices from the Far East—particularly from Indonesia, India, Japan, and Malaysia—but also from Madagascar, Pemba, Zanzibar, and Jamaica.

ADULTERATION. Spices are defined by the federal Food and Drug Administration[9] for advisory purposes only as "aromatic vegetable substances used for seasoning of food. From them no portion of any volatile oil or other flavoring principle has been removed." Spices are available whole or dried; some, dried and ground. A problem that has long been associated with the sale of spices in this country is adulteration—the addition of such materials as ground hulls, sawdust, ground fruit, seeds, and other waste material. Through the manufacturers' carelessness—or, sometimes, their deliberate intent to de-

11-6 *Pepper berries are the fruit of a climbing vine. Pepper is a popular and much used seasoning for food. (Courtesy of the American Spice Trade Association)*

[9] "Requirements of the U.S. Food, Drug, and Cosmetic Act," *Publication 2* (Washington, D.C.: U.S. Food and Drug Administration, rev. 1964).

11-8 *Paprika pepper plant. (Courtesy of U.S. Department of Agriculture)*

fraud—dirt, sand, twigs, and insects (dead or living) may also be present in fairly large amounts. Careful inspection and screening of the spices before packaging help to eliminate some of these adulterants. Microscopic and chemical tests can uncover less noticeable adulterating materials, such as starch.

Flavoring Extracts. Flavoring extracts are solutions of volatile oils in alcohol. These oils are derived from aromatic plants or from parts of plants (Table 11-5). These oils may also be called *ethereal* or *essential oils.* According to the Food and Drug Administration, a flavoring extract may not contain any artificial or imitation flavors unless it is so labeled. There are, however, many synthetic chemical compounds on the market that are suitable substitutes for the true extracts, for they closely duplicate the flavor of the natural extract.

Essential oils can be extracted from the plant source by a number of methods. Such extracts as vanilla and peppermint are prepared by macerating the raw plant material and extracting the essential oil with a suitable solvent (such as ethyl alcohol) by a method known as *percolation.* A

second method of obtaining an essential oil is *steam distillation,* which requires that a current of steam be passed through the plant material. This brings about the vaporization of the oil, which is subsequently condensed. The oil is then dissolved in alcohol of suitable strength. A third method of extraction is accomplished by the use of presses. This method, known as *expression,* is used mainly for oils of citrus fruit rinds.

Although most flavoring substances cannot have added materials, vanilla may be made with sugar, dextrose, or glycerine.

Flavor extracts are best stored in tightly closed containers in a cool place. Loose covers and excessive heat will increase the loss of volatile oils.

Chiefly because of their lower cost, synthetic flavors are used extensively in place of the natural flavoring extracts. The synthetic substances are similar in taste to the natural flavors.

Use of Condiments, Spices, and Flavoring. There are no hard and fast rules for the use of flavoring materials in cookery. A good procedure, however, when using spice, herb, or flavoring materials for the first time is to start with ⅛ tsp and to increase the amount gradually, checking the intensity of flavor. Herbs will lend a more characteristic flavor to a dish if they are chopped and cooked with a fat before being added. Prolonged cooking will cause a loss of the essential oils; consequently, the flavoring material should be added at the very last. Generally, in a cooked dish, it is not the condiment, herb, or spice that is intended to be the predominating flavor; therefore, such materials must be used in amounts that blend with the natural flavor of the foods.

SUMMARY

Sensory or organoleptic tests are used to measure the sensory qualities and general acceptability of a food. The three most common tests are those designed to reflect consumer preference, those intended to determine the influence of factors in production, and those intended to maintain quality at a given standard. The type of taste panel used depends on the information sought. Although the tests may not exclude personal prejudice or preference entirely, valua-

TABLE 11–4
Spices: Their Description and Uses

Spices and Herbs	Description	Flavor and Uses
Spices		
Allspice	Small berry, the size of a pea, dried to a dark-brown color	Has an aroma similar to a mixture of cloves, cinnamon, and nutmeg. Used whole in pickling and cooking meats and fish. Used ground in cakes, puddings, and preserves
Anise	Small dried ripe fruit of an annual herb	Has the flavor of licorice. Used in cakes, breads, cookies, and candies
Caper	Flower bud	Used in salad dressings and fish sauces
Caraway seed	Dried ripe fruit of an herb of the parsley family	Used in making breads, rolls, and cookies
Cardamom	Dried miniature fruit of a tropical bush	Used in cookies, breads, cakes, and preserves
Cayenne	Small hot red peppers, ground fine	Used in meats, stews, sauces, and salad dressings
Celery seed	Dried seedlike fruit of an herb of the parsley family	Has the flavor of celery. Used in meat and fish dishes, salads, and salad dressings
Chili powder	Ground chili pepper pods and blended spices	Very hot flavor. Used in chili con carne and other Mexican dishes
Cinnamon	Thin inner bark of the cinnamon tree	Used in stick form for fruits and preserves. Used ground for cakes, cookies, pies, and puddings
Clove	Dried flower buds of the clove tree, grown in East Indies	Used whole in meats, pickling, and fish. Used ground in cakes, cookies, and puddings
Coriander	Dried ripe fruit of an herb of the parsley family	Used whole in mixed pickle, poultry stuffing, and green salads. Used ground in sausages and on fresh pork
Cumin seed	Small dried fruit of a plant of the parsley family	Used whole in soups, cheese spreads, stuffed eggs, stews, and sausage. Used ground as ingredient in curry and chili powder
Dill seed	Small dark seed of the dill plant, grown in India and Europe	Sharp taste resembling that of caraway seed. Used in pickles, sauces, salad, soups, and stews
Ginger	Root of a plant resembling the iris, grown in India	Root (cracked) used in chutney, pickles, preserves, and dried fruit. Used ground in cakes, cookies, breads, and pot roasts
Mace	Orange-red fleshy covering of the nutmeg kernel, grown on nutmeg trees in Indonesia	Used in fish sauces, pickling, and preserving. Used ground in cakes, cookies, pies, and chocolate dishes
Mustard	Small, round seeds of an annual herb bearing yellow flowers	Pungent flavor. Dry mustard used in meat, sauces, gravies, and salad dressings
Nutmeg	Dried, hard, wrinkled seed or pit of the nutmeg fruit, grown in Indonesia	Aromatic, slightly bitter flavor. Used whole, grated as needed. Used ground in sausage, cakes, doughnuts, puddings, and eggnogs

TABLE 11-4 (Cont.)

Spices and Herbs	Description	Flavor and Uses
Paprika	Dried, ripe red pepper grown in middle Europe, United States, and Chile	Pleasant odor, mild sweet flavor. Excellent source of vitamin C. Used to season shellfish, salad dressings, and canapé spreads
Pepper	Peppercorn: dried small round berry of a tropical vine with small white flowers, extensively grown in India; white pepper: mature berry with black coat removed (usually ground)	Used whole in pickling, meats, and stews. Used ground for general seasoning of meats, fish, poultry, vegetables, and salads. White pepper used in dishes that require a less pungent flavor than that given by black pepper
Poppy seed	Tiny, dark gray seeds of the poppy plant, grown in the United States and Turkey	Used whole for toppings on rolls or fillings for buns. Oils used for salads
Sesame seed	Small, flat, oily seed of the sesame plant	Used on rolls, breads, cookies, and candies
Turmeric	Ground dried aromatic root of the turmeric plant, grown in the Orient	Slightly bitter flavor. Used ground in curry powder, meat, and egg dishes
Herbs		
Angelica	Green plant, grown in the United States	Leaves and stalks preserved and used for decorating cakes
Basil	Dried small leaves of an herbaceous plant	Used in stews, soups, and egg dishes
Bay leaf	Dried, aromatic small shiny leaves of the laurel tree, grown in Mediterranean countries and the United States	Used in soups, chowders, stews, fish, tomatoes, and pickles
Marjoram	Dried leaves and flowering tops of an aromatic plant of the mint family	Used fresh in salads. Used dried in meat and poultry seasoning
Mint	Leaves of the spearmint plant, grown almost everywhere	Used fresh for beverages. Used dried in sauces
Oregano	Dried leaves of a perennial herb of the mint family	Aromatic odor, slightly bitter flavor. Used dried in tomato sauces, pork, and egg dishes. Used as an ingredient in chili powder
Saffron	Dried stigma of a perennial plant closely resembling the crocus, grown chiefly in Spain, France, and Italy	Very expensive. Used mainly for its yellow color
Sage	Dried leaves of a perennial shrub of the mint family. Leaves covered with fine silky hairs	Used dried in sausage, meat products, fowl, and stuffings
Savory	Dried leaves and flowering top of an annual herb	Used fresh to flavor soups, salads, sauces, and gravies. Used dried in stuffings, salad dressings, and stews
Tarragon	Dried leaves and flowering tops of an aromatic herb, native to Siberia	An ingredient used in vinegar to develop special flavor. Used in fish sauces
Thyme	Dried leaves and flowertops of an annual herb with purple flowers, cultivated extensively in central Europe	Used dried in soups, sauces, stuffings, and cheese

TABLE 11-5
Flavoring Extracts: Their Description and Uses

Extract	Description	Uses
Almond	Prepared from oil of bitter almonds, free from hydrocyanic acid	Baked products and puddings
Lemon	Prepared from oil of lemon expressed from lemon peel	Baked products, puddings, candy, and ice cream
Orange	Prepared from oil of orange expressed from orange peel	Baked products, puddings, candy, and ice cream
Vanilla	Prepared from vanilla beans	By far the most widely used flavoring substance in baked products, puddings, and candy

ble information of product acceptability is gained.

Objective tests and measuring instruments have been designed to measure certain color and texture qualities of food. Sensory panel findings and objective tests and measurements should show good correlation to be useful guides for predicting food qualities.

The color of a food is caused by naturally occurring pigments in plant or animal tissues, but there are many color prejudices regarding food. A factor in food's acceptance or rejection, color is one way to judge quality. The main pigments of fruits and vegetables are classified as carotenoids, chlorophylls, anthocyanins, and anthoxanthins and in meat the principal color pigment is myoglobin. Changes in color occur in most foods during cooking; many are desirable, such as the browning of baked goods and meat, but some, such as the discoloration of green vegetables or the yellowing of white vegetables, are not. Maintenance of desirable color without nutrient loss is sought during cooking.

Types of color change are enzymatic browning, characterized by the darkening of bruised or cut portions of certain fruits or vegetables on exposure to air, and the browning or Maillard reaction, where a reaction between a protein and a carbohydrate may cause objectionable off-color and sometimes off-flavor in such foods as dried eggs and dried milk.

Tannins may also cause color discoloration in foods, and some processed foods undergo color change (Maillard reaction) during storage. To be acceptable, foods should have a uniform, natural-looking color. To meet this standard, pro-

ducers may sometimes add color, using natural coloring matters or coal-tar dyes tested and certified for safety.

Texture is as closely related to a food as its color or flavor—and any deviation from the usual or expected texture may result in rejection. Although it is difficult to measure texture, both subjective (taste panels and taste-difference tests) and objective (mechanical and physical measurements) methods are used in judging texture qualities. It is important in judging the eating quality of a food and in the evaluation of baked products, meats, and fruits, and vegetables.

Flavor, probably the most important factor in motivating food choices, is a total impression—a combination of the sensations of taste, smell, and touch. Stimulation of the taste buds produces taste sensations, generally accepted as sour, salty, bitter, and sweet. Far more acute than the sense of taste, the sense of smell is also chemical. Olfactory nerve endings in the nose, stimulated by the food's aroma, transmit an odor sensation to the brain. Hardness or softness of food, elasticity, gumminess, graininess, stickiness, and crispness—as well as such tingling sensations as come from pepper—are perceived by the tactile sense.

Flavor in food is difficult to measure, yet uniformity of flavor influences acceptability. Natural flavors may be modified or strengthened by the use of condiments, herbs, spices, and flavorings. Of these, salt is the most widely used. Monosodium glutamate, a flavor intensifier, is used to enhance flavor, especially in meat, fish, and vegetables, and combinations of these. Flavoring materials are added sparingly to food to achieve the desired intensity.

QUESTIONS AND TOPICS FOR DISCUSSION AND STUDY

1. Why is it difficult to taste food when you have a cold?
2. It has been said that people "eat" with their eyes. Give several examples of this from your own experience.
3. Discuss some observed food prejudices that may be based on color rejection. Suggest ways to help overcome the prejudice or prevent it from occurring.
4. Describe foods that are especially valued for their interesting textures. Give reasons for your selection.
5. From past experience, suggest interesting texture combinations in cooked dishes, such as casseroles, and in salads, soups, breadstuffs, and desserts.
6. What accounts for the characteristic flavors of spices and herbs?
7. Why do spices and herbs deteriorate on prolonged standing?
8. Make several specific suggestions for using one or several flavoring materials for food products.

SUGGESTED ACTIVITIES

1. Train yourself to identify flavors. Start with a salt solution and mix different combinations of salt and water ranging from no salt to high salt. Taste these until you are able to identify the concentrations correctly.
2. Repeat activity 1, using sugar.
3. Repeat activity 1, using lemon juice.
4. Train yourself to recognize different intensities of flavoring materials and of synthetic extracts. Mix a recipe for baked or stirred custard. Divide custard into 3-oz portions and bake or cook with different amount of flavoring. Taste and identify intensity; rank when the custard has cooled.
5. Compare gelatin products prepared with fresh fruit juice with a commercially prepared packaged gelatin. Write down your observations.
6. If possible, compare a jar of homemade fruit jam with a commercial product made from a similar fruit. Note whether color has been added to the commercial product.
7. Taste-test small amounts of several of the following foods: celery, water chestnut, mashed potato, avocado, vanilla pudding, persimmon, milk, and cooked okra.
8. Describe their feel in your mouth; note whether you instinctively swallow or chew the food.
9. Select several dried herbs you would like to become familiar with. Taste the herb in its dried form. Moisten it with a small amount of oil or water and taste it again. Compare this taste with that of the dry sample.
10. Add a small amount of monosodium glutamate to tomato juice. Try to describe the taste.
11. How can you explain the difference in taste between a whole strawberry and mashed strawberries?

REFERENCES

BOOKS

Color in Foods: A Symposium. Chicago: Quartermaster Food and Container Institute for the Armed Forces, 1954.

Crocker, E. C. *Flavor.* New York: McGraw-Hill, 1945.

Current Topics in Food and Nutrition, Proceedings of Workshop. Iowa City, Iowa: University of Iowa Press, 1968.

de Man, John. *Principles of Food Chemistry.* Westport, Conn.: Avi, 1976, Chaps. 6, 7, 8.

Farmer's World: The Yearbook of Agriculture. Washington, D.C.: U.S. Department of Agriculture, 1964, pp. 195–200.

Francis, F. J., and F. M. Clyesdale. *Food Colorimetry Theory and Applications.* Westport, Conn.: Avi, 1975.

Little, Arthur (sponsor). *Flavor Research and Food Acceptance.* New York: Van Nostrand Reinhold, 1958.

MacKinney, Gordon, and Angela Little. *Color of Foods.* Westport, Conn.: Avi, 1962, Chaps. 10, 11.

Merory, J. *Food Flavorings: Composition, Manufacture and Use.* Westport, Conn.: Avi, 1968.

Moncrief, R. W. *The Chemical Senses.* New York: Wiley, 1956.

Science for Better Living: Yearbook of Agriculture. Washington, D.C.: U.S. Department of Agriculture, 1968, pp. 304–307.

Texture in Food: A Symposium. London: Society of Chemical Industry (New York: Macmillan), 1960.

Objective Methods for Food Evaluation: A Symposium. Washington, D.C.: National Research Council–National Academy of Sciences, 1976.

Paul, Pauline, and Helen Palmer. *Food Theory and Applications.* New York: Wiley, 1972, Chap. 15, 16.

Rosengarten, Frederic, Jr. *The Book of Spices.* Wynnewood, Pa.: Livingston, 1969.

Safety and Suitability of Monosodium Glutamate for Use in Baby Foods. Washington, D.C.: National Research Council–National Academy of Sciences, 1970.

Schultz, H. W., E. A. Day, and L. M. Libbey. *Chemistry and Physiology of Flavors.* Westport, Conn.: Avi, 1967.

The Quality Control of Food: A Symposium. London: Society of Chemical Industry (New York: Macmillan), 1960.

Ockerman, Herbert, *Source Book For Food Scientists.* Westport, Conn.: Avi, 1978.

ARTICLES, BULLETINS, AND PAMPHLETS

Bayme, Barbara, Mary B. Allen, et al. "Sensory and Histological Characteristics of Beef Rib Cuts Heated at Two Rates to Three End Point Temperatures." *Home Econ. Res. J.* 2:29, 1973.

Berry, R. E., et al. "Orange Peel Color Extract: Its Use and Stability in Citrus Products." *J. Food Sci.* 36:367, 1971.

Carpenter, J. A., and J. O. Reagan. "Effect of Formulation Variables on Sensory Quality of Spiced Luncheon Loaves." *J. Food Sci.* 42:1356, 1977.

DeFelice, D., et al. "Fundamental Aspects of Meat Texture." Natick, Mass.: U.S. Army Natick Laboratories, U.S. Department of Commerce, August 1965.

Engler, Pamela, and Jane Bowers. "Eating Quality and Thiamin Retention of Turkey Breast Muscle Roasted and Slow Cooked from Frozen and Thawed States." *Home Econ. Res. J.* 4:27, 1975.

Halvarson, Dorothy, and Marion Jacobson. "Teaching Consumer Selection of Market Quality Beef by Observable Characteristics." *Home Econ. Res. J.* 5:190, 1977.

Henkin, R. I. "The Role of Taste in Disease and Nutrition." *Rev. Nutr. Res.* p. 28, 1967.

"Herbs: Culture and Use." *Farmer's Bulletin 1977.* Washington, D.C.: U.S. Department of Agriculture, 1946.

Malevski, Y., and L. Gomez. "External Color as Maturity Index of Mango." *J. Food Sci.* 42:316, 1977.

McKinney, Gordon, Angela Little, and Liza Brener. "Visual Appearance of Food." *Food Technol.* 20:60, 1966.

Mitchell, J. W. "Taste-Difference Testing." *Food Technol.* 12:476, 1957.

New York Academy of Sciences. "Flavor Potentiators." *The Sciences* 4:19, 1965.

Ockerman, H. W., and F. Leon Crespo. "Cooking of Fabricated Beef." *J. Food Sci.* 42:1410, 1977.

Sapers, G. M., et al. "Flavor Quality of Explosion Puffed Dehydrated Potato." *J. Food Sci.* 36:93, 1971.

Szcsesniak, Alina. "Texture Measurements." *Food Technol.* 20:52, 1966.

Watson, Ellen. "Tannins in Fruit Extracts as Affected by Heat Treatment." *Home Econ. Res. J.* 2:112, 1973.

Weaver, C., and H. Charley. "Enzymatic Browning of Ripening Bananas." *J. Food Sci.* 39:1200, 1974.

Wolford, Everett, and John W. Nelson. "Comparison of Texture of Carrots Frozen by Airblast, Food Freezant-12 and Nitrogen Vapor." *J. Food Sci.* 36:969, 1971.

Wrolstad, R. E., et al. "Color Quality of Frozen Strawberries." *J. Food Sci.* 35:448, 1970.

Management in Food Preparation

Good management is part of successful food preparation. The work of food preparation can be made easier by adequate planning of time, energy, and facilities. A scientific approach to cookery is only part of the story; well-prepared food requires planning. Recipes must be checked for accuracy, ingredients must be checked for quality and amount, and facilities necessary for accomplishing certain cookery processes must be on hand. The time and energy available for this activity are not unlimited; hence, much thought must be given to simplifying procedures.

Part Three suggests ways to organize the activities surrounding food preparation. Chapter 13 shows the importance of good physical facilities in efficient food management.

Part Three

Management Principles

Skillful management of time and energy and proper use and care of food materials and kitchen facilities will make it possible to get the most out of the time spent in preparing foods. An atmosphere of order and a precise work plan will minimize the time and energy required for the job and will help to release intellectual energy for the more creative aspects of cookery.

WORK SIMPLIFICATION

Time-and-motion studies conducted in industrial establishments and in private homes have proven that the application of work-simplification techniques to routine tasks is an effective way of decreasing the amount of time and energy necessary for those jobs. Although the findings of scientific motion and time studies were originally applied to industry, the individual working alone at any task can make his own application of work-simplification principles.

Principles of work simplification are based on four questions: What is to be done? Why is it to be done? Where is it to be done? How is it to be done?

The answers to these questions will show how

the production of highly acceptable food products is greatly dependent on good management. The answer to the first question—"What is to be done?"—requires setting a goal. In food preparation, this means setting a standard for the product to be prepared, knowing before starting what is wanted as the result of the work. Some knowledge of food standards, therefore, is important when approaching the task of food preparation. Standards can be based on good pictures, completed products that have been made for examination, or scorecard evaluations. Another way to discover what results are expected is to learn what a standard product is like in terms of shape, size, texture, color, and flavor. It should be borne in mind that the expert in the field of food preparation must be able to prepare and to identify quickly the standard products of all the foods likely to be encountered.

The following description of a muffin may be used as an example: A good muffin has an evenly browned crust and rounded top, a tender crumb, no tunnels or large air holes in crumb, a fine but not compact grain in crumb, and a good flavor.

The second question—"Why is it to be done?"—serves to point out whether or not every part of the job is necessary. When this question is asked about each step in the preparation of a food product, it offers an opportunity to discover ways of eliminating some of them. For example, from the standpoint of appearance and taste, there is every reason not to remove the skin of a good-quality salad apple; yet it is frequently removed out of habit. Similarly, young carrots may need only to be washed thoroughly before cooking; the scraping or peeling step may be eliminated. Observing other people at work will help the individual to discover ways of performing the same or similar tasks in less time with less expenditure of energy.

The third question—"Where is it to be done?"—helps the person who is performing the task to pick out the most convenient place available. Obviously, the area closest to the sink would be the most desirable for the washing and sorting of food, whereas the work area next to the mix center would be most suitable for measuring, mixing, and baking. Planning activities in the part of the kitchen unit that is best equipped for the job saves innumerable steps and much time.

The final question—"How is it to be done?"—suggests a careful analysis of the tools and motions to be used in accomplishing the task. To analyze the "how" of a cooking process, and to find the best way to do the job, the following questions can be used as guides:

1. Are both hands used whenever possible?
2. Are motions confined to the fewest muscles suitable for the work? (This is done by placing equipment and supplies near the point of first use. Hence, the vegetable brush should be at the sink area, as should paring knives, peelers, and other cleaning tools.)
3. Is the height of the work surface such that the task can be easily performed without stopping to rest?
4. Are all supplies placed in a semicircle in front of and near the worker before she starts the operation? (See Fig. 12-1.)
5. Is the preposition of all materials the best for the sequence of work to be followed?
6. Are all tools to be used especially designed for the job? (Dull knives, makeshift double boilers, and stirring spoons with short handles cut down on efficiency of motion and increase the time spent on preparation.)

12-1 *Prearranged measuring, mixing, and baking utensils and tools decrease total time spent in preparing a high-quality product. (Courtesy of Ralston Purina Company)*

USE OF TOOLS

Learning how to use a tool properly results in a saving of time and motion. Knowing which is the best tool to use for a particular task is crucial. Using a large-bowled wooden spoon instead of a fork to mix pastry may be the cause of a poor product. Baking biscuits in a cake pan rather than on a biscuit sheet may result in poorly shaped biscuits that brown unevenly. Each piece of equipment has its own use. To use each piece correctly, it is important to know how to handle it as well as to know the cooking processes for which it is suited.

STANDARDIZED RECIPE FORMS

One of the ways to develop the ability to recognize and to prepare a standard product is to use a *standardized recipe*. A standardized recipe is one in which the amounts and proportions of the ingredients and the methods of procedure will consistently produce a high-quality product. The ingredients are carefully balanced for the number of portions the recipe is to yield. A recipe has two important parts: the list of ingredients and the description of the method for putting them together. There are several distinct styles or patterns for writing recipes, and there are differences of opinion as to which is best. Actually, there is no one "right" way; a good recipe gives all necessary information in a form that is easy to understand and to use.

Old cookbooks contain recipes in which the measurements are vague and indefinite. They are very casual as to the exact amount of an ingredient. In one, for example, "a piece of butter the size of a walnut or duck's egg" is given as a "standard" measurement. Baking powder and sugar are described as measured out in "heaping" tablespoonsful. Obviously, these recipes cannot give consistent results. One person may not agree with another's concept of the size of a walnut. The practice today is to write exact recipes.

Standard Form. One of the most common patterns for writing recipes lists the ingredients, then gives the directions for combining them. The directions may be given in the imperative: "Sift flour and baking powder together"; "Cream fat and sugar together until light and porous." The exact measurements are given to help eliminate confusion. For example, the recipe will read 1 cup sifted flour, not 1 cup flour, sifted; or 3 cups packed brown sugar, not 3 cups brown sugar, packed. This recipe is used when there are many ingredients. An example of the standard form is as follows:

Cream Puffs

    1 cup water
    ½ cup butter
    1 cup sifted all-purpose flour
    4 eggs

1. Preheat oven to 400°F (205°C) (hot).
2. Heat water and butter in sauce pan until boiling.
3. Stir in flour; sitrring constantly for 1 minute until mixture leaves side of pan and forms a ball.
4. Remove from heat.
5. Beat in eggs one at a time until smooth and velvety.
6. Drop from spoon onto ungreased baking sheet.
7. Bake at 400°F (205°C) for 40–50 minutes.
8. Allow to cool slowly.

Action Form. Another very popular form of recipe is the action form, combining narration with ingredients in a stepwise order:

Cream Puffs

Heat to boiling point in saucepan
    1 cup water
    ½ cup butter
Stir in
    1 cup sifted flour

Stir constantly until mixture leaves the sides of the pan and forms a ball (about 1 minute). Remove from heat. Cool. Beat in one at a time
    4 eggs
Beat mixture until smooth and velvety. Drop from spoon onto ungreased baking sheet. Bake at 400°F (205°C) for 40–50 minutes. Allow to cool slowly.

Descriptive Form. In this format each ingredient is listed first, followed by the description of the ingredient. Sifted flour is read as flour, sifted and packed brown sugar as brown sugar, packed. The ingredients are listed in one column and the directions in another column parallel to the ingredients. This recipe form is often used in quantity cookery because of the ease with which it can be followed. The cream puff recipe can be rewritten as:

Water	1 cup	Preheat oven to 400°F (205°C).
Butter	½ cup	Add butter to water and heat until boiling.
Flour, sifted	1 cup	Stir in flour and continue stirring for 1 minute until mixture leaves sides of pan and forms a ball. Remove from heat.
Eggs, whole	4	Beat in one at a time until smooth and velvety. Drop from spoon onto ungreased baking sheet. Bake at 400°F (205°C) for 40–50 minutes. Allow to cool slowly.

Narrative Form. A different type of recipe uses a conversational form in which the directions and ingredients are given together: "Measure into a skillet 2 tbsp butter, 1 tbsp chopped onion, and heat until onions are golden brown." This style may prove confusing, especially to the beginning cook. It may, however, be used when the number of ingredients is few but the method is more complex. The cream puff recipe is this format reads:

> Preheat oven to 400°F (205°C) (hot). Heat together 1 cup water and ½ cup butter to boiling point in a saucepan. Stir in 1 cup sifted flour. Continue stirring for 1 minute or until the mixtures leaves the sides of the pan and forms a ball. Remove from heat and beat in 4 eggs one at a time until the mixture is smooth and velvety. Drop the mixture unto an ungreased baking sheet.
>
> Bake at 400°F (205°C) for 40–50 minutes. Allow to cool slowly.

HELPFUL HINTS IN FORMULATING RECIPES

Regardless of the pattern used, the recipe should be simple and easy to read, yet it should not lack interest for the reader. The Terminology Committee of the American Home Economics Association[1] has made a number of recommendations that have proved helpful in the formulation of recipes for publication. Some discussion of these recommendations follows.

The ingredients of a recipe should be listed in the order in which they are used. If space is available, abbreviations should not be used. If the ingredient is modified, the exact measurement should be given. For example: "2 cups sifted flour" is not the same as "2 cups flour, sifted." A good way to judge where the descriptive term should go is to ask if the process is to be carried out before or after measurement of the ingredient. The descriptive term is placed before the ingredient if the process is to be carried out before measurement; it is placed after the ingredient if the process is carried out after measurement.

Another important point in the construction of a recipe is the use of fractional measurements. Whenever possible, it is desirable to use simple

measurements. Because measuring cup sets come in ½-, ⅓-, and ¼-cup sizes, it is convenient to use these measurements rather than their equivalents in tablespoons or in difficult fractions (such as ⅞ cup). It simplifies matters to use weights instead of measures when they are of special value in understanding the recipe. Hence, uncooked meat, poultry, fish, cheese, and vegetables may be given by weight rather than volume. For example: "one 8-oz pkg. freshly processed cheese." For canned products, it is best to give both measure and weight if the entire can is to be used; otherwise, the measure will be sufficient. For example: "7¾-oz jar apricot applesauce (1 cup)."

In addition, a recipe that is well constructed specifies the particular type of ingredient to be used when another would affect the quality of the finished product. Thus, if cake flour is the preferred product, the recipe should read: "2 cups sifted cake flour." Similarly, distinctions should be made between light, medium, and dark brown sugars and between light and dark corn syrups.

Most published recipes do not use brand names; rather, they give the generic names of the ingredients to be used. Clear, understandable instructions for every step of combining and cooking ingredients are necessary. Short, clear sentences that give the necessary information help to make directions understandable. It is desirable to give up-to-date methods for handling and preparing the food involved.

The correct word should be used to describe a cooking process. *Mix* should not be used instead of *fold* or *beat*. Short descriptions of the manipulation of an ingredient or of the stage of preparation to which an ingredient is to be brought are helpful. For example: "Beat the eggs until they are thick and lemon-colored"; "Bake until the crumbs are golden brown and crisp."

Recipes are constructed not only to ensure good results but also to provide for the best order of work and the best use of time. For example, if all the dry ingredients are listed first, and all the liquid ingredients listed after, fewer bowls and measuring utensils will be used and less backtracking will occur during the preparation of the recipe.

Another factor affecting the success or failure of a product is the size of the baking pan or utensil used. A well-constructed recipe will

---

[1] *Handbook of Food Preparation* (Washington, D.C.: American Home Economics Association, rev. 1975).

specify the size of pan. For example: "9-in. round layer pans, 1½ in. deep." Also, clear information about the proper preparation of the pan (oiling, flouring, lining with wax paper) should be given.

Information regarding temperature and cooking time is important in obtaining successful results from a recipe. Often—because of variations in cooking utensils and in the heating range or size of ovens—a temperature range and time range may be given. For example: a recipe may give directions to bake the cake "for 20–25 min." The 5-minute difference is necessary to make up for these variations. Such a direction as "cook until 237°F or until a small amount of syrup spins a thread when dropped into water" is of great assistance. A statement that describes the stage at which the product should be removed from the oven is also very helpful. For instance: "The custard is done when a silver knife inserted in the center of the custard comes out clean."

Every recipe should indicate its yield in terms of average servings. It is best to give the exact size of a serving or the total volume to expect from the recipe. Thus, the yield of a recipe for rice pudding may be "four 1-cup servings"; the yield of a recipe for ice cream may be "1 qt".

Any special instructions concerning the product's characteristic appearance should be included in the recipe. These would include instructions for special garnishes or for ways of serving the product. Certain fruit dishes, for example, are not finished in appearance unless some contrasting bit of green is used to set them off. And such foods as soufflés, egg dishes, and griddlecakes must be served immediately if their appearance and flavor are not to be seriously impaired.

Extremely long recipes with many ingredients—some of which may be difficult to obtain—are less likely to attract users than recipes with fewer ingredients that do not appear time-consuming or expensive to follow. The suggestion of an inexpensive substitute for a very expensive ingredient is also excellent information.

Similarly, foreign or unfamilar cooking terms should be clearly defined or changed to readily recognizable equivalents. The term *marmite,* meaning "stock pot," is frequently used in recipes that are French in origin. This could be changed to *small casserole,* which is a much more meaningful term to most users of recipes in this country.

USE OF RECIPES

The use of tested recipes (Fig. 12-2) ensures food products of excellent quality, saves time and energy, and avoids waste of food materials. The time taken to read a recipe first in order to use it correctly is well spent.

The student approaching the study of foods for the first time will find many advantages in using a tested recipe. But the alert student will also become well acquainted with general proportions and up-to-date cooking methods so that she may be free to work without consulting the printed page for every step or detail. In short, basic proportions of ingredients for different food products must be learned and quickly recognized if a student is to make the best possible use of laboratory time. Once he learns the proportion of cornstarch necessary to thicken a liquid, he need no longer worry about this detail in a recipe. Confidence in one's knowledge of basic relationships to ingredients in a recipe permits the mind to create other combinations that are interesting and as trustworthy as those in the basic formula. The key to creative cookery is to gain sufficient competence so that the mind will be free to build pictures of palatable food combinations not yet experienced.

When the recipe is understood, the necessary ingredients and equipment should be checked to be sure all are at hand for its preparation. Any substitutions that have to be made should be thought out carefully before preparation begins.

The metric study group of the National Bureau of Standards has recommended that the United States change to the International System through a 10-year conversion program. In light of this, it has been suggested that recipes should be converted to the metric system as soon as possible. See the section "Metric System" in Chapter 15.

SUMMARY

Proper use of tools, understanding of cookery terms, use of a standardized, tested recipe, and thorough reading of the recipe prior to prepara-

12-2 *Home economists in a nationally known test kitchen perfect recipes for consumer use. (Courtesy of R. T. French Co.)*

tion are important factors in producing foods that meet the standards for the product. Good recipes are constructed not only to assure a good product, but also, by giving an efficient, orderly procedure for preparation, to minimize the time spent in preparation. Efficiency in food preparation can be increased by application of work-simplification principles, which analyze what is to be done, why, where, and how.

SUGGESTED ACTIVITIES

1. Observe a demonstration of food preparation. Write down your observations, summarizing what you observed about the use of time and energy and the handling of specific tools.
2. Familiarize yourself with the forms of recipes used in reference materials. Examine cookbooks and magazines and publications that feature recipes. Comment on different recipe forms.
3. Study the arrangement of the foods laboratory and make a diagram of the work space to which you have been assigned. Examine this diagram carefully so that you can plan, before each laboratory period, how to make the best possible use of space.

4. Find out where general supplies are kept and what laboratory facilities will have to be shared with other class members.
5. Work out the most efficient method for washing dishes (within the framework suggested by the instructor).

REFERENCES

BOOKS

Consumers All: The Yearbook of Agriculture. Washington, D.C.: U.S. Department of Agriculture, 1965.

Fonosch, Gail, and Elaine Kvitka. *Meal Management.* San Francisco: Canfield, 1978.

Gilbreth, L. M., O. M. Thomas, and E. Clymer. *Management in the Home.* New York: Dodd, Mead, 1962.

Kinder, Faye, and Nancy Green. *Meal Management.* New York: Macmillan, 1978.

Kramer, Mary, and Margaret Spader. *Contemporary Meal Management.* New York: Wiley, 1972.

McWilliams, Margaret. *Fundamentals of Meal Management.* Fullerton, CA.: Plycon, 1978.

Steidl, Rose, and Esther Bratton. *Work in the Home.* New York: Wiley, 1968.

ARTICLES, BULLETINS, AND PAMPHLETS

American National Standard Dimensions, Tolerances, and Terminology for Home Cooking and Baking Utensils: ANSI 26.1. New York: American National Standards Institute, 1970.

Fitzsimmons, Cleo, E. Gable, and G. Monhant. "Easy Ways." *Extension Bulletin 391.* Lafayette, Ind.: Purdue University Agricultural Extension Service, 1966.

Goodenow, M. "A Recipe Standardization Project." *J. Amer. Dietet. Assoc.* **39:**342, 1962.

Handbook of Food Preparation. Washington, D.C.: American Home Economics Association, rev. 1975.

Howard, Mildred, Genevieve Tayloe, and Russell Parker. "Beltsville Energy-Saving Kitchen." *Leaflet 518.* Washington, D.C.: U.S. Department of Agriculture, 1963.

Kornblueh, M., and H. C. Parke. "Use of Written Recipes." *J. Amer. Dietet. Assoc.* **43:**117, 1965.

Rice, Emma. "Baking, Cooking at High Altitudes." *Agricultural Experiment Bulletin 397R.* Laramie, Wyo.: University of Wyoming, 1961.

———. "High-Altitude Cookery." *Agricultural Experiment Station Bulletin MC136R.* Laramie, Wyo.: University of Wyoming, 1961.

Schlessinger, P., and B. Kennedy. "Metric Measurements in Food Preparation." *J. Home Econ.* **59:**120, 1967.

Steidle, Rose. "Affective Dimensions of High and Low Cognitive Homemaking Tasks." *Home Econ. Res. J.* **4:**121, 1975.

———. "Complexity of Homemaking Tasks." *Home Econ. Res. J.* **3:**225, 1975.

Kitchen Planning and Equipment

The principles of kitchen planning are extensively treated in the literature of home management. (Several good references are listed at the end of this chapter.) The purpose of this brief treatment is to orient the student of food preparation to the relationships between kitchen planning and the expenditure of time and energy.

The purpose of carefully planning where equipment and utensils will be placed in a kitchen is to ensure that the worker will be able to get maximum benefit from them as quickly and easily as possible.

In order to achieve this end, kitchen-planning principles stress the need to group together items that will be used together. Food operations—and the equipment used for them—fall into three groupings: storage and preparation, cleaning and cooking, and serving. Accordingly, all equipment used in storage and preparation of food should be placed to be in easy reach for use. But the work involved in all three categories is interrelated. Food is never just stored, or just cleaned, or just cooked. All operations take place in sequence or simultaneously; consequently, operational areas and different equipment must not be too widely separated but must form a compact work unit. The U-shaped kitchen[1] is frequently recommended by kitchen-planning specialists as the most efficient arrangement. However, other arrangements may be just as efficient, depending on the available floor space and the number of persons who are to use the facilities at the same time.

LAYOUT

The best use of kitchen space and equipment is achieved when range, sink, and refrigerator are fairly close to each other, with sufficient working surface and storage cabinets interspersed between them. Some extra space must be available to permit a worker to reach, bend, step backward, squat, or pass another person without being crowded or hampered. With these factors in mind, it is easy to see that many variations of arrangement are possible (Fig. 13-1).

In one convenient arrangement, the refrigerator is placed near the door through which

[1]Lenore Sater Thye, "A Step-Saving U-Kitchen," *Home and Garden Bulletin 14* (Washington, D.C.: U.S. Department of Agriculture, 1951).

13-1 *Center for food preparation and serving area are conveniently arranged in this attractive kitchen. (Courtesy of Young and Rubicam and General Electric Co.)*

groceries are brought in. It is recommended that one work area be placed on the side to which the refrigerator door opens and another work area between the refrigerator and the sink. At the other end of the sink a third work area is indicated, beyond which the range should be placed. Still another work area is needed beyond the range.

Suitable storage space should be part of each work area. Cabinets for storage of equipment and supplies are usually of wood, metal, or enameled metal. Whatever material is used, cabinets should be verminproof, and the exterior surfaces should be free of any projections on which clothing might catch.

Small equipment and supplies of food are stored at convenient places. Stored materials and articles should be kept at the point of first or most frequent use, and they should be within easy reach. Accordingly, a double boiler should be stored near the sink, mixing bowls near the refrigerator or mix center. Good storage facilities include separate storage space for special pieces of equipment. When unlike pieces of equipment are stacked together, some may have to be lifted or even taken out entirely before the desired piece can be reached. Cabinets can be designed for greater convenience by including such features as a vertical- or compartment-file section for trays and big platters, a sliding pan rack, shelves, drawers, or swing shelves. In a cabinet in which food supplies are kept, a section with

step-up shelves is suitable for storing spices. Storage space for small dishes is made more accessible by placing a shelf half the usual width between two other shelves, for the storing of cups, saucers, sauce dishes, and bread and butter plates. Drawers in cabinets may be partitioned for the storage of small utensils; one drawer can be designed for knives, with a slot for each knife.

WORK AREAS

Work areas are usually covered by such materials as hard wood, linoleum, Formica, stainless steel, and porcelain enamel. No one surface material is perfect; each has its advantages and disadvantages. Any material used, however, should be easy to clean.

The height of a work surface will affect the efficiency with which food preparation tasks can be performed. The rangetop, the sink bottom, and the work surfaces near the mix center are the important heights to be considered. Ideally, these should conform to the height of the person using the work surface, but average heights have been suggested: the top of a stand-up work surface 32 to 36 in. from the floor; the top of a lapboard, table, or sit-down work surface 24 in. from the floor.

A large array of equipment and tools for the preparation and serving of food is available. The equipment and tools finally chosen for a food

111

unit will depend on the kind of food preparation work to be done and the number of people who will be involved in it.

LARGE EQUIPMENT

The large equipment necessary for the proper preparation of food includes a range, a refrigerator, and a sink. When extra funds are available, a freezer and a dishwasher are desirable additions to the basic list.

Ranges. A majority of modern ranges use gas or electricity. To a great extent, the fuel used depends on local rates. Although ranges differ in size, shape, and special features, they all have some construction features in common. Most ranges have a sturdy frame covered with a long-wearing material. All ranges are equipped with surface units for top-of-the-range cookery, an oven for baking and roasting, and a broiler. Both surface burners and ovens have various temperature-control features.

Modern ranges provide certain oven controls that are very important to successful oven cookery. The oven should be moisture-tight, with enough insulation in the walls and door to keep the heat in the oven and to minimize the escape of heat into the room. Oven heat is controlled by a thermostat on which are marked the various degrees of temperature at which the heat may be maintained. Generally, ovens are large enough to hold several food items at one time (Fig 13-2).

A broiler is an essential part of a modern gas

13-2 *Built-in double oven in this kitchen offers expanded cooking facilities.* (*Courtesy of Young and Rubicam and General Electric Co.*)

or electric range. Its function is to cook food by exposing it directly to the source of heat. The broiler may be located at the top of the oven or underneath it with one source of heat supplying both oven and broiler. In some ranges, the broiler has a separate compartment. With the broiler at the top of the oven or in a separate compartment, a wide range of rack positions for low- or moderate-temperature broiling is possible. Broilers can be placed in a vertical position.

Electric-range oven units are of the tubular type. In some electric ranges, a metal sheet called a *baffle* is installed over the oven unit for even heat distribution. In some ranges, the baffle is a separate piece and is removable. Many electric and gas ranges have automatic clock controls that make it possible to place food in the oven and set the time desired for the cooking to start and stop. Not all foods may be so cooked.

Glass-ceramic smoothtop ranges are available

today (Figs. 13-3 and 13-4). Generally, they are more expensive than the conventional electric range. The glass-ceramic material used in smoothtop is break-resistant to falling objects and has high heat and cold tolerances. Spilled liquids will not cause damage. The heating elements are located beneath the surface of the smoothtop and the cooking areas are marked by permanent fired-in designs. When heated, only the cooking areas heat; the rest of the surface remains relatively cool. An "on" indicator light is provided for each unit and remains lit after the unit is turned off until the surface is cooled.

Microwave ovens (see Fig. 13-5) are gaining in popularity for home use (see also Chapter 45). Microwave ovens are electronic devices that heat food rapidly but are not related to radioactivity. These ovens are not all-purpose ovens, and some conventional auxiliary cooking units will be required, if the tabletop or counter model is used.

13-3 *This counterange by Corning combines a self-cleaning oven with a flat glass-ceramic rangetop that shows no heating units or burner openings.*

13-4 *The only visible surface on this rangetop is a smooth, flat sheet of glossy white glass-ceramic material. All electrical elements are sealed out of sight beneath the rangetop, and most spills can be wiped up with a damp cloth. (Courtesy of Corning Glass Works)*

Many free-standing ranges containing both microwave and conventional ovens are available today. A portable microwave oven plugs into any household outlet, but it does need its own 110/120-volt circuit to work efficiently. A full-size range needs a separate 220-volt line. Microwave ovens are designed to prevent microwaves from escaping outside the oven cavity by the FDA's safety standard limit. The amount of radiation that is considered safe is 5 milliwatts per square centimeter, measured at a distance of 2 in. from the oven door. The FDA safety standard requires that the oven be equipped with at least two separate safety interlocks to shut off radiation as the oven door is opened.

Electric and gas convection ovens are now available for home use. These ovens have a fan that constantly recirculates heated air throughout the oven chamber, channeling heat directly on to the food. The advantages of the convection oven are reduced cooking times and lowered oven temperatures for most foods. Instructions for adapting conventional recipes are included with the purchase of the convection range.

Both gas and electric ranges can be designed with self-cleaning ovens. Self-cleaning ovens use high temperatures to remove oven soils, and insulation keeps surface temperatures of the range at a safe level during cleaning.

Range Hoods. A vented hood for a range carries odors, grease, smoke, water vapor, and heat in the kitchen out of doors. If it is not possible to install a vented hood, nonvented range hoods are available. A combination of filters made of aluminum mesh, fiberglass, and charcoal will remove odors, grease, and smoke.

Refrigerators and Freezers. Every food-preparation area should be equipped with a refrigerator so that perishable foods may be quickly cooled and spoilage prevented. To be

13-5 *Some examples of microwave cooking utensils. (Courtesy of Corning Glass Works)*

efficient, a refrigerator must be well constructed and well insulated, for much of the heat that enters the refrigerator gets in through the walls. Warm air also enters when the refrigerator door is opened. The heat given off by the food placed in it is the third factor that contributes to raising the temperature of the refrigerator.

Convenience features on refrigerators are automatic icemakers and chilled water or ice dispensers. All icemakers must be connected to a cold water line and will add to the cost of operating the refrigerator.

Many modern refrigerators are of the combination refrigerator–freezer type, but individual freezer cabinets are also available for home use. There are two types of individual freezer cabinets: the upright type, which is like the refrigerator in appearance, and the chest type. The upright freezer takes up a minimum of floor space and is as convenient to use as a refrigerator. However, loss of cold air is more likely to occur with the upright freezer than with the chest type. This disadvantage may be overcome by the design of the cabinet interior, which should be divided into sections, each with separate doors, so that when one section is opened the others remain closed.

The materials used in the construction of freezer cabinets are similar to those used for refrigerators. Good insulation in a freezer is necessary for efficiency. Plastics are used for the door linings and breaker strips to ensure a tight fit and to prevent leakage of warm air into the freezer. The method of refrigeration in the freezer is similar to that in the refrigerator, but the temperatures maintained are considerably lower. The refrigerants used are adapted to very rapid freezing, and the evaporator coils are placed so that as much food as possible can be placed in direct contact with a cold surface.

The temperature required for freezing ranges from 0°F (-18°C) to -30°F (-34°C). The lower temperatures are more desirable.

Freezer cabinets are available in sizes of from 6 to 32 cu ft. The size purchased for a particular food-preparation unit depends on the number of persons to be serviced by it and the space available.

Sink. Modern sinks consist of a steel base with a finish of porcelain enamel or stainless steel. Monel metal is also used, but less frequently.

The sink is central to all food operations that require water; for cleaning, peeling, and cutting food; for removing waste; and for dishwashing. The sink should therefore be placed where it will be easily accessible. Its design should be as carefully planned as that of other large pieces of kitchen equipment. The proper height is important—too low a sink requires too much bending over and too high a sink means stretching. Convenience features that make for efficient work at the sink include double sinks and drainboards, a mixer faucet, a strainer outlet, and toe space at the baseboard. It has been suggested that if only a single drainboard is available, it should be at the left of the sink.

Dishwasher. Many kitchens are equipped with mechanical dishwashers. These may be built into the sink or placed under a counter-height work surface, or they may be portable appliances that can be stored anywhere in the kitchen and rolled to the sink area for use. Dishwashers are designed so that they have one or more washing cycles for normal full loads and one for rinsing small loads that are held until a full load has accumulated. Some models have heating coils or boosters to maintain the temperatures (140–160°F; 60–70°C) required for fast drying.

Food Waste Disposals and Waste Compactors. Food waste disposal units in homes must comply with local ordinances; some communities do not permit their installation because of water usage. Most disposals will grind small bones, fruit rinds, and seeds. Glass, metal, and china cannot be put into the unit. Waste compactors are helpful in reducing the volume of trash in a home. Bottles, cans, cartons, and waste paper can be compacted. The compactor is used after each addition of trash.

LABORATORY SEALS AND LABELS

An electrical appliance should carry an Underwriters Laboratories seal, which signifies that the product design meets safety requirements for fire and electrical shock. The American Gas Association blue star on gas appliances certifies that the appliance meets national safety standards and the Association of Home Appliance Manufacturers seal certifies that the refrigerated volume and shelf area of refrigerators and freezers are as stated.

APPLIANCE USE OF ENERGY

Appliances account for 20–30% of all energy used in the home.[2] Major appliances use most of this energy. Energy-efficiency labels are now appearing on refrigerators, refrigerator–freezers, ranges, ovens, and other major household equipment. Pilot lights use 5–10% of all natural gas used in homes. Today, new range models featuring electrical ignition eliminate the need for pilot lights. Well-insulated ovens will converve heat and will be more efficient in their use of energy when used to cook several foods rather than single foods.

Manual defrost refrigerators use the least amount of energy, while automatic defrost models use 55–60% more energy to operate than manual defrost models. Chest-type freezers are usually more economical to operate than upright models because they lose less cold air when opened.

Dishwashers with an energy-saving switch that automatically eliminates the use of heat during the drying cycle saves 20–40% of operating costs. Lacking a switch, the dishwasher can be turned off at the end of the rinse cycle and the door opened. Dishwashers should be run for full loads to conserve energy.

SMALL EQUIPMENT FOR FOOD PREPARATION

The right kitchen tools, utensils, and appliances must be available for the measuring, mixing, baking, and cooking of the ingredients (see Table 13-1 and Fig. 13-6).

Standard measuring equipment is essential for the accurate measurement of ingredients. The American Standards Association (ASA) has set standards for measuring cups and spoons, but not all measuring utensils sold meet these standards. Only pieces of equipment whose labels show they meet ASA standards should be chosen. Also

[2] "Energy Facts," Ithaca, N.Y.: New York State College of Agriculture and Life Sciences, Cornell University, 1977.

important in the selection of measuring equipment is the material from which it is made. Heavy-gauge aluminum and glass are good, but plastic and lightweight aluminum may bend out of shape and thereby impair the accuracy of the measure.

Standard measuring cups hold 8 fluid oz and are available for liquid and for dry ingredients. Cups for liquid ingredients are transparent, so that the contents can be seen. There should be a rim above the 1-cup line to prevent spilling, and a pouring spout. There are also 1-pt and 1-qt measures made of glass and constructed in the same manner as the 8-oz liquid measure. Fractions of a cup are marked on the sides of the cup as follows: ¼, ½, ¾, and ⅓, and ⅔, or marked off in milliliters.

The measure for dry ingredients has the 1-cup line at the top. Sets of nested cups are available. These are made in 1-, ½-, ⅓-, and ¼-cup sizes for measuring fractions of dry materials or fat. Sets of 50-, 125-, 250-ml are also available.

Standard measuring spoons are also essential for accurate measuring. These are made for measuring parts of one spoonful or combined spoonful. Sets of standard measuring spoons include 1 tbsp, 1 tsp, ½ tsp, and ¼ tsp. In combined spoonful, 3 tsp equal 1 tbsp. Metric measuring spoons come in sets of 25, 15, 5, 2, and 1 ml.

Utensils for Rangetop and Oven Cookery. Many different kinds of cooking utensils (see Fig. 13-8) are used for top-of-the-range cookery (see Table 13-2). These include saucepans, frying pans, Dutch ovens, steamers, pressure saucepans, and pressure canners. Such utensils are selected on the basis of the advantages of the various materials used in their construction and design, and the amount of work required to clean them. A cooking utensil that has a number of uses will offer a saving in cost and storage space.

Casseroles with and without covers of various sizes and materials are useful in oven cookery. Heat-resistant glass is especially desirable for casserole dishes. Small casserole dishes are known as *ramekins*.

Meat roasting pans are necessary utensils for oven cookery. Uncovered roasters with sides approximately 1 to 2 in. high are recommended (see Fig. 13-9).

Nonstick Finishes. Much of today's cook-

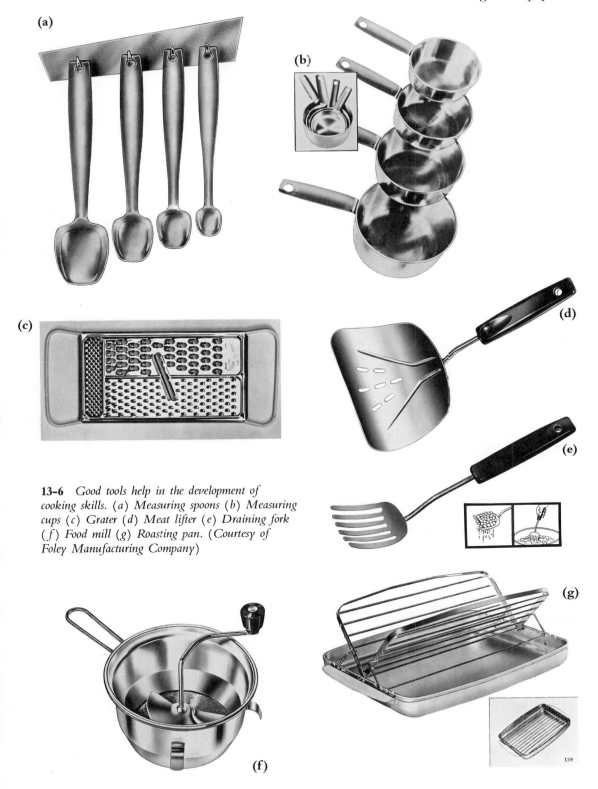

13-6 *Good tools help in the development of cooking skills. (a) Measuring spoons (b) Measuring cups (c) Grater (d) Meat lifter (e) Draining fork (f) Food mill (g) Roasting pan. (Courtesy of Foley Manufacturing Company)*

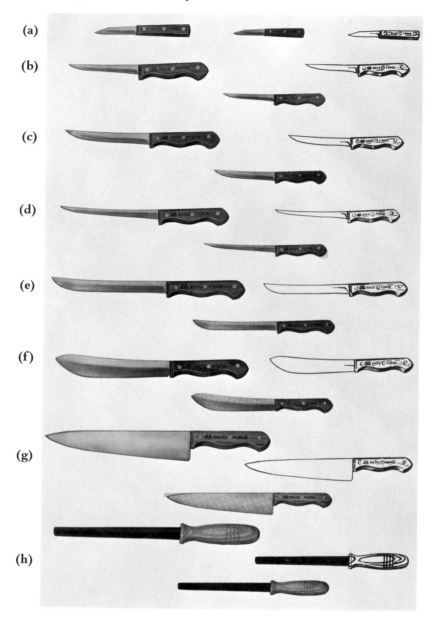

(a)

(b)

(c)

(d)

(e)

(f)

(g)

(h)

13-7 *A variety of well constructed knives for food preparation. (a) Paring (b) Boning (c) Utility (d) Fillet (e) Slicer (f) Butcher (g) Chef (h) Sharpening rod. (Courtesy of Ekco)*

ware has a nonstick-finished surface, thus eliminating the need for added fat in cooking, particularly in frying, and providing for easy, quick cleaning of pots and pans. Teflon, Boeclad, and Turfram are examples of nonstick finishes. Teflon is the finish most frequently used at this time.

Although Teflon is a hard coating, it can be scratched with metal utensils such as pancake turners. Breaking the surface coating interferes with the efficiency of the pans; actually, they lose their nonstick quality when the surface is broken. New Teflon-coated pans have several coatings, and newly designed lifting tools, such as spatulas, spoons, and pancake turners, are plastic or plastic-coated to prevent scratching.

When Teflon first appeared on the market, some concern was voiced that the fumes from

TABLE 13-1
Essential Tools for Measuring, Mixing, and Baking

Item	Description	Function
Measuring cup 8-oz (liquid)	Transparent, so contents can be seen; fractions marked on side of cup; rim above 1-cup line to avoid spilling; pouring spout; 500-ml cup sizes	Measuring liquids
Measuring cup 8-oz (dry)	1-cup line at top	Measuring dry ingredients
Nested cups	Made in 1-, $\frac{1}{2}$-, $\frac{1}{3}$-, and $\frac{1}{4}$-cup sizes; 50-ml, 125-ml, 250-ml cup sizes	Measuring fractions of dry ingredients or fats
Spatula	Wood or plastic handle; blunt flat blade	Leveling off measure of dry ingredients or fats
Sifter	Rotating wire, spring, or multiple-screen; fine or medium mesh	Sifting dry ingredients
Bowls	Glass, pottery, aluminum, enamelware, plastic, or stainless steel; come in 1-pt and 1-, 2-, and 3-qt sizes	For use in combining ingredients; heatproof bowls also used for baking
Hand beaters	Whisk, rotary, and turbine types	Beating (whisk not as efficient as rotary beater)
Wooden spoons	Handles of different lengths; paddle-shaped bowls are excellent	Mixing
Large metal spoons	Should have comfortable heat-resistant handle	Mixing
Pastry blenders	Wood or plastic handles; series of metal strips attached to handle in semicircular arrangement	Cutting shortening into flour
Rolling pins	Hardwood (maple); glass and metal also used	Rolling out dough
Cake pans	Available in bright aluminum, stainless steel, tin, or glass; smooth joinings; even heat distribution; round, square, or oblong	Baking cakes
Cookie sheets	Aluminum, tin, or stainless steel; at least one side open	Baking cookies
Measuring spoons	Heavy-gauge aluminum; sets include 1 tbsp, 1 tsp, $\frac{1}{2}$ tsp, and $\frac{1}{4}$ tsp; 1 ml, 2 ml, 5 ml, 15 ml, 25 ml	Measuring liquid or dry ingredients
Pie pans	Aluminum, tin, glass, stainless steel, or anodized aluminum; come in a variety of sizes	Baking pies
Muffin pans	Aluminum chiefly, tin also used; may have 6, 9, or 12 cups	Baking muffins, cupcakes, and rolls
Casserole baking dishes	Glass, pottery, stainless steel, or enamelware; range in size from 1 pt to 3 qt	Baking as well as serving
Custard cups	Glass or pottery	Baking custards, puddings, popovers, and individual servings of main courses

TABLE 13-1 (Cont.)

Item	Description	Function
Wire racks	Heavy wire; should be large enough to support a rectangular cake	Cooling cakes, cupcakes, cookies, and breads
Paring knife	Blade from 2½ to 3 in. long; comes in sharp, spear, and clip points	Paring fruits and vegetables
Utility knife	Longer than paring knife; blade 4–6 in.; cutting edge straight or curved	Cutting up fruit, large vegetables; slicing meat; any other operation requiring a flexible blade
Grapefruit knife	Blade curved and serrated	Cutting sections of grapefruit from rind
French cook knife	Straight-edged blade with firm, tapering point; handle designed so that hand does not interfere when knife is used for chopping	Chopping; slicing
Slicing knife	Thin narrow blade with tapered or rounded point	Essential for slicing thin pieces of large cuts of meat
Forks	Firm handles; sturdy tines that will not bend	Long-handled forks with two tines useful for handling large cuts of meat; smaller forks, with 3 or 4 tines, for smaller pieces of food
Kitchen shears	Designed to be used either in right or left hand	Cutting food; can be used to grip bottle caps
Can opener	Keen cutting edge; both hand and wall types; also screw-cap openers, punch types, pry-off types, and corkscrews	Opening round, square, or oval cans, removing vacuum lids and corks
Graters	Aluminum, stainless steel, plastic, or tin; various shapes, holes punched or drilled in sides	Grating food

Teflon-coated pans might be toxic because Teflon is a fluorocarbon and as such might produce harmful fumes at high temperatures. According to Dupont, the manufacturer of Teflon, there is little danger of toxicity from use of these products at cooking temperatures employed in the home. Manufacturers' directions for the initial use of Teflon-finished ware should be followed. Mainly, frying pans and some bakeware should be "conditioned" by oiling lightly before the first use. One authority recommends that in caring for nonstick-finished cooking utensils, extremely high temperatures should be avoided and pans should be removed from hot burners when the food is cooked.

Small Electric Appliances. A discussion of utensils used in food preparation would not be complete without some mention of small electric appliances (Fig. 13-10 and 13-11). (The references at the end of the chapter provide detailed information.)

There are two kinds of small electric appliances: those that produce heat and those that produce motion (see Table 13-3).

CARE OF EQUIPMENT

Utensils and equipment used for food preparation represent a large investment and should be

13-8 *Teflon-coated materials offer a nonstick surface for cooking. (Courtesy of Mirro Co.)*

wisely cared for. Care in the use and maintenance of equipment assures a high level of efficiency in use, durability, safety, and sanitation.

Manufacturers' direction booklets should be carefully studied and followed. Every appliance has one or more unique features that require special attention, and each manufacturer knows best how to care for and use his appliance. A reference file of such booklets is an aid to persons handling equipment that is new to them.

For overall care of the major pieces of equipment in the food unit, however, some general suggestions are pertinent.

Range. When a range is improperly used, the amount of time spent on its care increases. The first suggestion, then, is to avoid cooking methods that cause spillovers and splatterings of foodstuffs on the range surface and in the oven. Saucepans should not be filled to the brim; switches or burners should not be left turned on high heat for too long a time. Less cleaning of oven walls will be necessary if high oven temperatures are avoided.

Special metal finishes. stainless steel, and satin chromium should be cleaned with sudsy water. One recommendation always holds true: strong soaps and harsh abrasives should not be used on these surfaces. Removable oven racks may be taken to the sink, where some soaking in detergent and warm water will loosen most of the food particles adhering to them. Some electric oven units may be pulled out and wiped clean, but they should never be immersed in water.

Oven interiors of porcelain or chrome should be cleaned after the oven has cooled off. It is best to wipe the oven as soon as possible after use, so that spots do not burn on. Although chemical oven cleaners are effective, a neglected oven will take more time to clean, regardless of the cleaners used. Oven cleaners or ammonia should not be used in ovens that are aluminum-lined. If broiler pans are removed from the range immediately after use and soaked, the total cleaning job is reduced. Ranges with self-cleaning ovens are now on the market.

On an electric range, the flat coils of the surface unit are self-cleaning. Spillovers are burned off so that the surface can be wiped clean with a damp cloth when cool. Like units in the

13-9 *This easy-to-clean serving platter doubles as a broiler. (Courtesy of Corning Glass Works)*

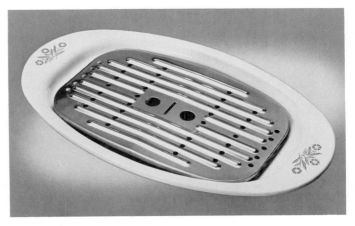

TABLE 13-2
Utensils for Rangetop and Oven Cookery

Item	Description	Use
Saucepans	Flat bottoms, slightly sloping sides, rounded corners between sides and bottom; well-placed spouts; tight-fitting covers; heat-resistant handles that fit comfortably into palm of the hand	Rangetop cookery
Saucepots	Similar to saucepans, but have handles on either side; saucepans and saucepots range in size from 1 pt to 8 qt; most useful sizes: $1\frac{1}{2}$–4 qt	Rangetop cookery
Double boilers	May serve as two pans for rangetop cookery; tops may also be designed for use as oven casseroles	Rangetop cookery
Pressure saucepans	Designed on principle of locking steam in the pan, thus raising temperature and permitting rapid cooking of food; one type has flexible cover that slips under rim of pan and is held in position with hook or clamp on handle; another type has lid that fits into grooves and locks in position; all have vent tube that permits escape of steam; in some, pressure is registered and controlled by weight placed over vent; all have safety valve or plug that automatically releases steam if pressure becomes excessive	All must be used in accordance with manufacturers' directions; look for Underwriters Laboratories seal as check on quality
Frying pans (or skillets)	Aluminum, stainless steel, cast or sheet iron, flameproof glassware; covers of same material or glass increase number of uses for frying pan; various sizes; 10–12-in. pan has many uses	Rangetop or oven cookery
Dutch ovens and chicken fryers	Have higher sides and dome-shaped covers; greater holding capacity than frying pans	Rangetop cookery
Casseroles	Various sizes and materials; heat-resistant glass especially desirable; most designed with covers	Oven cookery
Ramekins	Small casseroles	Oven cookery
Roasters	Aluminum, sheet iron, or stainless steel; oval, round, or rectangular (last most convenient to handle); uncovered roasters with sides 1–2 in. high recommended; should be fitted with rack or perforated tray to hold meat up from bottom of pan and prevent it from settling in fat drippings	Oven cookery
Oven thermometers	Used mainly where ovens lack regulators showing when correct baking temperature reached; should have sturdy base and be laboratory tested for accuracy	Oven cookery

TABLE 13-2 (Cont.)

Item	Description	Use
Coffeemakers	Various types, including percolator, vacuum, and drip; made of aluminum, enamelware, glass, or stainless steel for operation of all types; see Chapter 16.	Rangetop cookery
Meat thermometers	Used to determine temperature of meat and poultry at different stages of cooking	

electric oven, removable plug-in units should never be placed in water. But practically all reflector bowls on surface units are removable and can be washed in hot, soapy water. Wiping spills off rings and reflector bowls promptly will also minimize the total cleaning effort. The sensing device located on the thermostatic surface burner, like the electric units, should never be immersed in water.

Gas burners are easily taken out of the range for cleaning at the sink. Gas burners are made from cast iron, aluminum, or chrome, and are washable. Sometimes a chrome burner has blue-black discolorations that cannot be removed. Little can be done about these.

Refrigerator. Like the range, the refrigerator is in constant use and must be properly cared for. Modern frost-free and automatic defrosting refrigerators and refrigerator–freezer combinations require a minimum of defrosting care. However, there is still the cleaning job to be considered. Any spills or accumulations of food particles should be cleaned as they occur. As with all equipment, though, periodic cleaning is essential. The removable parts should be lifted out, washed, rinsed, and dried. Inside walls can be washed with clear water or with a solution of baking soda and warm water. Exteriors should be wiped off with clear, warm water and with a mild soap, if necessary, and wiped dry. Cleaner-wax polishes will help keep a clean finish on the exterior of the refrigerator. Good periodic care will help maintain the quality of the refrigerated food. If a refrigerator is to be left empty for long periods of time, it is best to remove all food, turn off the control, pull out the plug, and leave the door open.

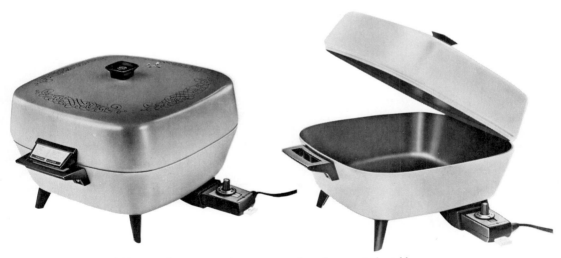

13-10 *An electric skillet provides an attractive way to cook and serve at the table.* (*Courtesy of General Electric Co.*)

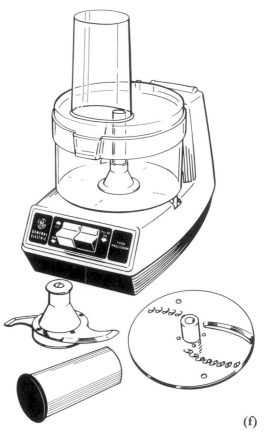

(g)

13-11 *Electric appliances and small equipment, if wisely chosen, are effective time-savers. (a) Egg poacher. (Courtesy of Wear-Ever Aluminum, Inc.) (b) Double boiler. (Courtesy of Wear-Ever Aluminum, Inc.) (c) Pressure cooker. (Courtesy of Mirro Aluminum Company) (d) Electric saucepan. (Courtesy of Wear-Ever Aluminum, Inc.) (e) A portable mixer that is easy to operate and clean. (Courtesy of General Electric Co.) (f) A food processor that slices, chops, shreds, grates—a fast work saver. (Courtesy General Electric Co.) (g) Heavy-duty stand mixer that can be used with dough hooks for mixing and kneading bread dough. (Courtesy of General Electric Co.)*

Freezer. The exterior of the freezer cabinet may be cleaned as is a refrigerator. The freezer should be completely defrosted and its interior cleaned at least once a year. The freezer must be disconnected (or the control turned to "Off" position) and removable shelves and baskets taken out of the cabinet. Frost-free units require only a cleaning with warm water. On the units that are not frost-free, as much frost as possible must be scraped off with a plastic frost scraper. Icepicks or sharp knives should never be used, for they may damage the liner.

Dishwasher. The inside of a dishwasher is porcelain enamel, which cleans itself each time dishes are washed. In hard-water areas, however, the tub should be wiped with a damp cloth. Of course, harsh abrasives should never be used. The exterior of a dishwasher, if porcelain enamel, needs only mild soap and warm water to be kept clean. A cleaner-wax polish may also be used to maintain the finish.

SUMMARY

The time and energy required to store, prepare, clean, cook, and serve food are directly related to kitchen planning and the positioning of equipment. Focal points in food operations are the range, sink, and refrigerator. They should be fairly close together, but work and storage areas adjacent to each unit are needed. Equipment and materials may be stored at the point of first or most frequent use. Heights of work surfaces affect efficiency.

The basic large equipment of sink, range, and refrigerator may be supplemented by a freezer and dishwasher. Essential features of ranges are the oven and broiler. For successful food preparation, the oven should be well insulated and moisture-tight. An efficient refrigerator or freezer is well insulated. Proper design and height are important considerations in selecting a sink.

Many small utensils, tools, and appliances are also required for efficiency in food operations. All equipment, large and small, should be used with care to assure high efficiency and long life. Practices that abuse equipment should be avoided, for example, spillovers and spatterings, accumulation of excessive frost, and use of harsh abrasives. Regular cleaning is essential.

SUGGESTED ACTIVITIES

1. Make a sketch of your home kitchen or of another kitchen with which you are familiar. Note all stored items—utensils, tools, food, cleaning supplies, linen, dishes, silver, and so forth. Suggest simple changes that would require little or no expenditure of money but would improve the efficiency of the kitchen.
2. Examine a range to determine the following: (a) size and control of surface burners or units; (b) construction of oven door—does it fit tightly? (c) operation of oven burner or oven bake unit—manual or automatic lighting of gas? (d) number of rack positions in oven; (e) way that racks slide into position (f) position of the broiler, operation of broiler

TABLE 13-3
Small Electric Appliances

Appliance	Essential Parts	Materials Used	Convenience Features
Electric toaster	Heating element insulated from frame; appliance cord may be permanently attached	Steel or copper plated with chromium or nickel; trim of thermoset plastic or synthetic rubber	Automatic device to control depth of browning; hinged bottom or removable crumb tray; pop-up ejector; small oven on bottom of toaster to keep toast warm
Waffle iron	Terminal studs on lower half of baker; connecting wires to upper unit pass through the hinge	Steel or copper plated with chromium or nickel; backing grids of cast aluminum	Interchangeable grids so the waffle baker can be changed into grids for grilling foods; signal light
Electric skillet	Heating element sealed in the bottom of skillet	Cast aluminum	Certain models may be submerged in water as far as the control on the handle without danger to the electric element (manufacturers' directions must be consulted)
Electric deep-fat fryer	Special compartment for the fat; heating element in lower portion of appliance; faucet near the base of fryer for draining fat from the well	Chromium-plated steel lining of heavy aluminum; base and knobs usually of plastic	Automatic temperature control, from simmer to 450°F (232°C); signal light
Food mixer (portable models also available)	Electric motor sealed in a housing; beaters; electric appliance cord	Bowls of glass or stainless steel; structural part of the mixer of enameled iron or steel; rubber feet on base of mixer; blades of stainless steel or nylon	Some have mixer head that can be removed from the base; variety of speeds; adjustable platform for holding bowls; beaters on mixers with stationary bowls have planetary action; may be supplied with a variety of attachments to eliminate hand cutting and mixing
Blender	Agitator blades that shred, grind, liquefy, chop, pulverize, and blend	Blades: stainless steel; motor housing: steel finished with chromium or in white baked-on enamel; container: glass	Two speeds are often provided; some have a two-piece top, so that ingredients can be added to the container without stopping the operation

burner or electric broil unit; (g) special features of the range—does it have a sensing unit, and oven thermometer, a self-cleaning oven, convenience outlets? How are these used?

3. What is the total capacity of the laboratory freezer?
4. Learn to operate the dishwasher.
5. Make a chart of the electric appliances in the laboratory. Read instruction books for each

appliance. Summarize important parts of appliances and special instructions for the use of each. Keep this information for permanent use.

6. Go over small equipment in laboratory. Be sure you can identify each piece of equipment by its proper name. Make a list of equipment, and give as many uses for each item as possible.

REFERENCES

BOOKS

Consumers All: The Yearbook of Agriculture. Washington, D.C.: U.S. Department of Agriculture, 1965.

Ehrenkranz, Florence, and Lydia Inman. *Epuipment in the Home.* New York: Harper & Row, 1973, Chaps. 4-8, 12, 13, 15.

Gilbreth, L. M., O. M. Thomas, and E. Clymer. *Management in the Home.* New York: Dodd, Mead, 1962.

Peet, L. J., and Mary S. Pickett. *Household Equipment.* New York: Wiley, 1970.

Steidl, Rose E., and Esther Crew Bratton. *Work in the Home.* New York: Wiley, 1968.

ARTICLES, BULLETINS, AND PAMPHLETS

American National Standard Dimensions, Tolerances, and Terminology for Home Cooking and Baking Utensils: ANSI 261.1. New York: American Standards Institute, 1970.

Baragar, Arnold. "Gas Cooking Top Thermostat Operation in Relation to Pan Material." *J. Home Econ.* **55:**437, 1963.

Burgess, Constance. "Choosing and Using Your Food Freezer," *Miscellaneous Bulletin 50.* Ithaca, N.Y.: New York State College of Home Economics, Cornell University, 1963.

Consumer Guide to Metal Cookware and Bakeware. Fontana, WI.: Metal Cookware Manufact. Assoc., 1977.

Housing and Household Equipment Committee. *Handbook of Household Equipment Terminology,* rev. ed. New York: American Home Economics Association, 1970.

Peters, Cheryl, and Fern Hunt. "Heat Disbribution and Heating Eficiency in Selected Pans on Conventional and Glass/Ceramic Surfaced Electric Range Units." *Home Econ. Res. J.* **5:**176, 1977.

Ruffin, Marilyn, and Katherine Tipper. "Service-Life Expectancy of Household Appliances: New Estimates from the USDA." *Home Econ. Res. J.* **3:**159, 1975.

Woodward Janice. "In Shopping, in Cleaning, Be Smart About Cookware." *Extension Bulletin 1182.* Ithaca, N.Y.: New York State College of Home Economics, Cornell University, 1967.

Preparation of Foods and Food Products

Part Four is concerned primarily with how to prepare food of uniformly high quality. It attempts to present the most advanced thinking on the selection, storage, preparation, and cooking of food.

Many ready-to-serve and partially prepared food products are used today in place of foods prepared entirely from the raw materials. The convenience foods require less time, space, and equipment to prepare. They may also be lower in cost than conventially prepared products. The person concerned with the production of food—whether in the home, in an institution, or in a commercial establishment—must be able to decide which foods are to be prepared from raw materials and which are to be purchased partially or wholly prepared. To make the best possible choice, the consumer should know what is involved in the production and preparation of both the conventional and the ready-to-serve products. Most meals today are prepared from a combination of raw materials, partially prepared foods, and ready-to-serve products.

Part Four

Food Preparation

The preparation of nutritious and appealing food that will be enjoyed by all who eat it is no small achievement. High-quality food is not only satisfying to the appetite and to the esthetic sense, it also plays an important role in good health. Food that is well prepared, perfectly flavored, and appropriately and attractively served is keenly anticipated and enjoyed.

It is generally agreed that cooking is an art as well as a science, but the esthetic principles are not so clearly defined as the scientific; nonetheless, they operate to a marked degree in the preparation of palatable food.

The esthetic values applied to the preparation of food originate in the mind of the person handling it. His attitude must be to treat food in such a way as to bring out only the very best in flavor, appearance, and texture. To achieve this end, a knowledge of the scientific principles underlying the preparation of food is certainly necessary. But there is need for an imagination that can create mental pictures of the food products to be prepared.

It is difficult to say what makes a good cook. Perhaps the catalyst that enables one person to produce an acceptable dish and another a superb dish is the fundamental attitude toward the materials being handled. The person who perceives the beauty in the food he handles will not destroy its natural qualities. Hence, the food itself—its shape, color, and form—suggests how it is to be used. This requires a study of the food before use, for carelessness can ruin good food.

The person who handles food creatively is never satisfied with an indifferent product: it must be a perfect example of what it could be, and—beyond that—it must have something that reflects his subjective feelings about each particular food.

There are, of course, aids that can be recommended to help in producing high-quality food. A few are discussed here to give some guidelines to follow in the development of competence in handling food. A sound understanding of how and why certain changes take place in food when it is cooked is essential, and the major portion of this book is devoted to the principles underlying these changes. But the factors discussed in this section, although they are not necessarily scientific, are nevertheless equally important.

PRINCIPLES OF FOOD PREPARATION

Selection of Food. The condition of the food when it is brought into the kitchen has a great deal to do with the results obtained. This does not mean that ingredients must be the most expensive on the market, but it does mean that all foods must be fresh and at the proper stage of maturity for cooking. Vegetables that have been kept too long, meat that has deteriorated, and oils that are slightly rancid cannot be improved during the cooking process.

Preliminary Treatment of Food. Only clean food is palatable. Surface dirt is apparent and is easily removed by thorough washing. It is essential, however, to learn the unique characteristics of each food that is to be prepared, so that a thorough cleaning may be given. For example, a soft brush may be necessary to clean thoroughly the spears of asparagus, which sometimes contain large amounts of sand that ordinary washing will not remove. Foods that are not thoroughly cleaned fail to make their true mark on the eater. In fact, violent food dislikes may develop because of a food that was not properly cleaned.

Another preliminary step in the preparation of food that affects the finished product is the mechanical treatment given it. Paring, cutting, slicing, dicing, and similar procedures must be planned for the particular food item handled. Excessive chopping or mashing may destroy natural texture and flavor. Unnecessary removal of beautifully colored skins of fruit and the cutting up of food into awkward sizes and shapes may have a fatal effect on the finished appearance. Soaking may be necessary for a few foods, such as dried fruit and dried legumes, but most fresh foods are not improved by it—they become soft and lose flavor as well as nutritive value.

In short, if care and planning go into the preliminary treatment of food, many food failures will be avoided. Poor preliminary treatment cannot be corrected later. Once the food is in the saucepan, the skillet, or the oven, early errors in preparation are bound to become more serious.

Seasoning. Some foods require little seasoning; others are improved by the addition of small amounts of seasoning materials. The purpose in seasoning food is to make it more enticing. It is obvious that overseasoned food is far from interesting; it may actually be offensive to some. But what constitutes overseasoning for one food is not overseasoning for another. For example, most fresh vegetables require little more seasoning than a dash of salt. On the other hand, a sauce intended to enhance the flavor of a bland food such as macaroni will require the most skillful seasoning technique. It is of the utmost importance to taste food as it is being cooked. Each recipe, regardless of the number of times it is prepared, will show small differences in flavor each time because the precise flavor of each ingredient making up the dish is never the same. Consequently, the food should be tasted at regular intervals so that the right amount of seasonings may be added. (Obviously, certain cooked dishes cannot be tasted before serving lest their form be impaired.)

COOKING TECHNIQUES

One of the keys to good cooking is understanding the composition and structure of the food and the chemical and physical changes that take place during cooking. Basic cooking principles must be observed for each group of food products if good results are to be obtained. Good food techniques—skill in handling food—are the result of the application of cooking principles to the preparation of food.

Some food techniques are more difficult to develop than others. A knowledge and application of the cooking principles for vegetables may be all that is necessary to cook vegetables properly. However, not only knowledge of cooking principles but practice as well are required to develop skill in making pastry.

Good Equipment. The use of proper equipment in top condition is of primary importance in the production of good food. Standardized measuring equipment, a variety of knives, accurate scales and thermometers, and well-insulated ranges all contribute to good-quality food.

Recipes. The use of standard recipes is a prime factor in producing good products. (See Chapter 12 for a full discussion.) They are particularly necessary to the person who is just beginning to develop skill in cookery. Once basic proportions and recipes are mastered, the inquiring student will find that they are general guides that can be varied within certain limits. It will soon become apparent that changing a recipe to conform to a new idea or a remembered taste is part of the art of cooking. Many interesting and palatable dishes have been created in this way.

Imagination. The magic ingredient in food preparation is imagination—that is, the ability to feel how others will feel about the food product involved. Imagination can be nourished by storing up a backlog of remembrances about the appearance, texture, and flavor of food through individual attention to all matters concerned with food. A texture change should always be tracked down, a new flavor investigated, a color change—as well as the sequence of events that led up to it—noted.

As is true in any other art, practice is essential, but the practice must be intelligently directed. There is little value in cooking without thinking. To become proficient in food preparation skills, the student must make the most of opportunities to handle food. The chance to prepare a special soup, to help make a salad, to direct the preparation of a community supper—all have value and require the use of creative resources. Competence will come with a minimum of practice if an inquiring attitude is brought to every cooking experience.

Serving Food. Not only must food be well prepared to be palatable, it must also be served with an eye to its color and appearance. No matter how simple it is, there should be something special about every food served. It is not always necessary to transfer the food from the baking or cooking dish to a platter or serving dish. Advance planning may suggest that the item should be cooked in a dish suitable for serving. A simple garnish effect can lift the dish out of the realm of the ordinary and make it a special creation.

Timing. To be most palatable and nutritious, food must be served as soon as possible after it has been prepared. Ideally, all food should be cooked in small quantities and for a relatively short period of time. Immediate service is fre-

quently possible when food is prepared for an individual or for a small group but relatively difficult when it is prepared for large groups. The successful handling of food in quantity is an area of food management that takes intensive study. Dishes that should be eaten cold are less than perfect if they are not served cold. Similarly, hot dishes, if they are served lukewarm and on cold plates, do not present the food to full advantage. Certain foods—such as omelets, soufflés, steaks, chops, and broiled fish—should be served immediately.

Dishes. When complementary colors are used as a background for food, they have a favorable effect on the person looking at it. In general, plates with simple background serve as a desirable field for showing off food. Dishes with tasteful designs in greens, yellows, light brown, and orange set off foods placed on them. The shape of the dish or container is all-important in providing the food with the proper background. A simple macaroni-and-cheese combination takes on a new dimension in a copper-colored casserole.

METHODS OF COOKERY

Although these are literally hundreds of recipes available for each food item, the methods of cooking food can be categorized into five or six groups; the characteristics desired in the finished product determine which method of cookery will be used for any given food.

Air, water, steam, and fat—or combinations of these—may be used as cooking media. Another method, microwave cooking, involves the generation of heat within the food; it is not a cooking medium.

Air. Cooking methods in which air is the principal cooking medium include roasting, baking, and broiling. Such cooking is called *dry-heat cookery*. Baking and roasting are now usually done in an oven, but at one time roasting meant turning the food on a spit before an open fire or covering it with hot coals. Food placed in the oven to bake or roast may be cooked partially by dry heat (convection currents of dry air and conduction of heat from the metal container to the food) and partially by moist heat, if the food is high in water content. The surface is cooked by dry heat, the interior by moist heat.

Roasting a piece of meat in the oven is largely a matter of cooking by convected air currents because little of the surface of the meat comes in contact with the heated roasting pan. On the other hand, a thin cookie bakes largely by conducted heat, although radiant heat is responsible for some of the surface browning of the cookie. If a food is placed in the oven in a glass container, most of it will be cooked by convection currents, but glass transmits some radiant energy; heat radiated to the surface of the food imparts to it a brown color.

Broiling is the cooking of food by exposing it to direct heat. The food on the broiler is cooked in part by conduction through contact with the hot broiler. But radiant energy also contributes to the cooking of broiled food.

Water. The cooking methods in which the cooking medium is water are well known and commonly used: boiling, simmering, and stewing. Boiling is the cooking of food in moist heat; water is the surrounding medium. The temperature of the water is usually 212°F (100°C). High altitudes and the presence of electrolytes in the water alter its boiling point. The boiling point of a liquid is reached when there are many bubbles of steam rising to the surface and breaking. Sometimes a food is *parboiled*—that is, it is boiled for a short period of time, removed from the water, and cooked further by another method. Foods that are cooked in water receive heat through convection currents and conduction. Simmering and poaching are the cooking of food by immersion in hot liquid maintained at temperatures just under boiling.

Steam. Steaming also involves moist heat. Food is said to be steamed when it is cooked in water vapor above water, or in a waterless cooker (in which cooking is done in the presence of a small amount of liquid and the steam it produces), and when cooked with steam under pressure. This method is known as *pressure cooking*. As a consequence of the fast elevation of temperature within the food under steam pressure, the cooking period is shortened. Wrapping food in aluminum foil before cooking it is another method of steaming.

In steaming, heat is transferred from the steam to the food. When the steam reaches the cold food, it condenses and gives off heat. Condensation of the steam continues until the heated food is brought to the same temperature as the steam (212°F; 100°C); then the condensation rate decreases.

Fat. Fat is used as a medium for cooking in several ways: sautéing, pan frying, and deep-fat frying.

Sautéing is the cooking of food in a lightly greased pan. The heat is transferred to the food mainly by conduction. Only thin pieces of food are sautéed, and these must be turned from one side to another to be completely cooked.

Pan frying differs from sautéing in that the food is cooked in a larger amount of fat—but not enough to cover it. The food must be turned on both sides for complete cooking. Heat is transferred to the food partially by conduction from the contact with the heated pan and partially by convection currents set up in the fat.

Cooking a food in deep fat is similar to boiling it. The fat receives heat from the bottom of the pan; the heat is transferred by conduction to the fat and is distributed through the fat by convection currents. Fats can be heated to a temperature higher than the boiling point of water. The smoking temperature of fat is an important consideration when choosing this medium (see Chapter 28). Fats and oils should not be heated to the smoking point because once the fat decomposes it no longer is suitable for frying purposes.

Combination Methods. Braising and fricasseeing are examples of use of a combination of cooking media: fat and water. The terms are used synonymously and their first step involves browning the surface of the food in a small quantity of fat. Then the food is slowly cooked in liquid or juices in a covered utensil. When a large piece of meat is cooked in this manner, the method is called *pot roasting*.

Direct Transference of Heat. When food is baked in a waffle iron or on a grill, the heat is transferred to it by conduction or by radiation. The waffle iron provides two metal surfaces through which the heat is transferred by conduction to the batter.

Electronic Transference of Heat. Microwaves can be absorbed, reflected or transferred. When microwaves are absorbed by food, internal friction caused by the agitation of water and fat molecules generates heat. Substances that reflect microwaves, such as paper, glass, and ceramics, do not become heated and are used as utensils. Metals are not used in microwave ovens because they reflect electromagnetic energy and may damage the oven. (See Chapter 45.)

SUMMARY

Preparation of food products that are the very best in flavor, appearance, and texture requires fresh, good-quality ingredients and a knowledge of the scientific principles underlying food preparation as well as creativity and imagination. Factors in achieving excellence include wise selection of foods at the peak of maturity, thorough cleaning, judicious seasoning, proper equipment, standardized recipes—and practice and imagination. To assure maximum enjoyment, foods must be attractively served on appropriate dishes at the proper temperature.

The characteristics desired in the finished product determine the method of cooking. Cooking media include air, water, steam, fat, and combinations of these. When a grill or waffle iron is used, the food is cooked by direct transfer of heat. In microwave cookery, heat is generated within the food. Microwave cookery is speedy and does not heat the cooking dishes (except by conduction from the food itself). General palatability compares favorably with that achieved by standard methods. Surface browning—considered desirable by many, especially for meats—does not occur, however, without a special browning unit. With this unit, the cooking vessels become hot.

QUESTIONS AND TOPICS FOR DISCUSSION AND STUDY

1. From past experience, describe instances in which you believe cooking improved some qualities of your food. Explain your feelings about it.
2. Suggest a number of interesting food combinations from the standpoint of color, texture, form, and taste. Give the reasons for your choices.
3. Explain how you believe food prejudices or preferences are formed.
4. Carefully compare an American cookbook with a foreign cookbook. What are the basic differences that you notice about the handling of raw food materials and the expected appearance of the finished product?
5. What factors do you believe make a food palatable? Which factor do you believe stands out above all others? Give the reasons for your answer.

SUGGESTED ACTIVITIES

1. Visit a fruit and vegetable market or the produce section of a supermarket. Note the items you look at first. Which fruits and vegetables capture your attention? Why do you think this is so? Watch other people. How do they react? Is it possible to make any generalizations about the relation between food preference and appearance of the food?
2. Compare the taste and flavor of a potato cooked in the following ways: baked, boiled, steamed, french-fried, sautéed and baked electronically. What are the disadvantages and advantages of each method? Is any one method perfect?

REFERENCES

Books

Consumers All: The Yearbook of Agriculture. Washington, D.C.: U.S. Department of Agriculture, 1965, pp. 441–481.

Food: The Yearbook of Agriculture. Washington, D.C.: U.S. Department of Agriculture, 1959, p. 495.

Food for Us All: The Yearbook Agriculture. Washington, D.C.: U.S. Department of Agriculture, 1969, p. 94.

Roosevelt, Nicholas. *Creative Cookery.* New York: Harper Row, 1956.

Vail, Gladys, J. Phillips, Lucile Rust, Ruth Griswold, and Margaret Justin, *Foods,* 7th ed. Boston: Houghton Mifflin, 1978, Chap. 20.

Van Zante, Helen J. *Equipment in the Home.* Englewood Cliffs, N.J.: Prentice-Hall, 1964.

Van Zante, Helen J. *The Microwave Oven.* Englewood Cliffs, N.J.: Prentice-Hall, 1973.

Measuring Techniques

The use of standard measuring equipment and standard measuring techniques will help to ensure successful products. For consistent results, identical measuring procedures must be followed each time a particular recipe is used. Every major ingredient, dry or liquid, requires a special measuring technique.

The purpose in measuring is to obtain a precise volume for liquid ingredients or precise weight for dry ingredients. Volume is measured in fluid (fl) ounces and weight in avoirdupois (avdp) ounces. Since the weight of a given volume will vary according to its mass, water has been designated as a standard. Water is the only substance in which fluid and avoirdupois ounces are equal. Similarly, in the metric system, water is the only substance in which a milliliter and a gram are equal. Foods with a lower specific gravity than water, such as oil, will weigh less than water. Those with a higher specific gravity such as milk, will weigh more. Although weighing is a more accurate measurement, it is also time-consuming and inconvenient to those without scales. Thus measurements in recipes for home use are given in volume measurements such as cups, tablespoons, or gallons.

ACCURACY OF MEASURING UTENSILS

Standards for volumes of measuring utensils are based on their metric equivalent. One measuring cup or 8 fluid ounces is equal to 236.6 milliliters; 1 tablespoon, 14.8 milliliters; and 1 teaspoon, 4.9 milliliters. The procedure for determining if the measuring utensil is accurate is to fill the utensil with tap water and then pour the water into a graduated cylinder. The volume in the graduated cylinder should match the number of milliliters designated for the particular utensil.

Since it would be very expensive for manufacturers of measuring utensils to produce products that have such exact measurements as 236.6 milliliters, the American Home Economics Association has proposed tolerances of 5% for household measuring utensils.[1] A measuring cup therefore can deviate by 5% of 236.6 ± 11.8

[1]A.S.A., *American Standard Dimensions, Tolerances, and Terminology for Home Cooking and Baking Utensils* (New York: American Standards Association, 1963).

136

milliliters. This small deviation is unlikely to produce a significant effect on the final product.

Flour. White flour is the most difficult ingredient to measure, for it has a tendency to pack—and the finer the flour, the more it packs. For this reason, it is recommended that flour be sifted before it is measured. Flour should be sifted once, then lightly spooned or scooped into a measuring cup, where it will peak up slightly. The excess is then leveled off with the straight edge of a spatula or knife. The cup should never be tapped to level off the flour; tapping will only pack down the flour and lead to using more than the amount required. Flour may also be sifted directly into the cup, but this is a less convenient and less accurate method because flour may

weigh less than that measured by the recommended method.

Presifted and "instantized" flours are designed to eliminate the necessity of sifting flour. It has been found that some adjustment in proportion must be made when presifted flour is used for standard recipes. Laboratory tests[2] show that the weight of a cup of unsifted, spooned flour can be adjusted to the approximate weight of a cup of sifted flour by removing 2 level tbsp. This adjustment is sufficient for all-purpose or cake flour.

Whole-grain flours and meals are not sifted before measuring. Instead, they are stirred with a

[2]R. H. Mathewes et al., "Sifted Versus Unsifted Flour," *J. Home Econ.* **55**:123, 1963.

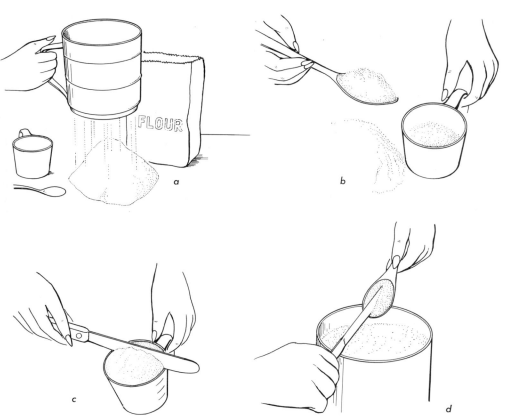

15-1 *How to measure flour. (a) Sift white flour before measuring. (b) Spoon flour into a dry measuring cup until the cup is more than full. (c) Level off the cup of flour with a spatula or the back edge of a knife. (d) To measure ½ tbsp. of flour or any dry material, first measure a tablespoon. Divide the amount in half and remove half.*

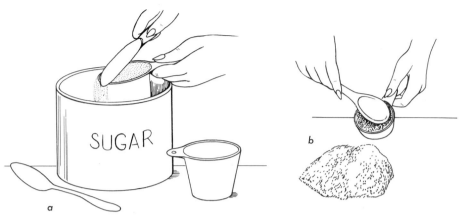

15-2 *How to measure sugar. (a) Spoon sugar into a dry measuring cup. Level off the cup of sugar with a spatula or the back edge of a knife. If lumpy, sift sugar before measuring. (b) Pack brown sugar into a dry measuring cup or fraction of a cup. It should hold its shape when it is turned out. Lumpy brown sugar can be put through a coarse sieve.*

fork or spoon and then—like white flour—are lightly spooned or scooped into a measuring cup.

Sugar. Usually, neither white nor brown sugar is sifted before measuring. White sugar, however, if it is at all lumpy (confectioners' sugar frequently is) should be sifted first, spooned into a dry measure, and leveled off with the edge of a spatula or knife. Brown sugar, on the other hand, must be packed into the cup so firmly as to keep the shape of the cup when it is turned out.

The moisture content of brown sugar is 2%. If it is not carefully sealed, it loses the moisture, dries out, and hardens. To protect against this,

brown sugar should be stored tightly wrapped in the refrigerator. If it does become lumpy, it can be rolled or sifted before measuring. Free-flowing brown sugar is poured into a cup or fractional cup and leveled (Fig. 15-2).

Fats. Fats are used either in solid or in liquid form. Solid fats should be pressed firmly (to eliminate air holes) into the measuring cup, then leveled with the edge of a knife (Fig. 15-3).

An alternative method to measure solid fats is the water-displacement method. If ¼ cup of fat is needed, a liquid measuring cup is filled to the ¾-cup marking with cold tap water. Fat is spooned in until it displaces the water to read 1

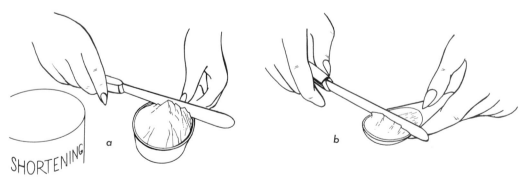

SHORTENING

15-3 *How to measure shortening. (a) Pack shortening in a measuring cup or fraction of a cup. Be sure all air spaces are pressed out. Level off with a spatula or the back edge of a knife. (b) When measuring a tablespoonful or teaspoonful, dip the bowl of the spoon into the shortening and level off with a spatula or the back edge of a knife.*

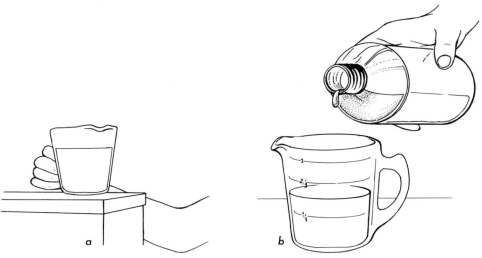

15-4 *How to measure liquids. (a) Pour the liquid to the desired line and check the measurement at eye level. (b) Pour thick liquids such as honey and molasses into the measuring cup or spoon. Use a rubber scraper to remove all the material from the cup.*

cup. The volume of fat that was added will equal $\frac{1}{4}$ cup. This method leaves a cleaner measuring cup but water adhering to the fat may alter the product if one is not careful to adjust for this.

In measuring fat that comes in bars or pound packages, it should be remembered that one $\frac{1}{4}$-lb bar equals $\frac{1}{2}$ cup. A liquid fat should be poured directly into the measuring cup, up to the desired level. Care should be taken in removing it from the cup so that none is left clinging to the sides.

Liquids. Liquids are measured in a standard liquid measuring cup, which has a rim above the 1-cup mark (Fig. 15-4). The cup should be set on a level surface before the liquid is poured in,

and any foam that forms on top of the liquid should be allowed to settle before the measurement reading is taken.

Syrups are poured into a measuring cup or measuring spoon (Fig. 15-6). Spoon measures should be level.

The liquid in a measuring cup tends to form a concave surface (the meniscus) from molecular attraction. The reading should be taken from the bottom of the meniscus.

Powdered Materials. Powdered food materials—such as baking powder, dried milk solids, salt, and soda—are stirred first if needed to break up any lumps. Then a dry spoon is dipped into the powder and taken up heaping. The excess is leveled off with the edge of a spatula or knife.

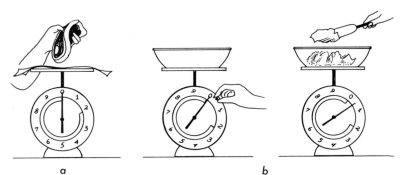

15-5 *How to use scales. (a) Place a piece of wax paper on the surface of the scale platform. Be sure the pointer is turned to zero on the dial. (b) When weighing food in a bowl, place the empty bowl on the scale platform and turn the pointer to zero on the dial.*

15-6 *Only standard measuring equipment should be used for measuring dry and liquid ingredients. Top: Liquid measuring cup, fractional measuring cups, and measuring spoons. (Courtesy of Corn Products Company) Bottom: Liquid ingredients are measured in a liquid measure. (Courtesy of Clabber Girl Baking Powder)*

Eggs. The measurement of eggs would be a fairly simple matter if all eggs were the same size, for most recipes give the number of eggs required. In such cases, medium-sized eggs are preferred. (It is possible that the difference between a small egg and a large one may be as much as the weight of another small egg.) If a recipe gives a cup measurement for eggs, it is wise to use that. If a recipe calling for one egg is cut in half and only half an egg is required, the egg is beaten thoroughly first. Then the beaten egg is measured in a cup and divided in half.

METRIC SYSTEM

In the United States, the Metric Conversion Act was signed into law in December 1975. The metric system (Tables 15-1 through 15-3) was developed in France at the time of the French Revolution. The system was based on the metre, a length defined as one ten-millionth the distance from the North Pole to the equator along the circle of earth from Dunkirk, France, to Barcelona, Spain. The United States changeover to the metric system of measurements will foster international trade, as a large portion of all world production is conducted in the metric system. The United States is the last industrialized nation to change to the metric system.

Food. The switch to metric is of prime importance when working with food. In the United States volume measures rather than scales will be used and the ingredients in recipes will be given in milliliters (ml) quantities. Measuring devices are available with metric measures, and in the future new cooking utensils such as casseroles and cake pans will be identified by liter. Biscuit and cookie sheets will be shown in centimeters (cm). Oven and cooking thermometers are available with both Fahrenheit and Celsius scale divisions. For large-quantity cooking, new scales or new dials for scales now in use will be needed.

Equipment. Cooking appliances such as conventional range ovens, some surface units, portable ovens, electric saucepans, and deep fat fryers now have Fahrenheit temperature markings on control dials. On new equipment control dials will be in the Celsius, not the Fahrenheit scale. There is, however, the possibility that both scales

TABLE 15-1
Base Units and Their Symbols

Quantity	Base Unit	Symbol
Length	meter	m
Mass	kilogram	kg
Temperature	degree Celsius	°C
Time	second	s
Electric current	ampere	A
Substance	mole	mol
Intensity of light	candela	cd

TABLE 15-2
Common Metric Units and Symbols

Quantity	1/1,000,000	1/1000	1/100	Standard	1000	1,000,000
Length	micrometer (μm)	millimeter (mm)	centimeter (cm)	meter (m)	kilometer (km)	megameter (Mm)
Volume		milliliter (ml)		liter (l)		
Mass	microgram (μg)	milligram (mg)		gram (g)	kilogram (kg)	megagram (Mg)
Energy				joule (J)	kilojoule (kJ)	megajoule (MJ)
Power				watt (W)	kilowatt (kW)	megawatt (MW)
Electromotive force		millivolt (mV)		volt (V)		
Temperature				degree Celsius (°C)		
Frequency				hertz (Hz)	kilohertz (kHz)	megahertz (MHz)
Electric current	microampere (μA)	milliampere (mA)		ampere (A)	kiloampere (kA)	
Time	microsecond (μs)	millisecond (ms)		second (s)	kilosecond (ks)	

Source: Handbook for Metric Usage (Washington, D.C.: American Home Economics Association, 1977), pp. 6–7.

will be used on some appliances. Recommendations are that control dials calibrated in Celsius be graduated in 10° intervals on a scale ranging from about 70 to 290°C, with values indicated at 20–40° intervals. Temperature controls on equipment such as dishwashers and refrigerators are not likely to undergo changes, as these controls are not marked with actual temperatures.

Food preservation equipment will come in for some special changes. A liter of freezing space should be allowed for 50 grams of unfrozen food placed in the freezer at one time. The present allowance is 3 pounds per cubic foot. Food processed in a home pressure canner is to be processed at 69 kilopascals (10 pounds per square inch) steam pressure. Other steam pressure recommendations will be converted to metric equivalents (Table 15.5).

Purchasing Food and Metric Recipes. Eventually consumers in this country will switch over to the metric system for buying food. The gram,

TABLE 15-3
Metric Prefixes and Their Values

Prefix	Symbol	Value
exa	E	10^{18}
peta	P	10^{15}
tera	T	10^{12}
giga	G	10^{9}
mega	M	10^{6} (one million times)
kilo	k	10^{3} (one thousand times)
hecto	h	10^{2} (one hundred times)
deka	da	10^{1} (ten times)
deci	d	10^{-1} (one tenth of)
centi	c	10^{-2} (one hundredth of)
milli	m	10^{-3} (one thousandth of)
micro	μ	10^{-6} (one millionth of)
nano	n	10^{-9}
pico	p	10^{-12}
femto	f	10^{-15}
atto	a	10^{-18}

TABLE 15-4
Conversion Factors

Quantity	Unit	Approximate Equivalent	
Length	inch	25.4	millimeters (exact)
	foot	304.8	millimmters
	yard	0.914	meter
	mile	1.609	kilometers
Mass (weight)	ounce	28.35	grams
	pound	453.59	grams
Volume	cubic meter	1000	liters
	liter	0.001	cubic meter
	fluid ounce	29.573	milliliters
	teaspoon	4.93	milliliters
	tablespoon	14.79	milliliters
	cup	236.58	milliliters
		0.237	liter
	pint	0.473	liter
	quart	0.946	liter
	gallon	3.785	liters
		0.0038	cubic meter
	cubic foot	28.317	liters
		0.0283	cubic meter
Temperature	degree Fahrenheit	$\dfrac{t_{°F} - 32}{1.8} = t_{°C}$	
Area	square inch	645.2	square millimeters
	square foot	0.0929	square meter
	square yard	0.836	square meter
	square mile	2.590	square kilometers
	acre	4046.9	square meters
	hectare	10,000	square meters
Energy, work, quantity of heat	British thermal unit	1055	joules
	kilocalorie	4.185	kilojoules
	horsepower-hour	2.6845	megajoules
	watt-hour	0.860	kilocalorie
		3.600	kilojoules
Power	British thermal unit per second	1.054	kilowatts
	horsepower	0.746	kilowatt
Pressure	pounds-force per square inch	6.895	kilopascals
	atmosphere (normal)	101.325	kilopascals
		760	millimeters of mercury
		14.696	pounds-force per square inch

Source: Handbook for Metric Usage (Washington, D.C.: American Home Economics Association, 1977).

kilogram, milliliter, or liter will be used. Many food labels now state their contents in both metric and customary U.S. units. This is called soft conversion. The hard conversion will come when containers of food are designed to hold metric units—for example, a liter rather than a quart of milk.

To be accurate, published recipes will have to

be retested when converted to metric measurements. The *Handbook for Metric Usage in Home Economics* recommends a procedure for adapting a recipe to metric measurements.[3] Table 15-4 shows conversion factors and Table 15-5 shows conversion tables that can be used in the changeover to metric units.

The International System of Units (SI). As the name implies (SI) is the common language of metrics. Its symbols are identical in all languages,

[3] *Handbook for Metric Usage* (Washington, D.C.: American Home Economics Association, 1977), p. 13.

but the unit names may be spelled differently. There are seven base units from which other units are derived. With the exception of Celsius, unit names are not capitalized unless they begin a sentence, and unit symbols are not capitalized unless the unit name is derived from the name of a person (e.g., A for ampere). Symbols of units are always in the singular and a period is used after a symbol only at the end of a sentence. Table 15-1 shows the seven base units and their symbols and Table 15-2 shows some common metric units and symbols. The names, symbols, and values for metric prefixes are given in Table 15-3.

TABLE 15-5
Conversion Tables

Volume

Unit	Approximate Replacement in U.S. Customary Units
1 milliliter (1 ml)	0.20 teaspoon
2 milliliters (2 ml)	0.40 teaspoon
5 milliliters (5 ml)	1.01 teaspoons
15 milliliters (15 ml)	3.04 teaspoons
	1.01 tablespoons
25 milliliters (25 ml)	1.69 tablespoons
50 milliliters (50 ml)	3.38 tablespoons
60 milliliters (60 ml)	0.25 cup
75 milliliters (75 ml)	0.32 cup
100 milliliters (100 ml)	0.42 cup
125 milliliters (125 ml)	0.53 cup
250 milliliters (250 ml)	1.06 cups
500 milliliters (500 ml)	2.11 cups
1000 milliliters (1000 ml)	4.23 cups
	1.06 quarts

Gauge Pressure at Sea Level and Boiling Point of Water

Pounds per Square Inch, psi	Kilopascals, kPa	°F	°C
1	7	216	102
5	34	228	109
10	69	239	115
15	103	250	121
20	138	259	126
25	172	268	130
30	207	275	135

Source: Handbook for Metric Usage (Washington, D.C.: American Home Economics Association, 1977).

SUMMARY

Standard measurements and uniform measuring practices are necessary for consistent and successful results in cookery. There is a special measuring technique for each major ingredient, dry or liquid, and special measuring equipment has been devised for dry and liquid products.

The International System of Units (SI) is the basis for metric measures in this country. In the United States, volume rather than scales will be used to measure food, and recipes will be given in milliliters. Cooking temperatures will be given in degrees Celsius (°C).

SUGGESTED ACTIVITIES

1. Practice measuring flour, sugar, fat, and liquid according to directions in this chapter. Do this until the weight of each of your measured ingredients corresponds to standard weights (Table A–2).
2. Measure weight of 125 ml of flour, sugar, fat, and water.
3. Compare the weight of a cup of sifted flour with that of one that has not been sifted. Can you conclude from this that one cup of flour is the equivalent of the other?
4. Measure $\frac{1}{3}$ cup of fat in a graduated 1–cup measure, and measure more of the same kind of fat in a $\frac{1}{3}$ fractional cup. Compare weights. Is one method more accurate than the other?
5. Determine whether the items of measuring equipment you are using in the laboratory are of standard capacity. Measure into them, from a graduated cylinder, the quantity of water they are supposed to hold. Compare your results with those of others in class.

REFERENCES

BOOK

Handbook for Metric Usage (Washington, D.C.: American Home Economics Association, 1977).

PAMPHLET

"Average Weight of a Measured Cup of Various Foods," *Home Economics Research Report No. 41.* Washington, D.C.: U.S. Department of Agriculture, 1977.

ARTICLES AND PAMPHLETS

Batcher, O. M., and L. A. Young. "Metrification and the Home Economist." *J. Home Econ.* **66:**1974, p. 28.

Miller, B. S., and H. B. Trimbo. "Use of Metric Measurements in Food Preparation." *J. Home Econ.* **64:**1972, p. 20.

Parker, F. J. "The Shift Toward Metric." *J. Home Econ.* **65:**1973, p. 15.

Beverages

COFFEE

The United States is the leading coffee-consuming nation in the world, accounting for half of the world's total exports. Most of its coffee is imported from Brazil, Colombia, and Africa with some small amounts coming from Puerto Rico, Hawaii, Costa Rica, Mexico, Arabia, and the East Indies.

Processing. The United States imports almost exclusively "green" coffee, which must be roasted before it is consumed. In the roasting process, the coffee is exposed to heat for a controlled period while the bean becomes drier and its oils, which give the beverage its distinctive flavor, become water soluble.

The coffee bean is obtained from the fruit of an evergreen shrub (Fig. 16-1). Each coffee berry contains two coffee beans enclosed in a parchmentlike membrane in the fruit pulp.

Fermentation of the bean helps to develop the proper flavor in the coffee berry and brings about partial decomposition of fermentable materials (carbohydrates). After fermentation, the beans are dried while still in the parchment lining.

All coffee must be roasted, the final step in its processing. Roasting is of utmost importance, for it develops the characteristic flavor and aroma of the coffee bean. When coffee is roasted, heat-liberating (exothermic) changes take place. Bean temperatures rise and there is an accompanying moisture loss. A tannin, chlorogenic acid (a nonvolatile acid), decreases during the roasting period. The fat content of the bean undergoes a change, developing a group of essential oils called *caffeol*. These volatile substances will go into solution with water, giving coffee its characteristic flavor and aroma. Carbon dioxide is formed in the coffee bean as it roasts. Some of it is given off during the process, but some carbon dioxide gas remains in the coffee even after grinding. This causes the coffee grinds to float in water. The color of the bean changes from green to brown, a change believed to be caused by the caramelization of the sugar in the bean.[1] Chemically, the caffeine is stable at roasting temperatures. Coffee oils are unsaturated in the green bean, and heating causes some hydrolysis to glycerol and fatty acids. Some volatile fatty acids

[1] Michael Sivetz, *Coffee Processing Technology,* Vol. 2 (Westport, Conn.: Avi, 1963), p. 121.

145

16-1 *The coffee tree may bear ripe and unripe berries at the same time; hence, the crop must be picked by hand. (Courtesy of the Pan-American Coffee Bureau)*

are driven off and may account for the oily surface and characteristic oily odor of the roasted bean.

The time required for roasting depends on whether the desired roast is to be light, medium, or dark, and depends on the variety of coffee. Preference in the United States is for a medium brown roast. French and Italian roasts are much darker. The best blends of coffee are made after the beans are roasted, because roasting time differs for each variety making up the blend. Underroasting or overroasting the coffee bean will result in a poor product.

Composition. The substances of consequence in the coffee beverage are tannins, caffeine, caffeol, caramelized sugar, and carbon dioxide.

Tannins are not completely extracted during coffee brewing, but the rate at which they dissolve in hot water increases as the temperature of the water reaches the boiling point. The longer the coffee has been in contact with water, the greater will be the amount of tannin in the beverage. Tannins make up in part the charac-

teristic flavor of coffee. Because the oils that give coffee its characteristic flavor are volatile, they escape quite rapidly if the coffee solution is boiled, leaving behind only the bitter taste of the tannins.

Caffeine gives coffee its stimulating and diuretic effect. It comprises 1.2% of the roasted bean. It is highly soluble in hot water; the greatest portion is extracted during the first few minutes of preparation.

The flavor and aroma of the coffee beverage are derived from chlorogenic acid, caffeol, and to a lesser degree, the tannins. The major organic acid in coffee is the slightly sour-tasting chlorogenic acid, which is noticeable in very weak coffee. It appears that the caffeol group of flavoring substances is produced by the breakdown of large molecules of fat during the roasting process. Green coffee is lacking in odor and has little of the pleasant taste of roasted coffee.

Nutritive Value. Most of the food value obtainable from coffee is that contributed by the addition of sugar and milk. Coffee itself contains a substance called *trigonelline*. When the bean is roasted, some of the trigonelline is converted to nicotinic acid, a B vitamin, in amounts averaging 0.5 milligram/cup. Since the recommended intake for this vitamin ranges from 14 to 20 milligrams/day, coffee should not be considered a significant source of this vitamin. The caffeine in the hot beverage is stimulating to both muscular and mental activity,[2] thus accounting for its popularity as a food adjunct. Excessive amounts of tannin and caffeine, however, may become irritating to the digestive tract.

Buying. Much coffee is bought by brand, and each brand of coffee is a particular blend (Table 16-1). Although a few consumers buy coffee whole beans which they grind at home, most of the coffee on the retail market is ground and packaged in sealed or vacuum-packed cans. Vacuum packing is a process that draws out the air before the cover is sealed and safeguards the

[2] S. C. Prescott and W. H. Ukers, *All About Coffee,* 2nd ed. (New York: Tea and Coffee Trade Journal Co., 1935), p.314.

coffee from the effects of dampness, light, air, and undesirable odors. Coffee packaged in paper containers frequently goes stale several days after grinding and roasting. Chicory or cereal may be added to coffee to give it bulk. In some parts of the South, chicory is added to the coffee as a valued flavor constituent.

Because coffee is a highly perishable product, it is desirable to purchase it in relatively small quantities. Once a container of coffee is opened and exposed to the air, the loss of carbon dioxide and caffeol is accelerated, with a corresponding loss of flavor in the coffee brew. The loss of flavor may be minimized by storage at refrigerator temperatures.

There are three coffee grinds on the market: regular (for percolators), drip (for dripolators), and fine (for vacuum coffeemakers). These different-sized grinds are necessary for the different methods of making coffee. A larger grind will have less surface area and thus require a greater amount of liquid in proportion to a smaller grind.

Care and Storage. Coffee purchased in paper bags should be transferred to metal or glass con-

TABLE 16-1
Some Common Kinds of Coffee Bought and Sold in the United States

Kind	Country of Origin	Characteristics
Santos	Brazil	Clear, sweet flavor (most popular of Brazilian coffees)
Bourbon Santos	Brazil	Smooth, sweet flavor
Rio	Brazil	Pungent flavor and aroma
Coatepec	Mexico	Mellow, rich-bodied, fine
Huatusco	Mexico	Mellow, rich-bodied, fine
Orizaba	Mexico	Mellow, rich-bodied, fine
Cobans	Guatemala	Aromatic, good blenders
Antiquas	Guatemala	Aromatic, good blenders
Medellin	Colombia	Good roasters, fine flavor and body
Monizales	Colombia	Good roasters, fine flavor and body
Longberry Harrar	Ethiopia	Heavy-bodied, useful for blending
Kona	Hawaii	Fine flavor, blends well with high-grade mild coffee
Costa Rican	Costa Rica	Rich-bodied, good blenders, mild flavor
Santo Domingo	Dominican Republic	Rich-bodied, good blenders, mild flavor
Haiti	Haiti	Rich-bodied, good blenders, mild flavor
Jamaica, Blue Mountain	Jamaica	Rich-bodied, good blenders, mild flavor
Java	Indonesia	Heavy-bodied, sweet
Mocha	Yemen	Heavy-bodied, generally blended with Java

Source: Joel Schapira, *The Book of Coffee and Tea* (New York: St. Martin's Press, 1975).

tainers with tight-fitting covers. Mason jars are satisfactory.

Loss of flavor and aroma occurs more rapidly when the bean is finely pulverized, because the grinding process breaks down cell walls in the coffee bean, releasing carbon dioxide and caffeol. Also, ground coffee is susceptible to oxidation when exposed to the air, with a resultant loss in flavor. A dull or stale flavor in the roasted coffee results in a beverage that is lacking in taste and smell. The loss of carbon dioxide and the oxidation of unsaturated oils are thought to be the direct cause of the loss of flavor. Storage in the refrigerator retards such losses.

Principles of Coffee Preparation. In making coffee, the goal is to extract the maximum amount of caffeine and flavoring substances (caffeol) but the minimum of tannin, and to have a clear infusion. Any particles of coffee remaining in the beverage give it a cloudy appearance.

Methods of making coffee differ in detail and in the type of utensils used, but all are based on the principle of bringing the ground coffee particles in contact with hot water to extract the soluble constituents.

The methods commonly employed in the making of coffee are drip, vacuum, percolation, and steeping. The drip and vacuum methods are highly satisfactory, for in these preparations caffeol extracts are dissolved into the hot water, and the tannins are kept at a minimum. Although a good coffee brew can be obtained by percolating or steeping, there is some danger that the temperature of the coffee infusion will be brought up to boiling, thus giving the coffee a bitter flavor. For best results, preparation should be based on the kind of coffeemaker used, the grind of the coffee, the proportion of coffee to water, and the cleanliness of the coffeepot.

Methods of Making Coffee. Porcelain, stoneware, glass, pyroceram, enamelware, and stainless steel are the preferred materials for coffeemakers. Some metals form compounds with caffeine and other soluble substances in coffee and give a metallic flavor to the beverage. Whatever type of coffeepot is used, it should be kept clean. The odor of stale coffee in a coffeepot will impair the flavor of any coffee brewed in the vessel. After

using, the pot should be disassembled, scrubbed, rinsed, and dried.

For maximum flavor, the coffee must be fresh and ground to the size appropriate for the method of preparation to be used.

The usual proportions for coffee of average strength, good color, and characteristic flavor are 2 level tbsp to $\frac{3}{4}$ cup of water.[3] Best results are obtained when the full capacity of the coffeemaker is used; making less than half the capacity of the pot will not bring forth a superior brew (Table 16-2).

Coffee is always at its best when it is freshly brewed. If it is cooled and reheated, it becomes bitter and unpleasant.

Because water comprises a large percentage (about 99%) of the total volume of the coffee beverage, the quality of the local water supply will have an important effect on flavor. In areas where the alkalinity of the water is high, there is some neutralization of the acids in the coffee, which may result in a loss of flavor. Sivetz suggests that the brew becomes flat and insipid.[4] Coffee will also taste flat if the water has been allowed to boil for any length of time before it comes in contact with the grinds. Boiling the water will cause a loss of dissolved air. Permanent water hardness and added chlorine also have an adverse effect on flavor.

The temperature of the water is another critical factor in determining the quality of the brew. The water must be hot enough (185°F; 85°C) to dissolve the flavor components. If it reaches the boiling point, it will overextract the soluble solids and be bitter. It will also lose most of its aroma. Thus, coffee that has been boiled rather than simmered will create a delightful aroma in the room but be lacking in taste in the beverage.

The drip coffeepot and the glass vacuum coffeemaker are used to make filtered coffee. In this method, the time during which the water and coffee are in contact is very short. Drip coffee is prepared by first heating the pot and then pouring boiling water over finely ground coffee held

---

[3] W. H. Ukers and S. C. Prescott, in *The Chemistry and Technology of Food and Food Products,* Morris B. Jacobs ed. (New York: Interscience, 1951), pp. 1677–1679.

[4] Sivetz, op. cit., p.241.

TABLE 16-2
Basic Coffee-to-Water Measure (Pan American Coffee Bureau)

Number of 5½-oz Servings	Approved Coffee Measures[a]	Measuring Tablespoons (Level)	Measuring Cups of Water[b]	Fluid Ounces of Water
2	2	4	1½	12
4	4	8	3	24
6	6	12	4½	36
8	8	16	6	48
For Large Quantities of Coffee				
20	½ lb coffee	1 gal water		
40	1 lb coffee	2 gal water		

[a] Equals 2 level measuring tbsp coffee.
[b] Three-fourths of a measuring cup (6 fl. oz) of water yields about 5½ oz of coffee, an average serving.
Source: The Coffee Brewing Center.

in a suitable sieve—such as a perforated, container—usually lined with a filter paper (See Fig. 16-2). When hot water is poured over the coffee, the coffee infusion filters into the lower container. This container may be kept over hot water to keep the beverage hot. Specially treated glass vessels can be placed over a low flame.

In the vacuum method, the measured water is poured into the lower part of the coffeemaker (Fig. 16-3). Vacuum coffeemakers generally have two bowls: an upper bowl contains the coffee, a lower bowl the water. There is a filter device in the upper bowl, which also has a cover. Finely ground coffee is placed in the upper bowl. As the water in the lower bowl is heated, steam is formed, the pressure of which forces the water

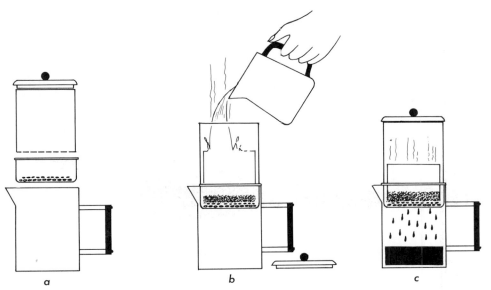

16-2 *The drip method: The dripolator consists of three parts: lower section, filter section, and upper section. The filter section with the coffee grounds is removed when dripping is completed. (a) Measure drip-grind coffee into filter sections. (b) Pour boiled water into the top section. (c) Allow coffee to drip into lower sections.*

149

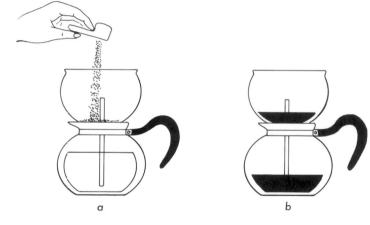

16-3 *In the vacuum method, the cold water is measured into the lower bowl. The coffee is measured and placed in the upper bowl. The coffeemaker is placed over the heat until the water rises into the upper bowl. After 1 to 3 minutes, the coffeemaker is removed from the heat and the coffee returns to the lower bowl. (a) Cold water measured in the lower bowl; coffee measured in upper bowl. (b) Heated water rises into the upper bowl.*

from the lower bowl into the upper bowl, where it mixes with the coffee. When the pot is removed from the heat, a vacuum is created in the lower bowl, drawing the clear infusion down into the bottom bowl. The coffee brew can be kept by placing it over a low flame or over hot water.

When a percolator is used, care should be taken to prevent boiling of the infusion. Medium-ground coffee is placed in the upper part of the percolator; the lower part is filled with fresh cold water (Fig. 16-4). Coffee is measured into the basket, and basket and stem are inserted in percolator. Heat is applied, and the heated water is forced up the tube of the percolator and sprayed onto the coffee in the perforated basket, where it slowly extracts the soluble materials. At no time does the entire amount of water come simultaneously into contact with all the grounds.

There may be some loss of coffee flavor with this method, for there is constant aeration of the brew as the liquid is forced up and sprayed over the grounds. The coffee should percolate gently throughout the cooking period (usually 7–10 minutes).

Steeped coffee is sometimes misnamed boiled coffee. Because boiling brings out the bitter substances in coffee, it is important to keep the water temperature slightly below the boiling point. Medium-ground coffee is placed in a pot with a tight-fitting cover and freshly boiled water is poured over the coffee (See Fig. 16-5). The coffeepot is covered tightly (to prevent the loss of volatile flavoring substances) and allowed to stand over low heat for 7–10 minutes. The coffee is then passed through a very fine strainer.

Electric coffeemakers—percolator and vacuum type—are growing in popularity (See Fig.

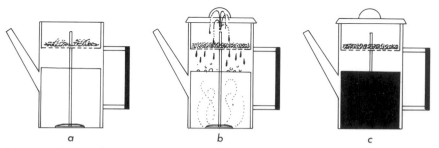

16-4 *In the percolator method, the measured amount of cold water is placed in the pot and the regular-grind coffee in the basket. The basket is removed before the coffee is served. (a) Cold water and coffee are measured into the pot and basket. (b) As the water is heated, it will be forced through the tube and into the coffee basket. (c) The coffee perks slowly for 6 to 8 minutes.*

16-5 *In the steeped method, the measured amount of cold water can be heated in any pot or pan with a cover. Regular-grind coffee is added to the water. Grounds should settle before the beverage is poured. (a) Measure cold water into a pot with cover. (b) Allow water to come to a boil, add coffee, and then let it steep.*

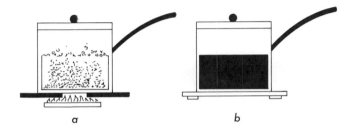

a   b

16-6). Generally, an electric coffeemaker is made of aluminum, of stainless steel, or of copper plated with nickel and chromium. Pyroceram, a ceramic material, is also used for electric coffee-makers. It has the same advantages as glass except for transparency. Electric percolators may be fitted with a valve that heats only the water directly above it. This reduces the amount of time that the already brewed coffee is in contact with high heat. This will reduce flavor loss and produces a beverage of good quality.

The automatic electric drip method is now very popular (see Fig. 16-7). Most of these coffeemakers use a paper filter designed to fit a brewing basket. The coffee of the recommended grind (drip) is put into the basket, which is positioned under the heated water outlet and the beverage receiver on the warming plate. Six ounces of freshly drawn cold water per serving is put into the water tank. The coffee machine is then switched on and brewing takes place almost immediately. The speediness and lack of bitterness of this method probably accounts for its current popularity.

16-6 *This well-designed electric coffee-maker brews coffee in 10 minutes. (Courtesy of General Electric Co.)*

16-7 *The automatic electric drip maker brews the coffee almost immediately.*

Once coffee has been made, it should be allowed to mellow for 3–5 minutes to allow blending of the flavors. After this time period it should be served immediately, as flavor deterioration will begin at that point. Since the grinds will absorb the aroma from the beverage, they should be discarded as soon as possible. If coffee is to be saved overnight or for long periods of time, refrigeration is suggested.

A double-strength brew can be made by using half the amount of water for the usual amount of ground coffee. To make iced coffee, hot coffee is poured over ice in tall glasses. After-dinner coffee, or demitasse, is traditionally a strong brew served without cream. Café au lait is made of equal parts of hot coffee and hot milk. For this beverage, the coffee is brewed double-strength lest the flavor be too weak to blend with the flavor of the milk.

Espresso coffee is now made in the United States as well as in Europe. It is usually drunk black with sugar and perhaps a twist of lemon. It is prepared by placing pulverized coffee on a filter (specially designed espresso coffeepots are available) and passing a measured volume of water and steam through the coffee. The extraction time for this method is very short.

Instant Coffee. Instant powdered coffee is made by adding water to ground roasted coffee to extract its principal ingredients and then evaporating the beverage until only the powder is left.

The advantages of instant soluble coffee are that it is convenient, its flavor is constantly being improved, and it is less expensive when compared on a cup-to-cup basis with brewed coffee. One of the disadvantages of instant coffee is that it lacks aroma; the less the aroma, the less the coffee tastes like brewed coffee. Some attempts are being made with a good degree of success to recover the essential coffee flavor in a concentrated form and reincorporate it into the instant coffee powder.[5]

FREEZE DRYING. Processing of freeze-dried coffee differs from processing of the conventional spray-dried product in that the concentrate is frozen at a very low temperature into a solid mass. The frozen mass is then broken up into fine particles that are placed on trays on hollow shelves in an airtight chamber designed to withstand vacuum conditions. Heat supplied by a hot liquid circulating within the hollow shelves sublimes the ice (changes it directly from the solid to the vapor phase without its becoming a liquid). The freeze-dried product may be packaged or blended with a spray-dried product.

Decaffeinated Coffee. Many people may like the taste of coffee but dislike the stimulating effects of the caffeine. Coffee consumed after an evening meal may have an adverse effect on sleep. This has created a demand for decaffeinated coffee, both in the ground and in the instant form. After decaffeination, the coffee bean is roasted, ground, and packaged in the usual manner. Decaffeinated coffee retains most of its characteristic aroma but loses up to 97% of the caffeine. There is also a slight loss in flavor, but this has been minimized by the freeze-drying method.

Imitation Coffee. The skyrocketing cost of coffee has led to an increasing number of homemade preparations of imitation coffee. The basic ingredients are grains that have been ground and roasted. Chicory is used as a flavoring agent to

[5] Ibid., p. 8.

add a slightly bitter taste. Molasses and licorice roots may also be added to disguise the grain taste and aroma. A pinch of salt is often added to counteract any overly bitter taste.

A typical recipe for imitation coffee is as follows:

Imitation Coffee

2 tbsp roasted ground oats
2 tbsp roasted ground wheat
1/2 tsp molasses
A pinch of chicory (optional)

Mix all ingredients. Perk as for regular coffee grinds. Serves six.

TEA

Tea is made from dried leaves of the tea bush, an evergreen shrub of the Orient (Figs. 16-8 and 16-9). Three kinds of tea are on the market: green, black, and oolong. The types of tea differ only in method of processing, not in the variety of the tea plant. A single plant may yield leaves to be processed for any one of the three kinds of tea.

Green tea is unfermented and is made by steaming and drying the fresh leaves. The high concentration of phenolic compounds give it its characteristic astringent taste. Green tea is divided into three groups; classification is based on the size of the leaf and its relative position on the stem. The smallest end leaves of tea are rolled into tight little balls during the drying process and are known as *gunpowder;* the medium-sized leaves are rolled lengthwise and are classified as *young hyson;* the largest leaves are rolled into balls and are designated *imperial.*

To make black tea, the fresh leaves are fermented or oxidized and then dried, a process that causes the leaves to turn dark brown. The fermentation of tea results from the activity of enzymes in the leaves rather than from microbial action.[6] Like green tea, black tea is classified

[6] A. E. Bradfield, "Some Recent Developments in the Chemistry of Tea," *Chem. Ind.* **26:**242–244, 1946.

16-8 *Tea plants are pruned to waist height to facilitate plucking the leaves by hand.* (*Courtesy of Tea Council of the U.S.A., Inc.*)

according to the size of leaves and their relative position on the plants. Orange pekoe and pekoe refer to the size of the leaf only. Orange pekoe has the longest leaves. Pekoe and souchong follow in descending order. The black teas are generally a blend of orange pekoe, which has a delicate flavor, and pekoe, which has a stronger, full-bodied flavor. The oxidation of the tannin in the leaf is carried further in black tea than in green tea, thus making it less astringent. Semifermented or oolong teas have some of the characteristics of both black and green teas. Some of the most tender leaves of the orange pekoe are scented with blossoms of other plants—usually chulan blossoms, which have a delicate fragrance. Experts value teas grown in mountain areas over those grown in the lowlands. The superior flavor of tea grown in mountainous areas is said to be the result of the mineral content of the soil.

Composition. The stimulant in tea is referred to as *theine,* a chemical identical to caffeine in coffee. Tannins are found in large amounts in tea. They dissolve slowly in hot water and impart a bitter, unpleasant taste. The amount of tannin going into solution depends on the length

16-9 *When the tea plant sends out new shoots or "flushes," it produces two tender leaves and a bud. (Courtesy of Tea Council of the U.S.A., Inc.)*

of time the tea and water are in contact with one another and on the temperature of the water. Tannins are more soluble at boiling temperature than at just below boiling.

The characteristic aroma and flavor of tea are imparted to the infusion by the slow dissolving of the essential oils in the tea leaves. These oils are volatile and are lost on boiling.

Nutritive Value. The constituents added to tea, such as sugar and milk, give it whatever nutritive value it has. However, tea is frequently consumed for its stimulating quality rather than as a necessary item of the diet.

Principles of Tea Preparation. In making the tea, the goal is to develop the flavor and to extract as little tannin as possible, so as to avoid a strong bitter flavor. To get good results, the water used should be fresh from the tap and brought to the boiling point before it is poured over the tea leaves. Water that has been boiled for a long time is flat-tasting and should not be used for tea. Tea should be allowed to steep from 3 to 5 minutes to develop the fine delicate flavor of the beverage. (Tea infuses more readily in soft water than in hard.) A suitable teapot is of china, glass, or pottery. These materials retain heat better than metal. One teaspoonful of tea or 1 teabag per cup (about $5\frac{1}{2}$ oz) of boiling water is the proportion recommended for a fine-tasting tea infusion.[7] Milk or lemon may be added to tea for body and flavor. The addition of sugar is a matter of taste.

A favorite American drink, iced tea, is made in the same manner as the hot brew. Half again as much tea is used in making the iced tea infusion to allow for the melting ice. Cloudiness may appear in the cooling tea because of precipitating tannins, but the tea can be restored to a clear color by adding a small amount of boiling water or acids such as lemon juice. The tea should not be refrigerated but kept at room temperature and poured over ice just before it is served.

Instant soluble tea powders are processed by preparing a highly concentrated brew of tea from which the water is removed by drying. The two types of instant tea available are (1) pure spray-dried tea, and (2) the vacuum-dried

[7]*Two Leaves and a Bud* (New York: Tea Council of the U.S.A., Inc. n.d.).

type, which contains carbohydrates as a flavor seal.

Buying, Care, and Storage. Black teas are most popular in America. Tea can be purchased in $\frac{1}{4}$-, $\frac{1}{2}$-, and 1-lb packages. Perhaps the most popular form of tea is the bag that contains enough tea for one cup of beverage. Tea is best kept in airtight packages, for, like coffee, it loses aroma and flavor on exposure to air. Although there is some loss of essential oils during the storage of tea, the process is a relatively slow one. Thus, tea can be kept longer than coffee.

The individual packaging of teas adds to the cost of the product, and special teas—flavored with spices and scented—are considerably higher in cost than unflavored teas.

COCOA AND CHOCOLATE

Europeans first became acquainted with chocolate in Mexico, where both cocoa and chocolate are made from the beans or seeds of the cacao tree, which grows in countries near the equator (Fig. 16-10). These two products of the cocoa bean differ from each other in that cocoa has had the greater part of the fat of the cocoa bean (*cocoa* implies the cacao bean) removed. Cocoa and chocolate are unlike tea and coffee in that they have considerable food value. Like tea and coffee, they are stimulants.

Processing. The manufacture of cocoa and chocolate is an important industry in the United States. The consumption of both products is high, for beverages from both are popular and easily made. Large quantities of cocoa and chocolate are also used in the production of other food products.

The fresh bean from the cocoa pod has a strong, bitter taste and must be treated to develop its flavor and color. The beans or chocolate "nibs"—up to 50 of them—are encased in a pulpy, almond-shaped fruit pod 6–14 in. in length. The first step in processing is to remove the beans from the mucilaginous substance in the pod. The beans are then fermented—to remove the pulp from the outside of the cocoa bean— and dried, at which time they develop their rich brown color from the oxidation of tannins. After drying, the beans are ready for roasting.

16-10 *Cocoa bean pods, which are the fruit of the cacao tree, contain many seeds or "beans."* (*Courtesy of Hershey Foods Corporation*)

The roasting process further improves the flavor of the cocoa bean and dries the husks or shells so that they can be easily removed. The beans are then cracked and separated from the germ of the seed—the cocoa nibs—which is the basis for the cocoa and chocolate products.

The nibs must now be ground at a temperature high enough to produce a smooth-flowing liquid chocolate. At this stage, the liquid chocolate is ready to be used as the foundation for such chocolate products as bitter or plain chocolate, sweet chocolate, and milk chocolate. If cocoa is to be made from the product, the chocolate is put into presses and part of the cocoa butter is removed. The pressed cocoa cakes are cooked, crushed to a fine powder, and packed in tins. Cocoas used in home and institutional cookery are breakfast and Dutch-process cocoas. The difference between the Dutch-process cocoa and the natural is that the former is less acid, less bitter, and darker in color. The Dutch-process cocoa has been treated with an alkali solution.[8]

[8] B. J. Zenlea, "There is a Cocoa for Every Use," *Food Ind.* **6**:402, 1934.

Dutch-process cocoa is partly responsible for the color of red devil's food cake.

In producing chocolate or a chocolate product, the manufacturer uses a blend of different cocoas. Each variety of cocoa contributes to the total quality and helps to maintain a standard product. Blends are hard to imitate, and in this fact lies the manufacturer's ability to claim a unique flavor for his product.

Bitter or plain chocolate contains 50% fat and is made by running the paste into molds and cooling it. Sugar, flavorings, and cocoa butter are added to the pure chocolate to make sweet chocolate. These ingredients are mixed together, aged, cooled, and molded into cakes of different sizes. Milk chocolate is made from either sweet or bitter chocolate by the addition of milk in one of its various forms and with or without cocoa butter and flavoring.

Composition. The stimulating agent in cocoa and chocolate beverages is *theobromine,* which is similar to caffeine in composition. Tannins are present in a soluble form, and they contribute to the color and flavor of the cocoa and chocolate products. Carbohydrates are present in fairly large amounts in the form of starch and sugar.

Nutritive Value. Table 16-3 shows that the nutritive energy value of both cocoa products is high. Chocolate is one of the most highly concentrated foods, yielding many calories per pound. Because of its high energy value and low bulk, it is a favored ration for explorers and military groups. For everyday use, milk is generally added to the cocoa or chocolate, so that the food value of both milk and the chocolate product is made available. Excessive eating of chocolate products, however, may prove to be irritating to the lining of the stomach.

Buying. Chocolate is available in cakes and packages of various weights. For ease in measuring, cooking chocolate—bitter or sweet—is marked off into 1-in. squares. Chocolate pieces are sold for cooking purposes, and a packaged cocoa-fat product that does not require melting is available. Cocoa, either natural or Dutch-process, is available in packages from ½ to 2 lb. One-pound containers are the most practical size for family use.

TABLE 16-3
Average Proximate Composition of Chocolate and Cocoa

	Chocolate (%)	Cocoa (%)
Water	5.9	4.6
Protein	12.9	21.6
Fat	48.7	28.6
Carbohydrates	30.3	37.7
Minerals	2.2	7.2

Source: C. Chatfield and G. Adams, "Proximate Composition of American Food Materials," *Bulletin 549* (Washington, D.C.: U.S. Department of Agriculture, 1940).

In the selection of cocoa or chocolate, the standards set by the Food and Drug Administration are worth noting. High-fat cocoa, which is called *breakfast cocoa,* must contain not less than 22% cocoa fat; a medium-fat cocoa will contain less than 22% but not less than 10%; low-fat cocoa can contain less than 10%.

Storage. The high fat content of chocolate and cocoa makes it necessary to store these products in airtight containers and in a cool, dark place at about 68°F (20°C). Heat and moisture cause powdered cocoa to lump and turn gray. Chocolate, too, will turn gray if stored in a room of high humidity, because moisture condenses on it and dissolves some of the sugar in it.

When the temperature is too cool, chocolate will "sweat" when brought to room temperature. When the temperature exceeds 78°F (25°C), the cocoa butter begins to melt and may appear as a gray coating known as "bloom." This does not affect the quality or flavor. Upon melting, the chocolate regains its original color.

Use in Cookery. There are many uses of cocoa and chocolate in cookery. Not only are they used in the preparation of the traditional chocolate-flavored beverages but also to flavor many kinds of desserts, including cakes, cookies, pie fillings, puddings, ice cream, and candy.

Because of its composition, chocolate sticks and burns readily. This tendency is easily controlled by heating the chocolate over hot water or by heating it at a low temperature. Both chocolate- and cocoa-beverage mixtures should be brought to the boiling temperature in order to cook the starch. When using chocolate or cocoa, it is desirable to find the brand suitable for the recipe involved, for another will alter the flavor and color of the finished product. A liquid chocolate product is also available for cooking.

The acid content of cocoas and chocolate is sufficient to enable baking soda to be used with them for leavening. The amount of soda used will depend on the acidity of the particular kind. Dutch-process cocoa, for instance, requires less soda because of its lower acidity.

The cocoa beverage should be a smooth, well-blended product, with the starch thoroughly cooked. The beverage contains milk and sugar as well as tannins, oxalic acid, acetic acid, theobromine, starch and coloring stubstances. The water-soluble materials are suspended materials that may separate out and form a sediment on standing. Cocoa blends readily with cold liquids because its fat content is fairly low; the lower the fat content of the cocoa, the greater its thickening power. Because of its high starch content, cocoa will lump if put directly into a hot liquid. The starch particles in the cocoa should be separated with sugar or mixed with a small amount of cold liquid before being combined with other ingredients. The cocoa should then be brought to the boiling point and held at that temperature until the cocoa syrup has thickened. Complete cooking improves both flavor and digestibility and produces a cocoa beverage with body and stability. Cooking holds the starch in suspension. Chocolate, on the other hand, has sufficient fat in it to separate the starch particles and therefore is easily blended when added to a hot liquid. It is best to add the chocolate to a hot liquid for the obvious reason that a low temperature hardens the fat in the chocolate, making it less easy to blend. Chocolate is frequently melted before being used in recipes. For substitutions in cooking, see Table A-7.

SUMMARY

Beverages popular in the United States include coffee, tea, cocoa, and chocolate. Neither coffee nor tea has nutritive value (except for added sugar, milk, or cream), but cocoa and chocolate have substantial food value. All contain stimu-lants. Temperature is an important factor in making beverages. Coffee should not be allowed to boil, but water for tea should be brought to the boiling point before being poured over tea leaves. Chocolate and cocoa beverages should be brought to the boiling point to cook the starch.

In making coffee and tea, the goal is a clear infusion with characteristic flavor but with a minimum of tannin, which imparts bitterness. A smooth blend is sought in cocoa beverages.

Coffee should be purchased in small quantities and stored in a container with a tight-fitting lid, because it is highly perishable. Tea may be kept longer, but there is loss of essential flavor materials during storage. Because of their high fat content, chocolate and cocoa should be stored in airtight containers in a cool, dark place. Cocoa and chocolate have many uses in cookery; coffee is sometimes used as a flavoring agent.

QUESTIONS AND TOPICS FOR DISCUSSION AND STUDY

1. Why does boiled coffee taste different from coffee that has not been boiled?
2. How can the components that give a bitter taste to tea and coffee be kept at a minimum?
3. Why should cocoa and chocolate be cooked in making beverages?
4. Which method of preparation of coffee gives maximum caffeol flavor and minimum tannin?

SUGGESTED ACTIVITIES

1. Prepare different varieties of tea—black and green. Compare them for color and flavor. Prepare soluble tea and compare for color and flavor with above.
2. Prepare coffee by using several different methods. Compare the results for color and flavor. Prepare soluble coffee and compare for color and flavor with above.
3. Prepare breakfast cocoa and Dutch-process cocoa. Prepare either breakfast or Dutch-process cocoa using nonfat dried milk solids, pasteurized homogenized milk, and evaporated milk. Compare the results for appearance and flavor.

157

REFERENCES

BOOKS

Cocoa. New York: Merrill Lynch, Pierce, Fenner and Smith, Inc., 1972.

Lee, Frank. *Basic Food Chemistry*. Westport, Conn.: Avi, 1975, Chaps. 15, 16, 17.

Minfie, Bernard. *Chocolate, Cocoa and Confectionery: Science and Technology*. Westport, Conn.: Avi, 1970.

Schapira, Joel. *The Book of Coffee and Tea*. New York: St. Martin's Press, 1975.

Sivetz, Michael. *Coffee Processing Technology*. Westport, Conn.: Avi, 1963.

Vail, Gladys, J. Phillips, Lucile Rust, Ruth Griswold, and Margaret Justin. *Foods,* 7th ed. Boston: Houghton Mifflin, 1978, Chap. 5.

ARTICLES AND PAMPHLETS

Harris, N. E. and S. J. Bishov. "Soluble Coffee: Shelf Life Studies." *J. Food Sci.* **39:**192, 1974.

Kaufman, C. W. "Recent Advances in Coffee Technology." *Food Technol.* **5:**154, 1951.

Lentner, G., and F. F. Deatherage. "Organic Acids in Coffee in Relation to the Degree of Roasts." *J. Food Res.* **24:**483, 1959.

Muller, John. "Freeze Processing of Coffee." *World Coffee Tea.* May 1966, p. 54.

Pangborn, R. M., I. M. Trabue, and A. C. Little. "Analysis of Coffee, Tea and Artificially Flavored Drinks Prepared from Mineralized Waters." *J. Food Sci.* **36:**355, 1971.

Segal, S., and B. E. Proctor. "The influence of High Temperature Holding upon the Components of Coffee Brew." *Food Technol.* **13:**679, 1959.

"Today's Coffee House." New York: Pan American Coffee Bureau (120 Wall Street, New York, N.Y. 10005), n.d.

Zenlea, B. J. "There Is a Cocoa for Every Use." *Food Ind.* **6:**402, 1934.

Fruits

The many varieties of fruit found today are the result of hundreds of years of selection and cultivation. The earliest cultivation of fruit is traced to two major areas. From the area stretching from the eastern Mediterranean to the Caspian Sea came apples, pears, cherries, figs, olives, plums, and grapes. From the area that stretches from China through Burma and eastern India southeast into the Malay Archipelago came peaches, apricots, bananas, mangoes, oranges, and lemons.[1]

As the inhabitants of these areas migrated to other parts of the world, they took with them cuttings from their favorite plants. In the early years of the settlement of this country, immigrants brought their finest seedlings with them for transplanting.

COMPOSITION

A fruit is the matured ovary of a flower, including its seeds and adjacent parts. The fleshy

portion of the pericarp makes up the chief edible part of the fruit. Fruits differ in structure according to the kinds of flowers from which they develop. Apples and pears, for instance, come from a simple blossom, and an aggregate fruit such as the strawberry develops from a flower with many stamens and pistils. Pineapple and figs are known as *multiple fruits* because many flowers have collected together to form them. Although nuts are botanically classified as fruits, they differ from the table fruits in that they yield a seed, rather than a fleshy pericarp, as the food portion.

As a group, fresh fruits are high in carbohydrates and water content. They are among the best food sources of minerals and vitamins. Different kinds of fruit, however, vary greatly in composition. (See Table A-12).

Two types of acids are found in fruit: volatile and nonvolatile. Volatile acids are those that are heat labile and easily pass off from the cooking liquid as vapor during heating. Nonvolatile acids may pass off into the cooking liquid but are not lost as vapor.

The characteristic colors of fruit are caused by the pigments they contain. The anthocyanins give rise to the blue, purple, red, and pink colors

[1]J. R. Magness, "How Fruit Came to America," *Nat. Geog. Mag.* **C3**:325, 1951.

in plums, cherries, grapes, and berries. Fruits such as bananas, peaches, and citrus fruits contain the yellow pigments xanthophyll and lycopene.

The framework of the fruit is made up of cellulose, which forms the walls of the plant cells and in which large amounts of water are held. Once the cell walls are broken and the water escapes, the firm structure of the fruit is altered.

NUTRITIVE VALUE

Most fresh raw fruits contain less than 100 calories per serving. A serving of fruit is considered to be a medium-sized apple, orange, or banana; two or three figs, apricots, or plums; or ½ cup fruit and liquid.[2] If sugar is added to the fruit to help retain its shape during canning or freezing, the calorie content is proportionately increased.

Fruits, as a group, do not contain large amounts of proteins and fats. The two notable exceptions to this are avocados and ripe olives, both of which are high in fat. Their fat content can range from 5 to 20% according to the species and harvesting maturity. Fruits are excellent sources of fiber. Fiber is the indigestible part of the plant composed of substances such as cellulose, hemicelluose, and lignin. These substances absorb water readily and swell to form an indigestible mass, which helps in maintaining regular gastrointestinal function.

Unripe fruit contains starch, which, with the right environmental conditions, is hydrolyzed to sugar. Bananas, for example, if chilled, cannot hydrolyze the starch to sugar and will not ripen properly. Thus, ripe fruit contains a higher percentage of sugar than unripe fruit does, and the sugar is chiefly in the form of sucrose, glucose, and fructose.

Sugars in fruit are in a form readily usable by the body. The minerals phosphorus and iron (as well as small but available amounts of calcium) are found in good quantity in fresh fruit. Bananas, oranges, and figs have high potassium values. Although there is variation of vitamin

content from fruit to fruit, most fruits in the raw state contain some ascorbic acid. Citrus fruits, berries, and melons are among the best sources of ascorbic acid. Three ounces of orange juice will meet the recommended daily allowance for ascorbic acid (45mg/day). If fruits are bruised, peeled, cooked, or exposed to air, alkali, or copper, large amounts of the vitamin may be oxidized. Ascorbic acid is best preserved if it is in an acid solution, such as orange juice. Carotene is present in good amounts in yellow fruits, such as apricots, peaches, and bananas. The B vitamins are present in only moderate amounts in fruits.

CHANGES DURING RIPENING

For the most part, only ripe fruit is good for use. Several important changes take place in fruit during ripening: the fruit develops to its full size, the pulpy edible tissue surrounding the seeds becomes soft and tender, the color changes, the starch content changes to sugar giving a mild, sweet flavor, and the full characteristic aroma of the fruit develops. These changes are brought about by the enzymes found in the plant tissues, and—by and large—these alterations enhance the overall eating quality of the fruit. However, the enzymes continue to function even after the fruit has reached its peak of maturity, and changes beyond this point cause spoilage and deterioration of texture and flavor.

The softening of fruit is retarded by decreasing the temperature at which it is kept, but excessive hardness is usually accompanied by a bitter, astringent flavor. Only fresh fruit that is to be cooked before eating can be considered as marketable while still hard and underripe. Although there are definite advantages in picking fruit while it is underripe, such fruit must be ripened artificially if its full succulence and flavor are to develop.

The starch content in green fruit is high but rapidly changes to sugar during ripening. (In peaches, the monosaccharides condense into sucrose as the fruit matures.) Fruits also contain considerable amounts of pectins. These substances, which occur in the slightly underripe fruit as protopectins, are responsible for the jellying quality of many fruits. As the fruit ripens, they change to pectic acid, which has less

[2]"Fruits in Family Meals," *Home and Garden Bulletin 125* (Washington, D.C.: U.S. Department of Agriculture, 1972), p. 1.

jellying quality. (For a fuller treatment of pectin material, see Chapter 41).

The acid content of most fruits decreases as the fruit ripens and becomes even softer. This is due to the increase (in most cases) of fruit sugar. Thus, the flavor of the fully ripe fruit is one of pleasant sweetness with a slightly acid overtone. Some fruits, such as bananas and apples, are very astringent when underripe, owing to the presence of tannins. As the fruit ripens, they become less soluble. The increase in the water content of some fruits during ripening may bring about a dilution of the acid and tannin content and a corresponding change in flavor.

The flavor components of fruit are essential oils—volatile acids in the form of organic salts called *esters*. The organic acids most commonly found in fruits that contribute to their flavor are malic, citric, tartaric, and oxalic. Malic acid occurs in apples, pears, peaches, apricots, cherries, and strawberries. Citric acid is present in fairly large amounts in citrus fruits, loganberries, and raspberries. Tartaric acid, as well as formic and succinic acids, are found in grapes, and traces of oxalic acid are found in ripe pineapples.

The amount of proteins, fats, and minerals in fruit does not change to any appreciable extent during the ripening period. It is likely, however, that vitamin content increases up to the peak of maturity.

Good produce management practices necessitate that a large percentage of many fruits be harvested while still underripe. Artificial ripening of the fruit may be controlled by carefully controlling the temperature and humidity of the surrounding air during the storage period. Ethylene is the gas responsible for ripening in most fruits. The gas stimulates the fruit to respire by inhaling oxygen and expelling carbon dioxide and the result brings about the discoloration of its green pigment, permitting the other colors to show. The artificial use of ethylene gas affects the permeability of the cell membranes and hastens the ripening process. Considerable use has been made of ethylene gas to accelerate ripening in a number of fruits and vegetables, particularly citrus fruits and tomatoes. Ethylene ripening of fruit is safe.

The development of an ethylene-generating chemical, known as *ethephon,* has shown good potential as an initiator of increased ripening and increased rate of skin coloration in apples. According to a recent report, ethephon may be a means for the apple processor to obtain early harvested ripe fruit. Since early harvested fruit is quite firm, a minimum of crop loss from bruising may be accomplished.[3]

ECONOMIC ASPECTS

Perishability, use of pesticides, weather conditions, consumer preferences, and the costs of packaging and storage are factors that greatly influence the cost of fruit to the consumer.

Many diseases and insects reduce the fruit crop. So far, the use of pesticides is the most effective method of control available. Pesticides—which include fungicides, insecticides, nematocides, and herbicides—are costly and very likely add to the cost of the fruit to the consumer. It is possible, however, that without the use of pesticides the crops would not be of the quality or quantity necessary to satisfy the nation's consumers. Even now there are no effective controls for many of the diseases and pests that attack fruit, and much fruit is still lost every year. (A very significant development in fruit crop management is the use of stop-drop sprays that strengthen fruit stems, so that the fruit does not drop from the tree as it becomes ripe[4].)

Shipping and handling practices play a part in the retail cost of fruit. Precooling of fruit lowers it temperature and cuts down on spoilage during shipping. Keeping the fruit sufficiently cooled during the journey requires refrigerated trucks. Truck hauling of fruit and other produce has provided a direct route for transporting fresh produce to the consumer. The refrigerated truck travels the highways in record time, avoiding the delays encountered in other forms of transportation and thus reducing spoilage losses.

Refrigeration plays an important part in marketing fresh fruit. Pentzer[5] notes that it would be difficult to find a fruit or vegetable that would not require refrigeration at some time of the year or at some step in moving it from the farm to the consumer. The marketing of bananas is a case in point. Bananas are harvested when green, transported to a port, and placed on refrigerated banana ships. The temperature of bananas when loaded is 75°–80°F (24–27°C), and they must be cooled to 55°F (13°C) in 12–14 hours in order to be at the proper carrying temperature. Warehouses for storing bananas just prior to their distribution to retail units are kept at temperatures between 55 and 70°F (13 and 21°C) and have a relative humidity between 85 and 90%. Fruits such as oranges, peaches, and grapes are subjected to precooling treatment before they are shipped or during storage. Refrigeration practices depend on the special temperature requirements for each kind of fruit.

The development of adequate storage methods permits some fruits to be made available any time of year. Of all the fruits marketed, apples and pears have profited the most by advances in knowledge about storage. Because of controlled-atmosphere storage, for example, McIntosh apples are available most of the year. These apples do well under storage conditions of 5% carbon dioxide and 3% oxygen at a temperature of 36–38°F (2 and 3°C). The important factor in this storage method is the slowing down of the processes in the living tissue, thereby extending the storage life of the fruit. Another new development has decreased pear loss through storage and extended the storage life of that fruit. Gas storage, such as described for the McIntosh apple, can delay the ripening capacity of pears, but it produces a fruit that never matures properly. To offset this shortcoming, a method was devised for sealing in the CO_2 given off by the pears during normal respiration and diminishing the oxygen in the atmosphere. The box in which the pears are packed is lined with a polyethylene film, the air is exhausted, the lining sealed, and the box closed and placed in cold storage rooms. When the pears are shipped from storage to the market, the film is torn so that the process of ripening—which was inhibited during storage—may resume.

Processed fruits are often less expensive than fresh fruits.[6] Frozen reconstituted orange juice is less expensive than canned, or store- or home-squeezed. Bottled lemon juice is less expensive than fresh lemon juice. Canned fruits such as cherries, pineapple, and grapefruit may be less than half the price of the fresh product. A probable reason for some fresh fruits costing more than processed ones are the losses that must occur during transportation, storage, and marketing of the fragile product.

Packaging Fruit. Most fruit is shipped in fiberboard containers. Some fruits are now packaged in plastic bags in family-size units. Prepackaging of fruits cuts down on loss of moisture and on loss of fruit from consumer handling and contamination by dirt and insects. The plastic bags have small perforations to permit the release of accumulated CO_2, thus retarding the softening of the fruit. Some fruits, such as pears, are placed in a special fruit wrapper that contains refined mineral oil and nonsoluble metal salts to protect the natural quality of the fruit.

Packaging affects the cost of fresh fruits. Although it is difficult to estimate just how much of the packaging cost is passed on to the consumer, many producers maintain that less handling leads to less waste, and thus keeps costs down.

Consumer preferences play a large part in determining the cost of fruit. Color and size of the fruit rather than flavor and nutritive value may determine the salability of the product. Giant-sized fruit is generally more expensive than average-sized fruit of the same variety; from the viewpoint of palatability and economics, it may be less desirable than the smaller fruit.[7] The shape of a fruit is also related to cost,

[5]W. T. Pentzer, "The Giant Job of Refrigeration," in *Protecting Our Food: The Yearbook of Agriculture* (Washington, D.C.: U.S. Department of Agriculture, 1966), p. 168.

[6]"Comparative Costs to Consumers of Convenience Foods and Home Prepared Foods," *Marketing Research Report 609* (Washington, D.C.: U.S. Department of Agriculture, 1963).

[7]"How to Buy Fresh Fruits," *Home and Garden Bulletin 141* (Washington, D.C.: U.S. Department of Agriculture, 1977).

for irregularities on the surface are directly correlated with waste.

SELECTION

Efficient selection of fruit involves a consideration of variety, size, and grade. Most cultivated fruits have a number of varieties, each with its special characteristics. One variety may be especially valued for its flavor, whereas another may have exceptional cooking qualities. The apple varieties are by far the most numerous. Apples are grown in many parts of the United States, making possible a long apple season and a relatively inexpensive fruit. Some varieties are good only for eating, some have excellent cooking properties, and a number of varieties combine both eating and cooking characteristics.

It is not possible to list the many varieties of all fruits, but the important characteristics of leading varieties of different fruits may be discussed briefly.

GRADES

There are permissive grades set up by the U.S. Department of Agriculture that may be used for the purchase and sale of fruit on the wholesale market. Grades of fruit are based on the size, uniformity of shape, color, texture, and freedom from defects. Little attempt is made to make fruit grades known to the consumer, although they are a good guide for purchase. U.S. grades in use for fresh fruits are the premium grades: U.S. Extra Fancy, U.S. Fancy, U.S. Extra No. 1, and the basic trading grades: U.S. No. 1 and U.S. No. 2.[8]

The lower grades are less expensive; they may be suitable for use, but waste may offset the price advantage.

As with other fresh produce, the largest fruit is not always the best buy. Fruit price is not an indication of quality or nutritive value but is determined by supply and demand. Fruit in season is generally cheaper and of better quality than fruit sold out of season. Fruits that are in short supply because of crop losses may be of very poor quality and yet be priced out of the reach of the average consumer.

Fruits deteriorate rapidly after they have ripened, and the practice of buying large quantities at one time is unsound, unless the fruit can be stored or preserved. Only apples and one or two varieties of pears may be kept for any length of time, in a cool, dry place in the home. And even these hardy fruits will lose some of their desirable qualities on long standing.

POMES

The group of fruits called *pomes* is characterized by an enlarged fleshy receptacle that surrounds the carpels.

Apples. The apple (Fig. 17-1) is a pome that is abundant and adaptable to many uses. It is thought that the apple is native to the temperature zone of Europe and Asia, because there is scarcely a temperate country in the world that does not grow some variety of the fruit.

More apples are produced in the United States than in any other country in the world. Most varieties of apples are spherical, but some tend to be slightly pointed at one end. They vary greatly in size and range in color from green to yellow to red (see Color Plate II). The apple core is made up of five carpels containing seeds that turn brown in color when the fruit is fully mature. The greatest apple-growing areas in the United States are in the Pacific Northwest, south and east of the Great Lakes, and in New York, Michigan, and Ohio. The crab apple is a small fruit, very acid, tough, and fibrous. In this country, crab apples are grown only for jelly making and pickling.

During the ripening of apples, there is considerable transformation of starch into sugar. Ascorbic acid is found in significant quantities in all varieties of apples but shows a steady decrease during storage.[9] There are so many varieties of apples that it is only possible to give a brief list of

---

[8]"Shopper's Guide to U.S. Grades for Food," *Home and Garden Bulletin 58* (Washington, D.C.: U.S. Department of Agriculture, 1966).

[9]Frank Lee, "Fruits and Nuts," in *The Chemistry and Technology of Food and Food Products,* Morris B. Jacobs, ed. (New York: Interscience, 1951), p. 1523.

17-1 *Top: The Rome Beauty is a popular variety of baking apple. Bottom: Golden Delicious apples are eaten fresh and made into various desserts. (Courtesy of Washington Apple Commission)*

the more important ones (see Table 17-1). (For a more complete treatment of apples, see the references at the end of this chapter.) If apples are ripe when purchased, they should be eaten within 1 month to avoid deterioration into a mealy product.

Pears. Although pears are grown extensively throughout the eastern part of the United States, the most valued varieties are grown in the mild, dry areas of California, Oregon, and Washington. Pears are an extremely important fruit crop in Europe—especially in France, Belgium, Germany, Italy, and Switzerland. Argentina and Australia are also pear-producing countries. The European pear has a buttery texture that is highly valued the world over, and imported pears from Europe and South America are sold in markets in the United States.

The pear is not unlike an apple in appearance: it is broad at the blossom or calyx end and tapers off somewhat toward the stem. Pears are harvested while still green. As they ripen, their color changes to yellow, yellow with a red blush, or brown (see Color Plate III).

Pears owe their characteristic flavor to malic and citric acids. They also have considerable amounts of sugar and are a fair source of ascorbic acid (a large part of which is lost during storage) and vitamin A.[10]

Usually pears are eaten raw, but they may also be canned, dried, or pickled (see Table 17-2).

DRUPES

Fruits classified as *drupes* have a single seed surrounded by a stony and fleshy pericarp. The fleshy pericarp is the soft, juicy, edible portion.

Apricots. Most of the apricots in the United States are grown in Washington, Oregon, and Utah.

The apricot looks like a small peach. Its skin is smooth and turns orange-yellow when ripe; the flesh is sweet and juicy. Malic and citric acids, as well as vitamin A, are found in apricots. Color

[10]D. D. Tressler and J. C. Mayer, "Changes in Vitamin C Content of Bartlett Pears in Cold and Gas Storage," *Food Res.* **6**:375, 1941.

TABLE 17-1
Characteristics of Some Leading Varieties of Apples

Variety	Size	Appearance	Season of Year	Use
Baldwin	Medium to large	Medium red, hard, crisp, juicy	Nov.–Apr.	Raw, cooking
Cortland	Medium to large	Red, white flesh, tart	Nov.–Jan.	Raw
Delicious	Medium to large	Red or golden, five knobs on blossom end, sweet, firm, tender	Oct.–Apr.	Raw
Jonathan	Medium to small	Tender, crisp, juicy, medium to high acid	Oct.–Jan.	Raw, general cooking
McIntosh	Medium	Medium red, hard, crisp, juicy, medium acid	Oct.–Mar.	Raw, general cooking
Northern Spy	Large	Bright-striped red, juicy, moderately tart, firm, crisp, tender	Oct.–Mar.	Raw, general cooking
Rhode Island Greening	Medium to large	Greenish yellow, firm, juicy, medium to low acid	Oct.–Mar.	Pies
Rome Beauty	Medium to large	Red-striped, firm, crisp, mealy when overripe	Nov.–May	Baking
Winesap	Small to medium	Dark red, hard, crisp, acid, medium juicy	Jan.–May	Raw, general cooking, pies

Source: Adapted from *Fruits and Vegetables,* Vol. 1 (Chicago: Quartermaster Food and Container Institute for the Armed Forces, 1946), p. 4.

pigments present in the fruit are carotene and lycopene, both yellow pigments.

Apricots are picked when yellow-green and ripened before marketing. If ripe when purchased, they should be stored in the refrigerator for use within 3–5 days. Large quantities of apricots are used fresh. They are also canned, dried, and made into jellies and other preserves that enjoy great popularity.

Plums. The plum has the general shape and size of an apricot. It may be red, yellow, green, or blue. Japanese plums are yellow and red, and the European varieties are green or blue. Wild plums are native to America, and wild plum trees are distributed throughout the United States. Large quantities of the fruit are gathered and used to make jams, jellies, butters, and homemade desserts. Prunes are plums suitable for drying purposes.

Plums are eaten fresh within 3–5 days of purchase. Large quantities are dried, canned, and made into preserves (see Table 17-3).

Peaches. In the United States, peaches grow best in California, along the Atlantic seaboard from Georgia to Massachusetts, and south and east of the Great Lakes.

The peach is spherical, with a groove on one side. The seed is strong, and the fuzzy skin—white or yellow with a red blush, depending on the variety—adheres firmly to the flesh of the fruit. Both malic and citric acids are found in peaches, and some ascorbic acid is also present. The carotenes are the color pigments identified in the fruit.

There are two basic types of peaches grown in the United States, freestone and clingstone. The clingstone is firmer, less expensive, and used primarily for canning. The Freestone variety does not hold its shape as well during processing and is used mostly for freezing and eating raw.

165

TABLE 17-2
Characteristics of Some Leading Varieties of Pears

Variety	Size and Appearance	Season of Year	Use
Anjou	Large, yellow	Late fall and winter	Raw, canning
Bartlett	Medium to large, yellow with red blush	July–Oct.	Raw, canning
Bosc	Medium to large, russet brown	Oct.–Apr.	Raw
Clapp's Favorite	Medium, green to light yellow	Aug.–Oct.	Cooking, canning
Comice	Large, light greenish yellow	Oct.–Mar.	Raw
Winter Nelis	Small, greenish yellow with dark brown	Oct.–Apr.	Raw
Seckel	Small, yellow	Oct.–Apr.	Raw, canning, pickling
Kieffer	Medium to large	Oct.–Dec.	Cooking, canning

Source: Adapted from *Fruits and Vegetables,* Vol. 1 (Chicago: Quartermaster Food and Container Institute for the Armed Forces, 1946), p. 9.

The latter is said to have a better peach flavor. A large part of the peach crop is frozen and canned, and significant quantities are used for desserts and preserves (see Table 17-4).

Nectarines. The nectarine, a peach with a smooth skin, is similar in shape and flavor to the peach, although it may have a more distinct flavor than the peach. Because it has a smooth skin, it may be easier to eat than a peach, but it is far more difficult to grow. The smooth skin makes it vulnerable to insects, disease, and cracking.

Cherries. In the United States, sweet cherries are produced in the dry western states, whereas the sour cherry thrives well in the area around the Great Lakes. Neither kind of cherry does very well in the southern part of the country.

The sweet cherry is round, with a light red or very dark red color, a rather firm flesh, and a sweet flavor. The sour cherry is red, soft-fleshed, and sour. The color pigment found in cherries is an anthocyanin, and the acids identified are mainly citric and malic. Sweet cherries are popular for dessert; they may also be bleached with sulfur dioxide and made into maraschino-type and creme de menthe cherries. Sour cherries are canned and frozen for pie making. Some cherry jam is made commercially (see Table 17-5).

BERRIES

A *berry* is a fruit in which the layers of the pericarp are pulpy and succulent, and seeds are contained in the mass.

TABLE 17-3
Characteristics of Some Leading Varieties of Plums

Variety	Size and Appearance	Season of Year	Use
Damson	Small, round, reddish blue, tart	Sept.–Nov.	Jams, jellies
Green Gage	Oval, yellowish green, sweet, juicy	June–Oct.	Dessert, canning
Italian Prune	Egg-shaped, purple or blue, sweet, juicy	Sept.–Nov.	Dessert, canning
Santa Rosa	Oval, red, juicy, slightly tart	June–Sept.	Dessert

Source: Adapted from *Fruits and Vegetables,* Vol. 1 (Chicago: Quartermaster Food and Container Institute for the Armed Forces, 1946), p. 17.

TABLE 17-4
Characteristics of Some Leading Varieties of Peaches

Variety	Size and Appearance	Season of Year	Use
Elberta	Large, oval, yellow with red blush flesh, freestone	Aug.–Sept.	Dessert, canning
Golden Jubilee	Medium, yellow, freestone	Aug.	Dessert, canning
Hale	Large, round, yellow with red blush flesh, freestone	Aug.–Sept.	Dessert, canning
Hiley	Medium large, white flesh, freestone	Aug.	Dessert, canning

Source: Adapted from *Fruits and Vegetables,* Vol. 1 (Chicago: Quartermaster Food and Container Institute for the Armed Forces, 1946), p. 15.

Blackberries. Wild blackberries are native to Europe and North America. The blackberry crop in this country, compared with that of other cultivated berries, is a small one. The blackberry is an aggregate of druplets loosely attached to the receptacles. The chief nonvolatile acid contained in blackberries is malic; there are traces of oxalic, succinic, and citric. The blackberry is a fair source of ascorbic acid but does not compare well with the strawberry in this respect. Blackberries are used mainly in jams, jellies, juice, and as a dessert fruit.

Blueberries. The blueberry is cultivated only in the United States and Canada. The wild blueberry, however, is believed to be the most widely distributed fruit in the world.[11] Blueberries and a related fruit, the huckleberry, are used and gathered as a crop both in the tropics and in the temperate regions of the world. Blueberries and huckleberries are somewhat alike, but there is a horticultural distinction: the blueberry is identified as having small inoffensive seeds; the huckleberry has large, conspicuous seeds. Only the blueberry is cultivated. An interesting historical note is that the Indians are said to have dried blueberries extensively for winter use.[12]

The blueberry is smooth and blue-black in color. The main nonvolatile acids found in it are citric and malic. Like many other berries, blueberries are used mainly for desserts, jams, and jellies. Fairly large quantities are frozen and canned.

Cranberries. The cranberry is a native of North America. Although a small wild variety is found throughout the temperate zone of Europe, it is not grown commercially there. Cranberries grown best in bog areas—flat land that can be flooded in winter. Massachusetts and New Jersey are the most productive cranberry-growing areas in the country, but some cranberries are also grown in Wisconsin. The cranberry is round or oblong and red. Like the strawberry and raspberry, it contains a color pigment that is classified as an anthocyanin. The nonvolatile acids are citric, malic, and benzoic. Cranberries are used for sauce, jelly, and juice.

[11]Magness, op. cit.

[12]Lee, op. cit., p. 1355.

TABLE 17-5
Characteristics of Some Leading Varieties of Cherries

Variety	Size and Appearance	Season of Year	Use
Bing	Large, dark red to purplish black, sweet	June	Dessert
Black Tartarian	Medium, purplish black, sweet	Early June	Dessert
Montmorency	Medium, light red, sour		Canning, pies
Royal Anne	Large, yellow with red blush, sweet		Canning

Source: Adapted from *Fruits and Vegetables,* Vol. 1 (Chicago: Quartermaster Food and Container Institute for the Armed Forces, 1946), p. 20.

Strawberries. Species of strawberries grow in all temperate regions of the world. The strawberry has no rival for popularity in the United States—it is grown everywhere in home gardens and commercially in Louisiana, Tennessee, Arkansas, Oregon, California, North Carolina, and parts of Maryland, Delaware, New Jersey, and New York. The strawberry season is very short and the fruit itself is short-lived. The berries vary in size from very small to well over an inch in diameter. Their characteristic color is red; the color pigment is an anthocyanin. The nonvolatile acids found in strawberries are malic and citric; the volatile compounds imparting flavor and odor are acetic, capric, formic, and benzoic esters. Fresh strawberries are rated as a rich source of ascorbic acid, but loss of this vitamin is rapid when fruit is capped or injured, cut, or juiced. Strawberries are used as a dessert berry and extensively, also, in the manufacture of jams, syrups, ice cream, and confections.

Grapes. The cultivation of grapes is the largest fruit industry in the world, and most grapes are used chiefly for making wine. American grapes are used mainly for juice, jams, and jellies; the European grape is cultivated in the southwestern states, mainly for wine products.

Grapes are berries with a fairly tough skin and ordinarily grow in bunches. The nonvolatile acids are a mixture of malic and tartaric acids. The pigment of the American grape is caused mostly by anthocyanins. American grapes are used for dessert purposes, and tons of grapes are pressed every year for bottled and frozen grape juice. Grapes are a poor source of ascorbic acid. Muscat and Thompson Seedless grapes are used for the manufacture of raisins. A small grape is

dried for currants; these are known as Zante currants and are grown in Greece, California, and Australia (see Table 17-6).

CITRUS FRUITS

Citrus fruits are grown and consumed in large quantities in the United States, and some are imported from the Mediterranean countries. The chief citrus products are citron, grapefruit, kumquat, lemon, lime, and orange.

Grapefruits. The grapefruit (Fig. 17-2) was developed from the shaddock, a thick-skinned East Indian fruit that was imported to the West Indies and from there to the United States. At the present time, grapefruits are grown extensively in Florida, California, Texas, and Arizona. Grapefruits are spherical, have a smooth yellow skin, and may be either heavily seeded or almost entirely without seeds. They have been crossed with a number of other kinds of citrus fruits. When a grapefruit is crossed with a tangerine, the hybrid fruit—called a *tangelo*—is juicy, thick-skinned, and easy to peel. White-fleshed grapefruits are the most commonly used, but the pink- and ruby-fleshed specimens are well known and highly valued.

The pigments in the flesh of the pink- and ruby-fleshed grapefruits have been identified as lycopene and carotene, and the pigments responsible for the color in the rind are carotenoids and chlorophylls. A natural characteristic of grapefruit is its high ascorbic acid content. The vitamin is found in greater amounts in the unripened fruit, but the gradual decrease in the concentration of ascorbic acid as the fruit ripens

TABLE 17-6
Characteristics of Some Leading Grape Varieties

Variety	Size and Appearance	Season of Year	Use
Concord (American)	Medium to large, black, seeds	Sept.–Nov.	Juice, jam, jelly
Emperor (European)	Large, dark cherry-red, seeds	Dec.–Feb.	Dessert
Niagara (American)	Yellow green, medium to large, seeds	Sept.–Dec.	Dessert
Thompson Seedless (American)	Small, yellow green, seedless	Aug.–Oct.	Dessert
Tokay (European)	Large, red sweet, seeds	Oct.–Dec.	Dessert

Source: Adapted from *Fruits and Vegetables,* Vol. 1 (Chicago: Quartermaster Food and Container Institute for the Armed Forces, 1946), p. 27.

17-2 *Fresh citrus rinds should be grated before extracting the juice from the fruit.* (*Courtesy of Sunkist Growers, Inc.*)

is more than balanced by the increased volume of the juice in the fruit. Thus, the total ascorbic acid content is greatest in the ripe fruit[13] (see Table 17-7).

Kumquats. The kumquat, a colorful little fruit, was brought to America from China and Japan.

[13]Ibid., p. 1387.

It is round or oval and resembles a miniature orange.

The rind as well as the pulp of the kumquat is good to eat. Like other citrus fruits, the kumquat has a high pectic content and is used in making preserves. Kumquats are also candied.

Lemons and Limes. Lemons and limes (see Fig. 17-3) are very similar in composition and use

TABLE 17-7
Characteristics of Some Leading Grapefruit Varieties

Variety	Size and Appearance	Season of Year	Use
Duncan	Light yellow, medium to small, 14 sections, 5 seeds	Jan.–June	Dessert
Hall	Large, light yellow, seeds, 14 sections	Feb.–Mar.	Dessert, canning
Marsh	Medium, light color, no seeds, 13 sections	Feb.–Mar.	Dessert
Walters	Pale yellow, 13 sections, seeds	Nov.–Mar.	Dessert

Source: Adapted from *Fruits and Vegetables,* Vol. 1 (Chicago: Quartermaster Food and Container Institute for the Armed Forces, 1946), p. 36.

17-3 *Preparing grapefruit. Using a sharp knife, peel grapefruit by cutting around the fruit with a continuous, sawing motion. To section the fruit, cut along each dividing membrane from outer edge to core. (Courtesy of Dudley–Anderson–Yutzy, on behalf of the Florida Citrus Commission)*

and therefore can be grouped together for discussion. Although most of the lemons and limes sold in the United States are of the acid variety, there are also available sweet varieties imported from Egypt. It is thought that both lemons and limes originated in eastern India. They thrive in warm humid climates and have adapted easily to the soils and climates of such countries and regions as Italy, Spain, Israel, and southern California. Lemons are picked while green and per-

mitted to ripen in cold storage. This ripening or "curing" process improves the flavor.

As with grapefruit, the color of the lemon rind is produced by chlorophylls and carotenoids. Lemon juice is high in ascorbic acid but has too sharp a flavor to be used as an undiluted beverage. Pale lemons usually have a high acid content; bright yellow lemons are generally sweeter. Lemon juice is used extensively as an ingredient of beverages, in many baked products, in jams and jellies, and in candies. Lemon peel is used in the manufacture of pectin products.

The lime is smaller and greener than the lemon and has a thinner skin. It is very acid in taste. The sour variety of limes is grown in Florida and imported from the West Indies. Both sweet and sour limes are imported from Egypt. Lime juice is popular as a flavoring in beverages and desserts, although in the United States fresh limes are less popular than fresh lemons.

Oranges. Oranges (see Fig. 17-4) constitute the leading citrus crop in the United States. Origi-

17-4 *A sharp knife with at least a 6" blade is an excellent tool for cutting citrus fruit. (Courtesy of Sunkist Growers, Inc.)*

nating in southeastern Asia, the cultivation of the orange spread to other parts of the world where the climate was suitable. Spain, Brazil, China, Japan, Italy, and Israel are among the chief producers of oranges. Florida leads the United States in orange production; California follows closely; and Texas, Arizona, Louisiana, and Mississippi are also considered good orange-producing states. The three major kinds of oranges grown are the mandarin, the sweet, and the sour or bitter. The sweet orange is the most important kind in the United States.

The varieties of sweet oranges found in the United States are Valencia, Hamlin, Parson Brown, and navel (see Table 17-8). The Temple orange is a cross between a sweet orange and tangerine. Valencia, Parson Brown, pineapple, and Hamlin oranges are grown in Florida. The navel orange (so named because of the "umbilical" mark on the blossom side of the fruit) is a seedless orange, grown mainly in California. The mandarin tangerine is grown in China and Japan. In the United States, the Satsumas variety—which has a lighter yellow peel than the mandarin—is popular. The third kind of orange, the bitter or sour, is not used extensively in the United States. It is grown in Italy, Spain, and Israel and is used mainly for making marmalade and beverages.

The Valencia orange, grown in Florida and in California, is generally known as the "juice orange" because of its thin skin and high juice content. The navel orange and the tangerine are dessert fruits. The navel has a thick skin that is fairly easy to remove, and the tangerine has a very loose skin and segments that separate very easily.

Citric and malic acids are present in oranges and contribute to their flavor. The ascorbic acid content of oranges is generally high. Vitamin content is fairly stable at storage temperatures of 32–35°F (0–2°C) but tends to decrease during prolonged storage under high temperatures.[14]

Oranges that hang on the tree during the winter months will turn orange before they are ripe. If the fruit is left to ripen on the tree until the summer months, the color will turn back to green. Regreening is thought to occur when the chlorophyll returns to the surface of the skin in response to warm ground temperatures. California oranges will turn orange again if they are gassed with ethylene. However, ethylene gas does not have a significant effect on Florida oranges, so dyes are often used to recolor the fruit orange. The orange will then be stamped "color added."

Oranges are used in large quantities as dessert fruits (see Fig. 17-5). They are also canned and frozen; the production of frozen orange concentrate is constantly increasing in order to meet rising needs.

The flavor of the orange juice is determined by the "Brix," the percentage of soluble solids in a given weight of the juice. It measures the sugar content, which has to be balanced against the acid concentration. Florida orange juice has a

[14]Ibid., p. 1348.

TABLE 17-8
Characteristics of Some Leading Varieties of Oranges

Variety	Size and Appearance	Season of Year	Use
Hamlin	Medium to small, no seeds	Oct.–Nov.	Dessert, slicing, juice
Navel	Large, round, orange to orange-yellow, no seeds	Dec.–Feb.	Dessert
Parson Brown	Medium, oblong, yellow to yellow-orange, seeds	Nov.–May	Dessert, slicing
Pineapple	Medium to large, deep orange, many seeds	Mar.–June (Fla.)	Juice
Valencia	Large, slightly oval, pale orange, few seeds	May–Nov. (Calif.)	Juice

Source: Adapted from *Fruits and Vegetables,* Vol. 1 (Chicago: Quartermaster Food and Container Institute for the Armed Forces, 1946), p. 31.

minimum Brix of 12.8 for reconstituted frozen concentrate and a Brix/acid ratio of 13:1.[15]

MELONS

Melons are generally divided into two classes: the *muskmelon,* which includes a number of varieties, such as honeydew, cantaloupe, and casaba; and the *watermelon* (see Fig. 17-6).

The muskmelon and its close relatives (Fig. 17-7) are almost spherical, with a grooved and netted surface. The honeydew has a hard, smooth surface. The flesh of the muskmelon and cantaloupe is dark yellow or orange; the flesh of the honeydew is greenish white, and that of the casaba yellowish white. *Phytofluene,* a yellow color pigment, is found in the cantaloupe. The watermelon is large, elliptical, green or green-striped, and smooth-skinned. The flesh is usually red or pink, but some varieties have a yellow flesh. Lycopene and carotene are the color pigments found in watermelon. Watermelon is a

17-5 *A serrated citrus fruit spoon may be used when serving halves of oranges or grapefruit. Kitchen shears are good for scalloping citrus shells. (Courtesy of Sunkist Growers, Inc.)*

[15]*The Care and Handling of Florida Orange Juice* (Lakeland, Fl.: Department of Citrus, 1975), p. 3.

17-6 *Melon varieties. (Courtesy United Fresh Fruit and Vegetable Association)*

(a)   **(c)**   **(b)**

17-7   *Melons available in our markets.* (*a*)
Honeydew (*b*) *Casaba* (*c*) *Persian* (*d*) *Cantaloupe.*
(*Courtesy of Western Growers Association*)

(d)

fairly good source of ascorbic acid, and, according to Clegg and Satterfield,[16] most varieties

[16]R. Clegg and G. Satterfield, "Average Ascorbic
Acid Content of Watermelons," *J. Amer. Dietet. Assoc.*
16:39, 1940.

have more ascorbic acid in the heart than immediately under the skin. Small amounts of watermelon rind are preserved or pickled.

With the exception of the watermelon, the
softening of the stem-end "eye" is an indicator
of ripeness. If the melon is not ripe when pur-

173

chased, it should be stored at room temperature until softened, then refrigerated. If the melon has been harvested unripe, the melon will soften but will not increase in sugar content or flavor.

OTHER FRUITS

Avocados. The avocado is native to Central America and Mexico. In the United States, avocados are grown in California and Florida. Avocados are pear-shaped, with a green or purplish skin (Fig. 17-8). Their color pigments are chlorophyll and carotene. They are high in fat content and have a pleasant, smooth texture. Avocados are usually firm and unripe when purchased and need to be softened at room temperature for 3–5 days before eating. Mashed with a bit of lime juice (to retard enzymatic browning) they are served as guacamole, a Mexican salad.

17-8 *Top: An avocado pear makes a pleasing first course or salad course. (Courtesy of United Fresh Fruit and Vegetable Association) Bottom: Avocados lend themselves to good combinations with other fruits and vegetables. (The California Avocado Advisory Board)*

Bananas. Bananas are the chief fruit grown in tropical lands throughout the world. They are an important export of most of the countries where production is high. The rapid growth of the banana tree, which is really a herbaceous plant, accounts in part for its economic importance. The banana plant grows quickly to a height of 15–30 ft, the bloom appears about 10 or 12 months after planting, and the fruit is mature 5 or 6 months later.

The banana commonly imported in the United States is yellow and finger-shaped. The bananas, or "fingers," are grouped together as "hands" and attached to a central stalk to form a bunch of bananas. Each bunch contains 10–20 hands of fruit and weighs about 50 lb. At present, most of the bananas imported to the United States come from Central and South America and the West Indies.

Bananas have high nutritive value. One banana contains as much as 22% carbohydrate and good amounts of vitamin A, ascorbic acid, and potassium. The fruit has a sweet, pleasant taste. Bananas that are to be shipped to market are picked green and stored in ripening rooms under carefully controlled temperature and humidity. The yellow color of the ripe banana skin is caused mainly by the carotenoid and chlorophyll pigments. When the fruit developes light brown flecks it is ready to be eaten.

In addition to their extensive use as a fresh dessert fruit, bananas are used in cakes, puddings, and cookies. They are canned, dried, and flaked for use as baby food.

Plantains are closely related to the banana, although about twice as large. Unlike bananas, they are not palatable raw, for they are still very starchy even when ripe. But they have a very pleasing flavor when boiled, baked, or fried. When fried it is difficult to distinguish them from french-fried potatoes; thus, they are often used as a substitute. The plantain is an important food in the tropics, forming the main portion of many meals.

Dates. The date has been cultivated for centuries in the North African countries. The date is actually a long berry, brown and with a somewhat wrinkled surface. Production is centered in areas having very dry summer and fall seasons. But the date palms require moist soil; hence, they thrive near underground springs, in oases, or in irrigated areas. The American date industry is located in the dry desert areas of southern California—the Coachella Valley—and Arizona.[17]

There are three varieties of dates: soft, semidry, and dry. The soft dates are excellent for flavor, but ship badly. They are used chiefly in date confections. The Deglet Noor, a semidry date, is the type grown in the United States. Dry dates are imported from Arab countries. Dates change from yellow green to a soft brown and become soft when ripe. The sugar content of this fruit runs as high as 47%. During ripening, the fruit becomes dehydrated and forms invert sugar. The fruit is then cured at constant temperatures that maintain it at the peak of maturity. The fruit is packed in moisture-proof containers or wrappers to reduce deterioration from the absorption of moisture during storage and the loss of moisture after storage.

Dates are used extensively as a dessert fruit and an ingredient in baked products and candy.

Figs. There are many varieties of figs grown both in the United States and in the area surrounding the Mediterranean. The fig is a pear-shaped fruit that has a very sweet flavor. In this country, it is grown in large quantities in California and to a lesser extent in some Southern states. Italy is the leading fig-producing nation. The chief varieties of figs are Adriatic, Black Mission, Calimyrna, and Kadota. The Black Mission fig is commercially the most important black fig in the United States.

Figs are eaten fresh in areas where they are grown, but they ship and handle poorly and must therefore be dried, canned, or preserved if sent to distant markets. Dried pressed figs are famous as a confection all over the world.

Pineapples. The pineapple is native to South America and ranks second to bananas in importance as a tropical fruit. The fruit is cylindrical and crowned with a tuft of stiff leaves. Although it is native to South America, it is produced chiefly in Hawaii. Florida, Puerto Rico, and Cuba also grow considerable amounts. Pineap-

---

[17]For detailed information on dates, see "Growing Dates in the United States," *Agriculture Information Bulletin 207* (Washington, D.C.: U.S. Department of Agriculture, 1959).

ples owe their color to the pigments carotene and xanthophyll. The flavor of the fruit varies according to the place where it is grown. Pineapple is ripened [by being stored at a temperature of 45°F (8°C)] after it is removed from the stem. A ripe pineapple is reddish brown to yellow and has a fragrant odor. Ripened fruit cannot be shipped very far as it softens and spoils very rapidly.

Pineapple rings can dress up a gelatin salad or add the finishing touch to a baked ham when held along the side by toothpicks. For other cooking purposes (cobblers, fruit syrup) broken or crushed pineapple is the more economical buy.

Pineapple in all forms—fresh, canned and frozen—is highly prized in this country. Large quantities of pineapple juice are packed for commercial use. The flavor of pineapple is mild and pleasantly sweet and blends well with a large variety of foods.

Pineapple juice contains the proteolytic enzyme *bromelin,* which is used in the preparation of meat tenderizers. For this reason fresh pineapple is never added to a gelatin salad. Canned pineapple which has undergone heat treatment sufficient to denature this enzyme must be used instead.

Mangoes. Although widely used in tropical countries, mangoes are not as well known in the United States. Mangoes in the United States are grown mainly in limited areas in Florida and, like the citrus fruits, are native to southeast Asia. The mango is a heavy, somewhat pear-shaped fruit, capable of growing up to 3 to 4 lb. A well-ripened mango (Fig. 17-9) is tender and juicy and has a flavor not unlike that of a peach. On the other hand, an inferior or unripe mango is fibrous, tough, acid, and has an unpleasant flavor. Canned mangoes are a rarity in the United States, but they are sold in Mexico and other mango-producing countries. They are normally eaten raw sprinkled with lime juice and hot chili powder. Indian chutney, made with mangoes, is sold here.

Papayas. Papaya is cultivated in India and the West Indies as well as other tropical areas. It is a large elongated fruit that is yellow or green in color. The flesh varies from pink to orange, and black seeds are encased in a central cavity.

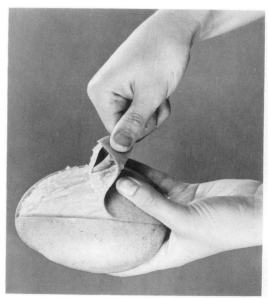

17-9 *Scoring the mango into quarters first and peeling with a sharp knife facilitates skin removal. (Courtesy of Calavo)*

Papain, a protein splitting enzyme, is obtained from the unripened fruit. The fruit is a good source of vitamin A.

PREPARATION OF FRESH FRUIT

Raw whole or cut fruit or a mixture of cut fruits is frequently served as an appetizer, as a salad, or for dessert. Fruits to be used as appetizers should be somewhat tart and need little or no sugar. Mixed cut raw fruits are usually chosen with a view to harmonious combination of appearance, flavor, and texture.

All fruits to be eaten must be washed in water that is safe for drinking purposes. Many fruits are sprayed with chemicals while in the growing stage, and although most of the residue is removed before the fruit is marketed, there is still a chance of contamination.

Uncooked fruits served whole are not an uncommon dessert. Most varieties of fruit, perfectly ripened and chilled, are most palatable and pleasing when served without alterations. Raw fruit that is to be sliced should be handled as little as possible. Sections of fruit that look ragged and worked over are not attractive. When citrus

17-10 *The papaya fruit is native to Central America and the West Indies. The plant contains the enzyme papain that is used to tenderize meat and to flavor beer. (Courtesy of Calavo)*

fruits are cut into sections or slices, a very sharp knife is needed to cut the fruit free of membrane or peel.

An easy way to peel citrus fruits is to steam them for 2–4 minutes. The fruit peel is scored into quarters without piercing the fruit and then peeled. The steaming loosens the membranes without injuring the flavor or nutritive value of the fruit. Apples and pears should be peeled by paring very thin slices away from the fruit with a potato peeler. Other fruits with skins that adhere to soft bodies such as ripe peaches and apricots should be blanched in boiling water for 45 seconds, then immediately cooled in cold water. The skin should slip off easily.

Fruit cups, appetizers, and salad plates are most appealing when the pieces of fruit used in the combinations have not lost their identity through excessive handling or chopping. The proper use of a garnish of a contrasting color will set off fruit colors.

With a few minor exceptions, raw fruit is more palatable and has a higher nutritive value than cooked and processed versions. Underripe fruit, however, is unpalatable, because many of the compounds contributing to its flavor are not completely developed until the fruit is ripe. Most cut raw fruits, except those with high acid content, turn dark on exposure to air. Discoloration

of cut surfaces is caused partly by the tannin compounds contained in the fruit and partly by enzyme action. Oxidizing enzymes may act on certain tannins and amino acids in the fruit causing a browning of the surfaces in contact with the air. (Darkening or browning occurs only when the fruit cells have been cut or injured.) Methods used to reduce or to slow down the rate of darkening of cut fruit are based on removing oxygen, changing the acidity (pH) of the fruit, preventing contact with oxygen, and destroying the enzymes. The most common practices are to immerse the cut fruit in an acid juice, such as lemon or orange, to increase its acidity. The ascorbic acid will retard browning until it itself is completely oxidized. When this happens, the chemical reaction continues, oxidizing the tannins. Another method is to cover it with sugar solution to prevent contact with oxygen. Dried fruits such as apricots are dipped in sulfur to retard browning. Freezing also tends to decrease the browning of cut fruits. Blanching will denature the browning enzyme, phenol oxidase, but will cause the fruit to lose its texture, and become mushy.

Osmosis and Cooking of Fruit. The force with which a liquid is drawn from a more concentrated solution through a semipermeable

177

membrane to a less concentrated one is called *osmotic pressure*. Fruits and vegetables have semipermeable membranes through which water molecules can pass.

PRINCIPLES OF COOKING FRUITS

Although most fruits are edible raw, cooking is necessary to soften the cellulose of some fruits and to cook the starch in underripe or very hard fruits. Fruit is cooked to provide variety in eating, and much fruit is canned for future use. The factors considered in the cooking of fruit are the amount and quality of cellulose, the degree of ripeness (related to protopectin content), and the amount of sugar and water used.

The amount of water used to cook fruit depends on its structure and water content. Berries, because they have little cellulose and will collapse quickly when cooked, are best cooked in little water. Apples and pears require sufficient water to soften their cellulose structure.

When fruit is cooked, the cell walls of the plant tissues become more permeable owing to the transformation of the protopectins to water-soluble pectin in the presence of the fruit's acids. The water passes in and out of the cell by diffusion. Since the cell wall is held together by the pectins, this weakens the wall and the cooked tissue becomes soft and limp. When fruit is cooked in a sugar syrup, water from the fruit is attracted to the more dense syrup—leaving the cells slightly dehydrated—and sugar is absorbed into the cells, making the fruit firm. Sugar from the syrup surrounding the fruit is found in higher concentration in the cell walls than within the cell.[18] There are a few fruits, however, that do not lend themselves to this practice: for example, the Kieffer pear and the quince, both hard fruits. The slow cooking of large pieces of fruit in a sugar solution will result in a lustrous, firm fruit that is highly palatable.

Texture Changes. The texture of fruit depends on the amount and character of cellulose in it. Cooking in moist heat will soften cellulose, but the addition of sugar strengthens the cellulose structure. Fruit that is to be served as a sauce or that is to be softened is cooked to tenderness before the sugar is added.

Color Changes. The color changes that occur during the cooking of fruit may be attributable to a change of acid content, or to the alkaline reaction of the cooking waters and their effect on the color pigment, or to the reaction of metals with the color pigment in the fruit. Red pigments, anthocyanins, react with iron to form ferrous iron salts, thus spotting the fruit with dull brownish discolorations. Some change in grapes and cherries may occur when these fruits have come in contact with tin salts. Red fruits, such as strawberries, may lose color when heated rapidly after storage in the refrigerator. Heating berries slowly so that the interior oxygen is used in respiration will help to keep the bright color of the berries.[19]

Many fruits and vegetables with anthocyanin pigments are processed in enameled lined cans to prevent discoloration of the food. The reaction of the acid of the fruits or vegetables processed in cans with a tin lining will produce metallic salts that change their color. To avoid discoloration, a number of fruits and vegetables are processed in lacquered containers.

Flavor Changes. Fruit cooked in syrup must be cooked longer to bring about evaporation of the water. A few fruits, such as strawberries and cherries, develop an off-flavor when cooked too long in a sugar syrup. These fruits should be quickly cooked in sugar rather than syrup. The flavoring substances in fruits include sugar and esters of organic acids. Some of the organic acids are volatile and are lost during cooking. Hence, fruits are cooked only for a short time. Esters of such acids as formic and caproic give the fruit its characteristic flavor and aroma.

Changes in Nutritive Value. The greatest loss in food value in cooked fruit is the loss of ascorbic acid through oxidation. Because this vitamin is unstable under heat, short cooking periods for

---

[18] Pauline Paul and Helen Palmer, *Food Theory and Applications* (New York: Wiley, 1972), p. 263.

[19] Belle Lowe, *Experimental Cookery,* 4th ed. (New York: Wiley, 1955), p. 133.

fruits ensure greater vitamin retention as well as greater flavor retention.[20,21]

METHODS OF COOKING FRUIT

Fruits are cooked by stewing or baking. The goal in cooking fruit is to improve its digestibility while retaining as much as possible of its flavor and color. In stewing fruit (a compote), the usual procedure is to cook it in water (if a sauce is desired) or in sugar or a sugar syrup (if the fruit is to retain its shape, as in a fruit compote). Fruits for stewing should be fresh, sound, and not overripe. Removing too thick a paring from apples and similar fruits is wasteful and detracts from the flavor, color, and nutritive value of the cooked product. Cooked fruit is most palatable when served immediately. Fruit sauces and pies are most delicious when served shortly after preparation.

Baked fruits are valued for their excellent flavor. Fruits with heavy skins such as apples and pears are good to bake because the peel serves as a protective covering and holds in the steam necessary to soften the cellulose and decrease the loss of volatile flavors. Such fruits as plums, peaches, and bananas may be baked in covered baking dishes. Rhubarb, although not a fruit but used like one, may also be prepared in this manner.

FRUIT BEVERAGES

Juice from canned, frozen, and fresh fruits is used for fruit beverages. Lemonade and orangeade and their many variations are the most commonly used fruit punches. When several fruit juices are combined in a fruit beverage, the combinations should be carefully planned so that an attractive color is obtained. For a red color, red or purplish juices should be used, with some lemon juice to maintain acidity. For a purple shade, purple and reddish-purple fruit juices are used singly or together, and no acid need be added. Canned pineapple juice keeps the purplish color dominant and does not impart red color to the reddish-purple juices as other acid fruit juices do. Lowe[22] suggests that the tin salts from the canned pineapple juice may be an important factor in this color reaction.

STORAGE OF FRESH FRUIT

Only a few fruits, mainly apples, can be stored for an extended period of time in cold or cellar storage. Controlled low temperatures must be employed to provide the best storage conditions for fresh fruit, to retard decay resulting from the natural respiration process of the fruit and from microbial spoilage. Each fruit must be stored at its own optimum temperature. Proper air circulation will ensure successful storage of fresh fruit. For holding a household supply of fresh fruit, the refrigerator or fruit cellar provides the required temperature.

Low temperatures [close to $32°F$ ($0°C$)] with a preferred relative humidity of about 85% furnish satisfactory conditions for commercial storage of fruit. If large quantities of fruit are to be stored, air circulation must be assured. Crates of fruit are stacked so that air can circulate around the sides, tops, and bottoms. Fruits stored in the home refrigerator tend to lose moisture. Some measures taken to prevent this loss include the use of ventilated covered containers and special fruit compartments. Fresh fruits absorb and emit odors, making it essential for space separate from other food storage to be provided.

Ripened bananas are not stored at low temperatures because of a color change in the skin when they are later removed to room temperature. Berries are not adapted to extended storage periods, either commercially or at home.

DRIED FRUITS

The preservation of food by drying is one of the most ancient methods of processing foods.

---

[20] G. E. Vail, "The Effect of Processing on the Nutritive Value of Food," *J. Amer. Dietet. Assoc.* **18**:569, 1942.

[21] E. Sondheinier and Z. I. Kerterz, "Participation of Ascorbic Acid in the Destruction of Anthocyanic in Strawberry Juice and Model Systems," *Food Res.* **18**:475, 1953.

[22] Lowe, op. cit., p. 127.

By removing a large portion of the water content from such foods as fruits and vegetables, their keeping qualities are extended well beyond normal storage life. Moreover, storage space is saved because the size of the food is reduced.

Although dried or dehydrated fruit is not necessarily accepted on equal terms with fresh fruit, there is a large consumer demand for certain dried fruit products. Prunes, figs, raisins, apricots, apples, pears, and dates are popular dried fruits and are valued for their sweet flavor, which is markedly different from that of the fresh fruit (Table 17-9).

Composition. The drying process removes more than 50% water and causes some destruc-tion of ascorbic acid. It also softens the cellulose and changes the starch to sugar. Volatile substances responsible for the flavor in fresh fruit are lost during drying, causing a marked change in the flavor.

Nutritive Value. Dried fruits are high in sugar and low in protein and fat. They may contain as much as 70% sugar; a 3–6% mixture of malic, citric, and tartaric acids; about 5% ash; as well as small percentages of certain vitamins. As a group, dried fruits are a good source of minerals.

Economic Aspects. Almost all the commonly used dried fruits are dried in California. Some prunes are dried in the Pacific Northwest and

TABLE 17-9
Varieties of Dried Whole and Cut Fruits

Fruit	Method of Drying	Principal Varieties Grown for Drying
Apples (slices, rings)	Evaporated	Many varieties of apples are dried; yellow or green-skinned apples are preferred to red-skinned ones, which leave traces of color on the skin
Apricots (cut pieces)	Usually sun-dried	Blenheim, best-quality dried fruit Royal (packed in Southern California) Moorpark (very large, round, reddish-orange variety)
Dates	Mature date is "dried" when picked	Deglet Noor
Figs	Partially dried on trees, sun-dried, dehydrated	Smyrna Adriatic Black Mission (only black-skinned fig grown in California)
Peaches	Usually sun-dried	Freestones (used mainly for drying) Muir (best-quality dried fruit) Lovell (larger than the Muir, yellow in color)
Pears (cut)	Usually sun-dried	Bartlett (produces best-quality fruit, and is only variety dried to any extent)
Prunes	Dehydrated	French (sold under the trade name of Santa Clara Italian)
Raisins (seedless, whole)	Sun-dried	Thompson Seedless
Muscat	Sun-dried	Muscat
Sulfur-bleached	Partly sun-dried and dehydrated	Thompson Seedless

Source: Adapted from *Fruits and Vegetables,* Vol. 1 (Chicago: Quartermaster Food and Container Institute for the Armed Forces, 1946), p. 4.

some apples are dried in almost every one of the apple-growing states. Fruit that is grown to be marketed fresh may be dried if there is a surplus crop, but most dried fruits are produced from crops grown solely for the purpose.

The economic advantages of dried fruits are the elimination of waste, the saving of freight and warehouse space, and the extended shelf life of the fruit. Uniformity in size is an added economic attraction, for accurate prediction of portions per unit of purchase can be made. These are concentrated foods, and their compact size and high nutritive value give them a priority rating as emergency items for storage.

Methods of Drying. Fruits are dried in the sun or by mechanical means. Fruit to be dried in the sun is washed, halved, and placed on trays with the cut surface up. All fruit that is cut is subjected to the fumes of burning sulfur, which acts to preserve the natural color of the fruit. Sulfuring also acts to prevent spoilage and to preserve certain nutritive qualities. This process causes a contraction of cell material and imparts a translucent, syrupy texture to the fruit in contrast to the dark color and rubbery texture of fruit dried without sulfuring.

Dehydrated foods are dried under controlled or partially controlled conditions of temperature and humidity until a large portion of the moisture is removed.

Dehydrating permits control over the product, a somewhat different state of affairs from that occurring in sun-drying. Also, the time required for dehydrating food is shorter and the method is more sanitary.

Practically all apples are dried by evaporation, using a form of artificial heat without controlled air flow and humidity. The driers are kilns in which drying rooms with slats in the floor are located over a heater. The fruit to be dried is cut and spread on the floor in layers; hot air is passed through the fruit and leaves by way of a roof vent.

Mechanical drying implies artificial heat. The usual method of dehydrating fruit mechanically is to subject it to drying in a tunnel drier. The tunnel drier is arranged so that moist fruits on trays or cars enter the tunnel at one end and pass out the opposite end as dried fruit. Hot air is circulated through the tunnel and blown over the fruit. The length of time the fruit remains in the tunnel depends on the system of blowing the air across the fruit, on the temperature and humidity, and on the kind of fruit.

A more modern approach to drying fruits is with a vacuum which can bring down the moisture content to 1–3%. This low moisture content considerably increases the shelf life of the product. This is called *dehydration* rather than drying. Although vacuum drying is more expensive, it is less likely to result in structural damage to the fruit. Fruits dehydrated in this manner are also much lighter, crisper, and less expensive to transport. They must be stored in containers without air or with nitrogen gas.

Foam-mat drying is used on fruit juices such as orange juice. Stabilizers are added to the liquid, which is whipped to a foam and dried as a thin film in a convection oven. The resultant dried product has a moisture content of only 1%.

Apples and blueberries are often puff-dried. In this process, called *explosive puffing,* the fruit is heated under pressure. As the pressure suddenly drops, the water leaves the fruit and a puff-dried fruit remains, which is dried further.[23]

Processing Dried Fruit. Prunes and raisins are treated by dipping them in a solution of sodium bisulfite or sulfur dioxide. Once the fruit is sulfured, the trays are arranged in single layers in a drying yard. Here the fruit remains from 2 days to 4 weeks, or until about two thirds of the water is removed from the fruit. Pears are kept until they are translucent.

Before prunes are dried in the sun, they are dipped in a hot alkaline solution for a very short time or in very hot water for just enough time to crack or "check" the skins. Checking the skins facilitates drying. From this point on, the trayed fruit is dried in a manner similar to that used in drying other fruit.

Unbleached raisins and currants usually are dried on wooden trays in the vineyard. The drying time is much greater than for sulfur-bleached raisins, which are spread out in the sun until the desired degree of bleaching is attained.

Although some drying of dates and figs may be necessary after harvesting, a considerable amount of drying occurs while the fruit is still on

[23] N. Eisenhardt, R. Eskew, and J. Cordig, Jr., "Explosive Puffing Applied to Apples and Blueberries," *Food Eng.* **36:**53, 1964.

the tree. Figs may be partially dried before pick-ing, and dates may need no further drying at all.

Fruits other than those discussed have been successfully dried either on a small scale or in experimental batches. Bananas, blueberries, and cranberries have been given trial runs as potential crops for drying. Of the fruits mentioned, dried bananas are the most popular of those finding their way to the market shelf. Bananas may be sun- or spray-dried. The peeled and sliced ba-nana is treated with a weak solution of sulfurous acid to prevent it from darkening before it is dried.

Buying. Dried fruits are generally packaged in 8-oz, 1-lb, and 2-lb cardboard cartons or bags for the retail market. Prunes are graded accord-ing to size: Extra large, Large, Medium, and Small. Large prunes run 40–50 to the pound; small prunes average 70–110 to the pound; me-dium-sized prunes average 50–70 to the pound.

The standards for grading are based primarily on quality and size. U.S. grades for dried apples, apricots, peaches, and pears are U.S. Grade A, U.S. Grade B, U.S. Grade C, and substandard.[24]

Cooking Dried Fruit. Many people enjoy eat-ing dried fruit without any preparation other than washing. Raisins, dates, figs, and apricots are often purchased for this use.

The goal in cooking dried fruits is to enable them to absorb a high percentage of the moisture lost through drying, without loss of flavor, tex-ture, or nutritive value. Dried fruits are soaked in hot water for a short time and then cooked in the same water. The fruit is cooked at simmering temperature in a covered pan. Specially treated dried fruits may not require soaking before cooking. When sugar is used in cooking, it is always added at the end of the cooking period so as not to toughen the cell walls or interfere with absorption of water. Actually, dried fruits are quite sweet and require very little additional sugar.

In addition to their use when fresh, frozen, and canned fruits are not available, dried fruits are used in pies, puddings, cakes, cookies, and candies. There is a trend toward the increased

use of dried fruits with a higher moisture con-tent because they require less cooking time and result in a product that is more acceptable to the consumer. These products are frequently of the right texture, flavor, and color for eating out of hand.

Spoilage. Dried fruits, like other dried foods, are perishable. Much dried fruit is stored for fairly long periods after processing. Conse-quently, several types of storage deterioration may take place that exact a heavy toll of the dried fruit stockpile. Darkening of fruit, insect infestation, and microbial deterioration are the chief causes of spoilage.

To prevent darkening from taking place, the fruit is held at fairly low temperatures. Insect infestation is controlled by drying the fruit under sanitary conditions and by using fumi-gants such as methyl bromide.

Microorganisms causing spoilage of dried fruit are produced by bacteria or mold spores. The surface of the fruit contains spores of the micro-organisms, and although washing and dipping the fruit in a lye bath before drying destroy many, a considerable number are likely to re-main on the surface of the fruit. The "sweating" of dry fruits may also engender some microbial growth. Pasteurization of fruit will destory a large percentage of the spoilage organisms.

FROZEN FRUIT AND FRUIT JUICES

From the large variety of frozen fruits and fruit juices on the market, it is apparent that these foods are much in demand. Frozen fruits are packed whole or cut up, and several fruits may be combined in one package. They may be packed with or without (dry) sugar or syrup. Frozen fruit juices are concentrates of the fruit juice. Various container sizes are now available, thus meeting the requirements of the small as well as the large family. Reconstituted frozen juice should be used within 2–3 days. Prices for frozen fruits and frozen fruit juices vary. The alert consumer will find that constant awareness of price differences within the frozen line of goods itself and with corresponding fresh and canned fruits and fruit juices will result in sav-ings. Of course, the amounts of frozen fruits and

---

[24] "U.S.D.A. Grade Names for Food and Farm Products," *Agricultural Handbook 342* (Washington, D.C.: U.S. Department of Agriculture, 1967).

fruit juices a consumer can use depend on food preferences, income, and available frozen-food storage space. Frozen fruit and fruit juices should be frozen solidly until purchased. Moving them rapidly from the store to home freezer is necessary if top quality is to be maintained. The usual grade names for frozen fruits are U.S. Grade A or Fancy; U.S. Grade B or U.S. Choice or U.S. Extra Standard; U.S. Grade C or U.S. Standard. Some processors use the grade standards in packing and selling the fruit but do not use the "U.S." in front of it on the labels. This is permissable as long as the quality of the food measures up to that indicated by the grade name. The "U.S." indicates that a government grader has examined the product. Processors using grade labels that do not reveal the true conditions within the container are liable to prosecution under laws on mislabeling.

CANNED FRUIT AND CANNED FRUIT JUICES

Canned fruits and fruit juices have many excellent uses and must be given high priority as convenience foods. Canned apple slices, blueberries, and sour cherries are notable examples of processed fruits that are popular convenience items used in making pies and other desserts. These is also a growing variety of canned fruit pie fillings on the market. Once again, grade labels give an indication of quality grades and are similar to those used on frozen-food containers. All grades are nutritious and have comparable food value, but it is best to select the grade that offers the quality best suited for use.

In canned fruits, the top grades have greater uniformity of size and color and high sugar syrup strength. Lower grades may be of irregular color and size and have a sugar syrup of medium strength but still be entirely suitable for many uses. Water-packed fruits are also available. These are used for cooking or dietetic purposes. Canned fruits and fruit juices should be stored in a dry place with temperatures under 70°F (20°C) but above freezing. Rusted, leaking, badly dented, and bulging cans are not suitable purchases. Bulging cans indicate gas formation resulting from food spoilage.

In a study to determine the effect of time and temperature on the ascorbic acid stability of orange juice—frozen, canned, and fresh—it was found that the ascorbic acid was very stable even after long periods of storage at room temperature. This was true provided that storage was in a tightly covered glass or plastic container. In view of these findings, it is fairly safe to assume that citrus fruit juices stored in the refrigerator in proper containers will retain a high degree of ascorbic acid.[25]

FRUIT DRINKS

Along with frozen and canned fruit juices, there are a number of fruit drinks to satisfy the consumer's demand for variety. These are available in powdered, bottled, canned, and frozen forms. They are made from natural or synthetic fruit juice or may be a combination of the two. A number of other ingredients are added to give the beverage a characteristic appearance and flavor. These may include natural or synthetic flavorings, color, sugar or artificial sweetener, vitamins—mainly ascorbic acid—and preservatives.

Fruit drinks have become popular convenience beverages, but they are not to be confused with or substituted for a fruit juice. There are five fruit drinks which are included in the federal standards.[26]

Lemonade. This drink must contain enough lemon juice to supply 0.70 g of anhydrous citric acid in 100 ml of the finished product. The sweeteners permitted are sugar, invert sugar, and the usual sugars and syrups made from corn.

Limeade. The standards for this drink are the same as for lemonade except that the juice and oil must be from limes.

Orange Juice Drink. Orange drink is the beverage prepared by adding water to one or more of the unfermented orange juice ingredients

[25] A. Lopez, W. A. Krehl, and E. Good, "Influence of Time and Temperature on Ascorbic Acid Stability," *J. Amer. Dietet. Assoc.* **50**:308, 1967.

[26] Definitions and Standards of Identity for Food: Code of Federal Regulations, *Title 21* (Washington, D.C.: U.S. Department of Health, Education, and Welfare, Food and Drug Administration, rev. 1971).

183

specifically given in the federal standards. They include fresh orange juice, frozen concentrate, canned orange juice, or orange juice solids.

Whichever product is used, the product must contain the equivalent of not less than 35% nor more than 70% single-strength orange juice or orange juice solids not less than 4.13% or more than 8.26%. Total solids must be 12%. Twelve additives may be permitted: nutritive sweeteners, organic acids, thickeners, stabilizers, clouding agents, emulsifiers, buffers, orange pulp, orange peel, natural and artificial flavor, natural and artificial color, and preservatives.

Orange Drink. This product is really a diluted orange juice drink. It must contain not less than 10% acid and not more than 35% equivalent of single-strength orange juice, or not less than 1.18% or more than 4.13% orange juice soluble solids; total soluble solids must be at least 10%. The permitted orange juice ingredients do not include fresh, frozen, and dehydrated orange juice. Other ingredients are the same as those in orange juice drink.

Pineapple–Grapefruit Juice Drink. This beverage is prepared from one or both of the pineapple juice ingredients specified in the federal standards. These ingredients are pineapple juice, concentrated pineapple juice, grapefruit juice, and concentrated grapefruit juice. The combined juice must constitute 50% of the final weight. The usual sugar products are permitted as sweeteners. Other additives are orange, lemon, or grapefruit oil; not less than 30 mg nor more than 50 mg of ascorbic acid in 4 fl oz (118.30 ml); and sodium citrate.

SUMMARY

Fruits, depending on the type of flower from which they develop and their seed structure, may be classified as pomes, drupes, or berries. As a group, fresh fruits are among the best food sources of minerals and vitamins. They are high in carbohydrates and water and, with few exceptions, contain little fat or protein. To be edible, most fruits must be ripe—and although many fruits must be harvested underripe, artificial ripening under controlled conditions is utilized.

Factors influencing the cost of fruit include perishability, crop yield, weather conditions, use of pesticides, packaging, storage, transportation, and consumer preference as to size and color, with larger sizes generally more expensive. Price, however, is not an indication of quality, or nutritive value, but reflects supply and demand.

Fruits are frequently used raw—as desserts, in salads, and as appetizers. Care should be taken in handling them to preserve an attractive appearance.

In cooking fruit, the amount and quality of the cellulose, the degree of ripeness, the water content, and the structure of the fruit must be considered in choosing the cooking method and in determining the amount of sugar and water to use. Fruits may undergo color and flavor changes during cooking and may lose some nutritive value. In the home, fresh fruits, except for bananas, may be kept in the refrigerator.

Some fruits—notably prunes, figs, raisins, apricots, apples, pears, and dates—are dried. Dried fruits are high in sugar but contain less ascorbic acid than their fresh counterparts. As a group, they are a good source of minerals. In cooking dried fruit, the goal is to enable the fruit to absorb much of the moisture previously lost without loss of flavor, texture, or nutritive value. Dried fruits have a number of uses in cookery.

Frozen and canned fruits and fruit juices are convenient, economical, and nutritious. Citrus fruit juices will retain a good amount of their ascorbic acid content if properly stored in containers of glass or plastic with tightly fitted covers. Fruit juice drinks are available.

QUESTIONS AND TOPICS FOR DISCUSSION AND STUDY

1. What may account for discoloration in fruit? What keeps fruits such as peaches from turning brown when combined with citrus fruits?
2. Why do fruits soften when cooked in water?
3. What happens when fruit is cooked in a syrup that makes the pieces translucent?
4. What is the purpose of soaking dried fruits before cooking? Must all dried fruits be soaked?
5. Why is sugar added to dried fruits (if needed) only after they are cooked?
6. What guides can be used in the selection of fresh fruit?

SUGGESTED ACTIVITIES

1. Use as many varieties of fresh fruits as possible in fruit cup and fruit plate combinations. Take care to cover fruits that brown quickly with a citrus juice or pineapple juice.
2. Prepare grapefruit for serving.
3. Prepare applesauce using a basic recipe. Compare the use of pared and unpared apples for color, flavor, and volume of the two products. Prepare applesauce from several varieties of apples using a basic recipe. Compare the various applesauces as to color, flavor, and appearance.
4. Bake different varieties of apples at the same temperature. Compare them for color, flavor, and appearance. Bake apples of the same variety at different temperatures (300–400°F; 150–200°C). Compare color, flavor, and appearance. Bake apples in containers with and without covers.
5. Prepare stewed fruit using a basic recipe. Note texture. (Firm fruit such as apples and pears may be used.)
6. Prepare dried fruit using directions on the package. Compare color, flavor, and appearance of fruits soaked before cooking with those of fruit not soaked before cooking.

REFERENCES

BOOKS

Braverman, J. B. *Introduction to the Biochemistry of Foods.* New York: Elsevier, 1963, Chap. 2.

Edlin, Herbert L. *Plants and Man.* Garden City, N.Y.: Doubleday, 1967.

Garard, Ira. *Introductory Food Chemistry.* Westport, Conn.: Avi, 1976, Chap. 15.

Jacobs, Morris B., ed. *The Chemistry and Technology of Food and Food Products.* New York: Interscience, 1951, Chap. 28.

Lee, Frank. *Basic Food Chemistry.* Westport, Conn.: Avi, 1975, Chap. 18.

Masefield, G. B. *The Oxford Book of Food Plants.* New York: Oxford University Press, 1973.

Paul, Pauline, and Helen Palmer. *Food Theory and Applications.* New York: Wiley, 1972, Chap. 6.

Vail, Gladys, Ruth Griswold, Margaret Justin, and Lucile Rust. *Foods,* 7th ed. Boston: Houghton Mifflin, 1978, Chap. 3.

ARTICLES AND BULLETINS

"Apples in Appealing Ways." *Bulletin 312.* Washington, D.C.: U.S. Department of Agriculture, rev. 1969.

Czerkasky, A. "Consumer Response to Color in Canned Cling Peaches." *J. Food Sci.* **36:**671, 1971.

Eheart, J., and B. Mason. "Sugar and Acid in the Edible Portion of Fruits." *J. Dietet. Assoc.* **50:**130, 1967.

Eitenmiller, R. R. "Mineral and Water-Soluble Vitamin Content of Rabbiteye Blueberries." *J. Food Sci.* **42:**1311, 1977.

"Fruits in Family Meals." *Home and Garden Bulletin No. 125.* Washington, D.C.: U.S. Department of Agriculture, 1972.

"Homemaker's Opinions About Selected Fruits and Fruit Products." *Market Research Report 765.* Washington, D.C.: U.S. Department of Agriculture, 1966.

"How to Buy Fresh Fruits." *Home and Garden Bulletin 141.* Washington, D.C.: U.S. Department of Agriculture, 1977.

Hsu, Debbie, and Marion Jacobson. "Macro Structure and Nomenclature of Plant and Animal Food Sources." *Home Econ. Res. J.* **3:**34, 1974.

Pederson, C. S., H. Beattie, and E. Statz. "Deterioration of Processed Fruit Juices." *Bulletin 728.* Geneva, N.Y.: New York State Agricultural Experiment Station, Cornell University, 1948.

"Processed Fruit and Vegetable Inspection at Your Service." *Bulletin PA-803.* Washington, D.C.: U.S. Department of Agriculture, rev. 1967.

"Storing Vegetables and Fruits." *Home and Garden Bulletin 119.* Washington, D.C.: U.S. Department of Agriculture, 1973.

Tatum, James, and Steven Nagy. "Degradation Products Formed in Canned Single-Strength Orange Juice During Storage." *J. Food Sci.* **40:**707, 1975.

Watson, Ellen. "Tannins in Fruit Extracts as Affected by Heat Treatment," *Home Econ. Res. J.* **2:**112, 1973.

Weaver, Connie, and Helen Charley. "Enzymatic Browning of Ripening Bananas." *J. Food Sci.* **39:**1201, 1974.

Wrolstad, R. E., et al. "Color Quality of Frozen Strawberries." *J. Food Sci.* **35:**448, 1970.

185

Vegetables

Like fruits, vegetables are edible forms of plant tissue. We classify as "vegetables" the roots, bulbs, stems, blossoms, leaves, seeds, or fruits of certain annual plants and the roots, stems, leaf stalks, or leaves of certain perennial nonwoody plants. A number of vegetables are native to America, but many of our important vegetables were introduced in this country by early explorers and settlers. Because Americans are true vegetable lovers who eat large quantities raw as well as cooked, the science of growing and developing many varieties of vegetables has grown extensively in this country. To trace the origin of every vegetable in common use today is a large order; however, a short treatment for each of the major vegetables is presented in this chapter. Most types of vegetable now grown here originated in lands adjacent to the eastern end of the Mediterranean. Most of the edible plants known and cultivated in Europe are undoubtedly Asiatic in origin, imported into the Western world by peoples migrating from the "Fertile Crescent" of the Near East, where civilization is thought to have had its beginning.

COMPOSITION

Compared to fruits, vegetables contain less sugar but more starch. This is especially true of tubers, roots, pods, and seeds, less true of stems, shoots, leaves, flowers, and vegetable fruits, the more succulent vegetables, the sugar content of which is closer to that of the fruits. The substances in vegetables that contribute to their flavor are sugar, organic acids, mineral salts, volatile sulfur compounds, and tannins.

The nonvolatile acids—malic, citric, oxalic, and succinic—found in vegetables also contribute to their flavor. The very strong flavors characteristic of such vegetables as cabbage, Brussels sprouts, turnips, and onions are caused by volatile sulfur compounds.

The same color pigments found in fruits are present in vegetables. The anthocyanin pigments give color to radishes and red cabbage. Chlorophyll is the predominant color pigment in green vegetables; the carotenoids and flavones are responsible for the yellow color in carrots, sweet potatoes, and corn.

186

The characteristic structure of vegetables is due to the cellulose, hemicellulose, and lignin, which form the indigestible fiber component of the plant. The walls of all plant cells are composed of cellulose, and between the cell walls is a material known as *protopectin*, which cements the cells together. In thin leaves, such as lettuce and spinach, the cellulose is very thin, and the plant cells can maintain their characteristic structure only through their water content. Without water, plants shrivel and wilt.

Similarities of composition among members of the same group make possible some general statements about the special contributions of the different groups of vegetables.

Roots, Tubers, Bulbs, and Stems. Certain vegetable plants store food in tap root, tuber root, or bulb. The best-known tuber is the white potato, the energy of which is stored largely in the form of starch; well-known root vegetables are sweet potatoes, beets, carrots, parsnips, and turnips. These vegetables are stable and, under proper conditions, can be stored for longer periods of time than any other group of vegetables. The bulbs—onions, garlic, and leeks—are used mainly for seasoning.

Stems are the pathways through which the nutrients are carried from one organ of a plant to another. They are valuable in the diet as sources of vitamins, minerals, and cellulose. Celery and rhubarb are well-known stem vegetables.

Leaves. Leaves are the manufacturing organs of a plant, where the life-giving process of photosynthesis takes place. In order to secure maximum exposure to air and sunlight, plant cells containing chlorophyll are spread out as a broad, thin surface. In these cells, photosynthesis transforms elements into carbohydrates, which are carried to other parts of the plant. The leaves in consequence are low in carbohydrate energy but do supply good amounts of riboflavin, calcium, carotene, ascorbic acid, and iron.

Vegetable Fruits and Flowers. As a group, vegetable fruits and flowers are high in carbohydrates in the form of starches and sugars. The fleshy or flowering portion of the plant serves as the repository for a large portion of the food material. Tomatoes, eggplant, squashes, and peppers are typical vegetable fruits; cauliflower, broccoli, and globe artichokes are classified as flowers.

Pods and Seeds. The seeds in the pods of legumes contain carbohydrates in the form of sugars and starches, as well as proteins, vitamins, and minerals. Green beans are eaten pod and all. The seeds of other legumes, such as peas and lima beans, are removed from the pod.

Sprouts. Seeds can be placed in water or damp soil to sprout. The young shoots can be used as a vegetable garnish, salad, or sandwich ingredient. Alfalfa, mung beans, soy beans, fenugreek, and sunflower seed sprouts are the most popular. All are excellent sources of ascorbic acid.

NUTRITIVE VALUE

All the food nutrients are present in vegetables, but they are especially rich in minerals and vitamins, and it is mainly for these nutrients that vegetables are recommended as daily foods. The nutritive value of a vegetable depends greatly on what part of a plant it is. Soil and climate may or may not affect the nutritive value of these foods.

The succulent vegetables are high in water and low in calories and vegetable proteins. Most boiled vegetables have fewer than 50 calories per half-cup serving. The starchy vegetables, such as potatoes, corn, peas, and lima beans will have up to 100 calories per half-cup serving. Vegetables are also high in vitamin and mineral value. Green leafy vegetables are good sources of calcium, carotene, ascorbic acid, riboflavin, and iron. The fruit and flower vegetables—tomatoes, peppers, eggplant, and cauliflower, among others—are low in caloric value. Tomatoes, green peppers, and broccoli are high in ascorbic acid; broccoli and cauliflower contain good amounts of calcium. The pod and seed vegetables are sources of incomplete proteins. Soybeans have a much higher percentage of protein (34%) than other vegetables (broccoli, for example, 3%), but the protein is incomplete since it is limited in its quantity of the essential amino acid methionine. The pod and seed vegetables are good sources of some B vitamins and excellent sources of trace minerals such as zinc and copper.

Roots, tubers, and bulbs have higher stores of

carbohydrates than stems, fruits, and flowers. White potato, a tuber, contains carbohydrate mainly in the form of starch; the sweet potato, a root, has large amounts of both sugar and starch. Potatoes are also excellent sources of ascorbic acid, averaging 30 mg/potato. Scurvy was almost eliminated in the nineteenth century when potatoes became a popular vegetable. Most other root vegetables—beets, carrots, parsnips, and turnips, for example—store their carbohydrate in the form of sugar.

ECONOMIC ASPECTS

The cost of vegetables to the consumer depends to a large extent on the size of the crop in any given year. Generally, fresh produce is cheapest when the supply is abundant, but there are exceptions to this. Despite the fact that storage of seasonal vegetables makes many of them available the year around, vegetables in season still offer a price advantage. The consumer purchasing vegetables expects a large selection from which to choose, a practice that forces added costs on the retailer and ultimately on the consumer.

Recent developments in techniques of harvesting, shipping, and storing vegetables have had a favorable effect on their quality and cost. Succulent vegetables are chilled, washed, packed, and refrigerated before shipment; modern refrigerated trucks, railway cars, and airplanes bring them to market areas within hours of harvesting. Root vegetables are harvested when mature, and after sorting and grading are stored under controlled temperature and humidity conditions. Reduction of waste in harvesting and the maintenance of high quality during storage have resulted in good quality produce to the consumer.

Improved methods of chilling and refrigerating vegetables have been of paramount importance in reducing the costs of shipping. This is clearly illustrated in the case of tomatoes. Heavy losses of tomatoes from decay in the ripening rooms was discovered to be a consequence of excessive chilling and refrigeration during transit. Present-day practice, based on research, is to cool tomatoes to not lower than 55°F (13°c). Savings to the consumer from this one change in the handling of tomatoes have been notable.[1]

Tomatoes are not the only fresh produce profiting from changes in refrigeration practices. Recent practice has been to keep refrigeration of each specific commodity at the optimum for that commodity rather than at the refrigeration specified by buyers, most of whom based their requirements on tradition rather than research. Many vegetables require fairly low temperatures, but others cannot be subjected to such temperatures without excessive decay and spoilage.

Vacuum cooling of leaf vegetables, such as lettuce, spinach, and cabbage, has undoubtedly reduced the cost of these commodities to the consumer. Vacuum cooling is achieved by placing the vegetable—usually packed in a fiberboard carton—in a sealed compartment in which is created a vacuum high enough to cause some evaporation of the water in the leaves of the vegetable. The evaporation of the water creates a quick and uniform temperature reduction. The vegetable thus precooled is then packed and shipped in carefully controlled refrigerated cars. Such vegetables as potatoes, which have little surface area but great mass, cannot be efficiently cooled by this method. Vegetables such as celery, asparagus, and sweet corn are adaptable to cooling with water in a process known as *hydrocooling*. This method, however, is not as rapid as vacuum cooling.

Packaging of fresh vegetables has also had its impact on the cost of these products. The trend is toward more prepackaging. Many vegetables are packed in perforated plastic bags—tomatoes, carrots, spinach, kale, potatoes, and soup and salad greens are thus packaged before they are displayed. The list grows longer as increased sales prove prepackaging to be a consumer-approved merchandising practice. The advantages in prepackaging fresh produce are decreased moisture loss, reduction of merchandising costs through less handling of produce, and protection of the food from insects and dirt. Prepackaging of vegetables also offsets excessive trimming wastes.

---

[1] W.T. Pentzer, "Marketing, Quality, and Cost," in *Food: The Yearbook of Agriculture* (Washington, D.C.: U.S. Department of Agriculture, 1959), p. 409.

One notable example is that of carrots. Retailing carrots with tops on was costly and wasteful. Today, prepackaged bunched carrots without tops are accepted without question, with a resultant saving in cost to the consumer.

Improved crop management has had its effect on vegetable costs. The use of pesticides has enabled the farmer to produce higher crop yields of high-quality vegetables. Despite the added cost of the pesticides, production costs passed on to the consumer would be higher still if they were not used, for many vegetables would be destroyed or of poor quality.

SELECTION

Standards for the selection of vegetables vary with the specific commodity. In general, freshness, uniformity of variety, size, color, degree of ripeness, and freedom from defects are the qualities most frequently used in selection. Vegetables, like fruits, should not be purchased simply because the price is low. Buying in season usually ensures a reasonable price. Unless proper refrigeration is available for the storage of surplus vegetables, the initial savings will be negated by subsequent loss of nutrients and palatability. It is well to keep in mind that undersized or oversized vegetables may not be of the best quality or the most economical. Each vegetable should be selected in terms of the use to be made of it; thus size may be an important factor for one purpose but not for another.

The amount of waste, such as skins, pods, peelings, leaves, seeds, membranes, pithy stems, and cores, should be taken into consideration when buying fresh vegetables. The percent of waste can be calculated by substracting the edible portion (E.P.) from the amount as purchased (A.P.). Some vegetables, such as globe onions, will have very little waste (9%), while others, such as green onions (63%), beets (60%), and corn on the cob (64%) will have high amounts.[2]

Suggestions for the selection of specific vegetables are given in Table 18-1.

GRADES

Standards for grades of vegetables have been established for almost all vegetable products by the U.S. Department of Agriculture. Grading is widely used and is a basis of trading on the wholesale market, but because grading is permissive, not compulsory, in most local communities and states, only a few of the fresh vegetables appearing in the retail market carry grades. The consumer benefits by the grading program only to the extent that wholesale transactions take advantage of grade standards. At the present time, little produce is marked with consumer grades in the United States.[3]

Among the important factors considered in establishing grades are ripeness, shape, color, and uniformity of size. Freedom from bruise spots, mold, and decay is also considered. The three wholesale grade levels that are important are U.S. Fancy, the highest grade, applied only to products of the very best quality; U.S. No. 1, the second grade; and U.S. No. 2, the third grade. U.S. No.1 is the wholesale grade most frequently seen on labels and tags attached to fresh vegetables in the retail market.

Consumer standards use alphabetical designations for grade names. U.S. Grade A and U.S. Grade B potatoes are further divided on the basis of size into eight designations, from "Small" to "Large." Consumer grades or standards have been established for broccoli, Brussels sprouts, carrots, celery, corn, kale, parsnips, potatoes, spinach, and turnips.

ROOTS

Botanically, vegetables are classified according to the part of the plant from which they are derived: bulbs, fruits, roots, shoots, tubers, leaves, stems, or flowers. The vegetables most commonly used are fruits, roots, leaves, stems, and flowers.

Root vegetables are the fleshy enlargement of the root end of the plant. The important root

[2]"Composition of Foods," *Agriculture Handbook 8* (Washington, D.C.: U.S. Department of Agriculture, 1963).

[3]"Shopper's Guide to U.S. Grades for Food," *Home and Garden Bulletin 58* (Washington, D.C.: U.S. Department of Agriculture, rev. 1966).

TABLE 18-1
Selection of Vegetables

Vegetable	Desirable Characteristics
Artichoke (globe)	Fresh, plump, and heavy globe; tight, fleshy leaves of a uniform green color. (Brownish leaves indicate age or injury; spreading leaves indicate overmaturity.)
Asparagus	Fresh, firm, straight shoots with closed, compact tips. (Spreading of tip indicates age; flat, angular stalks are apt to be woody and tough.)
Beans, lima	Well-filled, clean, shiny, dark green pods free of mold or rot. (Hard, tough, discolored skin denotes overmaturity.)
Beans, snap	Firm, clean, tender, crisp pods, velvety to the touch; seeds less than half grown. (Toughness, wilting, or discoloration indicates overmaturity.)
Beets	Smooth, firm roots of uniform size. (Appearance of beet top does not reflect the condition of root, but soft, flabby, rough, or shriveled roots indicate overmaturity.)
Broccoli	Fresh, clean compact bud clusters; firm and tender stems and branches. (Tough, woody stems and opened yellow or purple buds indicate overmaturity.)
Brussels sprouts	Hard, compact, fresh heads, green in color. (Wilted, puffy, or yellow leaves indicate overmaturity.)
Cabbage, Chinese	Primarily a salad vegetable, plants are elongated. Fresh, crisp green plants free from decay.
Cabbage, red	Hard, dark red or purple heads that may resemble domestic or Danish in shape. (Darkened, puffy leaves indicate overmaturity.)
Cabbage, Savoy	Crumpled leaves with developed round heads, dark green in color. (Yellow, flabby leaves indicate overmaturity.)
Cabbage, smooth-leaved green	Hard, tight-leaved, compact heads, greenish white in color. (Puffy, slightly yellow leaves indicate overmaturity.)
Carrots, mature	Hard, large roots, with a deep color and pronounced flavor. (Flabbiness and soft ends indicate poor quality.)
Carrots, young	Firm, fresh, smooth, well-shaped roots of a bright yellow to orange color. (Wilted, soft, flabby roots indicate poor quality.)
Cauliflower	Hard, clean, firm heads, with a compact curd encased in tender green leaves. (Rough, spreading leaves and yellow flowers indicate overmaturity.)
Celery	Fresh, clean, crisp, tightly packed stalks with good heart formation. (Yellowing and drying leaves indicate age.)

190

TABLE 18-1 (Cont.)

Vegetable	Desirable Characteristics
Chicory, endive, escarole	Used mainly in salads. Chicory and endive have narrow, notched edges and crinkly leaves. Belgian endive is a compact, cigar-shaped plant that is creamy white from bleaching. Escarole leaves are broader than those of chicory and curly endive. Look for freshness, crispness, tenderness, and a green color in outer leaves. (The Belgian variety is mostly white.)
Corn	Yellow or white kernels, depending on the variety, which are bright, plump, and mild, with little resistance to pressure. (Yellow, dry husk indicates overmaturity.)
Cucumbers	Firm, fresh, bright, well-shaped bodies and green color; firm, crisp, tender flesh; immature seeds. (Yellowing, withering, and hard seeds indicate overmaturity.)
Eggplant	Firm, heavy body of a uniform dark, rich purple color, free of scars or decay. (Wilted, flabby, soft fruit indicates overmaturity.)
Garlic	Young, plump, dry cloves with outer skin intact. (Sprouting, soft garlic is undesirable.)
Greens (chard, collards, kale, spinach)	Fresh, young, tender, green leaves. (Yellowing, flabby, wilted leaves are a sign of overmaturity.)
Lettuce, Boston (butterhead)	Tender, fresh, easily separated leaves, buttery to the touch. (Wilted, dry, or yellowing leaves indicate poor quality.)
Lettuce, iceberg (crisp head)	Hard, relatively large head with medium-green outer crisp leaves and crisp inner overlapping leaves. (Flabby, wilted leaves indicate overmaturity; rust spots and brown areas indicate poor quality.)
Lettuce, leaf	Tender, green, curled, loose leaves. (Drying, discolored leaves indicate overmaturity.)
Lettuce, romaine	Elongated, crisp, tender, green leaves. (Discolored and wilted leaves indicate poor quality.)
Mushrooms	Clean, fresh appearance and creamy-white color. (Dark or discolored caps indicate poor quality.)
Okra	Young, tender, fresh, small to medium-sized pods. (Dull, hard, discolored pods indicate overmaturity.)
Onions, dry	Bright, clean, hard, well-shaped globes with dry skins. (A thick, tough, woody condition indicates poor quality.)
Onions, green	Crisp, tender green tops. (Yellowing, wilted, or discolored tops are undesirable.)
Onions, green: leeks	Green fresh tops; crisp, young, tender bulbs. (Yellow tops indicate overmaturity.)
Onions, green: shallots	Crisp, straight stems; slight bulb development. (Tough or fibrous necks indicate overmaturity.)

TABLE 18-1 (Cont.)

Vegetable	Desirable Characteristics
Parsley	Bright, fresh, green tops, free of dirt. (Yellow, spreading tops indicate overmaturity.)
Parsnips	Smooth, firm, clean, well-shaped roots of uniform medium size. (Soft, flabby, or shriveled roots are usually pithy and indicate overmaturity.)
Peas	Young, bright-green pods, and well filled with well-developed peas. (Yellow or whitish color indicates poor quality.)
Peppers	Fresh, firm, bright appearance. (Soft, flabby, discolored peppers indicate overmaturity.)
Potatoes, white	(See Table 18-2.)
Radishes	Firm, smooth, crisp, tender roots, mild in flavor. (Pithy or spongy radishes are overmature.)
Rhubarb	Firm, crisp, tender, bright-colored stalks. (Coarse, fibrous, and stringy stalks are overmature.)
Squash, summer	Fresh, fairly heavy in relation to size. (Hard rind and hard seeds indicate overmaturity.)
Squash, winter	Firm body; bright-colored, hard rind. (Mold and water-soaked areas indicate overmaturity.)
Sweet potatoes	Smooth, well-shaped, firm roots, free of scars and decay spots. (Decay spots and a damp appearance may indicate poor quality.)
Tomatoes	Well-formed, firm, plump bodies, with a uniform red color. (Puffiness and discoloration indicate overmaturity.)
Turnips, white	Round shape, flat top; uniformly tender white skin with purple tinge. (Flabby, soft root indicates overmaturity.)
Turnips, rutabaga	Thick yellow or buff skin; crisp, fresh roots. (Hard-textured, woody, pithy, or hollow roots indicate overmaturity.)
Watercress	Fresh, young, crisp, tender leaves, medium green in color. (Toughening and yellowing of leaves indicate overmaturity.)

Source: Adapted from "How to Buy Fresh Vegetables," *Home and Garden Bulletin 143* (Washington, D.C., U.S. Department of Agriculture, 1967).

vegetables are beets, carrots, parsnips, turnips, rutabagas, and sweet potatoes.

Beets. Varieties of beets have been grown in America for over a hundred years. Easy to grow, they are commonly grown in home gardens. The garden beet is a taproot, medium in size, and usually of a deep red color. The sugar beet, a special variety, has a high sucrose content. It is grown for the manufacture of sugar. The carbohydrates of the garden beet are glucose, fructose, and sucrose, with some small amounts of raffinose. The pigment of the beet root is *betaine*. It is thought that the black spots often seen in canned beets are the result of a boron deficiency in the soil, a deficiency that can be corrected by proper soil management. Beets are usually cooked as a table vegetable, and large quantities are canned whole, quartered, and sliced.

Carrots. The carrot, like the beet, is a taproot. The shape of the carrot varies: it may be short and cylindrical, or long and tapering. Its characteristic color is orange-red to yellow. Carotene and lycopene are the pigments in carrots; the predominant carbohydrate is fructose. The color intensity and sweetness of carrots increase with the age of the vegetable, but the crude-fiber content remains fairly constant. Hence, carrots can be kept in storage for as long as 6 months without any appreciable deterioration. Storage temperatures, however, should be kept at 32–40°F (0–5°C). The principal loss during storage is water. Carrots are eaten cooked or raw. They are also commercially canned and frozen.

Parsnips. The parsnip looks like a white carrot; like the carrot, it is a taproot. The sweet flavor of the parsnip makes it very pleasant as a table vegetable. It is sometimes used as an ingredient in soup.(See Color Plate VI.)

Potatoes. It has been said that in the world as a whole the most important single vegetable is the white potato. In the United States, *potato* refers to the white or Irish potato.

Starch comprising some 65–80% of the dry weight of the white potato, is its most important nutritive component. In the raw vegetable, the starch is present as microscopic granules in the *leucoplasts,* cell-like compartments that line the walls of the parenchyma tissue. The starch granule is ellipsoidal and is much larger than the average starch granule of cereal grains. Striations on its surface give the granule an oyster-shell appearance. There is evidence that the size and distribution of the granules probably determine the character and quality of the cooked potato.[4]

The sugar content of potatoes ranges from slight traces to as much as 10% of the dry weight of the tuber. The two chief factors influencing sugar content of potatoes during storage are variety and temperature. Freshly harvested mature tubers may contain only traces of sugar, but some varieties, when harvested before they are fully mature, may have a fairly high percentage of sugar. The sugar concentration in the tuber potato increases when potatoes are stored at 50°F (10°C) or below; the lower the temperature, the greater the increase in sugar content. As is true of all higher plants, potatoes contain polysaccharides that are nonstarch materials. These substances are mainly crude fibers, cellulose, pectic substances, and hemicelluloses. Pectic acid in combination with calcium and magnesium is believed to make up the intercellular cementing substance. Hemicelluloses are cell-wall components.

The green color frequently seen immediately beneath the skin indicates the presence of chlorophyll. Much greening in potatoes is undesirable because of its association with a bitter taste and the possibility of the presence of *solanine,* a toxic substance that forms in the presence of light.

Nonvolatile organic acids—oxalic, malic, tartaric, and citric—give potatoes their flavor.

Many varieties of potatoes are grown in the United States, but only a few stand out as having market appeal. Some of the most important varieties for consumer use are presented in Table 18-2. (Also see Color Plate IV.)

Potatoes are classified as mealy, waxy, or new potatoes. If potatoes are placed in a container filled with brine made from 1 part salt to 11 parts water, some will float while others will sink. Mealy potatoes, owing to their high specific gravity, will sink while waxy potatoes, which have a low specific gravity, will float. The mealy potato is high in starch and low in sugar. When cooked, the high-starch cells will swell and burst, causing the granular dry cells to separate. Mealy potatoes such as the Russet, Bake-King, and Idaho varieties are best used for baking, mashing, and french-frying. The low sugar content permits them to be fried for a longer period before they will brown than waxy potatoes.

Being low in starch, when heated waxy potatoes become translucent, with the cells adhering together. This property is best taken advantage of for boiling, slicing for salads, and for use as scalloped potatoes. Maine are round, white potatoes of the waxy type. New potatoes are harvested before maturity. Their skins have not set and they are easily slipped off. They are used in

---

[4] A. Briant, C. Personius, and E. Cassel, "Physical Properties of Starches from Potatoes of Different Culinary Quality," *Food Res.* **10**:437, 1945.

TABLE 18-2
Potato Varieties

Variety	Description	Storage and Cooking Qualities	Uses
Cherokee	Medium, roundish with blunt ends; creamy white smooth skin, medium-deep eyes; white flesh	Cooking quality good	Potato chips
Chippewa	Large, elliptical to oblong; smooth, dark, creamy buff skin; shallow eyes; white flesh	Cooking quality good	General cooking; remains intact after boiling
Irish Cobbler	Large to medium, roundish with blunt end; shallow to deep eyes; white flesh	Storage quality good; cooking quality usually good	General cooking; potato chips
Katahdin	Large, elliptical to round; smooth skin, shallow eyes; dark cream to buff color	Keeping quality good; cooking quality fair to good; some tendency to discolor after cooking	General cooking; potato chips
Kennebec	Large, elliptical to oblong; smooth, buff-colored skin; shallow eyes; white flesh	Good storage and cooking qualities	General cooking
Red LaSoda	Semiround to slightly oblong; smooth, dark red skin; white flesh	Cooking quality fair	General cooking
Red Pontiac	Oblong to round, blunted ends; smooth red skin; red, medium-deep eyes; white flesh	Cooks very white	General cooking; commercially prepared french fries
Russet Burbank (mealy)	Long, cylindrical or slightly flattened; russeted skin; shallow eyes	Excellent for baking	Baking; potato granules; potato flakes; french fries; potato chips
Sebago	Large, elliptical to round; smooth ivory-yellow skin; shallow eyes; white flesh	Good cooking quality	Excellent for potato chips [provided they have not been stored below 50°F (12°C)]; resists after-cooking darkening
White Rose (mealy)	Large, long, elliptical; smooth skin; numerous white eyes; white flesh		Potato chips when freshly harvested in early spring months

Source: Adapted from N. R. Thompson, "Potato Varieties," in *Potato Processing,* W. F. Talbert and O. Smith, eds. (Westport, Conn.: Avi, 1959), pp. 46–69.

stews and creamed potatoes, because of their small size. Some new potatoes have been artificially colored red to increase their attractiveness to consumers.

Turnips. Most varieties of turnip are white-fleshed and of medium size. Turnips are gener-

ally eaten cooked because when raw they have a strong, bitter flavor.

Rutabagas. The rutabaga—sometimes called "Swede," or Swedish turnip—is believed to be a hybridization of some form of cabbage and a turnip. Its place of origin is not known, but its cultivation is confined to areas where there are long, cool growing seasons. (See Color Plate VI.)

This vegetable is fairly large, pear-shaped, and has yellow-colored flesh. It, too, is a root vegetable, but it grows considerably larger than the turnip or potato. In storage, rutabagas lose moisture at a rapid rate. Waxing the vegetable before marketing helps to cut down on moisture loss. The rutabaga is susceptible to brown-heart, thought to be a result of a lack of boron in the soil in which they are grown. Rutabaga is cooked as a table vegetable.

Sweet Potatoes. There are two kinds of sweet potatoes: one has yellow flesh and a dry, mealy texture; the other, which is sometimes called a *yam,* is moist, yellow to dark orange, and high in sugar. Both types have a brown skin. The sugars in the raw sweet potato are glucose, fructose, and sucrose. Both kinds contain a high percent-

age of starch and appreciable amounts of carotene, which is fairly stable during storage. Both kinds are cooked as a table vegetable or made into a sweet potato pie (similar to pumpkin pie). The dark, moist kind is popular in the South; in the North, the yellow, dry kind is preferred. A large portion of the sweet potato crop is canned, but some is frozen and some is dried as flakes.

BULBS

Bulbs are really stems holding a food reserve in the fleshy, overlapping leaves that give shape to the vegetable. Onions and garlic are the best-known examples of this vegetable group (see Fig. 18-1).

Garlic. The garlic globe is made up of several cloves, each covered by a thin white skin. The

18-1 *Varieties of bulb vegetables. (Courtesy United Fresh Fruit and Vegetable Association).*

cloves are easily separated from one another. The strong odor and flavor of garlic derive from sulfur compounds found in the volatile oil of the vegetable. To a limited extent, garlic is consumed raw, but it is extensively used the world over as a flavoring ingredient in cooked dishes. Because of its very strong flavor, it can be modified and used in the form of garlic salt.

Onions. Like garlic, the onion has an important place in history. Onions store well if properly prepared for long keeping. The onion is easy to cultivate and has a flavor that is pleasing to many. The shape of the onion globe—unlike that of garlic—varies: it may be round, spherical, flattened, or spindle-shaped. Onions also come in a variety of colors—silvery white, red, and yellow. Shape and color are frequently used as bases for classification of onions. Onions contain a high percentage of soluble sugars, the chief one being sucrose. Raw fresh onions contain some ascorbic acid; small ones contain more than larger onions of the same variety. Losses of ascorbic acid under home storage conditions run from 47 to 50% of the total amount found in the fresh vegetable. As much as 65% of the ascorbic acid in the raw vegetable may be lost in cooking.[5] The odor and taste of the onion are caused by the volatile sulfur compounds contained in the vegetable. During cooking, the volatile compounds are driven off in the steam, leaving the onion milder in flavor and odor.

The naturally milder onions are the Sweet Spanish and Bermuda, but both have a high moisture content and do not store well. Yellow onions are more pungent. These are excellent for storage because of their relatively low moisture content. Storage strengthens the onion's flavor and odor. This vegetable is used raw in much the same way garlic is used, but perhaps in greater amounts. Dehydrated onion flakes and onion salt are also used for flavoring sauces and other cooked dishes.

Shallots. Shallot bulbs physically resemble garlic globes in that several cloves are covered by a thin skin. The difference is that the shallot skin is the color of a yellow onion skin. Shallots have a mild flavor which tastes like a cross between an onion and garlic. They may also be sold in the plant form, in which they appear similar to green onions but lack swelling at the bulb. Shallots are frequently used in gourmet and European cookery. Once only available at specialty shops, they are beginning to be available at produce counters or in dried form in the spice section.

LEAVES AND STEMS

Vegetables that are classified as leaves or stems come from plants in which the leaf or stem becomes thick and serves as a reservoir for food material. Some important leaves, and stems are lettuce, spinach, kale, Brussels sprouts, cabbage, celery, kohlrabi, and rhubarb.

Lettuce. The important varieties of lettuce sold in the United States today are Iceberg, Butterhead, Romaine, and Leaf. Iceberg heads are large, round, and solid. Outer leaves are green, and inner leaves are lighter green. Butterhead lettuce is a small- to medium-head lettuce with soft tender leaves that are buttery to the touch. Boston and Bibb lettuce are varieties of Butterhead. Romaine lettuce is tall and cylindrical with crisp, dark green leaves. Leaf lettuce is made up of soft, tender green leaves. It is mainly grown in local gardens and sold locally. (See Color Plate V.)

Spinach. The large leaves of spinach are bunched near the ground and are smooth. The main color pigments found in spinach are chlorophyll and carotene; the soluble acids are citric, malic, and oxalic. Spinach contains considerable amounts of calcium, but the presence of oxalates renders its availability questionable.[6] Spinach is generally cooked and served as a table vegetable. Large quantities are canned and frozen.

Kale. *Kale*, a Scottish word, refers to a group of cabbage-like plants. Kale is especially adaptable to the long, cool growing season of Scotland. Cool growing weather and mild frost are essen-

[5] E. F. Murphy, "Ascorbic Acid Content of Onions and Observations on Its Distribution," *Food Res.* **6**:581, 1941.

[6] M. L. Finicke and E. A. Garrison, "Utilization of Calcium of Spinach and Kale," *Food Res.* **3**:575, 1938.

tial to give the vegetable its pleasing taste. The kale plant grows in an open structure rather than in heads, as cabbage does. The leaf is dark green, thick, and curly and contains chlorophyll and carotene pigments. Kale is used as a cooked table vegetable.

Greens. Any leaves used as a vegetable may be called greens (see Fig. 18-2). The most popular greens not discussed above are chicory, escarole, dandelion, watercress, collards, turnips, beet tops, and sorrel. The first five greens listed are often used as salad components. Chicory or endive has curly, crinkly edges on dark green outer leaves and "blanched" yellowish inner leaves. Escarole is similar to chicory, but the leaves are broader and smoother. Escarole is eaten raw or sautéed with garlic and oil and served chilled as a vegetable. The bitter taste of dandelion greens can be minimized with a salty vinegar dressing.

Collard, turnip, and sorrel greens are cooked for long periods of time, usually with a flavoring such as salt pork. Beet tops are best cooked in a minimum of water with a tight-fitting lid. (See Color Plate V.)

Kohlrabi. *Kohlrabi*, in German, means "cabbage turnip." Its flavor is similar to that of the turnip. It is a hardy vegetable that can be cultivated in fairly cool climates. Both white and purple kohlrabi are currently grown in America; the white (actually light green) is the more popular. The edible portion of this vegetable is its fleshy stem and the bulbular enlargement at the root end. Kohlrabi is used chiefly as a cooked vegetable. (See Color Plate VI.)

Rhubarb. Botanically a vegetable, rhubarb is used as a fruit in the United States, where it is sometimes called "pieplant" because of its popu-

18-2 *Varieties of greens. (Courtesy United Fresh Fruit and Vegetable Association)*

larity as a pie filling. Only the fleshy stalks of the rhubarb are edible; the leaves should not be eaten because they contain poisonous substances. (See Color Plate VI.)

Brussels Sprouts. Brussels sprouts thrive in a long, cool growing season. Brussels sprouts are formed from the buds in the axils of the leaves of the plant. The small heads resemble the cabbage in structure, characteristic flavor, and odor. They are served cooked as a table vegetable. Large quantities are frozen and canned. (See Color Plate VI.)

Cabbage. Most of the varieties of cabbage grown in the United States originated in Germany. Red cabbage, although known and used by Americans, is more extensively used in Europe. A cabbage head is formed by thick, overlapping leaves attached to a stem. In many instances, the leaves become quite large. Heads of cabbage may be either white or red and spherical, pointed, or flat, depending on the variety. Cabbage stores well and is extensively used both raw and cooked. Large quantities are used in the manufacture of sauerkraut. (See Color Plate VI.)

Asparagus. Asparagus is a fleshy green shoot vegetable which is picked before it is allowed to mature into a hard, woody plant. White asparagus does not have any chlorophyll because it was cultivated in the dark. This special cultivation increases the cost. Storage temperatures close to 33°F (0.5°C) appear to be most effective in preventing deterioration. When the butts of asparagus are stored on moist moss, the spears continue to grow. Asparagus is used as a table vegetable. It is commercially canned and frozen.

Celery. Celery is a fleshy stalk of the celery plant. Pascal and Utah celery, green in color, are the most commonly used varieties today, although the Gold Self-Blanching variety was once more popular. Until recently, it was thought desirable to bleach the green edible portion of celery, but this practice has fallen into disuse in America. Celery has a very high moisture content. Its low percentage of total solids is in the form of carbohydrates. Although it is generally eaten raw in this country, it is also used in many cooked dishes, such as stews and soups, for its flavor.

FRUITS

A number of vegetables—among them, cucumber, pumpkin, squash, eggplant, green pepper, okra, and tomato—are botanically classified as fruits.

Cucumbers. The cucumber is oblong, with a tender green skin and white flesh. Generally, it is used before it is ripe. The mature vegetable, yellow in color, is used for a special kind of pickle. Small, specially grown cucumbers are used for gherkins. Cucumbers have high moisture content and only 5% total solids, which consist of small amounts of simple carbohydrates and traces of minerals, vitamins, and proteins. Cucumbers are used as a raw salad vegetable. They are also manufactured into different kinds of pickles.

Pumpkins. The pumpkin is medium to large and round or spherical, with flattened ends. It is a member of the winter squash family. Its rind, which may be yellow, orange, or green, is tough. A soft, spongy flesh adheres to the outer rind, and the center of the pumpkin is hollow but partially filled with white seeds and strings of plant tissue. Fresh pumpkin contains sugar in the form of sucrose, glucose, and fructose. The immature pumpkin contains a higher percentage of starch than the ripe vegetable. During storage, much starch is lost, an alteration that changes the consistency of the vegetable. Pumpkin is canned commercially as pie stock. To assure a consistency desirable for baking, the pumpkin is canned just before it is ripe. For commercial packing, it is customary to use a mixture of pumpkin varieties so to assure the proper consistency for cooking.

Eggplant. The name *eggplant* stems from the fact that the plant bears colorful egg-shaped fruits. Although the eggplant is generally purple, yellow, brown, and ash-colored varieties have also been cultivated. It is a fairly large, oblong vegetable. In vegetable groupings, it is classified as a fruit; botanically, it is considered a berry. Eggplant has a tendency to "cook down" quickly, because of its high moisture content and the conversion of the protopectin into pectin materials during cooking. The darkening that frequently occurs during cooking is probably caused by the tannins present and the low acidity of the vegetable. Eggplant also tends to darken when brought in contact with iron in air.[7] It is used mainly as a cooked vegetable. (See Color Plate VI.)

Garden Peppers. In the United States, the nonpungent green variety is the most important type of pepper. In Spain, hot peppers are called *pimiento*. *Paprika* is the name given to a long, bright red pepper with nonpungent flesh. The garden pepper is classified botanically as a berry; it is bell-shaped, with a hollow center containing many seeds. The flavor is slightly pungent but very pleasant. Ripe bell peppers contain a high amount of ascorbic acid, most of it in the walls of the pepper. Fully mature peppers are very sweet and are a bright red color. Peppers are used mainly fried, stuffed, or raw in salads, but they are also used extensively to add flavor and color to sauces and other cooked dishes.

Squashes. Both summer and winter squashes are native to the Americas. (See Fig. 18–3.)

[7] C. W. Culpepper and H. H. Moon, "Composition of Eggplant Fruit at Different Stages of Maturity in Relation to Its Preparation and Use as Food," *J. Agr. Res.* **47:**707, 1933.

Summer squash, unlike winter squash, is ready for eating before the seeds or skin have toughened. The entire summer squash is suitable for eating. Summer squashes enjoy much popularity in Europe; Italians, for example, make extensive use of cocozelle and zucchini.

The varieties of summer squash differ in shape and size. The zucchini is elongated, with a dark-green tender skin; the white and yellow pattypan squash resembles a scalloped tart and has a smooth, rather tough skin. The straight-neck and crookneck squash, full at the blossom end but narrow in the neck, are usually light yellow or yellow and have a tender skin. The seeds of summer squash are small and tender and are generally cooked and eaten along with the other parts of the vegetable. Considerable amounts of summer squash are preserved by freezing.

The most frequently used varieties of the winter squash are the Hubbard and the Golden Delicious types. They are large, pear-shaped vegetables, with a tough, ridged, green or orange-yellow rind. The center of the squash is a hollow partially filled with seeds entangled in strands of the squash flesh. The starch content of the vegetable rapidly changes to sugar during storage. Squash stored in rooms with temperatures over 50°F (10°C) tend to shrink in weight because of this breakdown of carbohydrate. Ac-

18–3 *Varieties of squash.* (*Courtesy United Fresh Fruit and Vegetable Association*)

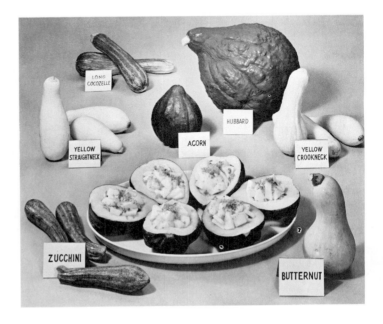

cording to Holmes and Spelman, squash remains a good source of carotene, riboflavin, calcium, iron, magnesium, and phosphorus even after 4 months of winter storage.[8] Like pumpkin, winter squash is cooked as a vegetable or used in the preparation of pie. It is also commercially canned and frozen.

Tomatoes. Botanically the tomato is a fruit, classified as a berry. It is spherical, somewhat flattened at the ends, or elongated and pear- or plum-shaped. Small cherry tomatoes are perfectly round. Tomatoes are usually red, but some yellow and purple varieties are known. During the ripening period, tomatoes increase in moisture, acids, and sugars; there is a corresponding decrease in total solids. Tomatoes may be ripened on the vine or by a commercial method entailing the use of ethylene gas. Unlike many other vegetables, tomatoes cannot be stored at low temperatures. Green tomatoes ripen slowly at $50°F$ ($10°C$) and can be kept at this temperature for several weeks without deteriorating. The color pigments found in the vegetables are carotene, lycopene, and chlorophyll; the organic acids are citric and malic. The ascorbic acid content of tomatoes is not greatly affected by the degree of ripeness after the fruit is mature green. But increases in ripe fruit when plants were transferred from shade to sunshine were reported by Hamner et al.[9]

Tomatoes are extensively used both raw and cooked. Tons of tomatoes are canned each year. Tomatoes are also used in the manufacture of catsup, chili sauce, tomato soup, tomato paste, and tomato juice.

Okra. Okra is a small pod-shaped vegetable made up of five or more cells or sections containing large numbers of seeds. It contains mucilaginous materials that impart a characteristic texture and taste to the vegetable. Okra is grown and used chiefly in the South. It is fried in corn-

---

[8] Arthur D. Holmes and Albert F. Spelman, "Composition of Squash After Winter Storage," *Food Res.* **11**:345, 1946.

[9] K. C. Hamner, L. Berstein, and I. A. Maynard, "Effects of Light Intensity, Day Length, Temperature and Other Environmental Factors on the Ascorbic Acid Content of Tomatoes," *J. Nutrition* **29**:85, 1945.

meal or used as a soup or gumbo ingredient. Small quantities are commercially frozen and canned. (See Color Plate VI.)

FLOWERS

Vegetables classified as flowers have small clusters of flowers on a stem of fleshy scales.

Artichokes. The thick receptacle known as the "heart" and the fleshy bases of the scales are the edible portions of the artichoke. Most of the artichokes in the United States are grown in California. The globe artichoke is the unopened flower bud of the thistle plant. The heart and the fleshy bases of the scales (peteles) are soft and pleasant-tasting. Carbohydrates, in the form of inulin, are stored in the fleshy portions of the vegetable. Artichoke is used as cooked table vegetable, an appetizer, or a salad (see Fig. 18-4). The peteles are picked off one at a time, dipped in a sauce such as butter, and then scraped between the teeth to obtain the fleshy portion. The fibrous outer part of the petele is then discarded. Young artichoke hearts are canned in oil or frozen plain.

The Jerusalem artichoke is not an artichoke; it is the tuberous root of a sunflower plant and resembles a small knotty potato. Inulin is also present in the Jerusalem artichoke.

Broccoli. The Italian word *broccoli* means "arm" or "branch." Broccoli has been used in the United States only in the last 25 years. Much of its popularity is undoubtedly the result of its extensive use among Italian-American families. Broccoli is a tall cabbage plant with clusters of small flowers on top of a tall stalk. Both stalk and flowers buds are green. A storage temperature of $32°F$ ($0°C$) is best for this vegetable. As in all green vegetables, chlorophyll is the important color pigment; malic and citric are the important acids, although some small amounts of oxalic and succinic acids are also present. Fresh broccoli is usually cooked and lightly seasoned. Large quantities are frozen.

Cauliflower. Cauliflower, like broccoli, is a type of cabbage in which flower buds are massed on short stalks. The stems and flowers grow into a head encompassed by green leaves. Cauliflower

18-4 *The artichoke has an interesting shape and lends itself to attractive plate arrangements. The illustration shows lobster newberg over a cooked artichoke. (Courtesy of The Stouffer Corporation)*

is stored best at temperatures close to 32°F (0°C). It contains malic and citric acids and considerable amounts of ascorbic acid. Cauliflower is used raw and cooked as a table vegetable and in the manufacture of mixed pickles. Large quantities of cauliflower are frozen.

Sweet Corn. Sweet corn consists of a long cob covered with white or yellow kernels surrounded by leafy husks. Tassels of silk extend from the distal end. The husks should remain on the cob until the corn is ready to be cooked. When sweet corn is ripe for eating purposes, the kernels of corn exude, when pierced, a milky liquid (a suspension of starch grains in liquid). The sugar content of young corn is high, but it decreases rapidly. Conversely, the starch content continues to increase as the corn ages. The corn kernel has a concentration of oil in the embryo and some small amounts distributed throughout the endosperm. The characteristic color of sweet corn is caused by carotene and cryptoxanthin. During the summer months, sweet corn is used fresh as a table vegetable. Large quantities are canned and frozen as whole kernel corn, creamed corn, and corn on the cob.

Sweet corn is a sweet maize. The word *corn* means "grain" of any kind, but in America the word is used for maize. Corn or maize was first grown in the Andean region of South America; from there, its cultivation spread northward. A wide range of sweet corn is grown in the United States. Among the best-known varieties are Golden Bantam, Country Gentlemen, and Towell's Evergreen.

LEGUMES

The pods and seeds of leguminous vegetables form an important group of vegetables.

Garden Peas. Many varieties of garden peas were developed in Europe during the eighteenth and nineteenth centuries. The plant was first cultivated only for its dry seed. Today the fresh vegetable is extensively used, and the dried version is also marketed in large quantities.

Fresh garden peas are spherical in shape; they grow in a shiny green pod from which they are easily removed. The garden pea, which is wrinkled (unlike the smooth-skinned field pea), has a characteristic sweet flavor as a result of its sucrose content. As the pea ripens, there is a decrease in sucrose and an increase in starch. Poor-quality peas are generally high in starch and low in sugar content. The decrease in sucrose begins immediately after harvesting; hence, long storage periods have adverse effects on the texture and flavor of peas. Peas are cooked and used as a table vegetable. Large quantities are canned and frozen.

Lima Beans. The lima bean is a flat seed encased in a broad flat pod. The chief varieties are the dwarf type and Fordhook (larger and more fleshy). Lima beans are an excellent table vegetable. They are also used in the preparation of soups and casseroles.

Stringbeans. Stringbeans are long and slender, with immature beans within the shell. Generally, short broken pieces of canned stringbeans cost less than whole pods, which are less expensive than the fancy "French-style" green beans. The cut of the green bean may have an aesthetic appeal but has no bearing on the flavor or nutritive value. Reports of studies made by Platenius et al.[10] show that snapbeans can be stored best at temperatures close to 40°F (5°C). Green and yellow fresh beans are used as a table vegetable and are extensively canned and frozen.

Dried Legumes. Dried legumes are the dried seeds of plants. In their fresh forms, they are used as succulent vegetables. The legume group includes navy, kidney, chili, pinto, lima, and great northern beans, and soybeans, lentils, and peas (black-eyed, cow, green, and yellow).

Dried legumes, with the exception of soybeans and peanuts, are low in fat and moderately high in carbohydrates and protein. The ash content is fairly high. As a group, dried legumes are good sources of proteins, but in general these proteins are not of as high a quality as those from animal sources. In general, legume proteins are low in certain essential amino acids. Hence, the proteins of the legume are more valuable when supplemented with small amounts of animal protein foods.

The use of vegetable proteins as meat substitutes is discussed more thoroughly in Chapter 25.

MUSHROOMS

Edible mushrooms are *saprophytes,* a group of fungi that lack chlorophyll. The gill mushroom (*Agaricus campastris*) is the most popular variety in the United States. In Europe, coral mushrooms and truffles are used. Some species of wild mushroom are poisonous and may be indistinguishable from an innocuous strain. Thus, it is best to limit mushroom picking to the supermarket. Mushrooms are used as an ingredient in or garnish for many cooked dishes. Large quantities are canned and used in the manufacture of cream of mushroom soup.

PREPARATION OF VEGETABLES

Like fruits, vegetables require careful washing (Fig. 18-5). Only thick-skinned vegetables, such as rutabagas, potatoes, and winter squash, require paring. Such vegetables as carrots, parsnips, and beets require only to be gently scraped or heavily scrubbed before cooking. Whenever possible it is best to cook vegetables with the skins intact since discarded peels will contain valuable nutrients. Damaged parts of the vegetables are best removed before cooking lest they show up as discolorations after cooking and impart an unpleasant flavor to the cooked vegetable. It is generally agreed that crispness is a desirable quality in the fresh vegetable. To restore this quality, wilted vegetables are sometimes soaked in cold water. But because nutritive material from the plant tissues is lost to the surrounding water, soaking is discouraged in modern cookery unless exceptional conditions exist. For instance, very sandy spinach or wormy cauliflower, broccoli, and cabbage may need to be soaked to remove the foreign substances.

Vegetables that are to be eaten raw can be restored to crispness by being kept in a cold section of the refrigerator for several hours. Embedding raw vegetables in ice will quickly bring about a crisp quality.

Size of Vegetable Pieces. The decision on whether or not to cut vegetables before cooking depends on how the cooked vegetable is to be served. Cutting raw vegetables into very small pieces is in most cases undesirable because large amounts of soluble nutrients from the cut cells will be lost to the cooking waters.[11] On the

---

[10] H. Platenius, F. S. Jamison, and H. C. Thompson, "Studies on Cold Storage of Vegetables," *Agricultural Experiment Station Bulletin 602* (Ithaca, N.Y.: College of Agriculture, Cornell University, 1939).

[11] F. O. Van Duyne, J. T. Chase, and J. I. Simpson, "Effect of Various Home Practices on Ascorbic Acid Content of Potatoes," *Food Res.* **10:**72, 1945; I. Noble and J. Worthington, "Ascorbic Acid Retention in Cooked Vegetables," *J. Home Econ.* **40:**129, 1948.

18-5 *Fresh vegetables should be washed to remove dirt and stored in a refrigerator. (Courtesy of U.S. Department of Agriculture)*

other hand, whole vegetables may take a longer time to cook, which may lead to a loss of color and flavor. A reasonable approach to this problem is to eliminate all waste and inedible portions of the vegetable (such as pithy stalks of asparagus, stems of broccoli, the ribs from the spinach leaf) before cooking. The vegetables may then be cut into pieces suitable for cooking. Because the more succulent vegetables require less cooking time than the roots and tubers, they may be cooked in whole pieces if desired. Roots and tubers will cook more quickly if cut into small pieces.

PRINCIPLES OF COOKING VEGETABLES

The goals in cooking vegetables are to retain nutrients and maintain a high level of palatability. Ideally, a cooked vegetable is tender but firm, its characteristic color is retained, and its flavor is pleasant. Because vegetables are important for their high nutritive value as well as for their pleasant taste, it is essential to use a method of cooking that will minimize loss of food value.

Nutrients are lost during cooking because some of the food materials dissolve in the cooking liquids. Sugar, water-soluble vitamins, and mineral salts are soluble and are lost in this man-

ner. Other losses are through the escape of volatile substances and the destruction of nutrients, such as ascorbic acid and thiamine, by heat.

Losses caused by the solubility of some food constituents in water are measurable and are of considerable importance economically and nutritionally. The dissolvable food materials are sugars, sodium, potassium, calcium, magnesium, phosphorus, sulfur, iron, ascorbic acid, and thiamine. Losses are increased with increases in cooking liquid, in the cut-surface area of the vegetable, and in cooking time. Losses are also increased by extremely high temperatures and by the degree of alkalinity or acidity in the water.

Research in vegetable cookery reveals important information about nutrient losses. Noble and Gordon report that green beans boiled in an open saucepan in enough water to cover retain less ascorbic acid than those cooked in a covered container with just enough water to cover and those cooked by steaming and in the pressure cooker.[12] Earlier studies by Noble and others[13]

[12] I. Noble and J. Gordon, "Ascorbic Acid and Color Retention in Green Beans," *J. Amer. Dietet. Assoc.* **32**:119, 1956.

[13] I. Noble and M. M. Hanig, "Ascorbic Acid and Dehydroascorbic Acid Content of Raw and Cooked Vegetables," *Food Res.* **13**:461, 1948.

showed that losses of ascorbic acid were greater in vegetables cooked in fairly large amounts of water than in those cooked essentially by steaming, as in a tightly covered kettle or steamer. These findings are supported by the work of Krehl and Winters.[14]

Loss of soluble constituents during cooking is increased as the total cut-surface area exposed to water is increased. For example, cooked French-cut beans showed almost twice as great a loss of nutrients as cooked beans that were cut into 1-in. pieces or left whole.[15]

The overcooking of vegetables increases ascorbic acid loss through oxidation and through leaching out into the cooking medium.

Green Vegetables. Good color retention in cooked vegetables is essential. The practice of adding soda to green vegetables to intensify their color is not recommended, because excessive amounts of soda are deleterious to ascorbic acid and produce a bitter flavor and a mushy texture in vegetables.[16] Acids released when the plant cells are heated are responsible in part for the change in color in vegetables. It is not known which volatile acids are given off during cooking, but it is throught that they are the low organic acids, such as formic, acetic, and propionic, and perhaps lactic acid.[17] The nonvolatile acids released in the cooking water are mainly citric, malic, and oxalic. Some traces of succinic, tartaric, and benzoic acids are also found.

The green pigment, chlorophyll, is held in *plastids*—cell-like compartments in the plant tissue surrounded by a semipermeable membrane. As the plant tissue is heated, the membrane becomes permeable, permitting acids to diffuse into the plastids and remove magnesium through hydrogen replacement from the chlorophyll molecule. The result is a drab olive-green color, caused by the formation of pheophytin. Alkalies

18-6 *Frozen vegetables should be plunged into boiling water without thawing. (Courtesy of U.S. Department of Agriculture)*

added to green vegetables neutralize the plant acids and produce a bright green color attributed to the chlorophylls in the vegetable. According to Halliday and Noble, the green color may be best conserved by keeping the cooking period short.[18] This can be accomplished by cooking the vegetable in small to moderate amounts of boiling water in a saucepan with a tight-fitting lid (Fig. 18-6). However, it is recommended that the lid be left off for the first 3 minutes of cooking to facilitate the loss of volatile organic acids. Color changes in green vegetables are not reversible. Little can be done to correct the poor color of improperly cooked products. Color and ascorbic acid retention were shown to be better when fresh green vegetables were cooked in small amounts of water with added ammonium bicarbonate (NH_4HCO_3) than when fresh green vegetables were cooked in large amounts of water. Texture of the green vegetables were improved when calcium acetate ($CaAc_2$) was added to cooking waters with NH_4HCO_3.[19]

Cooking water from municipal sources is usu-

[14] W. A. Krehl and R. M. Winters, "Effects of Cooking Methods on Retention of Vitamins and Minerals in Vegetables," *J. Amer. Dietet. Assoc.* **26**:966, 1950.

[15] Noble and Worthington, op. cit., p. 129.

[16] M. Sweetman and I. MacKellar, *Food Selection and Preparation,* 4th ed. (New York: Wiley, 1954), p. 237.

[17] L. Meyer, *Food Chemistry* (New York: Van Nostrand Reinhold, 1960), p. 275.

[18] E. Halliday and I. Noble, *Hows and Whys of Cooking* (Chicago: University of Chicago Press, 1946), p. 5.

[19] Dianne Oldland and Mary S. Eheart, "Ascorbic Acid Retention and Organoleptic Quality of Green Vegetables Cooked by Several Techniques Using Ammonium Bicarbonate," *J. Food Sci.* **2**:241, 1974.

ally slightly alkaline and may neutralize the plant acids in the water, thus helping to retain the green color of the vegetable. In a study to determine the effect of overcooking on the color and ascorbic acid content of green vegetables, it was found that the hues of all green vegetables progressed from yellow-green to yellow as the cooking period increased and all vegetables showed considerable color change with 5 minutes of overcooking in boiling water and 1 minute of overcooking in a pressure saucepan.[20]

Red Vegetables. The red and purple colorings in vegetables such as red cabbage and radishes belong to the anthocyanin group of color pigments. They are found dissolved in the cell sap and are highly soluble in cooking water. Their red color is intensified in an acid medium. If the medium in which the red vegetable is cooked is alkaline, color will change from red to purple, then to blue and green. This range of color is frequently seen in the cooking of red cabbage. Less change is noticed in the cooking of beets because they contain betaine rather than anthocyanin.

The addition of metals in soluble forms also brings about these color changes. The color change in the red vegetable is reversible: a small amount of dilute acid (such as vinegar or lemon juice) will bring back the bright red beet color. Red cabbage will not stay red during cooking unless some dilute acid is added. If the cooking water is extremely alkaline, the red cabbage will turn an unattractive green. Beets are more resistant to color change than red cabbage. Cooked peeled beets do not retain their red color as well as beets cooked in their skins. Less color will be leached into the cooking water if 1–2 in. of the tops of the stems remain attached. The purple red cooking water that results may be served as a soup called *borscht*.

For cooking red vegetables, boiling water and a covered saucepan are desirable. A small amount of vinegar or lemon juice will help prevent color changes.

Yellow Vegetables. The yellow color in vegetables is caused by the carotenoids. It is thought that they occur in the plastids of the plant cell.

These pigments are also present in green vegetables, but there the chlorophyll masks the yellow coloring matter. There are a number of carotenoids, including carotene (orange-yellow, found in such vegetables as carrots) and lycopin (orange-red, found in tomatoes). The carotenoids are not greatly affected by cooking conditions; they are almost insoluble in water, stable under heat, and not affected by the vegetable acids. Halliday and Noble suggest that the slight darkening of overcooked carrots is probably the result of the scorching of sugar dissolved in the cooking liquor rather than the decomposition of the yellow pigment.[21] Short cooking periods, in boiling water and in covered saucepans, are recommended for these vegetables.

White Vegetables. White vegetables, such as cabbage and cauliflower, contain the pigments *flavones,* also called anthoxanthins. The flavones are soluble in water and tend to turn a creamy yellow color in an alkaline medium. Upon prolonged overcooking, the creamy yellow color changes to dark brownish gray.[22] It has been suggested that the dark compound is formed by the combination of iron and sulfur or, possibly, by a combination of flavones and iron. Whatever its cause, the dark color develops only when the white vegetables are overcooked. Consequently, white vegetables should be cooked only until tender. Small amounts of acid added to the cooking water may help retain the white color. It will also toughen the plant tissue.

The initial pink discoloration that occurs when potatoes are cut is due to the activation of the phenol oxidase enyzme upon exposure to oxygen in the air. The enzyme acts on tyrosine to form the pigment melanin. This pigment will darken to brown and grayish black. Some cooks will soak peeled potatoes in cold water to prevent this discoloration of the cut surface by limiting the exposure to air. This is not necessary since the color will disappear with cooking. Soaking vegetables in water will also leach out water-soluble nutrients.

Another discoloration observed in potatoes is the stem-end blackening of certain species when cooked. This is due to a complex between the phenolic acids such as chlorogenic and the iron

[20] I. Noble, "Ascorbic Acid and Color in Vegetables," *J. Amer. Dietet. Assoc.* **50**:304, 1967.

[21] Halliday and Noble, op. cit., p. 9.
[22] Noble, op. cit., p. 306.

in the potato. Changing the pH of the water to slightly acidic will eliminate this problem.

Texture. Vegetables, properly cooked, are tender but firm. Mushiness indicates overcooking. "Tender but firm" means that something of the crispness of the raw vegetable is retained, whereas "mushiness" means that all the vegetable's crispness and form have been lost. Starchy vegetables, such as potatoes, should be cooked until they are mealy, but the sogginess that comes with overcooking must be avoided. Overcooking alters the form of the vegetable, reduces its nutritive value, and changes its color.

Changes that take place in the structural form of vegetables during cooking include the softening of the cellulose, the breaking down of hemicelluloses, the dissolving of pectins in solution, and the gelatinizing of starch. The lignin or woody component of the fiber in vegetables cannot be softened by cooking. It is useless to try to tenderize the woody stalks of mature asparagus. They should be snapped off prior to cooking. Plants containing large amounts of water also lose their crisp texture, as is demonstrated in the cooking of spinach. Sweetman[23] suggests that the resistance of the more mature vegetables to softening is probably the result of their increased fiber content and its interference with the hydrolysis of protopectin.

The addition of acids to vegetables during cooking increases their resistance to softening because—it has been suggested—they precipitate pectins. Vegetables such as beets, stringbeans, and cabbage, which may be served with acid sauces, should first be cooked in water to the proper degree of tenderness. The acidic sauce is added at the end of the cooking period.

Calcium ions will also increase the time of cooking. They may be naturally present in hard water or may be added as calcium salts. If a long cooking time is needed to develop the flavor of a vegetable (as in Boston baked beans), calcium as well as acid can be added. Molasses is often added since it contains high concentrations of calcium as well as aconitic acid. Ripe tomatoes which are canned will have calcium chloride or pectate added as a firming agent. The presence of phytates in the vegetable (peas, for example) will decrease the firming effect of the calcium ions due to formation of a calcium-phytate complex.

Flavor. Flavor changes are brought about in cooked vegetables through the contact of their cut surfaces with water, the amount of water used, and the length of the cooking period. Each vegetable has its own characteristic flavor, formed by plant acids, sugar, tannins, and volatile oils. Some of the flavoring materials are decomposed during cooking and driven off in the steam. Again, short cooking periods will minimize these losses and help to retain the flavor of the fresh vegetable.

As important as flavor loss is the development of an undesirable flavor, which may occur when vegetables are overcooked. Vegetables such as onions and those that belong to the cabbage family (Brussels sprouts, broccoli, turnips, and kale) contain sulfur compounds released by unfavorable cooking conditions. Upon application of heat, unpleasant sulfur components become pronounced.

The very strong flavor of some vegetables, such as onions, results from a volatile oil present in the raw vegetable. Upon cooking, however, onions lose their characteristic strong flavor as the oil passes off in the steam during cooking. Cooking onions in an uncovered saucepan in a fairly large amount of water will modify their flavor by promoting volatilization and solution losses.[24,25] The use of acid in the cooking water of vegetables containing sulfur compounds hastens their decomposition; hence, it is practical to add acids to these vegetables only at the end of the cooking period.

Bitterness in some vegetables such as eggplant and cucumbers can be minimized if cut slices of the raw vegetable are liberally sprinkled with salt and allowed to stand at room temperature for a period of time. The osmotic difference of the salt on the cut surface of the vegetable to the interior water will draw out the moisture containing the bitter substances. The beads of liquid that form on the cut slices are wiped off and the plant is ready to be used for cooking or in salads.

[23] Sweetman and MacKellar, op. cit., p. 243.

[24] Halliday and Noble, op. cit., p. 15.

[25] F. T. Maruyama, "Identification of Dimethyl Trisulfide as a Major Component of Cooked Brassicaceous Vegetables," *J. Food Sci.* **35:**540, 1970.

The intensified taste of freshly harvested vegetables may be related to the glutamic acid content, which decreases with the age of the plant. The salt of monoglutamic acid, monosodium glutamate, is used as a flavor enhancer in spices and cooking, particularly for vegetable cookery. Mushrooms and carrots, both flavor enhancers of many cooked dishes, naturally contain high levels of this amino acid.

It is generally suggested that flavor preferences be used as a guide for the time of adding salt. There seems to be little difference between adding the salt to the cooked vegetable and adding it to the cooking water.

METHODS OF COOKING VEGETABLES

Methods of cooking vegetables that are worthy of consideration because of their frequency of use are baking, boiling, steaming, and panning.

Baking. Sweet potatoes, white potatoes, squash, eggplant, tomatoes, and onions have sufficient water to form steam and keep moist when exposed to dry heat; hence, these vegetables are frequently baked. Baking a vegetable in its skin inhibits nutrient loss through solution, thus eliminating mineral loss and some vitamin loss. The skin holds in the steam while the vegetable cooks. Baking also develops a pleasant flavor. A covered glass or earthenware casserole can be used for baking vegetables. Although white potatoes require a high temperature of 425–450°F (219–232°C), a temperature of 350°F (177°C) is desirable for baking most vegetables.

Boiling. Boiling is by far the most common method of cooking vegetables but one that requires the most careful management. For best results in nutrient retention, taste, color, and texture, all vegetables should be cooked in a moderate amount of boiling water in a covered saucepan, using about 1 cup of water for four servings. The water should be brought to a full boil, the vegetable added, and the water brought back again to a boil. The flame can then be turned down to permit gentle rather than rapid boiling. Vegetables cook just as quickly in gently boiling water as in rapidly boiling water, because in both cases the temperature is 212°F (100°C).

Because green vegetables lose their color when cooked in an acid medium, the cooking procedure used for this group of vegetables is slightly different. The cover of the container should be left off for the first few minutes after the vegetables are added. This permits the volatile acids to escape and aids in the preservation of color. It should be noted, however, that this procedure also allows the loss of some of the volatile flavor substances, producing a cooked vegetable of rather mild flavor. Such a green vegetable as spinach may require only the water that clings to its leaves for cooking.

The cover need not be removed from the pan in cooking vegetables that require short cooking times.

Steaming and Pressure Steaming. Fresh, succulent vegetables—with the exception of most of the green vegetables—lend themselves to steaming (Fig. 18-7). In the home kitchen, steaming is usually accomplished by placing a perforated basket over a pan of boiling water so that the vegetable cooks in live steam. This method takes longer than boiling, but it has the advantage of conserving nutrients and retaining the shape of the vegetables. The color of the vegetables cooked by this method may be less desirable then when other cooking methods are employed. Gordon and Noble note that cabbage, cauliflower, and broccoli have a milder flavor when boiled than when cooked in steam.[26]

Cooking under pressure, as in the pressure saucepan, is the shortest method of cooking vegetables. A minimum of water is used in this method of cooking, and when timing is controlled the cooked vegetables compare favorably with those prepared by other methods. Krehl and Winters[27] studied the vitamin and mineral losses occurring in equal amounts of twelve vegetables cooked to the same degree of tenderness in different amounts of water. They concluded that the pressure saucepan method of cooking vegetables caused no greater loss than that ob-

[26] Joan Gordon and Isabel Noble, "Application of the Paired Comparison Method to the Study of Flavor Difference in Cooked Vegetables," *Food Res.* **25**:257, 1960.

[27] W. A. Krehl and R. M. Winters, "Retention of Vitamins and Minerals in Vegetables," *J. Amer. Dietet. Assoc.* **26**:966, 1950.

18-7 *Steaming the tops of asparagus retains their shape and flavor. (Courtesy of United Fresh Fruit and Vegetable Association)*

served in vegetables cooked in a small amount of water.

Panning. Panning is a method of cooking with very little water or with the steam formed from the vegetable's own juices. The liquid formed becomes a part of the flavorful liquor that is served with the vegetable. Shredded cabbage, kale, spinach, okra, summer squash, and young stringbeans are some of the vegetables amenable to this method of cooking. The vegetable is shredded or cut into small pieces and placed in a heavy-bottomed pot with a small amount of cooking oil or table fat. A tight cover is used to hold in the steam, and cooking time is a short 5–8 minutes, because the vegetables are cooked only until crisp and tender.

French Frying. Potatoes, sweet potatoes, eggplant, and breaded onion rings can be french-fried from the raw state. The starchy vegetables should be rinsed quickly and completely dried before frying to remove surface starch from the cut slices. Green peppers, carrots, broccoli, parsnips, and mushrooms must be parboiled and thoroughly dried and breaded before frying. When a variety of these vegetables are dipped in a flour-and-water batter and then deep-fried, they create a Japanese dish called tempura. The principles and techniques for french frying are discussed in Chapter 28.

Microwave Cookery. The use of the microwave oven for cooking vegetables is steadily gaining popularity. Cooking is effected by exposing the vegetables to the penetration of microwaves. According to recent studies, the colors of fresh and frozen broccoli are about the same when cooked in the microwave oven as when boiled on top of the range. Microwave cooking takes less time than the conventional method of boiling, and the vegetables have a high level of color and nutrient retention.[28]

Microwave is recommended as a favorable cooking method for fresh and frozen vegetables. Some measures must be taken to avoid overcooking and drying out of colored vegetables and those which are high in cellulose.[29] Timing is an important factor in all microwave cookery if superior color, flavor, and texture are to be retained. A recent study[30] rated microwave-

[28] V. Chapman, "Electronic Cooking of Fresh and Frozen Broccoli," *J. Home Econ.* **52:**161, 1960.

J. Gordon and I. Noble, "Comparison of Electronic vs. Conventional Cooking of Vegetables," *J. Amer. Dietet. Assoc.* **35:**241, 1959.

M. S. Eheart and C. Gott, "Electronic Cooking of Vegetables," *J. Amer. Dietet. Assoc.* **44:**116, 1964.

[29] Helen Van Zante, *The Microwave Oven* (Boston: Houghton Mifflin, 1973), p. 108.

[30] J. A. Maga and J. A. Twomey, "Sensory Comparison of Four Potato Varieties Baked Conventionally and by Microwaves," *J. Food Sci.* **42:**541, 1977.

baked potatoes as being inferior in all sensory properties to potatoes baked in a conventional oven.

METHODS OF SERVING VEGETABLES

Varying the method of serving vegetables as well as of cooking them can add interest, nutritive value, and palatability. There are a multitude of ways to serve vegetables, some more time-consuming than others. These methods of serving include the addition of a table fat with salt and pepper or the use of a plain or seasoned cream sauce (Fig. 18-8). Vegetables may also be scalloped and baked in a casserole dish or prepared in the form of croquettes, fritters, custards, or timbales. Cooked vegetables may be glazed, incorporated in soups and soufflés or stuffed and baked with various mixtures.

The simplest and most common method of serving vegetables is to add fat and seasonings

18-8 *Broccoli—a highly popular green vegetable—is frequently served with a cheese or hollandaise sauce. (Courtesy of United Fresh Fruit and Vegetable Association)*

while the vegetable is still hot. The cooking liquor must be completely drained off before the fat is added. Fats such as butter, margarine, bacon, salt-pork drippings, and salad oil may be used.

Scalloping. For variety, vegetables may be scalloped. The raw vegetable is sliced thin and placed in layers in a buttered baking dish. Each layer is sprinkled with flour, salt, pepper, and bits of fat. Some liquid—vegetable juices or milk— may be added, depending on the water content of the vegetable and on whether it has been cooked first. The vegetable is then baked in a slow oven until it is tender and golden brown. Starchy vegetables, such as potatoes, are very satisfactorily prepared in this manner.

Au Gratin. Vegetables served au gratin are placed in a baking dish. White sauce is added to the vegetable, which is usually cooked first, and the mixture is covered with buttered bread crumbs. The dish is cooked in a medium-hot oven for 10–15 minutes to brown the crumbs. Grated cheese is a frequent addition to au gratin dishes. It should be added between the layers of vegetables and white sauce or blended in with the white sauce.

Custards or Timbales. Vegetable custards or timbales are palatable, highly nutritious dishes. Cooked vegetables, diced, chopped, or puréed, are added to egg and milk to form a custard. This mixture is seasoned and placed in greased baking dishes or cups, which are then placed in a pan of hot water and baked in a slow oven. The finished product is of the same consistency as custard. A timbale is also a combination of vegetable, milk, and eggs, but it has more vegetable pulp than milk and has more of the characteristic taste of the vegetable than the vegetable custard does.

Glazing. On occasion, vegetables may be served glazed. Such vegetables as carrots, parsnips, and sweet potatoes lend themselves nicely to this form of preparation. Vegetables should be partially cooked, placed in a skillet, saucepan, or baking dish, and cooked in syrup until done.

Soufflés. A vegetable soufflé is made from a combination of vegetable pulp, white sauce,

18-9 *Peas in white turnip cups are eyecatching. This is a pleasing vegetable combination. (Courtesy of United Fresh Fruit and Vegetable Association)*

eggs, and seasoning. The entire mixture is baked in a slow oven until set.

Cream Soups. Creamed vegetable soups are palatable and nourishing. They are usually made by combining a vegetable purée with a thin white sauce, usually in equal parts.

Stuffing. One way to achieve an interesting combination of flavor and texture in serving a vegetable is to stuff it (Fig. 18-9). Mixtures of chopped meat, fish, or poultry, combined with starchy materials such as bread crumbs, rice or macaroni, and seasoned with herbs are stuffed into the centers of onions, tomatoes, squashes, cucumbers, mushrooms, potatoes, or green peppers. The stuffed vegetable is then baked in a moderate oven until tender.

PROCESSED VEGETABLES

In addition to the fresh variety, frozen, canned, and dried vegetables are commonly used. Vegetables frozen singly and in combination come in a variety of package styles and sizes. These enjoy a high degree of popularity not only because of their convenience but also because of their palatability when properly prepared. Be-

cause frozen vegetables are blanched before freezing, cooking times are much shorter than for the raw vegetable. Blanching of green vegetables will also cause the color to intensify to a bright green. This is thought to be due to the initial expulsion of air in the cells, which creates translucency in the vegetable. Package directions are the best guides for preparing frozen vegetables. Among the more recent frozen vegetables to make their appearance in the markets are mushrooms and onions. Grading of frozen vegetables follows that given for frozen processed fruits.

Despite a high volume of sales of fresh and frozen vegetables, there is still a demand for the canned variety. The important point in cooking canned vegetables is to be wary of overcooking. When the canned vegetable has considerable liquid accompanying it, the vegetable should be strained and the liquid cooked down to about a third of its volume. The vegetable can then be returned to the liquid and heated through. The liquid should not be discarded because it has high nutrient content.

Some dried vegetables such as beans, peas, and lentils do not require long soaking periods before cooking, as once was the practice. The method now recommended is to boil the dry legumes for 2 minutes and then allow them to soak for about

1 hour. The short boiling period softens the skin so that the hour is sufficient time for rehydration. Dry beans soaked and cooked in hard water remain tough because the minerals calcium and magnesium form insoluble salts with the pectic substances of the vegetables. To counteract this, a small amount of sodium bicarbonate, ⅛ tsp of soda for each cup of dry beans, is recommended. Care must be taken not to use too much soda, for an excess will promote loss of thiamine during cooking. Because a variety of means are employed in dehydration, package directions are important guides for cooking dried products.

SALADS

The term *salad* designates a variety of dishes prepared by the use of a single salad ingredient or a mixture of foods garnished with a salad ingredient and seasoned with a salad dressing (See Fig. 18-10). Traditionally, the salad green is an important part of the salad, and, with a few minor exceptions, a salad is served raw. It may be simply a mixture of greens (Fig. 18-11) or it can be composed of raw, cooked, or canned fruits, vegetables, meats, poultry, or fish (Fig.

18-12). Nuts, cheese, or eggs may also be used as one of the principal ingredients.

The varieties of lettuce frequently used include iceberg, Boston, Bibb, leaf, and romaine. Endive, chicory, cabbage, escarole, celery, tomatoes, cucumbers, onions, and cauliflower are other vegetables that frequently make up the contents of raw salads. Any number of vegetable green combinations are considered suitable as long as they are attractive in color and palatable in flavor. Some salad vegetables stand out as especially appropriate. Cabbage, for example, is an inexpensive nutritious vegetable that is available the year around. It is available in a variety of colors. and its crisp texture makes it a desirable vegetable to use as the basis for a light or heavy salad.

Tomatoes, too, may be used at almost any time of year as a salad ingredient. They may be served sliced, quartered, chunked, or whole, depending on their use in the salad. Cucumbers are another salad favorite—indeed, their chief use is as salad vegetable. They have a distinctive flavor that is not duplicated, even slightly, in any other vegetable. The crisp texture of the cucumber is a highly valued quality in salads. Crispness is preserved by keeping cucumbers in a cool place or by soaking them for a very short

18-10 *Red and Sovoy cabbage. These vegetables are in demand for salad as well as cooking purposes. (Courtesy of United Fresh Fruit and Vegetable Association)*

18-11 *Many nutritious greens are available for salads. Clockwise from the left: Scallions, romaine lettuce, iceberg lettuce, (above) Boston lettuce, (below) Bibb lettuce, curly endive, spinach, watercress, chives, and escarole. (Courtesy of Wish Bone Salad Dressings)*

period in ice water. Unpeeled cucumbers add considerable color interest to salads.

Preparation. Making salad is a fairly simple matter, but it requires some basic information about the flavor and texture of the materials used and an appreciative eye for pleasing color combinations. The possible combinations of salad materials are endless. One need only remember that something crisp and something green, tossed together with a pleasant-tasting salad dressing and chilled, will serve as either the basis for or the whole of an appetizing and palatable salad.

A few additional suggestions will help to create salad dishes of excellent quality. First, salad ingredients should have all moisture clinging to their surfaces carefully removed—in order both to keep the salad materials crisp and to enable the

18-12 *Fresh, crisp soybean sprouts add interest to a vegetable salad. (Courtesy of U.S. Department of Agriculture)*

Plate II: *Nine varieties of apples. (Courtesy of International Apple Institute.)*

Delicious, Golden

Delicious, Red

Gravenstein

Ida Red

Jonathan

McIntosh

Newton

Rome Beauty

Winesap

Plate III: *Three varieties of pears. From left to right: Anjou, Bose, and Comice. (Courtesy of Oregon-Washington-California Pear Bureau.)*

Plate IV: *The four basic potatoes. From left to right: Russets, Round Reds, Round Whites, and Long Whites. (Courtesy of The Potato Board and Kraft, Inc.)*

Plate V: *An assortment of salad greens. Starting top right: romaine, escarole (below), Belgian endive (below), red lettuce (above), Boston lettuce (below), iceberg lettuce (top), bunching lettuce (below), Chinese cabbage (below), Bibb lettuce (below), chard, Italian parsley (below). (Courtesy of Western Growers Association.)*

Plate VI: *A variety of vegetables. (Courtesy W. Atlee Burpee Company.)*

Brussel Sprouts

Chinese Cabbage

Red Cabbage

Belgian Endive

Eggplant

Kohlrabi

Okra

Parsnips

Rhubarb

Rutabaga

Salsify

Plate VII: *Herbs as they grow in the garden. (Courtesy of W. Atlee Burpee Company.)*

Basil

Dill

Marjoram

Mint

Oregano

Savory

Thyme

Plate VIII: *Retail cuts of beef. (Courtesy of The National Live Stock and Meat Board.)*

Shanks—cross cuts

Rib roast small end

Round rump—roast rolled

Chuck—blade roast

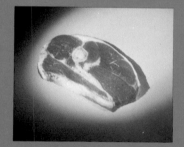

Chuck—arm steak

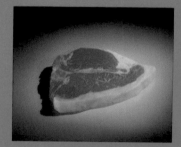

Porterhouse steak

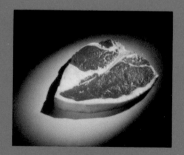

T-bone steak

Tenderloin steak

Flat-bone loin—sirloin steak

Plate IX: *Retail cuts of Pork. (Courtesy of The National Live Stock and Meat Board.)*

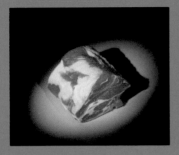

Loin—blade roast

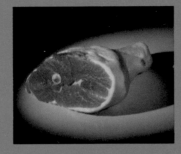

Leg—(fresh ham) shank half

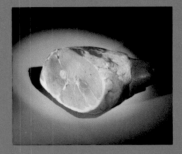

Smoked ham—shank half

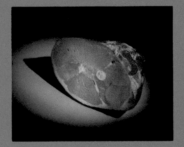

Smoked ham—rump half

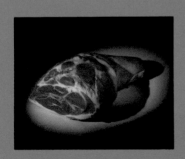

Shoulder—arm picnic

Spareribs

Loin-rib chop

1a Provolone (boccini style)
1b Provolone (salamini style)
2 Edam
3 Cheddar
4 Colby
5 Muenster
6 Gouda
7 Colby longhorn
8 Monterey Jack
9 Pasteurized process
10 Pasteurized flavored process

11 Port du Salut
12 Mozzarella
13 Brick
14 Swiss
15 Scamorze
16 Parmesan
17 Colby midget longhorn
18 Cheddar midget longhorn
19 Blue
20 Cold pack cheese food
21 Limburger

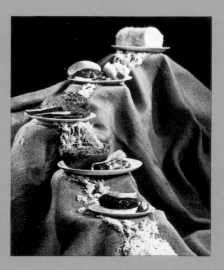

18-13 *Crisp vegetables combine well with foods of softer texture. This illustration shows a combination of rice, tunafish, celery, apples and peas. (Courtesy of Rice Council)*

salad dressing to cling to their surfaces (Fig. 18-13). A second point of importance is the adding of the salad dressing. For best results, the dressing should be added to the salad ingredients just before it is served. Generally, a tossed salad is mixed at the table, because the dressing tends to draw out the juices, causing the vegetable to lose its crispness. Marinating the basic ingredients of such salads as potato, macaroni, fish, and poultry with salad dressing is an effective way of blending flavors.

A third guide in salad making is to make the best possible use of the natural color and shape of the vegetables, fruits, and other materials being used. To achieve this, salad ingredients are handled as little as possible. The ingredients are cut into eating size, but not into pieces so small as to be unidentifiable.

STORAGE OF FRESH VEGETABLES

Vegetables continue to live after they are harvested, but that disturbance in the life process is the start of their loss of vitality and food value. The process of ripening in most vegetables involves complex physical and chemical changes. It is important, therefore, that consideration be given to the conditions of transit and storage that will hasten or delay the ripening process. To keep from decaying, the immature or ripe vegetable must continue to respire. This involves the consumption of oxygen, the metabolism of cell food materials, and the liberation of carbon dioxide, water, and energy. Most of the energy released is in the form of heat.

The process of respiration can be slowed down by low temperatures; hence, good storage facilities should provide optimum refrigeration for the specific vegetable.

Plant tissues change during storage. These changes are mostly the result of the loss of water, the modification of the fibers, and the change in the pectins. There is less loss of water in vegetables when they are stored in an atmosphere that is nearly saturated. Packing vegetables in ice or keeping them in moistureproof bags provides such an atmosphere. It has been found that removing the tops of carrots cuts down on the moisture loss because it decreases the total evaporating surface. The loss of water is reduced in some vegetables, such as rutabagas, by coating them with wax.

Succulent Vegetables. Succulent vegetables lose their rigidity and freshness through evaporation of water in the cell tissues, the continued action of enzymes that are responsible for the ripening process, and microbial action. Some vegetables, such as peas and corn, become less palatable during storage because their sugar changes to starch. Consequently, it is practical to buy these vegetables only in amounts that can be used at once. The succulent vegetables should be kept cold in a covered but ventilated container or in a dampened cloth bag.

The respiration of the cells in plants can be slowed down, and this will increase the life of the plant and the time that it can be stored. The environment of the vegetables can be altered to either decrease the oxygen content or to increase the carbon dioxide content. This controlled-atmosphere (CA) storage of vegetables such as lettuce, and fruits such as apples, has reduced quality losses.[31]

Roots. Roots and tubers may be stored for long periods in a cool, ventilated place. To delay moisture loss, tops should be removed from carrots, radishes, and beets. Only sound vegetables should be selected for storage; one or two spoiled specimens will contaminate the rest. Root vegetables may be stored in a cool place without refrigeration for long periods; temperatures of 38–50°F (4–10°C) are recommended in order to keep sprouting at a minimum.

Potatoes should never be stored at a temperature less than 40°F (5°C), because the decrease in metabolic activity decreases the rate at which the vegetable can use its natural sugar. The potato accumulates excess sugar, which has an unfavorable effect on cooking. The excess sugar may be eliminated if the potato is returned to room temperature for 1–2 weeks.

Potatoes are considered an excellent source of ascorbic acid. However, the length of storage time affects the vitamin content unfavorably. Studies show that longer storage periods result in greater losses of ascorbic acid.[32]

SUMMARY

The roots, stems, and leaves of certain annual and nonwoody perennial plants as well as the bulbs, blossoms, and seeds of other annual plants are classified as vegetables. With more starch and less sugar than fruits, vegetables contain large amounts of carbohydrates. They are recommended as daily foods principally because they are rich in minerals and vitamins. The nutritive value depends largely on which portion of the plant is edible.

Fresh vegetables are usually cheapest in season. Advances in methods of harvesting, shipping, and storage and improved crop management contribute to quality and lower costs. Grades for vegetables are widely used in wholesale trading. Factors for consumers to consider in vegetable selection include freedom from defects, degree of ripeness, uniformity of variety, size, and color.

Recommended methods of preparing and cooking vegetables are based on retention of nutritive value, maintenance of high palatability, and retention of good color and a firm but tender texture. Cooking methods include baking, boiling, steaming, pressure steaming, panning, and microwave cookery. Good results in boiling vegetables depend on using a moderate amount of water and controlled cooking time. Vegetables may be stuffed, glazed, scalloped, or may be served with sauces, au gratin, or as salads.

Succulent vegetables are highly perishable and should be stored for a short time only in a cold place in a ventilated container. Roots and tubers can be kept for longer periods when stored in a cool ventilated place.

Frozen, canned, and dried vegetables are frequently used in meals. When properly handled during storage and cooking, they provide excellent alternates for fresh vegetables. Package directions are the best guides for cooking frozen vegetables, and overcooking is to be avoided when heating canned vegetables.

QUESTIONS AND TOPICS FOR DISCUSSION AND STUDY

1. What are the types of cooking losses that occur in the cooking of vegetables? How can they be minimized?
2. To what is the color of green, yellow, white, and red vegetables, respectively, attributed?
3. To what is the flavor of vegetables attributed? How can the flavor of certain vegetables be modified? Which vegetables require this modification?
4. What is the effect of long cooking on colors of vegetables? On the flavor of such vegeta-

[31] B. Singh and C. C. Yang, "Controlled Atmosphere Storage of Lettuce," *J. Food Sci.* **37:**48, 1972.

[32] Jorg Augustin and R. McDole, "Ascorbic Content in Russet Burbank Potatoes," *J. Food Sci.* **40:**415, 1975.

bles as cabbage, onions, cauliflower, and turnips? On the nutritive value of vegetables? On the texture of vegetables?

5. How do vegetables come in contact with acids during cooking?

6. What are the advantages and disadvantages of cooking vegetables in a pressure saucepan? In a microwave oven? In boiling water in a covered saucepan?

7. What effects do long storage periods have on vegetables?

8. Summarize the important recommendations for preparing and cooking vegetables.

SUGGESTED ACTIVITIES

1. Select as many fresh vegetables as possible and cook by various methods: boiling, steaming, pressure cooker (use manufacturer's directions), and microwave oven. Compare cooking time and the color, flavor, and texture of the cooked vegetables. Reserve a small portion of the raw vegetable to compare with the cooked. (Allow at least ½ lb of vegetable for each cooking batch.) Compare a fresh cooked vegetable with a cooked frozen product. (Pound packages of frozen vegetables can be cut in half with a special saw for the purpose.)

2. Using some of the prepared vegetables, arrange an interesting vegetable-plate combination.

3. Using some of the prepared vegetables, prepare a scalloped or casserole dish.

4. Select a vegetable that is entirely new to you and prepare it in a manner that attracts you. Serve it as you would like to have it served at a meal. Ask your classmates for comments.

5. Prepare one or more of the following salads: fruit salad, gelatin salad, tossed green salad, or vegetable salad. Evaluate for appearance, flavor, and nutritive value.

REFERENCES

BOOKS

Griswold, Ruth. *The Experimental Study of Foods.* Boston: Houghton Mifflin, 1962, Chap. 6.

Halliday, Evelyn, and Isabel Noble. *Hows and Whys of Cooking,* rev. ed. Chicago: University of Chicago Press, 1946, Chap. 1.

Lee, Frank. *Basic Food Chemistry.* Westport, Conn.: Avi, 1975, Chap. 18.

Paul, Pauline, and Helen Palmer. *Food Theory and Applications.* New York: Wiley, 1972, Chap. 6.

Talburt, William, and Ora Smith (eds.). *Potato Processing,* 2nd ed. Westport, Conn.: Avi, 1967.

Vail, Gladys, J. Phillips, Lucile Rust, Ruth Griswold, and Margaret Justin. *Foods,* 7th ed. Boston: Houghton Mifflin, 1978, Chap. 5.

Van Zante, Helen. *Microwave Oven.* Boston: Houghton Mifflin, 1973, Chap. 11.

ARTICLES AND BULLETINS

Charles, V., and F. O. Van Duyne. "Palatability and Retention of Ascorbic Acid of Vegetables Cooked in a Tightly Covered Saucepan and in a Waterless Cooker." *J. Home Econ.* **46:**659, 1954.

Fung, A. C., Anthony Lopez and F. W. Cooler, "Essential Elements in Fresh and in Frozen Spinach and Collards." *J. Food Sci.,* **43:**897, 1978.

Goldsmid, Alfred. "Microwave Baked Potatoes in Large Scale Food Preparation." *J. Amer. Dietet. Assoc.* **51:**536, 1967.

Gordon, J., and I. Noble. "Comparison of Electronic vs. Conventional Cooking of Vegetables." *J. Amer. Dietet. Assoc.* **35:**241, 1959.

Heinze, Peter. "Cooking Quality and Compositional Factors of Potatoes of Different Varieties from Several Commercial Locations." *Technical Bulletin 1106.* Washington, D.C.: U.S. Department of Agriculture, 1955.

"How to Buy Vegetables." *Home and Garden Bulletin 141.* Washington, D.C.: U.S. Department of Agriculture, 1967.

Kylen, A., et al. "Microwave Cooking of Vegetables, Ascorbic Acid Retention, and Palatability." *J. Amer. Dietet. Assoc.* **39:**321, 1961.

MacLeod, A. J., and Glesui MacLeod. "Flavor Volatiles of Some Cooked Vegetables." *J. Food Sci.* **35:**734, 1970.

Sapers, G. M., et al. "Flavor Quality in Explosion Puffed Dehydrated Potato." *J. Food Sci.* **35:**728, 1970.

Sweeney, J. P. "Palatability and Nutritive Value of Frozen Broccoli: Effects of Cooking Time, Cooking Method, and Storage Time." *J. Amer. Dietet. Assoc.* **37:**357, 1960.

"Vegetables in Family Meals." *Home and Garden Bulletin 105.* Washington, D.C.: U.S. Department of Agriculture, 1971.

Cereals and Cereal Products

CHAPTER 19

Many grasses are grown for their edible seeds. These are known as the *cereal grains,* the most important of which are wheat (see Fig. 19-1), oats, corn (maize), and rice. Buckwheat, although not a true cereal because it is not a member of the grass family, is classified with cereals because of a likeness in structure. Sorghums are cultivated in the United States mainly for fodder. From the cereal grains are prepared various kinds of flour and meal, starch, dozens of kinds of breakfast cereals (Fig. 19-2), and dried pastes that are used in products such as macaroni, spaghetti, and noodles.

Maize is the only cereal known to be native to the western hemisphere. At the present time, cereal grains in some form are produced in every area of the world. Each area grows its own preferred cereal, generally the grain best adapted to soil and climatic conditions. Lacking cereals, the world could hardly feed its masses; no other food group can compare with cereals for their resistance to deterioration during storage, their high food value, and their low cost. In many countries, 80–90% of the food calories consumed are supplied by one single kind of cereal grain.

The per capita consumption of cereals in the United States has been steadily decreasing.[1] This may be related to a more affluent and weight-conscious public who considers breads and cereals as "fattening." People are often surprised to discover that these foods are not always that high in calories. A slice of white bread, for example, has only 68 calories. It is the foods that are eaten with it (butter, sugar, jam) that adds on the calories.

COMPOSITION

The chemical composition of dried cereal grains varies widely, especially in the amount of proteins, fats, and carbohydrates. But cereals have certain common characteristics as a food group.

Barley, buckwheat, oats, and rough rice have hulls; consequently, they have relatively high crude fiber and ash content. Corn and oats have a higher fat content than any of the other cere-

[1] "Food Consumption Prices Expenditures," *Supplement for 1975 to Agricultural Economics Report 138* (Washington, D.C.: U.S. Department of Agriculture, 1977), p. 21.

216

als. Of great importance to the manufacturer and the user of cereal products is the fact that the various components of the grains are not uniformly distributed throughout the kernel structure. Different parts of the kernel serve as reservoirs for the various components. The hulls and bran of the kernel are high in cellulose and minerals, the germ is characterized by its high fat and protein content, and the cereal hulls contain some sugars and minerals. The endosperm contains starch, is lower in protein content than the germ, and is also low in fat and minerals. Table 19-1 shows the composition of some cereal grains.

PARTS OF THE CEREAL GRAIN

The grain or kernel of cereal is like a nutfruit in structure. Each cereal kernel has three distinct portions: the *pericarp,* or bran layer; the *endosperm,* or inner portion, which consists largely of starch grains embedded in a matrix of protein; and, at one side or end, the *germ,* or embryo, which is the portion from which the new grain develops.

The outer coat of the wheat kernel, the bran layer, is really made up of three layers—the *epidermis,* the *epicarp,* and the *endocarp.* The bran layers are made up largely of cellulose and contain some protein and minerals. Their function is that of protection. The *aleurone* layer, which is the innermost layer of the bran or the outer portion of the endosperm, contains valuable nutrients. In milling, this part of the bran is removed with the outer layer. The endosperm is largely a storage place for starch grains. After the

cereal grain has been milled, the endosperm is left. The germ is rich in proteins, fats, sugar (chiefly sucrose), and minerals. Although it is the richest part of the grain, nutritionally speaking, it is also the most unstable portion. Because this portion of the cereal is largely responsible for the deterioration of cereal during storage, it is frequently removed during milling and sold as a separate food product.

NUTRITIVE VALUE

All cereals are excellent sources of energy. The energy value is mainly contributed by starch and fat. Starch is the main polysaccharide present in cereals; however, small amounts of dextrins are found after grinding. The cereal fats, which are located chiefly in the germ, consist of the fatty acids—oleic and linoleic—and lecithin. The fat is less stable in the unmilled grain than in the milled product. Because of the instability of the fat, the major processing methods have been designed to discard the germ. Although this practice may be effective in reducing deterioration in storage, it is very wasteful of nutritive value, for the germ portion of the cereal stockpiles proteins, minerals, and vitamins as well as fat.

Cereals belong to the incomplete protein group, lacking in either lysine, threonine, or tryptophan. The practice of eating cereals mixed with animal protein foods serves to bolster the total protein effect of the cereals. Cereal is often served with milk, so that the different proteins tend to supplement each other, and the cereals

TABLE 19-1
Composition of Some Common Cereal Grains

Grain	Water (%)	Protein (%)	Fat (%)	Carbohydrate (%)	Ash (%)
Barley	10.2	12.8	2.1	72.8	2.1
Buckwheat	12.0	12.4	2.4	71.6	1.6
Corn	11.0	10.0	4.3	73.4	1.3
Oats (oatmeal)	8.3	14.2	7.4	68.2	1.9
Rice	12.0	7.5	1.7	77.7	1.1
Rye	10.0	11.2	1.7	75.2	1.9
Wheat	8.7	11.7	2.0	75.8	1.8

Source: C. Chatfield and G. Adams, "Proximate Composition of Foods," *Circular 549* (Washington, D.C.: U.S. Department of Agriculture, 1940).

ENDOSPERM
. . . about 83% of the kernel

Source of white flour. Of the nutrients in the whole kernel the endosperm contains about:

70-75% of the protein
43% of the pantothenic acid
32% of the riboflavin   } B-complex
12% of the niacin   } vitamins
6% of the pyridoxine
3% of the thiamine

Enriched flour products contain added quantities of riboflavin, niacin and thiamine, plus iron, in amounts equal to or exceeding whole wheat—according to a formula established on the basis of popular need of those nutrients.

BRAN . . . about 14½% of the kernel
Included in whole wheat flour.
Of the nutrients in whole wheat, the bran, in addition to indigestible cellulose material contains about:

86% of the niacin
73% of the pyridoxine
50% of the pantothenic acid
42% of the riboflavin
33% of the thiamine
19% of the protein

GERM . . . about 2½% of the kernel
The embryo or sprouting section of the seed, usually separated because it contains fat which limits the keeping quality of flours. Available separately as human food. Of the nutrients in whole wheat, the germ contains about:

64% of the thiamine
26% of the riboflavin
21% of the pyridoxine
8% of the protein
7% of the pantothenic acid
2% of the niacin

19-1 *Structure of a kernel of wheat. (Courtesy Wheat Flour Institute and the Kansas Wheat Commission)*

then become valuable protein sources and form a significant part of the protein intake.

Cereals have good amounts of the B vitamins, but they contain almost no vitamins A, and D and ascorbic acid. Ascorbic acid may be found in grains that are sprouting. For this reason, sprouted grains are added to sandwiches and salads. The health food movement has increased the popularity of this practice.

Yellow corn, unlike other cereals, contains carotenes, which are convertible in the body to vitamin A. Because cereals are highly valued for their B vitamins, considerable work has been done on determining the distribution of these vitamins in the cereal grains. In a study of the riboflavin content of cereal grains, it was shown that cereals are a much poorer source of riboflavin than of thiamin (wheat, buckwheat, barley,

and rice contain much higher levels than corn, oats, and rye).[2]

The milling and heat processing that cereals are subjected to cause vitamin loss. Thiamin is especially unstable to heat.

All unmilled cereals contain good amounts of minerals, but these minerals may be unavailable, owing to binding by the large quantities of fiber and phytates present. The mineral content can be greatly reduced by the milling processes to which cereals are subjected. Calcium, phosphorus, and iron are the minerals present in the largest amounts.

[2] M. C. Kik and F. B. Van Landingham, "The Influence of Cooking on the Niacin, Riboflavin, and Thiamine Content of Rice," *Cereal Chem.* **17**:279, 1940.

ECONOMIC ASPECTS

In every country in the world, cereals make up a large portion of the diet of low-income groups. Cereal grains are the cheapest sources of food energy, and they constitute a large portion of the caloric and protein intake of human beings. When people have more money to spend for food, they tend to replace cereals with fruits, green vegetables, eggs, milk, and meat.[3] Fortunately for the world's population, cereal grains remain at a relatively low cost because they can be grown in many different climates and soil. Because they are not bulky, they can be stored in a fairly small space and transported cheaply over long distances.

Recent developments in agriculture have helped to increase yields per acre of cereal grains. Diseases such as rust, mildew, and rot can be controlled by chemical treatments. Also, genetic studies have given rise to methods of developing disease-resistant varieties of cereals.

ENRICHMENT

White flour and bread, as well as breakfast cereals, degerminated cornmeal, polished rice, and macaroni and spaghetti, all are frequently enriched. Enrichment is required by law in many states. In states that have no such legislation, enrichment proceeds on a voluntary basis. Federal law does not require enrichment of any cereal product, but there are provisions for Congress to establish standards of identity.[4] There are "required" and "optional" ingredients for enriched products. The B vitamins—thiamine, riboflavin, and niacin—and iron are required ingredients; all four must be included if the product is to be labeled "enriched." Calcium and vitamin D are optional ingredients and need not be included in the enriched product.

Cornmeal and wheat flour enrichment is added by vibrating feeders to the stream of flour or meal. Pasta products usually have the enrichment added in the mixer, and toasted breakfast cereals usually have the enrichment sprayed on after toasting to minimize losses during the heating process.[5]

Although it is generally accepted that cereal foods made from the cereal grains are relatively inexpensive, there are some differences in cost among the different types. Most of the home-cooked breakfast cereals cost less per serving than the ready-to-eat cereals. Many breakfast cereals have had nutrients put back into them, thus furnishing a food that has nutritional advantages over the milled products. These restored products may be higher in price than the unrestored ones, but generally the value returned to the user is greater. Larger packages of cereal usually cost less per serving. This is especially true of the ready-to-cook cereals.

DIFFERENT CEREALS

Wheat, rye, oats, barley, corn, rice, and buckwheat are the principal cereals used in the United States. The form in which they are used varies with the kind of cereal. Some cereals, especially wheat and rye, are ground into flour for use in making baked products. These and other cereals are used for a variety of breakfast foods.

Corn, Cornmeal, and Corn Grits. Next to wheat, corn is the grain most used in the United States. It occurs in the diet in many different forms—most frequently in the form of cornmeal, grits, or hominy.

Cornmeal, yellow and white, is produced by grinding the kernels of corn to a coarse mixture. It may be made from the entire corn kernel or from a refined product.

Cornmeal is used extensively for bread in the South. It has a lower protein content than white flour. Cornmeal, like wheat, can be prepared by grinding the whole grain, but the fat content of the germ portion makes storage difficult. (The meal will become rancid if kept too long.) The more generally used process entails removing the bran and germ before the endosperm is ground.

[3] M. Burke, "Pounds and Percentages," in *Food: The Yearbook of Agriculture* (Washington, D.C.: U.S. Department of Agriculture, 1958), p. 593.

[4] Code of Federal Regulations, *Title 21,* 1971.

[5] The Committee on Food Protection, Food and Nutrition Board, *Technology of Fortification of Foods* (Washington, D.C.: National Research Council–National Academy of Sciences, 1975), p. 41.

(a) *Barley.*　　**(b)** *Corn.*

(c) *Oats.*　　**(d)** *Rice.*

(e) *Wheat.*

19-2 *Today's large variety of ready-to-eat cereals are made from the grains—barley, corn, oats, rice, and wheat. (Courtesy of Cereal Institute, Inc.)*

This method produces a drier meal that contains less fat and has more starch than whole ground cornmeal. Both white and yellow corn are ground into meal. Yellow corn has the advantage of containing more vitamin A, in the form of carotene. Cornmeal can be cooked in water and served as porridge or cornmeal mush. If cheese and lard are added, it becomes an Italian dish called "polenta."

In the Central and Latin American countries, corn is usually soaked in an alkaline solution for 20–30 minutes. This softens the kernel and liberates the niacin (a B vitamin), which is bound to a protein, thus increasing its nutritive value. Limestone (calcium hydroxide), lye (sodium hydroxide), or wood ash (potassium hydroxide) is used to make the basic solution. The corn is then drained, rinsed, dried, and ground into a meal called *masa harina*. Masa is the basic flour for making tortillas, a flat, thin, round bread. Tortillas are served plain or fried and stuffed to create enchiladas or tacos.

Yellow and white corn grits of varying sizes are made by grinding this product to a much coarser consistency than cornmeal. Hominy is normally made from white corn, and it is pulverized into rather large particles, hence the name *pearl hominy*. It is also sold as canned whole hominy. Some corn is also used in the preparation of ready-to-eat breakfast cereals, cornstarch, corn oil, and corn sugar.

The law provides for the permissive enrichment of cornmeals and corn grits. Some southern states have mandatory enrichment laws for the refined products.[6]

Popcorn is corn that has had its moisture content adjusted to 11–15%. This moisture is most stable if the popcorn is stored in airtight containers or vacuum-packed. When the kernels are heated, the moisture in the endosperm expands to 20–30 times its volume so that its pops open. Best yields are obtained if all the popcorn is popped within 2 minutes of the initial popping.

Rye. Rye is used mainly for the commercial manufacture of bread; its popularity stems from

[6] The Committee on Cereals, Food and Nutrition Board, *Cereal Enrichment in Perspective* (Washington, D.C.: National Research Council–National Academy of Sciences, 1958).

the distinctive flavor it imparts to bread products. Rye is grown in quantities in Russia and the European countries. Breads made with rye flour are moist and less elastic in texture than those made from wheat flour. Because bread made with rye flour only is dense and compact, rye bread is frequently made of a combination of wheat and rye flours.

Triticale. Triticale is a hybrid cereal grain produced from parent species of wheat and rye. It combines the grain quality and disease resistance of wheat with the hardness and vigor of rye. Flour made from the triticale wheat can be used for bread, rolls, and pasta.[7]

Sorghum. Little sorghum is used as food in the United States, however, it is a very important world grain crop with only wheat and rice surpassing it. It is the chief food grain in Africa, parts of India, Pakistan, and China. In these areas sorghum grain is made into porridge, bread, or cakes. Sorghum products can be fortified with soy and cottenseed proteins to improve protein quality.[8]

Barley. Barley is used in soups, and some barley flour is used for baby foods. The lack of gluten prevents its formation into bread unless it is mixed with other flours (usually a 1:5 ratio). However, by far its most important use in the United States is in the production of malt. Sprouting the barley grain will produce an enzyme that changes the starch into maltose. The maltose of malt is roasted and dried. Most of the malt is used for the manufacture of alcoholic beverages, but some is reserved for food uses. Malt syrups are used for malted milk concentrates and enzyme supplements of breakfast foods.

Oats. Oats as food for human beings are used mainly in the form of breakfast foods. Much of the oat crop grown in the United States is used for fodder.

Oats are very little used for bread cereal in this country. However, Scotland's famous oatcake is sufficient evidence of their potential value for this purpose. Oatmeal is used in the preparation of bread much as cornmeal is. Some wheat flour is combined with oatmeal when it is used in the preparation of bread or cookies.

Oats, as they are commonly eaten, are a nutritious food (see Fig. 19-3) because the breakfast foods—rolled oats and oatmeal—are made from the whole grain, with only the husk removed. These foods are high in protein, fat, and energy value and rich in calcium, phosphorous, and iron. The B vitamins are also found in the oat grain.

Buckwheat. Buckwheat is a relatively minor crop compared with other cereals. Its main use in the United States is for the manufacture of pancake flour. The Silverhull buckwheat is the variety most commonly used for milling purposes because of its high endosperm yield. Some buckwheat groats are sold for use as a breakfast cereal.

Rice. Rice is an important food crop. It provides over one half the world's population with a low-cost, palatable, stable food. A very large percentage—over 90%—of the world rice crop is produced and consumed in Asia and on adjacent islands. Despite the large production of rice in the Far East, the United States exports rice to that area of the world, for it is one of the few

19-3 *Use of rolled oats in bread makes a nutritious loaf. (Courtesy U.S. Department of Agriculture)*

[7] K. Lorenz and J. Walsh, "Extrusion Processing of Triticale," *J. Food Sci.* **39**:572, 1974.

[8] G. N. Bookwalter and K. Warmer, "Fortification of Dry-Milled Sorghum with Oilseed Proteins," *J. Food Sci.* **42**:969, 1977.

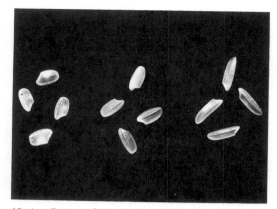

19-4 *Grains of rice. Left to right, short, medium, long. (Courtesy Rice Council)*

countries that does not use all the rice it produces.

The major areas of rice cultivation in the United States are Arkansas, California, Louisiana, Mississippi, and Texas, where the soil and temperature are conducive to the growth of the rice plant and where water for irrigation is readily available.

The rice varieties in the United States include long-grain, medium-grain, and short-grain types (see Figs. 19-4 and 19-5). The leading varieties in the long-grain group are Bluebonnet, Century, Patana, Rexoro Texas, Toro, and Rexark. In the medium-grain group, Zenith, Magnolia, and Blue Rose are the main types. The best-known short-grain varieties are Caloro and Caluso.

A small amount of wild rice, *Zizania aceritaca,* is marketed in the United States. It is actually the seeds of a reedlike water plant rather than a true rice. It must be harvested by hand in boats. The difficulty of its cultivation and harvesting is reflected in its extremely high price. The cost makes it a luxury item, usually reserved for stuffing small game or guinea hens. An economical way to serve wild rice is to stretch it with white or brown rice and seasonings. The grains are long, spotted with dark colors, and have a nutty flavor.

Each rice variety has its own characteristic cooking properties and cooking time; consequently, varieties should not be mixed when packaged.

It has long been known that in the processing of brown rice to white or polished rice, a large percentage of the protein, fat, minerals, and vitamins are lost. Because of these losses, several

19-5 *Rice is a pleasing accompaniment to a roast. (Courtesy of Uncle Ben's Foods)*

processing approaches have been devised that are designed to retain more of the B vitamins in the milled rice.

The first method widely considered to have reduced loss of nutritive value is the production of undermilled or "unpolished" rice. Rices that are undermilled do not have the customary white luster, and they are more subject to insect infestation and flavor deterioration than white rice is.

A second method is that of increasing vitamin retention by processing the rough rice prior to milling. This is done by parboiling the rough rice. Commercially, this type of rice is known as *converted rice*. This processing allows some of the B vitamins and minerals in the bran and hull to permeate the endosperm so that the content of the final milled product is enhanced.

Another means of remedying the losses occurring in the milling of rice is the artificial enrichment of the grain. A premix has been developed in which the rice is wetted with a solution of thiamine and niacin, then dried and covered with a protective coating. When this first layer of vitamin solution is dry, a second coating of iron pyrophosphate is distributed on the rice; this also is covered with a protective solution and dried. Riboflavin is not generally added because it turns the grains yellow. So far as practicability for use is concerned, the rice premix is presumably highly resistant to washing, cooking, and storage losses. Today many of the convenience forms of rice are used.

Quick-cooking rice is in demand. The rice is cooked to gelatinize the starch and subsequently dried. The processed rice has a porous structure that will permit rapid rehydration, usually within 5 minutes. Quick-cooking rice does not produce long, separate grains and thus has the tendency to congeal.

CEREAL BREAKFAST FOODS

Breakfast cereals appear in many shapes and forms. They are grouped into two major types: those that require cooking before serving and those that have been cooked and are ready to serve. The first group is the older type of cereal breakfast food. Whole or partially ground, cereal lends itself to being cooked in water or milk to a thick mush. Uncooked cereal breakfast foods are manufactured from cereals such as corn, rolled oats, and wheat. Two things happen to breakfast cereals when they are manufactured: the grain is pulverized, reducing the particle size, and some of the tough fibrous outer coatings are removed. Reducing the size of the particles makes it possible for the cereal to be cooked in a reasonable amount of time and also improves the texture of the grain.

Bulgur. Bulgur is either soft or hard wheat that has been soaked in water and cooked in steam or water under pressure or at normal air pressure. After the water treatment, it is dried and the bran partially removed. The kernels are either left whole or cut to suitable size, fine, medium, or coarse. These processed wheat particles are glassy-looking and hard. Bulgur is an excellent alternative breakfast cereal product to use with those of the refined type. It takes longer to cook than the refined cereals, and for some uses the bulgur may have to be soaked prior to its incorporation in a cooked dish. Bulgur has been likened in texture and taste to wild rice.

Uncooked Wheat Cereal. The important wheat cereal is farina. This product is made from the wheat middlings, which are chunks of endosperm free of bran and germ. When pulverized, middlings become flour. A hard wheat is used to manufacture farina in order to achieve a product that does not become pasty upon cooking. Most farina on the market is enriched with vitamins and minerals, permissible amounts having been established by federal specification. Some farina products have disodium phosphate added to increase the speed at which they cook. At present, there are instant farina products on the market. Presumably, if directions are carefully followed, the cereal is ready to serve after about 1 minute of boiling time. Apparently, the instant product has been treated with proteolytic enzymes during processing, thus opening up pathways for the easy penetration of water. Other forms of farina are the malt- or cocoa-flavored types. Chiefly, these are made of farina middlings and flavoring materials.

Farina is made from the refined wheat kernel, but there is also a very limited demand for the whole-grain products. Whole-wheat meal, cracked wheat, and flaked wheat are sold in very small quantities.

Oat Cereals. The most popular oat cereal is rolled oats, but ground oats and steel-cut groats also enjoy some popularity. The oat grain with its hull removed is called a *groat*. Quick oats are flakes made from particles of the whole groat; they cook in about 5 minutes. Regular oats are flaked whole groats and must be boiled for 10–15 minutes. The advantage of the regular oats is that they will not lose their chewy texture upon standing. Steel-cut oats—those that are not flaked—are the most resistant of the oat products to overcooking. Instant oatmeals are also available. They provide a wholesome cooked cereal in a short time.

Corn Cereals. Cornmeal and hominy grits are used as hot breakfast cereals in some parts of the country. Cornmeal fortified with ground whole soybean meal can be made into acceptable tortillas, an important Mexican and Mexican American ethnic food.[9]

Rice Cereal. An instant rice cereal is on the market. It consists of milled rice with particles about the size of those in farina. It requires no heating other than the addition of boiling water.

Ready-to-Eat Cereals. New ready-to-eat cereals appear on the market every day. They appear to have unlimited popularity because of their flavor, convenience, and marketing appeal to children. Ready-to-eat cereals differ in the kind of grain used, the part of it used, and the method of processing. They may be flaked, extruded, puffed, shredded, toasted, and coated with sugar. The cereals are usually ground and made into a slurry mixed with flavorings, salt, sugar, vitamins, and minerals. Corn flakes are flattened by a flaking mill and subsequently toasted. To make shredded wheat, the mixture is put through a shredding machine and baked. Puffed cereals have been heated under pressure

[9] Franz Day, "Tortillas Fortified with Whole Soybeans Prepared by Different Methods," *J. Food Sci.* **40:**1275, 1975.

and the pressure suddenly released. This expands or puffs up the grain, which is later dried.

PRINCIPLES OF COOKING CEREALS

In cooking cereals, the essential action is gelatinization of the cereal starch. Starch gelatinizes as it absorbs water; hence, enough water is used in cooking cereal so that it will form a soft starch gel. Penetration of the water through the tough outer coat of the cereal is accomplished by heating.

The heat of cooking forms steam that penetrates to and causes irruption of the starch granules. The release of soluble starch paste causes the cereal to thicken as it cooks. Cooking also brings about a change in the flavor of the cereal, probably as a result of the conversion of starch to dextrin and sugars.

The various cereal grains vary in the amount of water required to form a finished cereal gel of the right consistency. Gelatinization of starch granules takes place very quickly when the temperature is sufficiently high.

During cooking, rice grains swell and become tender without breaking. The goal is to achieve dry, fluffy grains of rice that stand apart. Grains that are sticky or gummy and split down the middle are not desirable. The changes that occur during cooking include a softening of the cell-wall component materials and a gelatinization of the starch. Although cooking does not cause any decomposition of cellulose, the application of moist heat softens the fibrous material so that the rice kernels become easy and pleasant to chew.

METHODS OF COOKING CEREALS

The goal in cooking cereal is to achieve a mixture that forms a soft, not sticky, gel free of uncooked lumps of starch and having a pleasant flavor.

Cereals must be cooked long enough to cook the starch, to form a starch paste or gel, and to develop the flavor. Because of modern methods of cereal processing, long, slow cooking is not necessary. Studies by Hughes and others have shown that the starch may be completely gelatinized when the cereal is boiled over a direct flame for 1 or 2 minutes and then cooked over hot water for 10–15 minutes.[10]

The type and form of the cereal have a good deal to do with the amount of water required. Finely ground cereals tend to lump when they are cooked. To prevent these lumps from forming, the cereal should be combined with enough cold liquid to form a paste before it is added to the remainder of the liquid, which has been brought to the boiling point.

Another way to cook cereal free of lumps is to sprinkle the cereal slowly into rapidly boiling water to which 1–2 tsp salt for each quart of liquid have been added. For the first few minutes, the cereal is cooked directly over the heat. The cooked cereal can be held over hot water.

Soluble nutrients, especially thiamine, will leach out and be dissolved in the cooking water; hence, cooking methods that include discarding the cooking water are undesirable.

Rice. Because rice is cleaned before packaging and because washing rice tends to increase the loss of soluble nutrients, it is neither necessary nor desirable to wash it before cooking. It is accepted today that methods recommending the use of excess water for cooking rice are to be avoided, for nutrients may be discarded with the excess cooking water. In the Far Eastern rice markets, rice is often washed or sprinkled to keep the starch dust minimal. This also washes away valuable nutrients. Recipes for Spanish rice may include the procedure in which rice is soaked and washed in water several times to remove the starch. Although this does produce a product with completely separate rice grains, it is at the expense of its nutritive value. This same result of separate grains can be achieved if the rice is sautéed very briefly in hot fat to seal in the starch. If chicken or beef broth is then added as a cooking liquid, it becomes a *pilaf*. The amount of water and cooking time will vary with different types of rice, but generally the volume of water should be 2 or 2.5 times that of the rice. With

this amount, most all the cooking water will have been absorbed and some will have evaporated by the time the rice is cooked, and none will remain to be discarded. A small amount of fat or oil is added to reduce foaming.

FACTORS AFFECTING COOKING. Each rice variety has certain specific processing and cooking characteristics. Most long-grain types tend to cook dry and fluffy; the cooked grains remain intact and do not stick together. Short-grain types cook more firmly than the long grains and tend to be more cohesive. (See Fig. 19-6.) Medium-grain rice varieties seem to be somewhere in the middle with regard to these qualities. In judging the desirability of a specific type for cooking, a rice that gives a clear translucent grain is preferred to grains having an opaque appearance or chalky centers. The number of broken grains can be reduced if the rice is stirred only once when the water first comes to a boil.

QUICK-COOKING RICE. Forms of precooked rice are now available that cook in 2–15 minutes. The rice has been precooked in water and dried under closely controlled conditions, sometimes under dry heat. One popular commercial method shortens the cooking time of both brown and white rice by heating the dry grains in a current of air at high temperatures. Another form of quick-cooking rice is produced by precooking white rice and then either drying the

19-6 *Rice pudding is an adaptable dessert—easy to serve warm or cold, plain or with colorful garnishes such as fruit or dessert sauces. (Courtesy Rice Council)*

[10] O. Hughes, E. Green, and L. Campbell, "The Effect of Various Temperatures and Time Periods on the Percentage of Gelatinization of Wheat and Custard and of Cereals Containing Those Starches," *Cereal Chem.* **15:**795, 1958.

kernels rapidly in a current of hot air or drying them slowly. The drying process is followed by application of heat, which causes an expansion of the dried grains.

MACARONI PRODUCTS

Macaroni products, sometimes called *pasta* or *alimentary pastes,* include such products as macaroni, spaghetti, vermicelli, and egg noodles (see Fig. 19-7). The main ingredient in the macaroni group of products is a special durum flour of high gluten content well suited to the manufacture of this product. Macaroni products are widely used throughout the country, and the trend is to increased per capita consumption.

Composition. The standard of identity established by the U.S. Food and Drug Administra-

19-7 *Macaroni shapes. Clockwise from top: Cantelli, medium egg noodles, lasagna, manicotti, folded fine egg noodles, margherita, jumbo shells, linguine, egg rings roaa marino, mafalde, fancy egg rings, rigatoni, spaghetti, egg bows, curly lasagna, elbow macaroni, occhi di lupo, and riccini.* (*Courtesy of National Macaroni Institute*)

tion for macaroni products allows for these basic raw materials: semolina, durum flour, farina, flour, or any combination of two or more of these, and water. Permitted optional ingredients are egg white solids (from 0.5 to 2.0% by weight of the finished food), disodium phosphate, onions, celery, garlic, bay leaf, salt, or other seasonings. Gum gluten can be used in such quantities that the protein content of the macaroni is not more than 13% by weight.[11]

Whole wheat, milk, soy, and vegetable macaroni products are permitted by standards of identity, but they are manufactured in small quantities.

Noodles. Noodles or egg noodles are macaroni products to which eggs have been added. These products are defined as having a ribbon shape and as containing solids of egg or egg yolks not less than 5.5% by weight of the total solids. Green noodles will have approximately 3% spinach solids added.

Manufacturers of macaroni products use enrichment processes as a way of improving the nutritive value of an otherwise refined food. The enrichment is in the form of the B vitamins and iron. Either yeast or synthetic mixtures can be used to provide the necessary amounts.

Basic Ingredients. Durum wheat is most commonly used in the manufacture of macaroni products because of its adaptability to the processes involved. Macaroni products are made from durum semolina (the purified middlings of durum wheat, ground to a certain sieve size). Macaroni products made from durum have a characteristic yellow color, which has become associated with good quality in macaroni products. The color is imparted to the wheat by the carotenoid pigments xanthophyll and taraxanthin. Durum wheat also lends a hardness and translucency to the finished product that is highly valued by manufacturers and users of macaroni foods. However, a dough made from durum semolina is less tough than dough prepared from hard wheat; hence, dough made from durum wheat extrudes through a small hole at a lower pressure than dough made from

[11] Code of Federal Regulations, *Title 21,* 1971.

hard wheat. Durum semolina is the preferred material for making macaroni products, but durum granular and durum flour are two other durum products that can be used successfully in this operation. The durum granular product is a semolina to which flour has been added; durum flour is the pulverized middlings. Durum flour makes a dry macaroni, resistant to breakage, smooth, and of a clear yellow color. In contrast to the semolina product, it is stronger mechanically, more uniform in color, and takes less time to cook. However, the semolina product is more resistant to overcooking and causes less cloudiness in the cooking water.

Products made with durum granular have properties that lie between those of the flour products and the semolina products.

Eggs. The second raw material used in macaroni products is egg. Egg noodles, egg spaghetti, egg macaroni, or any macaroni product that has the word *egg* added must contain egg solids. These egg solids may be added to the product as frozen, dried, or fresh egg yolks or whole eggs. Frozen and dried eggs are used more than fresh eggs, and usually only the egg yolk is used, because the egg white dilutes the natural yolk color and yields a lighter-colored product not as salable as the products made with yolks. The egg ingredients in noodles cost almost as much as the flour, even though they represent only 5.5% of the total solids in the product; thus, egg noodles cost more per pound than other macaroni products.

All macaroni products are cooked in gently boiling salted water to a standard called "al dente" (to the tooth). They are quickly drained and not rinsed. Strands of macaroni should be tender, firm, and distinct, not mushy, starchy, or matted. Products that have had disodium phosphate added to them will cook slightly faster than those that have not. The disodium phosphate increases the alkalinity, enabling the starch grains to gelatinize faster.

SUMMARY

The edible seeds of grasses, cereal grains, include wheat, oats, corn, and rice; buckwheat, although not a true cereal, is classified with them. Cereal grains are excellent and inexpensive sources of energy, principally because of their starch and fat content, but they vary widely in the amount of protein, fats, and carbohydrates they contain. Cereal proteins are incomplete, but when combined with animal protein foods they form a significant part of the protein intake. Enrichment, required by law in many states, restores B vitamins and iron to white flour and bread, breakfast cereals, degerminated cornmeal, polished rice, macaroni, spaghetti, and noodles. When eggs are added to noodles, they are called egg noodles.

The grains are used in various ways: wheat principally for flour, durum wheat for the manufacture of macaroni products, with a small amount used for wheat breakfast cereals; corn for cornmeal, grits, hominy, ready-to-eat breakfast cereals, cornstarch, corn oil, and corn sugar; rye principally in bread manufacture; barley for malt; oats for rolled oats and oatmeal; buckwheat for pancake flour; rice as a diet staple and small amounts as instant rice cereal.

Breakfast cereals are of two major types: those that require cooking and those that are ready to serve. In cooking cereals and rice, to prevent nutrient loss the amount of water used should be only what will be absorbed. Cooked rice should be dry and fluffy; a cooked cereal should be soft, free of uncooked lumps, and have a pleasant flavor. Macaroni products are cooked until tender and then drained.

QUESTIONS AND TOPICS FOR DISCUSSION AND STUDY

1. Why do directions for rice, especially the enriched and converted varieties, recommend not washing or rinsing it before cooking?
2. Is a long-grain variety rice always superior to the short-grain variety for cooking purposes?
3. Why do the amounts of water recommended for the cooking of different kinds of cereals differ?
4. What is meant by enriched cereal?
5. What changes in cooked cereal take place when stirring is excessive?
6. Why is durum wheat considered the most desirable form of wheat for macaroni products?
7. What happens when a macaroni product is constantly stirred during cooking?

SUGGESTED ACTIVITIES

1. Prepare and serve a cooked cereal. Through tasting, train yourself to recognize the cooked flavor of the cereal.
2. Prepare instant cereal. Compare for time of preparation, flavor, and appearance with the product cooked in the conventional manner. Compare cooked lots of long-grain, short-grain, converted, and instant rice as to volume, appearance, texture, and flavor. Compare the results of steaming and baking rice. (Use a long-grain variety).
3. Prepare one or more of the different kinds of macaroni products—spaghetti, macaroni, or noodles. Prepare a sauce to serve with these products.

REFERENCES

BOOKS

Edlin, H. L. *Plants and Man*. Garden City, N.Y.: Doubleday, 1967, Chap. 3.

Garard, Ira. *Introductory Food Chemistry*. Westport, Conn.: Avi, 1976, Chap 13.

Hoskins, Charles M., and G. William. "Macaroni Production." In S. Matz (ed.), *The Chemistry and Technology of Cereals as Food and Feed*. Westport, Conn.: Avi, 1959.

Storck, John, and Walter Teague. *Flour for Man's Bread*. Minneapolis, Minn.: University of Minesota Press, 1952.

ARTICLES AND PAMPHLETS

Houston, D. F., and G. O. Kohler. "Nutritional Properties of Rice." Washington, D.C.: National Academy of Sciences, 1970.

Kies, C., M. R. Peterson, and H. M. Fox. "Protein Nutritive Value of Amino Acid Supplemented and Unsupplemented Precooked Dehydrated Oatmeal." *J. Food Sci.* **37**:306, 1972.

The Committee on Cereals, Food and Nutrition Board. *Cereal Enrichment in Perspective*. Washington, D.C.: National Research Council–National Academy of Sciences, 1958.

The Committee on Food Protection, Food and Nutrition Board. *Technology of Fortification of Foods*. Washington, D.C.: National Research Council–National Academy of Sciences, 1975.

From Wheat to Flour. Chicago: Wheat Flour Institute, 1965.

Starch

CHAPTER 20

Starch is the main form in which plants conserve their energy; it is found in greater amounts in seed, tuber, and root vegetables than in other types of vegetables, but some starch is found in all vegetable tissue. The storage form of glucose in animals is called glycogen. Starch is a polysaccharide made up of many glucose molecules with one molecule of water removed for every molecule of glucose in the union. The number of glucose molecules ranges from 40 to several hundred thousand. As the size of the molecule increases, its solubility decreases. Most starches are mixtures of approximately three-fourths amylose and one-fourth amylopectin. *Amylose* is a linear polysaccharide that is linked together by α-1,4 linkages. Amylopectin is a branched-chained polysaccharide that has α-1,6 linkages every 20–30 glucose units in addition to the linear α-1,4 linkages. The proportion of these two polysaccharides in different foods is determined by genetics. Their relative proportion is a major factor in the way a starch behaves during cooking.

Waxy starches from corn, rice and barley cereals contain little or no amylose but large amounts of amylopectin. They have excellent thickening properties and do not undergo retrogradation. Cornstarch, which is made from ordinary hybrid corn, is about 80% amylopectin and 20% amylose.

Representation of Amylose and Amylopectin molecules.

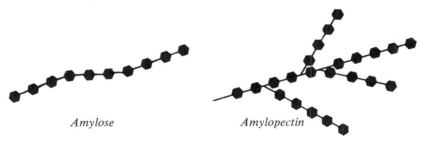

Amylose   *Amylopectin*

PROPERTIES OF STARCHES

Starches used in the preparation of food are cornstarch, rice starch, wheat starch (flour), tapioca starch, potato starch, arrow root, and sago starch. Sago starch is prepared from the pith of the East Indian sago palm. Although similar in overall characteristics, these starches differ sufficiently to warrant specialized use. In the United States, the most abundant sources of starch are corn, wheat, and rice. White and sweet potatoes are also used for the manufacture of starch if surpluses are available. A good bit of tapioca, which is prepared from the root of the South American plant manioc (cassava), is manufactured for use in the preparation of desserts. Such properties as swelling, gelatinization, temperature, and viscosity of pastes formed are different for the various starches.

Changes During Cooking of Starch. Any starch is more digestible cooked than raw. During the cooking of starch mixtures, several important changes take place that are significant in the preparation of typical starch products.

When starch granules (see Fig. 20-1) are added to cold water, a temporary suspension is formed, with the starch tending to settle out as soon as the mixture is allowed to stand. The starch granules do not dissolve, but when the mixture is heated, the water begins to penetrate the starch granules, causing them to swell and soften, forming a paste. This is gelatinization, and the change transforms the temporary suspension into a more permanent one. The suspension may form a gel when reaching high temperatures, but if not and if it is sufficiently concentrated, it forms a gel on cooling. The starch mixture does not change its physical form

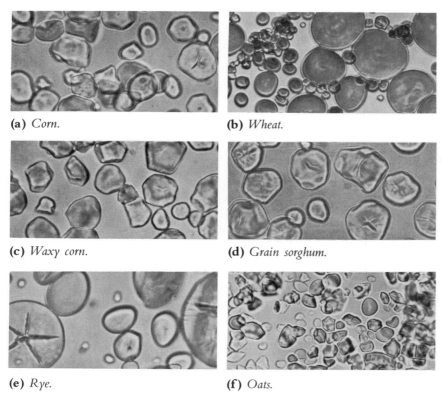

(a) *Corn.* **(b)** *Wheat.*

(c) *Waxy corn.* **(d)** *Grain sorghum.*

(e) *Rye.* **(f)** *Oats.*

20-1 *Ungelatinized starch granules (magnified 500 times). (a) Corn (b) wheat (c) waxy corn (d) grain sorghum (e) rye (f) oats. (Matz, Samual,* The Chemistry and Technology of Cereals as Food and Feed, *1959, p. 570. Courtesy of the Avi Publishing Company, Inc.)*

immediately upon being heated, but gradually increases in viscosity and translucency as the temperature rises. A starch mixture will start to thicken somewhere between 165 and 190°F (74 and 88°C), but complete gelatinization does not occur until the mixture is close to or at the boiling point. This will vary with the type of starch and size of the starch grain. Potatoes, waxy corn, and tapioca thicken at much lower temperatures than do regular corn and wheat starch. The increase in the viscosity of the heated starch mixture is caused by the action of the enlarged starch granules bumping against each other, trapping the water and inhibiting its free flow. Once a starch mixture has reached the temperature at which gelatinization takes place, the mixture need only be held at that temperature until the flavor of the uncooked starch has disappeared. Usually, this occurs only a few minutes after gelatinization. Completely gelatinized starch should not be stirred unless necessary, since the swollen grains are easily broken. Broken grains and fragments will thin out the mixture. As a cooked starch mixture cools, there is a marked increase in the stiffness of the gel formed. This is due to the decrease in kinetic energy, which keeps the molecules from reassociating. There is also a loss in translucency as the amylose recrystallizes. Starches that do not gel, such as tapioca and waxy cornstarch, do not lose their translucency and remain clear because of the lack of amylose.

The thickening power of starch makes it a very valuable material for preparing food products that require some agent to change a predominantly liquid mixture into a solid form. Cornstarch puddings, cream sauces, and gravies are foods prepared by the use of the various starches.

In using starch to thicken a food mixture, it is important to know the proportion of starch that should be used to obtain the desired thickness in a given amount of liquid. Equal substitutions of one starch for another cannot be made, for the different starches have different thickening powers. Flour and cornstarch are the two starches most commonly used to thicken puddings and gravies. To thicken gravies, sauces, and soups, flour is most frequently used; for puddings and fruit juices, cornstarch gives an excellent product.

Pregelatinized starches are used in such food products as instant puddings and pie fillings. These processed starches are subjected to heat treatment, which results in the breaking up of the large swollen starch granules into smaller particles. When the pregelatinized starch mixture is heated, the fragmented or smaller particles become hydrated and increase the viscosity of the mixture. However, the mixture does not become as viscous as when the hydrated starch granules have not been subjected to heat. Hence, a greater weight of pregelatinized starch than of untreated starch of the same kind is used for the same viscosity.

Principle of Cooking Starches. When starch is cooked, the goal is to obtain the full value of its thickening power. This can be accomplished only when there is sufficient heat and water to hydrate the starch granule. Heating the starch mixture above the gelatinization temperature results in the continued swelling of the granule. The granule becomes very swollen and fragile, making its movement past the other starch grains difficult. The mixture is viscous and translucent at this state, approximately 194–203°F (90–95°C) for wheat starch. When the mixture cools, it forms a gel. The gel may be thought of as an interlacing network of the polysaccharides amylopectin and amylose, and water molecules held together by intermolecular bonds. Tapioca is an exception; since it gelatinizes at a much lower temperature, heating it to high temperatures decreases its viscosity rather than increases it.

Lumping. When dry starch is mixed with warm or hot water, the exterior portion of the starch granules becomes sticky and the granules cling together in lumps. Heating does not help to separate the granules; once formed, the lumps tend to remain intact. If one of these lumps is broken open, raw starch is found inside. Lump formation may be prevented in three ways. The first method is to create a slurry of the flour in cold water which has the desired consistency of the final product. The slurry is added to the hot liquid wth continuous stirring. The second way consists of surrounding and separating the flour with a fat. This fat–flour mixture is cooked briefly over moderate heat to decrease the taste of raw starch and liquid is then added. The last method, used in making puddings, is to separate the starch grains with sugar. The blending of the starch with sugar, liquid, or fat must be complete to achieve a smooth mixture.

Effect of Sugar and Acids. Sugar has a tenderizing effect on a starch gel. If it is not used in extreme amounts, it will also protect the swollen starch grains from rupturing from mechanical damage such as stirring. This keeps the starch paste thick. In a study on behavior of starch during cooking, it was found that concentrations of 20% or higher of all sugars or syrups used caused decreases in gel strength of the starch paste.[1] If too much sugar is used, the starch gel will lose its gelatinized structure and turn into a thick runny mass. It has been suggested that this change of viscosity results from competition of the sugar for the liquid, which lowers the amount available for the swelling of the starch.

When acids are cooked with a starch mixture, they have the effect of decreasing the thickening power of the starch. In the presence of an acid, some of the starch granules are broken down into smaller particles, and the reduced starch particles have less thickening power. To avoid this, such mixtures as lemon puddings and other acid-containing starch mixtures are more satisfactorily prepared if the starch and liquid mixture is cooked and thickened before the acid is added. It should be noted, however, that a too-soft or "runny" lemon pie filling may be caused by the degree of coagulation of the egg ingredient rather than by the thickening effect of the starch.[2]

Another theory suggests that the high sugar concentration of a lemon pie filling retards the swelling of the starch, resulting in insufficient cooking and a too-thin filling.[3]

Effect of Dry Heat. Dry heat also brings changes to starch granules through a process known as *dextrinization*. If starch or a product containing starch is subjected to dry heat, carbohydrate compounds called *dextrins* are formed. When these substances are dissolved in water, they have a sweet taste. Slow toasting of bread and toasting of commercially prepared breakfast cereals will change a portion of the starch to dextrins.

The flavor developed in foods by the formation of dextrins is highly pleasing. This is well illustrated in the crusts formed on baked breads and in the crusty exterior of baked vegetables. The appealing flavor and color of brown gravies are, in part, also the result of dextrinization of starch. If extensive dextrinization of flour occurs, as in browning of flour, the thickening power of the flour is lessened.

Retrogradation. After a starch gel has cooled or chilled, the starch becomes less soluble and recrystallizes. This is known as *retrogradation* of starch. It is more likely to occur in starches with a high proportion of amylose. Amylopectin does not gel when cooled. This can be used to advantage when thickened but not gummy or gelled liquid is desired, as in fruit toppings or pies. Amylopectin starches are used in commercial sauces and pie thickeners to avoid the retrogradation problem. Retrogradation of a starch gel is greatly accelerated by freezing. When a starch gel is thawed, water is lost because it is unable to rebind to the fragile spongy mass. Because of this, frozen products that require thickened sauces or gravies are prepared with starch or flour from a waxy cereal (waxy corn, sorghum, or rice). When a cooled starch gel that has been standing for a while is cut, there is a leakage of liquid. This leakage is called syneresis, or weeping.

Modified Starches. A modified starch has been treated with chemicals, resulting in starches that have suitable properties for use in the food industry. Acids used to treat starches bring about granule disintegration and a corresponding lowered viscosity; however, the gel that is formed is rigid. Some starches are modified (oxidized starches) by treatment with sodium hypochlorite, which is used in place of an acid. The results are similar, but the oxidized starch yields a less rigid gel. Cross-bonded starches are made by reacting starch suspensions with phosphorous oxychloride or water-soluble metaphosphates.

[1] M. L. Bean and E. Osmon, "Behavior of Starch During Food Preparation," *J. Food Res.* **24:**665, 1959.

[2] H. J. Neilson, J. D. Hewitt, and N. K. Fitch, "Factors Influencing Consistency of a Lemon Pie Filling," *J. Home Econ.* **44:**782–785, 1952.

[3] A. M. Campbell and A. M. Briant, "Wheat Starch Pastes and Gels Containing Citric Acid and Glucose," *J. Food Res.* **22:**358, 1957.

The cross-linked waxy starches are used for thickening in frozen food products because of their stability in an acid medium and their lack of gel formation. These are used in prepared fruit pie fillings and salad dressings.

Pregelatinized starches are used in packaged "instant" puddings and cream pie fillings. A pregelatinized starch has been precooked and hot-roller-dried. Natural and modified starches can be pregelatinized. A product made with pregelatinized starch has a different texture than those made with the raw starch of the same kind.

METHODS OF PREPARING STARCH DISHES

White Sauce. White sauce is the basis for many frequently prepared foods such as cream sauces, soufflés, croquettes, and scalloped dishes. White sauce is a mixture of flour and milk, with some fat added for flavor. When cooked, it has the consistency of cream. Sometimes cream is substituted for part of the milk. This fact and the cooked appearance of the finished white sauce account for its often being called a *cream sauce.*

A white sauce is thick, with a smooth satiny appearance free of lumps. The taste is pleasant and without any suggestion of uncooked starch. The consistency depends on the proportion of thickening material to liquid used. Different thicknesses of sauces are required for different food products (Table 20-1). Thus, a sauce used in a cream soup is generally in the proportion of 1 tbsp flour to 1 cup of milk and is called a thin white sauce. Creamed and scalloped dishes usually require a medium white sauce; croquettes and soufflés, a sauce thick enough to bind the other materials.

The goal in making white sauce is to combine the flour with the liquid and fat so that a smooth, creamy mixture results. The lumping of starch grains in a white sauce is the most common cause of an unpalatable product. To avoid this, the starch grains must be separated before they are heated, lest the heat penetrate unevenly and thus cause the starch granules to stick together. There are a number of ways to separate the starch granules in the making of white sauce. In the first method, if as much fat as starch is used, melted fat or a liquid fat is used to separate the grains. The starch (usually flour) is stirred into the fat until a stiff paste is formed. To this the hot liquid is added, and the mixture, called a *roux,* is cooked until it is thick and smooth. Cooking can be done directly over the heat or over boiling water in the top of a double boiler. Or cold liquid may be used as the separating material. The cold liquid and starch are mixed together to form a paste and heated, and the fat is added just after the sauce thickens. Another method consists of heating the milk and fat in the top of the double boiler, leaving out a small portion of the cold liquid to mix with the starch. The mixture of starch and cold milk is added to the hot mixture as it is stirred constantly. (The first method described is used most frequently

TABLE 20-1
Proportions for Starchy Sauces

Sauce	Liquid (1 cup)	Thickening Agent (tbsp)	Fat (tbsp)	Seasonings	Uses
Thin white	Milk or thin cream	1	1	Salt	Cream soups
Medium white	Milk or thin cream	2	2	Salt	Creamed dishes
Thick white	Milk or thin cream	3	3	Salt	Soufflés
Very thick white	Milk or thin cream	4–5	4	Salt	Croquettes
Brown	Water, meat, or vegetable stock	1–3 (browned flour)	1–3	Salt, pepper	Meat sauces, gravies
Sweet	Cream, milk, or fruit juice	1–1½ (cornstarch) or 2–4 (flour)		Salt, sugar, extracts	Puddings, sauces

because it produces a white sauce of fine flavor and good consistency.) Instant-blending flours on the market combine readily with liquids and have been recommended for use in making sauces.

Gravies. Gravies are prepared in a similar manner to a medium white sauce. The starch is separated by coating with meat fat or by suspending it in cold water to make a slurry. Gravy is different from white sauce in using meat drippings (which may be diluted with hot water) as the liquid rather than milk. Comparison of the two methods has shown that the *roux* method results in a thicker product.[4] If the meat drippings are somewhat sparse, hot chicken or beef bouillon cubes can be added to increase the flavor. A dark brown color can be achieved by the addition of a commercial gravy color additive.

Cream Soups. Cream soups are thin white sauces to which vegetable juices, vegetable purée, or pieces of meat, poultry, or fish are added. Freshly prepared, canned, frozen, or leftover foods may be used to prepare a great variety of these highly nutritious and palatable soups. The steps followed in making cream soups are few and vary only slightly. Usually, equal parts of solid pulp and thin white sauce are combined, heated, seasoned to individual taste, garnished in numerous ways, and served hot. If a starchy vegetable pulp is used, the amount of flour used in the white sauce may be reduced, but it can never be omitted entirely because it surrounds the fat globules and helps to keep them from precipitating out and settling on top of the mixture. The vegetables preferred for cream soups are potatoes, tomatoes, celery, cauliflower, spinach, corn, and green beans. Special attention must be given to the making of cream of tomato soup, perhaps the most popular of all cream soups, because the acid of the tomatoes tends to curdle the proteins in the milk. A good method of preventing curdling is to thicken the tomato juice or purée as well as the milk and to add the thickened tomato juice to the thin white sauce

very slowly, stirring constantly. This soup must be served immediately. A few other vegetables—namely, asparagus, stringbeans, peas, and carrots—also cause some small separation (curdling) of the white sauce. Usually, such vegetables as cabbage, spinach, and cauliflower can be used in cream soups and no curdling occurs.[5]

The acceptable standard for all cream soups includes a creamy consistency, a smooth and uniform texture, and the pleasant characteristic flavor of the vegetable, fish, or meat used in its preparation.

Puddings. Milk or fruit juice thickened with a starchy material forms the main ingredient in a number of very popular desserts. Cornstarch, rice, tapioca, cornmeal, and sago are frequently used for this purpose. These must be added in different proportions when used to thicken a mixture; therefore, it is more practicable to discuss the different dessert products separately. However, for general use it might be helpful to keep in mind that 1 tbsp of flour is equivalent to about one-half the amount of cornstarch, potato starch, rice starch, or arrowroot starch or to 2 tsp quick tapioca.

CORNSTARCH PUDDING. In making a cornstarch pudding, as in making a white sauce, it is necessary to separate the granules of starch before they are added to the liquid. A simple solution to this, if equal quantities of cornstarch and sugar are used, is to mix the two before the hot liquid is added. Otherwise, it is best to mix the starch with a little cold liquid before adding it to the hot liquid. The amount of starch can be varied according to the consistency desired. The standard proportion of cornstarch to milk that will produce a suitable consistency for molding is 1½ to 2 tbsp cornstarch to 1 cup liquid. To this, 2 tbsp sugar is added. Starch puddings flavored with vanilla are known as *blancmanges*. For a chocolate pudding, between ½ and 1 square of chocolate to 1 cup milk is used. Cocoa may be used as a substitute for chocolate. Chocolate is heated with the milk, and cocoa is added to the sugar and cornstarch. When cocoa and chocolate are used, only the minimum amount of cornstarch need be added because the flavoring ma-

---

[4] H. B. Trimbo and B. S. Miller, "Factors Affecting the Quality of Sauces (Gravies)," *J. Home Econ.* **63**:48, 1971.

[5] Belle Lowe, *Experimental Cookery,* 4th ed. (New York: Wiley, 1955), p. 311.

terials themselves contain starch. Egg yolks are sometimes used as part of the thickening for these puddings; beaten egg whites may be added to the mixture to give it a light fluffy texture.

Cornstarch puddings may be cooked until thick over direct heat or over very hot water. If cooked over a direct flame, the mixture will need constant stirring to keep it smooth as it thickens. After the mixture has thickened, it should be cooked over hot water for 5–10 minutes to improve the flavor.

Other than cornstarch and flour, tapioca, rice, and cornmeal are the thickening materials most used in preparing desserts that are essentially thickened liquids.

TAPIOCA. Tapioca, like cornstarch and flour, is bland in flavor and is usually combined with other materials for variety and interest. In the manufacture of tapioca, the tuberous roots of manioc (cassava) are ground and the starch is removed from the fiber and dried. In the preparation of this product, some of the starch granules are ruptured when heated, partly cooking the product. Tapioca can be purchased in pearl and granule forms. Pearl tapioca is in the form of round balls of various sizes. Granulated tapioca is known as "minute" tapioca.

Pearl tapioca takes longer to cook than the granular product (which has been specially treated to allow shorter cooking periods), and the large pearl tapioca may need to be soaked before it is cooked. Tapioca products are used either to thicken fruit fillings for pies or to thicken liquids in puddings. Added to water or a fruit juice, tapioca makes a clear liquid.

Tapioca fruit puddings are prepared by pouring the partly cooked tapioca over the fruit (whole, crushed, or sliced). Sugar and seasonings are added, and the mixture is baked or cooked until the flavor of the raw starch has disappeared. Tapioca custards differ from fruit tapiocas in that they contain milk and eggs. This product is called a *tapioca cream*.

OTHER PUDDINGS. One of the most famous of all thickened milk puddings is rice pudding, which is a mixture of one part of rice to about eight parts milk. To these ingredients, sugar, flavoring, raisins, and occasionally eggs are added. The mixture may be baked in the oven for several hours (the preferred method) or cooked in the top of a double boiler until thick. Another famous, typically American pudding is Indian pudding, a mixture of milk and cornmeal with molasses and spices added.

Bread pudding may be classified as a starch-thickened pudding because of the high content of wheat starch in the bread. It is prepared very much as rice pudding is. The flavoring ingredients are frequently varied for interest. Leftover cake may be used as a substitute for bread in this type of pudding.

SUMMARY

Various starches are used in food preparation, including cornstarch, rice starch, wheat starch (flour), tapioca starch, potato starch, and sago starch. Because of their thickening power, they are used in soups, sauces, puddings, and other foods. To avoid lumping, dry starch is usually first mixed with cold water to form a paste. Sufficient heat and moisture then secure the maximum thickening of the starch. Sugar and acids tenderize a starch gel. Methods of preparing starch dishes vary according to the characteristics of the other ingredients.

QUESTIONS AND TOPICS FOR DISCUSSION AND STUDY

1. What causes a starch paste to thicken as it cooks?
2. Why do starch lumps form in cooked mixtures?
3. Why does the cornstarch settle out of a mixture of cold water and starch?
4. Why is a starch mixture cooked beyond the point at which it thickens?

SUGGESTED ACTIVITIES

1. Prepare white sauces using various forms of milk—nonfat dried milk solids, whole fluid milk, homogenized milk, and evaporated milk. Compare the sauces for flavor, texture, and consistency. Use the sauces to prepare a cream of vegetable soup.
2. Prepare vanilla, chocolate, and butterscotch cornstarch puddings. Compare results for flavor and appearance with those of a corresponding pudding mix.

235

REFERENCES

BOOKS

Paul, Pauline, and Helen Palmer. *Food Theory and Applications.* New York: Wiley, 1972, Chap. 4.

ARTICLES

Elbert, Elizabeth. "Starch: Changes During Heating in the Presence of Moisture." *J. Home Econ.* **57:**197, 1965.

————, and Robert L. Witt. "Gelatinization of Starch in the Common Day Pea, *Phaseolus vulgaris.*" *J. Home Econ.* **60:**186, 1968.

Hood, L. F., and A. S. Seifried. "Microstructure of Modified Tapioca Starch Milk Gels." *J. Food Sci.* **39:**117, 1974.

————"Effect of Frozen Storage on the Microstructure and Syneresis of Modified Tapioca Starch–Milk Gels."*J. Food. Sci.* **39:**121, 1974.

Trimbo, Henry, and Byron Miller. "Factors affecting the Quality of Sauces (Gravies)." *J. Home Econ.* **63:**48, 1971.

Eggs

Eggs and egg products constitute an important part of family meals. The economic importance of the egg to agriculture and industry, its multiple uses in the preparation of many food products, and its excellent nutritive qualities have stimulated scientific scrutiny into the nature of the egg.

STRUCTURE AND COMPOSITION

The egg is composed of a living center surrounded by large amounts of food substances, The whole protected by several membranes. The chief parts of the egg are the *yolk,* the *albumen* (the white), and the *shell* and *shell membranes* (Fig. 21-1).

The yolk is the life center of the egg. Its uppermost surface, the *blastoderm,* is the germinative portion of the fertilized egg. (In the unfertilized egg, the *blastodisk* is the corresponding structure.) The yolk is the nutritive material that supports the growth of the embryo. It is located near the center of the egg and, in fresh eggs, tends to rise to the top of the albumen that surrounds it. The albumen is a clear, viscous material with a greenish-yellow cast caused by the pigment ovoflavin. The albumen is surrounded by two shell membranes firmly cemented to each other—except at the blunt end of the egg, where an air cell intervenes between the two membranes. At each end of the yolk is a ropelike structure called the *chalaza,* anchoring the yolk to the membranes surrounding the albumen. The shell of the hen's egg is porous, translucent, and hard, and consists almost wholly of calcium carbonate.

Water in the egg is the medium in which the chemical and physical changes take place. The proteins found in the egg yolk are mainly conjugated proteins. A conjugated protein combines a simple protein and a nonprotein group such as phosphoric acid. Vitellin is a phosphoprotein; livetin is a sulfur-containing protein. The proteins in the egg white are in the form of simple proteins and glycoproteins (proteins combined with sugars). Ovalbumin, ovoconalbumin, and ovoglobulin are the simple proteins, whereas ovomucoid and ovomucin are conjugated proteins containing a carbohydrate group.

The proteins include a small amount of the protein, avidin, which binds biotin and makes it unavailable. However avidin is inactivated by heat.

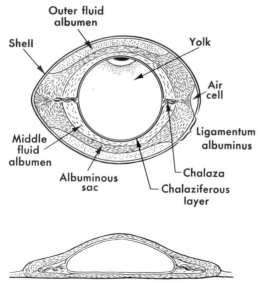

21-1 *The gross structure of an egg, after Romanoff,* Food Res., **8:***286, 1943.* (*Courtesy of* Food Research, now Journal of Food Science)

The carbohydrate content of eggs is in the form of glucose, mannose, and galactose. The fatlike substances of the egg are concentrated in the yolk. Frequently referred to as *lipids,* these fatlike materials are in the form of true fats, or glycerides, and compounds made up of fat and another material (such as phosphorus, nitrogen, or sugar). Cholesterol, which is contained in the yolk, is kept in a colloidal state by the naturally occurring emulsifier lecithin.

Pigments. The egg yolk contains orange, red, and yellow pigments that belong to the carotenoid group. Carotenoid pigments derive from carotenoid-rich plants, such as yellow corn, green grass, and alfalfa. If the hen is allowed access to these plant foods, the yolks will be darker in color. These pigments are related to vitamin A, and large amounts of vitamin A in the hen's feed will increase the level of vitamin A in the yolk. Although the egg yolk contains a number of pigments, the egg white contains only ovoflavin.

The carotenoids are by far the most important pigments of the yolk, but others derive from the feed consumed by the hen. The occurrence of other color pigments will reduce the marketability of the egg. The presence of a green pig-

ment in the egg yolk results in an olive-colored yolk. This may be brought about by gossypol, a toxic constituent in the cottonseed meal fed to chickens, and by unidentified substances in alfalfa. Pimiento pepper contains the pigment capsanthin, which when fed to hens yields an egg yolk of red-orange color. To some degree, the riboflavin content of the egg white reflects the amount of riboflavin in the diet of the hen.

Minerals. Calcium is the most abundant mineral in the whole egg, but it is concentrated in the shell. Phosphorus is the most abundant mineral in the yolk, with calcium, magnesium, chlorine, potassium, sodium, sulfur, and iron contributing small but significant amounts of ash to the total mineral content of the yolk. In the egg white, sulfur, potassium, sodium, and chlorine are present in the greatest amounts, and phosphorus, calcium, magnesium, and iron are found in much smaller amounts. It should be noted, however, that eggs are considered an important source of iron in the American diet.[1] Most of the iron is found in the yolk. The sulfur in the egg white causes the dark stains of silver sulfide that appear on silver utensils that come in contact with it. There is a strong relationship between the mineral content of the hen's diet and the concentration of minerals in the egg.

ECONOMIC ASPECTS

Most of the eggs marketed as food are infertile. Although fertile eggs are marketed as food, the quality of such eggs suffers in consequence of embryo development. In the United States, White Leghorns, Plymouth Rocks, New Hampshires, and Rhode Island Reds are the egg-producing breeds. Other breeds are used for meat.

Size and Color. The factors that affect egg size are the size of the hen, the age at which she commences laying, the season of year, the temperature of her environment, and the nature of her feed. The color of the egg shell is related to the breed of the hen; there is *no* connection between the color and the quality of an egg. The

[1] F. A. Johnston, "Iron Content of Eggs," *J. Amer. Dietet. Assoc.* **32:**644, 1956.

color of the shell, however, assumes economic importance in areas where consumers show a marked preference for one color rather than another. Because the color of the shell has no relationship to the egg's nutritive value, there is no reason to pay a premium price for a particular color.

Breeding experiments have demonstrated that egg quality is determined to a large extent by inheritance; hence, the elimination of low-quality layers will improve the quality of the total egg crop.[2] It has also been found that the nutrients in eggs can be increased to some extent by adding nutrients to the hen's ration.[3]

Because the price of eggs varies from one season to another, it is important to compare the prices of different-sized eggs in the same grade or same-sized eggs in different grades (Table 21-1). The U.S. Department of Agriculture suggests that for eggs of the same grade, if there is less than 7 cents difference between the sizes, it is more economical to buy the larger size.

Occasionally, blood spots will be found in graded eggs when they are broken open (Table 21-2). These are usually caused by the rupture of a blood vessel during egg formation. Approximately 1% of all eggs will have these blood spots, which are usually detected and removed during grading. However, when the egg is very fresh, it is more difficult to detect this flaw and it may go undetected. Although these flaws may

be objectionable to the consumer, in most cases it is not necessary that the egg be discarded.

Measuring the Quality of a Broken-Out Egg. For experimental purposes, there are two methods used to judge the quality of a broken-out egg: the eye-scoring method and the conversion of the height of the white (or the yolk) into an index number.

The eye-scoring method involves breaking an egg onto a flat surface and comparing it with a set of pictures. The egg is then given the score of the egg picture it most nearly matches. The two charts used for this type of quality scoring are the U.S. Department of Agriculture Chart and the Van Wagener chart (Cornell chart).[4]

If the index method is used, the height of the thickest portion of the white or yolk—whichever is being measured—is divided by the diameter of the egg (Fig. 21-2). This measure gives the yolk index or the thick white index.

BUYING EGGS

Sorting. Eggs are sorted by size and quality. The practice of sorting and grading the eggs is a desirable one for the consumer, for classification provides some indication of the internal quality of the egg. To grade eggs, a candling device is used that enables an observer to see through the egg. The broad end of the egg is held up to an opening in the device. Behind the opening, there is a strong light bulb. As the egg is rotated, the

---

[2] A. Brant and L. Shrader, "How to Measure EGG IQ," *PA202,* (Washington, D.C.: Bureau of Animal Industry, U.S. Department of Agriculture, 1952).

[3] R. E. Hodgson, "Livestock Production," in *Food: The Yearbook of Agriculture* (Washington, D.C.: U.S. Department of Agriculture, 1959), p. 334.

[4] Available from Service Press, Inc., Hartford, Conn.

TABLE 21-1
Economical Cost of Eggs

Price/Dozen[a]	Price/Pound	Cost/2-Egg Serving
60	40	10
69	46	11.5
78	52	13
90	60	15
99	66	16.5

[a]Large eggs weighing 24 oz/dozen.
Source: J. C. White, "Texas Eggs," *TAP-B75* (Austin, Tex.: Texas Department of Agriculture, 1975).

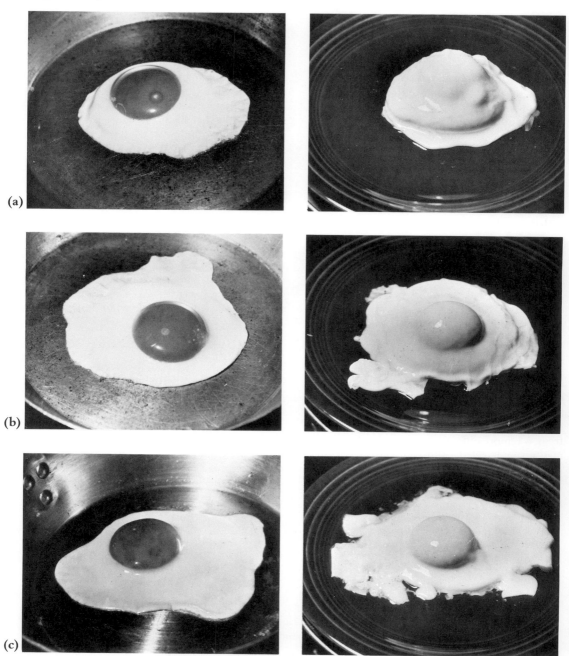

21-2 *Standards for quality for each of three grades of eggs. On left are fried eggs; on right, poached. (a) Grade AA—quality covers a small area, the white is very thick and stands high, and the yolk is firm and well centered. (b) Grade A quality covers a moderate area, the white is reasonably thick, and stands fairly high, the yolk is firm, high, and well centered. (c) Grade B quality covers a wide area, has a small amount of thick white, the yolk is somewhat flattened, enlarged and off center. (Courtesy U.S. Department of Agriculture)*

TABLE 21-2
Egg Flaws

Flaw	Causes	Use in Cookery
Blood clot (mostly on the surface of the yolk)	Rupture of a small blood vessel while the egg is being formed	Small blood clots can be easily removed and the egg used for general cookery
Bloody egg	Large blood clot covers most of the white, giving it a pink appearance	Unfit for consumption
Meat spot	Tissue from the oviduct enclosed within the shell during egg formation	Small meat spots can be removed and the egg used for general cookery
Large meat spot	Large piece of tissue from the ovary or oviduct encloses in the shell during formation	Unfit for consumption
Body check	Shell appears to have been cracked while in the uterus before shell completely formed	Weakened shell only; the egg may be used for general cooking
Black rot	Usually occurs in eggs with advanced embryo development; decomposed egg contents are gray or black in color	Unfit for consumption
Olive-colored yolk	Caused by the hen's eating Shepherd's purse, a barnyard weed; some discoloration of this kind may be caused by cottonseed meal in the hen's ration	Can be used for general cooking if discoloration is not too great
Black or grayish areas	Mold developments within the egg shell or along cracks in the shell	Unfit for consumption
Crusted yolk	Advanced deterioration (the yolk is covered with a light crust, the egg has a putrid odor when opened)	Unfit for consumption

light passes through the egg, enabling the observer to see its contents. Candling reveals the quality of shell, air cell, yolk, white, and germ. Eggs with thin, porous, or cracked shells are easily identified and separated from sound eggs. (In good marketing practice, cracked eggs are not packed with sound eggs for shipping.) The air cell should be fixed in position with no tendency to bubble or to move about. A bubbly air cell may be an indication of staleness or a weak membrane. In a fresh egg, the yolk is seen only as a slight shadow. In an egg of poor quality, the yolk moves more freely and casts a darker shadow because it floats nearer the shell. In a top-quality egg, the egg white is firm, clear, and so viscous that it holds the yolk firmly in place. Any germ development in an egg takes it out of the high-quality grade; the greater the germ development, the lower the quality.

GRADES AND WEIGHTS

U.S. Department of Agriculture grades AA, A, and B for eggs describe egg quality (see Fig. 21-3). Grade AA eggs are the best-quality eggs for all purposes. The height of the egg as well as the firm centering of the yolk gives the egg a superior appearance. The thick egg white is best for poaching, frying, and cooking in the shell. Grade A eggs are not as satisfactory for poaching but are still excellent for frying and cooking purposes. If the appearance of the egg does not matter, as in blended cooked foods or scrambled eggs, grade B eggs are generally the best buy. Regardless of the grade, the nutritive value of the egg remains the same. These grades may be applied to any of the size or weight categories of eggs, which are Jumbo, Extra Large, Large, Medium, Small, and Peewee (Table 21-3).

TABLE 21-3
Sizes and Weight of Eggs

Classification	Minimum Weight (oz)
Jumbo	30
Extra Large	27
Large	24
Medium	21
Small	18
Peewee	15

21-3 *U.S. grade label for eggs. (Courtesy of U.S. Department of Agriculture)*

These weight categories represent minimum weights/dozen, which are, respectively, 30, 27, 24, 21, 18 and 15 oz/dozen (Fig. 21-4). Jumbo and Peewee eggs are normally not found in the average supermarket. Recipes are based on medium-size eggs. If smaller or larger eggs are substituted in a recipe, adjustments must be made for size differences to maintain the quality of the product.

The grade and size of eggs may be marked directly on the carton, or on a sticker, or on the tape sealing the carton (Fig. 21-5). Although quality and size are both marked on the carton, one is not related to the other. Eggs of any size may be of any grade.

Table 21-4 gives the standards for quality of grades of eggs. The Haugh unit given in the tables indicates the height of the thick white.

The Egg Products Inspection Act. The Egg Products Inspection Act became law in 1970. It assures wholesome, unadulterated, and truthfully labeled egg products for the consumer and restricts the use of certain types of shell eggs. It provides for the mandatory continuous inspection of plants processing egg products, whether shipping in intrastate, interstate, or foreign com-

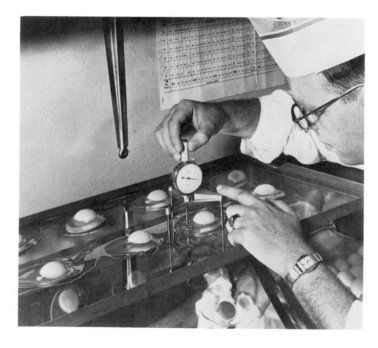

21-4 *One method of determining interior egg quality is by the break-out test shown here. Height of egg white is measured. (Courtesy of U.S. Department of Agriculture)*

21-5 *U.S. weight classes for eggs, showing the minimum weight per dozen for each size. (Courtesy of U.S. Department of Agriculture)*

merce. The act requires that certain types of restricted eggs (incubator rejects and inedible, loss, or leakage eggs) be destroyed to prevent their use as human food and that checked and dirty eggs be shipped to an official egg products plant where proper segregation and disposition can be made by an official inspector. It also requires that imported egg products be inspected and meet the same requirements as domestic egg products. Imported shell eggs are also controlled.

The act provides for cooperation with State governments to carry out its provisions. State standards for shell eggs must be no different from Federal standards. The law is administered by the Poultry Division, Consumer and Marketing Service, United States Department of Agriculture.

HOME CARE

Eggs subjected to varying temperatures deteriorate far more quickly than eggs held at a constant temperature. For best quality, only eggs that have been refrigerated should be bought and they should be kept refrigerated until used. For best quality eggs should be used within 1 week of purchase. Egg cartons may be used to hold eggs in the refrigerator. They should be placed so that the broad ends of the eggs are up, thus preventing movement of the air cell up toward the yolk. Because eggs pick up odors and flavors from other foods, they should be kept covered in the carton to prevent absorption of off-flavors.[5] The normal flavor of the hen's egg is bland and any off-flavor is immediately noticeable. The hen herself, the environment, the feed, or the exposure of the egg to unusual odors are all contributing factors to taints which may be absorbed through the egg shell.

If the egg has been broken (Fig. 21-6) and

[5] Alexander MacLeod and S. Jane Cave, "Absorption of a Taint by Eggs," *J. Food Sci.* **42**:539, 1977.

TABLE 21-4
Summary of United States Standards for Quality of Individual Shell Eggs
(Specifications for Each Quality Factor)

Quality Factor	AA Quality	A Quality	B Quality
Shell	Clean; unbroken; practically normal	Clean; unbroken; practically normal	Clean to very slightly stained; unbroken; may be slightly abnormal
Air cell	$\frac{1}{8}$ in. or less in depth; practically regular	$\frac{3}{16}$ in. or less in depth; practically regular	$\frac{3}{8}$ in. or less in depth; may be free or bubbly
White	Clear; firm (72 Haugh units or higher)	Clear; may be reasonably firm (60–71 Haugh units)	Clear; may be slightly weak (31–59 Haugh units)[a]
Yolk	Outline slightly defined; practically free from defects	Outline may be fairly well defined; practically free from defects	Outline may be well defined; may be slightly enlarged and flattened; may show definite but not serious defects

[a]If they are small (aggregating not more than ⅛ in. in diameter).
Source: "Shell Egg Grading and Inspection of Egg Products," *Marketing Bulletin 30* (Washington, D.C.: U.S. Department of Agriculture, 1964).

21-6 *Steps in separating whites from yolks of eggs. (a) Crack the egg with the sharp edge of a knife. (b) Hold it over a small bowl or dish and break the egg apart. (c) Let most of the white drain into the bowl, keeping the yolk in the lower part of the shell. (d) Put the yolk in a separate bowl. (Courtesy of American Egg Board)*

only part of it used, leftover raw eggs yolks or whites may be stored in the refrigerator. Leftover whites may be stored covered for no more than 2–4 days. Egg yolks should be covered with oil and used within a day or two. Eggs should not be washed. The shells are porous but the pores are usually filled with organic material that prevents the invasion of microorganisms.[6]

[6] D. V. Vedehra, "Bacterial Penetration of Eggs," *Food Life Sci. Quart.* **5:**9, 1972.

PRINCIPLES OF EGG COOKERY

The basic principle of egg cookery centers around the ability of the proteins in both the yolk and the white to coagulate when heated. The thickening or coagulation of an egg mixture is brought about because protein molecules attract and hold about them large quantities of water. Solid particles held suspended in a liquid result in a gel formation. This quality of eggs makes them usable for thickening such food products as custards and puddings, and for coating food materials.

Because the proteins of the egg yolk differ from those of the white, the temperatures at which they coagulate differ, too. However, temperatures no higher than 165°F (74°C) will thicken both white and yolk. Undiluted egg white, when heated slowly, will coagulate at about 145–148°F (61–64°C). Egg yolk begins to thicken at a temperature close to 158°F (70°C).

Coagulation of Egg Proteins. When heat is applied, the egg white changes from a transparent viscous mass to a soft, white, opaque material. If the heating of the white continues past the optimum coagulation temperature of 148°F (64°C), the white becomes tough and porous. Excessively high temperatures cause the egg white to lose water, shrink, and toughen. Because of its fat content, undiluted egg yolk has less tendency to toughen; rather, it becomes crumbly in texture when heated beyond the optimum temperature. In cookery, egg proteins are often mixed with other food materials. In these instances, the egg mixture will coagulate at a different temperature than the whole or separate parts of the undiluted egg. Coagulation temperature will depend on the concentration or dilution of the egg and the kind of materials added. Dilution of egg protein raises the temperature at which a mixture thickens, and concentration of the egg protein lowers it.

Sugar. The addition of sugar to an egg mixture elevates the temperature at which coagulation takes place; the more sugar, the greater the heat required to bring about coagulation.

Salt. The addition of salt to an egg mixture lowers the temperature at which it coagulates. In a typical egg mixture, curdling may result from stirring the protein gel; hence, it is better to add salt to the mixture before heating.

Acid. Any acid material added to an egg mixture will produce a firmer gel and lower the coagulation temperature of the mixture. Prolonged heating of an acid egg mixture, however, will bring about *peptization* (a term used to indicate the breaking up of large aggregates of mol-

ecules into smaller ones) of the protein and a corresponding thinning out of the mass. This action—the acid dispersion of protein—is swift and accounts for the thinning out of cooked salad dressings and pie fillings to which acid has been added.

Starch. Some food mixtures, such as cream pie fillings and cooked salad dressings, make use of the coagulation of egg proteins and the gelatinization of starch to bring about the thickening of the mixture. Because the coagulation and gelatinization temperatures of the eggs and starch differ, it is best to bring the starch mixture to its maximum thickness before adding the uncooked egg.

USES OF EGGS IN COOKERY

Binding and Coating. Egg used in such food mixtures as meat loaf or croquettes is distributed through the mixture. Upon heating, the proteins coagulate, binding the food into a cohesive mass of a desired form. This is why croquettes, for example, retain their shape during the cooking process.

Frequently, an outer coating of flour, bread crumbs, cereal, or batter is added to a food to enhance its appearance, texture, or flavor. An egg batter provides a binder for added coatings.

Leavening. A foam is created when egg white is beaten. The foam is made up of air bubbles surrounded by a thin, elastic film of egg white. When the foam is incorporated into a mixture, it provides leavening for such products as omelets, soufflés, sponge cakes, and meringues. When these products are heated, the air bubbles expand and the egg white film hardens. The volume of egg yolk increases when beaten, but the presence of fat in the yolk makes its foaming power considerably lower than that of the egg white.

Egg White Foam. Egg white foams are used in many foods to make them light and porous. An egg white foam is a colloid of bubbles of air surrounded by part of the albumen that has been denatured by the beating of the egg white. The denatured albumen is stiff and gives stability to the foam. As egg white is beaten it loses its elasticity, but some elasticity is necessary in an egg white foam used in such dishes as soufflés and cakes so that the air cells can expand without breaking down the cell walls. This expansion occurs in the heated oven before the albumen becomes rigid.

The addition of sugar to egg white makes a stable, smooth foam—one that will not collapse and drain quickly. Although more beating is required when sugar is added, a sugared egg white foam is less likely to be overbeaten than egg white alone. A more stable foam is formed when sugar is added early in the beating process, for overbeating the egg white before adding the sugar will cause drainage or leakage of the egg white. The addition of even a small amount of egg yolk or other food material containing fat (such as milk, oil, cream, or butter) interferes with the formation of the foam. Water added to egg white increases its foam but decreases its stability.

An egg white foam is formed and reaches greater volume more quickly when egg whites are at room temperature rather than at refrigerator temperature. This is probably because of the lowered surface tension of the warmer egg whites. The stability of egg whites beaten at room temperature is not as great as that of colder egg whites. Studies have shown that the thin egg white can be beaten into foam more readily than the thick egg white. Volume is also greater from the less viscous white than it is from the thick egg white.

A foam can be formed by beating air into an egg white with a wire whisk, a rotary beater, or an electric mixer. While the egg white foam is increasing in volume, the air bubbles become smaller and more evenly distributed, the translucence changes to an opaque whiteness, and the elasticity of the foam decreases as it becomes stiffer. An egg white foam beaten to the dry stage lacks elasticity, tends to break down into small dry clumps, and rapidly diminishes in volume. There is also an increase in drainage. For best results in cookery, egg whites should be beaten only until peaks that stand straight and bend slightly at the tips are formed (Fig. 21-7). At this stage, the foam still has a shiny, moist appearance. When the foam is beaten past this stage, its total volume diminishes.

Underbeaten egg whites do not retain their rigidity, lose volume very rapidly, and allow the liquid and whatever materials have been added to the egg white to separate out to the bottom of the utensil.

Salt decreases the stability of an egg white foam; limited amounts of acids, such as cream of tartar, increase it. For meringues, no more than

21-7 *For best results, egg whites are beaten only until they stand up in glossy peaks that bend slightly at the tips. (Courtesy of U.S. Department of Agriculture)*

⅛ tsp salt per egg white is used. The stage to which an egg white foam is beaten depends on the food product being prepared.

Meringues. Soft meringues are made with 2 tbsp of sugar for each egg white. Studies[7] on methods of making soft meringues for pastry show that topping the fillings while they are still hot and baking the pies at 375°F (190°C) until the meringues reach a light color yield a stable meringue and reduce the amount of liquid (called *leakage*) collecting under the meringue and the tendency of the meringue to slip from the surface of the pie. The meringue should be spread to touch the crust all around the surface of the pie to help hold it in place. The cause of leakage on baked meringued pies is not known. It has been suggested that the liquid formed may be due to undercoagulation of the egg white. The amber beads that frequently appear on the surface of meringues are caused by overcoagulation of the protein, with an attendant loss of absorbed liquid.

Hard meringues have a much higher proportion of sugar to egg white. As much as ¼ cup of sugar per egg white may be used. Since sugar retards the denaturization of the egg proteins, a longer whipping time is necessary. Hard meringue can be shaped into objects such as baskets, hearts, pie shells, or animal figures. The baking temperature is very long (1½ hours) and very low (275°F; 135°C).

Emulsifying Agents. Eggs are used to form stable emulsions, mayonnaise, for example. Oil and vinegar separate out unless the oil droplets are coated with a substance that keeps them from running together. Egg yolk is often effective in accomplishing this. Eggs are used as emulsifiers in ice cream, cakes, and creampuffs.

Interfering Substances. Beaten egg whites will act as an "interfering" substance in mixtures to be frozen, such as sherbet. Tiny bubbles of air trapped in egg prevent ice crystals from coming together and creating large masses of icy material. Egg white and, at times, egg yolk perform a similar service in the making of candy: an egg white added to candy such as divinity interferes with the formation of large sugar crystals.

Clarifying Agents Raw eggs may be added to hot broths and coffee. When the proteins in the egg coagulate, they trap the loose particles in the liquid and clarify it.

Custards, Puddings, and Pie Fillings. A custard may be cooked over hot water and stirred as it is cooked (soft custard) or it may be cooked without stirring (baked custard). Both types can be made from the same basic recipe. Generally, the liquid ingredient in a custard is milk, and either the yolk, the white, or the whole egg may be used to thicken the mixture. Sugar, salt, and flavoring are usually added. Stirring a soft custard during the cooking period prevents the formation of a coagulated mass, or gel. When properly cooked, the soft custard has a uniformly smooth texture and is the consistency of cream. The coagulation of the soft custard takes place at about 160°F (70°C). If in making a soft custard the mixture is held at the coagulation temperature for too long, or if the temperature exceeds this level, the protein is overcooked, the mixture thickens unevenly, and the finished product will be curdled. The curdled mixture cannot be changed back to a smooth, uniform sauce unless it is vigorously beaten so that the overheated protein curds are divided into small uniform particles. The perfectly coagulated soft custard is superior to the custard that has been "saved." For good results, rapid heating of the custard mixture should be avoided, the mixture should be stirred while cooking, and it should be cooked only until a thick layer of the mixture coats the spoon. A soft custard that is undercooked will not thicken upon cooling; it will be thin and lacking in body.

A baked custard is cooked without stirring in an oven at 350°F (176°C). General instructions for baking a custard recommend placing the mixture to be baked in a pan of water, which serves to equalize the temperature, thus preventing the outside of the custard from being overcooked while the heat penetrates to the center. A baked custard is done when a knife inserted into the center of the mixture comes out

[7] S. A. Felt, K. Longree, and A. M. Briant, "Instability of Meringued Pies," *J. Amer. Dietet. Assoc.* **32**:710, 1956; E. E. Hester and C. J. Personius, "Factors Affecting the Beading and Leakage of Soft Meringues," *Food Technol.* **3**:236, 1949.

clean. The overcooked product will curdle, and "weeping" will occur. Flavorings must be added to the custard before cooking.

The liquid ingredient in custard is milk. Homogenized milk in custards produces a lighter color throughout the mixture than nonhomogenized milk does. Use of homogenized milk increases the time required for coagulation but produces custards with high gel strength.[8] The time required for a custard to cook can be decreased if the milk is scalded prior to mixing with the other ingredients. Care should be taken that the milk is not hot enough to curdle the egg. This can be avoided if a small quanity of warm milk is beaten into a blended egg. The rest of the eggs are then added to the diluted egg, followed by the remaining warm milk. Custards made with evaporated milk have an excellent texture and a distinctive flavor and color.[9] Nonfat dry milk can also be used successfully in making custards.

Custards made with frozen eggs compare favorably with those made with fresh eggs.[10] Some adjustment must be made in the recipe if frozen egg yolks to which sugar is added before freezing are used.

Dried egg powder of top quality has also been used successfully in making custards. In the author's experience, however, custards in which dried egg solids of unknown age were used in place of fresh eggs had an "eggy" flavor and a tough, dark layer approximately ⅛ in. thick. Under the tough layer, the mixture was thin and watery. But egg solids that had been refrigerator-stored for only a short period were a satisfactory substitute for fresh eggs in custards and custardlike puddings.

CUSTARD PIE. The soggy crust of the custard pie creates a baking problem that requires special consideration. A satisfactory method that elimi-nates a poor baked crust is to bake the filling and the pie crust separately. To do this, two pie pans of the same size must be used. For good results, the crust of the pie should be baked upside down on the back of the pie pan. The pan with custard filling is baked in a pan of hot water. The baked custard is cooled until warm and them loosened around the edges of the pan with a sharp knife. When the pan is gently tilted, the custard slips out of the pan into the crust.

CREAM PIE FILLINGS AND PUDDINGS. In coconut, banana, chocolate, butterscotch, and lemon pie fillings, the thickening of the mixture depends on the coagulation of the egg proteins and the gelatinization of the starch. The procedure for cooking the mixture must allow first for optimum cooking time for the complete gelatinization of the starch and thickening of the mixture, and then for a lowering of the cooking temperature to allow maximum coagulation of the egg proteins to take place. A watery filling will result if after the egg yolks are added, the mixture is not cooked for several minutes at a high enough temperature to coagulate the egg proteins.

METHODS OF COOKING EGGS AND EGG DISHES

Eggs are served in many different ways. Although commonly thought of as a basic breakfast food, they are frequently served at other meals. Eggs are fairly simple to prepare, and adherence to the basic principles of protein cookery will enhance the appearance and palatability of egg dishes. Eggs and egg mixtures should always be cooked at low to moderate temperatures. High temperatures will inevitably result in unevenly cooked, rubbery eggs and egg dishes.

Eggs in the Shell. Eggs cooked in the shell may be either soft-cooked (1–3 minutes) or hard-cooked (15 minutes). Regardless of the length of time that they are cooked, eggs should never be boiled but simmered to prevent rubberiness. Either cold water or water that has been brought to the boiling point may be used to cook eggs in the shell. Putting eggs to cook in cold water is not as precise a method as putting them in water just below the boiling point and will not give

[8] R. E. Carr and G. M. Trout, "Some Cooking Qualities of Homogenized Milk," *Food Res.* **7**:7, 1942.

[9] D. B. Hussemann, "Effect of Altering Milk Solids Content on the Acceptability of Certain Foods," *J. Amer. Dietet. Assoc.* **27**:583, 1951.

[10] G. A. Miller, E. M. Jones, and P. Aldrich, "A Comparison of the Gelation Properties and Palatability of Shell Eggs, Frozen Eggs and Whole Egg Solids in Standard Baked Custards," *J. Food Res.* **24**:584, 1959.

consistent results. It is best to place the eggs into boiling water and turn the heat off or turn it down to simmer. It must be borne in mind, however, that cooking time will be slightly altered for very large, very cold, or very small eggs. Cracking of eggs during simmering can be prevented by making a small hole at the larger end of the shell.

Once cooked to the hard stage, eggs may be peeled easier if they are rolled in the hands to loosen the shell. Peeling should begin at the large end of the air cell. Peeling under running water is often helpful in removing difficult pieces.

FERROUS SULFIDE. Eggs cooked and held in their shells for longer than 15 minutes often show a greenish discoloration at the intersurface of the yolk and egg white. Eggs cooked at a high temperature for a long time may also show a green edge forming around the yolk. The geenish color is produced by the formation of ferrous sulfide as hydrogen sulfide in the white combines with iron in the yolk. Although nothing can be done to reverse the color change once the ferrous sulfide is formed, it is possible—by immersing the cooked eggs in cold water—to keep the development of the green color at a minimum. The quick lowering of the temperature of the egg tends to reduce the amount of hydrogen sulfide gas evolved by the white diffusing toward the yolk. The reason for this is that the gas pressure within the egg is also lowered and the hydrogen sulfide diffuses to the surface of the egg rather than to the yolk. It has been suggested that advanced deterioration of some eggs may account for the fact that among eggs of the same size that have been cooked for the same amount of time, some may show discoloration whereas others do not.

Poached Eggs. An egg is poached out of its shell in enough hot water to cover (Fig. 21-8). For good results, only the best-quality eggs should be used. If the egg white is thin and watery, it will not properly veil the yolk. In a poached egg, the white sets but remains tender and opaque, and the yolk is slightly set and perfectly covered with a tender layer of white. The general outline is oval and compact. For poached eggs, temperatures close to boiling are used so that the outer white of the egg sets just as soon as the egg is immersed in the water, thus preventing it from dispersing. Boiling water is undesirable, since it will disrupt

the shape and toughen the egg protein. Because any treatment that tends to flatten the egg before it is slipped into the hot water will lessen the compactness of the poached egg, it is desirable to break open each egg to be poached just before placing it in the liquid. Although the addition of salt, vinegar, or lemon juice to the water will hasten coagulation, it may cause the surface of the egg to pucker and shrivel. It takes from 3 to 5 minutes to poach eggs to the desired consistency.

Fried Eggs. To fry eggs, enough fat is used to keep the eggs from sticking. Usually about 1 tbsp per egg and oils as well as other solid fats may be used. The fat is heated until it is moderately hot. After breaking the eggs into a small dish (one at a time) they are slipped into the pan, being careful not to break the yolk. They are slowly cooked until firm. Fat is spooned over the tops or a cover is placed over the pan and cooked for 2 or 3 minutes until a white film covers the complete surface of the egg. To cook on both sides (easy over), omit the basting and turn the egg carefully over when the egg white is firm.

A low-fat method of frying eggs has been developed. In this method ½ to ¼ tsp of fat per egg is melted over low heat and the egg is slipped on top of the fat. One tablespoon of water is added per egg and the pan is tightly covered for 3–4 minutes. The egg may be basted with the steaming water once or twice. The egg is cooked by a combination of frying and steaming. Many prefer this method, since the egg is less greasy.

Scrambled Eggs. To scramble eggs use 1 tsp of fat for each egg. The whole eggs are broken into a dish and beaten together until a uniform mixture is formed (Fig. 21-9). Milk, cream, or water (1 tbsp/egg) may be added to the mixture as well as seasonings such as salt and pepper. If more than 1 tbsp per egg is used, they are likely to become watery and the egg mixture itself will form small firm masses instead of thick, soft, creamy curls.

Baked Eggs (Shirred Eggs). An easy way to cook eggs, particularly for a large number of people, is to bake them in the oven. The eggs are slipped into buttered individual ramekins or shallow baking dishes. They are put into a 325°F (160°C) oven for 12–15 minutes. The dishes

249

(a)

(b)

(c)

21-8 *Steps in poaching eggs.* (a) *Fill a saucepan with hot water to cover eggs by 1 in. Add salt (1 tsp. to 1 qt. water) Bring to boil; then turn down to simmering. Break each egg into a saucer and slip into the water. Slide egg toward the side of the pan to keep yolk in center.* (b) *Cook at below simmering for from 3 to 5 minutes.* (c) *Lift eggs from water with a slotted spoon and serve at once.* (*Courtesy of American Egg Board*)

may be placed in a pan of water to help equalize the heat transferance. If bacon is desired as an addition, it may be partially fried and held in place surrounding the inside of the dish while the egg is slipped into the center of the dish. This creates an attractive dish for company.

Omelets and Soufflés. Omelets and soufflés are similar in that the main ingredient in both products is egg. Omelets may be either plain or foamy. The plain omelet is made without separating the white from the yolks: the whole egg is beaten together with the liquid ingredient and flavoring materials. A plain omelet requires 1 tbsp of liquid for each egg used. It is cooked in a frying pan but is not stirred or broken up in any way. (Milk, water, or tomato juice may be used as the liquid ingredient.) The mixture is

cooked over low heat until it will no longer flow and the bottom turns a golden brown. The omelet is removed from the pan and rolled or folded.

The foamy omelet is prepared by beating the whites and yolks separately. If liquid is used, 1 tbsp for each egg is beaten into the egg yolks. The whites are beaten until stiff (salt is added when whites become frothy) and then folded into the yolk mixture. The foamy omelet is cooked in the same way as the plain omelet. After the bottom if browned, the omelet should be placed in a moderate oven or under a low broiler flame until its surface dries out. All omelets may be spread with fillings before they are folded. A main-dish omelet may be spread with small pieces of poultry, fish, meat, or cheese, or with a combination of vegetables; a dessert ome-

(a)

(b)

(c)

21-9 *Steps in scrambling eggs. (a) Beat eggs. (b) Lift cooked portions of egg at edges so uncooked portions flow underneath and (c) cook until eggs are thickened throughout but still moist. (Courtesy of American Egg Board)*

let is generally spread with a sweet mixture, such as jam.

To combine beaten egg whites and beaten egg yolks when preparing omelets or similar dishes, the yolk is spread over the surface of the whites. With a spatula, the material is blended into the egg white by lifting the egg white and folding it over the yolks. Folding is stopped as soon as the two materials are blended. The egg white must be completely blended with other materials to prevent the liquid from leaking out of the omelet during cooking.

A soufflé is a baked omelet with cream sauce added. The sauce is made light and fluffy by the addition of beaten egg whites. Flavoring materials, such as cheese, fish, meat, poultry, or puréed vegetables, are added to the basic mixture for main-dish soufflés. Sugar, chocolate, and puréed fruit are added to the principal ingredients for a hot dessert of unusual texture and flavor. A prune soufflé is a popular example of this kind of dessert.

The white sauce used in a soufflé is either thick or very thick (a minimum of 3 tbsp flour to 1 cup liquid). The white sauce is cooked before being added to the egg whites. For soufflés, the egg whites are beaten until the peaks are fairly stiff and their tips slightly rounded. The beaten egg yolks and added materials are then folded into the stiff egg white. The best method of combining the flavoring materials is as follows:

1. For a cheese soufflé, add the cheese to the white sauce and blend these with the egg yolks. Without further cooking, fold the cheese–white sauce–egg yolk mixture into the egg whites.
2. If vegetable pulp, meat, or fish is to be added to the soufflé, cook the sauce and egg yolks over hot water until the eggs have coagulated. Fold this mixture into the egg whites, then fold in the flavoring materials.

Soufflés are best when baked at a temperature of 350–375°F (175–190°C) in a pan of water for about 40–50 minutes. A higher temperature can be used, but the resultant product is not as stable.

As foamy omelets and soufflés cool, the volume of air incorporated into the product will contract and some shrinkage will take place. If not sufficiently cooked, the product will fall rapidly and lose considerable volume. A properly baked soufflé will not shrink to any great extent, unless it is cooled too rapidly.

DETERIORATION

Flavor and overall appearance are at their best in the freshly laid egg; the process of deterioration commences immediately thereafter. The rate of deterioration is related to quality. A highly perishable food, eggs are markedly affected by unfavorable storage conditions. They deteriorate rapidly at room temperature, but proper refrigeration can prolong the life of the egg as long as 6 months. This is essential in modern-day egg production since there are seasonal lows in egg laying (May to October) and seasonal highs in consumer demands (Easter).

Shrinkage. Loss of water from within the egg will result in some shrinkage, the amount of which is usually measured by the size of the air cell as it is seen in candling. The rate at which the shrinkage progresses depends on the temperature and humidity of surrounding air and the porosity of the shell. Low temperature is an important practical means of controlling egg quality generally and shrinkage in particular.

Having a high humidity of 85–90% will retard loss of moisture.

Because of the shrinkage found in older eggs, the peeling of hard-cooked eggs becomes easier.

Liquefaction. Not all the reasons for liquefaction are understood; however, some of the physical changes that occur are known. When the egg is held at a high temperature, water passes from the white into the yolk. To accommodate the incoming water, the vitelline membrane stretches and is thereby weakened. With the increase in water, the yolk is made more fluid. This increased fluidity of the yolk, plus the decreased viscosity and impaired mechanical support of the white, causes a flattening of the egg when it is opened.

Alkalinity. Although fresh egg white is nearly chemically neutral (pH 7.6), loss of carbon dioxide from the egg white turns it alkaline. The rate of liquefaction and shrinkage and the rate of change from neutral to alkaline of the egg white are all directly proportional to storage temperature. The change in pH will decrease the thickness of the egg white. As it grows older and more alkaline, it will turn yellowish and eventually cloudy.

There is a loss of carbon dioxide from the time the egg is laid, with the greatest rate of loss occurring when the egg is first laid. The loss of carbon dioxide from the egg white can be controlled during storage by the introduction of carbon dioxide into the room.

Another method to retard aging is thermostabilization, dipping the eggs in a hot liquid. This will kill microorganisms and cause a thin layer of the egg white to coagulate on the inside of the shell. Eggs treated in this manner may adhere to the shell when broken and are more difficult to create a foam.

Oil or plastic coatings are often applied to eggs within 24 hours after laying to prevent loss of carbon dioxide and thus retard aging and moisture loss. This may create a cloudy or milky white egg white with no effect on flavor. As the gas eventually escapes, the white of the egg will become clear.

Bacterial Decomposition. As an egg ages, the porosity of the shell increases, making possible the infiltration of bacteria. Molds and bacteria have been found in eggs. The source of the microorganisms entering the egg may be fecal matter from the hen or the soil, or contamination from unclean washing water used to clean egg shells. If eggs are fertile, serious chemical changes take place at temperatures above 85°F (30°C). The alkalinity of the egg white and an antibacterial substance in egg white, *lysozyme,* serve to reduce the spoilage caused by microorganisms.

PRESERVATION

The purpose of preserving eggs is to hold at a minimum the physiochemical deterioration and to prevent microbial spoilage. Preservation makes possible the availability of eggs throughout the year.

Cold Storage. Studies show that eggs held in cold storage or at refrigerator temperatures are more successful in producing cakes and custards of good flavor than eggs held at room temperature, and that all stored eggs are inferior to fresh eggs for poaching purposes.[11] These same studies show that neither the temperature nor the length of storage of the eggs greatly affects the baked custards made from eggs held at refrigerator temperatures or in cold storage.

Eggs held under cold storage conditions are refrigerated at 29–30°F (−1 to −2°C) and at humidities of 85–90%. Cold storage of eggs is no longer as large an operation as it once was. Freezing and drying of broken-out eggs are the main methods used to preserve a portion of the eggs produced annually.

Freezing. Freezing eggs keeps the development of microorganisms at a minimum. Modern methods of freezing also ensure the retention of flavor. Because the flavor of an egg is the substance of its value as an ingredient in many manufactured food products, frozen eggs can easily be substituted for fresh eggs by bakers, candy manufacturers, and makers of ice cream or mayonnaise. At present, large food industries are the top users of frozen eggs. The eggs cannot be frozen in the shell, since the egg shell would crack with expansion of the liquids when frozen. Instead, the whites and yolks are removed and mixed together before they are frozen. Separated egg whites and egg yolks are also frozen. Egg yolks will lump and separate if frozen plain. To prevent this, 1 tbsp of corn syrup or sugar or ½ tsp of salt is blended with 1 cup of egg yolks before freezing. The choice of a sweetener or salt is dependent on the use of the thawed product. If the egg yolks are to be incorporated into baked goods, sugar is used. If they will be used in products containing salt, salt may be used. Egg whites may be frozen plain. Frozen whole eggs are best blended with 1½ tsp sugar or corn syrup or ½ tsp salt to each cup of blended whole eggs. A convenient way to freeze individual servings of eggs is in ice-cube trays. Eggs are generally frozen at temperatures from 0 to −20°F (−18 to −28°C). Liquid egg is sold in the cans in which it was frozen. Freezing of eggs within 7 seconds may be achieved by feeding the liquid egg in a thin film to a refrigerated roll.

PHYSIOCHEMICAL CHANGES IN FROZEN EGGS. There is little apparent change in the egg albumen as a result of freezing, except that there is more liquid in it after thawing. In contrast, marked changes take place in the frozen yolk that become apparent when the yolk is thawed. It is thought that the freezing process may result in lipoprotein destabilization and aggregation. This aggregation results in the formation of a more viscous yolk.[12] Because of the yolk content, the whole egg, too, is altered. During the freezing of the egg yolk, water separates out of the yolk solids, leaving the solid portions of the yolk free to bunch together in hard clumps. The water freezes into ice crystals. The defrosted egg does not reabsorb the moisture, and the yolk remains thick and lumpy. It is necessary, therefore, to add edible substances, such as sugar, salt, or glycerine, that increase the osmotic pressure and lower the freezing point of liquid egg. As a practical result of adding these substances, the egg solids retain sufficient water to prevent them from precipitating and lumping.[13] When the egg thaws, moisture is reabsorbed, and the original consistency of the egg is restored. Dextrose and levulose are more effective than sucrose in preventing precipitation. Glycerine does not preserve the consistency of frozen egg yolk or whole egg as well as salt or sugar does. In the freezing of liquid eggs, some—but not all—bacteria are destroyed. This presents a danger during or after the thawing period, for the outer portion of egg material may reach a temperature that will support bacterial growth before thawing is completed. A frozen egg of good quality is odorless, regardless of length of storage; a decomposed egg, on the other hand, smells putrid or sour. The availability of home freezers has stepped up the freezing of eggs and use of frozen

[11] R. Jordon, A. T. Barr, and M. L. Wilson, "Shell Eggs: Quality and Properties as Affected by Temperature and Length of Storage," *Bulletin 612* (Lafayette, Ind.: Purdue University Agricultural Experiment Station, undated).

[12] R. J. Hasiak and D. V. Vadehra, "Effect of Certain Physical and Chemical Treatments on the Microstructure of Egg Yolk," *J. Food Sci.* **37**:913, 1972.

[13] D. Tressler and C. Evers, *The Freezing Preservation of Foods* (Westport, Conn.: Avi, 1968), p. 873.

eggs in the home, but the practice is still far from popular.

Dried Eggs. In drying eggs, 99% of the water is removed by evaporation in the presence of heat. Albumen is usually pan-dried (which yields a flaked product), and whole egg and egg yolk are spray-dried (which yields a powered product). Consumers may purchase either 5- or 8-oz containers of dried egg solids. Each ounce of the dried whole egg solids is equal to 2 large eggs. Eight ounces of the dried egg yolks is equal to 27 egg yolks and 8 oz of the dried egg white is equal to 50 egg whites.

The heat required for drying may destroy many of the properties of the liquid egg and thus reduce its reconstitution properties. Mainly, the egg will suffer some loss of solubility and, during storage, may change in color and develop an unpleasant taste.

The practice of pasteurizing liquid eggs is required by law to cut down on the contamination of dried egg powders with the microorganism *Salmonella*. Dried eggs may be stored in the refrigerator for up to 1 year in a tightly closed container to prevent them from taking up moisture from the air and absorbing flavors from other foods. If dried eggs are allowed to take up moisture, they will become lumpy and will not mix rapidly with liquid.

USE OF DRIED EGGS IN COOKERY. Although dried eggs are used mainly in the production of commercial products, they are available to some extent for institutional and to a limited degree for home use. Dried whole eggs can be used in place of shell eggs in thoroughly cooked products, such as baked breads, long-cooked casseroles, baked scrambled eggs, cakes, and baked desserts. They should not be used in uncooked or slightly cooked products such as egg–milk drinks, salad dressings, and stovetop custards and omelets.

When dried eggs are used with products that have several other dry ingredients, the dry egg is sifted with them. The water needed to replace the water removed from the egg in drying is added to the liquid in the recipe. For baked scrambled eggs and omelets, the egg is reconstituted by blending with the amount of water needed to replace that removed in drying. For a cooked salad dressing, in which flour or other starchy ingredients are used to thicken the mix-

ture, the dry ingredients and the liquid are cooked first. This mixture is then added to the reconstituted dried egg. The procedure is similar to that used for shell eggs. Dried egg that has been reconstituted with water should be used within an hour.

The amount of reconstituted egg used in a basic recipe appears to have marked effect on the finished product. Longree and others[14] found that when the amount of reconstituted whole egg solid was as low as 17.7% (based on the weight of the milk), the custards were soft in consistency as compared to those made with 31.6% dried whole egg solids. Other studies in the same series on the use of whole egg solids showed that large batches of plain cheese, and vegetable soufflés made from the dried whole product were of acceptable color, flavor, height, and texture.[15]

When dried egg whites are blended with water, they can be beaten to the same stiffness as whites from shell eggs, and they give results in cooking that compare favorably with those of fresh egg whites. Excellent angel food cakes can be made with dried egg whites.

Dried egg yolks are also available. They may be used alone or with dried egg white, in recipes for baked dishes that call for yolks or for separated eggs. A recent study showed that the addition of freeze-dried egg white would minimize the determental effects of egg whites with limited amounts of egg yolk (04.%).[16]

Table 21-5 indicates the amounts of dried egg, dried egg yolk, and dried egg white to be used in place of the fresh product.

IMITATION EGGS

Concern over the high cholesterol content of eggs (275 milligrams of cholesterol/egg yolk)

[14] K. Longree, M. Jooste, and J. White, "Time–Temperature Relationships of Custards Made with Whole Egg Solids," *J. Amer. Dietet. Assoc.* **38**:147, 1961.

[15] K. Longree, J. C. White, and B. Sison, "Time–Temperature Relationships of Soufflés," *J. Amer. Dietet. Assoc.* **41**:107, 1962.

[16] E. A. Sauter, "Effects of Adding 2% Freeze-Dried Egg White to Batters of Angel Food Cakes Made with White Containing Egg Yolk," *J. Food Sci.* **40**:869, 1975.

TABLE 21-5
Equivalent Amounts of Fresh and Dried Eggs

Fresh Product	Dried Product, Sifted	Lukewarm Water
Fresh egg whites		
1	2 tsp	2 tbsp
6	¼ cup	¾ cup
Fresh egg yolks		
1	2 tbsp	2 tsp
6	¾ cup	¼ cup
Fresh shell eggs (large eggs weighing 24 oz per dozen)		
6	1 cup	1 cup
1	2½ tbsp	2½ tbsp

Source: "Eggs in Family Meals," *Home and Garden Bulletin 103* (Washington, D.C.: U.S. Department of Agriculture, 1967), p. 31.

has increased the popularity of imitation eggs made from milk solids or soy protein. There are two types of egg substitutes on the market. The first is a complete egg substitute made from soy or milk proteins, but this is gradually being replaced by the second type. The second type is a partial egg substitute in which only the yolks have been replaced; the egg whites remain.

Egg substitutes have about half the fat and calories of natural eggs. There is also a significant reduction in the sodium content. Since the fat has been replaced with vegetable oil (usually corn oil), there is a much higher ratio of polyunsaturated fats to saturated fats (*P/S* ratio). The *P/S* ratio is approximately 0.4, compared to 1.4 for whole fresh eggs. The shelf life of the product is 10 weeks if unopened and stored in the refrigerator and 2 weeks if opened.

There is a distinct flavor difference in imitation eggs which may be masked if they are incorporated into multiingredient cooked dishes. If using the egg substitutes that have been completely replaced with milk proteins, they should not be added to recipes where the addition of egg is necessary for its thickening quality. This is because the milk protein casein is not coagulated by heat during normal cooking conditions.

SUMMARY

A valued and popular food, eggs are also an important component of many food products. Generally an economical source of high-quality protein, eggs are also valued for their mineral (especially iron) and vitamin content. Shell color has no bearing on egg quality, but yolk color is influenced by the diet of the hen. Eggs are graded for quality and are classified by size. Price comparisons by grade and size indicate best buys. Quality is determined by candling. Eggs require continuous refrigeration to retard deterioration.

Low to moderate temperatures, as in other protein cookery, should be used in egg cookery. The temperatures at which proteins of the white and yolk coagulate differ, however; the white coagulates sooner. Sugar raises the coagulation temperature, salt reduces it, and acid, on prolonged heating with an egg mixture, peptizes the proteins, causing thinning. In cookery, eggs are used for binding, coating, leavening, emulsifying and as an "interfering" substance, as in sherbert or some candies. Popular egg products include meringues, custards, puddings, pie fillings, omelets, soufflés, and sponge cakes.

Ferrous sulfide often forms on the intersurface of the yolk in hard-cooked eggs. Development of the green color can be held to a minimum by immediate cooling. Preparation of egg white foams requires that egg whites be beaten until stiff but not dry.

Eggs are preserved for future use by holding in cold storage, freezing, or drying. Frozen eggs can be substituted for fresh eggs in commercial food operations. Dried eggs are used mainly in preparation of commercial products, with limited use in institutions and homes.

QUESTIONS AND TOPICS FOR DISCUSSION AND STUDY

1. Why does a dark gray-green color sometimes form on the surface of the yolk of cooked eggs? How can this be avoided?
2. What property of egg protein makes it possible to use eggs as a thickening agent?
3. Is there a difference in the thickening powers of the whole egg, the egg white, and the egg yolk?

4. What causes the curdling of a custard?
5. At which stage of beating is it best to add sugar to an egg white foam?
6. How do the gels that are formed in a custard differ from those formed in a cornstarch pudding?
7. Does the grade of an egg make a difference in the quality of the cooked product?

SUGGESTED ACTIVITIES

1. Break open and place in saucers three eggs, one each of Grades AA, A and B. Compare them for appearance and odor. Fry the eggs separately. Compare their appearance and flavor.
2. Prepare eggs in any one or more of the following forms: poached, cooked in the shell, fried, scrambled, in an omelet, and baked. Evaluate the finished products.
3. Prepare a soufflé, baked custard, and soft custard. Use standard for product to evaluate it.
4. Compare baked custards made from whole milk, homogenized milk, and evaporated milk for flavor, color, texture, and length of time required for coagulation.
5. Compare baked custards made from fresh and frozen eggs for flavor, color, texture, and length of time required for coagulation.

REFERENCES

BOOKS

Paul, Pauline, and Helen Palmer. *Food Theory and Applications.* New York: Wiley, 1972, Chap. 9.

Romanoff, A. L., and A. J. Romanoff. *The Avian Egg.* New York: Wiley, 1949.

Stadelmare, W. J., and O. Y. Cotterill. *Egg Science and Technology.* Westport, Conn.: Avi, 1973.

Vail, Gladys, J. Phillips, Lucile Rust, Ruth Griswold, and Margaret Justin. *Foods,* 7th ed. Boston: Houghton Mifflin, 1978, Chap. 11.

ARTICLES, BULLETINS, AND PAMPHLETS

Chang, C. W., and W. D. Powrie. "Microstructure of Egg Yolk." *J. Food Sci.* **42**:1193, 1977.

"Cooking with Dried Eggs." *Home and Garden Bulletin 50.* Washington, D.C.: U.S. Department of Agriculture, 1956.

"Eggs in Family Meals." *Home and Garden Bulletin 103.* Washington, D.C.: U.S. Department of Agriculture, 1971.

Felt, S. A., K. Longree, and A. M. Briant. "Instability of Meringued Pies." *J. Amer. Dietet. Assoc.* **32**:710, 1956.

Ijichi, K., H. H. Palmer, and H. Lineweaver. "Frozen Whole Eggs for Scrambling." *J. Food Sci.* **35**:695, 1970.

Janek, D. A., and D. M. Downs. "Scrambled Processed Eggs." *J. Amer. Dietet. Assoc.* **55**:578, 1969.

Klippenstein, Ruth. "The Versatile Egg." *Cornell Extension Bulletin.* Ithaca, N.Y.: Cornell University, rev. 1963.

"Know the Eggs You Buy." Washington, D.C.: U.S. Department of Agriculture, 1969.

Morgan, J. K., K. Funk, and M. E. Zabik. "Comparison of Frozen, Foam Spray Dried, Freeze Dried and Spray Dried Eggs, Soft Meringues Prepared with a Carrageenan Stabilizer." *J. Food Sci.* **35**:699, 1970.

Reagan, J. G., and I. R. York. "Improved Methods for Determination for Certain Organic Acids in Pasteurized and Unpasteurized Liquid and Frozen Whole Eggs." *J. Food Sci.* **36**:351, 1971.

"Shell Egg Grading and Inspection of Egg Products." *Agricultural Marketing Service Bulletin 30.* Washington, D.C.: U.S. Department of Agriculture, 1964.

Yadav, N. K., and D. V. Vadehra. "Mechanism of Egg White Resistance to Bacterial Growth." *J. Food Sci.* **42**:97, 1977.

Milk

Milk is the secretion of the mammary glands of mammals. No other food known to man can match milk in nutritive value and utility in cookery and manufacture of food products. The unqualified term *milk* implies cow's milk. All other milk bears a description, such as *human milk, goat's milk,* and *camel's milk.*

COMPOSITION

The chemical composition of cow's milk is given in Table 22-1.

Butterfat. Butterfat occurs as extremely small fat globules that tend to clump together in larger aggregates when milk is agitated, but the individual fat globules in the larger fat particle retain their separate structures. The tendency of milk to cream is a result of the lower specific gravity of the butterfat compared to that of the milk serum. During creaming, the fat globules rise as clumps, not as individual particles.

Butter is made from cream separated from whole milk. When the cream is churned at the proper temperature, the fat globules clump to-gether, forming large masses of fat clusters distributed through the water phase. At a certain point, the fat-in-water emulsion breaks and the fat separates from the surrounding liquid to form a solid: butter. In butter, water is dispersed through the fat or oil mass (in the raw milk, the fat was dispersed in the water phase). Certain fat-soluble substances are generally present in small amounts in butterfat. Among the principal ones are the yellow coloring substances carotene

TABLE 22-1
Proximate Chemical Composition of Cow's Milk

Constituents	Whole Milk (%)
Water	87.0
Protein	3.5
Fat	3.8
Carbohydrate	4.8
Minerals	0.65

Source: C. Chatfield and G. Adams, "Proximate Composition of Foods (Edible Portion)," *Circular 549* (Washington, D.C.: U.S. Department of Agriculture, 1940).

and xanthophyll; the sterols, in the form of cholesterol, phospholipids, lecithin, and cephalin; and the fat-soluble vitamins A,D,E, and K. The yellowing coloring substances are passed on to the milk through vegetable matter consumed by the animal (the animal cannot synthesize these substances). The natural yellow tint of butter stems from the yellow-tinted pigments found in the milk. Carotene is a precursor of vitamin A and adds considerably to the vitamin A value of milk.

The fatty acid composition of butterfat is relatively high in the number of short-chained, saturated fatty acids. The cholesterol content of butterfat is rather high, these substances being soluble in fat. The phospholipids are fat substances containing phosphorus groups or choline. The choline-containing substances are the lecithins, which are significant in the development of the "fishy" odor that frequently occurs in butter and dried milks of high moisture content. It is believed that oxidation of choline produces a gas, trimethylamine, which at ordinary temperatures has a pronounced "fishy" odor.

Milk Sugar: Lactose. The carbohydrate in milk is in the form of lactose, or milk sugar. Cow's milk contains about 4.8% lactose (which is less sweet than sucrose). Lactose is not very soluble; sometimes it settles out during the heat treatment of condensed milk, imparting a granular texture to the finished product. In the souring of milk, lactic acid bacteria convert lactose into lactic acid, thus giving the soured milk its characteristic flavor. Milk also contains very small amounts of glucose, a simpler sugar than lactose.

Proteins. The main protein of milk is casein, which is present in the average amount of 2.7%. In addition to casein, milk contains small quantities of the proteins lactalbumin (0.5%) and lactoglobulin (0.05%). In fresh milk, the casein is in the form of a salt, calcium caseinate. When casein is acted on by the enzyme rennin, it is precipitated out in the form of calcium paracaseinate, whereas the lactoglobulin and lactalbumin remain in the whey (hence they are sometimes referred to as the "whey proteins"). A factor in the lactoglobulin is believed to be responsible for the inhibition of milk on the volume of yeast bread. This factor can be deac-

tivated if the milk is scalded. Casein is coagulated by rennin.

Mineral Salts. The elements contained in milk are calcium, phosphorus, magnesium, potassium, sodium, chlorine, and sulfur. The chief mineral of milk, calcium, is in the form of calcium phosphate. Some of these minerals are present in true solution, some are organically bound to the proteins of milk. The salt content of milk is significant in that small amounts are necessary for the coagulation of products (such as custards) made with milk.

Pigments. Fresh whole milk has a faint ivory cast caused by the refraction of light in the dispersed particles in the milk. Skim milk, by contrast, has a bluish cast. The carotene in milk gives it a slightly yellow tinge, and lactoflavin, another milk pigment, imparts a green tone.

Flavors. Normally, milk has a mild sweet flavor. Any marked variation from its characteristic taste greatly decreases its palatability. The flavor may be affected by the physical condition of the cow and by the composition of her feed. Off-flavors are chiefly caused by pasture weeds, such as wild onion, garlic, mustard, and stinkweed, Some rancid or bitter flavors are caused by old or moldy feed; unclean or "barny" flavors are the result of the exposure of drawn milk to unsanitary external conditions.

NUTRITIVE VALUE

Milk contains most of the substances known to be essential to good nutrition. The proteins in milk, which include casein, lactalbumin, and lactoglobulin, are of high quality. They are complete, and can be eaten as the only proteins in the diet. They supplement cereal proteins when milk and cereals are eaten in combination. Milk fat is in an emulsion; it is palatable, highly digestible, and assimilable. Lactose (milk sugar) is less sweet than cane sugar and milk is the only food in which lactose is found naturally.

Calcium is the mineral of greatest importance in milk. It is present in good quantity and in a readily assimilable form. Milk and milk products are by far the most important source of calcium in the diet; hence, use of milk in cookery is of great nutritional significance. Milk also contains phosphorus and iron.

Vitamins. Milk is a rich source of both fat-soluble and water-soluble vitamins. Whole milk, cream, and products made from cream or whole milk are excellent sources of vitamin A. According to some reports, the vitamin A content of milk is highest during the summer in milk from cows on green pasture; the amount present varies with the amount of green food available to the cow.

Whole milk does not contain very large amounts of vitamin D, but the nutrient is added to the food (400 U.S.P. units per quart) to make it a rich vitamin D source. The amounts of this vitamin contained in the milk vary with the feed and with the amount of sunlight to which the cows are exposed.

Although milk is only a fair source of some B vitamins, it is an excellent source of riboflavin. When exposed to sunlight, however, it loses riboflavin and develops "sunlight" flavor in a short time.[1] A water-soluble vitamin, riboflavin is abundant in the nonfat portion of the milk. Thiamine and niacin are also water-soluble vitamins of the vitamin B group found in milk in fair quantities. Although the niacin content is small, milk proteins contain considerable tryptophane, an amino acid that can serve in place of niacin.

Small amounts of ascorbic acid are present in raw milk, although generally dairy products are not very reliable sources of this vitamin. Ascorbic acid is highly unstable, and much of it is lost in the handling and processing of milk. The ascorbic acid content of milk is known to be uniform immediately after milking and it tends to decrease quite rapidly during storage[2]; pasteurized milk has from one-third to one-half the quantity originally present in the raw milk.

[1] D. Josephson, L. H. Burgwald, and R. B. Stoltz, "The Effect of Route Delivery on the Flavor, Riboflavin, and Ascorbic Acid Content of Milk," *J. Dairy Sci.* **29**:273, 1946.

[2] A. Dahlberg, H. Adams, and M. Hald, *Sanitary Milk Control and Its Relation to the Sanitary, Nutritive, and Other Qualities of Milk* (Washington, D.C.: National Research Council–National Academy of Sciences, 1953), p. 89.

ECONOMIC ASPECTS

Milk is used as a daily beverage by all age groups and is also used as the liquid ingredient of many prepared dishes. Nutritionally, milk is an excellent buy; hence, liberal amounts of various forms of milk are included in recommendations for family meals.

Of prime importance in the production and distribution of milk are the costs incurred by producers, dealers, and others in meeting the sanitary requirements set down for the handling of milk. These costs make up part of the total expenses of production and distribution and affect the cost of milk and milk products to the consumer.

Milk delivered to the door adds to the cost of milk; often the cost is less when the consumer carries it home himself. The growing practice of selling milk in large containers also reduces the cost per quart.

Although fresh fluid milk enjoys universal popularity because of its excellent food value and high palatability, evaporated milk, skim milk, buttermilk, and nonfat dry milk solids may be more economical forms. A combination of equal volumes of whole milk and reconstituted nonfat dry milk will create a product that has the taste of whole milk but at a less expensive cost. Evaporated milk, when diluted with an equal volume of water, has nutritive value comparable to that of fresh whole milk. The milk fat is removed from skim milk, buttermilk, and nonfat dry milk solids, thus leaving them low in fat, vitamin A, and energy value. However, the products remain high in proteins, minerals, and the water-soluble vitamins found in whole milk.

Improvement of the quality of milk placed on the market is one of the indirect ways in which the consumer gets a better return for his money. Generally, cows of a given breed have a tendency to secrete milk of a uniform composition.

Breeding research has recently turned attention to producing a milk cow that will milk with a high proportion of protein to fat.[3] Such an

[3] R. E. Hodgson, "Livestock Production Transition," in *Food: The Yearbook of Agriculture* (Washington, D.C.: U.S. Department of Agriculture, 1959), p. 334.

alteration in basic composition will offer the consumer an excellent protein food with lower energy value.

The easily stored canned and dried forms of milk are excellent alternatives to whole fluid milk for cooking and in beverages.

SANITARY CONTROL AND GRADES

In most municipalities throughout the United States, the production and distribution of milk are surrounded by rigid sanitary controls administered by local health departments. The ordinances and laws governing milk production and distribution in a local community serve as the basis for the legal structure of sanitary milk controls. The main purpose of sanitary milk controls is to insure a safe milk, free of disease-producing bacteria, toxic substances, and foreign flavors. In addition, sanitary controls help to produce milk that has an initial low bacterial count, good flavor, satisfactory keeping quality, and high nutritive value. These regulations are not uniform from community to community. The U.S. Public Health Service, however, has formulated a milk ordinance and code that may be used as a model by states and communities.[4] The code is revised periodically. Adoption of the code is up to individual state legislatures.

Pasteurization. Milk cannot be safely marketed raw because of the possibility that it may be a carrier of gastroenteritis, tuberculosis, diptheris, and typhoid, undulant, and scarlet fever. Almost all fresh fluid milks are pasteurized. Pasteurized milk has been heated to a high temperature below boiling by one of two methods: the flash method or the holding method. In the flash method, the milk is brought to 160°F (71°C) and held there for not less than 15 seconds. In the holding method, the milk is brought to a temperature not lower than 143°F (62°C) and held there for not less than 30 minutes. Both methods destroy disease-producing bacteria and keep less harmful strains of bacteria to a minimum. The lower than boiling temperatures

eliminate the undesirable flavor milk acquires when it is boiled.

The adequacy of pasteurization can be measured by the activity of phosphatase, a natural enzyme found in milk. When it is deactivated, the milk has been heated sufficiently to also destroy pathogenic microorganisms. By this test, unpasteurized milk can be detected if added to unpasteurized milk at concentrations as small as 0.01%.

The nutritive value of pasteurized milk is similar to that of raw milk except for a slight decrease in the heat-labile vitamins, thiamine, and ascorbic acid.

Milk Grades. The bacterial count of fresh milk is the basis for its grading, the highest grade—Grade A—having the lowest bacterial count. Generally, states and municipalities use the grade standards for milk that are recommended by the Public Health Service, but there is some variation according to locality. Although Grade A has the lowest bacterial count, Grades B and C are also safe and wholesome. In some areas, only one grade of milk is sold. According to the code, the allowable bacterial counts per cubic centimeter are Grade A pasteurized, 30,000; Grade A raw, 50,000; Grade B pasteurized, 50,000; and Grade B raw, 1,000,000.

The U.S. Department of Agriculture has established grades for nonfat dry milk solids: U.S. Extra Grade and U.S. Standard Grade. Grade A dry milk powder means that the powder has been made from milk that meets Grade A standards set by the U.S. Public Health Service. At present, these grades are used for commerical trading and to a very limited extent for retail packages of milk.[5]

KINDS OF MILK

Whole Fluid Milk. Milk for common consumption must be free of pathogenic bacteria. The essential process for insuring this condition is efficient pasteurization. Although bacteria are destroyed by pasteurization, it is sound public

---

[4] "Milk Ordinance and Code," *Public Health Bulletin 229* (Washington, D.C.: U.S. Public Health Service, 1965).

[5] "Shoppers Guide to U.S. Grades for Food," *Home and Garden Bulletin 58* (Washington, D.C.: U.S. Department of Agriculture, rev. 1966).

health policy to recommend that the raw milk itself have a minimum of pathogenic bacteria. The principal factors that help to assure the production of milk of low bacterial count are clean healthy cows, proper sterilization of utensils, prompt cooling of milk, and minimum storage time. Some cities and municipalities forbid the sale of raw milk. Fluid milk contains at least 3.25% butterfat, which accounts for its rich, satisfying taste.

Certified Milk. The high cost of producing certified milk limits its distribution. Certified milk may be homogenized and may have added vitamin D. The sanitary standards for the production of this milk are very high, and their maintenance is carefully upheld by American Association of Medical Milk Commissions. It is used chiefly by doctor's recommendation in special cases of infant and invalid feeding.

Homogenized Milk. Homogenized milk on the market is whole, fresh pasteurized milk treated so that its fat globules are broken to the extent that there is no separation of fat from the milk serum even after 2 days' storage. Homogenization is a mechanical process that reduces the size of particles of matter and ultimately mixes them. Because the homogenizing process decreases the size of the fat particles and increases their number, there is a corresponding increase in total surface area of the fat globules. This brings about a stabilization of the milk emulsion, which prevents the rising of the cream.

Homogenization of milk alters its cooking properties. There is a increase in the cooking time believed to be the result of a longer time required for heat pentration. Although using homogenized milk gives products a creamier texture, it also produces more rapid curdling.

CANNED WHOLE MILK. Whole milk that is homogenized, sterilized at 270–280°F (132–138°C) for 8–10 seconds, and canned aseptically is available chiefly for use on ships or for export.[6] It can be stored at room temperature until opened, after which it requires refrigeration.

FROZEN WHOLE MILK. Homogenized, pasteurized whole milk can be quickly frozen and kept below − 10°F (− 23°C) for 6 weeks to 3 months. Like concentrated frozen milk, it must be used soon after defrosting. At the present time, it is not ordinarily available in retail markets, being used mainly for overseas military installations.[7] On thawing, frozen milk has a tendency for the fat to separate, and particles of precipitated protein may be visible on the glass (freezing denatures the protein).

VITAMIN D MILK. Whole fluid milk may have vitamin D added. The possibility of irradiating the milk with ultraviolet light (which transforms the cholesterol compounds of the milk into vitamin D) was discarded due to the formation of toxisterols. Instead, vitamin D is added directly to the milk or the cows are fed feed that has been irradiated. Milk is normally fortified with 400 I.U. of vitamin D per quart.

Chocolate Milk and Related Products. Chocolate milk is made from whole milk. If the chocolate beverage is made with skim milk, it must be labeled chocolate drink, because it does not meet the butterfat standards for whole milk. In addition to chocolate or cocoa syrup, chocolate beverages contain vanilla, salt, and a stabilizer (vegetable gum, starch, or tapioca). If cocoa or chocolate syrup made with cocoa is used instead of chocolate, the product must be called chocolate-flavored milk or chocolate-flavored drink.

Fluid Skim Milk. Fluid skim milk is like fresh fluid whole milk except that it contains almost no fat, vitamin A, or vitamin D. It is recommended to reduce fat and total calories in the diet. Although it lacks fat and vitamins A and D, plain skim milk is an excellent source of calcium, B vitamins, and protein. There is a limited distribution of fortified skim milk to which vitamins A and D have been added.

Fluid Low-Fat Milk. *Low fat, partly skimmed,* and *2 % milk* are terms used in some markets to describe a fresh fluid product having a fat content of 2% instead of the usual 3.5%. A product known as *2%–10%* contains 2% milk fat and 10% nonfat milk solids (usually 8.5% milk solids is present). This product differs from the standard fluid skim milk in that it has a heavier

---

[6] *Newer Knowledge of Milk,* op. cit., p. 13.

[7] Ibid.

consistency and richer taste than skim milk. Fat-free milk (99%) has 1% fat.

The lower fat content of skim and low-fat milk has made these popular among those who are concerned with the amount of cholesterol and/or calories in the diet.

Cultured Milk. Cultured or fermented milks have a pleasant, sour flavor as a result of the breakdown of lactose into lactic acid. This change is brought about by bacterial action. The food value of fermented milk is equal to that of the milk from which it is prepared. The main fermented milks in the United States are buttermilk, yogurt and acidophilus milk.

BUTTERMILK. Buttermilk was originally a by-product of butter making, the liquid left after the fat had been removed from the cream by churning. Buttermilk is similar to skim milk in composition, except that it contains acid. It also contains the phospholipid membranes, which surrounded the fat droplets before they were broken. The buttermilk distributed today is chiefly made from pasteurized skim milk or partially skimmed milk treated with a culture of lactic acid bacteria. Cultured buttermilks are smooth and mild in flavor and are slightly less expensive than fresh pasteurized milk. There is some variation in the butterfat content of this type of fermented milk; natural buttermilk has approximately 0.55% butterfat; cultured buttermilks may have as low as 0.1%; cultured buttermilks with added cream or butter usually contain 1–2%.

Buttermilk is often used in cooking for its acid content. If none is available, a subsitute may be made by adding 1 tbsp of either lemon juice or vinegar to 1 cup of sweet milk. It will be ready to use after 5 minutes of standing.

YOGURT. Yogurt is a coagulated milk product with a custardlike consistency. It may be made with skimmed, partially skimmed, or whole milk and be fortified with 3% nonfat dry milk. It is heated and homogenized. Heat treatment involves holding the milk at 180–185°F (82–85°C) for a constant amount of time and cooled to 113°F (45°C). The heat treatment is important for the protein coagulation and the starter organisms. The cooled milk is inoculated with a mixture of *Streptococcus thermophilus, Bacterium bulgaricus,* and *Plocamo bacterium yoghouri.* This mixture is placed in individual containers and held for several hours at 106–108°F (41–42°C). Fruit preserves or fruit essence may be added to the mix to mask the slightly acid flavor.

Yogurt is more expensive than milk, generally costing twice that of the milk from which it was made. The nutritive value is also similar to the milk used, except there is a small amount of lactic acid formed from the lactose in the milk. Dieters should note that the addition of sugar-flavored fruits will increase the caloric content to be greater than that of whole milk.

Frozen yogurt is becoming more popular because of a weight-conscious public. Its calorie content is approximately one-third that of ice cream. Unfortunately, sugar is added to the frozen product, which subsequently also increases its caloric value.

Concentrated Milks. As has been noted, fresh fluid milk has a high water content. This makes fresh milk a large-bulk food—which presents problems of storage and refrigeration. To meet these problems, excellent methods have been devised to remove all or part of the water and leave a highly concentrated milk product.

EVAPORATED MILK. The evaporation of milk is accomplished by removing a considerable amount of water from whole fluid milk. The official definition of evaporated milk, upheld by the U.S. Food and Drug Administration, is "sweet whole cow's milk, evaporated so that it contains not less than 7.5% by weight of milk fat and 25.5% of total milk solids." About 60% of the water is removed. The evaporated milk must be sealed in a container and sterilized at about 239°F (115°C) for 15 minutes, thus preventing bacterial spoilage. If a stabilizer is used, it must be not more than 0.1% by weight of total milk solids. Stabilizers such as sodium citrate, carrageen, disodium phosphate, and calcium chloride are used to obtain a smooth evaporated milk product.

Evaporated milk can be enriched by irradiation or by the addition of an oil rich in vitamin D. All evaporated milks containing vitamin D are so labeled. Two consumer can sizes can be purchased: 13 fl oz (approximately 1⅔ cups); 5.33 fl oz (approximately ⅔ cup).

In the production of evaporated milk, the milk is preheated to a higher than pasteurization temperature in stainless steel steam-jacketed kettles. The milk is then passed into vacuum pans, where evaporation occurs. Evaporation is facilitated by reducing the atmospheric pressure so that the milk boils at 130–135°F (74–77°C), which prevents the undesirable changes caused by overheating from taking place. The light brown color of the milk is due to the reaction of the sugar (lactose) and the proteins in the milk when heated (the Maillard reaction). Under normal atmospheric conditions, milk boils at 212.3°F (100°C). As evaporation takes place and solids become more concentrated, a higher temperature is required for the milk to boil.

EVAPORATED SKIM MILK. Evaporated skim milk with vitamin D added is similar to evaporated milk but it is made with skim milk instead of whole milk. When diluted with an equal amount of water, it is used like fresh skim milk.

SWEETENED CONDENSED MILK. Sweetened condensed milk is obtained by evaporating fresh milk sweetened with sucrose or dextrose (or both) to a point where the finished product contains not less than 28% total milk solids, not less than 8.5% milk fat, and 44% sugar. The amount of sucrose or sucrose and dextrose used is sufficient to prevent spoilage. Corn syrup may be used as part of the sweetening ingredient, replacing dextrose.

Sweetened condensed milk is processed in the same way that evaporated milk is, except that sugar is added before evaporation takes place and the heated mixture is cooled rapidly, with agitation. Sweetened condensed milk is used to make sweetened desserts. If lemon juice or another acid is added to the milk, it will thicken without heating to form a pudding or cream pie filling.

DRY MILK. Dry milk is available as dry whole milk and nonfat dry milk. To obtain dry whole milk, water is removed from fresh sweet milk. Dry whole milk contains butterfat, milk proteins, minerals, milk sugar, and vitamins. In the manufacture of nonfat dry milk solids, most of the water and butterfat are removed from fresh whole milk, leaving milk proteins, minerals, milk sugar, and vitamins (except vitamin A).

The methods used to dry milk are the spray process and roller process. In spray drying, the water in the milk is removed under pressure and blown as a fine spray into a heated vacuum. Spray-dried products are fine and powdery and are generally preferred over roller-dried solids, for they are easily dissolved when handled according to directions. Roller-dried milk solids form coarser granules than the spray-dried milk solids and are not readily soluble.

There is a tendency for dry milk solids to lump when added to water. If the solids are exposed to moisture, the fine powder forms crystals that bring the water-soluble lactose to the surface of the crystal. These crystals instantly dissolve when mixed with water.

Instant nonfat dry milk crystals (Fig. 22-1) are almost instantly dissolved when mixed with water. Instant dry milk crystals cannot be substituted exactly for spray-dried milk in a recipe; package directions should be followed for reconstitution. The quick dehydrating characteristic of the instant milk solids is the result of a second drying step that imparts a porous, spongelike structure to the particles.

Filled Milk. Filled milk is a combination of skim milk and vegetable fat or of nonfat dry milk, water, and vegetable fat. The fat may be either coconut oil or hydrogenated soybean and corn oils. It is illegal to ship it out of the state in which it is manufactured.

Imitation Milk. Imitation milk is a combination of several nondairy ingredients made in the semblance of milk. The ingredients include vegetable fat (generally coconut oil), protein such as sodium caseinate or soy, solids, corn syrup solids, flavoring agents, stabilizers, emulsifiers, and water.

Cream and Related Foods. Cream is milk that is extra rich in fat droplets. If milk is not ho-

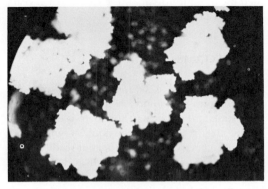

22-1 *Microscopic view of instant nonfat milk particles.* (*Courtesy of Carnation Company*)

mogenized, the fat droplets will rise to the top to form a layer of cream. When the fat droplets are homogenized to a very small size, they are unable to aggregate and remain in solution. Some milks, such as goat's milk, do not cream, since the fat droplets are naturally present in a small size.

Heavy cream or whipping cream contains not less than 36% fat; it is not homogenized. Coffee cream is also known as *light cream* or *table cream* and is often homogenized. It contains about 18–20% butterfat. Half and half is a mixture of milk and cream, usually containing 10–12% butterfat. Sour cream (or cultured sour cream) is made from light cream that has been soured by lactic acid produced from a bacterial culture. Since sour cream will easily curdle, owing to its acid content, it is usually added at the end of cooking a product. Pressurized whipped cream is a mixture of cream, sugar, stabilizers, flavors, and emulsifires packed in aerosol cans under pressure.

Cream Substitutes. The cream substitutes are the coffee whiteners, and dry whipped topping mixes; also, most of the whipped toppings in pressurized cans are made from nondairy products. A recent product on the market is an imitation sour cream. The substitute products are generally composed of corn syrup solids, vegetable fat, sodium caseinate, buffers, anticaking agents (coffee creamers), emulsifiers, and artificial flavors and colors.

In general, the substitute product is less expensive than the corresponding dairy product they replace. The shelf life of the imitation dairy product may be longer, owing to the vegetable fat content. For example, coffee creamer has a shelf life of 6 months at 100°F (38°C) or 2 years at 70°F (21°C).

MILK FOAMS

When a liquid is whipped, the air may be trapped into the liquid to form a foam. The formation and stability of the foam is dependent on the surface tension of the liquid. Owing to its high surface tension, water does not readily foam unless an emulsifying agent such as detergent is added. When milk products are whipped, the air is trapped as bubbles surrounded by thin layers of protein with fat interspersed to act as stabiliz-

ers. Thus, the higher the fat content of the foam, the greater the degree of stability.

Whipped Cream. The fat content of cream to be whipped may range from 22 to 36%. Although the higher fat cream produces a more stable product, it is most economical to use cream with a fat content of 30%. Cream with a lesser fat content may by used but results in a less desirable product. An exception to this is when cream is to be used as a filling in pastry. A high-fat cream will have a lower water content and thus allow a drier, less soggy pastry.

Since the ease of incorporation of the cream into a foam is partially dependent on the ability of the fat droplets to aggregate, homogenized cream is difficult to whip. It can be used satisfactorily if it is scalded and chilled prior to beating.

The temperature at which cream is whipped is very important. Since fat droplets will clump more easily when they are in a hardened rather than softened state, cream should be between 35°F (2°C) to 40°F (4°C) when whipped. It is also helpful to chill the bowl and beaters to allow as little dissipation of heat as possible. If cream is allowed to warm to room temperature (70°F, 20°C) whipping may be difficult, if not impossible.

It is easy to overwhip cream. Only a few extra seconds with an electric beater may turn it into an irreversible buttery product. The chance of overbeating can be reduced if sugar is folded in at the end of the whipping period. Sugar should not be added prior to this, since it will increase the beating time as well as decrease the volume. The volume of the final product will be 2–3 times that of the cream from which it was made.

Stabilizers may be added to retard the collapse of the foam. Either 2 tsp of instant nonfat dry milk solids or 1 tsp of 10% limewater (calcium hydroxide) may be added to 1 cup of cream before whipping. Refrigerating the finished product will also reduce its tendency to collapse.

Finished shaped portions of whipped cream may be frozen unwrapped on waxed paper. Once solid, they may be placed into a container to be stored for future use. Only a few minutes are required for thawing.

Whipped Evaporated Milk. Although the flavor and texture of whipped evaporated milk is not as acceptable as that of whipped cream, it is still popular, owing to its lower cost. The methods for whipping evaporated milk are basically the same as for cream. However, since it does not form as stable as foam as whipped cream, the viscosity must be increased. This is done by chilling the milk in the freezer until ice crystals are formed. An acid that denatures the protein, such as lemon juice, may be added. Two tablespoons of lemon juice are added to 1 cup of evaporated milk. This may produce an acid taste in the product. The addition of gelatin or vegetable gums are other ways to increase the viscosity without affecting the taste. Instead, the texture is affected resulting in a stiffer product.

Whipped Nonfat Dry Milk. Partially reconstituted nonfat dry milk may also be whipped into a foam. An advantage to this product is the lower calorie content and inexpensive cost. The methods for whipping and increasing viscosity are similar to that for evaporated milk. It is made by adding 2 tbsp of lemon juice to ½ cup nonfat dry milk and ½ cup water or fruit juice. If instant crystals are used, the ratio is ½ cup crystals to ⅓ cup liquid.

PRINCIPLES OF COOKING MILK AND MILK PRODUCTS

In cookery, milk is treated as a high-protein food. Both the flavor and the odor of milk are adversely affected by prolonged heating and by high temperatures. Heated milk forms a precipitate thought to be albumin, which covers the bottom of the cooking pan. This coagulated material tends to scorch unless the milk is heated in a double boiler or stirred while heating. When milk is heated in an uncovered pan, a surface skin forms. It is thought that the skin consists of coagulated milk proteins (casein), fat, and minerals and results from a drying out of the top of the milk. The skin is tough, forming a tight steamproof film over the milk, causing it to foam and boil over. Skin formation can be prevented by using a covered container, by stirring the milk during the heating process, or by beating the mixture with a rotary beater to form a foamy layer on the surface of the mixture.

When milk is served warm, as in hot chocolate, the skin formation is unappetizing. It can be covered by serving the beverage with whipped cream or marshmallows floating on top. It may

also be made unnoticeable if the beverage is whipped into a foam.

Milk proteins are coagulated not only by heat but also by the enzyme rennet and by acids. The importance of rennet in the cheese industry is widely recognized. When added to heated milk, rennet brings about the clotting of casein as in the following reaction:

calcium phosphocaseinate $\xrightarrow{\text{rennin}}$

calcium caseinate

The gel-like clot formed is tough and rubbery and contains most of the calcium. This curdling of the milk into curds and whey creates clabbered milk. The curds are then pressed into cheese if desired. Boiling, and an alkaline reaction in the milk, will retard the action of rennet, thus preventing clotting.

When acid is added to milk or the pH falls below 5.2, casein will no longer stay in solution. Casein salts (such as casein chloride and casein lactate) are formed and the milk curdles. This is shown in the following reaction:

calcium phosphocaseinate $\xrightarrow{\text{H}^+ \text{(acid)}}$

neutral caseinate

In this reaction the curd is soft and fragile. Most of the calcium will remain in the whey.

The most frequent example of this is the behavior of milk in the preparation of cream of tomato soup, in which vegetable acids may cause the separation of the milk proteins. A cream soup made with asparagus, stringbeans, peas, and carrots is more likely to curdle than one made with such vegetables as cabbage, cauliflower, and potatoes. Neutralization with baking soda can prevent curdling, but it adversely affects flavor and nutritive value.

If only a small amount of acid is added or formed, as in the case of milk beginning to sour, it may decrease the stability of the colloid proteins without clabbering. If this unstable and consequently sensitive milk is heated, it will readily curdle. This occurs when slightly sour milk is added to hot coffee.

METHODS OF COOKING MILK AND MILK PRODUCTS

When milk is used in a white sauce or as a basis for such dishes as soufflés, custards, milk puddings, and beverages, low heat should be applied.

To prevent curdling of milk when acid is added, either the milk or the acid can be thickened with starch before being combined with the other ingredient. This treatment will hold the casein in suspension and prevent it from coagulating. When fruit juices and fresh fruit are added to milk, clotting of the casein often occurs. Generally, this is due to the acidity of the fruit. (If pineapple juice is used, the enzyme bromelin may cause clotting.) These clots, however, become very soft and are easily dispersed.

USE OF DRY MILK SOLIDS

Generally, whole or nonfat dry milk may be substituted satisfactorily for fresh milk in most recipes, and dry milk solids may be added to many commonly used food products to increase their food value. Dry milk solids are usually sifted with the other dry ingredients when used in a recipe for baked products. For use in beverages, soups, custards, and sauces, dry milk solids are reconstituted and used as fluid milk. Nonfat dry milk increases the viscosity of chocolate puddings and starch sauces such as white sauce. This can be adjusted by reducing the amount of cornstarch or flour used for thickening.

The dry milk product is converted to fluid form by combining ½ cup to ⅔ cup dry milk with 1 pt water. Water and milk solids are mixed together until a smooth mixture is obtained. Manufacturer's direction may give a slightly different proportion of milk solids to water.

Nonfat dry milk solids are added with the dry ingredients to mixtures for prepared dishes. Baked products fortified with extra amounts of dry nonfat milk solids are a deeper golden brown than those baked with standard amounts. They are also more convenient to use in bread making than whole milk since they do not have to be scalded. Adding extra nonfat dry milk to food mixtures is an economical way for the consumer to increase the amount of good-quality protein.

For home use, nonfat dry milk, mostly instantized, is available in many package sizes; there are bulk packages in cardboard and glass containers and packages with envelopes containing just enough for 1 qt reconstituted milk.

USE OF EVAPORATED MILK

Evaporated milk is less likely than whole milk to curdle when combined with acid ingredients. It tends to form more stable gels when used in puddings and custards. Evaporated milk may be used as it comes in the can only for recipes developed specifically for such use. For general use in cookery, evaporated milk is diluted with an equal volume of water and used as a substitute for fresh whole milk. In a study of the cooking qualities of different forms of milk, it was found that sauces made with evaporated milk were thicker than those made with fresh whole milk, dry whole milk, fresh skim milk, or nonfat dry milk solids.[8]

CARE OF MILK

For best retention of quality, fluid milk should be stored in the refrigerator no more than 1 week. It should be taken out only long enough to pour what is needed and immediately returned to the refrigerator. Covering or capping milk containers protects the milk from dust, bacteria, and undesirable odors and flavors. The mixing of milks from containers whose histories differ may increase the total bacteria content of the product. Milk should not be exposed to sunlight. Ascorbic acid and riboflavin losses are high in milk so exposed, and flavor of the milk deteriorates in a short time.

Storage of Dry Milk. It is important to store dried whole milk at temperatures not higher than ordinary room temperature, even when the package is airtight. If storage temperatures do not exceed normal room temperature, milk products should last at least a year without signs of deterioration. Once the container has been opened and exposed to room temperature, a lower storage temperature is desirable. This is especially true for the whole milk products, because of their fat content.

To reduce the changes caused by deterioration packages should be tightly closed or put in con-

[8] R. Matthews et al., "Functional Qualities of Different Forms of Milk," *J. Amer. Dietet. Assoc.* **40:**23, 1962.

tainers with tight-fitting covers to keep out the air and moisture.

Because of its high moisture content, reconstituted milk is subject to the same kind of spoilage as whole milk and should be refrigerated as soon as it is reconstituted if it is not immediately used.

Storage of Evaporated Milk. Unopened cans of evaporated milk may be stored at room temperature. Once the can is opened, however, the milk should be refrigerated to prevent spoilage. Cans of evaporated milk stored at room temperature for long periods of time should be turned over every few months. It is a good practice to store the milk in a dry, ventilated place to prevent rust formation on the can. Rusting may result in perforations, which could cause the milk to spoil.

Storage of Sweetened Milk. Like evaporated milk, cans of sweetened milk may be stored at room temperature until opened. The opened can should be refrigerated at a temperature close to 40°F (5°C).

SUMMARY

Milk when so identified refers to cow's milk. It is unmatched by any other food for nutritive value and has many uses in cookery. Milk contains complete proteins of high quality, is an important source of calcium, and has good amounts of phosphorus, iron, and both fat- and water-soluble vitamins. Whole milk and cream are excellent sources of vitamin A. Through enrichment, milk is made an excellent source of vitamin D. Although fresh whole milk is most in demand, evaporated milk, skim milk, buttermilk, and nonfat dry milk solids are more economical. Where the milk fat has been removed, as in buttermilk, skim milk, and nonfat dry milk solids, the milk is low in vitamin A and has reduced energy value but remains high in proteins, vitamins, and minerals.

The U.S. Public Health Service has recommended sanitary controls for the production and distribution of milk. Many states and local communities have adopted this code. Milk grades reflect bacterial count; the highest grade—Grade A—has the lowest bacterial count.

The various kinds of milk include pasteurized milk, certified milk, skim milk, chocolate milk, fermented milks, including buttermilk and yogurt, homogenized milk, vitamin D enriched milk, evaporated milk, sweetened condensed milk, and dry milk.

Low to moderate heat is used in cooking milk products. Special handling is required for milk-acid mixtures because of their tendency to curdle. In using the various forms of milk, minor adjustments in cooking time or method may be required.

Fresh milk should be refrigerated as quickly as possible because it is highly perishable. Canned milks and dry whole milk should be refrigerated after opening.

QUESTIONS AND TOPICS FOR DISCUSSION AND STUDY

1. In what ways do the nutritive values of non-fat dry milk solids and evaporated milk differ from those of whole milk?
2. Why does milk sometimes curdle in the following products: cream of asparagus, bean, or tomato soup; lemon sauce?
3. Why does an acid curdle milk?
4. What happens when rennet is added to luke-warm milk?
5. Why is it necessary to pasteurize milk?
6. What accounts for the formation of a surface film (skin) when milk is heated? How can it be avoided?

SUGGESTED ACTIVITIES

1. Compare the use of different forms of milk—nonfat dry milk solids, evaporated milk, and whole homogenized milk—in a cream soup for cost, time required for preparation, appearance, and flavor.
2. Prepare junket, using prepared mix and rennet tablet. Compare texture and flavor.

REFERENCES

Books

Garard, Ira. *Introductory Food Chemistry*. Westport, Conn.: Avi, 1976, Chap. 11.

267

Lee, Frank. *Basic Food Chemistry.* Westport, Conn.: Avi, 1975, Chap. 13.

Paul, Pauline, and Helen Palmer. *Food Theory and Applications.* New York: Wiley; 1972, Chap. 10.

ARTICLES PAMPHLETS

"Federal and State Standards for the Composition of Milk Products (and Certain Non-Milk Fat Products) as of January 1, 1974." Agriculture Handbook 51. Washington, D.C.: U.S. United States Department of Agriculture.

How Americans Use Their Dairy Foods. Chicago: National Dairy Council, 1967.

Kirkpatrick, Mary. "Use of Different Market Forms of Milk in Biscuits." *J. Home Econ.* **53:**201, 1961.

Modler, H. W., et al. "Physical and Chemical Stability of Soybean Oil-Filled Milk." *J. Food Sci.* **35:**302, 1970.

Newer Knowledge of Milk, 3rd ed. Chicago: National Dairy Council, 1968.

The Composition of Milk. Washington, D.C.: National Research Council–National Academy of Sciences, 1953.

Cheese

CHAPTER 23

Cheese is a milk product in a solid or semisolid form. Cheese is a convenient way of preserving the valuable constituents of milk, for although fresh milk is a highly desirable food product, it spoils easily.

Cheese manufacture in America is closely bound to the European art, having been brought to this country by European immigrants. The cheeses most easily recognized are those named after their place of origin: Cheddar, Roquefort, Brie, and Muenster are only a few of these. Cheddar is the most popular cheese sold in America. It has numerous uses and is by far the most important cheese for cooking purposes.

Tables 23-1 and 23-2 list the classes and principal varieties of cheese sold in the United States.

COMPOSITION

The great variation in the moisture content of the different classes of cheeses makes it difficult to give approximate compositions for all kinds. Ripened cheeses made from whole milk are approximately one-fourth protein, one-third fat, and one-third water. American Cheddar, for example, has 23.9% protein, 32.3% fat, 39% water, and 3.1% ash. Cottage cheese, however,

TABLE 23-1
Examples of Different
Classes of Cheese

Class	Name of Cheese
Hard grating	Parmesan (Caciocavallo), Romano
Hard	Cheddar, Swiss, Edam
Semihard	Brick (Lagerkaese), Muenster
Soft unripened (uncured)	Cream, Neufchatel (as made in America), cottage
Soft ripened (cured)	Camembert, Brie, Bel Paese

TABLE 23-2
Domestic and Foreign Varieties of Cheeses Commonly Sold in the United States

Name, Country of Origin	Description and Use
Bel Paese (Italy)	Soft to semisoft, with a yellow inside and gray surface; made from cow's milk; usually sold in 1-lb units; requires about 3 months to ripen; eaten as purchased
Blue vein (France)	Similar to Roquefort; semihard white cheese made from cow's milk; has a green mold; requires about 2 months' cure to develop flavor; usually sold by the pound but also comes in 5-lb units; eaten as purchased
Brick (Lagerkaese) (U.S.)	A sweet curd cheese made from cow's milk; semihard, with a creamy yellow inside and a straw-colored surface; can be cured from 2 to 9 months (sweetish taste becomes sharper with additional curing); eaten as purchased
Caciocavallo (Italy)	Hard cheese, light inside and gray outside; smoked; molded in the shape of a tenpin and is usually hung by a small rope around its neck; curing time from 2 months to 2 years; made in 2–5-lb molds; may be eaten as purchased or grated and used for flavoring
Camembert (France)	Soft, mold-ripened, with a grayish surface and creamy, waxy color inside; made from cow's milk; almost creamy in texture when cured; cured for approximately 4 weeks; used as purchased
Chantelle (U.S.)	Semihard, with a yellow inside and a red surface; creamy texture; usually eaten as purchased
Cheddar (England, U.S.)	Hard, white to orange inside; mild to sharp flavor; waxed surface; ripening lasts from 2 months to 2 years; most commonly used cooking cheese in the United States
Cheshire (England)	Cheddar-type cheese with very sharp taste; made from cow's milk; usually cured for 8–10 weeks; molded in 50–70-lb units; used for cooking as well as for general eating purposes
Colby (U.S.)	Cheddar-type cheese; mild, mellow, or sharp, depending on cure; used for cooking and for general eating purposes
Cottage (Germany)	Soft, large curd; made from cow's milk; high moisture content; requires no curing; very perishable; eaten as purchased
Cream cheese (U.S.)	Soft, uncured, smooth; white to creamy; made from cream or a mixture of cream and one or more ingredients such as skim milk and suet (a thickening agent such as gelatin or algin may also be used)
Edam (Holland)	Hard, ball-shaped cheese with a yellow inside and a red wax surface; made from cow's milk, partly skimmed; cured for 1 to 3 months; comes in 2–6-lb molds; can be used for cooking, grating, and general eating purposes
Gorgonzola (Italy)	Semisoft or soft; yellow with green inside, gray surface; in U.S., made from cow's milk; in Italy, made from a mixture of cow's and goat's milk; very sharp flavor; cured from 3 months to 1 year; eaten as purchased
Gruyere (Switzerland)	Processed Swiss cheese, soft inside; sold in triangular portions; eaten as purchased

TABLE 23-2 (Cont.)

Name, Country of Origin	Description and Use
Harz (Germany)	Semihard; sharp odor and taste; sold in 4-oz packages; eaten as purchased
Jack (U.S.)	Soft; whitish inside and out; cured about 6 weeks; sold primarily on the West Coast; used in cooking and for general eating purposes
Liederkranz (U.S.)	Soft; creamy inside, russet outside; bacteria-ripened; strong flavor resembles that of Limburger but is not as sharp
Limburger (Belgium, Germany)	Soft-textured cheese; very distinct flavor and odor; cured from 1 to 2 weeks; creamy white inside, grayish outside; bacteria-ripened; used for general eating purposes
Muenster (Germany)	Semihard mild cheese made from cow's milk; creamy white inside and yellowish surface; slight cracks or holes in body of cheese; cured for about 2 months; used for general eating purposes
Mysost, Primost (Scandinavia)	Semihard; generally made from cow's whey; sweet flavor; buttery texture; brown inside and out; cured for 6 to 8 months; used for general eating purposes
Neufchatel (France)	Soft, mild; similar to cream cheese; creamy white in color; requires no curing; spoils quickly; eaten as purchased; may be used in cooking
Parmesan (Italy)	Very hard; yellowish-white inside and green surface; cured for several years; used mainly for cooking in grated form
Pineapple (U.S.)	Hard, Cheddar-type; deep yellow inside, orange surface; cured for 6 to 8 months; used for general purposes
Port du Salut (France)	Semisoft, sharp; creamy yellow inside, deeper yellow surface; cured for 5 to 6 weeks; used for general purposes
Provolone (Italy)	Hard, smoked; light yellow inside, light tan surface; requires 2 to 3 months' curing; has rope marks on outside; used for general purposes
Ricotta (Italy)	Soft white curd made from whey and skim milk; salty to taste; no curing necessary; spoils easily; used principally for cooking
Romano (Italy)	Very hard; creamy yellow inside and black surface; made from cow's milk; in Italy made from sheep's milk; cured from 1 to 4 years; excellent for flavoring and cooking; usually used in grated form
Roquefort (France)	Semihard, sharp, with a green mold; made from sheep milk; requires 3 to 9 months' curing; eaten as purchased
Royal Stilton (England)	Semisoft; very sharp-tasting; made from cow's milk; creamy color, with green mold inside; requires 6 months to 2 years' curing; eaten as purchased
Sap Sago (Switzerland)	Hard, green-colored, flavored with clover leaves; usually sold in the shape of a cone; requires 6 months to 2 years' curing; used for cooking in grated form
Swiss (Switzerland)	Hard; light yellow cheese made from cow's milk; sweet-tasting; gas holes are formed from bacteria; requires from 3 to 10 months' curing; may be eaten as purchased; excellent for cooking when cut or ground

has approximately 74% water 1% fat, 19.2% protein, and 1.7% ash.[1]

NUTRITIVE VALUE

Cheese, a highly concentrated form of milk, is rich in nutrients. Approximately 10 lb of milk goes into 1 lb of cheese. For practical purposes, a round figure of 5 oz American cheese is given as the equivalent in food value to 1 qt of milk. Because the proteins of milk are complete, they are excellent body-building material. The chief protein in cheese is casein; there is also a small but significant amount of albumins. In some cheeses, the ripening process is rather extensive, causing much of the casein to be broken down to amino acids and ammonia. The energy value depends mainly on the fat and water content of the particular kind of cheese. The amount of cholesterol in the cheese will depend on its variety. Uncreamed cottage cheese will have only 7 mg of cholesterol/100 grams while others, such as cream cheese, will have as much as 110 mg/100 grams. The cheeses that have rennet-formed curds are excellent sources of calcium and zinc, retaining about 80% of the total amount present in the milk; the cheeses whose curd is formed by acid coagulation retain only about 20% of the original calcium content of the milk. Hence, Cheddar cheese, a rennet-formed curd cheese, has a high percentage of calcium retention; cottage cheese and Neufchatel, acid-formed curd cheeses, lose considerable amounts of calcium salts which split off into the whey during manufacture. Cheese is easily digestible since lactose is generally left in the whey during curd formation. Residue amounts which remain are acidified to lactic acid by bacteria during ripening. Cheeses made from whole milk are good sources of vitamin A and riboflavin.

ECONOMIC ASPECTS

The higher-priced varieties of cheeses are not necessarily those with the highest food value. The more expensive cheeses are valued for their

[1] C. Chatfield and G. Adams, Proximate Composition of Foods (Edible Portion)," *Circular 549* (Washington, D.C.: U.S. Department of Agriculture, 1940).

flavor. Early methods of making cheese evolved as a means of preserving the valued nutrients of milk. Local methods of making cheese were not standardized, and the milk curds were set aside to develop flavors that were characteristic of the environment in which they were stored. These methods, although hit-and-miss, established flavor standards that are still used today as one of the factors in grading cheese. Of very practical importance to the consumer is the fact that low-cost cheese may easily have a nutritive value equal or superior to that of more expensive cheeses. The length of time the cheese ripens also adds to its cost. Domestic varieties of foreign cheeses are generally less expensive than the imported varieties.

Cheese should be selected in terms of the use to be made of it. Cheese for cooking should have excellent blending qualities as well as good flavor. Some knowledge of cost, grade, and flavor will serve as a guide to selection.

GRADING

Federal grades for cheese are available for wholesale buyers' use. Some of the cheese packaged for retail trade also carries government grades. Grading is based on the factors of flavor, body, and texture. In addition, Swiss cheese is rated on "eye" formation. U.S. grades are a valuable guide to cheese flavor. Plants using the grading service must operate under regulations for sanitation and packing specified by the U.S. Department of Agriculture. No U.S. grades have been established for processed cheese and cheese foods, but a good amount processed under federal inspection in accordance with specifications prepared by the U.S. Department of Agriculture is being marked with the official inspection emblem. The grades for Cheddar cheese include U.S. Grade AA, U.S. Grade A, U.S. Grade B, and U.S. Grade C. Those for Swiss cheese are U.S. Grade A, U.S. Grade B, U.S. Grade C, and U.S. Grade D. Most of the graded cheese on the market is Cheddar cheese marked "U.S. Grade A." The official grade label or inspection mark on cheese assures the customer of a dependable quality. Cheddar cheese is labeled "mild," "medium" or "mellow," or "aged" or "sharp." The sharp or aged flavors are usually better for cooking and eating. The increased cost of the longer curing time required for the development of flavor is reflected in the price that the consumer pays.

CHEESE MANUFACTURE

Modern American methods of making cheese draw more heavily on the science of microbiology and the role of microorganisms in the development of flavor than on the older trial-and-error methods that were used in Europe. In America, the cheese industry has become important chiefly through scientific research. At present, practically any variety of the 800 natural cheeses can be manufactured in the United States. Although different types of milk (sheep, goat, buffalo) may be used to manufacture many types of cheese, in the United States the most common milk used is cow's milk.

There are two basic ways to produce cheese. The first involves acidifying the milk (whole or skim) to form a soft gel-like curd (see Chapter 22). This forms the soft, unripened cheeses with a high moisture content, such as cottage and cream cheese. The second method involves forming a curd from the enzyme extracted from calf's stomach, rennin. This produces a tough, rubbery clot with a low moisture content. Depending on the time and conditions of ripening, hard cheeses such as cheddar and Swiss are manufactured by this method.

American Cheddar is the principal variety of cheese manufactured and sold in this country (Fig. 23-1). Frequently, this cheese is simply called American cheese.

Manufacture of Selected Cheeses. CHEDDAR CHEESE. Cheddar cheese is made from whole pasteurized milk. The milk is placed in large rectangular vats, heated to 86°F (30°C), and treated with *Streptococcus lacti* bacteria. The bacteria are allowed to ferment 30 to 60 minutes to acidify the milk to pH 5.8. Coloring matter (usually annatto) is added. The milk is heated to 99°F (37°C) and sufficient rennin added to bring about coagulation of the proteins. The temperature at which rennin is coagulated is sensitive. Slightly below this temperature, too soft a curd will form; above 149°F (65°C), the clot will be too hard; and below 50°F (10°C), curds will not form. The coagulated milk is

23-1 *Grade label shows that this Wisconsin natural cheese has been graded and packed under the supervision of the U.S. Department of Agriculture. (Courtesy of U.S. Department of Agriculture)*

heated until the curd reaches a consistency of sufficient firmness to form the cheese body. The curd is cut into small pieces to expel the whey and to shrink the curd. After the curd is cut, there is considerable shrinkage of the curd and a corresponding loss of water.

After the curd is formed, the whey is removed by gravity flow. The curd becomes a firm homogeneous mass that is further cut and stirred until all the whey is removed. At this time, the cheese "cheddars"—that is, the curd mats together. The cheese is again broken up, salted, mixed, and packed into cheesecloth-lined hoops. The hoops will be of various sizes, depending on the style of cheese desired. The hoops are put into cheese presses, which with increased pressure will expel the remaining whey and form the shape.

The cheddaring process is very important, for if this is not accomplished properly, the curd will have a soft, open texture. The moisture that collects in these holes is apt to cause rot while the cheese is curing. At this stage of processing, the cheese is called *green cheese*. The pressed green cheese is dried for several days and is then coated with hot paraffin to prevent moisture loss during the curing process.

The final step in the manufacture of Cheddar cheese, and the principal one with regard to flavor development, is the curing of the green cheese. The green cheese is placed in a ventilated room on racks for 2 months to 1 year. The temperature range is 40–65°F (5–13°C). The longer the curing period, the more developed the flavor.

PASTEURIZED PROCESSED CHEESE. Processed cheese is in high demand because of its uniform and blending characteristics. A processed cheese without a variety name means processed Cheddar cheese, although Cheddar is not the only variety of processed cheese. Processed Cheddar cheese is made by blending, usually in the proportion 6 parts of heavily cured Cheddar cheese to 1 part green cheese. The blended cheeses may have only 1% more moisture than the cheeses from which it was made. The cheese is cleaned, trimmed, cut into large pieces, and passed through a huge grinder in which the first mixing of the cheese takes place. It is heated (pasteurized), after which no further ripening occurs. The cheese is then mixed with a small amount of water and salt. An emulsifier or plasticizer is added to the mixture. Commonly used emulsifiers are disodium phosphate and sodium citrate. The plasticizers are essential to the production of a completely uniform cheese product. Only the emulsifiers permitted by the U.S. Food and Drug Administration are used.[2] The mixture is stirred and heated for 10–15 minutes at a temperature of 150–170°F (66–77°C). This incorporates air into the mixture and pasteurizes the cheese. The hot cheese mixture is then poured into greaseproof wrapper–lined molds and salted. Much of the original character of the cheese is lost in the manufacture of processed cheese; the heating of the mixture reduces the danger of mold fermentation, but it also stops the ripening of the cheese and the resultant development of flavor. Processed cheese is very popular, however, for its sliceability and good blending characteristics.

The cheese from which a processed cheese is made may be smoked, or the processed cheese itself may be smoked. The cheese product may contain chemical substances prepared by condensing or precipitating wood smoke.

The emulsifying agent used for plasticizing the processed cheese is never added in amounts greater than 3% of the weight of the processed cheese. Optional ingredients added to the cheese are acids, cream, water, coloring, and spices.

As yet, no grades have been established for processed cheese and cheese foods. They may be processed under federal inspection and are marked with an official inspection emblem.

PASTEURIZED PROCESSED CHEESE FOODS. When pasteurized processed cheese foods are prepared, milk or milk products are added to the pasteurized processed cheese. The milk is added to create a softer product and to develop a milder taste.

Pasteurized processed cheese foods with added fruits, vegetables, or meats, or a mixture of these, must (with few exceptions) meet the same standards of identity prescribed for pasteurized processed cheese.

PASTEURIZED PROCESSED CHEESE SPREADS. Pasteurized processed cheese spreads have a higher moisture content (ranging from 47 to 60%) and a lower milkfat content than pasteurized processed cheeses. A cheese spread is a packaged cheese that may be easily spread with a knife at ordinary room temperature. Among the cheese spreads are a moist, spready processed cheese and processed American Cheddar cheese to which whey and dried skim milk have been added. These products are prohibited by federal Food and Drug legislation from being labeled and sold as cheese, and are sold under trade names. They are identified as spreads on their labels.

COLDPACK CHEESE. Coldpack cheese or club cheese is a blend of one or more varieties of fresh and aged natural cheese. The difference between coldpack cheese and processed cheese is that the former is mixed into a uniform product without heating. The flavor is the same as that of the natural cheese used—usually "aged" or "sharp." The body is soft and spreads easily. Coldpack cheese may be packed in jars or rolls. Coldpack cheese food is prepared like coldpack cheese but may include nonfat dried milk or whey solids and water. Some sweetening agent such as sugar or corn syrup may be added. The flavor is milder than that of the cheese from which it is made.

COTTAGE CHEESE. Cottage cheese is made

---

[2] Code of Federal Regulations, rev. 1971.

from pasteurized skim milk that has been inoculated with lactic acid bacteria and a small amount of rennin. The curds formed are drained, washed, and salted. The curd is not worked, so the curd granules may be varied in size up to ½ in. in diameter. It may be sold as country style (small curd) or popcorn style (large curd).

Cream is usually added to the mixture so that it contains not less than 4% milkfat and not more than 80% moisture. The percentage of milkfat should appear on the cottage cheese label. Uncreamed or dry curd cottage cheese does not have any cream added to the drained curd. It is made in the same way as cottage cheese, but it contains not less than 0.5% milkfat and not over 80% moisture. Lowfat cottage cheese is different from the dry-curd type in that it contains between 0.5 and 4.0% milkfat and not over 82.5% moisture. Direct-set cottage cheese has had special food-grade acids added to it to coagulate the milk to form the cheese curd. The label should read "Direct Set" or "Curd Set by Direct Acidification."

Baker's cheese is cottage cheese in which the curds are drained of the whey but are not cooked, washed, or worked. Salting is optional. It is given this name because it is often used in baked products, such as cheese cake, pies, and pastries.

CREAM CHEESE. Cream cheese is an unripened cheese made from cream with 10-12% milkfat. It is started by a lactic acid bacteria which acidifies the milk to produce curds. It is then stirred, heated, salted, and centrifuged. It is worked until it is a smooth paste, often with the help of emulsifiers such as gelatin, agar, and other vegetable gums. Owing to its high moisture (55%) and high fat (33%) content, it is marketed soon after manufacture. If cream with a lower fat content is used, it is called neufchatel cheese.

AMERICAN SWISS CHEESE (RINDLESS). Swiss cheese is made from clarified, partially skimmed milk that has been ripened by *Lactobacillus bulgaricus* and *Streptococcus thermophilus* at 88–94°F (31–35°C). The eyes or hole of the Swiss cheese is due to the propionic acid fermentation of a third microorganism, *Propionibacterium shermanii*. When the milk has been acidified, rennin is added to form a curd. The curd is cut into very small pieces and heated while being stirred constantly for 1 hour at 125–129°F (46–54°C).

This mixture is subject to pressure and the whey is gradually drained off. The pressed cheese is cut into 80- to 100-lb blocks, salted, and allowed to dry for a few days. It is then wrapped in plastic film, held for a few days at cool temperatures, and then put into a room-temperature environment. In less than 1 month, the eyes of the cheese will have developed, but best flavor is reached if it is allowed to cure at lower temperatures for a few months.

WHEY CHEESE. When curds are formed, the whey retains many of the important nutrients, such as lactose, whey proteins, vitamins, and minerals. Whey can be made into cheese by two methods. The first is to concentrate whey by boiling, then cooling to a firm sugary consistency. Mysost or Primost are examples of whey cheeses made in this manner. They are very hard cheeses, owing to their low moisture content, and have a long storage life.

Ricotta cheese, which resembles cottage cheese, is made according to the second method. The whey protein is coagulated from whole milk, skimmed milk, or skimmed milk and whey. The type of milk used determines its final fat content. Heat and acid is used to coagulate the protein and the curd is skimmed off and pressed into hoops.

DRIED WHEY. Sweet whey processed and dried under sanitary conditions is being used in increasing amounts as a component of food products such as candies, cheese spreads, and salad dressings.

Ripening. During ripening, some chemical and physical changes take place in the cheese that are of prime importance in its manufacture. These changes affect the appearance, flavor, and texture characteristics of the cheese. The proteins (calcium caseinate) hydrolyze and are more soluble. Considerable breakdown of the fat also occurs. The fats are hydrolyzed into volatile fatty acids which contribute much to the sharper flavor of aged cheese. These volatile fatty acids are easily digestible. There is also an increase in B vitamins formed during ripening of some cheese varieties. Physically, the cheese changes from a tough, rubbery mass to a soft and sometimes crumbly solid.

Flavor. Flavor in cheese is principally caused by the fatty acids and their compounds, the ammonia substances formed during ripening from the breakdown of casein, and the salt added to the curd. The breakdown of the nitrogenous material of cheese is brought about chiefly by the action of enzymes originally present in the cheese or by microorganisms that cause fermentation.

The flavor of the cheese is best appreciated if it is served at room temperature. It normally takes 30 minutes to 1 hour for refrigerated cheese to warm to room temperature. Only soft unripened cheeses such as cottage and cream cheese should be served chilled.

CHEESE CLASSIFICATION

Although there are literally hundreds of names for cheese, domestic and foreign, there are really only about 18 varieties (see Color Plate X). These varieties are differentiated according to their flavor, body, and texture. This will vary with the type of milk used, quantity of salt and other seasonings, bacterial species and molds used for manufacturing inoculation, and manufacturing and processing methods.[3] The environmental conditions during the ripening process, such as temperature, humidity, and curing time, can also make a major difference in the final product. Cheeses are classified as hard grating cheese, hard cheese, semisoft cheese, soft uncured cheese, and soft cured cheese.

Hard grating cheeses are made principally from partly skimmed cow's milk. Fat is removed from the milk in the making of these cheeses, but some fat is necessary for the development of desirable flavor. In order to develop sufficient flavor, hard grating cheese must contain at least 32 per cent milkfat in the solids. Hard grating cheese is fairly low in moisture content. Because this kind of cheese has a sharp flavor, the minimum curing time required to develop the characteristic flavor is 6 months. Most grating cheeses have a much longer curing time than other cheeses and are rennet-curd cheeses.

The hard or firm ripened cheeses are made from pasteurized milk and subjected to the action of lactic acid bacteria, which bring about the proper acidity of the mixture for curding. The procedure in the making of a hard cheese is similar to that described for making Cheddar cheese. The shaped curd is cured for from 2 months to 2 years, and the flavor becomes increasingly sharp. Cheddar, Colby, Edam, Gouda, Provolone, and Swiss are examples of firm ripened cheeses. They have a moisture content of approximately 40%.

Semisoft or ripened cheeses are those with a moderate moisture content of 35 to 45%. Brick, Muenster, and Port du Salut are manufactured much as the hard cheeses are, but the curd may not be cut or heated. Semisoft cheese may be cured with molds for from 4 weeks to several months.

Soft uncured or unripened cheeses such as cottage, cream, and neufchatel cheese are made from cream or from a mixture of milk, skim milk, and concentrated skim milk. To the cream mixture, lactic acid bacteria (with or without rennin) are added. The coagulated mass is drained, and the curd is pressed, chilled, and seasoned with salt. The soft uncured cheeses have a lower fat content than other cheeses.

Soft cured or soft-ripened cheeses are made much like semisoft cheese, but a mold or bacteria culture is used to effect the cure and to develop the necessary flavor. Brie, Camembert, and Limburger are soft-ripened cheeses. The cheese cures on these cheeses move from the surface to the interior of the cheese. Since the microorganisms must diffuse throughout the cheese, the size of these cheeses is limited.

The blue-vein (ripened) cheeses are made with a mold culture characteristic of each variety. A culture of bacteria such as *Penicillium roqueforti* is mixed with the cheese before it is shaped. As it ripens (for 2–12 months) it spreads throughout the cheese, hydrolyzes fats to free fatty acids, and produces flavor and texture changes. Blue, Gorgonzola, Stilton, and Roquefort are common blue-vein mold varieties.

Excellent domestic varieties of most of the cheeses listed in Table 23-2 can be purchased in the United States.

Low-Fat, Low-Cholesterol Cheeses. A low-cholesterol cheese that meets the flavor and cooking standards of natural cheeses has been developed. The milkfat has been replaced with corn oil to form a pasteurized process filled cheese food. The cheese has 95% less cholesterol than regular cheese and a *P/S* ratio of 4.5:1.

[3] "How to Buy Cheese," *G193* (Washington, D.C.: U.S. Department of Agriculture, 1971).

A low-calorie, 99% fat-free cheese has recently come on the market. In this type of cheese spread product, all but 1% of the milkfat has been removed. It is high in protein and has 65% fewer calories than ordinary cheddar spread. A spreadable form packaged in a plastic tub is also being marketed. For those who are on low-sodium diets, a cheese reduced in sodium content as well as cholesterol has appeared on the market.

PRINCIPLES OF COOKING CHEESE

Like the proteins of meat and eggs, cheese proteins coagulate when subjected to heat and become tough and rubbery when overheated. Cheese proteins, however, do not exude water when overheated, for they are emulsified with fat and water. At cold temperatures, the fat in the cheese is solid. As it is allowed to warm to room temperature, the fat will soften and so will the cheese. During heating, the fat will melt and, if overheated, the emulsion will sometimes break and the fat separate out from the other constituents. This loss of water will cause the cheese to shrink and toughen. Overcooking may be caused by prolonged cooking or cooking at excessively high temperatures.

METHODS OF COOKING CHEESE

Some cheeses blend more easily than others. Cream cheese combines very easily with other ingredients and is used in a number of main dishes and deserts. Processed cheese lends itself well to cooking because it is made of several cheeses blended together and therefore contains emulsifiers and other materials that prevent the separation of fat during heating. Cheddar is the chief cheese used for cooking, but it has a tendency to stringiness and separation when cooked alone. When Cheddar is used in cooked dishes, it is a good practice to modify its texture by adding a white sauce or some other starchy ingredient to keep the fat emulsified. (See Fig. 23-2) The Cheddar cheese that has the most satisfactory cooking qualities has a normal, not low, fat content and a high moisture content.[4]

A green cheese is difficult to use in cooking because it does not blend well with other materials and brings little of the characteristic flavor of the cheese to the cooked dish. Cheeses that have had a ripening period of 12 months have cooking qualities superior to those of cheeses ripened for shorter periods of time. A cheese to be used in cooking should have been ripened for at least 3 months.

Cheese should be chopped or grated before being added to a sauce or cooked dish. The division of cheese is important, for it increases the surface area of the cheese for emulsification.

[4] C. Personius, E. Boardmore, and A. R. Aushermore, "Some Factors Affecting the Behavior of Cheddar Cheese in Cooking," *Food Res.* **9**:304, 1944.

23-2 *A delectable cheese soufflé may be served for luncheon or supper. (Courtesy of American Egg Board)*

The addition of an acid to a cheese dish may increase the tendency of the cheese to separate and become stringy.

Processed cheese appears to have better cooking qualities than natural cheese. It combines well with white sauce, possibly because of the addition of emulsifying salts to the cheese blend and added water. It is thought that the emulsifiers may render the casein more soluble, which would minimize the tendency of the cheese to toughen when heat is applied.

CARE AND STORAGE

Soft unripened cheese will spoil quickly and must be placed in a covered container and refrigerated until consumed. It should be eaten within a few days of purchase.

Hard and semihard cheeses should also be stored at low temperatures to avoid deterioration. It is best to store the cheese in the original wrapper. When it is cut, the cheese should be carefully covered with a moist cloth or plastic wrap to prevent drying out. If the cheese must be stored for a long period of time, the cut surface should be sealed with hot parafilm wax. Any mold that forms on old cheese is unappetizing rather than harmful. If it is scraped away with a knife, the cheese is safe to eat. Grated cheese has less of a tendency to dry out in a covered jar in the refrigerator than when stored at room temperature. Strong-flavored cheese such as Limberger should also be stored in this manner.

Large pieces of hard grating cheese, such as Parmesan, will be difficult to grate unless they are kept covered during storage.

Normally, cheese should not be allowed to freeze, as this may cause it to become dry and crumbly. Small pieces—weighing 1 lb or less and not over 1 in. thick—of certain varieties (Brick, Cheddar, Edam, Gouda, Muenster, Port du Salut, Swiss, Provolone, Mozzarella, and Camembert) can be successfully frozen, however, for as long as 6 months. They should be used as soon as possible after thawing.

White deposits on fully ripened cheeses are not mold but crystals of the amino acid tyrosine. Tyrosine is not very soluble, and as the proteins are hydrolyzed into amino acids, tyrosine will accumulate and precipitate.

SUMMARY

A highly concentrated form of milk, cheese is produced in a solid or semisolid form, with about 5 oz American cheese considered the equivalent in food value of 1 qt milk. When made from whole milk, cheeses are good sources of vitamin A and riboflavin. Calcium content varies according to the method of production used. Flavor and the time required for ripening—rather than nutritive value—determine the price of cheese. Domestic cheeses are generally less costly than imported cheeses. Intended use should determine selection.

Some cheese is marked by grade for the retail trade. Either a grade label or an inspection mark assures dependable quality. Through scientific research, virtually any variety of cheese can be manufactured in the United States, but American Cheddar is the principal one made and sold here. Manufacturing methods and the milk or milk and cream combination differ according to the cheese variety being produced. There are about 18 basic kinds of cheese. These are classified as hard grating, hard, semisoft, soft uncured, and soft cured.

Overheating or prolonged cooking causes cheese proteins to become tough and rubbery, and occasionally the fat will separate from the other constituents of the cheese. Processed cheese lends itself particularly well to cooking.

Cheese should be stored at low temperatures to prevent spoilage. It should be covered and wrapped to prevent drying. Small pieces of some types of cheese may be frozen successfully for periods of 6 months.

QUESTIONS AND TOPICS FOR DISCUSSION AND STUDY

1. Why do some cheese dishes become semiliquid and stringy when heated? How can this be avoided?
2. What accounts for the fact that cubed or grated processed cheese may blend more quickly with milk than a cubed or grated Cheddar cheese?
3. Why is cheese a good substitute for milk?

SUGGESTED ACTIVITIES

1. Prepare one or more of the following cheese dishes: cheese rarebit, cheese soufflé, macaroni and cheese, cheese fondue. Set up a standard for each dish and evaluate it.
2. Select a cheese dish and cut the recipe in half; prepare one half with processed cheese; prepare the other half with Cheddar. Compare for ease of blending cheese, time required for preparation, cost, flavor, texture, and appearance.

REFERENCES

BOOKS

Garard, Ira. *Introductory Food Chemistry*. Westport, Conn.: Avi, 1976, Chap. 11.

Kosikowski, Frank. *Cheese and Fermented Milk Foods*. Published by the author. Ithaca, N.Y.: Cornell University, 1970.

Shopper's Guide: The Yearbook of Agriculture. Washington, D.C.: U.S. Department of Agriculture, 1974.

Webb, Byron, and Arnold Johnson. *Fundamentals of Dairy Chemistry*. Westport, Conn.: Avi, 1965, Chap. 12.

ARTICLES, BULLETINS, AND PAMPHLETS

"Cheese in Family Meals." *Home and Garden Bulletin 112*. Washington, D.C.: U.S. Department of Agriculture, 1966.

"How to Buy Cheese." *G193*. Washington, D.C.: U.S. Department of Agriculture, 1971.

Newer Knowledge of Cheese, 2nd ed. Chicago: National Dairy Council, 1972.

Sanders, G. "Cheese Varieties and Descriptions." *Handbook 54*. Washington, D.C.: U.S. Department of Agriculture, 1969.

Scott, C. R. and H. O. Smith. "Cottage Cheese Shelf Life and Special Gas Atmospheres." *J. Food Sci.* **36:**78, 1971.

Meat

CHAPTER 24

The United States produces more meat than any other country, and its people consume almost the total output. Americans have an appetite for meat, especially beef. Pork, lamb, veal, and mutton also are important meats in the American diet.

STRUCTURE AND COMPOSITION

Structure. The flesh from any meat-producing animal is composed of *muscle fibers, connective tissue,* and *adipose* (fatty) *tissue.* Bone is an essential part of the gross structure of the meat animal.

MUSCLE TISSUE. Bundles of fibers or muscle cells held together with connective tissue make up the lean portion of meat (Fig. 24-1). The thickness of the muscle fibers, the size of the fiber bundles, and the amount of connective tissue binding them together determine the grain of the meat. When the fibers and the bundles are small, the meat is fine and velvety—top quality.

The individual muscle fiber is a specialized, multinucleated, elongated cell, varying in size with function and amount of use. The muscle cell has an outer covering of membrane and an inner filling of small rodlike structures called *fibrillae.* The fibrillae are dense protoplasm enmeshed in a semifluid muscle material.

CONNECTIVE TISSUE. Although the muscle tissue gives meat its characteristic appearance and—to some extent—its flavor and texture, it is the connective tissue of meat that determines tenderness. Connective tissue in meat forms the walls of the muscle fibers, binds them into bundles, surrounds the muscles as a membrane, and makes up the tendons and ligaments that attach the muscles to the bones. Some connective tissue is loose (e.g., that which lodges between organs) and some is very compact (for example, that in cartilage and tendons).

FAT. Fat is distributed throughout meat in small particles or in large masses. The pattern formed by the uniform distribution of fat in small "lakes" throughout the muscle or lean flesh is call *marbling* and is considered an important factor in contributing tenderness and flavor to muscle tissue. An exterior layer of fat is known as *cover fat* or *separable fat* and serves to retain the moisture of the muscle or lean tissue and to protect the flesh from the action of microorganisms. Although it is generally agreed that the presence of fat adds to the flavor and possibly the

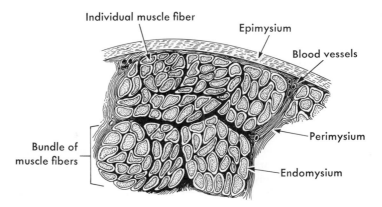

24-1 *Diagram of a cross-section of muscle showing bundles of individual muscle fibers.*

Labels in figure: Individual muscle fiber, Epimysium, Blood vessels, Bundle of muscle fibers, Perimysium, Endomysium

tenderness of meat, efforts in animal breeding have been aimed at reducing the fat.[1] Consumer demand for lean, nutritious cuts of meat has motivated research in this area.

BONE. The condition of the bone is an indication of the age of the animal. In young animals, the chine, or backbone, is soft and has a reddish tinge; in fully mature animals, the bones are flinty and white. A high proportion of bone to meat increases the cost of meat; therefore, the carcass with a high proportion of meat to bone is the most desirable. The shape of the bone is an excellent guide for identifying the various cuts of meat.

Composition. Meat is made up of proteins, fats, minerals (phosphorus, iron, and calcium), some carbohydrates, nitrogenous and nonnitrogenous extractives, pigments, enzymes, vitamins, and water (Table 24-1).

PROTEINS. The amount of protein (approximately 15–20%) in any particular cut of meat is directly related to the amount of lean tissue in it. Hence, the amount of protein in a cut of meat decreases as the fat and bone content increase. The principal proteins in meat are the muscle-cell or protoplasmic proteins actin and myosin and the extracellular proteins collagen and elastin, which are abundant in the connective tissue. Actin and myosin together form the contractile component of muscle. Actin can exist in either of two forms: G–actin or F–actin. Actomyosin is a complex of the proteins F–actin and myosin. It

is found in this form in the voluntary muscles of an animal.[2]

FAT and CARBOHYDRATES. Fatlike substances known as *sterols,* substances essential to cell metabolism, are found in the fluids of the fat cell. Adipose tissue, considered to be a specialized form of connective tissue, appears late in the development of the organism. The fat cells begin to store droplets of fat only after the available nutrients exceed the amount necessary for organ production. Obviously, a meat-producing animal must attain a certain age and level of nutrition before fat cells develop.[3]

Two forms of carbohydrate are found in meat: glycogen, which is stored mainly in liver, and glucose, which is found in blood.

[1] S. Hoover, "Quality in Animal Products," in *Food: The Yearbook of Agriculture* (Washington, D.C.: U.S. Department of Agriculture, 1959), p. 331.

[2] J. W. Giffee et al., "Chemistry of Animal Tissues," in *The Science of Meat and Meat Products* (San Francisco: Freeman, 1971), p. 75.

[3] M. Birkner and E. Auerback, "Microscopic Structure of Animal Tissues," in *The Science of Meat Products,* op. cit., p. 20.

TABLE 24-1
Proximate Composition of Meat

Constituents	Beef Muscle (%)
Water	67
Protein	19
Fat	13
Carbohydrate	—
Minerals	1

Source: C. Chatfield and G. Adams, "Proximate Composition of Foods (Edible Portion)," *Circular 549* (Washington, D.C.: U.S. Department of Agriculture, 1940).

PIGMENTS. Myoglobin and hemoglobin are the two pigments that contribute to the red color of meat. Hemoglobin transports oxygen in the bloodstream, and myoglobin holds it in the muscles for contraction. The organ meats have more hemoglobin than skeletal muscles have, because of their greater blood supply.[4] When meat is cut and left exposed to the air, it becomes a bright red at first, but the surface quickly dries out and becomes a darker red. When the meat is first cut, the oxygen of the air combines with the protein pigment myoglobin to produce oxymyoglobin, and the slow oxidation of the oxymyoglobin produces the brown color, which is metmyoglobin. This chemical change occurs by oxidation of the iron of myoglobin from the ferrous to the ferric state. High temperatures hasten spoilage and the darkening of meat, and all meat should be displayed or stored under conditions of adequate refrigeration.

ENZYMES. Protein-splitting enzymes may be responsible for increasing the tenderness of meat during its ripening or aging.

MINERALS. Phosphorus and iron are the chief minerals in meat. Both are found in different combinations in the muscle tissue. Potassium is also found in the muscle fiber or dense material, and sodium is more concentrated in the fluids.

EXTRACTIVES. Lactic acid is always present in the muscle tissue of animals. This chemical is an intermediary product of carbohydrate metabolism. There is always an increase in lactic acid in the muscle tissue after rigor mortis sets in. The nitrogenous extractives found in muscle tissue are the end products of protein metabolism. Some authorities regard the nitrogenous extractives as the source of meat flavor, although attempts to isolate the compounds responsible have not been successful.

NUTRITIVE VALUE

A universally popular food, meat has outstanding nutritive value, contributing substantial amounts of high-quality proteins and essential minerals and vitamins to the diet.

The proteins of meat are well utilized by the body, thus ensuring a supply of essential amino acids necessary for growth and maintenance.

[4] Ibid., p. 88.

Meat contains enough iron, phosphorus, zinc and copper to rate as an important source of these minerals. A significant nutritional fact is that a large share of the iron found in meat is located in the liver, an organ constituting only a small protion of the carcass.

As far as vitamins are concerned, vitamin A, thiamine, and riboflavin are present in the liver, the kidneys, the heart, and the sweetbreads (the pancreas or the thymus). Lean pork is an outstanding source of thiamine, and all lean meats contain some niacin, riboflavin, and thiamine.

Meat also is relatively high in energy value. The calorie content of a cut of meat depends on the amount of fat it contains.

ECONOMIC ASPECTS

Meat packing is the largest of all American food industries and has played an important part in the economic development of the nation. The meat industry in the United States provides not only edible meats but inedible by-products as well. The constant challenge to livestock growers and meat packers to keep costs within the buying range of the consumer has brought change and progress to the meat-packing industry.

Recent animal breeding research has brought about the production of animals with a higher percentage of lean meat.[5] The meat-type hog, for example, has less back fat and a higher proportion of lean flesh and, on the average, is heavier per 100 lb of feed consumed than the hog bred for both lard and pork. Recent developments in breeding suggest that such economically important carcass traits as depth of back fat, marbling, length and quality of loin muscle, juiciness, and tenderness are heritable and can be bred into animals. Crossbreeding has brought about an increase in yield of preferred cuts of lamb. Researchers concerned with beef cattle have demonstrated that efficiency of feed utilization and the characteristics of the area of the rib eye in beef cattle are heritable.[6] These find-

[5] G. D. Wilson, "Factors Influencing Quality of Fresh Meat," in *The Science of Meat and Meat Products,* op. cit., p. 261.

[6] R. E. Hodgson, "Livestock Production in Transition," in *Food: The Yearbook of Agriculture,* op. cit., p. 334.

ings have opened the way for selection of beef animals to improve salable areas of the carcass. As with pork and lamb, the goal of beef breeding is to produce a meat-type animal that yields a good percentage of preferred beef cuts and has less fat than is now the case.

Improvements in the handling of meat animals have also contributed to increased production of meats. The use of antibiotics as feed adjuncts for control of disease has been a factor in keeping the level of production high.[7]

Animal feeding practices today put stress on balanced rations that animals can utilize to a maximum extent. Too much or too little of any one nutrient makes an imbalance, and the feed is not used efficiently. An animal usually eats more of a balanced ration than of one that is not balanced.[8]

BUYING MEATS

The price of meat varies, depending on market supply and demand and the price of feed. The average consumer shows a preference for the tender cuts of meat, such as roasts, steaks, and chops, and pays a higher price for these cuts than for the tougher cuts from the shoulder, neck, shank, and breast of the animal. Price is also affected by the grade or quality of the carcass. The better the grade, the higher the price. Hence, a rib roast graded U.S. Prime commands a higher price than a rib roast graded U.S. Good. The higher grades are more tender and have better flavor than the lower grades.

Lean beef, veal, pork, and lamb have about the same protein value. One pound of lean meat from a rib roast is equal in nutritive value to 1 lb of lean meat from the chuck. The difference lies in the tenderness of the cut and the cooking method required to make the meat palatable. The less tender cuts and the medium and low grades of meat are generally excellent meat buys for family use.

[7] J. Cunha, "Antibiotics for Swine, Beef Cattle, Sheep, and Dairy Cattle," in *First International Conference on Antibiotics in Agriculture* (Washington, D.C.: Research Council–National Academy of Sciences, 1956).

[8] *After a Hundred Years: The Yearbook of Agriculture* (Washington, D.C.: U.S. Department of Agriculture, 1962), p. 284.

From the standpoint of cost, the organ meats—liver, heart, and kidneys—are good buys. Unlike skeletal cuts of meat, organs have no waste in the form of bone or fat. There may be a small amount of fat in kidneys: otherwise, the edible portion of the meat is approximately the weight as purchased. Organ meats have high food value. All kinds of liver are especially good sources of high-quality protein, and vitamin A, iron, thiamine, riboflavin, and niacin.

The price per pound of meat does not always reveal its true cost. Some cuts of meat have a large proportion of waste that must be taken into consideration when calculating the price per pound of edible meat (Table 24-2). A cut of meat that has a very high proportion of bone and fat may prove to be expensive regardless of how low the price per pound. Conversely, boned meat with no fat waste that is high in price per pound may turn out to be an economical purchase. In general, the size of the cut has a direct effect on the price of meat; a large cut, such as a leg of veal or a ham, will be considerably less per pound than a slice of veal cutlet or ham steak. Similarly, individual chops are higher per pound than a loin from which they are taken. A worthwhile practice for the consumer is to buy a large piece and have it cut into smaller ones for future use. Most homes today have adequate refrigeration for this kind of meat purchase.

New uniform retail meat identity standards have been developed to end consumer confusion over retail cuts of meat. Before these were instituted, there were dozens of popular and local names for a single cut of meat. Recipes were confusing and consumers could easily be misled when buying at the meat counter. The standard nomenclature is now in effect for the approximately 300 retail cuts of beef, pork, lamb and veal.[9] Local or popular names may still be on the price–weight label, but these must be accompanied by the proper identification.

MEAT INSPECTION

Every animal that is to be slaughtered in meat-packing establishments engaged in inter-

[9] *Uniform Retail Meat Identity Standards* (Chicago: National Live Stock and Meat Board, 1973), p. 1.

TABLE 24-2
Amounts of Meat to Purchase for Average Servings

Cut	Amount (lb)	Approximate Number of Servings
Boned or ground meat: Flank, clod, beef roll, tenderloin, boneless loin, sirloin butt, sirloin strip, heel of round, liver, heart, kidneys, brains, sweetbreads, tongue, sausages, wieners	1	3–4
Meat with a medium amount of bone: Rib roasts, rump roasts, chuck, chops, steaks, ham slices, loin roasts, leg of lamb	1	2–3
Meat with a large amount of bone: Short ribs, neck, breasts, brisket, plate, shank, shoulder cuts	1	1½

Source: L. Houlihan, "There's More Than Steak for Your Meat Dollars," *Food Marketing Leaflet 4* (Food Marketing Program Extension Services of the State Colleges of Agriculture and Home Economics of New York, New Jersey, and Connecticut, undated).

state commerce is inspected (see Fig. 24-2). The purpose of the inspection, which is administered by the Agricultural Research Service under the Meat Inspection Act, is to protect consumers against bad meats, unsanitary conditions, and deceptive and fraudulent practices.

The Wholesome Meat Act of 1967 provides for federal inspection of meat plants in any state not meeting federal standards. Many states are developing their own programs for inspecting meat plants that sell within the state.

The inspection procedure includes a close

24-2 *Meat inspections.* (*a*) *Animals are examined before slaughter. Healthy animals are passed, but those that show any sign of disease are separated and tagged for special handling.* (*b*) *After slaughter, every carcass is examined by a federal inspector. (Courtesy of Meat Inspection Division, U.S. Department of Agriculture)*

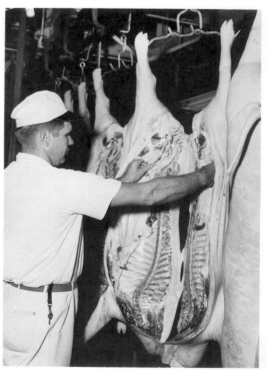

(*a*)

(*b*)

24-3 *Federal meat inspection stamp. (Courtesy of U.S. Department of Agriculture)*

scrutiny of the animals in the pens; those that are unfit for human food are identified and properly disposed of. This is known as the *antemortem inspection.* Then as the animals passed on the antemortem inspection are slaughtered, each carcass with its parts—including the internal organs—is inspected for symptoms of disease or other conditions that would make the meat unsafe for food. The third part of the inspection has to do with the examination of processed meats: ham, bacon, lard, sausage, canned meat, and other food products from the meat and organs. Meats that pass federal inspection are marked with a round stamp stating that they have been inspected and approved (see Fig. 24-3). When the products examined are not satisfactory, they are marked "Condemned." The condemned material is then sent to a separate area in the plant, where it is converted into nonfood products, such as fertilizer.

All inspections are made by trained veterinarians who are regularly employed by the U.S. Department of Agriculture and by a smaller number of trained lay inspectors (Fig. 24-4).

Worm Parasites. The roundworm (nematode) *Trichinella spiralis* is considered the most dangerous worm parasite transmissible from domestic animals to man. When *Trichinella spiralis* worms

24-4 *U.S. Department of Agriculture Marketing Service meat inspectors check side of beef. (Courtesy of U.S. Department of Agriculture)*

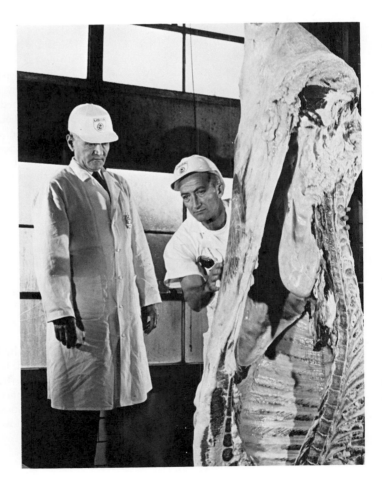

are present in sufficient numbers in a suitable host, they produce trichinosis. Because infected pork eaten raw or imperfectly cooked is the main source of human trichinosis, the proper handling and cooking of pork products is of significant importance in reducing the incidence of human infection. The regulations governing meat inspection by the U.S. Department of Agriculture stipulate that no article of any kind prepared to be eaten without further cooking shall contain any muscle tissue of pork unless this meat has been subjected to a temperature sufficient to destroy all live trichinae. For practical application, this indicates that all meat food products containing pork must be heated until all parts attain a temperature of at least 137°F (58.5°C). Present practices tend toward processing temperatures as high as 169°F. (76°C). Trichinae can also be killed if the meat is frozen at 5°F (−15°C) for a minimum of 20 days. Special curing methods used to dry and smoke sausages and ham will also eliminate trichinae.

GRADING

Grade markings of meat (see Fig. 24-5) for retail sale are optional but where employed are a valuable protection for the buyer. Beef can be graded for either of two factors: "quality" and "cutability." The quality factor includes appearance and general palatability of the meat. The cutability factor has to do with the amount of edible lean meat available in a cut. A packer who wishes to use the U.S. Department of Agriculture system of grading pays for the services of a federal meat grader. Frequently, packers use brand names to identify different grades of meat. In any case, only one grade marking appears on a piece of meat—the government's grade or the packer's grade. Meat and meat products not sold across state lines come under the jurisdiction of state and local inspection laws. For veal, calf, yearling mutton, and mutton, the kind of meat is added to the grade of meat. Cattle are separated into beef, veal and calf groups for grading, and the ovine animals are grouped as lamb, yearling, and sheep. The federal grades found on wholesale and retail cuts of meat are shown in Fig. 24-6.

The grading of meat is carried out by a qualified inspector who carefully evaluates the carcass. The factors on which quality grading is based are as follows:

Conformation has to do with the bulk and general form of the animal. A full, stocky, well-developed carcass is said to have good conformation. Retail cuts from an animal with good conformation will be juicy and have a good amount of meat surrounding the bone.

Finish has to do with the appearance of fat and its distribution in meat. Fat that is creamy, not yellow, in color; waxy, not brittle, in texture; and uniformly distributed through the lean, not bunched in large clumps between muscle tissue, indicates good finish.

Quality refers to the probable tenderness and palatability of the meat when it is cooked. The best-quality meat has a velvety or silky feel—very smooth and soft to the touch. A small amount of connective tissue is evident, and its color is characteristic of the kind of meat being graded.

In 1975, the Federal Grade Standards for beef were revised. Conformation (the bulk and general form of the animal) is no longer considered in grading, since it is not believed to be related to eating qualities. Minimum marbling requirements were lowered for prime and choice cattle, thereby increasing the number of cattle in these grades.

24-5 *Stamps for U.S. meat grades of beef.* (*Courtesy of U.S. Department of Agriculture*)

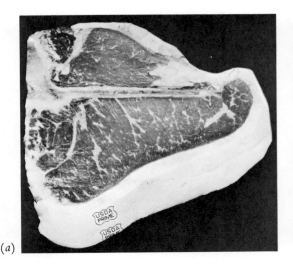

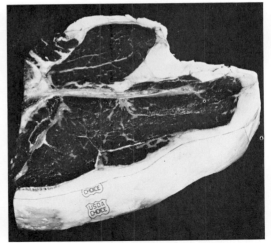

(a)

(b)

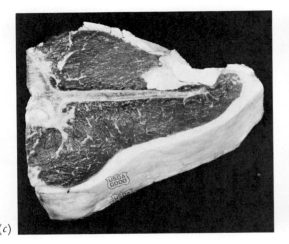

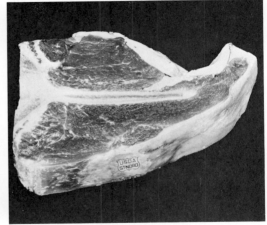

(c)

(d)

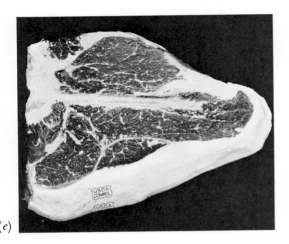

(e)

24-6 *U.S. graded beef (all cuts shown are porterhouse steaks). (a) U.S. Prime grade meat is the very best in tenderness, juiciness, and flavor. It is produced from young animals and has a liberal amount of marbling. (b) U.S. Choice is the grade of meat in greatest supply and is the one most commonly sold in the retail stores. It has less marbling than Prime but still is of very high quality. This grade of meat comes from young animals. (c) U.S. Good grade meat is leaner than the higher grades and is economical. (d) U.S. Standard grade meat has a high proportion of lean meat and is also economical. (e) U.S. Commercial grade meat is produced only from older animals and lacks juiciness. It has good flavor and can be made into satisfactory, economical dishes, but cuts require slow cooking with moist heat to make them tender. (Courtesy of U.S. Department of Agriculture)*

POSTMORTEM CHANGES IN MEAT

After slaughter, meats are cooled and kept at slightly above freezing temperatures for 2–3 days. During this time, enzymes within the muscle tissue and microorganisms bring about physical and chemical changes that alter the structure and chemical composition of the meat. Eight hours or so after slaughter, the muscles of the animal become rigid (rigor mortis) owing to the contraction of the actin and myosin to actomyosin. If meat is cooked during this contraction period, it is very tough. The sugar (glycogen) is synthesized to adenosine triphosphate (ATP) until its supply is exhausted. The ATP will then begin to break down. The lactic acid that is produced during this conversion lowers the pH of the meat to approximately 5.3. The lactic acid acts on connective tissue, rendering the muscle tissue more tender. The holding of chilled meat for at least 48 hours after slaughter has a tenderizing effect on the meat. This is known as *aging*.

Meat will have a low glycogen content at slaughter if the animal has been subject to stress or exhaustion. If the level is low, insufficient lactic acid will be formed, resulting in a darker color and less flavor and texture to the meat.

TENDERNESS IN MEAT

Connective Tissue. It is generally agreed that the amount of connective tissue is directly related to the tenderness of meat. Cuts of meat with much connective tissue are tougher than those containing little connective tissue.

There are two types of connective tissue: collagen and elastin. The white connective tissue is composed of collagen, a protein that is hydrolyzed into gelatin at ordinary cooking temperatures. Elastin is yellow and does not break down into gelatin at ordinary cooking temperatures; it may soften if the temperature is sufficiently high. Because white connective tissue will change into gelatin during the cooking process and gelatin is readily dispersed in the liquid medium in meat tissue, the change in structure of the white connective tissue makes a more tender meat product. Change in the structure of elastin probably contributes little to the tenderness of meat because of the high temperatures required for its conversion to gelatin and because only a small amount of elastin occurs in muscle tissue. Other factors affecting the tenderness of meat are the fat content, the age of the animal when slaughtered, and the water-holding capacity of the muscle proteins.[10]

Fat. It is thought that a good marbling of fat throughout the muscle tissue increases tenderness, but it is still not known whether factors other than fat are responsible for degrees of tenderness. A possible explanation for the tenderizing effect of fat is that it may separate and dilute connective tissue fibers and make them more available to heat treatment.[11]

Age. Generally, meat from younger animals is more tender than that from older ones. Once again there are many exceptions to this general rule. It would seem, however, that the lack of muscular development in the young animal is a significant factor. The tenderness of muscle decreases as the diameter of the muscle fiber increases, and the diameter of the fibers increases with the age of the animals. Older animals, with greater muscle development, have increased connective tissue.

Location. The location of the cut is an indication of its tenderness. The least-used muscles, such as are found in the loin and rib cuts, are more tender than those that are more fully developed, those found in neck, chuck, and round cuts.

Temperature. The temperature to which meat is cooked will alter its tenderness and affect the contraction of the meat fibers. High temperatures and overcooking cause toughening of the meat. Whether or not cooking tenderizes meat depends on the relationship between the hydrolysis of collagen and the coagulation of the muscle proteins. If hydrolysis of collagen predominates, the meat may become more tender. If hardening of the muscle proteins is the dominant process, the meat increases in toughness.

[10] Frank Lee, *Basic Food Chemistry* (Westport, Conn.: Avi, 1975), p. 370.
[11] Pauline Paul, and Helen Palmer, *Food Theory and Applications* (New York: Wiley, 1972), p. 348.

According to the work of Dawson[12] and others, tenderness of beef does not increase consistently with increased hydrolysis of collagen. This suggests that collagen hydrolysis is not the only significant factor in tenderizing meat.

Muscle tissue that is tender, such as that from the loin of the animal, may actually become tough and stringy when braised because the muscle fibers have little connective tissues to hold them together. It is thought that the muscle tissue of a bottom round cut responds to braising by becoming softer and more tender when braised for a longer period.[13]

Grinding and Pounding. Grinding breaks and cuts the muscle fibers and connective tissues, making it possible for all ground meat to be prepared in a fashion similar to that used for the tender cuts. This has great practical application for all cuts of tough meats. Pounding is used to tenderize the meat; this process breaks and tears only the surface meat fibers and connective tissue.

Aging. Aging is an important method of tenderizing meat. When rigor mortis occurs in an animal's carcass, the muscle is hard and the muscle proteins actin and myosin react to form actomyosin. As a result of this, some muscle fibers contract as alternating fibers are stretched. As aging continues, after the onset of rigor mortis, the muscle softens and the muscle fibers appear to straighten out with noticeable breaks. It is believed that the fiber breaks are caused by enzymatic action on the proteins. Because of discoloration of the meat and moisture loss, only cuts of meat such as ribs and loins with thick coverings of fat that can be cut off are suitable for aging.

Lamb is occasionally aged; pork is never aged because of its high fat content; veal does not have the proper finish and protective fat covering for the aging process.

Dry Aging. Meat is held at 34–38°F (1–3°C) for 3–6 weeks.[14] The humidity may be relatively low (70–75%) to keep the cut surface dry or relatively high (85–90%) to purposely develop mold growth. If the latter method is used, evaporative moisture loss is decreased. Meat purchased by restaurants and hotels has usually been aged by this method.

Fast Aging. This is a faster method in which the meat is held for 2 days at a temperature of 70°F (21°C) at high (85–90%) humidity. Microbial growth is retarded by the use of ultraviolet light. Most of the meat marketed in retail stores has been aged in this manner. Additional aging occurs in the 6–10 days that it takes for meat to be transported, marketed, stored, and cooked.

Vacuum Packaging. The weight loss and surface spoilage that occurs with aging can be lessened if the meat is packaged in a moisture and vaporproof film. Meat vacuum-packaged for 1 or 2 weeks shows no loss in tenderness, juiciness, and flavor but has a significant reduction in weight loss.[15]

Freezing. The effect of freezing on the tenderness of meat has been widely investigated.[16] The majority of studies conclude that it makes little or no difference.

Enzymes. Meat can be made tender by the use of proteolytic enzymes such as papain, an enzyme found in papaya leaf. An unsolved problem concerning meat tenderizers is that of uniformly distributing the enzyme throughout the cut of meat. When the tenderizer is forked or injected into the meat, there is no way to assure uniform distribution. In large cuts, only the surface of the meat is affected by the application of the tenderizer. A negative factor: studies to date indicate a loss of flavor and juiciness when tenderizers are used.[17]

Although most commercial tenderizing prep-

---

[12] E. Dawson et al., "Factors Influencing the Palatability, Vitamin Content, and Yield of Cooked Beef," *Home Economics Research Report 9* (Washington, D.C.: U.S. Department of Agriculture, 1959).

[13] S. Cover, "Scoring for Three Components of Tenderness to Characterize Differences Among Beef Steaks," *Food Res.* **24**:564, 1959.

[14] *Lessons on Meat* (Chicago: National Live Stock and Meat Board, 1974) p. 58.

[15] D. Minks, and W. C. Stringer, "The Influence of Aging Beef in Vacuum," *J. Food Sci.* **37**:736, 1972.

[16] D. Tressler and C. Evers, *The Freezing Preparation of Foods* (Westport, Conn.: Avi. 1968), p. 681.

[17] Dawson, op. cit., p.26.

arations contain papain, bromelin and ficin are also being used. The enzymes are mixed with salt and used as a dry mixture or as a liquid dip.

The enzyme tenderizes the meat by breaking down the outer covering of the muscle fiber and the collagen and elastin material found in the muscle tissue. If tenderizers are to be effective, however, they must have time to act.[18] Enzyme activity is slow at room temperature; it is most active in the range 140–160°F (60–70°C). Hence the action of the tenderizer takes place during the cooking of the meat. Cooking the meat until it is well done deactivates the enzyme—but cooking it short of the well-done stage may permit the continued activity of the enzyme in the muscle fiber by hydrolyzing actomyosin.

[18] H. Wang et al., "Studies on Enzymatic Tenderization of Meat," *Food Res.* **23**:423, 1958.

Recently, attention has been directed to the antemortem introduction of enzymes to achieve uniform tenderness.[19] The tenderizing solution (papain) is introduced into the jugular vein of the animal for even distribution throughout body tissue. This tenderizing process has been approved as successfully increasing the tenderness of beef. At present, beef subjected to the antemortem enzyme process is being produced commerically and marketed as "ProTen"[20] (Fig. 24-7). Tough cuts of meats that have been treated by this process may be cooked by dry heat methods.

[19] H. E. Robinson and P. A. Goeser, "Enzymatic Tenderization of Meat," *J. Home Econ.* **54**:195, 1962.

[20] ProTen is the trademark, owned by ProTen, Inc., that identifies quality beef produced from animals subjected to this new tenderizing process.

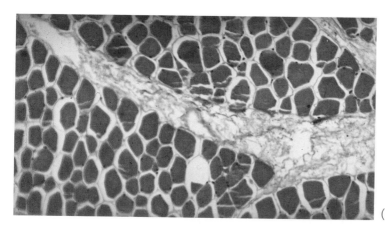

(a)

(b)

24-7 *Meat tissue (a) Pro-Ten-cooked beef, tenderized by the antemortem enzyme process. (b) Control-cooked beef. (Courtesy of Swift & Company)*

Acid Material. Studies concerned with the effect of adding acid materials to meat to increase its tenderness have indicated little or no difference in the degree of tenderness of various cuts so treated. Dawson[21] found that neither soaking meat in vinegar for 48 hours nor braising it increased tenderness.

PRINCIPLES OF COOKING MEAT

The goals in cooking meat are to improve its flavor, change its color, make it more tender, and destory harmful organisms. Generally, constant low-temperature heat improves palatability and appearance and lessens loss in weight and nutritive value.

Low-temperature cooking for home and institutional use is a fairly uniform practice today. Extensive research comparing low and high heat in cooking meats proved the practicality of constant low temperatures to prevent losses in cooking and to produce a tender product.

According to Cline and her associates, a constant low temperature of 325°F (165°C) is convenient for all home roasting of meats.[22] Roasting temperatures of 230, 257, 325, 376, 424, and 500°F (110, 125, 163, 191, 218, 260°C) were used to roast ribs of beef until rare. The cooked roasts were compared, and results showed that low oven temperatures result in more tender, juicier, and better-flavored roasts than high oven temperatures. Cover also worked with roasts and came to somewhat the same conclusions.[23] Her studies added the information that increased tenderness in the roasts is associated with slow heat penetration, for when there was little or no difference in speed of heat penetration there was no noticeable difference in tenderness. Oven temperatures as low as 176°F (80°C) were effective in producing more tender meat. However, it would seem that unusually low oven temperatures are not practical. Long cooking times are required, and if the roast is cooked to well done it becomes dry and stringy.

Because of rapid penetration of heat, high temperatures cook meat in a relatively short time; considerable shrinkage of the meat also occurs. High temperatures toughen protein and squeeze out the juices. There is consistent agreement in meat studies that constant low temperatures cook meat more uniformly than high temperatures. There is also less shrinkage and more retention of nutritive value.

The internal temperature to which meat is cooked alters the cooking time and has a noticeable effect on shrinkage. Numerous studies have shown that cooking losses of roasts are increased when there is an increase in cooking time. Marshall and others compared top rounds of beef of different grades cooked at a constant temperature of 300°F (150°C) to internal temperatures of a range of 140 to 176°F (60–80°C).[24] They concluded that cooking losses increase with degree of "doneness" up to the well-done stage, and that large and heavier roasts have less total preparation losses at all degrees of doneness (except rare) than smaller roasts.

Physical and Chemical Changes. During cooking, the protein of the muscle fibers starts to coagulate and toughen. At the same time, the collagen is hydrolyzed and softens. Heat is conducted from the surface of the meat to the interior.

COLOR CHANGES. The characteristic color of meat is caused by the muscle pigment myoglobin. Heat brings about color changes that range from pink to brown or gray. The surface of the cooked meat browns as a result of the partial breakdown of its proteins, fat, pigments, and other constituents. The amount of time required for the color change from red to gray varies somewhat among different roasts, according to the age and grade of the meat and the length of time it has been stored. This explains the difference in the color of beef roasts cooked to the same interior temperature of 140°F (60°C). Although beef and lamb undergo a color change from red to brownish gray, the color change for

[21] Dawson, op. cit.

[22] A. Cline, "How Certain Methods of Cooking Affect the Quality and Palatability of Beef," *Missouri University Agricultural Experiment Station Bulletin 293*, 1930.

[23] S. Cover, "Effect of Temperature and Time on the Tenderness of Roasts," *Texas Agricultural Experiment Station Bulletin 542*, 1937.

[24] N. Marshall, L. Wood, and M. Patton, "Cooking Choice Grade Top Round Beef Roasts: Effect of Size and Internal Temperature," *J. Amer. Dietet. Assoc.* **35**:569, 1959.

pork is from pink to white. Veal changes from light red to gray—and changes more rapidly than beef does. Most authorities agree that the color change in meat is complete when the meat has reached an internal temperature of 160°F (70°C).[25] The color of the internal fat may change very little during the time the color changes in the lean take place. Beef is the only meat that is acceptable when served bright red (rare). Lamb may be served medium rare (pink), but pork and veal are always served well done.

FLAVOR CHANGES. Heating changes the flavor of meat through loss of volatile substances, caramelization of carbohydrate, melting and decomposition of fat, and coagulation and breakdown of proteins. The characteristic flavors of the various meats are mainly the result of differences in fat composition. Generally when the surface of the meat browns, flavor is intensified. The greater the amount of air circulating around the surface of the meat, the faster the rate at which decomposition of the meat proteins, fats, and carbohydrates takes place.

The loss of soluble materials, such as phosphates and sodium chloride, to the juices of meat changes its flavor. Careful analysis shows that most of the flavor of meat is in its juices. The length of cooking time and the cooking temperature affect the flavor of meat. Weir notes that cuts of meat cooked until well done have a less desirable flavor than those cooked for a shorter period of time.[26]

In a review of current meat research, Paul states that compounds linked to meat flavor that have been isolated from muscle tissue are a number of amino compounds including amino acids and some containing phosphorus; simple sugars such as ribose and glucose; mono- and dicarbonylaldehydes having 2–18 carbons, free fatty acids, saturated and unsaturated, having 1–18 carbons; ammonia; hydrogen sulfide; inosine; creatinine; hypoxanthine; and a glycoprotein containing glucose.[27] Heat is required for the development of the flavor of meat; hence, the components mentioned are considered as flavor precursors.

ODOR CHANGES. Cooked meat also undergoes a loss of aromatic and volatile substances. Without this loss it would be hard to identify a meat flavor, for a large part of the flavor is made up of a combination of compounds that produce the fragrant odor.

Meat is done when the heat necessary to bring about desired changes in color, texture, and flavor has penetrated to the center of the piece. The time required for heat to penetrate a given piece of meat depends on several factors: the cooking temperature, the stage to which the interior of the meat is to be cooked, the size of the piece, the composition of the meat, and the temperature of the meat at the beginning of the cooking period.

METHODS OF COOKING MEAT

Methods of cooking meat are grouped into two classes: those that use dry heat (roasting, broiling, pan broiling, and frying) and those that use moist heat (braising, stewing, and simmering). To a large extent, the method selected for cooking a given cut of meat depends on the tenderness of the cut and on the available cooking facilities. Cultural and regional cooking patterns may also influence the choice of method for preparing the meat.

Regardless of the method, a few general principles are common in the preparation of meat. Meat is not usually washed; it is wiped clean with a damp cloth. It is not washed because it is believed that extractives that contain both nutrients and flavor will be leached out of the meat tissues. If salt is used before cooking, it will penetrate to a depth of about ½ in. For large roasts cuts, the salt may be added before or after cooking. The salting of certain cuts of meat, such as chops, thin steaks, and stew meat, may cause increased drip loss because of the increase in osmotic pressure at the surface of the meat. For meats that are served with their juice, the addition of salt before cooking matters little, for the dish is enhanced by the increased flavor of the meat juices.

Dry Heat Methods. ROASTING. Any tender cut of beef, veal, pork, or lamb is suitable for

---

[25] Committee on Preparation Factors, National Cooperative Meat Investigations, *Meat and Meat Cookery* (Chicago: National Live Stock and Meat Board, 1942), p. 86.

[26] Weir, op. cit., p. 215.

[27] Pauline Paul, "Current Research on Meat," *J. Amer. Dietet. Assoc.* **46**:468, 1965.

roasting—that is, cooking by dry heat, usually in an oven. Some of the less tender cuts of beef, such as chuck or round, may be roasted or broiled if they are of the best grade. Good marbling and little connective tissue in chuck and round cuts indicate the possibility of using dry heat.

Veal is from a young animal. It lacks fat but has considerable connective tissue. Roasting is one of the methods used to cook veal. To soften the connective tissue in veal, it should be cooked slowly to the well-done stage. Veal may be larded—that is, strips of fat may be inserted into the muscle with a larding needle in order to keep the meat from drying out.

Compared with cuts of veal and beef, lamb cuts are small; cuts from mutton are somewhat larger. With the exception of neck and shank cuts, all lamb is tender, and the dry-heat methods—roasting and broiling—are generally used. Removing the fell (a thin, parchment-like covering over the lamb and mutton carcass) before roasting detracts from the general shape of the cut. Lamb and mutton are cooked to medium or well done. The unpalatable "muttony" taste associated with lukewarm lamb or mutton is caused by the partial congealing of fat. The melting point of lamb and mutton fat is high, and unless the meat is served very hot the fat will be of a pasty consistency.

All cuts of pork are tender, largely because of their good distribution of fat and the young age of the hogs slaughtered. Large cuts of pork, both fresh and cured, are roasted. Pork must always be well cooked to minimize the danger of contamination from trichinae.

In roasting, the meat is placed, fat side up, on a rack in a shallow roasting pan. (The rack keeps the meat out of the drippings and the melting fat on top bastes it.) A meat thermometer is inserted so that the bulb reaches the center of the thickest muscle of the roast (Fig. 24-8). The meat thermometer should not touch bone or be embedded in a lymph gland or in fat. The roasting pan is left uncovered and no water is added. (If water is added, the cooking method becomes one of moist heat.) The meat is roasted in a slow oven (325–350°F; 163–177°C) for the entire roasting period. The higher temperature (350°F; 177°C) is used mainly for pork roasts to insure complete cooking. The lower temperature (325°F; 163°C) is more satisfactory for the majority of cuts. When the meat thermometer indicates that the correct temperature for the desired degree of doneness has been reached, the meat can be removed from the oven (Table 24-3).

The distance the heat travels to reach the center of the thickest part of the cut is a significant factor in cooking meat to the stage of doneness desired. It is important to keep two things in mind: the larger the piece of meat, the greater the weight in proportion to the volume; and the farther the heat must travel to the center

24-8 *To roast a standing rib roast of beef, place the roast in a shallow roasting pan without water or cover. Use a meat thermometer to indicate degree of doneness. (Courtesy of the National Live Stock and Meat Board)*

TABLE 24-3
Standards for Doneness Set Up by Committee on Preparation

Meat	Color	Description	Internal Temperature °F	Internal Temperature °C
Beef	Rare	Rose red in the center, pinkish toward the outer portion, shading into a dark gray; brown crust; juice bright red	140	60
	Medium	Light pink; brown edge and crust; juice light pink	160	70
	Well done	Brownish gray in center; dark crust	176	80
Lamb	Medium	Light pink; juice light pink	160	70
	Well done	Center brownish gray; texture firm but not crumbly; juice clear	175–180	80–82
Veal	Well done	Firm, not crumbly; juice clear, light pink	165	74
Pork, rib and loin	Well done	Center grayish white	170	77
Pork, shoulder chops and fresh hams	Well done	Center grayish white	185	85

Source: Adapted from *Meat and Meat Cookery* (Chicago: National Live Stock and Meat Board, 1942), p. 102.

of the thickest part of the meat, the greater the total time for the cooking. Thus, large cuts will generally require fewer minutes of cooking per pound than smaller cuts of the same type, and a thin, wide piece of meat will take fewer minutes of cooking per pound than a small, thick roast of the same weight.

Charts showing required cooking minutes per pound for desired degree of doneness of a cut of meat can only furnish approximate cooking times. The meat thermometer is the only accurate guide to the degree of doneness and to the internal temperature of meat, roasts, and large, thick steaks. In the less tender cuts of meat, such as stew and pot roast, a fork may be inserted to test resistance to that pressure. This is a fairly reliable way of testing doneness in these cuts of meat.

Roasts continue to cook at the center after they are removed from the oven. This occurs because heat continues to be transferred from the surface of the roast to the interior, each fiber of meat conducting the heat to adjacent fibers.

Usually, at the end of the roasting period, there is a difference in the temperature of the meat halfway between the surface and the center of the roast and the temperature of the meat at the center. The transfer of heat from the areas of higher temperature to those of lower temperature causes the postoven cooking. If roasts are to stand for any length of time before being served, they should be removed from the oven when they are still a few degrees below the temperature suggested. (In very thin pieces of meat, the interior temperature does not rise after the cooking process is stopped.)

It has long been recommended that pork roasts be cooked to an internal temperature of 185°F (85°C) to ensure well-done meat throughout the cut. Investigations made on fresh rib and loin pork roasts demonstrated that for optimum quality an internal temperature of 170°F (77°C) for roast pork rib and loin is desirable. Roasts cooked to this end temperature have lower cooking losses, are higher in juiciness, require less cooking time, and are comparable in flavor to roasts cooked to 185°F (85°C).[28]

Studies have shown that the end-point temperature of 170°F (77°C) was at least 30°F (17°C) above the temperature required to kill *Trichinella spiralis*.[29] Recommendations for thorough cooking of pork are made because pork may be infected with trichinae, which can be the cause of trichinoses in human beings who have eaten the meat when insufficiently cooked. Bramblett's[30] study shows that an internal temperature of 170°F (76°C) is a satisfactory end point for roasting boned and tied fresh hams and shoulders at 325°F (163°C).

BROILING. Broiling is cooking by direct radiant heat. The parts of the meat touching the broiler pan are cooked by conduction. Broiling is another dry-heat method of cooking and is suitable for tender cuts of meat, such as rib and loin lamb chops, steaks, lamb, ham slices, and bacon. Cuts of meat not generally considered suitable for broiling can be treated with tenderizers or mechanically treated by grinding or scoring then broiled.

It has been noted that high temperatures are

---

[28] A. Carlin, D. M. Bloemer, and D. K. Hotchkiss, "Relation of Oven Temperature and Final Internal Temperature to Quality of Pork Loin Roasts," *J. Home Econ.* **57**:442, 1965.

[29] Ibid., p. 444.

[30] V. D. Bramblett et al., "Cooking Pork Roasts," *J. Amer. Dietet. Assoc.* **57**:132, 1970.

---

sometimes used to broil meat without apparent toughening of muscle tissue. This may be due to fast cooking and tenderness of the meat muscle involved.

Manufacturers' direction for broiling in gas and electric ranges differ—the door of the gas range is closed but that of the electric range is partially opened. The reason for the latter procedure is to minimize the formation of steam, because less air circulates in the electric range. Too much steam in the oven will prevent browning of the meat. The heat is transferred by conduction to the surface of the meat from the heated air circulating around the piece of meat to be broiled.

Broiling is infrequently used to cook pork chops, for broiling to the well-done stage dries out the chop.

A good thickness for steaks and chops is 1 to 1½ in. A ham steak ½ in. thick will also broil satisfactorily.

Directions for broiling: Wipe the chops, steak, or ham with a damp cloth, and cut the fat edge in several places to prevent curling of the meat. Place the meat on the rack of a broiler pan and adjust the rack so that the top of the meat is 2 to 5 in. from the source of heat (Fig. 24-9). Cuts of meat that are 1 in. or less in thickness need only be 2 in below the broiler flame. Broil at 350°F (176°C) until top side is brown. (The meat should be approximately half done by the time it is browned on top.) Season with salt and pepper,

24-9 *To broil porterhouse steak in an oven, place the steak on the rack of the broiler pan, with the tip of the steak 2 to 3 in. from the heat, and insert a meat thermometer in the side of the steak. (Courtesy of the National Live Stock and Meat Board)*

turn, and brown the other side. (Turn meat carefully with tongs or two spatulas. Do not pierce with a fork.) Aluminum foil placed on the broiler rack may cause the retained hot fat to catch on fire. The rack should always permit fat drippings to drop into the broiler pan or the meat will fry.

When very thick chops and steaks are broiled, a meat thermometer can be used for determining exactly when the meat has reached the desired stage of doneness. The thermometer should be inserted into the steak or the chop so that the center of the bulb is in the center of the largest muscle.

Regulating a gas oven for proper broiling temperatures is important. To insure constant moderate temperature, the broiler rack may be placed further from the heat. If the space in the broiler does not permit lowering the broiler rack, adjustments in temperature will have to be made by regulating the thermostat. The evidence is overwhelmingly in favor of a moderately low boiling temperature. If the temperature is too low, meat will not brown. Experimental work has shown that moderately low temperatures (300–350°F; 149–177°C) produce more tender, more uniformly cooked, and juicier chops, and steaks than higher temperatures do.[31] It is also apparent that shrinkage is greater when broiling temperatures are increased.

PAN BROILING. Tender cuts of meat that are commonly oven-broiled may also be pan-broiled or griddle-broiled. This may be a preferred method for small, thin cuts of steaks or chops because of the ease of using simple equipment. In this case, heat is conducted from the metal to the surface of the meat.

Directions for pan broiling: Place the meat in a heavy frying pan and cook it slowly. Do not cover pan or add water. Turn the meat to obtain even browning. (Be sure not to pierce the meat when turning.) Pour off fat as it accumulates in the frying pan. (If meat is allowed to cook in its own fat, it will fry instead of broil.)

FRYING. Although frying is a widely used method of cooking meat, there is very little research information available on it. Frying, or

cooking fat, may be used successfully to cook thin pieces of tender meat or meat that has been ground or cut up in small pieces. The use of small amount of added fat or accumulations of fat from the meat itself as it cooks is called pan frying or sautéing. Heat is indirectly transferred to the surface of the meat from the metal of the pan. When the meat is completely immersed in fat and cooked, it is considered to be deep-fat fried. Often, meat that is to be fried in deep fat is first coated with egg and crumbs or with a cover batter to increase browning and to add crispness and flavor.

PAN FRYING. It is most satisfactory to use a heavy frying pan in order to ensure even distribution of heat. Use of an electric fry pan or the thermostatic surface burner helps maintain constant cooking temperatures.

Directions for pan frying: Heat a small amount of fat. Place the meat in the pan and cook at a moderate temperature until it is golden brown on both sides.

If water is then added or the pan covered, the method of cooking is braising. Braised meat may be more tender, but it is also less crisp and lacks the characteristic color of fried meat. Little information is available about the amount of time required to pan-fry meats. Because the cuts fried are usually thin, it is fairly safe to assume that the meat will be done when the outer coating or surface is a crisp brown.

DEEP-FAT FRYING. When a very crisp surface is desired for tender meats (such as liver, sweetbreads, or brains), they are coated, generally with a protective covering of crumbs or some similar material, and fried in deep fat heated to 300–325°F (149–163°C). This method of frying can only be used with tender cuts of meat, because the cooking time involved is short.

Directions for deep-fat frying: Use a deep pan with a wire basket in which to place the meat while cooking. Heat the fat to the desired temperature (use a frying thermometer to determine when the fat is sufficiently heated). Lower the basket with a few pieces of meat at a time into the fat. Cook until the meat is golden brown. (For more detailed information on deep-fat frying, see Chapter 28).

Moist Heat Methods. The less tender cuts of meat are generally cooked by moist heat. It has long been held that tough cuts of meat subjected

[31] Committee on Preparation Factors, National Cooperative Meat Investigations, *Meat and Meat Cookery,* op. cit., p. 103.

(a)

(b)

(c)

24-10 *Braising is a method for cooking less tender meats. (a) Brown meat on all sides in heavy utensil. (b) Add vegetables during the last hour of cooking. (c) Make a sauce or gravy from the liquid in the pan. (Courtesy of Armour Food Company)*

to moist heat become less tough as the collagen (the protein of the white connective tissue) softens. Moist cooking methods provide for variety in the preparation of meat. Well-done, tender pieces of meat served in their own well-seasoned juices, clear or thickened, are highly acceptable meat dishes.

BRAISING. Braising is a method generally accepted for the less tender cuts of meat (see Fig. 24-10). In practice, it is also used for tender cuts of meat. It is used for the preparation of pork chops, veal chops, round steaks, cutlets, and organ meats. In the main, the less tender cuts of meat braised are tough cuts of beef and cuts lacking in fat (such as veal). Long, slow cooking to the well-done stage softens the connective tissue and develops the flavor. Pot-roasting meat is combining braising with browning.

Although many authorities still hold that moist cooking is required to break down collagen to make meat tender, others believe that collagen breakdown can be accomplished through dry heat. Because the development of tenderness by using this method requires low temperatures and takes so long a time, it hardly seems a practicable recommendation. The tenderizing effect of low oven temperatures is possibly caused by slow penetration of heat rather than the low heat itself.

Directions for braising: Braise meat by slowly cooking it in a small amount of liquid or steam in a covered utensil. It may or may not be browned. The meat is browned in its own fat or in a small amount of added fat. (For small amounts of meat, a surface burner may be used; for large amounts, a very hot oven may be more convenient.) After the meat is browned, some liquid may be added. Additional liquid, however, is not essential and should be kept to a minimum in order that the full, characteristic flavor of the meat may develop in its juices. Cover the cooking utensil tightly and continue cooking (low heat) until the meat is tender but not too stringy. Tough cuts of meats cooked for prolonged periods beyond the stage of little fork resistance become stringy, lose flavor, and are difficult to cut.

Experimental work with moist methods of cooking meat is not extensive, and recommended methods rest to a large extent on the work done with tender cuts. The shrinkage in meats cooked with moist heat parallels that in meats cooked with dry heat.

SIMMERING. Simmering is the cooking of cuts of meat in heated water until they are sufficiently tender to cut and chew. This method is particularly effective when preparing tough cuts of meat. In keeping with more recent developments in the field of meat cookery, recommendations for simmering emphasize the importance of keeping the temperature of the water below boiling. In the preparation of meat stews, cuts of meat such as brisket, neck of beef, and neck and breast of veal and lamb are cut into cubes and simmered in water. Large cuts of cured meats may also be prepared by simmering.

Directions for simmering: Place the meat in a kettle with enough water to cover. Cover the utensil tightly and adjust the temperature to below boiling. Cook the meat until tender. (For large cuts of meat, such as corned beef, smoked tenderloin, and tongue, cooking time may be 3–4 hours.)

PRESSURE COOKING. Pressure cooking, or cooking with steam, brings about the same changes in meat as do other methods of cooking with moist heat. Cuts of meat that are usually treated by moist heat can also be cooked in the pressure cooker. The unique quality of pressure cooking is the marked decrease in cooking time. Pressure-cooked meats will lack some of the color or flavor produced by the initial browning of the meat, but flavor and color can be added in the form of other food material.

STEAMING IN ALUMINUM FOIL. Wrapping meat in aluminum foil and cooking it in an oven is another method of steaming meat. The tight-fitting foil retains steam as effectively as a covered pan. In experimental work, foil-wrapped roasts lost more weight during cooking and were considered less juicy, less tender and less flavorful than roasts cooked by dry heat.[32]

Cooking Frozen Cuts of Meat. The increasing emphasis on freezing as a convenient and safe method of preserving meat has motivated some investigations into such problems as the difference in cooking time, the shrinkage, and the loss of palatability associated with cooking frozen or thawed cuts of meat. There is little difference between the tenderness, juiciness, and flavor of meats cooked in the unthawed state and after thawing; hence, the usual cooking methods may be used for both. However, extra time must be allowed for the cooking of unthawed frozen meat. Large frozen roasts should be cooked one and one half times as long as unfrozen roasts of the same size and general shape. Frozen steaks, chops, and roasts develop browner surfaces during cooking than do corresponding unfrozen cuts under similar cooking conditions. Increasing the oven temperature above that usually recommended does not shorten cooking time for cooking beef roasts from the frozen state.[33]

Frozen meat may be thawed in the refrigerator, at room temperature, in running water, or by forced convection currents. Although thawing takes three times as long in the refrigerator as it does at room temperature, refrigerator thawing is the more feasible method for household and institutional use.[34] It is also the safest method of those described and the one that results in the most uniform thawing and the best appearance of the meat.

Meat Stock. The flavor of the meat can be extracted as a stock from the bones and/or tough pieces of meat. Large bones are usually cracked to allow greater ease of penetration of the liquid into the marrow. Meat is cut into small pieces to increase its surface area. Stock is made when the meat and bones are simmered for three to four hours with continual removal of any scum that forms. Vegetables and spices such as onions, carrots, garlic, leeks, parsley, bay leaf, celery, salt, and thyme are added towards the end of the cooking period to more fully

---

[32] M. P. Hood, "Effect of Cooking Method and Grade on Beef Roasts," *J. Amer. Dietet. Assoc.* **37:**363, 1960.

[33] Diane Ferger, et al., "Lamb and Beef Roasts Cooked from the Frozen State by Dry and Moist Heat," *J. Food Sci.* **37:**226, 1972.

[34] B. Lowe et al., "Defrosting and Cooking Frozen Meats," *Research Bulletin 385* (Ames, Iowa: Agricultural Experiment Station, Iowa State College, 1952).

develop the flavor of the broth. The broth is strained and may be degreased by chilling.

A brown stock is distinguished from a white stock in that the bones or meat have been roasted or browned in order to develop the flavor and color. If brown stock has been clarified by egg white it is called *bouillon*. A *consommé* is also a clarified broth but is generally a light stock made from a mixture of meats.

Microwave Cooking. Meats cooked in a microwave oven require much shorter cooking time than those cooked in the conventional oven. (For a full discussion, see Chapter 45.) The absorption of microwave energy by the meat causes a rearrangement of molecules that, in turn, produces heat. A medium-sized roast will cook in a microwave oven in approximately one-eighth the time that would be required in a conventional oven. This is the prime advantage of microwave cooking. There is greater shrinkage in roasts cooked by microwave energy than in roasts cooked by the conventional oven. Also, cooking may not be uniform, because microwave energy heats the outer portion of the meat quickly but fails to penetrate very deeply. The center of the roast, therefore, cooks more slowly, by the conduction of heat from its surface.

Marshall found that meat roasted to the well-done stage in a microwave oven took only 10.7 minutes per pound as compared with 45.4 minutes for that prepared in the conventional oven.[35] However, the palatability rating for the microwave cooked meat was low, and the meat fibers were hard and dry. Dripping losses in the microwave cooked meat were excessive compared to those from meat roasted by conventional methods. When more than one roast is cooked at the same time, cooking time is increased.

Meat cooked by microwave lacks surface browning. The browned surface of a conventionally cooked roast or chop is a universal standard; cooked meat that does not come up to this standard may be rejected. Some microwave ovens are equipped with conventional broiling units that can be used to brown the surface of the meat. Use of plastic covers decreased the cooking time of a number of meat products cooked in the microwave oven. However, caution is required in their use because of melting, bubbling, and breaking of plastic film during cooking.[36]

SELECTION OF DIFFERENT KINDS OF MEAT

Beef. Beef is the flesh of mature cattle. For transportation and convenience in marketing beef carcasses are quartered. The meat is then ready to be divided into wholesale cuts—that is, the tender portions are separated from the tough. Cutting practices depend on the bone structure of the animal, but the Chicago style is the most common (see Fig. 24–11). The wholesale cuts are then divided into retail cuts for the consumer. (See Color Plate VIII.)

TENDER STEAKS. The tender steak cuts come from the beef loin. These are suitable for broiling and pan broiling. Club steaks are triangular, the smallest steaks in the short loin, and the first cut from the rib end of the loin. There is no tenderloin muscle in this steak.

A rib steak is cut from the rib wholesale cut (light end). It contains the rib eye and rib bone.

T-bone steaks are cut from behind the club steaks; they are fairly large steaks containing a piece of the tenderloin muscle and more fat than club steaks have. T-bone steaks are usually cut ¾ to 1½ in. thick for broiling and are sometimes used in place of porterhouse steaks.

Porterhouse steaks are cut from the end of the short loin. They are the largest steaks in the short loin and have more tenderloin muscle than T-bone steaks. The porterhouse is considered a very desirable steak.

Pin-bone steak is cut behind the porterhouse steak from the loin end. It contains the pin bone (the forward end of the hip bone), a piece of the tenderloin muscle, and the tough tail muscle. This is considered the least desirable of the sirloin steaks.

The double-boned sirloins have a good pro-

[35] N. Marshall, "Electronic Cookery of Top Round Beef," *J. Home Econ.* **52**:31, 1960.

[36] G. Ambruster, and C. Haefele, "Quality of Foods After Cooking in 915 and 2450 Hz Microwave Appliance Using Plastic Film Covers," *J. Food Sci.* **40**:721, 1975.

BEEF CHART

RETAIL CUTS OF BEEF — WHERE THEY COME FROM AND HOW TO COOK THEM

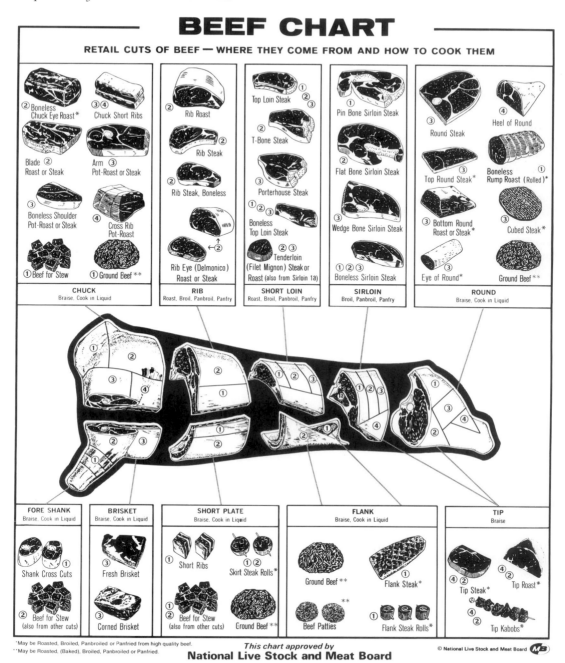

24-11 *Retail cuts of beef. (Courtesy of the National Live Stock and Meat Board)*

portion of lean meat to fat and bone. They are very suitable for family use. These steaks, cut about 1½ in. thick, weigh approximately 2 lb. The round-bone sirloins come from the end of the loin near the round; they are tender and of

excellent flavor. The wedge-bone sirloins come from the loin end next to the round. They differ from the round-bone steaks only in the shape of the bone. Tenderloin steaks are cut from stripped-out tenderloin muscle. This muscle is part of the porterhouse and sirloin steaks because it is not stripped out of all beef but only the lower-grade carcasses. It is considered the most tender cut of meat and costs more than other steaks.

TENDER ROASTS. Rib cuts are the most popular beef roasts because of their flavor and tenderness. The wholesale rib cut includes ribs 6 to 12 (see Fig. 24-11). The ribs next to the loin (8 to 12) are considered the best. A rib roast should have at least two ribs. A rib roast may also be boned and rolled. This roast requires longer cooking time.

A blade-rib roast contains the sixth and seventh ribs. It is not so tender as the rib roast from the lighter end, but it is an economical cut and has an excellent flavor.

THE LESS TENDER STEAKS. The less tender steaks are taken from the round, chuck, and flank. These are cooked by braising. Round steaks are round or oval, with a small round bone, and have a high proportion of lean to fat and bone. Although not as tender as the steaks from the loin, they may be just as high-priced because of the lean-meat content.

The muscles in the round steak vary in tenderness: the top muscle is considered the more tender, the bottom muscle less so. The sirloin tip end is more tender than the eye of the round.

A chuck-blade steak is the first steak taken from the rib end of the chuck. The eye muscle of this cut tends to be tender. This is an economical cut, and very tasty.

Shoulder arm steaks come from the lower portion of the chuck. They have excellent flavor and are very palatable when braised. The bone is shaped like that in a round steak, but the muscle structure is different: a small round muscle near the bone is surrounded by connective tissue.

The flank steak is an oval boneless steak weighing ¾ to 1½ lb. These steaks lie inside the flank, one on each side of the animal. They are stripped out rather than cut. The muscle fibers are coarse and run lengthwise. As is true of other tough steaks, flank steaks are best prepared by moist heat, although they are occasionally cooked by dry heat. The steak is broiled for a very short time on either side, then sliced diagonally. When cooked in this manner, it is called London broil.

THE LESS TENDER ROASTS. The rump is a triangular portion between the loin and the round. It contains sections of the hip bone and the ball-and-socket joint. Rump roasts are tough but have many meaty portions. The recommended cooking method for this cut is moist heat.

The top round roast is popular because it is the most tender portion of the round. This cut consists of one round muscle; it is usually braised.

The bottom round roast is distinguished from the top round by having two muscles. The cut is economical because of the small ratio of fat and connective tissue to lean meat, and there is no bone.

The chuck or blade roast is the first cut taken from the rib end of the chuck. In higher grades of meat, the eye muscle of this cut tends to be tender. The shoulder arm roasts come from the lower portions of the chuck and are prepared in the same manner as round roasts.

The brisket is a less tender cut of meat. It has layers of lean and fat and pieces of breast bone.

GROUND BEEF. Ground beef is ground only from muscle that has been attached to the skeleton. This excludes any organ or variety meat. It may be labeled "ground beef" or have the name of the primal cut on the label, as in "ground chuck" or "ground round." The lean/fat ratio is an important factor in the selection of the meat and has a minimum lean of 70%. If it is labeled not less than 75% lean, this is the same as 25% fat. Ground beef that has this high fat content is recommended for hamburgers, chili, and spaghetti sauce.[37] A higher proportion of lean to fat (75–80%) is best used for meat loaf, meat balls, noodle and rice casseroles, and Salisbury steak. Low-calorie patties and combination dishes should use ground beef labeled 80–85% lean.

SHANK. Fore and hind shank bones are used for soup. They contain a high percentage of cartilage and connective tissue. The cooked meat is frequently used in making croquettes or hash.

BONES. The names of meat cuts are frequently related to the bone structure. (See Fig. 24-12.) Bones are also a clue to a cut's tenderness. The muscles along the backbone are generally more tender than those in the shoulders, legs, breasts, and flanks. The bones in the four major meat animals are almost identical in ap-

---

[37]*Be a Smarter Shopper . . . A Better Cook* (Chicago: National Live Stock and Meat Board, 1974), pp. 12, 13.

BONES IDENTIFY SEVEN GROUPS OF RETAIL CUTS

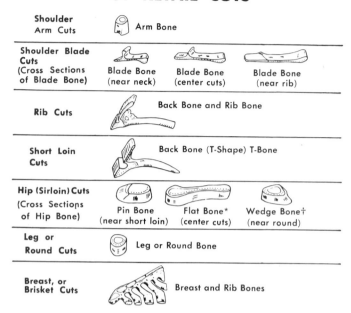

Shoulder Arm Cuts	Arm Bone
Shoulder Blade Cuts (Cross Sections of Blade Bone)	Blade Bone (near neck) Blade Bone (center cuts) Blade Bone (near rib)
Rib Cuts	Back Bone and Rib Bone
Short Loin Cuts	Back Bone (T-Shape) T-Bone
Hip (Sirloin) Cuts (Cross Sections of Hip Bone)	Pin Bone (near short loin) Flat Bone* (center cuts) Wedge Bone† (near round)
Leg or Round Cuts	Leg or Round Bone
Breast, or Brisket Cuts	Breast and Rib Bones

*Formerly part of "double bone" but today the back bone is usually removed leaving only the "flat bone" (sometimes called "pin bone") in the sirloin steak.

†On one side of sirloin steak, this bone may be wedge shaped while on the other side the same bone may be round.

24-12   *Bone Identification. (Courtesy of National Live Stock and Meat Board)*

pearance. The seven bone groups shown in Fig. 24–12 are the major ones the average shopper needs to know.

Suggested Cooking Guide. The use of an appropriate method of cooking is essential to bring out the desirable eating qualities of the specific cut and grade selected. Table 24–4 suggests the most generally accepted method of cooking retail cuts of beef of some grades (see Fig. 24–13). All grades of flank, plate, brisket, foreshank, and the heel of the round should be prepared in the same manner. These less tender cuts are used for stewing, braising, pot roasting, or simmering, or are ground for use in meat loaves and similar dishes.

Veal. Veal is the flesh of bovine animals not more than 1 year old (see Fig. 24–14). The wholesalers' use of the term *veal* is limited to the flesh of 12- to 14-week-old calves; meat from any beef animal not more than 1 year old is

called *calf.* For all practical purposes, the term *veal* will be applied to this meat.

Veal may be split into fore and hind saddles by cutting between ribs 12 and 13 (counting from front to back), or it can be cut in a manner similar to beef. The lean portion of veal is light pink, and the bone ends are pliant, porous, and red. There is very little covering tissue of fat, and no marbling in the lean tissue.

Veal Roasts. In general, veal roasts are tender and may be cooked by dry heat.

The leg of veal is comparable to the round and rump in beef. The leg may be roasted whole, or the rump portion may be removed to make a small roast. The leg contains a good proportion of lean meat.

Veal shoulder roasts are frequently used for their palatability. They may be square-cut, with the shoulder bone removed and the backbone cut between the ribs for ease in carving, or shoulder may be completely boned and stuffed

TABLE 24-4
Cooking Different Cuts
and Grades of Beef

Cut	Prime	Choice	Good
Bottom round	Braise, pot roast	Braise, pot roast	Braise, pot roast
Top round	Broil, pan fry, braise	Broil, pan fry, braise	Braise
Rump	Roast, pot roast	Roast, pot roast	Pot roast
Sirloin	Broil, roast	Broil, roast	Broil, roast
Porterhouse	Broil	Broil	Broil
T-bone	Broil	Broil	Broil
Club	Broil	Broil	Broil
Rib roast	Roast	Roast	Roast
Blade chuck	Roast, pot roast	Roast, pot	Roast, pot roast
Shoulder arm roast	Roast, pot roast	Pot roast	Pot roast

Source: "U.S. Grades for Beef," *Marketing Bulletin 15* (Washington, D.C.: U.S. Department of Agriculture, 1960).

to form a cushion shoulder, or it may be rolled with or without stuffing.

Veal rib roast is similar to standing beef roast. It has much less fat than a beef roast and is quite light in color.

Breast of veal is a thin, flat cut containing rib ends and breastbone. A pocket may be cut and stuffing put in between the ribs and lean meat, or the cut may be boned and rolled. Basically an economical cut, it may be roasted or braised.

VEAL STEAKS. A veal steak is also called a *cutlet*. It is cut from the round and contains a cross-section of the thigh bone.

VEAL CHOPS. A loin veal chop has a good proportion of lean meat and is tender. These chops, which correspond to the porterhouse and T-bone steaks, are generally braised to keep them from drying out.

Rib chops contain a much smaller proportion of lean meat to bone and connective tissue than loin chops do. They also contain rib eye and rib bone, and they are generally braised.

SHOULDER CHOPS. Shoulder chops contain blade bone and rib bone. They usually cost less than loin and rib chops and have an excellent flavor. Braising is recommended.

Lamb. Lamb and mutton come from the ovine family of animals (see Fig. 24-15). Lamb is the meat of the young sheep, mutton the flesh of the mature sheep. Although there is no definite age division between the two, *lamb* usually refers to the flesh of animals not more than 14 months of age. The term *mutton* is used for the flesh of older sheep. Lamb carcasses are lighter in weight than mutton. Lamb also has a softer bone, lighter-colored flesh, and softer fat. Meat handlers agree that the break joint is a good indication of the age of lamb. The break joint in a young lamb has four sharp ridges that are moist, red, and smooth. In mature animals, the break joint is more porous and hard. At the mutton stage, the forefeet must be taken off at the round joint, below the break joint.

Lamb cuts are very similar to those of veal, although the carcasses are smaller and the cover fat more abundant. Small cubes of lamb cut from the shoulder are served as shish kabob. The meat is marinated, skewered with tomatoes, onions, and peppers, and then broiled.

LAMB ROASTS. A leg of lamb is an excellent cut for roasting. It may be trimmed and sold as Frenched leg or it may be sold as longcut loin. A

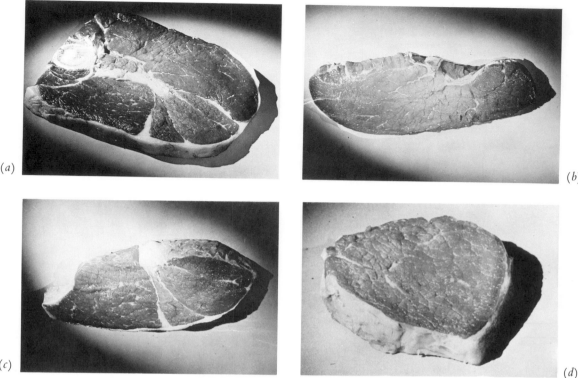

(a)

(b)

(c)

(d)

24-13 *Retail cuts of less tender cuts of meat (a) Round steak—full cut, (b) bottom round (c) hip cut and (d) eye of the round. (Courtesy of National Live Stock and Meat Board)*

leg of lamb generally weighs 6–8 lb. Shoulders of lamb may be prepared in a manner similar to veal. They, too, may be stuffed, or boned and rolled. Two intact sections of ribs with the back bone removed may be curved to form a crown roast of lamb. It is served with stuffing in the center of the crown and the bone ends are decorated with paper frills.

LAMB CHOPS. Lamb chops may be cut from the loin, rib, or shoulder and are suitable for broiling. Loin chops are preferred because they are the most tender and have a good flavor. The English chop is a double loin chop. Saratoga chops are boneless chops from the shoulder which are rolled and fastened together.

Pork. Pork is the flesh of swine (see Fig. 24-16). Most pork comes from animals not more than 1 year old and generally has more fat than other meats. Because of these characteristics, pork is a tender cut of meat. The color of young lean

pork is light pink, changing to rose as the animal matures. The lean is firm, well marbled, and covered with a firm white fat; the cut surface of the bones is red. Cutting practices for pork differ from those for beef, veal, and lamb. Practically all pork is separated into cuts at the packing plant. A number of pork cuts are cured, and some pork is used for sausage.

CUTS OF PORK. (See Color Plate IX.) The pork cuts most frequently used for fresh meat are the spare ribs and the loin. The spareribs, taken from the belly portion of the animal, contain a large proportion of bone to lean. The pork loin is a long cut that extends along the backbone of the animal. This may be cut into smaller loin roasts: the shoulder end of the loin, containing rib bones and blade bones, and the loin end (the preferred cut), containing the section with the rib eye and tenderloin muscles.

Pork chops are cut from the loin. The loin chops have a piece of the back muscle and the

VEAL CHART

RETAIL CUTS OF VEAL — WHERE THEY COME FROM AND HOW TO COOK THEM

SHOULDER

(Large Pieces) (Small Pieces)
①②③ for Stew*
— Braise, Cook in Liquid —

③ Arm Steak ② Blade Steak
— Braise, Panfry —

②③ Boneless Shoulder Roast

③ Arm Roast ② Blade Roast
— Roast, Braise —

RIB

④ Boneless Rib Chop

④ Rib Chop
— Braise, Panfry —

④ Crown Roast

④ Rib Roast
— Roast —

LOIN

① Top Loin Chop

① Loin Chop

① Kidney Chop
— Braise, Panfry —

① Loin Roast
— Roast —

SIRLOIN

Cubed Steak **

① Sirloin Chop
— Braise, Panfry —

① Boneless Sirloin Roast

① Sirloin Roast
— Roast —

ROUND (LEG)

①③④ Cutlets ①③④ Rolled Cutlets

Cutlets (Thin Slices) ③④ Round Steak
— Braise, Panfry —

Boneless Rump Roast

② Rump Roast ③④ Round Roast
— Roast, Braise —

SHANK

⑤ Shank

⑤ Shank Cross Cuts
— Braise, Cook in Liquid —

BREAST

⑥ Breast ⑥ Stuffed Breast
— Roast, Braise —

⑥ Riblets ⑥ Boneless Riblets ⑥ Stuffed Chops
— Braise, Cook in Liquid — — Braise, Panfry —

VEAL FOR GRINDING OR CUBING

Rolled Cube Steaks ** Ground Veal* Patties*
— Braise — — Roast (Bake) Braise, Panfry —

Mock Chicken Legs* * City Chicken Choplets*
— Braise, Panfry —

*Veal for stew or grinding may be made from any cut.
**Cube steaks may be made from any thick solid piece of boneless veal.

This chart approved by
National Live Stock and Meat Board

© National Live Stock and Meat Board

24-14 *Retail cuts of veal. (Courtesy of the National Live Stock and Meat Board)*

tenderloin muscle. End chops contain more bone; shoulder chops contain pieces of the shoulder bone; sirloin chops contain pieces of the hip bone.

CURED PORK. Cured and smoked hams are sold whole or in halves or slices. They are also available with none, some, or all of the bone and with all or part of the skin and fat removed.

305

LAMB CHART

RETAIL CUTS OF LAMB — WHERE THEY COME FROM AND HOW TO COOK THEM

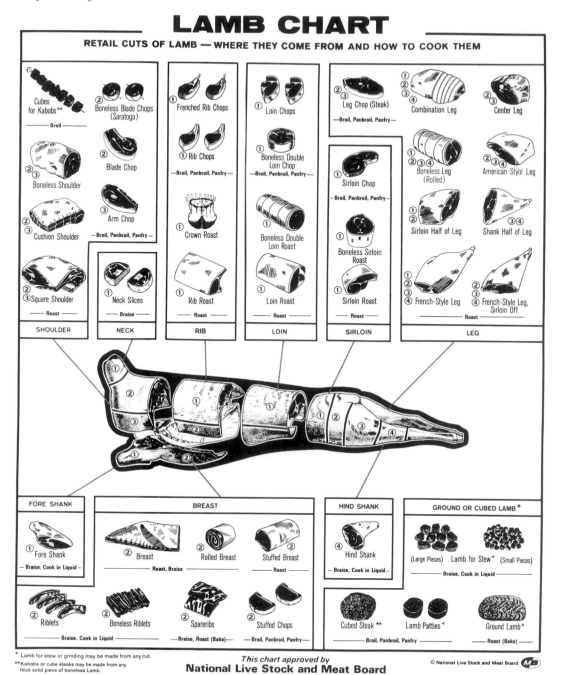

24-15 *Retail cuts of lamb. (Courtesy of National Live Stock and Meat Board)*

Bacon is cut from the belly portion of the hog carcass and is comparable to the plate and brisket of beef. It is cured and sold in slices or slabs. Canadian-style bacon is a loin cut that has been boned, rolled, and cured. It may be broiled or baked. Jowl bacon, cut from the jowl, has a high percentage of fat. Picnic hams are usually cured. Cut from the lower portion of the shoulder of

PORK CHART

RETAIL CUTS OF PORK — WHERE THEY COME FROM AND HOW TO COOK THEM

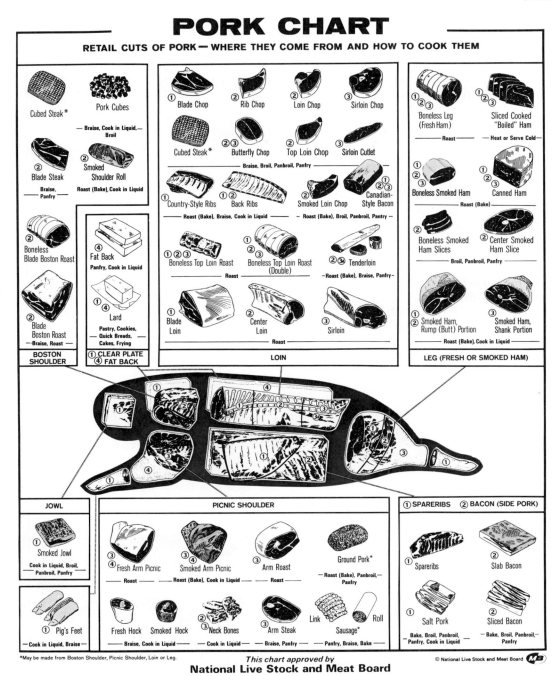

24-16 *Retail cuts of pork. (Courtesy of the National Live Stock and Meat Board)*

the animal, they are smaller than true ham cuts and have more bone in proportion to lean meat. This cut may be boned before cooking to make it easier to slice.

The Boston butt is cut from the upper shoulder. It is boned before curing, has a compact shape, is easy to slice, and generally has a good proportion of lean to fat.

Variety Meats. Variety or specialty meats are the internal organs of meat animals. They include liver, kidneys, heart (Fig. 24-17), tripe,[38] sweetbreads (Fig. 24-18),[39] brains, and lungs (Table 24-5). Some meat users also group oxtail and pork feet (pig's knuckles) with the internal organs.

Variety meats may be tough or tender and are cooked accordingly. Brains, sweetbreads, liver (Fig. 24-19), and kidneys from young animals are tender and may be cooked by any form of dry heat. Tongue, heart, tripe, oxtails, and beef and pork kidneys and beef liver are less tender and therefore require moist heat for cooking. Variety meats should be cooked until well-done to minimize the danger of transmitting the parasitic organisms found in them.

Fabricated Beef. This is a shaped frozen beef product prepared from boneless beef pieces, chopped meat trimmings, salt, and phosphate prior to freezing. The product is used for sliced beef sandwiches.

Sausages. Over 200 varieties of sausages (Fig. 24-20) are made from ground or minced meat

[38] Tripe is the stomach lining of beef animals. The two kinds of tripe available are honeycomb, the preferred kind, and smooth. The former is from the lining of the second stomach of the animal; the latter is the lining of the first stomach.

[39] Sweetbreads are the thymus glands and pancreas of young beef, veal, and lamb. As the animal matures, the thymus gland atrophies.

24-18 *Sweetbreads from different animals. Left to right: lamb, veal, and beef. (Courtesy of the National Live Stock and Meat Board)*

that has been salted, seasoned, and stuffed into casings. Fillers or extenders in the form of cereals, starches, flour, and dry milk solids may be added up to 3.5% of the product. Sausages can be classified as fresh, fresh smoked, cooked, cooked smoked, dry and semidry, and ready-to-serve (luncheon meats) (Fig. 24-21). Examples of fresh sausage are fresh pork sausage, Italian pork sausage, bockwurst, and bratwurst. Fresh sausage must always be refrigerated and thoroughly cooked before eating. If the fresh sausage has been smoked, it still needs to be refrigerated and cooked. Country-style pork sausage, mettwurst, and Roumanian sausage are fresh smoked. Cooked and cured meats are liver sausage, braunschweiger, and veal sausage. Cooked smoked sausages which are ready to eat but benefit in flavor from heating are kielbasa,

24-17 *Hearts. Left to right: beef, veal, pork, and lamb. (Courtesy of the National Live Stock and Meat Board)*

24-19 *Liver is the most popular variety meat. Clockwise from left: beef, veal, pork, and lamb. (Courtesy of the National Live Stock and Meat Board)*

TABLE 24-5
Variety Meats

Organ	Animal	Identifying Characteristics
Brains	Calf, lamb, pork, beef	Grayish; soft; delicate flavor
Heart	Calf, lamb, pork, beef	Brownish; fairly tough and muscular (beef heart is less tender than lamb, pork, or veal heart); pronounced flavor and texture
Kidneys	Calf, lamb, pork, beef	Brownish; beef and pork kidneys are stronger flavored and tougher than lamb or veal kidneys
Sweetbreads	Beef, veal, lamb	Grayish; soft; delicate flavor
Tongue	Beef, veal, pork, lamb	Light pink to red; beef and veal tongue are the most frequently used because of size; may be purchased fresh, pickled, corned, or smoked (pork and lamb tongue are usually purchased ready to serve)
Tripe	Beef	Yellowish white; muscular
Liver	Beef, lamb, calf, pork	Beef liver is less tender than lamb, calf, and pork; calf and lamb liver are milder in flavor than pork and beef

frankfurters (weiners), knockwurst, and bologna. Dry and semidry sausages that have a long shelf life due to their low moisture content are salami, chorizos, pepperoni, cappicola, and summer sausage. Refrigeration will prolong the life of any sausage even if it is not required.

PRESERVATION AND STORAGE OF MEAT

Commercial Methods. CURED MEAT. The curing of meat is a means of preserving it. Cur-

ing is altogether confined to beef and pork cuts: hams (pork), bellies (bacon), brisket (beef), and navel (beef). Accessory meats, such as tongue and ham hocks, are also processed. Ground or chopped meat may be cured in such products as sausage. A cured meat product may be dried and smoked and treated with salt, sodium nitrite, and/or sodium nitrate, sugar, and sometimes spices and vinegar, and phosphates.

During curing the nitrite reacts with the myoglobin pigment of the meat to produce the pink nitrosomyoglobulin. There is concern that it may also react when heated with amine groups

24-20 *The 12 lanes of wieners leaving the production line represent a continuous process. (Courtesy of Oscar Mayer and Co.)*

24-21 *Ready-to-serve meats (Clockwise: veal loaf, New England ham, "boiled" ham, pepper loaf, souse, pickle and pimiento loaf, summer sausage, bologna, liver sausage). (Courtesy of the National Live Stock and Meat Board)*

to form nitrosamine, a compound that has been found to be carcinogenic. This is discussed in Chapter 43.

Salt is added to retard microbial growth as well as for flavor. Sugar is added to counteract the saltiness. Phosphates are often used for their water-retaining ability, which keeps the meat juicy.

The curing agents may be applied dry to the surface of the meat. Or the meat may be immersed in a water solution of the curing agents (pickling). Or the solution of curing agents may be pumped through the vascular system of the piece of meat (vein pumping). Pumping is the method most frequently used today, for it provides the most rapid and even distribution of the curing agents.

When a curing solution is pumped into a ham, it increases its weight. To avoid deception, the ham must be labeled "water added" if it has up to 10% more weight than the fresh ham and "imitation ham" if it increases the weight by more than 10%. Consumers may be wary of these labels, but the addition of the watery curing solution generally increases the juiciness and flavor of the ham.

"Virginia" or country-style ham is dry-cured and does not require refrigeration. The curing solution is rubbed into the ham and allowed to cure the meat for approximately 1 day per pound of ham. The hams are smoked naturally without chemicals and allowed to age for up to 1 year. Owing to the high salt content, these hams must be soaked and boiled before cooking.

In curing, sugar is used principally to provide flavor, salt to dry out the meat, sodium nitrite

and nitrate to stabilize the color pigment so that the cured meat retains its redness. Sodium nitrite is a source of nitric oxide, a specific color fixative. It is the interaction of nitric oxide with the hemoglobin that forms the stable pigment nitrohemoglobin.[40] The addition of sugar to brine makes it a sweet brine or pickle. Cured meat smoked in federally inspected establishments is truly wood-smoked; a smoked taste is otherwise achieved by chemical treatment.

A new requirement that cured meat products be labeled with an ingredient statement became effective early in 1973. All cured products are required to have on their labels a list of all ingredients used in curing; this includes the labels of products such as frozen dinners containing ham.

DEHYDRATED MEAT. There is a limited amount of dehydrated meat available; that which is processed is used mainly for export or as provision on exploratory expeditions. There is little merit in the flavor and texture of dehydrated meat compared to that of other forms of meat, but it does offer a notable saving in space. The method of drying that seems to offer possibilities for the future is freeze drying. The chief disadvantage of freeze drying is the cost. A steak takes 24 to 30 hours drying time. As is true of other freeze-dried foods, meat retains its original shape and, rehydrated, looks and tastes much like the fresh item.

[40] Department of Agriculture regulations require the lowering of nitrates in bacon as of June 1978. See Chapter 43.

FROZEN MEAT. Most commercially marketed frozen meat is quick-frozen. Freezing inhibits microbial growth, limiting the action of the most destructive spoilage agents.

CRYOGENIC FREEZING OF MEAT. A rapid freezing method that employs the use of condensed gases is called *cryogenic*. Some meat and poultry are frozen in this manner. The low temperature, $-315°F$ ($-195°C$), of liquid nitrogen makes it an excellent coolant. In the vaporization of 1 lb of liquid nitrogen, 86 Btu is absorbed; in addition, the cold gas can absorb an additional 90 Btu in warming to $41°F$ ($5°C$). The very low initial temperature of the liquid nitrogen freezes the food. Nitrous oxide and dry ice are also used in cryogenic freezing.

Cryogenic frozen meats have very small ice crystals. For this reason, there is little piercing of cell walls by ice crystals and consequent damaging of meat tissue so that cryogenic freezing produces a product very close to the unfrozen meat. The lighter color of the surface of cryogenically frozen meat is caused by reflectance of light from the well-distributed small ice crystals.

IRRADIATED MEAT. Irradiation-sterilizated meat appears to have possibilities but is not on the market. The radiation preservation process involves exposing food to electrons or gamma rays. There is a rise in temperature of only a few degrees, so food is not cooked in the process. The changes in color, flavor, texture, and odor that occur in the sterilization of meat are still being investigated.[41] Proctor and Goldblith[42] reported good results in using irradiation to reduce spoilage caused by microbial action. Mehrlich and Sin[43] believe that recent experiments in low-temperature irradiation of meat show substantial benefits over earlier studies. When boneless beef roasts were exposed to sterilizing doses of radiation at a liquid nitrogen

temperature of $-300°F$ ($-150°C$), it was found that fresh meat sterilized at such low temperatures are superior in color, texture, flavor, and nutritional value to those treated at room temperature.

HOME STORAGE OF MEAT. Fresh, cured, and ready-to-eat meats are perishable foods; they may be held in home storage at refrigerator temperatures just above freezing for a short period. The meat is chilled at the processing plant and shipped to wholesale and retail markets in refrigerated cars. Once purchased for use, meat must receive good care if it is to retain its freshness. Meat that has been scored or ground is more susceptible to spoilage because a larger surface area has been exposed to contamination from air, human handling, and equipment. Ground meat should be used within 24 hours of purchase. Organ meats, too, are easily contaminated and should be promptly used after purchase. Skin serves to protect the interior of the meat, despite the fact that microorganisms grow on it.

It is best to store meat products at temperatures slightly above freezing (33 to 36°F; 1–2°C) to inhibit the growth of microorganisms. The coldest part of the refrigerator is the best place for the meat storage box. Wrappings and containers used to prepackage meats help to protect the meat from further contamination, but they also help to maintain the moist surface of the meat. This moistness encourages the growth of microorganisms. Tight wrapping should be removed if meat is kept longer than 2 days.

Fresh beef, not prepackaged, should be removed from the market wrapping paper, wrapped loosely in waxed paper or aluminum foil and refrigerated for not longer than 2 days.

Cured meats present a different storage problem: the fat will quickly become rancid if the meat is exposed to light and oxygen. Consequently, cured meats should be stored in the refrigerator in their original wrappings. But if the original wrapping is removed and only a small portion of the meat is used, the package should be rewrapped. Cured and smoked meats can be refrigerated for 7 days.

Leftover cooked meats should be covered and immediately placed in the coldest part of the refrigerator to prevent spoilage.

[41] I. J. Somers and J. M Reed, "Developments in Food Preservation," *J. Amer. Dietet. Assoc.* **35**:235, 1959.

[42] B. E. Proctor and S. A. Goldblith, "Preservation of Food by Irradiation," *Amer. J. Pub. Health* **47**:439, 1957.

[43] F. Mehrlich and R. G. Sin, "Military and Space Operations," in *Protecting Our Food: The Yearbook of Agriculture* (Washington, D.C.: U.S. Department of Agriculture, 1966).

SUMMARY

Meat provides high-quality complete proteins and also contains important amounts of iron, phosphorus, and copper. Pork is especially high in thiamine. All lean meats contain thiamine, riboflavin, and niacin. The organ meats are also rich in vitamin A. The amount of protein in any particular cut depends on the amount of lean tissue in it, whereas calorie content varies with the amount of fat. Connective tissue and the distribution of fat affect tenderness. Largest of all American food industries, the meat-packing industry seeks to find uses and markets for the inedible by-products and thus reduce costs per pound of meat. Research strives to meet consumer demand for lean meats. Meat prices reflect supply and demand, but true cost per pound is determined by the percentage of edible meat, pound for pound of lean meat. Less tender cuts and lower grades of meat are just as nutritious as higher-grade, higher-priced tender cuts.

All meat crossing states lines is federally inspected before and after slaughter. The Wholesome Meat Act of 1967 mandates that states provide meat inspection equal to federal standards. Quality may be indicated by federal grade markings for beef ranging from U.S. Prime (top quality to U.S. Canner grade. Beef can be graded on the basis of "cutability," which is the amount of lean meat available in a cut. Cutability is graded from 1 to 5. Some beef, and occasionally lamb, is aged to improve its flavor and tenderness.

Meats with small amounts of connective tissue and good marbling of fat may be cooked by dry heat, whereas less tender cuts are cooked by moist heat. Enzymes may be used to tenderize meat, and they make it possible to use dry-heat methods for tough cuts of meat. Unthawed meat may be cooked by the usual methods, but extra cooking time must be allowed. The microwave range cooks meat quickly, but shrinkage loss is greater and there is no surface browning without a special unit.

The principal kinds of meat used in the United States are beef, veal, lamb, and pork—and the variety or organ meats of each. Beef carcasses are quartered and then divided into wholesale cuts, whereby tender portions are separated from the tough. Veal may be cut similarly, or it may be split into fore and hind saddles. Lamb carcasses are smaller than veal, but cuts are similar. Pork is usually divided into retail cuts at the packing plant. Variety meats may be tender or tough, and a suitable cooking method should be selected. All should be cooked to well done to minimize transmission of parasitic organisms.

Meats may be preserved by curing, dehydration, and freezing. In the home, meat should be stored, loosely covered, in the coldest part of the refrigerator. Cured meats may be left in their original wrappings, stored in the refrigerator but not in the freezer.

QUESTIONS AND TOPICS FOR DISCUSSION AND STUDY

1. What are the advantages of moderate- to low-temperature meat cookery?
2. What cuts of meat can be cooked by dry heat? Why cannot all meats be so cooked?
3. What changes does heat bring about in meat?
4. What happens when meat is cooked in the oven in a covered pan?
5. What constituent of meat causes toughness?
6. Distinguish between dry and moist methods of cooking.
7. How can a tough cut of meat be made tender by cooking?
8. What factor must be considered when cooking frozen meat?
9. Why must pork be cooked until well done?
10. What are the variety meats? In what way do they contribute to the diet?
11. What accounts for the color of cured meat?
12. When a roast is taken out of the oven, there is usually a rise in internal temperature. Why?

SUGGESTED ACTIVITIES

1. Observe a meat-cutting demonstration to learn how to identify various cuts of meat.
2. Study the meat charts in this chapter. Identify wholesale cuts and retail cuts from beef, veal, pork, and lamb carcasses.
3. Prepare one or more tender cuts of meat: roasts, steaks, and chops. Use a meat ther-

mometer and roast or broil meat to a predetermined stage—rare, medium, or well-done. Weigh roasts at different stages of doneness to determine cooking losses.

4. Prepare one or more less tender cuts of meat: Swiss steak, stuffed flank steak, stew, and pot roast. Evaluate for tenderness, juiciness, and appearance.

5. Prepare one or more of the variety meats: heart, liver, sweetbreads, tongue, kidneys, and brains.

6. Cut a boned and rolled roast in half and roast one half in a conventional oven, the other in a microwave oven. Compare for cooking time, appearance, tenderness, and flavor.

REFERENCES

Books

After a Hundred Years: The Yearbook of Agriculture. Washington, D.C.: U.S. Department of Agriculture, 1962, pp. 276–286.

American Meat Foundation. *The Science of Meat and Meat Products.* San Francisco: Freeman, 1971.

Lee, Frank. *Basic Food Chemistry.* Westport, Conn.: Avi, 1975, Chap. 17.

Paul, Pauline and Helen Palmer. *Food Theory and Applications.* New York: Wiley, 1972, Chap. 7.

Articles, Bulletins, and Pamphlets

"Beef and Veal in Family Meals." *Home and Garden Bulletin 118.* Washington, D.C.: U.S. Department of Agriculture, 1975.

Campion, D. R., and J. D. Crouse. "Predictive Value of U.S.D.A. Beef Quality Grade Factors for Cooked Meat Palatability." *J. Food Sci.* **40:**1225, 1975.

Cover, S., and R. Hostetler. "An Examination of Some Theories About Beef Tenderness by Using New Methods." *Texas Agricultural Experiment Station Bulletin 947.* College Station, Tex.: University of Texas, 1960.

Dawson, E., et al. "Factors Influencing the Palatability, Vitamin Content, and Yield of Cooked Beef." *Home Economics Research Report 9.* Washington, D.C.: U.S. Department of Agriculture, 1959.

Deethardt, D., and H. J. Tuma. "Effect of Cooking Methods on Various Qualities of Pork Loin." *J. Food Sci.* **36:**626, 1971.

Greene, B. E., et al. "Retardation of Oxidative Color Changes in Raw Ground Beef." *J. Food Sci.* **36:**940, 1971.

"The Inspection Stamp as a Guide to Wholesale Meat." *Agricultural Information Bulletin 92.* Washington, D.C.: U.S. Department of Agriculture, 1952.

Kennick, W. H. "Effect of Marbling and Other Variables on Case Life of New York Steaks." *J. Food Sci.* **36:**767, 1971.

"Lamb in Family Meals." *Home and Garden Bulletin 124.* Washington, D.C.: U.S. Department of Agriculture, 1971.

Lind, Martha, Dorothy Harrison, and Donald Kropf. "Freezing and Thawing Rates of Lamb Chops." *J. Food Sci.* **36:**629, 1971.

Marketing and Labeling Program of the Meat Inspection Division. Washington, D.C.: U.S. Department of Agriculture, 1965.

Marsh, B. B. "The Basis of Tenderness in Muscle Foods." *J. Food Sci.* **42:**295, 1977.

Marshall, Nancy. "Electronic Cookery of Top Round Beef." *J. Home Econ.* **52:**31, 1960.

"Meat, Fish, Poultry, and Cheese: Home Preparation Time, Yield, and Composition of Various Market Forms." *Home Economics Research Report 30.* Washington, D.C.: U.S. Department of Agriculture, 1965.

Ockerman, H. W., and Leon Cresp. "Cooking of Fabricated Beef." *J. Food Sci.* **42:**1410, 1977.

Paul, Pauline. "Current Research on Meat." *J. Amer. Dietet. Assoc.* **46:**468, 1965.

Penfield, M. P., and B. H. Meyer. "Changes in Tenderness and Collagen of Beef Semitendinosus Muscle Heated at Two Rates." *J. Food Sci.* **40:**150, 1975.

"Pork in Family Meals." *Home and Garden Bulletin 160.* Washington, D.C.: U.S. Department of Agriculture, 1975.

Rey, C. R. "Effect of Fluctuating Storage Temperatures on Microorganisms on Beef Shell Frozen with Liquid Nitrogen." *J. Food Sci.* **37:**865, 1972.

Tappel, A., D. S. Miyada, C. Sterling, and V. P. Maier. "Meat Tenderization. 2. Factors Affecting the Tenderization of Beef by Papain." *Food Res.* **21:**375, 1961.

Toepfer, E., C. Pritchett, and E. Hewston. "Boneless Beef: Raw, Cooked, and Served." *Agricultural Research Series Technical Bulletin*

1137. Washington, D.C.: U.S. Department of Agriculture, 1955.

Tuomy, J. M., R. G. Lechnir, and T. Miller. "Effect of Cooking Temperature and Time on the Tenderness of Beef." *Food Technol.* **17**:1457, 1963.

"U.S. Department of Agriculture Grade Names for Food and Farm Products." *Agricultural Handbook 342*. Washington, D.C.: U.S. Department of Agriculture, 1967.

"U.S. Grades for Beef." *Marketing Bulletin 15*. Washington, D.C.: U.S. Department of Agriculture, 1960.

Vegetable Proteins as Meat Substitutes

The practice of using vegetable proteins as substitutes for meats and meat products is rapidly increasing in popularity. Meat has always been an important component of our food supply because of the protein content. However, certain vegetables that contain substantial amounts of protein can with the proper combination and quantity adequately substitute for meat in the diet (see Fig. 25-1.)

REASONS FOR SWITCHING TO VEGETABLE PROTEINS

Supply and Demand. In 1650 the world population was approximately 500 million and rose to an estimated 4 billion in 1976. By 2000 it has been estimated to increase to as high as 6.2 billion.[1] Thomas Malthus speculated that the world would eventually starve because its population would increase faster than its food production. In some underdeveloped countries (Bangladesh, India, Pakistan, the Sahel in Africa,

and parts of Central America) this prediction has become a reality. In order to feed the increases in population, the demand for food in 1985 will be 40% more than it was in 1962.[2] Agricultural and food technological achievements have been enormous but they are simply unable to keep up with the expanding populations. Consequently, much of the world suffers from malnutrition and will continue to do so unless population growth is stabilized and unconventional food sources as well as agricultural production are developed to the maximum.

Availability of Protein. In the United States enough animal products are produced to supply far in excess of the Recommended Daily Allowance for protein (56 grams for males, 46 grams for females). In countries such as Ceylon, India, Ecuador, Iran, Morocco, Pakistan, and the United Arab Republic, the per capita availability of protein from animal sources is less than 15 grams.[3] In order to meet the dietary require-

---

[1] *1976 World Population Data Sheet.* Population Reference Bureau, Inc. N.D.

[2] S. Johnson (ed.), *The Population Problem* (Newton Abbott, England: David and Charles Ltd., 1973).

[3] *The State of Food and Agriculture* (Rome: Food and Agriculture Organization, 1968).

25-1 *All of these protein-containing foods have the equivalent of 20 grams of protein (one 3 oz. serving of meat): 7 slices of whole wheat bread, 2 cups of sunflower seeds, 3 oz. of Swiss cheese, 1 pint of milk, ½ cup of uncooked beans, 1½ cups of oatmeal, ¾ cup of whole unshelled almonds, 3 eggs, 4 ears of sweet corn.*

ment for protein, diets must be based on cereal grains, legumes, and tubers. Unfortunately, many of the dietary staples available in these countries are poor sources of protein. In Costa Rica and the Dominican Republic, sugar, which has no protein, is the main source of calories. In Africa, Brazil, Paraguay, and Haiti, the main dietary staple, cassava meal, contains only 1% protein.[4] Thus, the type of protein that is consumed in the diet is limited to that which is available to the buyer.

Economic Cost of Vegetable Versus Meat Proteins. Protein derived from meats, poultry, and seafood is more expensive than protein of vegetable origin. If the price of a food product is compared to its protein content, the cost of the protein can readily be calculated (see Table 25-1). In general, vegetable proteins are less expensive than animal proteins, milk and cheese and other dairy products are less than meat and poultry products, and raw agricultural products are less than processed foods.

[4] Marion Arlin, *The Science of Nutrition* (New York: Macmillan, 1977), Chap. 18.

Proteins of animal origin are more expensive because it takes more acres of land to produce the product. An acre of land will only produce 53 lb of edible protein when fed to cattle and 97 lb as milk. The same land when cultivated with wheat will yield 180 lb of edible protein, 323 lb from corn, or 500 lb from soybeans. The price of the final product is therefore dependent on the cost of agricultural production.

Religious, Ethical, and Spiritual Beliefs. Many societies abhor the violence of killing animals and choose instead to practice vegetarianism. The Hindus believe that life, whether it is in human or animal form, is sacred and should not be destroyed. Others forgo consumption of only certain meats, owing to religious restrictions. The Muslims are forbidden to eat swine and meat from animals that have been killed violently or without the name of God mentioned during slaughtering.

More recently, concern over the limited food supply for the world has increased the number of vegetarians, particularly in the Western world. If more of the world's acreage was utilized for production of grain for human con-

TABLE 25-1
Comparative Cost of 100 Grams of Animal and Vegetable Protein Foods

Food	Cost/Unit[a]	Protein/100 g	Cost/100 g Protein
Pinto beans	$0.25/lb	22.3	0.25
Peanut butter	0.85/18 oz	25.2	0.42
Split peas	0.49/lb	24.2	0.45
Eggs, large	0.65/dozen	12.9	0.66
Milk, nonfat dry	1.79/25.6 oz	35.9	0.69
Oatmeal	0.57/18 oz	35.9	0.79
Rice, white, raw	0.29/lb	6.7	0.95
Wheat germ	0.79/10 oz	26.6	1.05
Hamburger, raw	0.89/lb	17.5	1.12
Hot dogs, raw	0.65/lb	12.5	1.15
Beef chuck roast, raw	0.87/lb	16.2	1.18
Cheddar cheese	1.37/lb	25.0	1.20
Tuna, canned	0.63/6¾ oz	24.2	1.36
Chicken, fried, frozen	2.39/lb	30.6	1.72
Swiss cheese	2.21/lb	27.5	1.77
Yogurt	0.25/8 oz	3.4	3.25
Beef, porterhouse steak, raw	2.41/lb	14.8	3.59
Bacon, raw	1.45/lb	8.4	3.81
Pork chop, loin, raw	1.79/lb	16.4	3.45
Ham, luncheon meat	1.05/4 oz	19.0	4.87

[a]cost based on food prices in Austin, Texas, in October 1977.

sumption rather than for fattening cattle, world supplies of foods would increase. This does not, however, take into account the protein produced from cattle and sheep that graze on land unsuitable for agricultural production.

NUTRITIONAL QUALITY OF VEGETABLE PROTEINS

Proteins are composed of 22 amino acids. Eight of these, called the *essential* amino acids, cannot be manufactured in the body and must be supplied in the diet for normal growth and maintenance. They are phenylalanine, valine, tryptophan, threonine, isoleucine, lecucine, methionine, and lysine.

Protein Quality. For a protein to be of high quality it must have the eight essential amino acids not only in sufficient quantity but also in the right proportions. If a protein has a pattern of amino acids which is similar to that needed by humans, it becomes a high-quality protein. Egg protein most nearly matches the perfect protein, and for this reason is used as the reference to

which all other proteins are compared (Table 25-2). High-quality proteins include those of animal origin: meat, poultry, and seafood, with the exception of gelatin.

Vegetable proteins are considered poor-quality proteins because they lack one or more of the essential amino acids, either in quantity or in unfavorable ratios. The amino acid lacking in a protein is called the *limiting* amino acid (Table 25-3). For example, corn lacks tryptophan, wheat lacks lysine, and soybeans lack methionine.

Soybeans and other legumes have a higher quality than the other vegetable proteins and can more easily be substituted for animal proteins (see Fig. 25-2). However, other vegetable proteins can contribute important amounts of protein to the diet if eaten with other foods.

Protein Supplementation. The quality of vegetable proteins may be improved if the limiting amino acid is supplied. This can be achieved through enrichment of the vegetable protein or product with the addition of synthetic amino acids. The biological value of sorghum can be greatly improved if lysine and threonine, the

25-2 *Isolated soy protein. (Courtesy of Ralston Purina)*

first and second limiting amino acids, are supplemented in the diet and/or combined with other food sources.[5] Methionine, the limiting amino acid in soybeans, can be added to soy flour to improve the nutritional quality of soy products.

A practical way of supplementation for the consumer is to combine the soy flour with another protein vegetable which has higher amounts of methionine. Thus, corn, which is low in lysine and tryptophan but higher in methionine, can be combined with soy flour, which

is adequate in lysine and tryptophan. This combination of proteins if consumed at the same meal, will provide all eight essential amino acids in the right quantity and proportion to create a high-quality protein pattern.

Other vegetable combinations that can yield high-quality proteins are rice and beans, peanut butter and whole wheat bread, beans and nuts, rice and peas, corn and beans, and legumes and leafy vegetables with cereals. Multiple combinations such as whole grains, soybeans, and sesame seeds and soybeans, peanuts, brown rice, and bulgur are even more effective.

Small amounts of animal protein combined with vegetable proteins are another easy way to increase the biological value of the vegetable. Milk can be combined with cereal, cheese with macaroni, and small amounts of meat or fish with rice. This allows the meat protein to "stretch" the value of the vegetable protein. Cooking by combining protein foods may be the only way poor societies can survive without animal proteins.

Fiber. The dietary component that protein-containing vegetables have that meats do not is the indigestible combination of hemicelluloses, celluloses, and lignins called fiber. Fiber decreases the digestibility of the protein-containing vegetables to approximately 70%. Large amounts of vegetables (and consequently fiber) may cause abdominal bloating, diarrhea, and flatus owing to fermentation of the fiber by the intestinal bacteria and subsequent production of gas.

[5] M. Briley et al., "The Nutritional Quality of Proteins in Sorghum," *J. Food Sci.* **41**:1082, 1976.

TABLE 25-2
Comparative Amounts of the Essential Amino Acids

Amino Acid	Reference Protein (egg)	Comparative Proteins			
		Beef	Corn	Wheat	Soybean
Isoleucine	6.6	5.2	4.6	4.0	5.4
Leucine	8.8	8.2	13.0	6.3	7.7
Lysine	6.4	8.7	2.9[a]	2.6[a]	6.3
Methionine	3.1	2.5	1.9	1.4[a]	1.3[a]
Phenylalanine	5.8	4.1	4.5	4.6	4.9
Threonine	5.0	4.4	4.0	2.7	3.9
Tryptophan	1.6	1.2	0.6[a]	1.2	1.4
Valine	7.4	5.6	5.1	4.3	5.2

[a] represents a limiting amino acid for the protein.
Source: Adapted from *"Amino Acid Content of Foods,"* *Home Economics Research Report 4* (Washington, D.C.: U.S. Department of Agriculture, 1966), Table 1.

THE VEGETARIAN DIET

The 1970s have brought an increasing popularity of the vegetarian diet, as a result of genuine concern over the world food crisis, rejection of our affluent society, and/or spiritual beliefs of purification through avoidance of animal foods. The types of vegetarians can be classified as follows:

1. *Lacto-ovovegetarian.* Dairy products are readily consumed but all meats, poultry, and seafood are avoided.
2. *Lactovegetarian.* Milk and cheese are used, but eggs and other animal products are eliminated from the diet.
3. *Vegan.* There is a complete restriction of all food of animal origin, including dairy and egg products.
4. *Fruitarian.* Belief that the spiritual cleansing of the body will occur if all foods are eliminated except fruits, nuts, honey and olive oil.

Nutritional Adequacy. Studies have shown that eating proper combinations of plant proteins and sufficient amounts of calories can make the vegetarian diet nutritionally adequate. The exception to this is the fruitarian diet, which is not recommended by nutritionists. It is important that the calorie content of the diet be high enough so that proteins are used for growth and repair of body tissue rather than converted into energy.

When dairy products are used to supplement an all-vegetable diet (the lacto-ovo- and lacto-vegetarian diets), it is relatively easy to secure an adequate protein combination. To supplement vegetable proteins only with other vegetable proteins becomes more difficult. Thus, the vegan diet is more likely to produce nutritional problems, particularly among growing children and pregnant and lactating women. Great care must be taken to provide proper combinations of plant proteins to ensure optimal growth and health.

If no foods of animal origin are consumed for extended periods of time, the lack of vitamin B_{12} (only found in animal foods) may result in deficiency symptoms of anemia, sore tongue, and irreversible nervous disorders. Thus, vegans must supplement this diet with a source of vitamin B_{12} (desiccated liver is most commonly used).

Vegetarians have been reported to have decreased serum cholesterol levels. In a study of Seventh-Day Adventists the incidence of heart disease was only 60% that of the average population.[6] Whether this is an effect resulting from decreased cholesterol levels or from below-normal body weights commonly reported (10–20 lb) is still unknown.

The high fiber content of the vegetarian diet, while being somewhat uncomfortable, has been implicated as important in the prevention of diverticulosis and cancer of the colon.[7] It has also been suggested that the high fiber content may limit absorption of trace minerals in the intestine, leading to problems in zinc status.[8]

Changing Menus to Fit Vegetarian Diets. Meals can be planned to ensure an adequate diet if the basic four food groups (meats–protein, milk, bread, and fruits and vegetables) serve as guidelines with slight modifications. Since plant foods are high in bulk but low in calories, a major problem in the vegetarian diet is securing sufficient number of calories unless the meals are well planned. If adequate calories are not ingested, the body will use the protein in the diet to supply its energy. Thus, a vegetarian diet adequate in protein but too low in calories becomes a diet low in proteins also.

The following guidelines should be used when planning a vegetarian menu (Table 25-4):

1. Meat proteins must be replaced by generous quantities of nuts, whole grains, legumes, or meat analogs developed from soybean and other plant protein mixtures. Careful combination of supplemental plant proteins is essential to yield high-quality protein mixtures. The daily menu should include six or more servings of these foods, to provide adequate intakes of protein as well as zinc.

---

[6] F. R. Lemon and R. T. Walden, "Deaths from Respiratory System Disease Among Seventh-Day Adventist Men," *J. Amer. Med. Assoc.* **195**:117, 1966.

[7] A. Tunaley, "Constipation—The Secret National Problem," *Nutrition* **28**:91, 1974.

[8] J. Freeland et al., "Changes in Zinc Absorption Following a Vegetarian Diet," *Fed. Proc.* **37**:253, 1978 (abstract).

TABLE 25-3
**Calorie, Fiber, and Protein Content of Protein-Containing Plants
with Their Respective Limiting Amino Acids[a]**

Plant	Quantity/100 grams			Limiting Amino Acid		
	Calories	Fiber (g)	Protein (g)	Lysine	Methionine	Tryptophan
Legumes						
Beans, common, cooked	118	1.5	7.8		*	*
Beans, lima, immature, cooked	111	1.8	7.6		*	*
Beans, mung sprouts	35	0.7	3.8		*	*
Lentils, cooked	106	1.2	7.8		*	*
Peanuts, roasted with skins	582	2.7	26.2	*	*	*
Peas						
black-eyed, cooked	76	1.0	5.1		*	
Green split, cooked	115	0.4	8.0		*	*
Soybeans						
Cooked	130	1.6	11.0		*	
Curd (tofu)	72	0.1	7.8		*	
Milk	33	0.0	3.4		*	
Nuts						
Almonds, roasted	627	2.6	18.6	*		*
Brazil nuts	654	3.1	14.3	*		*
Carob flour	180	7.7	4.5			*
Cashews	561	1.4	17.2	*	*	
Cocoa	265	4.3	17.3	*	—	
Coconut	346	4.0	3.5	*		
Hazelnut (filbert)	634	3.0	12.6	*	*	
Pecans	687	2.3	9.2	*		
Pistachio	635	1.9	13.0	*		*
Walnuts, English	651	2.1	14.7	*		*
Seeds						
Pumpkin	553	1.9	29.0	*	—	
Sesame	563	6.3	18.6	*		
Sunflower	560	3.8	24.0	*		
Grains						
Barley, scotch, raw	348	0.9	9.6	*		
Buckwheat, raw	335	9.9	11.7	*		

TABLE 25-3 (Cont.)

Plant	Quantity/100 grams			Limiting Amino Acid		
	Calories	Fiber (g)	Protein (g)	Lysine	Methionine	Tryptophan
Grains (Cont.)						
Bulgur, white, parboiled	357	1.7	10.3	*		
Corn, sweet, cooked	83	0.7	3.2	*		*
Rice, cooked						
Brown	119	0.3	2.5	*		
White	109	0.1	2.0	*		
Rye, meal, raw	334	2.0	12.1	*		*
Wheat flour						
Whole	333	2.3	13.3	*		
White	364	0.3	10.5	*		
Germ	363	2.5	26.6			
Green leaves						
Greens, cooked						
Beet	18	1.1	1.7	*	*	*
Collard	33	1.0	3.6			
Mustard	23	0.9	2.2	*	*	
Turnip	23	1.0	2.5		*	
Kale	28	1.1	3.2	*	*	
Swiss chard, cooked	18	0.7	1.8	*	—	*
Watercress	19	0.7	2.2		—	

[a] An asterisk represents a limiting amino acid in the protein;—indicates that data are not available.
Source: B. Watt and A. Merrill, "Composition of Food," *Handbook 8* (Washington, D.C.: U.S. Department of Agriculture, rev. 1963; M. Orr and B. Watt, "Amino Acid Content of Foods," *Home Economics Report 4* (Washington, D.C.: U.S. Department of Agriculture, 1957).

2. To ensure adequate intake of vitamin B_{12} as well as to "stretch" the nutritive value of plant proteins, at least two or more servings of milk (three for children) and other dairy products is recommended. If no foods of animal origin are consumed, a source of vitamin B_{12} either from desiccated liver or yeast grown in vitamin B_{12}-rich nutrient solution should be included.

3. If milk and other dairy products are avoided completely, servings of beans, seeds, and greens (broccoli, spinach, turnip, etc.) should be eaten daily. Although a cup of greens on a weight basis will have the same calcium content as a cup of milk, oxaltes and phytates in the vegetables may bind calcium and thus limit the availability of it and other minerals.

Soymilk which has not been fortified cannot be relied on as the only source of calcium since it contains only 25% of that found in whole milk.

4. Large quantities of fiber should be avoided since they may cause discomfort as well as bind trace minerals, making them unavailable

TABLE 25-4
Typical One-Day Vegetarian Menu

Breakfast	Noon Meal	Evening Meal
Orange juice—4 oz	Soy patties with tomato	Vegetable soup—1 cup (200 g)
Cooked oatmeal—1 cup	sauce—2	Sandwich
Milk (LV)[a] 4 oz	Baked potato—1	Whole wheat bread—2 slices
Soymilk (PV)[b] 4 oz	Margarine—1 pat	Garbanzo-egg filling (LV)
Whole wheat toast—1 slice	Cooked fresh or frozen	Savory garbanzos (PV)
Peanut butter—1 tbsp	peas—⅔ cup	Sliced peaches—½ cup
Clear hot cereal beverage,	Shredded carrot salad—	Walnut-stuffed dates—4
if desired	½ cup, scant	Milk (LV)—8 oz
	Dressing—½ tbsp	Soymilk (PV)—8 oz
	Wheat roll	
	Margarine—1 pat	
	Strawberries, fresh or	
	frozen without sugar—	
	¾ cup	
	Milk (LV)—8 oz	
	Soymilk (PV)—8 oz	

[a] LV = lacto-ovo-vegetarian.
[b] PV = pure vegetarian.
Source: U. D. Register and L. M. Sonnenberg, "The Vegetarian Diet." Reproduced by permission from *The Nutrition Crisis,* Theodore LaBuza, ed. Copyright © 1975, West Publishing Company. All rights reserved.

for absorption in the body. This reduction of fiber intake can be achieved by limiting the consumption of fruits and vegetables to four servings each day and including adequate amounts of milk, cheese, yogurt, and eggs in the diet. Sources of vitamin C (citrus fruits) and vitamin A (dark green leafy vegetables) should be eaten every day.

SOYBEANS

The high protein content of the soybean has made it the most widely used replacement for animal proteins. Although the bean is normally associated with oriental cooking (soy sauce, tofu), the United States is the world's leader in agricultural production, growing 75% of the world's crop.[9] Before 1925, soybeans in the United States were practically nonexistent, but today they are an important part of the oil, margarine, and meat and poultry industries.

The Whole Bean. There is very limited canning of immature beans still enclosed in the pod (similar to string beans). However, this product is not very successful commercially. The Occidental method of cooking mature whole beans has also not achieved popularity in the United States, probably because of the long cooking time (3–4 hours), the bitter flavor, and the associated indigestion. Raw beans are never used, because they contain a trypsin inhibitor that interferes with proper growth and metabolism.[10]

Soy Milk. A milk substitute can be created by grinding the softened beans in water and draining off the fluid. This fluid soy milk contains most of the beans's protein, oil, and other solids. Attempts to market the milk have in the past met with failure, owing to the bitter, beany taste. The off-flavor is due to the presence of lipoxidase, which is released when the bean is ground. Recent advances in soymilk processing have devised methods that inactivate lipoxidase,

[9] F. Clydesdale and F. Francis, "Potential Sources of Protein," in *Food, Nutrition and You,* F. Clydesdale and F. Francis, eds. (Englewood Cliffs, N.J.: Prentice-Hall, 1977), p. 190.

[10] *Toxicants Occurring Naturally in Foods* (Washington, D.C.: National Academy of Sciences, 1973), p. 282.

thus eliminating the bitter taste.[11] It was known that lipoxidase could be denatured or inactivated at temperatures of 180°F (82°C), but when the ground beans were added to hot water the protein became insoluble and milk could not be produced. A new procedure was developed in which the softened beans were ground while in hot water, allowing deactivation of the enzyme and production of an acceptable product.

Soy milk has only 25% as much calcium as cow's milk. Therefore, to be nutritionally equivalent in this nutrient, it is necessary to fortify it with calcium salts, such as calcium carbonate. It is also good practice to add a small amount of vitamin B_{12}, to provide a source of this vitamin for the vegan. Before purchasing commercial soy milk, consumers should always check the label to make sure that it has been fortified.

Fermented Products. Soy milk can be made into a cheese by an acid hydrolysis that precipitates the curd. The cheese is squeezed to remove the whey and then pressed into blocks. The resulting cheese is called tofu and may be fried in combination with vegetables, made into patties, or used in sandwiches. It can be stored for extended periods of time by drying.

The most popular fermented product of soybeans used in the United States is soy sauce. This sauce originates from defatted soy flakes which are mixed with wheat. The mixture is salted and allowed to ferment after the microorganism *Aspergillis oryzae* has been added. After 8–12 months the mixture develops into soy sauce, which is used to flavor oriental cooking.

Another fermented product that takes a shorter time to develop is tempeh. The manufacture of tempeh requires inoculation of cooked soybeans with *Rhizopus oligospores* and fermentation for 24 hours. Tempeh may be used in a manner similar to tofu.

Flour. As an oilseed, the soybean differs in structure from cereal grains. The cereal grain is composed of a bran covering and a rather large high-starch, low-protein endosperm which surrounds a small embryo, the germ. In oilseeds, the major part of the bean is instead the germ with only a surrounding thin layer of endosperm. The germ contains the oil and protein for which the soybean is known.

The process of obtaining flour from these seeds, or milling, begins when the seeds are heated to inactivate destructive enzymes and subsequently dried. It is then a simple process to crush the seed and extract the oil with a solvent. The flour is defatted since elimination of fat which is subject to rancidity will extend the shelf (storage) life of the flour considerably.

The high-protein flour may be used in baking to make doughnuts, breads, rolls, cakes, cookies, and other products. It is also used in the production of textured vegetable protein foods.

Soy grits are simply larger particles of soy flour that have not been ground as thoroughly as has soy flour. The pieces of soybeans are heated to inactivate enzymes, which results in a product with a slight crunch to it. These are used as toppings or to provide texture to foods.

Soy Concentrate. If all the oil and most of the soluble carbohydrates are removed from defatted soy flakes, a protein concentrate of approximately 70% is formed. Concentrates in granular form are used in ground-meat products and in powdered form in sausage products, baby foods, cereals, and snacks. In addition to increasing the protein content of these foods, the soy concentrate will absorb the fat, resulting in less loss of flavors (which are fat-soluble).

Soy protein also has the tendency to gel when heated. This is used to advantage in the manufacture of pet foods and creamed soups. Soy protein is added to liquid product before it is canned. During the canning process the temperature creates a gel, which gives the product its final consistency.

Soy Isolate. A more purified form of isolated soy protein (approximately 90%) may be prepared from defatted soy flour. The flour is treated with alkali, which dissolves the protein and permits the insoluble residues to be removed. The mixture is then acidified, resulting in the precipitation of a curd. The curd is redissolved to form the basic material utilized in the extrusion process. The products are used in the manufacture of texturized vegetable proteins (see Color Plate XI).

[11]M. Bourne, "Recent Advances in Soybean Milk Processing Technology," *Protein Advisory Group Bull.* **10**:14, 1970.

TEXTURIZATION

Extrusion. Vegetable protein can be texturized by the process known as extrusion. Extrusion is used in the manufacture of granules which are marketed as *texturized vegetable protein* (TVP). The process by which it is made is similar to that in making breakfast cereals. A slurry of proteins, water, vitamins, flavor, and color is heated, subjected to pressure, and put into an extruder. As the material passes out, it puffs up and granules are formed. The granules are dried to a low moisture content and vacuum-packed to ensure stable shelf life.

Texturized Vegetable Protein (TVP). The market for consumer use of TVP is growing rapidly. Dried granules are commonly sold as a grocery product which requires storage in a cool dry place. Before it can be used, TVP must be rehydrated with 1.5–2.5 times its weight in water. Once hydration is complete, it may be added to ground-meat items such as hamburger, meat loaves, chili, and spaghetti sauce. It is commonly used in fast-food hamburgers and frozen convenience products. (See Color Plate XI.)

If the TVP is mixed with meat at home or is purchased already in combination with meat at the supermarket, it should be stored under the same conditions as the meat to which it has been added. When using this vegetable protein–meat combination, it should be remembered that the cooking time will be shortened somewhat. There will also be less shrinkage, because the juices are absorbed by the extender. While this may keep the fat-soluble flavor components in the food, it will also cause greater sticking in the pan.

In macaroni products the opposite occurs when soy proteins are added to the durum wheat dough. When the macaroni is cooked in water, the water absorption is decreased, thus allowing a firmer product which will keep its shape longer. Maintenance of a firm shape is important in canned products in which macaroni is an essential component. Alphabet soup and macaroni and beef in tomato sauce are examples of this. Macaroni that has been supplemented with soy protein is available commercially as high-protein macaroni. However, the increased cost of this product, which traditionally has been economical, has caused its success to be rather limited.

The advantage of using texturized plant protein as an extender is that it provides more protein at a lower cost than would be possible if extra meat were added. The nutritive value of TVP is lower than that of meat, owing to the low methionine content of soybeans. When TVP is used in combination with a meat product, the methionine present in the meat will supplement the nutritive value of the soy protein.

A cost-conscious consumer who adds TVP to meat products at home is adding extra protein to the meal in the most economical way possible. Similarly, the food industry's use of TVP in the production of meat and meat products also results in economical benefits for the consumer.

The low cost of TVP has made it attractive for dietetians who plan school lunches. The U.S. Department of Agriculture has approved the addition of textured meat alternatives in amounts not to exceed 30% of the weight of the combined plant protein–meat food product. The textured meat alternatives used must meet the specifications of the Food and Nutrition Service.[12] These include nutrient requirements, definition of texture, a minimum 18% protein level for hydrated products, and labels identifying the product as acceptable to the U.S. Department of Agriculture.

ENGINEERED FOODS

Texturized vegetable protein is used in the formulation of fabricated foods. An engineered food is composed of a variety of natural and/or synthetic ingredients which have been texturized and modified to simulate the appearance and taste of a particular food product. The food product may substitute for a familar natural product, such a nondairy coffee cream in place of cow's milk cream, or imitation eggs for chicken eggs. It may; instead, be an entirely new concept in foods, as is Pillsbury's Space Food Sticks, which are based on food products developed for astronauts.

[12] *Federal Register* **39:**11296, 1974.

Engineered foods have the advantage of being consistent in their year-round availability, appearance, taste, and nutrient content. They often have a long shelf life as a result of their packaging, and are easy to prepare. A powdered orange juice substitute breakfast drink is an example of an engineered convenience food that has all these qualities. Not only is it extremely easy to prepare, but small or large amounts can be easily mixed. Thus, little waste will result.

The question to be answered is whether engineered foods can completely substitute for natural products. A completely fabricated food may not have all the essential vitamins and minerals that the natural product has. Nutritional studies in human beings have been conducted utilizing soy protein foods as the sole source of protein in the diet for 6 months.[13] No adverse physiological or biochemical findings were reported, and the subjects appeared to be in good health. Other studies have resulted in similar conclusions.

Successful experiments to date on the nutritional adequacy of engineered foods do not, however, rule out the possible detrimental effects that might result from long-term ingestion over a life span. Since it is not feasible to use human beings as subjects for such long-term experiments, animal data must suffice. No known hazards have been found to be associated with animal consumption of fabricated foods, and on this basis it is assumed that these products are relatively safe. However, it is suggested that generous servings of natural agricultural products also be included in the diet whenever possible.

Meat Analogs. Extruded isolated soy protein is blended with other vegetable proteins, fats, carbohydrates, vitamins, minerals, flavors, and colors to form various textured products which resemble meat and meat products. These meat analogs contain approximately 50% protein. This is quite high when compared to meats, which generally range from 15 to 30% protein. Although the amino acid composition is dependent on the type of proteins that are blended together, meat analogs, because of their basic soy protein content, are low in the essential amino acid methionine (see Fig. 25-3).

If methionine is added to the meat analog, the protein quality, expressed as the protein efficiency ratio (PER), can be increased to approach that of the standard animal protein, casein (PER of 2.5). In comparison, ham analogs have a PER of 3.1; plant protein weiners, 2.5; textured vegetable sausage, 2.4; and chicken analog, 2.3.[14]

The quantity of fat in vegetable meat analogs is only one-third that found in the meat simulated. The types of fats found in animal foods are saturated fats and cholesterol. Since vegetables do not have cholesterol, there is none present in the subsequent vegetable protein product. There is also a reduction in the amount of saturated fats with a concommitant increase in unsaturated fats.

Some of the typical ingredients found in meat analogs are texturized and hydrolyzed vegetable proteins (wheat gluten, soy, yeast), water, oil (soybean, corn, cottonseed), egg albumin, sodium caseinate, oats, salt, onion and garlic powder, modified cornstarch, rice starch, spices, sugar, sorbitol, emulsifiers and stabilizers (glycerin, carrageenin, xanthum gum, mono- and diglycerides), sodium triphosphate, disodium guanylate, disodium inosinate, vitamins, minerals, and artificial colors and flavorings.

Many consumers are unaware that they are using meat analogs. The products may look and taste the same as the substituted product. The only noticeable difference to the consumer may be the name, packaging, and labeling. The names may be only slightly different. For example, a texturized vegetable protein sausage is marketed as Breakfast Links, a ham analog as Breakfast Patties, and pieces of simulated bacon as Bacos.

Seafood Analogs. Seafood analogs are also formulated from extruded soy. This analog has a seafoodlike texture and a bland taste. It is used to blend with crabmeat, tuna, lobster, fish, or shrimp. It can replace from 30 to 50% of the seafood with good retention of the basic flavor. Preparation for the analog may include grinding, cubing, chopping, or flaking. The main ingredi-

---

[13] S. Koury and R. Hodges, "Soybean Protein for Human Diet? Wholesomeness and Acceptability," *J. Amer. Dietet. Assoc.* **52**:480, 1968.

[14] R. Robinson, "What Is the Future of Textured Products?" *Food Technol.* **26**:59, 1972.

(a)

(b)

25-3 (a) *Breakfast strips made from vegetable proteins.* (b) *Breakfast patties, slices and links made from vegetable proteins.* (*Courtesy of Miles Laboratories Inc.*)

ents in this analog may be soy protein isolate, water, corn oil, egg white solids, salt, monosodium glutamate, carrageenan, and artificial colors. Since the analog does not change appreciably when heated, it reduces the weight loss and shrinkage of the cooked seafood product. The cost of the analog is much less than the crab, shrimp, lobster, and other expensive seafoods to which it has been added, thus allowing an economical product to be produced.

Use of meat analogs will undoubtedly increase in the future. It has been estimated that by 1985, meat and seafood analogs and extenders will comprise 10% of the meat consumption in the United States.[15]

Genetic Manipulation. Manipulation of the genes of a plant can change its nutrient content as well as its appearance. In the 1960s a high lysine corn called opaque-2 was developed by plant geneticists.[16] The limiting amino acids in the corn, lysine, and tryptophan were increased, thereby greatly improving its nutritive value. Unfortunately, the hybrid corn was not very resistent to disease and had a different appearance which did not please consumers. In addition, the farmers who grew the corn were unhappy because it produced lower yields, and mill prices were higher for milling nonstandard maize into flour. In 1971, a new mutant of opaque-2 was harvested which was greatly improved. Hopefully, worldwide dissemination of these improved seeds will provide a better-quality vegetable protein for those populations who consume corn as a dietary staple.

Other grains that have been manipulated genetically to produce better nutritional content, higher yields, and greater disease resistance include dwarf indica rice; dwarf wheat; high-protein, high-lysine barley; triticale; hybrid upland cotton; hybrid sorghum; and hybrid millet.

Vegetable Blends. The problem in devising a vegetable protein product to feed the populations of underdeveloped countries is the cost.

What we would consider to be very economical (a meat analog pattie for 50 cents per serving) would be prohibitive for a family of eight who lives on an annual income of $500. Families such as these cannot afford to spend more than a few cents a day per person. This limited amount of money available for food negates the purchasing of meat and makes consumption of vegetable protein a necessity.

If only one dietary staple, such as corn or rice, is eaten, gross nutritional deficiencies develop. To avoid protein deficiency, a combination of plant proteins must be available in the right amounts at a low cost. The Institute of Nutrition in Central America and Panama (INCAP) has devised such a blend of vegetables, called Incaparina. Its cost per day is less than 4 cents. It is composed of locally grown plants, such as ground maize and sorghum, cottonseed flour, and tortula yeast, and is fortified with calcium carbonate and vitamin A. Daily consumption of this mixture will prevent nutritional deficiencies and allow adequate nutrients for growing children.

CSM is another vegetable blend being sold throughout the world. It is a combination of cornmeal, soy flour, nonfat dry milk, vitamins, and minerals. This is also available in the United States through the U.S. Department of Agriculture's Commodity Distribution Program. Pro-Nutra in Africa, Multi-Purpose Food in India, and Cerealian in Brazil are other examples of vegetable blends. The success of these special blends of vegetable protein foods will depend on their acceptance by consumers.

SINGLE-CELL PROTEINS (SCP)

The demand for protein in the future will lead to increased use of unconventional sources of protein. An expanding population that must feed off a limited supply of acreage will necessitate that protein be derived from sources other than those that utilize land. The use of microorganisms or single-cell proteins (SCP) may be the answer to this problem. An acre of land capable of producing 450 lb of protein could be used to produce 2 million pounds of yeast protein per year.[17]

[15] T. Hammonds and D. Call, "Utilization of Protein Ingredients in the U.S. Food Industry," *Department of Agriculture and Economics Research 320 and 321* (Ithaca, N.Y.: Cornell University, 1970).

[16] T. Wolff, "Maize: 'Super Grain' of the Future?" *War on Hunger* **10**:15, 1976.

[17] R. J. Flannery, "Nonagricultural Sources of Food," *Food Technol.* **29**(8):64, 1975.

Algae, yeast, bacteria, and fungi all have high concentrations of protein that could be used as a protein source for animal feeds or human foods. The feasibility of utilizing SCP as a protein source will depend on the price and availability of the products (substrates) used to feed them. The price of the nitrogenous and phosphorus sources that must be added to the substrate are also considerations. Additional expenses result from the energy and labor involved, as well as the construction and maintenance of the facilities to produce SCP. Then the total expenditure of producing SCP must be compared to the price and availability of alternative proteins. Thus, what seems like a simple solution to the world protein problem may be more complex than was originally thought.

Advantages and Disadvantages. The exponential growth rate of microorganisms, combined with their rapid doubling time (3–5 hours), can produce enormous quantities of SCP in a relatively short time. Those that are produced photosynthetically from carbon dioxide and sunlight or from processing waste products can be marketed inexpensively. However, these substrates may be seasonal and thus not always available.

Another disadvantage of using SCP products for food is that they may be digested poorly and have toxic substances which must be removed prior to human consumption. There is also a high nucleic acid content in SCP, which could lead to the formation of gout in humans. Although these problems can be eliminated by mechanical and chemical technology, they do increase the cost of the final product.

SCP from Petroleum Products. For years it was known that bacteria, yeast, and fungi grew in oil, paraffin, methane, and other petroleum products. These were simply considered a nuisance until the possibility of their use as a food was proposed. Oil companies began building plants to grow microorganisms on their petroleum. This was a new and exciting food source when petroleum was thought to be unlimited and sold very cheaply. The skyrocketing cost of petroleum and the realization of its limited supply dampened the enthusiasm for this alternative food source. Production was essentially halted in 1973 when consumer groups raised the issue of the carcinogenic residues that had been detected in the resultant SCP.

Emphasis then shifted to the production of SCP from methanol and ethanol, by-products of petroleum refining. Of these two, ethanol is preferable because it is already manufactured in the fermentation of alcoholic beverages. In addition, methanol derived from petroleum refining can be toxic, and it is hard to completely eliminate all residue from the dried SCP grown on it. However, methanol may become an important food source for SCP if proposed large-scale manufacturing plants are built to produce methanol as a fuel additive. In this case, methanol would become a readily available, inexpensive, residue-free substrate.

SCP from Algae. Algae in the form of seaweed has been an essential part of Oriental cookery for centuries. It is harvested from the sea and lakes or may be easily grown with carbon dioxide, sunlight, and minerals in a water bath.

In the early 1960s, enthusiasm was generated for large-scale cultivation of algae as a protein source. Initial tests in the laboratory produced excellent results. However, the expense of artificial light in an indoor plant made it necessary for cultivation to be accomplished outdoors, by natural sunlight. This limited the geographical areas for its cultivation to where sunlight was available most of the year (below 35° latitude). Furthermore, the expense of harvesting, recovery, and purification was too great to be competitive with other protein sources.

SCP from Cellulose Waste Products. Agricultural and forest-product processing wastes have been investigated as substrates for SCP. Bagasse from sugarcane milling, barley straw from feed-lot residues, and cellulose and sulfite from pulp and paper mills may soon be an inexpensive source of food for microorganisms. Other waste products that can be used to grow microorganisms include coffee waste, collagen meat-packing waste, corn and pear waste, and potato processing. The expense of collecting and transporting these wastes to a SCP production facility must be reasonable for this to be economically feasible.

SCP from Sugars and Starches. The advantage of using sugar and starches as food for SCP production is that they are easily renewable. Yeast can be produced from molasses (primary dried yeast), the lactose sugar in whey, the by-product of cheese manufacture (dried fragile yeast), and from the carbohydrates in the brewing of alcoholic beverages (brewer's yeast).

UNCONVENTIONAL SOURCES OF PROTEIN

Leaf Protein Concentrate (LPC). The most abundant source of supply of protein in the world is leafy green plants. Green leaves have been considered as an unconventional source of protein, owing to their high productivity and low cost. Extraction of the protein from green leaves to create LPC has been done primarily in alfalfa, since it is a readily available inexpensive source. The process of producing LPC is a simple one in which the alfalfa is ground into a green slurry, heat-treated to coagulate the protein, and pressed into fibrous cakes. Although the biological value of the protein is high, the bitter taste, the dark green color, and the high fiber content has limited its appeal for human use. The foods to which it is added have an unattractive green color. It may be feasible only in foods that are naturally highly colored, such as the greenish-yellow Indian curries.

A process called Pro-Xan has been developed in an attempt to further purify the protein of leaf concentrate.[18] In this process an alkaline slurry is heated to coagulate protein, and centrifuged to form a brown liquid supernatant. The brown wheylike juice is heated again to coagulate cytoplasmic proteins, which are filtered off. The remaining liquid is dried and may be pressed into the original press cake. The pressed curd may then be granulated, extruded, or pelleted. Since the green color of the final product is still undesirable, a new process called Pro-Xan II has been developed. This results in a separate green and white LPC. The spray-dried white LPC has possible uses for human consumption.

Protein Derived from Seeds and Cereals. Drought-resistant seeds indigenous to North America have been suggested as an important

[18] G. Kohler and B. Knuckles, "Edible Protein from Leaves," *Food Technol.* **31**(5):191, 1977.

protein and oil source. Seeds of the okra plant, different types of gourds, and of the cotton plant may in the future be utilized as alternative proteins.

Cottonseed meal is currently fed to cattle but is unfit for human consumption because of a toxic yellow pigment called gossypol. This toxic pigment can be degraded by heating, but this lowers the quality of the protein. Geneticists have developed a low-gossypol cottonseed, but the cotton fibers produced are not of high quality. Until this problem is solved, the future of cottonseed protein is in doubt.

Other seeds and cereals that have been proposed as potential sources of protein include sesame seeds, sunflower seeds, wild rice, buckwheat, and triticale (a hybrid of wheat and rye).

SUMMARY

The high cost and increased demand for protein has led to the substitution of meat and meat products by vegetable proteins. In general, vegetable proteins are more economical than those of animal origin. Protein quality is determined by the quantity and ratio of the eight essential amino acids. Vegetable proteins lack one or more of these amino acids and thus have limiting amino acids. The quality of vegetable proteins can be improved if the limiting amino acid is supplied by combination of grains and legumes, nuts and legumes, or vegetable proteins with small amounts of animal products.

The four types of vegetarianism include the lacto-ovovegetarian, the lactovegetarian, the vegan, and the fruitarian. With the exception of the fruitarian diet, the vegetarian diet can be nutritionally adequate if it is based on four major food groups—protein, cereals, dairy and fruits, and vegetables.

The high protein content of soybeans has made them a replacement for animal protein. Some popular soy products are soy milk, tofu, tempeh, flour, grits, TVP, soy concentrate, and soy isolate. Soy and other vegetable proteins can be texturized by extrusion and fiber spinning, used to create meat extenders and analogs.

Genetic manipulation of protein and blending of vegetable proteins are ways of improving the nutritive value. Unconventional sources of protein which will become greater in importance in the future include single-cell protein derived from petroleum products, algae, cellulose and sugar or starch waste, leaf protein cencentrate, and seeds and cereals.

QUESTIONS AND TOPICS FOR DISCUSSION AND STUDY

1. Why are vegetable proteins considered to be incomplete proteins?
2. How may an adequate diet be planned if only vegetable proteins are available?
3. Why are vegetable proteins less expensive than animal proteins?
4. What are the advantages and disadvantages of vegetarianism?
5. Explain how vegetable proteins are texturized.
6. Name some engineered foods and describe how they are formulated.
7. Which of the unconventional sources of protein do you foresee as being economically feasible by the year 2000?

SUGGESTED ACTIVITIES

1. Using Table 25-1, plan a vegan menu for 1 day. Use the proper combination of plant proteins to ensure adequate protein intake.
2. Compare the cost of different proteins in your diet. What changes could you make to decrease the cost while maintaining the nutritive value?
3. Prepare two meat loaves, one made with hamburger and the other with 30% TVP. Compare the two baked products for weight loss, drippings, flavor, tenderness, and cost.

REFERENCES

BOOKS

"Amino Acid Content of Foods." *Handbook 4.* Washington, D.C.: U.S. Department of Agriculture, 1966.

Arlin, Marion. *The Science of Nutrition.* New York: Macmillan, 1977, Chap. 18.

Bernard, Melvin. *The Chemicals We Eat.* New York: McGraw-Hill, 1975, Chap. 6.

Clydesdale, F., and F. Francis, eds. *Food, Nutrition, and You.* Englewood Cliffs N.J.: Prentice-Hall, 1977, Chaps. 7, 8, 9, 10.

Martin, Ethel Austin. *Nutrition in Action.* New York: Holt, Rinehart, and Winston, 1971, Chap. 7.

Register, U., and L. Sonnenberg. "The Vegetarian Diet." In Theodore LaBuza, ed., *The Nutrition Crisis.* New York: West, 1975.

Robertson, Laurel, Carol Flinders, and Bronwen Godfrey. *Laurel's Kitchen. A Handbook for Vegetarian Cookery and Nutrition.* Petuluma, Calif.: Nilgiri, 1976.

ARTICLES AND BULLETINS

"A Storage Study of Six Commercial Soy Protein Ingredients Combined With Ground Beef," *Technical Report Natick TR-77-020.* Natick, Mass.: United States Army, 1977.

Breene, W. "Problems in Determining Textural Properties of Textured Plant Protein Products." *Food Technol.* **31**(5):95, 1977.

De, S. S. "Technology of Production of Edible Flours and Protein Products from Soybeans." *Agricultural Series Bulletin 11.* Rome: Food and Agricultural Organization, 1974.

Litchfield, J. "Single Cell Proteins." *Food Technol.* **35**(5):175, 1977.

Miller, G., and P. LaChance. "Protein: Chemistry and Nutrition." *Food Prod. Develop.* **7**(10):23, 1973.

"Some Aspects of Protein Nutrition." *Dairy Council Dig.* **43**:3, 1972.

Poultry

Poultry includes chicken, turkey, duck, goose, Cornish hen, guinea hen, squab, and pigeon. Of this group, chicken and turkey are most commonly used. Because of the high level of production of palatable birds, chicken and turkey are fast becoming daily, year-round foods. The broiler–fryer chicken has the highest production rate of all poultry classes.

NUTRITIVE VALUE

The nutritive value of poultry is similar to that of other meat (Table 26-1). The proteins

TABLE 26-1
Proximate Chemical Composition of Chicken, Turkey, and Duck

Constituents	Chicken	Turkey	Duck
Water	55.9	55.5	61.0
Fat	25.0	22.9	19.0
Protein	18.0	21.1	18.3
Ash	1.1	1.0	1.3

Sources: C. Chatfield and G. Adams, "Proximate Composition of Foods (Edible Portion)," *Circular 549* (Washington, D.C.: U.S. Department of Agriculture, 1940).

supplied by poultry are complete and contain the amino acids that are essential for building body tissues. In addition, poultry is a very good source of the B vitamins—thiamine, riboflavin, and niacin. There is little fat in the meat of young birds, but the range of fat among the different kinds of poultry is wide. An average serving of chicken or turkey contains fewer calories than an average serving of most other meats.

ECONOMIC ASPECTS

Poultry today is a highly satisfactory and economical food (Table 26-2). It is readily available chilled or frozen throughout the year. Broilers and fryers are inexpensive yet tender and can be cooked in a relatively short time. Whole turkeys are good buys for large families, and turkey halves, quarters, and parts are available for the small family. Poultry has increased in sales in the last two decades.

Production. Scientifically balanced rations and the use of antibiotics to improve the nutritional status of the birds and to prevent characteristic poultry diseases have been important factors in

TABLE 26-2
Cost of Chicken, Whole and Parts (in cents)

If the price per pound of whole fryers, ready to cook, is:	Chicken parts are an equally good buy if the price per pound is:				
	Breast Half	Drumstick and Thigh	Drumstick	Thigh	Wing
27	38	35	33	36	21
29	41	37	36	39	23
31	44	40	38	41	25
33	47	42	41	44	26
35	49	45	43	47	28
37	52	47	46	49	29
39	55	50	48	52	31
41	58	53	50	55	33
43	61	55	53	57	34
45	63	58	55	60	36
47	66	60	58	63	37
49	69	63	60	65	39
51	72	65	63	68	41
53	75	68	65	71	42
55	78	71	68	73	44

Source: Reprinted from "Your Money's Worth in Foods," *Home and Garden Bulletin 183* (Washington, D.C.: U.S. Department of Agriculture, 1973), p. 12.

developing a table bird that has a good percentage of palatable meat. The soft plump chickens and turkeys found in the supermarket are superior to those sold 20 years ago.

Feeding small amounts of such common antibiotics as penicillin and tetracycline appears to have a growth-promoting effect on poultry. The increased growth probably is the result of the antibacterial action of the antibiotics in the intestinal tract, which improves the health and rate of growth of the poultry.[1] The use of antibiotics in poultry rations appears to have practically eliminated the harmful bacteria in the environs in which poultry are raised. Some antibiotic residues are found in the liver and the fat of the poultry.

A new, fast-growing broiler bird, developed through breeding experiments, has brought marked changes to the poultry scene. The scientifically bred broiler of today reaches market weight in a much shorter time than the broiler

of 20 years ago. This increase in rate is achieved without any increase in feed consumed. Breeding experiments have been successful in improving such appearance qualities as color of skin and conformation of flesh.

The Beltsville white turkey, a heavy-breasted, compact, palatable bird, was developed by government researchers. This fairly small, meaty bird has brought many changes to the turkey market. The Beltsville turkey has a sizable amount of sliceable white meat and is also highly acclaimed for flavor. The broad-breasted Bronze turkey attains greater weight than the Beltsville; some Bronze turkeys weigh as much as 60 lb.

Inspection. The Wholesome Poultry Products Act of 1968 parallels the Meat Inspection Act. Under this law, all poultry and poultry products sold in the United States must be inspected for sanitary condition. A federal or state inspector is empowered to set standards of sanitary conditions in plants engaged in interstate commerce, to inspect live poultry before slaughter, to inspect eviscerated poultry before further processing, and finally to label properly all inspected poultry. Individual states must provide inspection for products sold within the state.

[1] G. F. Coombs, "Mode of Action of Antibiotics in Poultry," in *First International Conference on Antibiotics in Agriculture* (Washington, D.C.: National Research Council, National Academy of Sciences, 1956), p. 107.

THE INSPECTION MARK. The label used on inspected poultry includes the class of the product, its net weight, the name of the packer or distributor, and the official inspection mark. It usually is attached as a tag to the wing of a bird, printed on the wrapper, or printed on the wrapper enclosing the giblets. Poultry products such as canned boned poultry, frozen dinners and pies, and speciality items like poultry à la king must be prepared under inspection. Government regulations also require the label to list the common name of the product, the net weight, the name and address of the packer or distributor, the official plant number and inspection mark, and a list of ingredients in order of their proportion in the product, the ingredient present in the largest amount being listed first.

RETAIL PREPARATION

The home slaughter of poultry has declined with the increase of urban life. However, the procedures are still used by those who hunt wild birds, such as pheasant, quail, turkey, and geese. Fasting birds are hung by the feet to decrease their activity. The jugular vein is cut so that the heart will pump out all the blood. Birds that have not been well bled will have an undesirable taste. An alternative, cleaner method is to wring the neck (popping the neck up and twisting) without breaking the skin so that the blood will accumulate under the skin around the neck. The feathers are loosened by dipping the bird into hot water (138–140°F; 52–54°C) for 45 seconds. This brief exposure to this temperature does not damage the outer skin. Home-slaughtered birds are plucked by hand, but processed birds have the feathers rubbed off with machines having rubber projections. After the feathers are removed, the birds are eviscerated, drawn, and chilled. Rigor in chickens disappears in 4–5 hours and in turkeys, in 12 hours.

GRADING

Grading poultry is optional and may be carried on in conjunction with inspection, but the grade mark may be used only on inspected poultry (Fig. 26-1). The qualities used for grading poultry are conformation; fleshing; fat; freedom from pinfeathers; freedom from cuts, tears, and other skin and flesh blemishes; and freedom from disjointed or broken bones (Fig. 26-2). Six kinds of poultry are graded: turkey, chicken, duck, goose, guinea, and squab.

BUYING POULTRY

Poultry may be sold chilled or frozen (Table 26-3). A large amount of the ready-to-cook poultry on the market is drawn, packaged, and frozen where it is bred. The "class" of the bird appears on the label; it is a guide to tenderness and suggests a method of cookery. Chickens of the roaster, broiler, or fryer class are tender and are suitable for roasting, broiling, and frying. Stewing chickens require slow, moist cooking. Chicken and turkey rolls and smoked poultry are available.

Turkey ham is turkey thigh meat that has been commercially processed and flavored to simulate ham. It has the taste and pink appearance of ham and can be used as its replacement in recipes. The fat content and the cost is lower than that of ham.

The color of poultry is not an indicator of its quality but is related to the presence of xanthophyll and carotene pigments in the diet. If a bird is fed a diet of yellow corn or supplemented with a xanthophyll source such as gold marigold petals, its fat will be the yellow color that seems to be preferred by consumers.

26-1 *The grading and inspection stamps for poultry may be combined. (Courtesy of U.S. Department of Agriculture)*

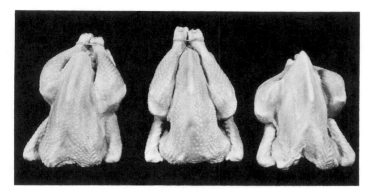

26-2 *Grades of poultry. Left to right: U.S. Grade A, U.S. Grade B, U.S. Grade C. (Courtesy of U.S. Department of Agriculture)*

Amounts to Buy. It is difficult to determine exact amounts of poultry to buy for an average serving. The following findings are helpful guides.

Cooked edible meats amount to 51.3% of the ready-to-cook weight of broilers. One pound of cooked edible meat may be obtained from approximately 2 lb of ready-to-cook weight or 2.35 lb of dressed weight.[2] Three quarters of a pound to 1 lb of ready-to-cook poultry per serving is a good allowance.

Winters and Clements recommend amounts shown in Table 26-4 of ready-to-cook poultry

[2] J. Tadle et al., "Cooked Edible Meat in Parts of Chicken," *J. Amer. Dietet. Assoc.* **31**:597, 1955.

TABLE 26-3
Poultry Classification—Ready-to-Cook Weight

Type	Description
Chicken	
Rock cornish	Not over 2 lb
Broiler–fryer	All-purpose chicken that comes to the market at the age of 9 weeks, averaging 2½ lb.
Roaster	Young chicken, usually about 6 months of age, averaging 4–5 lb
Capon	Young, desexed male chicken; used mainly for roasting 4–8 lb
Hen	Chicken over 1 year old 2½–5 lb
Fowl	Old chicken, either male or female, 2½ to over 5½ lb
Turkey	
Fryer	Young bird, usually 4–8 lb
Roaster	Young bird, 8–16 lb
Hen	Female bird, 18 to over 24 lb
Tom	Male bird, 18 to over 24 lb
Duck	
Broiler or fryer duckling	3 to over 5 lb
Roaster duckling	3 to over 5 lb
Mature or old duck	3 to over 5 lb
Geese	
Young goose	6–8 lb
Mature or old goose	8–12 lb
Pigeons	
Squab (young)	8 to over 14 oz
Pigeon (mature)	8 to over 14 oz

Source: Handbook of Food Preparation, rev. ed (Washington, D.C.: American Home Economics Association, 1975).

TABLE 26-4
Pounds of Ready-to-Cook Poultry That Will Supply 1 Pound of Cooked Meat

Type	Weight
Whole poultry	
Large turkey	1.76
Small turkey	1.85
Chicken, broiler	1.94
Goose	2.42
Duck	2.6
Poultry parts	
Turkey breast	1.5
Broiler breast	1.6
Goose breast	2.1
Duck breast	2.3
Turkey legs and thighs	1.8
Broiler legs and thighs	1.9
Goose legs and thighs	2.1
Duck legs and thighs	2.3

Source: A. R. Winters and P. Clements, "Cooked Edible Meat in Ready-to-Cook Poultry," *J. Amer. Dietet. Assoc.* **33**:800, 1957.

to supply 1 lb of cooked meat. In a more recent study, Fulton et al found that the mean yield of cooked meat from frozen and thawed cooked turkeys was 42 to 43%.[3]

PRINCIPLES OF COOKING POULTRY

The changes that take place in cooking poultry are similar to those that take place in other meat. Intense heat will toughen the protein and cause considerable shrinkage and loss of juice; low to moderate heat is best for tender, juicy, uniformly cooked poultry.

Raw chicken has little or no flavor; with chicken, the flavor develops during cooking. It is thought that the flavor may be due in part to glutathione, glutamic acid, cysteine, and glycine.

AGE

For best results, poultry should be cooked with age and fat distribution in mind. Young

[3] L. H. Fulton, G. Gilpin, and E. Dawson, "Turkeys Roasted from Frozen and Thawed States," *J. Home Econ.* **59**:728, 1967.

birds are more palatable when cooked by dry heat; older birds are best cooked by moist heat. With regard to older birds, it is of interest that Hanson's studies showed that older chickens and turkeys subjected to moist-heat cookery are most acceptable for precooked frozen products. The older chickens, for example, were superior in flavor to the younger ones. Roasting the turkeys had no advantage over moist cookery for imparting a turkey flavor to creamed products.[4]

BASTING, STUFFING, AND USE OF THERMOMETER

According to Lowe, basting does not decrease cooking losses, but it does improve the desirability of the lean meat of both thigh and breast.[5] Young chickens, which are totally lacking in fat, are much improved in flavor, palatability, and appearance when they are basted. In short studies in the author's laboratory, broilers basted with butter were superior in appearance and palatability to those broiled and basted with margarine, corn oil, or cottonseed oil. The differences were small, however, and probably not significant for all practical purposes.

Cooking Breast-Side Down. Chickens cooked in dry heat, breast-side down in the pan, are slightly more tender and juicy than those roasted breast-side up.[6] Because chicken has much less fat than other meat, there is little chance for self-basting. Prolonged exposure to the dry heat circulating around the breast will tend to dry it out. Hence, the breast-down position offers some protection for this portion of the bird. With turkeys, the breast-up position of roasting is considered to be as satisfactory as the breast-down position.

Stuffing. Chickens and turkeys should be stuffed immediately before roasting so that the

[4] H. L. Hanson, H. M. Winegarden, M. B. Horton, and H. Lineweaver, "Preparation and Storage of Frozen Cooked Poultry and Vegetables," *Food Technol.* **4**:430, 1950.
[5] Belle Lowe, *Experimental Cookery*, 4th ed. (New York: Wiley, 1955), p. 249.
[6] Ibid., p. 249.

danger of bacterial action is minimized. It is undesirable to fill the cavity completely with stuffing because the stuffing tends to swell and fill the air spaces and thus may not thoroughly cook in the center.

A temperature of 185°F (84°C) should be achieved in the center of the turkey stuffing to assure adequate destruction of organisms there. The rate of heat penetration to the interior of the stuffing is slower for a large bird than for a small one. Hence, longer roasting periods are necessary for large birds. Adequate roasting time for a frozen stuffed bird is about twice as long as that required for birds that are not frozen. Commercially frozen stuffed poultry must not be thawed before cooking. It is recommended that consumers *not* stuff and home-freeze poultry, because of the possibility of bacterial contamination.

Use of a Thermometer. A thermometer (Fig. 26-3) is the most accurate way of determining when the interior of the bird has reached the desired stage of doneness. It is inserted into the thigh muscle, the breast muscle, or the stuffing. A temperature of 185°F (84°C) for both muscle and stuffing indicates the bird has been sufficiently cooked. If no thermometer is available, pressing the fleshy side of drumstick is useful for testing doneness. If the bird is done, the drumstick will move easily.

METHODS OF COOKING POULTRY

All poultry must be washed before cooking. The cooking methods used for the preparation of poultry are the same as those for other meat (see Chapter 24). Any number of poultry dishes are simply variations of these methods. Briefly, all young poultry is either broiled, roasted, fried, or braised; all older birds must be cooked in moist heat to assure tenderness. The darkened bone seen in some cooked young chickens that were frozen before being cooked is caused by the oxidation of the hemoglobin that has filtered from the bone marrow through the porous bone wall. This in no way affects the flavor or the texture of the meat.

The most acceptable roasting temperature for poultry is 325°F (163°C) (Table 26-5). Esselen et al[7] report that roasting unwrapped birds at 325°F (163°C) in an open pan according to

[7] W. B. Esselen et al., "Adequate Roasting Procedures for Frozen Stuffed Poultry," *J. Amer. Dietet. Assoc.* **32:**1162, 1956.

26-3 *A meat thermometer is frequently used to determine doneness in cooking poultry. (Courtesy of U.S. Department of Agriculture)*

TABLE 26-5
Roasting Guide for Stuffed Poultry

Kind of Bird	Ready-to-Cook Weight (lb)	Approximate Roasting Hours at 325°F (163°C)
Chicken		
Broilers or fryers	1½–2½ lb	1–2
Roasters, stuffed	2½–4½ lb	2–3½[a]
Capons, stuffed	5–8 lb	2½–3½[a]
Duck	4–6 lb	2–3
Goose	6–8 lb	3–3½
	8–12 lb	3½–4½
Turkey		
Fryers or roasters (very young birds)	6–8 lb	3–3½
Roasters (fully grown young birds), stuffed	8–12 lb	3½–4½
	12–16 lb	4½–5½
	16–20 lb	5½–6½
	20–24 lb	6½–7
Halves, quarters,	3–8 lb	2–3
and half-breasts	8–12 lb	3–4
Boneless turkey roasts[b]	2–10 lb	2–4

[a]Poultry without stuffing may take less time.
[b]Internal temperature of boneless roasts when done is 170–175°F (77–79°C).
Source: Handbook of Food Preparation, rev. ed. (Washington, D.C.: American Home Economics Association, 1975).

conventional procedure results in a high-quality cooked product of attractive appearance (Fig. 26-4). In the same study, birds roasted in aluminum foil appeared to be stewed rather than roasted. One or two cups of juice accumulated in the foil, causing the stewing. Also, turkeys wrapped in foil with the bright side facing out took a few minutes longer to cook than did those wrapped in foil with the dull side out.

For whole and half turkeys, a temperature of 325°F (163°C) was found to be satisfactory for roasting. The turkeys were roasted to an end point of 195°F (90°C).[8]

Cooked poultry should always be eaten as soon as possible after being removed from the heat. If it is to be used in such dishes as chicken pies, stews, or casseroles, it should not be handled excessively, but refrigerated in a shallow container for the necessary holding period.

[8]G. Goertz and S. Stacey, "Roasting Half and Whole Turkey Hens: Effect of Varying Oven Temperatures," *J. Amer. Dietet. Assoc.* **37**:458, 1960.

Microwave Cooking. Some attention has been given to microwave cooking of chickens. Studies have shown that ovens appear to be satisfactory for the cooking of chicken and chicken dishes and their use results in a considerable saving of time.[9] However, external appearance and color are better in conventionally cooked chicken. Bone darkening in frozen poultry appears to be lessened when cooked with microwaves and compared with electronically cooked chicken that had been thawed prior to cooking.[10]

PRESERVATION AND STORAGE

Commercial Methods. FREEZING. Chicken, duck, and turkey as prepared for commercial

[9]L. Phillips, I. Delaney, and M. Mongel, "Electronic Cooking of Chicken," *J. Amer. Dietet. Assoc.* **37**:462, 1960.
[10]Helen Van Zante, *The Microwave Oven* (Boston: Houghton Mifflin, 1973), p. 94.

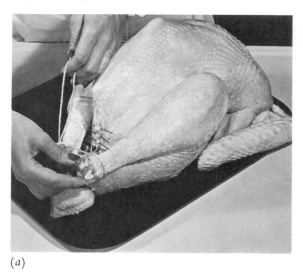
(a)

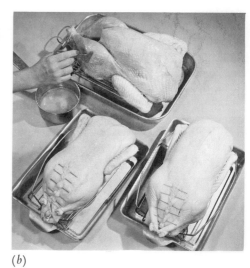
(b)

26-4 (a) *Preparing turkey for oven.* (b) *Turkey, duck, goose ready for oven.* (*Courtesy of Armour and Company*)

freezing are eviscerated and washed. The giblets are wrapped in parchment or a bag and placed in the abdominal cavity. Each chicken is wrapped in a moistureproof film and is quick-frozen. Small poultry, such as chicken, may be placed in a waxed carton before freezing. If the skin of poultry dries out enevenly, it discolors and mottles, thereby disfiguring the frozen bird. This condition is commonly known as *freezer burn*. Storage temperatures below 0°F are recommended for poultry to retard oxidation and the resultant rancidity of the fat. (Rancidity is much more noticeable in frozen turkey than it is in chicken.)

CHILLING. Chilling poultry for storage purposes serves to protect it from spoilage for only a short period. Poultry can be chilled with cold air or by direct contact with ice or ice water. The closer the temperature to freezing, the longer the poultry can be stored.

Home Storage. Poultry is a source of *Salmonella* bacteria, which occur in the intestinal tract as a rule and may spread to the surface of the poultry through processors' handling.

The wrappings of chilled, tightly packaged poultry are suitable for short-term refrigerator or freezer storage. Giblets should be removed from the bag and covered loosely before refrigerating. Chilled poultry may be held for 1–2

days. Hard-frozen poultry may be stored at a holding temperature of 0°F, or lower, for a period of 4–6 months. Once defrosted, poultry—like other meat—should not be refrozen.

Frozen turkeys over 18 lb may take as long as 3 days to thaw in the refrigerator. Those less than 18 lb may require from 1 to 2 days. Chickens 4 lb or over require 1–1½ days to thaw; small ones will complete thawing within a day. Frozen poultry should be thawed in the refrigerator until pliable.

Poultry leftovers (meat, stuffing, broth, and gravy) should be refrigerated immediately and stored not longer than 1–2 days. Large poultry, such as turkey, presents a problem in this regard. The size of the carcass, the use of a moist dressing, and the difficulty in quickly reducing the temperature of leftover parts increase the chances for multiplication of *Salmonella*. Leftover stuffing should always be removed and refrigerated or frozen separately.

SUMMARY

Readily available throughout the year, poultry is an economical food comparable in nutritive value to other meat. Poultry, as a class, consists of chicken and turkey (the most commonly used), duck, goose, Cornish hen, guinea hen, squab, and pigeon. Improved poultry management has bettered the quality and quantity of poultry produced. Poultry and poultry products are federally inspected. Grading is optional; there are Grades A, B, and C. Most poultry is marketed chilled or frozen and ready to cook.

Low to moderate heat is recommended for poultry, as it is for other meat. Age and fat distribution are important in determining cooking method. Because poultry is a source of *Salmonella* bacteria, it is essential that the interior of the bird (and the stuffing) reach a temperature of 185°F (84°C). Commercially, chicken is stored mainly by freezing or chilling. In the home, poultry should be refrigerated in loosened wrappings and not held for more than 24 hours. Hard-frozen poultry may be stored at 0°F (−18°C), or lower, for 4–6 months. Frozen poultry is best thawed in the refrigerator.

QUESTIONS AND TOPICS FOR DISCUSSION AND STUDY

1. How has the use of antibiotics in poultry management affected the market situation?
2. There are similarities between the cooking of poultry and other meat. Give examples of these similarities and the reasons for them.
3. Explain the method of cooking involved when poultry is wrapped in aluminum foil and baked in the oven.

SUGGESTED ACTIVITIES

1. Prepare poultry in one or more of the following ways: broiled, fried, roasted, creamed, fricasseed, in chicken pie, and in chicken paprika. Evaluate each product for cost per serving, flavor, texture, and appearance.
2. Watch a demonstration of the disjointing of

poultry and practice by cutting up whole poultry.

REFERENCES

BOOKS

After a Hundred Years: The Yearbook of Agriculture. Washington, D.C.: U.S. Department of Agriculture, 1962.

Paul, Pauline, and Helen Palmer. *Food Theory and Applications.* New York: Wiley, 1972, Chap. 8.

Van Zante, Helen. *The Microwave Oven.* Boston: Houghton Mifflin, 1973.

ARTICLES AND BULLETINS

Breclaw, E. W., and L. E. Dawson. "Smoke-Flavored Chicken Rolls." *J. Food Sci.* **35**:379, 1970.

Deethardt, D., L. M. Burrill, K. Schneider, and C. W. Carlson. "Foil-Covered Versus Open Pan Procedures for Roasting Turkey." *J. Food Sci.* **36**:624, 1971.

Engler, Pamela, and Jane A. Bowers. "Eating Quality and Thiamin Retention of Turkey Breast Muscle Roasted and 'Slow-Cooked' from Frozen and Thawed States," *Home Econ. Res. J.* **4**:27, 1975.

Goertz, G. E., D. Meyers, B. Weathers, and A. Hopper. "Effect of Cooking Temperatures on Broiler Acceptability." *J. Amer. Dietet. Assoc.* **45**:526, 1964.

Hatch, Vaughn, and W. J. Stadelman. "Bone Darkening in Frozen Chicken Broilers and Ducklings." *J. Food Sci.* **37**:850, 1972.

MacNeil, J. H., and P. S. Dimick. "Poultry Product Quality." *J. Food Sci.* **35**:191, 1970.

Phillips, L., I. Delaney, and M. Monge. "Electronic Cooking of Chicken." *J. Amer. Dietet. Assoc.* **37**:346, 1960.

"Poultry in Family Meals." *Home and Garden Bulletin 110.* Washington, D.C.: U.S. Department of Agriculture, 1971.

Fish

The 20,000 different species of fish may vary in size from ½ in. long at maturity (goby) to as long as 50 feet (whale shark). Some fish will live only a few weeks or months, but most fish have a life span of 10–20 years. The age of a fish can be determined by the number of growth rings that appear on the scales for each year of its life.

Edible fish are categorized as either finfish or shellfish. The term *finfish* refers to fishes that have bony skeletons. *Shellfish* is used to designate both the mollusks and the crustaceans. The mollusks have hard, hinged shells and include oysters, clams, scallops, and mussels. The crustaceans—lobsters, shrimps, and crabs—have segmented, crustlike shells. Most finfish come from salt water; however, the Great Lakes and inland rivers add considerable amounts to the total catch. Edible shellfish are mainly saltwater fish. Anadromous fish are born in fresh water, swim to the sea for their adult life, and return to their birthplace to spawn. Salmon, sturgeon, smelt, and striped bass are anadromous.

COMPOSITION

The composition of fish varies, reflecting to a large extent its variable fat content. In fish such as cod, haddock, whiting, rockfish, and sole, the amount of fat is less than 1%; in salmon, mackerel, lake trout, and butterfish, the fat is as high as 25%. The fat content of the flesh will vary with its location and the color of the muscle. Red muscled sections in the belly flap area will have the maximum amount of oil, followed by the flesh near the head. If the lowest fat content is desired (as in low-calorie diets), sections from the white-muscled tail should be used.[1]

The protein content of fish is approximately 20%, the mineral content about 1.5%. Shellfish have less fat and more carbohydrate than finfish.

To a limited extent, pigments occur in the flesh and oil of some species of fish. The red pigment astacin is found in salmon and lobster. The reason lobster turns red when cooked is due to the stability of astacin. The other green and brown pigments that darken the shell of the live lobster are destroyed when heated. The yellow pigment found in pilchard oil is fucoxanthin (the pilchard is a member of the herring family).

Like meat, fish contains some glycogen in muscle tissue. In the live fish, glycogen is a source

---

[1] M. E. Stansby, "Polyunsaturates and Fat in Fish Flesh," *J. Amer. Dietet. Assoc.* **63:**625, 1973.

of stored energy. Oysters are notable for their high content of glycogen, averaging 2–3%.[2]

NUTRITIVE VALUE

The protein of fish is of excellent quality and can be readily used as an alternative for meat protein. Fish contains both saturated and unsaturated fatty acids and the total fat content of raw fish, in general, is less than the fat content of an equal amount of raw poultry or meat. Because fish are not high in fat or carbohydrate, they are not classified as high-energy foods. It is a common practice, however, to add food materials such as fat, milk, flour, bread crumbs, and cornmeal to fish during its preparation. These added food materials are intended to enhance flavor, but they also add to the energy value.

The vitamin content of fish also varies according to its fat content. High-fat fish, such as salmon and mackerel, are good sources of vitamin A. Vitamins A and D occur in high concentrations in fish liver oils and in fish viscera. Fishroe is an excellent source of thiamine and riboflavin. All fish are good sources of thiamine, riboflavin, and niacin; they also contain good amounts of calcium, phosphorus, and iron. Ocean fish are excellent sources of iodine. Fish canned with the bones in (notably sardines) are good sources of calcium and phosphorus. Oysters are very good sources of iron and copper.

Surprisingly, there is very little salt in the flesh of edible fish with the exception of shark meat. The sodium content of fresh fish is only slightly higher than that of meat.

On the whole, iodine is the most important element in saltwater fish and occurs there more abundantly than in any other of nature's products.

ECONOMIC ASPECTS

Fish falls far below meat in per capita consumption, yet there are 240 varieties of fish and shellfish sold in the United States today.[3] With modern methods of transportation, a good supply of fresh, frozen, and canned fish is available throughout the country—not only in coastline areas but in the interior as well—the year around.

There is an unevenness about the fish industry, however, that appears to discourage a national increase in the utilization of a greater variety of seafoods. Most people are familar with only about six or seven varieties of fish and are reluctant to try unfamiliar species. Consequently, a very large percentage of the total catch sold for food is tuna, salmon, haddock, cod, mackerel, herring, whiting, pollack, and flounder. However, halibut, trout, swordfish, carp, bluefish, catfish, shad, bass, and red snapper are found fresh or frozen in good supply in some localities at certain seasons of the year. Prejudice against shark or perhaps fear of its poisonous liver has limited its acceptance in this country. In England a form of shark (dogfish and school) is often used to make the famous "fish and chips." The strong taste of its meat is reduced by icing for 24 hours and soaking in brine for 2 hours. Sardines are any of a number of small herringlike fish.

Trout either fresh or frozen is fast becoming a popular item on the American menu. The U.S. Trout Farmers Association anually supplies about 5–5.5 million pounds of fresh and fresh-frozen trout to the market.[4]

Lobsters are expensive not only because their number is limited but because the contain so little meat. It takes an average of five 1-lb lobsters to yield 1 lb of lobster meat. The lesser-known varieties of finfish and shellfish lend themselves to interesting, nutritious, and economical dishes.

GRADING

The Fishery Products Inspection Program of the U.S. Department of Commerce's National

[2] M. Stansby, "Fish, Shellfish, and Crustacea," in *The Chemistry and Technology of Food and Food Products,* Morris B. Jacobs, ed. (New York: Interscience, 1951), p. 954.

[3] "Let's Cook Fish!" *Fishery Market Development Series 8* (Washington, D.C.: Fish and Wildlife Service, U.S. Department of the Interior, n.d.), p. 6.

[4] Donald Spencer, "Protecting the Sportsman's Paradise," in *Protecting Our Food: The Yearbook of Agriculture* (Washington, D.C.: U.S. Department of Agriculture, 1966), p. 48.

TABLE 27-1
Oyster Classification

Grade	Number per Gallon	Use
Eastern or Gulf		
Counts, or Extra Large	160	Fried, baked
Extra Selects, or Large	161–210	On the half-shell, fried
Selects, or Medium	211–300	Stews
Standards, or Small	301–500	Stews, casserole
Standards, or Very Small	500 and over	Stews, casserole
Pacific		
Large	64 or less	Fried, baked
Medium	65 to 96	Fried
Small	97 to 144	Stews
Extra Small	Over 144	Stews

Marine Fisheries Service is a voluntary program providing inspection and certification service on a user-fee basis. Processors desiring the service must request and pay for it. It is available for use by processing plants for all types of processed fishery products (i.e., fresh, frozen, canned, and cured). The program is based on the application of official U.S. quality standards and specifications for fishery products, as well as minimum sanitary and operating requirements for participating plants. Fishery products produced in a sanitary plant under inspection and meeting wholesomeness requirements and applicable quality standards may be identified with a "U.S. Grade A" or other inspection shield on the product label. This shield indicates to the consumer that the product was produced under good sanitary conditions and has a good flavor and odor, as well as a high rating in other important quality factors.

Grades (Tables 27-1 and 27-2) for fresh shellfish are useful guides for purchasers of large quantities. Oysters, clams, scallops, lobsters, crabs,

and shrimp are sold fresh, frozen, and shucked. Oysters, it should be noted, must bear a certificate showing that they have been produced in oyster beds that have passed inspection by health authorities. This is a necessary safeguard, because oyster beds are in shallow water and may become polluted by waste products from surrounding areas.

BUYING FISH

Finfish. Table 27-3 shows some popular species of finfish on the market.

Fish that are fresh can be easily identified by noting the following qualities: the eyes should be bright, clear, and bulging; the gills a reddish pink; the surface free of dirt or slime; the flesh firm to the touch, with no traces of browning or drying around the edges. A "fishy" odor means that deterioration (oxidation of the polyunsaturated fats and bacterial growth) has begun. Truly fresh fish will not have a fishy odor.

There is a good variety of frozen fish of high quality available the year around. Such fish—properly processed, packaged, and held at 0°F (−18°C) or lower—will maintain good quality for relatively long periods of time.

Frozen fish may be purchased whole or dressed and as steaks, fillets, chucks, portions, and sticks.

The flesh of frozen fish should be solid when purchased. There should be little or no odor; the wrapping should be moistureproof, and there

TABLE 27-2
Fresh Shrimp Grades

Size	Number per Pound
Jumbo	Less than 25
Large	25–35
Medium	30–42
Small	42 and over

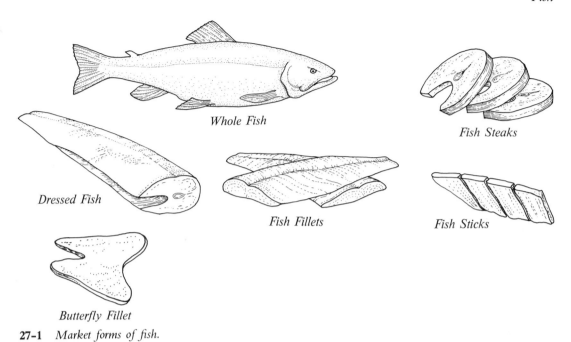

Whole Fish

Fish Steaks

Dressed Fish

Fish Fillets

Fish Sticks

Butterfly Fillet

27-1   *Market forms of fish.*

should be little or no air space between the fish and the wrapping.

The popular forms for retailing fish are shown in Table 27-4 and Fig. 27-1.

Mollusks and Crustacea. OYSTERS. The eastern oyster is cultivated on the eastern coast of the United States, south of Cape Cod, with the main growing area centering around Chesapeake Bay. Oyster beds are also found in the Gulf of Mexico off the Louisiana coast. The Pacific coast yields up the small Pacific or Japanese oyster. Oysters in this country are cultivated much as farm crops are. A suitable area is selected and oyster larvae spawned by the female oyster are "planted." The larva grows by attaching itself to a large hard object, such as a rock or shell. When the developing oyster reaches the seed-oyster stage, it is removed to different oyster grounds with appropriate conditions for growth. The oyster is mature after 2 years and is then usually moved to another area to develop flavor. Oysters are dug up with rakes or tongs and are graded according to size. A large percentage of oysters are sold shucked and fresh.

Oysters sold in the shell must be alive when purchased and the shells must be tightly closed. Shell oysters may be held in the refrigerator at temperatures less than 40°F (50°C) for only a short time before they are eaten. Shucked oysters are commonly sold by the dozen and may be fresh, chilled, or frozen. The liquid content of this bivalve should be used along with the meats. Oyster are graded for size after thay are shucked.

CLAMS. Clams (Table 27-5 and Fig. 27-2) may be of the hard-shell or surf-clam varieties. Hard-shell clams are embedded—as deep as 50 feet—along the coast. Clams close to the tidal zone are dug by hand or with handrakes; more deeply embedded clams are dredged up. The surf clams soft- or long-necked, are found along the coast, buried only a few inches deep in the sand.

Clams may be sold alive in the shell or shucked. Like oysters, clams in the shell should be alive when bought. With hard clams, the shells should be tightly shut, but soft clams may have partially opened shells, because of the long siphon extending from the interior. Shucked clams are plump and contain a fresh, clear liquor.

SCALLOPS. Scallops are highly prized because of their buttery texture and delicate flavor. The bay or cape scallop grows in shallow waters; the sea scallop is dredged up from deep waters. Scallops are similar to clams, oysters, and mussels in that they have two shells, but they differ in

TABLE 27-3
Some Popular Species of Finfish on the Market

Fish[a]	Weight (lb)	Market Form	Preparation
Brook trout (l)	¾–8	Whole	Broil, bake, fry
Butterfish (f)	¼–1	Whole	Broil, bake, fry
Carp (f)	2–8	Whole	Stuff and bake
Cod (l)	3–20	Fillets, steak	Broil, bake, steam
Flounder (l)	¼–5	Whole, fillets	Broil, bake, fry
Haddock (l)	1½–7	Whole, fillets	Stuff and bake, broil, steam
Halibut (l)	8–100	Steak	Broil, bake, steam
Herring (f)	¼–1	Whole	Fry, bake, marinate
Lake trout (f)	2–8	Whole	Bake, fry
Mackerel (f)	¾–3	Whole, fillets	Stuff and bake, broil
Pollack (l)	1½–4	Fillets	Bake
Pompano	1	Whole, fillets	Broil, bake, fry
Porgy (l)	½–1	Whole	Bake
Red snapper (l)	2–15	Whole, fillets, steaks	Bake
Rosefish (l)	¾	Fillets	Bake
Salmon (f)	3–30	Whole, steaks, fillets	Bake, broil, steam
Shad (f)	1½–7	Whole, fillets	Bake
Smelts (f)	⅛–1	Whole, fillets	Fry, bake
Whitefish (f)	1½–4	Whole, fillets	Broil, bake

[a](f) = fat, (l) = lean.
Source: Adapted from "Applied Cookery," *Navsanda Publication 277* (Washington, D.C.: Bureau of Supplies and Accounts, Department of the Navy, 1955).

that they are capable of swimming freely through the water. The large muscle that controls the shell's movements is the portion removed for food purposes. Called the eye, it makes up only a part of the meat. There appears to be little reason, other than custom, for discarding the rest.

Scallops are sold shucked, fresh, or frozen. The bay scallops measure about ½ in. in diameter and are light tan in color; deep-sea scallops measure 2 in. in diameter and are white. Scallops are sold by the pound.

MUSSELS. Mussels are a little-known shellfish found along the Atlantic coast, usually in rocky coastal areas. The demand for mussels in this country is limited to areas where they live. Restaurants specializing in foreign foods have created a very small commercial market for this unfamiliar mollusk.

CRABS. The blue crab of the Atlantic coast and the Dungeness crab indigenous to Pacific waters make up the major portion of the crab catch in the United States. Rock crabs found in New England coastal waters are reported to have an excellent flavor and a high proportion of meat to shell. But they have not yet become

27-2 *Clams. Left to right: two soft clams and two hard clams. (Courtesy of Bureau of Commercial Fisheries, U.S. Department of the Interior)*

TABLE 27-4
Amounts of Fish to Buy per Person

Market Form	Amount (lb)
Whole, round (as caught and taken from the water)	¾
Drawn (the whole fish, with entrails removed)	¾
Dressed (whole fish, with scales, entrails, and fins removed)	½
Steaks (cross-section slices cut from large dressed fish; cross section of the backbone is generally included)	⅓
Fillet (boneless sides of fish cut lengthwise away from backbone)	⅓
Butterfly fillets (the two sides of the fish cut lengthwise away from the backbone and held together by the uncut flesh and skin of the belly)	⅓
Raw breaded fish portions (portions are cut from frozen fish blocks, coated with a batter, breaded, packaged, and frozen; raw breaded fish portions weigh more than 1½ oz, are at least ⅜ in. thick, and must contain not less than 75% fish; they are ready to cook as purchased)	⅓
Sticks (uniform sticks cut from a large block of frozen fillets, weighing approximately 1 oz each)	⅓

Source: Adapted from "Let's Cook Fish!" *Fishery Market Development Series 8* (Washington, D.C.: Fish and Wildlife Service, U.S. Department of the Interior, n.d.).

popular. Chesapeake Bay is the principal crab-producing area in the United States, with the Gulf states of Louisiana and Florida making a fairly good contribution to the total catch. On The Pacific coast, Oregon, home of the Dungeness crab, has a crab industry of some importance.

Soft-shell crabs are hard crabs that are molting. Soft crabs are caught during the summer months, hard crabs during the winter. Crabs may be caught on baited lines or dredged up.

Much of the catch is sold cooked and picked. The crabs are steamed, picked by hand, and packed in tin cans or in waxed cardboard containers. The containers are shipped in boxes of crushed ice. Crabs must be kept chilled until used. Some fresh crabmeat is pasteurized before being shipped [the cans are heated for 1 minute at 170°F (77°C)].

The Alaskan king crab fishing grounds lie off the northern Pacific coast. This crab is about 5 feet long and weighs 7 to 10 lb. It has a small

TABLE 27-5
Origin and Use of Clams

Clams	Origin	Use
Butter	Pacific coast	Chowder, fried, baked
Cherrystone	Atlantic coast	On the shell
Little Neck	Atlantic coast	On the shell
Pisino	Pacific coast	Chowder, fried, baked
Quahog (hard)	Atlantic coast	Chowder
Razor	Pacific coast	Chowder, fried, baked
Soft	Atlantic coast	Steamed, chowder

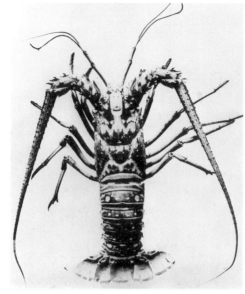

27-3 *The lobster is one of the largest of shellfish. The spiny lobster can be distinguished from the northern lobster by the absence of large, heavy claws, the presence of many prominent spines on its body and legs, and its long, slender antennae.* (*Courtesy of Bureau of Commercial Fisheries, U.S. Department of the Interior*)

(*a*) *Northern lobster.*   (*b*) *Spiny or rock lobster.*

(*c*) *South African spiny lobster tail.*

(*d*) *Western Australian spiny lobster tail.*

(*e*) *Cuban lobster tail.*

body and long legs. King crab may be frozen or canned.

Both soft and hard crabs must be alive when cooked. The meat from cooked hard crab is separated into lump meat, flake meat, and claw meat.

LOBSTERS. Lobsters (Fig. 27-3) are taken from the Atlantic waters from Labrador to South Carolina. The biggest share of the catch comes from the New England area. Lobsters are caught in lobster pots, wooden boxes that are really one-way traps from which they cannot escape once they enter. Lobsters must be kept alive and in sea water until cooked. If they cannot be kept alive, the meat will keep longer if the head, which includes the viscera and gills, is removed.

Lobsters usually range in size from ¾ to 2½ lb.

Lobsters over 2½ lb are jumbos. If lobsters are sold cooked, they are carefully refrigerated below 40°F (5°C) and kept only for a short period of time.

The green sac that appears with cooking is *tomalley*, the lobster's liver. It is considered a delicacy. Coral or red-colored masses found in cooked lobster are the eggs of the female.

SHRIMP. In the United States, all members of the *Natantia* group are called shrimp. In Europe the larger-sized ones may be called "prawns." A "crayfish" or "crawfish" may be as small as a shrimp but has a structure and flavor similar to the spiny lobster. Shrimp come principally from the Atlantic coast and the Gulf of Mexico, 10 to 15 miles offshore. Louisiana is the center of the shrimp industry. About 50% of the shrimp catch is canned; the rest is frozen and marketed fresh or dried. Shrimp to be canned is iced until processed. Fresh shrimp are known as *green shrimp,* and the head and thorax are removed before packing. Fresh shrimp grades (shown in Table 27-5) are helpful as purchasing guides. Some shrimp are sold cooked.

FABRICATED SHRIMP PRODUCTS. Fabricated shrimp products (frozen) are available to the consumer. These are composed of small or broken pieces of raw or cooked shrimp combined with a binding agent such as textured vegetable protein and then mechanically shaped.[5]

The quantity of shellfish to buy depends on the recipe, but Table 27-6 suggests minimum amounts to purchase per person.

PRINCIPLES OF COOKING FISH

Because fish has little connective tissue, it requires a much shorter cooking time than meat and poultry. Fish is cooked at moderate temperatures long enough for its delicate flavor to develop, for protein to coagulate, and for the very small amounts of connective tissue present to break down. The flesh of fish is sufficiently cooked when it falls easily into clumps of snowy-white flakes when tested with a fork. Cooking fish at high temperatures or cooking it

[5] H. M. Soo, and E. H. Sander, "Textural and Mechanical Shaping Characteristics of Comminuted Shrimp-Binding Matrix Agent Compositions," *J. Food Sci.* **42**:1522, 1977.

TABLE 27-6
Shellfish: Minimum Amounts per Serving

Type	Amount
Crabs	
Hard	
Live	1–2 lb
Cooked	3 oz
Dungeness	
Live	1 lb
Cooked	3 oz
Lobsters	
Live	1 lb
Cooked	3 oz
Oysters and clams	
In shell	½ dozen
Shucked	
Scallops, cooked	⅓ lb
Shrimp	
Headless fresh or frozen	¼ lb
Cooked	3 oz

Source: Adapted from *Fish Cookery for One Hundred, Test Kitchens No. 1* (Washington, D.C.: Fish and Wildlife Service, U.S. Department of the Interior, 1950).

too long will cause the muscle protein to shrink, leaving the fish tough, dry, and lacking flavor.

Fish can also be "cooked" by coagulating the proteins with an acid such as lemon or lime juice. Raw fish that has been marinated in acid will turn white and is served as cerviche. Only fresh fish that has been carefully inspected for parasites should be used.

METHODS OF COOKING FISH

Fish is usually cooked by dry heat—broiling, baking, and frying. Moist heat (see Fig. 27-4 and 27-5) is also effectively employed to protect the delicate flavor of fish. Fish such as salmon, shad, bluefish, mackerel, herring, and swordfish contain some fat and require very little additional fat in cooking. Other fish, such as cod, haddock, halibut, bass, trout, and flounder contain very little fat and require added fat during cooking. If the fish is seasoned, lightly floured and sautéed in butter, it is served as *à la meuniere.* Shellfish, particularly lobster, is often served with drawn butter (melted, clarified, and sometimes thickened).

347

27-4   *Poached fish. The liquid used in poaching may be lightly salted or seasoned water. (Courtesy of Bureau of Commercial Fisheries, U.S. Department of the Interior)*

Finfish may be poached in water or court bouillon, a highly seasoned stock that enhances the flavor of the fish. In order to keep the flesh from falling apart while it cooks, it is best to tie the fish in cheesecloth or parchment paper before immersing it in the hot water. Shellfish (see Fig. 27-6) need only be plunged into the simmering salt water, but care must be taken to keep the water from boiling so that the fish meat

27-5   *Steamed fish. Steaming is a method of cooking fish by means of the steam generated from boiling water. Any deep pan with a tight cover is satisfactory. In place of a steaming rack, anything that prevents the fish from touching the water may be used. (Courtesy of Bureau of Commercial Fisheries, U.S. Department of the Interior)*

remains juicy and tender. Shellfish cooked in the shell is said to retain its flavor better. (See Fig. 27-7)

In a study of baked salmon steaks, Charley found 400°F (205°C) to be a suitable oven cooking temperature.[6] In a later study on pieces of salmon weighing 2 lb, results showed that shrinking of the meat and blistering of the skin were markedly less at lower oven temperatures.

The fish was cooked to an internal temperature of 158°F (70°C) at oven temperatures of 350°F (177°C), 400°F (205°C), 450°F (232°C), and 500°F (260°C). Cooking times were decreased as oven temperatures increased. Differences in oven temperatures did not affect palatability ratings.[7]

Fish that is oven-baked enclosed in a sheet of oiled paper is called *en papillote*. Other ways in which fish is baked are with butter and almonds (almandine); with garlic, bread crumbs, and butter (de jonghe); with spinach (florentine); with tomatoes, garlic, and onions (provençale), or with mornay sauce, a mixture of butter and Gruyere and Parmesan cheeses. (See Figs. 27-8 and 27-9.)

Unlike meat and poultry, cooked fish tends to break up easily, thus requiring careful handling during cooking and serving. When fish is to be cooked from the frozen state, cooking time is increased to allow for thawing during the process. If fish is to be cooked stuffed or rolled, it must be thawed first. Because broiling fish tends to dry it out, frozen fish that is to be broiled should be thawed and basted with a fat before placing it under a broiler. As a general guide, the fish can be placed 3–4 in. from the source of heat, with the thicker cuts farther from the heat than the thinner ones.

Fish soup or chowder is a mixture of fish with a milk or tomato base. A bisque has a richer cream base. A bouillabaise is a more elaborate fish chowder which often has the more expensive shellfish, such as shrimp, lobster, and clams, included. It may be flavored with wine.

[6] H. Charley, "Effects of Internal Temperature and of Oven Temperature on the Cooking Losses and the Palatability of Baked Salmon Steaks," *Food Res.* **17**:136, 1952.

[7] H. Charley and G. E. Goertz, "The Effects of Oven Temperature on Certain Characteristics of Baked Salmon," *Food Res,* **23**:17, 1958.

(a)

(b)

(c)

27-6 *Steps in cooking shrimp. (a) Boiling is the basic method of cooking raw shrimp. (b) Drain shrimp and peel (1½ lb. shrimp yield about ¾ lb. cooked, peeled, and cleaned shrimp). (c) Remove sand vein. (Courtesy of Bureau of Commercial Fisheries, U.S. Department of the Interior)*

PRESERVATION AND STORAGE

Canning. Only a few varieties of fish are canned, but the canning industry is an important one on both the Atlantic and Pacific coasts.

Salmon, tuna, sardines, mackerel, herring, lobster, crab, clams, shrimp, and mussels are canned. Of these salmon and tuna are the most popular by far. Almost all canned salmon is processed in and around Alaska and along the Pacific coast. Tuna is canned in Oregon and southern California; sardines are canned in California and Maine.

Canned shellfish may become dark or discolored during storage. This discoloration is thought to be caused by iron sulfide formed by the hydrogen sulfide released from the fish and the iron in the can. The use of a special enamel can containing zinc is effective in preventing this discoloration (zinc sulfide forms a white substance). However, the color changes in canned tuna are the result of a lack of vitamins in the flesh. Ascorbic acid and nicotinamide, a vitamin B, are effective in returning the flesh to its normal pink color.

BUYING CANNED FISH. Salmon, tuna, sardines, shrimp, and crabs are the principal canned fish sold. There are hundreds of excellent recipes available for these highly nutritious and palatable canned products. Many of them were developed by the Fish and Wildlife Service of the U.S. Department of the Interior and are published in the *How to Cook Fish* series.

There are five species of canned salmon on the market. They differ from each other in color, texture, and flavor. Canned salmon and tuna are graded by the industry—there are no government grades available for these fish as yet. Industry grades are quite helpful to the consumer in selecting canned fish. All grades of tuna and salmon are of good quality and can be used interchangeably in recipes. The grades refer to the type of meat and the color in the pack.

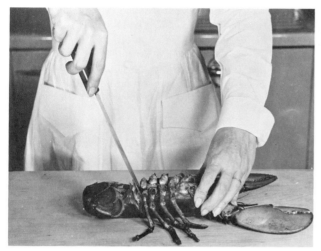

27-7 *Steps in cooking lobster. (a) Place the lobster on its back and insert a sharp knife between the body shell and the tail segment, cutting down to sever the spinal cord. (b) Cut the lobster in half lengthwise and remove the stomach and the intestinal vein. (c) Lay lobsters as flat as possible on a broiler pan and brush with butter. (Courtesy of Bureau of Commercial Fisheries, U.S. Department of the Interior)*

(*a*)

(*b*)

(*c*)

27-8 *A bread stuffing for fish. Fish should be stuffed loosely and the opening sewn with needle and thread or closed with skewers. (Courtesy of Bureau of Commercial Fisheries, U.S. Department of the Interior)*

Federal Food and Drug officials inspect canned fish to be sold over state lines.

Shellfish is sometimes dipped in acetic, citric or tartaric acid before it is packed. This increases the acidity of the fish and reduces the possibility of iron sulfide formation. Crabmeat may de-

27-9 *Fish is baked in a moderate oven (350°F) until it flakes easily when tested with a fork. (Courtesy of Bureau of Commercial Fisheries, U.S. Department of the Interior)*

velop a blue discoloration caused by a copper–ammonia complex formed by the combination of the copper in the crab's blood and the ammonia in its flesh. These discolorations are not harmful.

SALMON. Salmon canneries are close to the fishing grounds, so the fish require little or no refrigeration before canning. Once at the cannery the fish are graded according to species, and sometimes according to color of flesh and place of origin. The fish are machine-cleaned and -washed. They are then cut into can-size pieces. The cans of salmon are processed at 10 lb of steam pressure for varying lengths of time, depending on the size of the container.

Grades of salmon are sold by their name, which indicates differences in type of meat. Grades are given in Table 27-7 in descending order of price. Higher prices are charged for the varieties that have deep red color and higher oil content.

Unlike salmon, tuna is frozen when caught. (Tuna fishermen may be away for weeks, so some method of preserving their catch is necessary.) The true white canned tuna is albacore.

Canned oysters and shrimp are graded for size, sardines for size and number. Smoked clams, oysters, and shrimp are graded for both size and number. For shrimp, the kind of pack—wet or dry—is indicated on the label. Tuna, salmon, and sardine can labels indicate the kind of oil used.

STRUVITE. Struvite crystals are found in canned fish—mainly tuna and shrimp. Struvite crystals may appear to be glass but are harmless particles composed of magnesium ammonium phosphate hexahydrate; they are natural constituents of fish and shellfish made up of mineral elements of seawater in which they live. The crystals form as the result of the sterilization of the seafoods in their processing. Struvite crystals can be crushed to a powder with the thumbnail or can be dissolved in a few minutes by boiling them in a little vinegar or lemon juice. Glass is not soluble in such weak acids.

Chilling. Because the enzymes that cause spoilage of fish are active at low temperatures, and because fish oils become oxidized at fairly low temperatures, fish catches subjected to temperatures above freezing are given to fast deterioration. The entire fish catch is usually chilled

TABLE 27-7
Salmon and Tuna Grades

Salmon Grades	Tuna Grades
Chinook (King)	Fancy or Solid (large pieces of meat packed in oil)
Sockeye	Chunk (convenient-sized pieces packed in oil)
Coho	Flaked (flakes packed in oil, no large pieces)
Pink	Grated (packed in oil, no large pieces)
Chum	Shredded (no large pieces)

aboard the fishing vessel by packing in crushed ice or by mechanical refrigeration. Although only a temporary method, chilling does keep spoilage at a minimum. The use of antibiotics and other preservatives in the crushed ice retards bacterial action to some extent.

Freezing. The freezing of fish greatly extends the period of storage and is effective in keeping the fish in a condition similar to that of fresh fish. Large fish may be frozen by the *sharp freeze,* a comparatively slow freeze. Smaller fish are quick-frozen, the more acceptable of the two methods from the consumer's standpoint, for quick-frozen fish thaws to a more attractive product. Freezing kills some microorganisms in the fish and deactivates others. When the fish thaws, those organisms that were not killed revive and resume their growth.

Finfish are usually frozen as fillets and steaks, with or without skin. Recently, there has been a good demand for brook trout frozen whole. For the most part, only the common varieties of fish are frozen and packaged. Fillets of cod, pollack, sole, haddock, rosefish, and whiting are the most popular. Swordfish, turbot, salmon, and halibut are frozen in steak form. Large quantities of shellfish are also frozen in the United States. Scallops, clams, shrimp, lobsters, lobster tails, langouste (crayfish or prawn), squid, oysters, and crabs are available in frozen form.

PROTEIN DENATURATION. The time taken to freeze fish influences the size of the crystals formed and the extent of protein denaturation. Considerable denaturation of the protein takes place during the freezing process, mainly because of the loss of moisture from the flesh. As the water freezes in the fish, the salt concentration of the muscle tissue increases. The highly concentrated salt solution that prevails while the water is going into crystalization denatures the protein, making it tough and rubbery. This is an irreversible action; the protein remains tough and stringy upon thawing. Not all denaturation of muscle protein takes place during the freezing process; considerable alteration occurs while the frozen fish is stored.

DESICCATION. Another effect of freezing is desiccation (drying out). Drying is caused by the transfer of moisture from the surface of the fish to the cold metal surfaces on which the fish rest during freezing. It may also be caused by air currents: the air close to the fish in the storage room is warmer than the refrigeration pipes and is able to absorb large amounts of moisture from the fish. As the warm air moves into contact with the refrigeration pipes, its temperature drops and its capacity to hold water is reduced. The excess moisture is deposited on the refrigerator coils. Despite the protective wrappers designed to hold the moisture in the fish desiccation can occur if air pockets are left in the cartons or between the fish and the wrapping. When this happens, the surface of the fish gives up moisture to the air pocket; the moisture is formed into ice crystals that are deposited on the inside of the package. Many quick-freezing processes freeze fish under pressure to eliminate the formation of air pockets.

Another, less controllable form of desiccation is caused by the evaporation of water from the frozen fish flesh into air interstices within the muscle fibers.[8] This evaporation may be reduced by covering the fish with a dilute brine that fills in the interstices.

Frozen fish undergo undesirable oxidation changes. In general, fatty fish react with oxygen and become rancid much more quickly than lean fish do. The rate of oxidation is related to the properties of the fish oil. Cutting out the dark or red muscles, which contain fat that oxidizes easily (creating a rancid flavor), will

[8] Maurice Stansby, in *The Chemistry and Technology of Food and Food Products,* 2nd, ed. Ed. Morris Jacobs (New York: Interscience, 1951), p. 961.

enable the fish to be frozen for a longer period of time. Oxidation can be retarded by packaging the fish so that no air spaces form between the surface of the fish and the wrapping.

Curing. Both finfish and shellfish are preserved by curing. There are smoked, salted, dried, and marinated products. Smoked whitefish, kippered salmon, salted cod, and herring in vinegar (pickled) are a few examples. Fish is salted in either dry salt or brine. Smoked fish is made by exposing salted fish to a smoking period of short duration.

Home Storage. Fish spoils quickly and should be used as soon as possible after purchase. It should be kept covered in a cold part of the refrigerator for no longer than 2 days. Prepackaged fish and shellfish can be refrigerated in the original package for a short time. Fish wrapped in butcher paper should be taken out and wrapped in aluminum foil or plastic wrap. Frozen fish maintains good quality when placed in the freezer immediately after purchase. Freezer temperatures of 0°F (−18°C) or lower are necessary to prevent loss of color, texture, flavor, and nutritive value. Cured fish is best kept covered in the refrigerator; open canned fish should be used up immediately or refrigerated.

SUMMARY

Two general classifications are used for fish: finfish (those with bony skeletons) and shellfish, which include both mollusks, such as oysters, clams, scallops and mussels, and the crustaceans, lobsters, shrimps, and crabs.

Although fish contains complete proteins and can be alternate for meat in the diet, fish consumption per capita is far lower than for meat. Finfish may be designated as fat or lean types, depending on their fat content, which may range from less than 1% in sole or haddock to as high as 25% in salmon or trout. Shellfish contain less fat than finfish, and neither group is considered a high-energy food. Freshwater and saltwater varieties are a good source of iodine. Fish liver oils are high in vitamins A and D.

An optional inspection and grading system is in use in the fish industry under the supervision of the U.S. Department of Commerce. Only firms that process fishery products under continuous inspection are permitted to use the U.S. shield. Oyster beds must pass inspection of health authorities.

Clams and oysters in the shell and hard and soft crabs must be alive when cooked. Shrimp is marketed frozen, fresh, dried, or canned, and scallops are sold shucked, fresh, or frozen.

Fish can be broiled, poached, baked, or fried and should be cooked at a moderate temperature long enough for the protein to coagulate and for the minimal amounts of connective tissue to break down. Shellfish is plunged into simmering salted water.

Canned fish accounts for an estimated 40% of the total fish consumption, with tuna and salmon the most popular. Federal Food and Drug officials inspect canned fish to be sold over state lines. There are industry grades for canned tuna and salmon.

Fish is subject to rapid deterioration, because enzymes that cause spoilage are active at low temperatures; it is held by chilling or freezing. Fish kept in the home refrigerator should be used within 2 days.

QUESTIONS AND TOPICS FOR DISCUSSION AND STUDY

1. Why is less cooking time required for fish than for meat?
2. What are the main differences between shellfish and finfish?
3. What happens to fish when it is overcooked?
4. What are the characteristics of fresh fish? Why does fish spoil more quickly than other fresh foods?

SUGGESTED ACTIVITIES

1. Examine publications of the Fish and Wildlife Service, U.S. Department of the Interior. Make a chart of many interesting ways basic fish cookery can be varied.
2. Prepare fish in one or more of the following ways: baked and stuffed, scalloped, and deep-fat fried.
3. Simmer or poach a piece of fish according to directions found in the recipe section or in a cookbook. Try modifying the flavor of the

fish by serving it with small amounts of white sauces with different seasonings.

REFERENCES

BOOKS

Food: The Yearbook of Agriculture. Washington, D.C.: U.S. Department of Agriculture, 1959, pp. 353–370.

Food for Us All: The Yearbook of Agriculture. Washington, D.C.: U.S. Department of Agriculture, 1969, pp. 127–138.

Paul, Pauline, and Helen Palmer. *Food Theory and Application.* New York: Wiley, 1972, Chap. 8.

Protecting Our Food: The Yearbook of Agriculture. Washington, D.C.: U.S. Department of Agriculture, 1966, pp. 123–139.

Tressler, Donald, and Clifford Evers. *The Freezing Preservation of Foods.* Westport, Conn.: Avi, 1968, Chap. 19.

Vail, Gladys, Jean Phillips, Lucile Rust, Ruth Griswold, and Margaret Justin. *Foods,* 7th ed. Boston: Houghton Mifflin, 1978, Chap. 13.

BULLETINS

Burtis, J., and R. Kerr. "How to Cook Shrimp." *Test Kitchen Series 7.* Washington, D.C.: Fish and Wildlife Service, U.S. Department of the Interior, reprinted 1964.

Carson, Rachel. "Food from the Sea." *Bulletin 33.* Washington, D.C.: Fish and Wildlife Service, U.S. Department of the Interior, 1941.

National Oceanic and Atmospheric Administration (NOAA). *Food Fish Facts No. 1–62.* Chicago: National Maritime Fisheries Services, n.d.

Fats and Oils Used in Cookery

The terms "fat" and "oil" do not refer to different substances; they only indicate different physical states of the same group of substances. A fat that is liquid at normal room temperature is called an *oil*, whereas one that is solid or semisolid is referred to as a *fat*. All oils solidify when sufficiently cooled, and all fats liquefy at elevated temperatures. Solid fats may contain a relatively large proportion of liquid oil but still be classified as fats because they remain solid at room temperature. The temperature at which a fat changes to an oil is called the *melting point* of the fat; the melting point varies for different fats.

COMPOSITION

Fats are composed of carbon (C), hydrogen (H), and oxygen (O). They are built up by a linking together of a number of individual fatty acids chemically combine with glycerol. The union of one molecule of glycerol and one molecule of a fatty acid forms a *monoglyceride*. In the process, one molecule of water is freed.

Glycerol   Fatty acid

Monoglyceride   Water

*Designates any one of a number of hydrocarbons chains.

If two fatty acids are attached to glycerol it is called a *diglyceride*. Chemically, fats may be generally defined as *triglycerides*—glycerides containing three fatty acid radicals. When the three

355

fatty acids are of the same kind, the fat is a *simple triglyceride*. If the fatty acids are different, as is normally the case in natural fats, the fat is called a *mixed glyceride*. Partially hydrolyzed fats contain monoglycerides and diglycerides. Natural fats in foods are made up mostly of triglycerides, but traces of monoglycerides and diglycerides are also present.

NUTRITIVE VALUE

Fats are essential in the diet because they provide a source of linoleic acid, an essential fatty acid. They are also important as a concentrated source of energy, furnishing 2.25 times as much energy (9 calories/gram) as carbohydrates (4 calories/gram) or protein (4 calories/gram). They are necessary for palatability in the diet since flavors are usually fat-soluble. The satiety of the meal is dependent on fat, since the presence of fat in the stomach will delay its emptying rate and decrease hunger pangs. The hungry feeling that occurs so quickly after Chinese food or a meal of vegetables is due to the low fat content of these meals. Even in weight-control diets, a certain amount of fat is necessary.

Fats are also necessary as carriers of the fat-soluble vitamins, vitamins A, D, E, and K. Vitamin A is present in butter in amounts depending on the diet of the cow and the season of the year. Margarine, which is manufactured from fats and oils, does not contain vitamin A unless it is fortified. (In some states, fortification of margarine is mandatory.) Margarine fortified with 15,000 units of vitamin A per pound, to match the average vitamin A content of butter, is available in most parts of the country, and some margarine is fortified with vitamin D as well. Vitamin E is found in vegetable oils and wheat germ oil.

Concern has risen about the high fat content of the American diet (40–50% of total calories). The U.S. Dietary Goals proposed by the Senate Select Committee on Nutrition and Human Needs in 1977 suggested a reduction in the overall fat consumption to 30% of total calories. It recommended a reduction in saturated fat to 10% of the total energy intake, balanced with a 10% intake of both polyunsaturated and monounsaturated fats. Another goal was the reduction of the cholesterol content (a fatlike substance) in the diet. These proposed changes have been advocated since many nutritionists feel that the excessive intake of saturated fats and cholesterol may increase the incidence of elevated blood lipids (fats), arteriosclerosis, and coronary heart disease. The fat in beef, lard, butter, milk, cheese, and chocolate contains a large percentage of saturated fatty acids. Polyunsaturated fats are found in most vegetable oils (corn, safflower, soybean), poultry, and fish. High-cholesterol-containing foods are organ meats, egg yolks, butter, cheese, cream, and shellfish.

KINDS OF FAT

Most fats contain mixtures of different fatty acids. There are a number of natural fatty acids in food; however, only a few of them are present in abundance. These are myristic, caproic, capric, palmitic, stearic, oleic, and linoleic acids (see Table 28-1). Fats differ in composition. A fat may have two long-chain fatty acids, such as the 18-carbon linolenic or oleic acid, and one short-chain fatty acid, such as the 4-carbon buytric acid. Some fatty acids are saturated, which means they have no double bonds between the carbon atoms. Fatty acids with double bonds are unsaturated. Some—linoleic acid, for example, which has two double bonds—are more unsaturated than others. The place in the chain where the unsaturation occurs can also vary. These differences in chemical structure—chain lengths, double bonds, and position of double bonds—explain the differences in the properties of fats.

The carbon chain of saturated acids is

$$
\begin{array}{ccccccc}
H & H & H & H & H & H & H \\
| & | & | & | & | & | & | \\
-C & -C & -C & -C & -C & -C & -C- \\
| & | & | & | & | & | & | \\
H & H & H & H & H & H & H
\end{array}
$$

An unsaturated acid chain is

$$
\begin{array}{cccc}
H & H & H & H \\
| & | & | & | \\
-C & -C & =C & -C- \\
| & & & | \\
H & & & H
\end{array}
$$

The degree of unsaturation also has much to do with the reaction of fats with oxygen at ordinary temperatures. Double bonds provide points in the molecule for the addition of oxy-

TABLE 28-1
Fatty Acid Content of Fats and Oils (Range of Values)

Source of Fat	Oleic (%)	Linoleic (%)	Stearic (%)	Palmitic (%)	Caproic (%)	Capric (%)	Myristic (%)
Butterfat[a]	18.7–33.4			26–41	1.4–3.0	1.7–3.2	5.4–14.6
Olive oil	65–85	4–15	1–3	7–16			
Coconut oil[b]	5–8	tr–2.5	1–3	8–11		6–10	13–19
Lard	41–51	2–15	5–14	20–28			1–4
Palm oil	38–52	5–11	2–7	32–45			5–6
Peanut oil	53–71	13–22	3–6	6–9			
Corn oil	19–49	34–62	2–5	8–12			
Cottonseed oil	23–35	42–54	1–3	20–23			
Safflower	13–21	73–79	1–4	3–6			
Soybean oil	15–33	43–56	2–6	7–11			

[a]Contains 3.2% butyric acid.
[b]Contains 51% lauric acid.
Source: Daniel Swern, *Bailey's Industrial Oils and Fat Products,* 3rd ed. (New York: Wiley, 1964), Chap. 6.

gen, hydrogen, iodine, or other reactive substances (hence the term *unsaturated*).

The higher the proportion of saturated acids, the harder the fat; the higher the proportion of unsaturated fatty acids, the softer the fat (see Table 28-2).

Saturated fatty acids or unsaturated fatty acids may be attached to the glycerol. The unsaturated fatty acids may be either in a linear configuration called *trans,* or bent at the position of the double bond, called *cis.*

Trans form of a fatty acid (stearic)

Unsaturated fatty acids exist naturally in the *cis* form, in which case the linearity of the molecules is disrupted at the double bond, as shown:

Cis form of a fatty acid (oleic)

The cis or trans form of the double bond has an effect on the melting temperature. The cis-form fatty acids have a much lower melting point than do the trans forms. The melting temperature is also lower for unsaturated fats than for saturated fats. Stearic acid, a saturated fat, has a melting point of 157°F (69°C) compared to monounsaturated oleic acid, 61°F (16°C) and triunsaturated linolenic acid, 12°F (−11°C).

The length of the fatty acid chain is another factor influencing the melting point. Long-chain fatty acids such as stearic (C_{18}) have a much higher melting point than do short-chain fatty acids such as butyric, found in butter (C_4, 18°F or −8°C). The melting points of solid fats are variable as a result of the mixture of the saturated and unsaturated fatty acids; the cis and trans forms; and the monoglycerides, diglycerides, and triglycerides. This mixture of fats will melt very slowly as the temperature increases as a result of the mixture of melting points.

Most of the vegetable and animal fats and oils used for food are close to 100% fat (Table 28-3). In butter, margarine, bacon, and salt pork, water and other nutrients are present in varying amounts. Lard, hydrogenated fat, and vegetable oils are 100% fat.

Flavor. The flavor of butter is highly valued. It is frequently preferred over other fats for cooking. Many people consider the flavor of margarine equal to that of butter. Bacon fat, because of its availability and pleasant taste, is frequently used for frying vegetables.

Olive oil, corn oil, cottonseed oil, and peanut oil are used for cooking. Of the oils commonly

TABLE 28-2
Fatty Acids Commonly Found in Food (Saturated and Unsaturated)

Saturated	Number of Carbon Atoms	Unsaturated	Number of Carbon Atoms[a]
Butyric (C_3H_7COOH)	4	Oleic ($C_{18}H_{34}O_2$)	18 (1 double bond)
Caproic ($C_5H_{11}COOH$)	6	Linoleic ($C_{18}H_{32}O_2$)	18 (2 double bonds)
Caprylic ($C_7H_{15}COOH$)	8	Linolenic ($C_{18}H_{30}O_2$)	18 (3 double bonds)
Capric ($C_9H_{19}COOH$)	10		
Lauric ($C_{11}H_{23}COOH$)	12		
Palmitic ($C_{15}H_{31}COOH$)	16		
Stearic ($C_{17}H_{35}COOH$)	18		

[a]The number of double bonds indicates the degree of unsaturation (that is, number of places for the addition of other atoms).

Source: L. Stanley and A. Cline, *Foods: Their Selection and Preparation* (Boston: Ginn, 1950), p. 137.

used in salad dressings and for cooking and baking, only olive oil has a characteristic flavor. Olive oil is used mainly in the sautéing of foods. Cottonseed oil, corn oil, peanut oil, and soybean oil because of their bland flavor, are excellent for salad dressings.

All fats, mild-flavored or bland, tend to accentuate the flavors of the foods to which they are added.

FAT CRYSTALS

The solid fats are mixtures of microscopic crystals that may trap liquid inside the crystalline formation. Unlike water, fat molecules will become more dense when crystallized. Consequently, when the fat is melted, the volume will increase. An equal volume of melted fat will weigh less than that volume of solid fat.

There are four types of crystals: alpha, beta prime, intermediate, and beta. Alpha crystals are very fragile and transparent. These are the small, unstable crystals that are formed in frozen desserts and candies. The beta prime crystals are somewhat larger and more stable in cooking. This crystal is best for cooking purposes. There is an intermediate form that occurs as the beta

prime crystals change into beta crystals. The beta crystals are coarse and grainy and give these characteristics to the food product. These occur when fats are cooled slowly or stored for a length of time.

ECONOMIC ASPECTS

The cost of a fat or oil depends on the original cost of the product in which it is found and on the processing involved. The supply of and demand for the fat also play an important role in its cost. Modern food technology has brought about dramatic changes in fat and oil production in the United States. New techniques of oil refinement have made possible improved supplies of fats and oils extracted from meats, grains, cottonseed, soybeans, peanuts, olives, and coconuts. Agricultural research has been effective in improving the acreage yields of oil seeds and grains and in producing meat animals with high fat content. Recently, there has been a change in the consumption of fat in the United States. One noticeable difference is the increased substitution of margarine for butter and the increased consumption of cooking and salad oils. Also, Americans have increased their consumption of total

TABLE 28-3
**Fatty Acids in Some Animal and Plant Products (Grams per 100 Grams
of Total Fatty Acids)**

Source of Fat	Saturated			Unsaturated		
	Total	Palmitic C_{16}	Stearic C_{18}	Oleic $C_{18} - 2H$	Linoleic $C_{18} - 4H$	Other Un-saturated
Separated fats and oils						
Butter	59	27	12	35	3	3
Cacao butter	59	24	35	38	2	1
Corn oil	12	8	3	30	55	3
Cottonseed oil	26	23	2	22	51	1
Lard	40	32	8	48	11	1
Linseed oil	10	(8)	(2)	22	18	50
Margarine	27	22	3	60	9	4
Olive oil	12	9	2	80	8	—
Palm oil	48	41	5	42	8	2
Peanut oil	19	8	6	50	31	—
Safflower oil	8	3	4	15	76	1
Sesame oil	15	9	5	40	44	1
Shortening, hydrogenated	24	15	7	68	8	—
Soybean oil	18	9	6	21	55	6
Sunflower oil	12	6	5	21	66	1

Source: Collie Mae Coons, "Fats and Fatty Acids," in *Food: The Yearbook of Agriculture* (Washington,
D.C.: U.S. Department of Agriculture, 1959), p. 85.

fats, and are getting more of their calories from
fat and less from carbohydrates than they did 50
years ago.[1]

The costs of fats with near or comparable
food values vary. Margarine is less expensive
than butter, and lard is as expensive as—or only
slightly less expensive than—hydrogenated fats.
Olive oil is generally more expensive than other
vegetable oils; imported olive oils are far more
costly than those produced in the United States.

PRODUCTION OF FATS

Fats are extracted from animal products by a
process called *rendering*. There are two methods
of rendering fats, steam and dry. In steam rendering, steam for 15 seconds is used to extract
the fat from pulverized meat and meat products.

In dry rendering, the fat is heated in a closed
vacuum container to prevent its contact with
oxygen. Lard is manufactured in this manner
because it produces a more cooked flavor.

The oils from plant products are extracted
with a solvent after the seed or grain has
been heated and crushed. Contaminants such as
protein are coagulated and filtered or centrifuged out.

Contaminants and undesirable fatty acids
present in the fat will cause it to deteriorate
faster. They are removed by refining, a process
in which the oil is made into an alkaline emulsion, heated, extracted, and washed. This process
is repeated until the fats are approximately
99.5% pure. Bleaching and deodorizing finalize
the refining process.

Fluid oils and soft fats can be solidified by
hydrogenation. This is a process utilizing heat
and nickel as a catalyst in which hydrogen atoms
are added to the double bonds present in unsaturated fats. The hydrogenated fat is cooled to
65°F (20°C) and subjected to pressure with
nitrogen gas for 30 seconds while being stirred.

[1] B. Friend and F. Clark, "Changes in Sources of
Nutrients," in *Food: The Yearbook of Agriculture*
(Washington, D.C.: U.S. Department of Agriculture,
1959), p. 602.

The pressure is suddenly released, which disperses the nitrogen throughout the liquid. The fat is then tempered at controlled temperatures for several days to produce small crystals. These small crystals are stable, even at fluctuating temperatures. During the hydrogenation process, some of the cis forms of the fatty acids are converted to the trans form. This conversion helps in the solidification of the fat.

BUTTER

According to federal regulations, butter must contain 80% butterfat. The other constituents of butter are water, salt, and some natural milk constituents. Butter is a good source of vitamin A, and its popularity stems from its good flavor. It is made by the separation of butterfat from cream through mechanical agitation (churning). Ripened (sour) cream or sweet cream is used, and salt and coloring matter (carotene) may or may not be added. Before the cream is made into butter, its acidity is adjusted by the addition of an alkali and it is pasteurized and ripened. The ripening process starts after the introduction of starters, such as lactic acid bacteria. The churning of the cream reverses its oil-in-water system to a water-in-oil system (butter). The butter is then washed, and worked to press out the buttermilk. Most butter is salted at this stage. Whipped butter has been whipped with air to increase its spreadability. Each tablespoon has only one-half the weight and calories (50) than unwhipped butter (100).

Butter contains both saturated and unsaturated fatty acids. Approximately 40% are unsaturated. The following fatty acids are found in butter: palmitic, stearic, butyric, lauric, and capric. Oleic and linoleic acids are the unsaturated fatty acids present in largest amount. Butterfat contains more butyric acid than any other known fat.

Federal grading of butter is not compulsory, but the U.S. grade label on the outside of the carton or wrapper carries the assurance that the butter within has been tested by a government grader at the request of the packer or processor (see Fig. 28-1). A grade label without the federal stamp means that the processor has tested the butter and found it up to federal standards for the grade indicated. Government standards for

28-1 *U.S. grades for butter appear on cartons. Grades may also be found on paper wrappers of pound, half-pound, or quarter-pound packages. (Courtesy of U.S. Department of Agriculture)*

grading butter are based on flavor, body or texture, color, and salt content.

A water-soluble dry packaged form of butter has recently appeared on the market. Sweet cream butter is saponified and esterified to produce butter esters and derivatives which are later dried. The powder is reconstituted by mixing with hot water and has the flavor of fresh melted butter. It is recommended for use wherever melted butter is needed. When this reconstituted butter is incorporated as part of the food as in baking or cooking, it must be supplemented with real fat to increase the weight and cooking qualities.

Storage. Butter absorbs odors so rapidly that it must be stored covered. Like other fats, butter needs protection from heat, light, and air. The best temperature range for short storage periods is 32–35°F (0–1°C). Because freezing does not cause any deterioration in butter, it may be stored for from 5–6 months at 0°F (−18°C). Unsalted butter is more perishable than the salted form, since the salt is not present to act as a preservative.

MARGARINE

Margarine is prepared by blending highly refined animal and vegetable fats (or vegetable fats alone) with salt and properly cultured and ripened skim milk. Ground soybeans may also be added as part of the nonfat solids. Additional additives may include the following: diacetyl for butter flavor, sodium benzoate or benzoic acid for preservation, mono- and diglycerides or lecithin for emulsification, yellow coloring matter, and vitamins A and D. The label must state the fats and other ingredients used. Margarines reduced in calories are marked *imitation margarine;* they contain about half the amount of fat real margarine must contain.

Many consumers mistakenly believe that all margarines are high in polyunsaturates. However, during the hydrogenation process, monosaturates, which do not function as do polyunsaturates, are formed. The shifts from the cis to the trans forms of the fatty acids also decreases the effectiveness of the polyunsaturated fatty acids. Regular margarines generally have a polyunsaturated/saturated (P/S) ratio of $0.2:1.5$. Special margarines are produced that are high in polyunsaturates and have a P/S ratio of $1.0:2.4$. These special margarines are labeled as such and usually cost almost as much as butter.

HYDROGENATED FATS

Vegetable shortenings are fats manufactured from refined, bleached vegetable oils that have been changed to a plastic state by hydrogenation. These fats are whipped or aerated to give them added plasticity and a whiter appearance. Most shortenings on the market are superglycerinated. All-purpose shortenings are used commercially. Superglycerinated shortenings—all-purpose shortening to which about 5% of monoglycerides and diglycerides have been added to improve the emulsifying properties—are used in making cakes. There are some hydrogenated fats that contain both animal and vegetable fat. This information is given on the label.

OILS

Vegetable oils are designated either by the name of the vegetables from which they are made or by trade names. The important edible oils are corn oil, cottonseed oil, peanut oil, and soybean oil.

Corn oil is expressed from the germ of the corn grain. Most of the corn oil produced in the United States is sold as salad oil. Cottonseed oil—expressed from the seed of the cotton plant—solidifies at temperatures of 40–45°F (5–7°C), so it must be "winterized" to produce a salad oil. The process of winterizing an oil consists of chilling it to a temperature of 40–50°F (5–7°C) and removing, by filtration, the precipitated solid crystals. Corn oil is a natural winter oil, very suitable for the preparation of salad dressings. Soybean oil does not need to be winterized.

Olive oil is of great importance because of its excellent flavor. The highest-quality olive oil is *virgin oil,* that oil expressed first under light pressure and not further refined. Most olive oil on the market is expressed under heavy pressure and undergoes further treatment. When olive oil is blended with other oils, the contents of the blend must be clearly stated on the container. Olive oil will easily oxidize into an oil with a strong flavor. Careful protection from light and heat will increase its shelf life considerably.

Peanut oil is expressed from peanuts and can be used for all purposes, although it is used mainly as a salad oil. Soybean oil—expressed from soybeans—is subject to flavor reversion and must be deodorized in the manufacture of hydrogenated fats. Packaging oils in dark glass containers offers protection from light and decreases the possibility of rancidity.

LARD

Lard varies in composition and general characteristics according to the feed given the hog and the parts of the animal from which the lard is obtained. Lard from hogs fed on soybeans or peanuts is much softer than lard from corn-fed hogs, and lard made from the fat adhering to the organs of the animal is firmer than that made from the fat of other parts of the carcass.

Prime steam lard comes from the fat that is stripped from the internal organs of the animal at the time of slaughter or trimmed from the various market cuts. The fatty tissue is heated in a closed tank under 30–60 lb of steam pressure and then rapidly cooled to assure a smooth texture.

Dry-rendered leaf lard is made from the internal fat of the hog (except that which adheres to the intestines). It is firmer than other lards and slightly grainy because of the slow chilling it undergoes. It also keeps better than other kinds of lard.

Hydrogenated lards—lards to which hydrogen has been added chemically, thus raising their melting point—are marketed under trade names.

Rearranged Lard. The beta prime fat crystals in lard have the tendency to convert to the coarse, grainy beta crystals with storage. This is prevented by rearranging (interesterifying) the position of the fatty acids on the glycerol molecule. Heating the lard with a catalyst will cause the fatty acid radicals to recombine with glycerol in a heterogenous fashion, making the lard crystals smaller. The creaming properties of the rearranged lard are greatly improved by this process and may be used as a product that takes the place of hydrogenated shortening.

PEANUT BUTTER

At present, peanut butter is the only nut butter manufactured in significant quantity in the United States and is made by grinding roasted blanched peanuts and adding salt. To this mixture a stabilizer can be added to prevent the oils from separation. Its excellent nutty flavor and good spreadability enhance its importance. Peanut butter blends very easily with other foods and is frequently used as a substitute for other fats in cakes, cookies, and hot breads. It contains about 50% fat, which accounts for its high caloric content (2,635 calories/lb).

INVISIBLE FATS

Many foods contain large amounts of fats that are not apparent by their appearance. Avocados are 16% fat; egg yolk, 31%; sweet chocolate, 35%; prime beef, 41%; almonds, 58%; pound cake, 30%; Cheddar cheese, 32%; and mayonnaise, 80%. The high caloric content of these foods is directly attibutable to the high fat content.

USES OF FAT IN COOKERY

Fats and oils have numerous uses in cookery. They add flavor and nutritive value to a food, prevent particles of food from sticking to one another or to pans, serve as a cooking medium in which to fry foods, and enhance flour mixtures by imparting a shortened quality to batters and doughs, thus tenderizing them. And in cakes, fats hold in air incorporated during the beating of the mixture. They also serve as a chief ingredient in preparing foods that form emulsions. Some fats are suitable for all purposes, but some—because of their physical properties—have limited uses.

Frying. In pan-frying, the fat serves as a lubricant and as a heat-transfer medium. Pan-fried food develops a brown crust and absorbs some of the flavor of the fat. Deep-fat fried foods are golden brown and crisp.

SMOKE POINT. A suitable fat for frying food is one that has a fairly high smoke point (Table 28-4). This quality is of prime importance in deep-fat frying because the temperatures reached are higher than in pan frying. When fat begins to smoke, its chemical breakdown begins and free fatty acids and acrolein are formed from glycerol.

Glycerol　　　Acrolein　　Water

If the fat is permitted to smoke for any period of time, the acrolein causes irritation of the eyes and nostrils. Because the highest temperature necessary for the cooking of any food is close to 390°F (199°C), any fat used should have a smoke point well above that. A smoke point of about 420°F (216°C) is considered good for oil

TABLE 28-4
Smoke Points of Some Fats and Oils

	Smoke Point	
Fats	°F	0°C
Corn oil, cottonseed oil, or peanut oil[a]	450	232
Shortenings (containing[b] no emulsifiers)	450	232
Lard[b]	360–400	182–204
Shortenings (containing monoglyceride emulsifiers)[c]	300–350	149–177

[a]*Source:* K. Mattil, F. Norris, A. Stirton, and D. Swern, *Bailey's Industrial Oils and Fat Products,* 3rd ed., ed. D. Swern (New York: Interscience, 1964), p. 123.
[b]*Source:* B. Lowe, S. Pradhan, and J. Kastelic, "The Free Fatty Acid Content and Smoke Points of Some Fats," *J. Home Econ.* **50:**778, 1958.
[c]*Source:* Private correspondence, Lever Bros. Co., January 1968.

and shortenings that do not contain emulsifiers.[2] Studies show that the higher the content of free fatty acids in a fat, the lower the smoke point.[3]

Cooking oils and all hydrogenated fats decompose at a higher temperatures than lard, butter, and mixtures of animal and vegetable fats. The smoke points of lards vary. Lard is used in deep-fat frying because of the flavor and luster it imparts to foods, but some lards have smoke points below those of vegetable oils. For practical purposes, it is important to note that the smoke point of a fat, although related to free fatty acid content, also varies with the handling accorded the fat. A fat that has had repeated or prolonged use will begin to smoke at a temperature too low for frying.[4] Shortenings that contain emulsifiers (used to improve baking quality) have a lower smoke point.

The smoke point of a fat is also lowered with increases in the number of food particles dispersed through the fat, as in the frying of foods coated with flour or bread crumbs. Small particles of food break off, increasing the total surface of food exposed to the fat.

Cooking utensils, too, have an effect on the smoke point of the fat. Fats heated in shallow, wide pans with slightly sloping sides begin to smoke at lower temperatures than do those heated in smaller pans with vertical sides.

Thus, the smoke point of each fat may vary within fairly wide limits, depending on the amount of free fatty acids present, the relative amount of surface exposed to the fat, the presence of foreign particles, and the addition of such emulsifiers as monoglycerides and diglycerides.

Fried foods that absorb a good deal of fat are considered unpalatable. In flour mixtures, such as doughnuts, the proportions of sugar, liquid, and leavening affect the amount of fat absorbed. The absorption of fat increases as the proportion of each of these ingredients is increased.[5]

Different foods require different temperatures for frying. Table 28-5 provides a time and temperature chart as a guide for deep-fat frying.

French-fried potatoes must be carefully prepared. The utensil in which potatoes are fried must not be overloaded. The amount of fat in the frying kettle should be adequate for the amount of food to be cooked but should not fill the pan more than halfway, since fat will expand and foam with heating. When too many potatoes are immersed in the fat, the temperature drops, cooking time is prolonged, and the potatoes become soggy and grease-soaked. Soaking

[2] F. C. Martin, "Processing of Soybean Oil for Edible Purposes," Regional Oil Conference, Teheran (Saudi Teheran, Iran: Soybeans Council of America, 1964), p. 39.
[3] Belle Lowe, S. Pradhan, and J. Kastelic, "The Free Fatty Acid Content and Smoke Points of Some Fats," *J. Home Econ.* **50:**778, 1958.
[4] M. Bennion and F. Hanning, "Decomposition of Lard in the Frying of French Fried Potatoes and of Fritter-Type Batters," *J. Home Econ.* **48:**184, 1956.

[5] Belle Lowe, *Experimental Cookery,* 4th ed. (New York: Wiley, 1955), p. 535.

TABLE 28-5
Time and Temperature Chart for Deep-Fat Frying

Product	Temperature of Fat °F	Temperature of Fat °C	Time Required to Brown 1-In. Bread Cube (sec)
Chicken	350	177	60
Doughnuts, fritters, oysters, scallops, soft-shell crabs, fish	350–375	177–191	60
Croquettes, eggplant, onions, cauliflower	375–385	191–196	40
French-fried potatoes	385–395	196–202	20

Source: Terminology Committee of Food and Nutrition, *Handbook of Food Preparation,* rev. ed. (Washington, D.C.: American Home Economics Association, 1971).

the cut potatoes in cold water before frying removes some of the sugar content and prevents overbrowning. The water must be carefully drained before the potatoes are immersed in the fat so that the fat will not bubble and foam. After a fat has been used for frying, it can be strained through several thicknesses of cheesecloth and stored in the refrigerator. For efficient reuse, some fresh fat should be added to the filtered fat.

SHORTENINGS

To shorten a flour mixture is to tenderize it by limiting the amount of long gluten strands that can be formed.

The shortening effect is brought about by the formation of fat layers that serve to separate the starch and gluten particles, thus reducing their tendency to adhere to one another. Lard and vegetable shortenings are used extensively in the preparation of flour mixtures. Vegetable shortenings, because they hold in most of the air that is incorporated during mixing, seem to be preferred for cake products; lard, being softer, is somewhat superior in shortening value and is frequently used in making pies, biscuits, and shortcakes.

Vegetable shortenings may be of the compound or blended variety, or of the hydrogenated type. The compound, a blend of vegetable and animal fats, is not as stable as hydrogenated shortening. Generally, hydrogenated shortenings cost more than the compounds because their manufacture is more expensive; they are made by partially hydrogenating all the oil or by

treating part of the oil until it is about hardened and adjusting the mixture with small amounts of unhardened oil. (Complete hydrogenation of an oil would make the fat too hard.) Superglycerinated shortenings are made by adding about 2–5% monoglycerides and diglycerides to hydrogenated shortening so as to improve baking and emulsifying properties.

Shortening Agents. Shortening agents are fats characterized by their plasticity, which enables them to combine readily with the ingredients in flour mixtures. The purpose of using shortening in such mixtures is to make the baked product tender and—in some cases—flaky. When a fat is selected for baking, careful consideration must be given to its flavor, odor, and plasticity. All shortenings used in the preparation of flour mixtures should be completely devoid of strong flavors or odors.

Shortening Value. Products such as butter and margarine which are 80–85% fat, do not have as high a shortening value as do products that are 100% fat.

The shortening value of a fat is defined as its ability to tenderize baked products; this ability is commonly measured by the Bailey Shortometer, an instrument that measures the amount of weight required to break pastry or cookies of definite size and thickness.

SALAD DRESSING

Salad dressings contain fat in the form of a permanent or semipermanent emulsion. The fat may be any oil or a well-flavored solid or semisolid fat. Although occasionally a single food, such as vinegar or sour cream, may be used as a salad dressing, the term is used to designate products that have acid, fat, and seasonings as the basic ingredients. Lemon juice and vinegar are the acids most often used in a salad dressing, and seasonings such as salt, pepper, paprika, red pepper, onion, mustard, sugar, and a number of herbs may serve to add flavor to the product. The condiments in a salad dressing help to bring about temporary emulsification of the mixture.

Salad dressings may be a simple oil and vinegar mixture, French, cooked, mayonnaise, or a variation of these.

French dressings and mayonnaise depend for proper consistency on the ability of the salad oil used to form an emulsion. In both mayonnaise and French dressing, the oil is dispersed in a small amount of water, and small amounts of acids and flavoring materials are added to the fat and water to help form either a temporary or a permanent emulsion. Mayonnaise is an example of a permanent emulsion; French dressing is a temporary emulsion.

Oils Used in Salad Dressing. The fat used in making a salad dressing may be a vegetable oil—such as corn oil, cottonseed oil, peanut oil, olive oil—or a combination of these. The important factor in the selection of an oil for a salad is a bland or mild flavor. An oil that is used in the preparation of salad dressings should be easy to pour from its container when cold and should not crystallize and break the emulsion of mayonnaise-type salad dressings. Cottonseed oil solidifies at rather high temperatures, making it undesirable for use as a salad oil unless it is "winterized."

Mineral oil should never be used as a salad oil because it interferes with the absorption of fat-soluble vitamins.

Mayonnaise. Mayonnaise is a semisolid emulsion of vegetable oil, egg yolk or whole egg, acid, and seasonings. The emulsifying agent in this mixture is the egg yolk protein (vitellin), which serves as a protective colloid by lowering the surface tension of the liquids. The films formed around the droplets of oil stabilize the emulsion. The egg yolk is itself an emulsion and is the nucleus around which the mayonnaise emulsion forms. The egg white is frequently included, and

although it has no function in the emulsification of the mayonnaise, it lightens the finished product. Fresh and frozen egg yolks may be used to make this type of salad dressing. The vinegar used in making mayonnaise constitutes most of the liquid in the emulsion. The acidity of this material may reduce the tendency of the oil to become rancid. White distilled, malt, or cider vinegars may be used in making mayonnaise. Mustard is frequently included as a flavoring material. (Becher[6] suggests that the finely divided mustard aids in the stabilization of the emulsion.) Other spices are added to taste.

The oil most used in making mayonnaise is corn oil or cottonseed oil. It is desirable to use a winterized oil so as to prevent crystallization of fatty acids and subsequent interference with the emulsion. By law, mayonnaise must contain 65% oil. Commercial levels run as high as 75%.

French Dressing. The products known as French dressings are mixtures of vinegar and vegetable oils with salt and spices added. The ingredients are combined by agitation, which breaks up the oil into small particles and disperses them evenly throughout the acid ingredient. Although this emulsion is not as stable as that formed in mayonnaise, it is more stable than an ordinary oil-in-water emulsion. The dry ingredients used as flavoring materials tend to remain in solution as particles, thus helping to keep the fat globules apart. In a home-style French dressing, the acid/oil ratio is 1:3.

In commercially prepared French dressing, condiments, eggs, tomato sauce, and other materials are used to aid in emulsification. The emulsions formed are thus likely to be more stable than those of French dressings made at home. Commercial French dressings must contain not less than 35% oil.

Cooked Salad Dressings. Cooked salad dressings are mixtures of egg, vinegar, starch, fat or salad oil, and seasonings. Milk may also be a part of the liquid content. The liquid ingredients are thickened with egg or with a combination of egg and starch. Usually, flour is the thickener employed. The fat used may be butter, margarine,

[6] Paul Becher, *Emulsions: Theory and Practice* (New York: Reinhold, 1965), p. 345.

or cream. When both starch and egg are used as thickeners, the water and starch must be heated to the boiling point before the egg is added. Cooked dressings may be varied by using fruit juices in place of vinegar, milk, or water. Other sweetening may be used in place of sugar, and cream may be used in place of butter or margarine.

Cooked salad dressings are properly stored in a covered container in the refrigerator. They are susceptible to spoilage from mold. Commercial cooked dressings must contain not less than 30% oil.

FAT RANCIDITY

Deterioration of fat is attributed chiefly to oxidation and enzyme action. When fats are exposed to air, they readily take up oxygen and lose a hydrogen.

$$\underset{\text{Unsaturated fatty acid}}{-\overset{\text{H}}{\underset{\text{H}}{C}}-\overset{\text{H}}{\underset{\text{H}}{C}}=\overset{\text{H}}{C}-\overset{\text{H}}{\underset{\text{H}}{C}}-} \xrightarrow[\text{oxygen}]{\text{catalyst}} \underset{\text{Activated peroxide fatty acid}}{-\overset{\text{O-O·}}{\underset{}{C}}-\overset{}{\underset{\text{H}}{C}}=\overset{}{C}-\overset{\text{H}}{\underset{\text{H}}{C}}-}$$

The activated peroxides that are formed will pick up another hydrogen from other unsaturated fatty acids to form a hydroperoxide.

$$\underset{\text{Activated peroxide fatty acid}}{-\overset{\text{O-O·}}{C}-C=C-C-} + \underset{\text{Unsaturated fatty acid}}{-C-C=C-C-} \longrightarrow$$

$$\underset{\text{Hydroperoxide}}{-\overset{\text{O-OH}}{C}-C=C-C-} + \underset{\text{Free-radical fatty acid}}{-C-C=C-C-}$$

The free radicals are autocatalytic and begin a chain reaction repeating this process, quickly turning the fat rancid. The degree to which fat becomes oxidized depends mainly on their degree of saturation, because hydrogenation increases the fat's resistance to rancidity. Oxidation is accelerated by high temperatures, light, and the presence of pro-oxidants (such as copper, iron, and nickel). The iron-containing protein in meat, hematin, is responsible for fatty acid oxidations in meat. If this process has begun, it will continue even if the meat is frozen to a limited degree. This limits the storage time of meat. Control of these factors and the addition of antioxidants will serve to retard rancidity.

Enzymatic activity causes a particular type of rancidity. The action of the enzyme lipase causes hydrolysis of the fat, freeing fatty acids and glycerol. Lipase is more active at room temperature than chilled, explaining why fats such as butter turn rancid at room temperatures. This rancidity creates an objectionable odor and a soapy flavor. On the other hand, the enzyme catalase has been reported to inhibit oxidation.

Reversion. Reversion is an undesirable "beany" or "fishy" flavor which develops prior to rancidity. It occurs primarily in oils that have a high proportion of linolenic acid. This reaction is catalyzed by metals, ultraviolet light, and heat. Soybean oil is particularly susceptible to flavor reversion, owing probably to the trace amounts of iron and copper that it contains. The addition of sequesterants such as EDTA has improved this problem.

Certain microbes cause spoilage in such fat-rich foods as butter, margarine churned in milk, meat fat, and salad dressing. The enzymes given off by bacteria and molds are capable of decomposing the fatty acids contained in these foods, causing them to smell and taste badly.

Antioxidants. Antioxidants prevent oxidation from taking place in one of two ways. They may be oxidized themselves and donate their hydrogen to the fat. Or they may sequester (bind up) catalytic factors such as metals. A number of antioxidants occur naturally in fats and oils. The best-known of these is a group known as the *tocopherols* (vitamin E). The higher stability of vegetable oils, as compared with animal oils, is the result of their greater tocopherol content. Lecithin, a fatlike substance, gum guaiac, and seasamol (found in sesame oil) also possess antioxidant properties. At present, the antioxidants mentioned, and several others, such as butylated hydroxyanisole (BHA), butylated hydroxytoluene (BHT), propyl gallate, and gallic acid, are permitted by federal law to be used in animal fats. Often a synergistic compound is added to increase the antioxidant effect. Citric acid, ascorbic acid, EDTA (ethylenediaminetetraacetic acid), and phosphoric acids are common synergistic compounds.

Oxidation can also be retarded by protecting fat from light and air, and by storing it at a cool temperature. Colored glass and wrappers have been found to be effective in reducing the penetration of wavelengths active in catalyzing oxidation.

SUMMARY

Fat and oil are different physical states of the same group of substances. An oil is liquid at room temperature, whereas fat is solid or semisolid. Raising or lowering temperatures will change the physical state of both. A concentrated source of energy, fat adds a satisfying quality and palatability to meals, and a certain amount is desirable in a well-rounded diet. Butter contains varying amounts of vitamin A. In most states, margarine is fortified with vitamins A and D. Composed of carbon, hydrogen, and oxygen, fats contain mixtures of different fatty acids. The fatty acids with no double bonds are saturated; those with double bonds are unsaturated. The higher the proportion of saturated acids, the harder the fat. Differences in chemical structure—chain lengths, double bonds, and position of double bonds—explain the differences in the properties of fat.

Fats most commonly used in foods are butter—valued for its flavor and nutritive value and required, by federal regulation, to contain 80% butterfat—margarine, olive oil, corn oil, cottonseed oil, peanut oil, lard, and hydrogenated fats. The cost of a fat or oil reflects the cost of the product from which it comes and the amount of processing required.

Butter may carry either an industry label or a U.S. grade label. Vegetable oils are designated by trade names or by their plant source. Hydrogenated shortenings made from refined, bleached vegetable oils and plasticized by hydrogenation may be all-purpose or superglycerinated. Margarine may be a blend of vegetable oils only or a blend of vegetable and animal fats. Other materials added are listed on the label. The characteristics of lard vary according to the part of the animal from which it is obtained and the feed given the animal.

In cookery, fats and oils add flavor and nutritive value, serve as a cooking medium, provide a lubricating action, prevent sticking of food particles, and incorporate air into and tenderize flour mixtures. Their specific use depends on their physical properties. Salad oil is bland or mild in flavor, pours easily when cold, and should not crystallize or break the emulsion of mayonnaise-type dressings.

Fats oxidize quickly when exposed to air. The rate of oxidation depends on their degree of saturation. Enzymatic activity may also cause deterioration. Addition of antioxidants and control of factors accelerating oxidation will retard rancidity of fats. Careful storage of butter is required because it absorbs odors rapidly.

QUESTIONS AND TOPICS FOR DISCUSSION AND STUDY

1. What is the difference between a fat and an oil?
2. What causes rancidity in a fat?
3. Explain hydrogenation. How does the process of hydrogenation alter a fat?
4. What fats are generally used in the manufacture of margarine?
5. What are antioxidants?
6. Why do some fats have a higher melting point than others?
7. Some oils become cloudy when stored in the refrigerator. Explain how winterizing prevents this from occurring.
8. What are the desirable characteristics of a fat used for deep-fat frying?
9. What material is formed when fat begins to smoke?
10. How does reusing fat affect its smoking point?
11. How do low temperatures affect the amount of fat absorbed in deep-fat frying?
12. What is the purpose of coating foods that are to be deep-fat fried?
13. Compare the composition of cooked salad dressing with that of mayonnaise.
14. What happens when a mayonnaise separates?
15. Which materials in salad dressings stabilize the emulsion?
16. Why is mechanical agitation important in breaking up the oil particles when making mayonnaise?

SUGGESTED ACTIVITIES

1. Prepare one or more of the following: mayonnaise, French dressing, and salad dressing. Use on salads.
2. Read the labels on as many cooking fats and table spreads as possible. Find the names of the common emulsifiers.
3. Compare different fats and oils for use in deep-fat frying. Rank them in order of your preference.
4. Prepare one or more of the following: french-fried potatoes, croquettes, fritters, and deep-fat fried chicken. Evaluate each for appearance and palatability.

REFERENCES

BOOKS

Becher, Paul. *Emulsions: Theory and Practice,* rev. ed. New York: Reinhold, 1965.

Food: The Yearbook of Agriculture. Washington, D.C.: U.S. Department of Agriculture, 1959, pp. 74–88.

Lee, Frank. *Basic Food Chemistry.* Westport, Conn.: Avi, 1975, Chap. 5.

Paul, Pauline, and Helen Palmer. *Food Theory and Applications.* New York: Wiley, 1972, Chap. 5.

Swern, Daniel. *Bailey's Industrial Oil and Fat Products,* 3rd ed. New York: Wiley, 1964.

ARTICLES AND BULLETINS

Bennion, M., and F. Hanning. "Decomposition of Lard in the Frying of French Fried Potatoes and of Fritter-Type Batters." *J. Home Econ.* **48:**184, 1956.

Bennion, M. and R. L. Park. "Changes in Fats During Frying." *J. Amer. Dietet. Assoc.* **60:**308, 1968.

Fleischman, A. I., et al. "Studies on Cooking Fats and Oils." *J. Amer. Dietet. Assoc.* **42:**394, 1963.

Kilgore, L., and M. Bailey. "Degradation of Fats During Frying." *J. Amer. Dietet. Assoc.* **56:**130, 1970.

"Know Your Butter Grades." *Bulletin 264.* Washington, D.C.: U.S. Department of Agriculture, rev. 1960.

Lowe, B., S. Pradhan, and J. Kastelic. "The Free Fatty Acid Content and Smoke Points of Some Fats." *J. Home Econ.* **50:**778, 1958.

Matthews, R. H., and E. H. Dawson. "Performance of Fats and Oils in Pastry and Biscuits." *Cereal Chem.* **40:**291, 1963.

Okos, Linda, and Rachel Hubbard. "Use of Low Fat Dairy Spread." *J. Home Econ.* **63:**266, 1971.

"Soybean and Cottonseed Oils Used in Shortening and Salad and Cooking Oils." *Market Research Report 898.* Washington, D.C.: U.S. Department of Agriculture, 1970.

Pastry

CHAPTER 29

The term *pastry,* used to designate a group of desserts, includes such baked products as pie, Danish pastry, and pastries made from puff paste. In America, few desserts are as popular as pie. The success of a pie depends mainly on the quality of the crust. Frequently, pie crust dough is used for products other than dessert pies—meat, fish, and poultry are sometimes prepared with a pie crust, casserole dishes of various kinds may be finished off with bits of pie crust, and small rounds of pie crust cut out with a biscuit cutter are used as the base for finger foods.

A plain pastry is generally used for pies. Baked, it should be golden brown in color and tender enough to cut with a fork, but not crumbly, and its surface should be flaky and "blistered" rather than compact and smooth.

The term *pastry* will refer to pie crust in the following discussion.

COMPOSITION

Although making pastry requires skill and judgment, the only ingredients used in this mixture are flour, salt, fat, and water.

All-purpose flour is generally used for plain pastry, but in some cases a pastry flour manufac-tured from a soft wheat flour is used to make a more tender mixture.

Instant-blending flours can be used; however, dough made with instant flour look and handle differently than those prepared with all-purpose flour.

Any one of the cooking fats may be used in pie crust, but some are easier to handle in the preparation of the dough and may therefore produce a more acceptable pie crust. Lard is more pliable and workable over a range of temperatures than other fats are. It is less brittle than refrigerated butter, margarine, and hydrogenated fat. The kind of shortening used in a pie crust or plain pastry depends to a large extent on the experience and personal preferences of the maker. Oils do not yield a flaky pastry, but they do make one that is mealy and tender. They are not easy to manage in the mixing of the pie dough, for they tend to soak up flour and leave little free flour for the addition of water. The resultant product is dry and greasy. (A certain amount of water is necessary to hydrate the starch and gluten and leaven the pastry.)

Fat Shortening Ability. The choice of a fat for pie dough is related to a number of factors: flavor, cost, and tenderness. Flavor and cost are

369

personal considerations. Tenderness is of such critical importance to the success of the product that many investigations have been undertaken to compare the shortening values of fats and oil. It has been suggested[1] that the shortening power of fat is lessened or increased according to its ability to cover a small or large surface area. And because the unsaturated fats (oils) are liquid, they are able to cover a much greater area than the saturated ones and thus have a greater shortening power. When other factors remain unchanged, the shortening power of a fat is increased as its concentration is increased. The concentration of the fat depends on the amount of water in its composition. The reaction of the fat to elevated temperatures is also important. Although low temperatures lessen the fat's ability to spread and cover a large area of the other ingredients, chilling the fat is often recommended because the gluten developed in flour absorbs water quickly at high temperatures and becomes attenuated, thus creating a larger surface area for the fat to cover. Laboratory experiments indicate that more tender pastry is produced when the ingredients are kept at room temperature (68–75°F; 20–24°C).

The fat ingredient in pie crust not only determines the flakiness or mealiness of the baked product, it also affects the flavor and color. To enhance flavor and color, butter and margarine (which have less shortening power than other plastic fats) are frequently used. When butter or margarine (both slightly over 80% fat) is the only shortening used in the pastry, the amount of water used must be reduced and some other adjustments made. When butter or margarine is substituted for a 100% fat such as lard, at least one-eighth more butter or margarine is needed.

Lard has long been recommended and used for pastry because of its excellent shortening power as well as its plasticity—thought to be essential for flakiness.[2] Moreover, many people prefer the flavor of pie crust made with lard.

Hydrogenated vegetable shortenings—because of their uniformity with respect to such qualities as plasticity, shortening power, and blandness of flavor—are frequently used in making pastry.

---

[1] Belle Lowe, *Experimental Cookery,* 4th ed. (New York: Wiley, 1955), p. 536.
[2] L. Stanley and A. Cline, *Foods: Their Selection and Preparation,* rev. ed. (Boston: Ginn, 1950), p. 148.

Superglycerinated hydrogenated fats are not necessary for pastry but can be used.

Water. Water is an important ingredient in pie crust. The function of water is to bind the dough by hydration of the gluten. The amount of water used in the basic pastry recipe is not constant; it varies with the proportion and composition of the shortening, the protein content of the flour, and the method of mixing. Too little water will result in an overcrumbly pastry; too much water will produce a tough and shrunken dough.

Salt. Salt is used to bring out the flavor of the crust. If it is omitted, the result is a bland, insipid crust.

Miscellaneous Ingredients. Commercial bakers use baking powder to reduce crust shrinkage, but the amount is limited to less than 1% of flour weight. Some bakers also use small amounts of corn syrup or nonfat dry milk solids to improve the color of the pie crust.

Proportions. Plain pastry or pie dough is very stiff. Most recipes use from one-third to one-half as much fat as flour. Using one-third as much fat as flour produces a very palatable crust. Salt is used in the proportion of ½ tsp to 1 cup flour, but adjustments should be made for salted butter or margarine. The liquid proportion is approximately 3 tbsp water to 1 cup flour. (The exact amount of water varies with the kind of flour and the amount of fat.)

PRINCIPLE OF PASTRY MAKING

The goal in making pastry is to manipulate the basic ingredients, which are in proper proportion to each other, so that the gluten strands formed are short. A pastry that has short strands of gluten will be tender when baked. Development of gluten strands can be decreased by avoiding overhandling of dough. Too much mixing and rolling make a tough crust.

METHODS OF MIXING

The techniques used for the manipulation of the ingredients in the dough determine the success or failure of the baked products. An entirely satisfactory product may be made by using one of several methods. One of the main points is to avoid overmixing.

The most common technique employed in mixing pie dough is to cut the fat into the flour and salt until the fat particles are about the size of peas and coated with flour (Fig. 29-1). This may be done with a pastry blender, fork, two knives, or fingertips. After the fat is incorporated into the flour, the water is added gradually so that it is distributed evenly among the fat–flour particles. Best results are obtained when the water is added gradually and stirred into the other ingredients with a fork. As the ingredients are tossed together, the dampened part of the dough mixture should be brought in contact with as much of the dry portion as possible. As soon as the flour mixture is dampened sufficiently to form a soft pliable ball of dough, it is ready to be placed in the refrigerator for a short time before rolling.

Rolling. When the ball of dough is ready to be rolled into a crust, it is placed on a lightly floured board or on a pastry cloth. Only enough pastry for one crust is rolled at a time. The rolling pin and the board must be lightly floured to prevent the dough from sticking. (A canvas cover on the board and a stockinette cover on the rolling pin will also prevent dough from sticking.) It is important to start with a smooth ball of dough, flat on top. Short strokes from the center of the pastry toward the edge in every direction will keep the round shape. Repeated strokes over the same area of dough will tend to make a tough crust. If possible, turning pastry over should be avoided, unless its tendency to stick is very great. For excellent results, pastry should be rolled to a ⅛-in. thickness before it is transferred to the pan for baking.

Variations of Mixing Methods. A flaky pie crust can be achieved by using a modified method of distributing the fat and water throughout the flour: a portion of the flour is blended with the water to form a paste, which is then added to the fat and flour mixture.

The hot-water method of mixing pastry produces a mealy but tender crust. Boiling water is poured over the fat and the two are beaten together until creamy. The blended fat and water are then stirred into the flour and salt mixture and tossed together with a fork until a ball of dough is formed. This dough must be chilled several hours before it is rolled.

Another pastry variation involves removing 2 tbsp of flour–fat mixture before the water is added and then sprinkling it over the rolled-out pastry. The pastry sheet is rolled up and then rolled out to fit the pie pan.

Oil is also used in making pastry. It is recommended that the oil and water be stirred together and added to the flour and salt. Some recipes call for milk instead of water as the liquid ingredient. Incomplete blending of liquid and dry ingredients makes the dough difficult to handle.

KINDS OF PIES

Pies are either of the one-crust or the two-crust variety. In a one-crust pie, the pie shell may be baked separately or together with the pie filling; in a two-crust pie, the filling (usually fruit) is placed between the crusts and all are baked together. Custard pies and variations are examples of one-shell pies that are baked with the filling in them. Chiffon and cream pies are examples of one-crust pies that are baked before the cooked or prepared filling is added.

One-Crust Pies. Custard and cream preparations are the principal kinds of fillings used in one-crust pies.

Cream fillings are usually made of a custard base in which the both egg and starch or flour are used to thicken the mixture. Usually, only the yolks of the eggs are used in the filling; the whites are reserved for the meringue. Milk, water, and fruit juice are the liquids used for making the typical cream filling. The right proportions and proper method of combining the ingredients are necessary to attain a palatable cream filling stiff enough to hold its shape when the pie is cut. Most fillings are cooked in a double boiler to prevent uneven cooking and scorching.

Because eggs coagulate at a lower temperature than that at which starch gelatinizes, it is necessary to cook the starch mixture thoroughly before cooking the eggs. If butter or margarine is added to the mixture, it is usually added when

(a) Stir flour and salt together in a mixing bowl. With a pastry blender, cut in the shortening thoroughly. Particles should be the size of tiny peas.

(b) Sprinkle water into the flour, a tablespoon at a time. Mix lightly with a fork after each tablespoon of water until all the flour is moistened.

(c) Mix the dough thoroughly until it cleans the sides of the bowl. At this point, just the right amount of gluten is developed.

29-1 Steps in preparing pie crust.

(d) Gather the dough together with your hands and press firmly into a ball. If the dough does not hold together, 1 to 2 tbsp. water may be added.

(e) To roll the pastry, use of a pastry cloth into which flour has been rubbed and a stockinette-covered rolling pin. Run the rolling pin across the floured board.

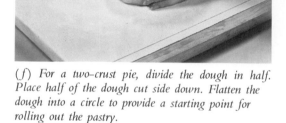

(f) For a two-crust pie, divide the dough in half. Place half of the dough cut side down. Flatten the dough into a circle to provide a starting point for rolling out the pastry.

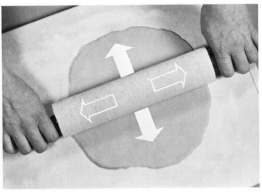

(g) *Roll from the center to the outside edges in all four directions. For even thickness, lift the rolling pin toward the edge. If edges begin to break, pinch together at once.*

(h) *Keep the pastry circular and roll it about 1½ in. larger all around than the inverted pie pan.*

(i) *Unfold. To prevent stretching, ease the pastry gently into the pan and press toward the center of the pan with fingertips. Stretching causes shrinkage during baking. (Courtesy of Betty Crocker of General Mills)*

the eggs have thickened. The cooked mixture is poured into the baked crust and covered with a meringue.

LEMON MERINGUE PIE. Lemon meringue is one of the most popular of the cream pies, but it presents several problems. When milk is used as the liquid ingredient, there is a slight tendency for it to curdle when the lemon juice is added. This is often avoided by using water instead of milk or by thickening the milk with the starch and cooling the mixture before adding the lemon juice. Another problem is the thinning effect of the lemon juice on the cooked starch mixture. To minimize the thinning of the starch gel, the starch paste–egg yolk mixture should always be cooked long enough to bring about extensive coagulation of the protein of the egg yolks for greater firmness in the filling before the acid is added.[3] The extra sugar is needed to add flavor and the additional starch to compensate for the thinning effect of lemon juice and sugar.

Cream pies are usually topped off with a meringue. This may be made with 2–3 tbsp sugar to each egg white used (2½ tbsp of sugar seems to be the measurement that produces best results). The egg whites are beaten with the salt, and the sugar is added gradually. The mixture is then beaten until it is stiff enough to hold its shape. The meringue is spooned over the hot pie filling and spread out to meet the crust around the edge of the pie. The continuous surface of meringue and crust prevents excessive shrinkage of the meringue during baking. The meringue-covered pie is placed back in the oven and baked at a temperature of 325°F (163°C) until the topping is a delicate brown.

Honey, syrup, or jelly (1 tbsp per egg white) may be used in place of sugar.

Hard meringue is used for meringue cases, which are hollow shells that are used to hold ice cream or fruit. A hard meringue is made with at least 4 tbsp sugar to each egg white, and it is baked slowly until dry. The proportion of sugar to egg white and the long, slow baking give the mixture a crisp crust.

The usual method of mixing meringue is to beat the whites until frothy, add the salt and cream of tartar, then continue beating, adding

[3] H. J. Neilson, J. D. Hewitt, and N. Fitch, "Factors Influencing Consistency of a Lemon Pie Filling," *J. Home Econ.* **44**:782, 1952.

the sugar gradually. For hard meringues, the mixture is shaped with a spoon or pastry bag into the desired size and shape on a baking sheet covered with unglazed brown paper. Meringues are baked slowly at 225–325°F (107–163°C) until they achieve the necessary crispness. A meringue torte is baked in a buttered spring pan to achieve the desired shape. (See Chapter 21 for additional information on baking meringues.)

CUSTARD PIES. Custard pies are prepared by pouring uncooked custard mixtures into an unbaked pie shell and baking the two together. There is a problem, however: when the oven temperature is set for baking custard, the crust bakes very slowly, absorbs liquid, and becomes soggy; on the other hand, if the temperature is high enough to bake the crust properly, it causes the custard filling to become tough and watery. Several solutions have been devised. One method is to set and brown the crust by placing it in a hot oven of 450°F (232°C) for 3–5 minutes before adding the warm custard filling. The filled pie is returned to the oven and baked for 10 minutes at 425°F (218°C), then at 325°C (163°C) until done. The most satisfactory method involves baking the crust and custard filling separately in pans of identical size and depth. When set, the custard filling is gently eased out of the pie pan into the cooked baked shell. (When this method is used, it is best to bake the pie shell upside down on the back of the pie pan to allow for the small difference in size between filling and crust that is desirable for a good fit.) Flavorings such as orange, lemon, vanilla, and maple may be added to custard pies.

Pumpkin pie is a variation of custard pie. Its chief ingredients are pumpkin, brown sugar or molasses, spices, milk, and eggs. Sweet potato, squash, and carrot pies are much like pumpkin pies with respect to method of preparation and palatability. The pecan pie is also considered to be a pie with a custard basis. The liquid ingredient, however, is syrup or molasses. A sour cream raisin pie is another rich variation of custard pie, as are some cheese pies.

CHIFFON PIES. A chiffon pie consists of a baked shell with a filling that has a gelatin or custard cream base. This type of pie filling should hold its shape when the pie is cut. Whipped cream or a soft meringue is used as a topping for chiffon pie.

Two-Crust Pies. Two-crust pies are made by placing the filling between two uncooked layers of dough. The filling is usually fruit and fruit juice, with sweetening and a thickener added. The top crust of a fruit pie may be solid, or it may be crisscrossed or latticed. Any form of fruit may be used—fresh, frozen, cooked, dried, or canned. The vast majority of fruit pie fillings make use of a thickening agent such as flour, cornstarch, or tapioca to give a light consistency to the mixture. Tapioca and cornstarch thicken the juice but leave it clear; flour thickens the juice but turns it slightly opaque. The proportions are 2–3 tbsp thickener to 1 qt of fruit filling. Many recipes direct that the fruit filling be precooked, thereby reducing the actual baking time for the pie. Other recipes suggest that only the juice and thickener be precooked. Still others recommend that neither fruit nor juice be precooked, but that the thickener be added to the filling just before the top crust is put on.

Baking. Before baking, a one-shell pie crust is pierced with a fork to allow the steam to escape. It is baked on the inside or on the outside of the pan for 15–18 minutes (or until light brown) at a temperature of 450°F (232°C). The pie dough should be fitted loosely into the pan. If the dough is stretched too tightly over the bottom, the shell will be too small and will not retain its shape. The temperature at which fruit pies are baked depends on the type of filling, the condition of the fruit, and the amount of sugar used in the filling. Generally, fruit pies are placed in a hot oven (425°F) (218°C) so that the lower crust will bake before the filling has had time to soak in and make it soggy. Fresh fruit pies—such as apple, rhubarb, and peach—are generally baked at 425°F (218°C) for 10 minutes, then at 350°F (177°C) (to give the fruit sufficient time to tenderize) until done. Fruit fillings should be adequately cooled before being poured into the bottom crust; warm fillings will tend to melt the shortening that is dispersed within the dough in layers, causing it to be absorbed by the dough. This will result in a mealy rather than a flaky pastry. Hot fillings may also cause the crust to become soggy. On the other hand, cold fillings may require longer than average baking time, so that the outer portion of the crust browns before the inner side is properly baked. Best results are obtained if the fillings are brought close to room temperature before being used.

BOILING OUT OF FRUIT FILLINGS. The tendency of fruit fillings to boil over in the oven is a common and trying problem. One way of preventing fruit juice spillover is to avoid an excessively low oven temperature and the resultant long baking time. Fillings that have insufficient solid contents, in the form of sugar or fruit, have a tendency to boil out before the pie is adequately baked. Another cause of spillover is insufficient thickening material. Too much sugar in a filling will cause the starch gel to break down and the thin and watery juice to boil out. This may be avoided by reducing the amount of sugar used in the pie filling.

Juice spillover may also be caused by certain techniques in handling the dough. If the dough is stretched over the bottom of the pie pan, the crust will inevitably shrink when it is baked and the filling will boil out. To prevent this, enough dough should be used for the bottom crust so that it extends well over the edge of the pie pan. The extra allowance is turned over onto the top crust to seal the edges and prevent the escape of juices. If the edge of the top crust is dampened before the bottom crust is folded over the edges will seal more securely. The sealed edge may then be fluted with the fingers or crimped with a fork.

MICROWAVE OVEN. Two crust pies and pastry shells can be baked in the microwave oven but they do not brown.[4]

PIE PANS

Aluminum, tin, and glass pie pans and dishes are suitable for the one- and two-crust pies. Peet and Thye[5] point out that aluminum pans with a dull gray alumilite finish rapidly absorb heat and that heat-resistant glass dishes absorb radiant energy extremely well. Both are especially desirable for oven use, although oven temperatures may have to be reduced for glass dishes.

[4]Helen Van Zante, *The Microwave Oven* (Boston: Houghton Mifflin, 1973), p. 109.
[5]L. J. Peet and L. S. Thye, *Household Equipment*, 4th ed. (New York: Wiley, 1961), p. 35.

PASTRY MIXES

The demand for pie crust mixes, like that for other prepared mixes, increases steadily. Pie crust mix is classified as an unleavened product made with soft wheat flour, or a mixture of hard and soft wheat flours, as the major ingredient. Various shortenings are used in pie crust mixes. They include completely hydrogenated vegetable oils, prime steam lard, and partially hydrogenated shortenings. The type of shortening used depends on the mixing methods used by a given manufacturer and on the total fat content of the given mix. The fat is sometimes "shattered"—that is, dispersed throughout the mixture in the form of fine granules. The flavor of the shortening is of basic consideration to the manufacturer. Completely deodorized, tasteless fats are frequently used to eliminate the occurrence of any flavor reversion. Some manufacturers, however, prefer the flavor and texture imparted to the crust by lard. The goal of the manufacturer is to produce a mix that resists rancidity yet produces a good pie crust.

Many varieties of fruit pies are commercially frozen and sold on the retail market. These differ greatly in quality, and each must be tested and carefully evaluated in terms of cost and palatability. Antioxidants are used in fillings and crust to maintain quality.

SUMMARY

Pastry is a baked product such as pie, Danish pastry, and puff pastry. Pies are the most popular form of pastry consumed in the United States. The quality of the crust is a chief factor in the success of a pie. Flavor, cost, and shortening power influence the choice of fat for pastry. The fat ingredient determines the character of the pastry, with oils yielding a mealy and tender crust and lard frequently recommended because of its shortening power and plasticity. When butter or margarine alone is used, the proportion of fat must be increased and the amount of water decreased.

Techniques of combining and handling and proportions of ingredients are important in producing successful pastry. Several methods will produce good results, but overmixing will result in tough pastry.

One-crust pies may be baked before filling—or the pie, as is the case with custard pies, may be filled before baking. But because oven temperatures, for the crust and filling are incompatible, some modification of method may be necessary. In two-crust pies, a filling, usually of fruit in any form, and often juice and a thickener, is placed between two uncooked layers of pastry. Temperature for baking depends on the form of the fruit and the amount of sugar used in the filling. The goal is to bake the lower crust before it can become soggy. Fruit fillings may be prevented from boiling over by avoiding an excessively low oven temperature and the resultant long baking period, by using adequate thickening—correct proportion of sugar to fruit and thickening material—and by handling the bottom crust carefully, in order to avoid stretching and resultant shrinkage. It may be necessary to reduce oven temperature for glass pie pans.

Various fats are used in pie crust mixes; the goal in manufacture is to produce a mix that will yield a good pie crust but will not become rancid quickly.

Many varieties of frozen pies are available—baked or ready for baking. There are great quality variations, and product evaluation is desirable.

QUESTIONS AND TOPICS FOR DISCUSSION AND STUDY

1. Explain the effect on pastry of using too great an amount of water in proportion to the other ingredients.
2. On what do the flakiness and the tenderness of pastry depend?
3. Why is it preferable to use a plastic fat if a flaky pastry is desired?
4. How does the excessive handling of ingredients affect the tenderness of pastry?
5. What are the possible reasons for juice spillover in a fruit pie?
6. Why is meringue baked at a low temperature?
7. Why, in mixing pastry, is it important to add the fat to the flour before adding the liquid?

SUGGESTED ACTIVITIES

1. Prepare pastry dough and make a one-crust or two-crust pie.
2. Compare lard, hydrogenated shortening, butter, and margarine for flavor, texture, and ease of handling in pastry dough.
3. Prepare pastry dough with oil as the shortening ingredient. Compare the dough with that made with plastic fats for flavor, texture, and ease of handling.
4. Prepare one or more of the following pies: fruit (fresh or canned), custard, pumpkin, pecan, and chiffon.

REFERENCES

BOOKS

Department of Foods and Nutrition, Kansas State University. *Practical Cookery,* New York: Wiley, 1966, p. 184.

Halliday, Evelyn, and Isabel Nobel. *Hows and Whys of Cooking,* rev. ed. Chicago: University of Chicago Press, 1946, Chap. 7.

Hughes, Osee. *Introductory Foods.* New York: Macmillan, 1962, Chap. 10.

Paul, Pauline. *Food Theory and Applications.* New York, Wiley, 1972, Chap. 5.

ARTICLES AND BULLETINS

"Finished Foods—A Third Report: Pie Crusts—From Recipe and Mix." *J. Home Econ.* **54**:767, 1962.

Rose, T. S. "Supplementary Study on Pastry Methods." *J. Home Econ.* **45**:337, 1953.

Rose, T. S., M. E. Dresslar, and K. A. Johnston. "The Effect of the Method of Fat and Water Incorporation on the Average Shortness and the Uniformity of Tenderness of Pastry." *J. Home Econ.* **44**:707, 1952.

Snow, P. R., and A. M. Briant. "Frozen Fillings for Quick Lemon Meringue Pies." *J. Home Econ.* **52**:350, 1960.

Tinklin, G. L., and A. K. Perry. "A Comparison of Quality, Acceptability, and Cost of Frozen Chocolate Cream Pies." *J. Home Econ.* **58**:808, 1966.

Wellmore, W. "Safeness and Servability of Meringued Pie." *J. Amer. Dietet. Assoc.* **43**:43, 1962.

Flour

CHAPTER **30**

WHEAT

The common wheat types grown in this country are hard winter wheat in the Southwest, hard spring wheat in the Northwest, hard and soft wheat in the Pacific Northwest, soft wheat in the area east of the Mississippi River, and durum wheat in North and South Dakota.

Hard red winter wheats are planted in the fall in regions where the winters are dry and not too cold. The wheat begins to grow before the onset of cold weather, becomes dormant during the winter, and resumes its growth in the spring. It attains maturity and is harvested in early summer. Hence, there is no spring delay caused by waiting until the fields become dry enough to cultivate. Kansas produces the most hard red winter wheat.

Hard red spring wheats are planted in the spring, as soon as the ground is dry. They are grown in a number of states in the Midwest. Minnesota, North Dakota, South Dakota, and Montana lead in the production of this wheat.

Durum wheats are grown in the Dakotas and Minnesota. They are seeded in the spring, as soon as the soil is dry. One fact that gives farmers less incentive to grow durum is that the yield per acre is lower than that for spring and winter wheats.

Soft red winter wheats require a greater amount of rainfall than hard wheat. They are grown in an area that lies east of the Mississippi River.

White wheats, like red wheats, are of two varieties: spring and winter. The principal areas for the production of soft white wheats are Oregon, California, and Washington, although some are grown in Michigan and New York. The character of white wheats is similar to that of the soft red winter wheats.

Uses. The hard wheat varieties are used principally for flours designed for the production of yeast-leavened bread. The soft wheats are particularly suited to making such baked products as cakes, pastries, and cookies. Durum wheats are used in making macaroni products.

FLOUR

Flour is used principally in making bread, pastry, cakes, cookies, and macaroni products. Refined wheat flour is generally used, although some whole-wheat and rye flours are also used.

Seventy percent or more of the milled flour in the United States is used for the production of bread flour; the remaining 30% is used for the production of cakes, cookies, pastries, and related products. A flour is carefully selected for its purpose: a wheat milled into a bread flour has a protein content of 11% or more; wheat milled into flour for cakes, cookies, and pastry has 8–11% protein content.

MANUFACTURE

The flour yield from any batch of wheat milled will be approximately 70–75%, because it is not possible, in the milling process, to obtain all the endosperm as flour. The remaining 25–30% of the grain is used for animal feed. If a grain shortage were to develop (as during World War II), it would be possible to obtain a higher flour yield, but the flour would be darker and the products baked with it would show a difference in color, texture, and volume.

Before wheat is crushed and separated into its various parts, it is scoured and brushed and conditioned by the addition of water and the application of heat. Conditioning makes it easier to separate the bran from the endosperm and to grind the endosperm to flour.

Breaking. The cleaned and conditioned wheat is treated to a series of grinding operations. The first grindings are designed to exert a crushing and shearing action, commonly known as *break-ing.* The purpose of breaking is to bring about the separation of the tough bran from the endosperm, which is easily pulverized. This part of the grinding process is carried out on break rolls, which revolve in opposite directions at different speeds. The first break crushes the wheat into fairly coarse particles called *middlings,* separates some of the bran from the endosperm, and produces some fine flour (*break flour*). At each successive break, the flour is separated from the middlings and the middlings are progressively reduced in size. The middlings still have some particles of bran clinging to them when fed to the break rolls, but sifting and further crushing remove the bran almost completely.

Reduction. After breaking, the middlings are sent to the reduction rolls, which reduce the endosperm middlings to flour. Reduction rolls are smooth and are capable not only of grinding the middlings into flour, but also of removing remaining bits of germ and bran.

Sifting. After each reduction, the flour is sifted and classified by particle size. Oversized particles are sent back to the reduction rolls for further processing.

Feeding the wheat and subsequent middlings through break and reduction rolls produces many flour streams. These streams derive from different portions of the endosperm and differ in degree of refinement. The final flour product is made by blending several streams of flour; the grade of a flour depends on the streams that were blended to produce it. If all the streams are combined, a *straight flour* is obtained. When the more refined streams are kept separate, they are called *patent;* the flour that is left over from a patent is designated *clear flour.*

Patent flours, composed mainly of the streams that come from the reduction of the middlings, are known as *long* or *short* patents, depending on how much of the total flour milled they contain. The term *85% patent* indicates a flour that contains 85 percent of the total milled wheat meal. Short patents may contain as little as 60% of the total flour, long patents as much as 95%. The short patent flours are the highest grade and the most refined.

The *clear flours, left over after the patent flour is removed, are classed as fancy clear, first clear,* and *second clear.* The clear flours are more refined than straight flour.

Flour Quality and Strength. The qualities most carefully appraised in evaluating a flour are strength, water-absorption capacity, and color.

STRENGTH. The strength of flour is determined by the ratio between the rates of carbon dioxide production and loss in the fermenting dough.[1] Gas production is related to the sugar content in the dough, gas retention to the quantity and quality of the gluten and the manner in which it develops during mixing and fermentation.

The purpose to which a flour will be put in

[1] E. J. Pyler, *Baking Science and Technology,* Vol. 1 (Chicago: Siebel, 1952), p. 225.

baking depends on the quantity and quality of the gluten (see Fig. 30-1) formed when it is made into dough. Hard or strong wheat flours have a relatively high protein content that forms a tenacious, elastic gluten with good gas-retaining properties. These flours are suitable for the production of yeast-leavened breads. On the other hand, soft wheat flours have poor gas-retaining properties and are more satisfactorily used for tender quick breads, cakes, and cookies.

WATER ABSORPTION. The water-absorbing capacity of the flour is an important factor in determining its quality. The flours used for making bread can absorb a high percentage of water and, in so doing, produce a dough that gives a high yield of bread. In contrast, soft flours have relatively low water-absorbing capacity. Within each flour classification, there are degrees of water-absorbing capacity that account for differences in the amounts of liquid required to obtain standard products.

COLOR. Normally, milled flour has a yellow pigment imparted by the carotenoid pigments, xanthophyll and carotene. But a white crumb is the standard set for baked products in this country and the slightly colored flour is converted to a nearly pure white by the addition of small quantities of bleaching agents.

Bleaching Agents. Before the use of bleaching agents, the carotenoids were rendered colorless by storing the flour for several months and permitting the oxygen in the atmosphere to react slowly with the color pigments. This was known as "aging," and during this period the flour not only changed color but also showed a marked improvement in baking characteristics.

However, the long storage periods required were costly and gave manufacturers an incentive to find new methods of aging.

The artificial bleaching methods that have been developed bleach out the color in flour within a few moments. Also, a number of bleaching agents have been developed that not only bleach the flour but also "age" it so that the artificially treated product is similar in these respects to the flour that underwent the natural maturing process. The bleaching agents most commonly used are chlorine, chlorine dioxide, and potassium bromate. Chlorine and chlorine with nitrosyl and benzoyl peroxide are used for bleaching as well as maturing; potassium bromate is used only for maturing the flour.

Chlorine gas, used mainly in the treatment of cake flours, causes a mellowing (dispersing or tenderizing) of the proteins. It should be noted that bleaching is not used to cover up flour defects. No treatment of this kind will improve a flour of poor quality.

DIFFERENT KINDS OF FLOUR

Wheat Flours. Wheat flours of various types are available for home and commercial use. They vary in composition according to the variety of wheat used, the part of the wheat grain used, and the selection and blending of the flour streams. Definitions and standards of identity for wheat flour and related products have been established under the Food and Drug Administration.

Whole-wheat flour, graham flour, and *entire wheat* are terms used to designate products ground

30-1 *Gluten balls—raw and baked. The baked gluten balls form light porous balls. The insoluble protein can be separated from flour by adding water to form a stiff dough and kneading in water to wash away starch. (Courtesy of Wheat Flour Institute)*

from cleaned whole wheat (other than durum or red durum). Malted wheat, malted wheat flour, and malted barley flour may be used to supply enzyme materials that are lacking, and some provision is made for the addition of a bleaching agent. If one is used, however, the flour must be labeled "bleached."

Flour, white flour, wheat flour, and *plain flour* are terms used to designate products prepared by milling cleaned wheat (other than durum and red durum). They are made up chiefly of the endosperm of wheat, with a moisture content of not more than 15% and an ash content of not more than 0.05% of the protein plus 0.35. Provision is made for the addition of bleaching and/or maturing agents. To make up for any deficiency in diastatic enzymes, malt preparations may be used in limited amounts. If a bleaching agent is used, the flour must be labeled accordingly.

Enriched flour designates flour that conforms to the definition for white flour and contains certain enrichment ingredients. To each pound of flour are added 2.0–2.5 mg thiamine, 1.2–1.5 mg riboflavin, 16.0–20.0 mg niacin, and 13.0–16.5 mg iron. Calcium and vitamin D are optional enrichment ingredients.

Phosphorated flours must conform to the standards prescribed for flour except that monocalcium phosphate is added in a quantity not to exceed 0.75 percent of the total weight of the finished phosphorated flour.

Self-rising flours designate products that conform to the standards prescribed for flour and contain additions of sodium bicarbonate, the acid-reacting substances monocalcium phosphate or sodium acid pyrophosphate (or both), and salt. The acid-reacting substance is added in a quantity sufficient to neutralize the sodium bicarbonate.

Durum or macaroni flour designates flour milled from durum wheat, which has a high protein content. It is used for macaroni products.

Bread flours, like durum flours, are fairly high in protein. They are milled from blends of hard spring and hard winter wheats, are rather granular to the touch, and are slightly off-white in color. Bread flours are used mainly for baking products leavened with yeast. Although used mainly in the commercial production of bread, they are also suitable for home use.

All-purpose flours or *family-type flours* are made from a blend of hard wheats or soft wheats. In the North they are usually a blend of hard wheats, and although they are used as a general flour for home baking, they are specifically suited to such products as yeast breads. In the South they are usually blended from soft wheat. This blend, too, is excellent for all-purpose baking, but its slightly lower protein content makes it desirable for the quick bread type of flour mixture that is so popular in the South. All-purpose flours are lower in strength and lighter in weight and color than bread flours.

Pastry flour is chiefly used by commercial bakers for making pastry, although some is used in home baking. It is made of soft wheat and is fairly low in protein. Finely milled and not so granular as all-purpose and bread flour, pastry flour is suitable for all baked products other than breads.

Cake flours are also ground from soft wheats and are very fine in texture. Usually, they are short patent flours that may have had bleaching agents added to whiten their color and soften and mellow their proteins. Cake flour is very finely pulverized and is almost silky to the touch. This flour is used for the finest cake products.

Instantized flours are the instant-blending flours. They are made by a special agglomerating procedure, whereby a number of individual flour particles are combined into readily pourable particles.

Naturally Aged Flours. Unbleached flours and certain breads made of unbleached flour are available on the American market. These products are preferred by some consumers because of the effects of the chemical changes in the bleached flours brought about by the bleaching agents. It is thought that the bleaching chemicals have an effect on the essential unsaturated fatty acids and the antioxidant substances found in the freshly milled flour.

OTHER CEREAL GRAINS

Rye and corn are the two other grains that are milled into flour or meal. Rye flour contains some protein, which, unlike the protein of wheat, does not form an elastic dough. Hence, bread products made with rye flour may be small and compact unless some wheat flour has been added.

Rye Flours. Rye is a hardy plant, and it is commonly cultivated in cold climates. Although some rye is used in the production of bread in the United States, it is not as important a bread cereal as wheat flour is. In northern Europe, however, rye is the leading bread cereal. Rye flours are classified as white, medium, or dark—the darker the color, the higher the bran content. Pumpernickel rye is made from a dark all-rye flour. The rye dough is fermented to produce a sour dough that gives a characteristic flavor to the bread. But the rye bread more popular in this country is that made with a mixture of flours.

Cornmeal. Corn contains some protein, but it has little capacity for retaining gas and forming an elastic dough. Cornmeal is used extensively for such baked products as corn muffins and cornbread. When cornmeal is used in a leavened product, it is mixed with a large proportion of wheat flour.

Sorghum. Sorghum is the chief food grain in much of Africa and parts of India, Pakistan, and China. In the United States, the sorghum crop is used principally for animal feed. Some use is made of products such as sorghum starch or its derivatives. Sorghum is one of the cereal grains that has great potentiality for increased human use if the need arises to increase a country's cereal production. Because it is an important food in large parts of Asia and Africa, its use in other areas of the world is conceivable. The starch manufactured from sorghum yields a waxy paste when cooked.

Special Flours. Small amounts of flours made from barley, rice, potato, cassava, and peanuts are manufactured and sold in this country.

SUMMARY

Flours used in producing yeast-leavened bread come principally from hard wheats, whereas flours that are used for cakes, pastries, and cookies come from soft wheats. Durum wheats are used for macaroni products. Flour is carefully selected for its intended purpose. A wheat milled for bread flour has a protein content of 11% or more; wheats milled for flours for cakes, cookies, and pastry have a protein content of from 8–11%.

The terms *straight flour, patent flour,* and *clear flour* describe the streams of flour coming through the reduction rolls during milling. The grade of a flour depends on the streams blended to produce it. The short patent flours are the highest grade and the most refined. In evaluating a flour, the qualities most carefully appraised are strength, water-absorption capacity, and color.

The quantity and quality of the gluten formed when flour is made into a dough determine its use in baking. Yeast-leavened bread requires a flour with relatively high protein content that forms a tenacious, elastic gluten with good gas-retaining properties. Soft wheat flours have poor gas-retaining properties and are used for cakes, cookies, and quick breads.

Hard wheat flours have a high water-absorbing capacity (a requisite for high yield of bread), whereas soft wheat flours have relatively low water-absorbing capacity.

To achieve the white crumb, standard for baked products in this country, small quantities of bleaching agents are added to milled flour. Definitions and standards of identity for wheat flour and related products have been established under the Food and Drug Administration.

Also milled into flour or meal are rye, corn, and oats. Rye flour, unless combined with wheat flour, produces bread of small volume because its protein does not form an elastic dough. Cornmeal is widely used for corn muffins and cornbread.

QUESTIONS AND TOPICS FOR DISCUSSION AND STUDY

1. Why do some flours have higher absorptive powers than others?
2. What is the action of bleaching agents of flour?
3. How does bread flour differ from cake flour and pastry flour?
4. What accounts for the different weights of equal measures of whole-wheat, all-purpose, cake, and pastry flours?
5. Explain the term "enriched flour."
6. Why is wheat flour used in making bread?

REFERENCES

BOOKS

Aykroyd, W. R. *Wheat in Human Nutrition.* Rome: Food and Agriculture Organization, No. 21, 1971.

Halliday, Evelyn and Isabel Nobel. *Hows and Whys of Cooking,* rev. ed. Chicago: University of Chicago Press, 1946, Chap. 2.

Lee, Frank. *Basic Food Chemistry.* Westport, Conn.: Avi, 1975, Chap. 12.

Metz, Samual, ed. *The Chemistry and Technology of Cereals as Food and as Feed.* Westport, Conn.: Avi, 1959.

Paul, Pauline. *Food Theory and Applications.* New York: Wiley, 1972, Chap. 11.

ARTICLES

Bookwalter, G. N., et al. "Dough Conditioners for 12% Soy-Fortified Bread Mixes." *J. Food Sci.* **41:**67, 1976.

Schoppet, E. F., et al. "Enrichment of Pasta with Cottage Cheese Whey Proteins." *J. Food Sci.* **41:**297, 1976.

Leavening Agents

A leavening agent aerates a mixture and thereby lightens it. Leavening action may be produced by physical, chemical, or biological means; the common leavening agents are air, steam, and carbon dioxide.

AIR

Air is introduced into a mixture through sifting dry ingredients, creaming and mixing batters, and incorporating beaten egg whites. To some degree, all flour mixtures—yeast-leavened breads, quick breads, cakes, and cookies—depend on air for leavening, but usually air is not sufficient and other leavening agents are used as well. The basic formula for shortened cake usually directs that some chemical leavening agent be used, although extensive creaming of the fat and sugar is recommended for aeration. This creaming action leads to the formation of air cells into which the carbon dioxide gas formed by the baking powder can diffuse. When foam cakes—angel food and yellow sponge—are heated, the air trapped in the cells expands and the volume of the cake increases. Angel food cakes are leavened by the incorporation of air

cells into the mixture by beaten egg whites, and air is beaten into egg yolks or whole eggs for yellow sponge cakes. Chiffon cakes depend on beaten eggs for a large part of their leavening, but baking powder is also used.

STEAM

Although the steam produced during baking causes the mixture to expand, steam alone cannot leaven a mixture. Its action must be combined with that of air and/or carbon dioxide. Some products—popovers and creampuffs, for example—depend almost entirely on the steam produced during baking to increase their volume.

When steam is used as the leavening agent, high temperatures must be achieved so that the boiling point of the mixture can be quickly reached.

CARBON DIOXIDE

The principal means of leavening flour mixtures is by the formation of carbon dioxide,

383

generated by the action of chemical leaveners or produced from sugar by the action of yeast microorganisms. The chemical leaveners generally used include baking powders, baking soda (which depends on the presence of an acid ingredient, such as sour milk, to give off its carbon dioxide), and ammonium carbonate. By far the most important of these chemical agents is baking powder.

BAKING POWDER

The U.S. Department of Agriculture defines baking powder as the leavening agent produced by the mixing of an acid-reacting material and sodium bicarbonate, with or without the addition of starch or flour. Permissible acid ingredients are tartaric acid or its acid salts, acid salts of phosphoric acid, compounds of aluminum, or any combination of these acids in substantial proportions.[1]

Baking powders may be classified by their acid component. Accordingly, baking powders are frequently referred to as *tartrate powders, phosphate powders,* and *combination powders* (sodium aluminum sulfate and monocalcium phosphate). Baking powders are also classified according to their action rate. The fast-acting powders give off most of their gas volume during the first few minutes of contact with liquid. When such powders are added to a mixture, the mixture must be handled quickly to avoid loss of carbon dioxide and volume.

On the other hand, the slow-acting powders give up very little of their gas volume at low temperatures—they require the heat of the oven to react completely.

The double-acting baking powders are so called because they begin reacting at low temperatures and give some smoothness and viscosity to the batter, but they do not go into complete reaction until they are exposed to high temperatures. Double-acting or slow-acting baking powders are more popular for cake baking.

Most published recipes today use slow double-acting baking powder.

[1] L. H. Bailey, "Development and Use of Baking Powder and Baking Chemicals," *Bulletin 138* (Washington, D.C.: U.S. Department of Agriculture, 1940).

The rate at which a baking powder gives off carbon dioxide depends on the solubility of its acid-reacting component in cold water. When the acid component is soluble in water at room temperature, the baking powder reacts at room temperature; when the acid component is insoluble in cold water, the baking powder will not react completely until elevated temperatures are reached. The double-acting baking powders (combination powders) have two acid ingredients: one is soluble in cold water, the other is soluble only at high temperatures.

A baking powder must be so balanced that its baking soda and acid ingredients will form a salt when the powder is combined with a liquid. Federal standards also require that the proportion of constituents of baking powders be such that the powders will yield not less than 12% of available carbon dioxide. (Most commercial powders yield 14–17%, to allow for a possible loss of strength during storage.)

Baking powders also contain an inert filler, usually cornstarch or powdered calcium carbonate. The filler acts as a buffer between the active ingredients and prevents their going into reaction when exposed to moisture. It also serves to standardize the strength of the powder. In order to yield a standard amount of carbon dioxide, the weight of the soda is held constant while the weight of the different acid components is varied according to the amount needed to release the necessary amount of carbon dioxide. To standardize the powder, the differences in weight are corrected by the use of a filler.

Fast-Acting Baking Powders. Cream of tartar and tartaric acid baking powders are fast-acting powders, for the reaction between the acid and alkali components takes place at low temperatures in the presence of moisture.

The tartaric acid ingredients in tartrate baking powders are used in limited amounts (usually in combination with cream of tartar) because the reaction of tartaric acid with soda is very quick.

The chemical reactions between cream of tartar and bicarbonate of soda and between tartaric acid and bicarbonate of soda are as follows.

Potassium acid tartrate plus soda yields potassium sodium tartrate plus water plus carbon dioxide:

$$KHC_4H_4O_6 + NaHCO_3 \longrightarrow$$
$$KNaC_4H_4O_6 + H_2O + CO_2 \uparrow$$

Tartaric acid plus soda yields sodium tartrate plus water plus carbon dioxide:

$$H_2C_4H_4O_6 + 2NaHCO_3 \longrightarrow$$
$$Na_2C_4H_4O_6 + 2H_2O + 2CO_2 \uparrow$$

The residue of the reaction between acid and alkali consists of two salts, tricalcium phosphate and disodium phosphate. The acid component, monocalcium phosphate, reacts rather rapidly with sodium bicarbonate at slightly elevated temperatures and can be classified as a fast-acting powder.

Monocalcium phosphate plus soda yields tricalcium phosphate plus disodium phosphate plus water plus carbon dioxide:

$$3CaH_4(PO_4)_2 + 8NaHCO_3 \longrightarrow$$
$$Ca_3(PO_4)_2 + 4Na_2HPO_4 + 8H_2O + 8CO_2 \uparrow$$

Slow-Acting Baking Powders. A slow-acting powder of the monocalcium phosphate type is widely used. The acid ingredient is an anhydrous monocalcium phosphate. The phosphate is in the form of small crystals with a water-insoluble coating that protects against decomposition in the presence of moisture, retards reaction with sodium bicarbonate in the presence of moisture, and retards reaction with sodium bicarbonate in the presence of water at low temperatures.

Combination Powders. The combination powders contain two acid-reacting ingredients and are classified as slow-acting. An example of such a baking powder is one in which the acid components are monocalcium phosphate and sodium aluminum sulfate. Besides the reactions of each acid with the soda, there is probably also a reaction between the two acids.[2] The sodium sulfate component of this baking powder imparts a bitter aftertaste if excess amounts of powder are used.

Sodium aluminum sulfate plus water yields sodium sulfate plus aluminum hydroxide plus sulfuric acid:

$$2NaAl(SO_4)_2 + 6H_2O \longrightarrow$$
$$2NaHSO_4 + 2Al(OH)_3 + 2H_2SO_4$$

[2] Ibid.

Sulfuric acid plus sodium bicarbonate yields sodium sulfate plus water plus carbon dioxide:

$$H_2SO_4 + 2NaHCO_3 \longrightarrow$$
$$Na_2SO_4 + 2H_2O + 2CO_2 \uparrow$$

Proportions Used. When tartrate baking powders are used, the mixture must be handled quickly, for as much as 90% of the carbon dioxide will be evolved at room temperature. Unlike the fast-acting powders, double-acting powders require no hasty handling of the mixture, for their reaction requires the high temperatures of the oven to be brought to completion.

It has been recommended that 1½ to 2 tsp of the fast-acting powders or 1 to 1½ tsp of the slow-acting powders be used for each cup of flour. There is sufficient evidence, based on wide practical experience, that a compromise quantity of any baking powder can be used in a recipe, most satisfactory being 1½ tsp to 1 cup flour.

Ammonium bicarbonate and ammonium carbonate are also used as leavening agents in the baking of cookies and crackers. Both compounds, when subjected to heat, decompose into ammonia, carbon dioxide, and water and leave no solid residue.

BAKING SODA

One of the earliest chemical methods of leavening is the combination of bicarbonate of soda and an acid ingredient to produce carbon dioxide. This method is still used, but exact amounts of soda must be used, for an excess of soda will result in an unpalatable product with yellow spots on its surface. Sour milk and buttermilk are the acids most frequently used. When fruit is used in batters and doughs, some soda is generally added to neutralize the acid content of the fruit juice.

When sodium bicarbonate is heated, it breaks down into sodium carbonate, water, and carbon dioxide:

$$2NaHCO_3 \longrightarrow Na_2CO_3 + H_2O + CO_2 \uparrow$$

A residue of sodium carbonate in a flour mixture gives a disagreeable flavor. Therefore, when soda is used, a suitable quantity of an acid is added so that a more neutral residue is formed.

Baking powder and baking soda are sometimes substituted for one another. Equivalent measures are ½ tsp soda and 2 tsp baking powder.

YEAST

Yeast is a microscopic unicellular plant that reproduces rapidly under suitable conditions of food, warmth, and moisture. The leavening action of yeast is brought about through fermentation. Fermentation takes place when the enzyme zymase is released or extracted from the yeast cells. The action of zymase converts sugars into alcohol and carbon dioxide. (The starch present is also susceptible to fermentation after it has been broken down to glucose.) In a yeast-leavened flour mixture, the carbon dioxide released by fermentation is retained in the gluten structure of the dough; the alcohol is driven off during baking.

Compressed Yeast. Yeast is available in either compressed or dry form. Compressed yeast is a moist mixture of yeast and starch. The manufacture of yeast involves the selection of strains of yeast that have desirable gas-producing qualities. The yeast is introduced into a solution of molasses, mineral salts, and ammonia and permitted to grow under very carefully controlled conditions. After growth ceases, the yeast cells are separated from the solution by filtration or centrifugation, mixed with a small amount of starch, and compressed into cakes.

Compressed yeast must be refrigerated in order to retard deterioration. Dried-out, dark, compressed yeast cakes with a cheesy flavor may be ineffective and may render the product unpalatable. Some compressed yeast is still used for household preparation of yeast-leavened products, but dry yeast is more popular.

Dry Yeast. The main difference between dry yeast and compressed yeast is that dry yeast is less moist and thus less susceptible to deterioration during storage. The manufacture of dry yeast is similar to that of compressed yeast. After the yeast is washed and filtered, it is extruded in short noodle form onto a conveyor belt that passes through a dryer. The drying cuts moisture content of the yeast to about 8%, renders the

yeast cells dormant, and makes refrigeration during transportation unnecessary. The yeast cells are then mixed with cornmeal and packaged. The real advantage of using dry yeast lies in the fact that it need not be refrigerated and—although the yeast cells do not remain active indefinitely—it is far more durable than compressed yeast. Dried yeast cells become inactive after prolonged storage. Packaged dry yeast has an expiration date stamped on the package. It should not be used after the date indicated.

BACTERIA

Certain species of bacteria, under controlled conditions of temperature and moisture, grow and act on sugar, breaking it down into carbon dioxide and hydrogen. These bacteria are used to leaven the products known as *salt-rising breads*.

SUMMARY

A leavening agent aerates and lightens a mixture. The principal leavening agents are air, as utilized in the beaten eggs in angel and sponge cakes, and the partial aeration achieved by sifting of ingredients and the creaming of fat and sugar in other baked products; steam produced during baking, as in popovers and creampuffs; and carbon dioxide, which is formed by the action of either chemical leaveners or biological agents. Of the chemical leaveners, baking powder is the most important. A mixture of an acid-reacting material and sodium bicarbonate with or without starch of flour, baking powders may be classified as to their action rate—fast-acting, slow-acting, or double-acting. Baking powders must be so formulated that the baking soda and acid ingredients will form a salt when combined with a liquid and that they yield a minimum of 12% of the available carbon dioxide.

Fermentation produces the leavening action of yeast, a microscopic unicellular plant that reproduces rapidly under suitable conditions of food, warmth, and moisture. Yeast is available either compressed or dry. Compressed yeast must be refrigerated to retard deterioration. More durable than compressed yeast, dry yeast must be dissolved in hot water before use.

Salt-rising breads are leavened by the use of

bacteria that break sugar down into carbon dioxide and hydrogen.

QUESTIONS AND TOPICS FOR DISCUSSION AND STUDY

1. Explain physical, chemical, and biological leavening agents.
2. In what types of batter can steam be used as a leavening agent?
3. Why is baking soda alone not a good leavening agent?
4. What is the role of starch in baking powder?
5. How is air incorporated into a flour mixture?
6. What are the acids used in baking powders? How do these affect the rapidity with which baking powders react?
7. What is the reaction of baking soda when heated in the presence of moisture? (This may be given as a word equation.)
8. Why are high temperatures used in baking when steam is the leavening agent?
9. What is the most desirable temperature range for growth of yeast?
10. What is the process of fermentation?
11. What causes yellow spots in the crumb of biscuits?

REFERENCES

Books

Garard, Ira. *Introductory Food Chemistry*. Westport, Conn.: Avi, 1976, Chap. 13.

Paul, Pauline, and Helen Palmer. *Food Theory and Application*. New York: Wiley, 1972, Chap. 12.

Flour Mixtures: Quick Breads

The ingredients used in different flour mixtures vary in kind and amount. The least complex of these mixtures, a simple cracker dough, contains nothing more than flour and a liquid. Other mixtures include ingredients that impart tenderness, texture, flavor, and food value to the product. Fat, for example, is used to make a product tender, but it also has some effect on the product's flavor and appearance. Sugar, added mainly for flavor, also affects the texture and color of the baked food. Salt is nearly always added for flavor.

CLASSIFICATION

Flour mixtures lend themselves to general classification based on the amount of liquid used. The two main classifications are *batters* and *doughs;* the batters contain more liquid than do the doughs.

Batters. Batters are flour mixtures that contain enough liquid to be beaten or stirred. Batters vary in stiffness and can be subdivided into *pour batters* and *drop batters.* A pour batter has approximately ⅔–1 cup of liquid per cup of flour, whereas a drop batter has about ½–1 cup flour. Popover batter is an example of a pour batter; muffin mixtures are typical of drop batters (see Table 32-1).

Doughs. A dough has less liquid in proportion to flour than a batter has and is of a consistency to be handled or kneaded. For a soft dough, about ⅓ cup of liquid is used per cup of flour. Baking powder biscuits and related products are examples of soft doughs. A stiff dough has about ⅛–⅙ cup of liquid per cup of flour. Stiff doughs (such as pie crust dough) are somewhat resistant to handling and rolling.

A knowledge of the basic proportions of ingredients required for the various flour mixtures is essential. And an understanding of the function of these ingredients and the chemical and physical changes that take place when they are combined will serve as a basis for predicting results. Once the basic proportions of essential ingredients are known, skill can be developed in varying the ingredients to make interesting and different products. Other factors affecting the final baked product are the techniques used in the manipulation of the basic ingredients and the utensils and temperatures used in baking.

TABLE 32-1
Proportions of Ingredients for Batters and Doughs

	Baking Temperature		Flour[a] (cups)	Liquid (cups)	Fat	Leavening	Eggs	Sugar (tbsp)	Salt (tsp)
	°F	°C							
Pour batters									
Popovers[b]	450	232	1	1 (sweet milk)	0–1 tbsp	Steam	2	0	¼
Timbales[b]	360	182	1¼	1 (sweet milk)	0–1 tsp	Steam	1–2	0–½	¼
Griddle cakes[b]	—	—	1⅓–1½	1 (sweet milk)	1 tbsp	1½–2 tsp baking powder	1	0–1½	½
Waffles[b]	—	—	½	1 (sweet milk)	2 tbsp	1½–2 tsp baking powder	2	0–1½	½
Drop batters									
Cakes[c] (cake flour)	375	190	2½–3	1 (sweet milk)	½ cup	2½–4½ tsp baking powder	2	1–1½ cups	¾
Muffins[b]	425	218	2	1 (sweet milk)	2 tbsp	2–3 tsp baking powder	1	0–3	¼
Drop cookies[c]	375	190	1½–2	1 (sweet milk)	2–8 tbsp	2 tsp baking powder	1	1 cup	½
Creampuffs	425	218	1	1 (water)	½ cup	Steam	4	—	½
Soft doughs									
Biscuits[b]	425	218	2	⅔–¾ (sweet milk)	2–5 tbsp	2–3 tsp. baking powder	—	—	½–1
Yeast breads[d]			2	½ (water or milk)		½ pkg. yeast	0–1	1	½
Rolls	375	190	2	½ (water or milk)	2–4 tbsp	½ pkg. yeast	0–1	1–2	½
Sweet rolls	425	218	2	½ (water or milk)	4 tbsp	½ pkg. yeast	1–2	2–4	½
Stiff doughs									
Pastry	425	218	2	4–6 tbsp (water)	½–¾ cup	Steam, air	—	—	1
Cookies, rolled[c]	375	190	2	—	½ cup	1½ tsp baking powder	1	1 cup	⅛

[a] All-purpose, unless otherwise specified.
[b] Muffin or biscuit method of mixing generally used.
[c] Conventional or quick-mix methods of mixing.
[d] Straight dough, sponge, or cool-rise method.

389

COMPOSITION

The basic structure of the flour mixture and the quality of the baked product depend on all or some of the following ingredients; flour, liquid, leavening agent, shortening, eggs, and sugar.

Flour. The proportions of ingredients in batters and doughs and the methods of combining them are related to the kind of flour used in the mixture. Flour provides the materials that form the framework of the baked product. When water is added to flour, a structural framework called *gluten* (see Fig. 32-1) is formed. The swollen protein molecules come in contact with each other and line up around a lipoprotein core. The protein molecules are held in place by interstitial water. In order for the gluten to form, the flour must be hydrated. It must also be kneaded to allow the protein molecules to slide past one another and line up in position. Kneading will develop the gluten from a sticky mass to a stretchable, smooth, satiny-finished dough.

The gluten can be separated from the dough by washing it with cold water. This removes the starch. Two types of proteins make up the gluten mass, *gliadin* and *glutenin*. Gliadin is very thin and gives elasticity to the dough. Glutenin gives strength to the gluten. Starch that becomes enmeshed in the gluten matrix also gives structure to the dough. The quality of gluten formed will affect the finished product (see Chapter 29). For instance, when the gluten strands are continuous, the dough is soft and elastic. For quick breads, a flour that has a medium to strong protein content is desirable. The gluten formed from such flours will have sufficient strength to retain air, steam, and carbon dioxide, thus enabling the baked product to attain good volume.

All-purpose flour and cake flour are the ones most commonly used for baking quick breads. The all-purpose flour has a better ability to form gluten of sufficient strength than cake flour does.

Such flours as rye lack gluten strength and are usually combined with wheat flour for baking. Products made with all whole-wheat flour are smaller in volume than those made with white flour. It is often the practice to substitute white flour for part of the whole-wheat flour to provide the necessary volume.

INSTANT-BLENDING FLOUR. Instant-blending flour may be used in the preparation of baked products. This is a free-flowing flour that does not pack. It is also referred to as *agglomerated flour*. To manufacture it, regular flour that originally met standard granulation specifications is exposed to hot water or steam to combine individual particles into agglomerates. A recent study showed that adjustments in volume of flour when using instant flour in place of sifted regular flour in a batter or dough recipe are needed to assure a good-quality baked product. When the weight of instant flour was adjusted to the weight of sifted regular flour, muffins, drop biscuits, waffles, coffee cake, plain cake, cream-puffs, and plain cookies received acceptable ratings. Yeast rolls, popovers, and pastry, however, did not show up satisfactorily when adjustments in flour were made. The implication of this

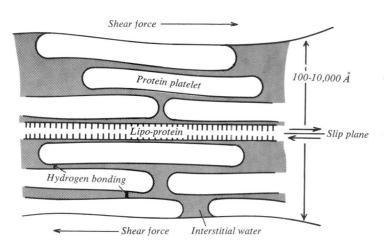

32-1 *Proposed model of a gluten strand. (Reproduced by courtesy of Dr. J. C. Grosskreutz, "A Lipo-protein Model of Wheat Gluten Structure,"* Cereal Chem. **38:**347, 1961)

study is that new formulations for these products are necessary.[1]

Liquids. Liquids are responsible for many of the physical and chemical changes that take place in flour mixtures upon mixing and baking. In addition to serving as solvents for solid ingredients, they serve to hydrate proteins (necessary for gluten formation). Liquids also aid in the gelatinization of starch and are essential to the reaction of chemical leaveners.

The amount of liquid used in a flour mixture depends on the desired consistency of the flour mixture and on the strength of the flour. The amount and kind of liquid used have a decided effect on the texture and appearance of the various products. When water is substituted for milk—in bread, for instance—a little less is used.

The liquid most commonly used in flour mixtures is milk. It is preferred because of its nutritive value and because it contributes to the browning of the product. Fresh whole or skim milk, evaporated milk, and whole or nonfat dry milk are satisfactory for this purpose. Dry milk may be reconstituted to form a liquid first, or it may be added dry directly to the other dry ingredients, with the required amount of water added later. Nonfat dry milk is more likely to be used than dry whole milk. Fruit juices are sometimes used as the liquid ingredient in certain types of cake.

An ever-increasing amount of nonfat dry milk is being used for industrial and home purposes. One of its special and beneficial uses is as a nutritious supplement. Studies[2] indicate that 2–4 times the usual amount of milk solids can be used for chocolate cakes, and 5 times the usual amount for plain cakes. Two to four times the usual milk solid weight can be used with 10 ml additional liquid when more than 3 times the normal level is used. Muffins received good ratings when 1 cup nonfat dried milk replaced 1 cup whole milk. (This is approximately 3 times

the normal milk solid level.) Yeast rolls, however, were not improved in texture or tenderness with fortified amounts of milk.

Leavening Agents. All quick breads—which include such products as muffins, baking powder biscuits, griddle cakes, waffles, popovers, fritters, and dumplings—depend on air, steam, and/or a chemical leavening agent, such as baking powder or baking soda and sour milk, to make them light and porous. A greater amount of baking powder is usually needed for thin batters than for stiffer ones. The reason for this is that carbon dioxide is not retained so well in the thin batters, which lack gluten development.

Fat. The shortening used in a flour mixture is usually one with a pleasant flavor and color; a wide range of fats and oils are permissible. The addition of a fat to a flour mixture gives a shorter or a more tender dough and also aids in leavening it. Fat makes a flour mixture tender by coating the flour particles and keeping them separated, thereby reducing the tendency for the mixture to form heavy, continuous bands of gluten. Fat also helps to leaven the product by its capacity to cream. The creaming process mixes air into the fat, which leavens the whole mixture. Oils, of course, cannot be creamed and therefore cannot be counted on to contribute to the leavening of a product.

Eggs. Eggs are used in flour mixtures for leavening, color, shortening action, flavor, and nutritive value. When eggs are used to introduce air into the flour mixture, they actively supply the necessary leavening for the product. Eggs also provide protein, which is extensible and will stretch as the gas volume in a mixture expands. The heat of the oven coagulates the egg protein, which is in a network of protein film and capable of maintaining the increased volume of the mixture. Egg yolk, because of its emulsification properties, helps to distribute the shortening in the mixture, thus helping to achieve a tender texture in the product.

Most flour-based products may be made with dried eggs. On the whole, such products compare favorably with those made with fresh eggs; however, sponge cakes made with dried whole eggs are compact and lack resiliency. (See Table 21–5 for substitution of dried egg for fresh egg.)

[1] R. Matthews and E. Bechtel, "Eating Quality of Some Baked Products Made with Instant Flour," *J. Home Econ.* **58:**748, 1966.

[2] L. Harper, M. Collins, and D. LeGrand, "The Fortification of Batters and Doughs with Nonfat Dried Milk," *Technical Bulletin 149* (Blacksburg, Va.: Virginia Agriculture Experiment Station, August 1960).

Sugar. The function of sugar in a flour mixture is principally to sweeten the mixture, to tenderize the flour structure by reducing the gluten strength, and to develop color and crispness. Finely granulated sugar is recommended for cake mixtures because it can be more evenly dispersed than medium or coarse granules. Sweeteners such as corn syrup, maple syrup, and sorghum may be used as a substitute for sugar. Generally, an equal volume of syrup is substituted for the sugar and the liquid ingredient is reduced by one-third. When brown sugar is used in a recipe, it lends a special color and pleasing flavor to the product. The free-flowing type of brown sugar must be measured according to directions on the package. (See Table 35-1 for equivalent weights of brown sugars.)

PRINCIPLES OF PREPARATION

The important principles involved in the preparation of quick breads are (1) the proper manipulation of ingredients so that the right amount of gluten formation takes place to make the product light and porous, and (2) the addition of the correct proportion of ingredients such as leavening, eggs, sugar, shortening, and liquid to modify gluten structure.

METHODS OF MIXING

Success in achieving baked products of excellent quality depends not only on the kind and proportion of ingredients used in the flour mixture, but also on the way they are combined.

The main goal in the preparation of a flour mixture is the uniform distribution of all ingredients. The method of combining the ingredients has a marked effect on their distribution. The forms of manipulation that are commonly used in combining batters and doughs are designated as stirring, creaming, beating, kneading, cutting in, and folding in.

Stirring involves moving a spoon or similar utensil with a rotary motion, through the contents of the bowl. Bowls with slightly sloping sides make this much easier. Stirring, although not an especially vigorous action, does succeed in incorporating some small amounts of air into the mixture. Its primary purpose, of course, is to evenly distribute the ingredients of the mixture.

Creaming involves working a food, such as fat, with a hand implement or an electric mixer until it is soft and creamy. Large amounts of air are incorporated in the mixture in this way.

Beating a mixture introduces some air into it. It is a vigorous and rapid motion with a wooden spoon, a rotary beater or wire whisk, or an electric mixer. Its object is to distribute the ingredients of the flour mixture until it is smooth.

Kneading a dough makes it smooth and even. It involves working the dough with the hands on a board that may or may not have been slightly floured. To knead dough, the hands are placed palms down on the dough with the fingers curved over the farthest edge, which is then folded over until it is almost even with the front edge. The layers are pressed together with the palms of the hand and pushed back to the center of the board. Then the ball of dough is given a quarter of a turn. These motions are repeated until the dough is of the desired smoothness. To keep dough from sticking, a slight coating of flour is usually sprinkled over the board. Care must be taken not to use too much flour, lest the basic proportion of the recipe be changed.

Cutting in is the technique used to incorporate a solid shortening into a flour mixture. This is done by placing the fat in the bowl containing the dry ingredients and using either a pastry blender, two knives, or two spatulas to cut through the mixture, stroking the blades against each other. These motions are continued until the fat is uniformly divided and of the desired particle size.

Folding in involves combining beaten egg white with a mixture. The object is to combine two materials or mixtures without losing the air that is in one of them. This technique is used mainly for angel food and sponge cakes. In the folding-in process, the mass of beaten egg white or beaten yolks is incorporated into the flour mixture by use of an egg whip, a spatula, or a spoon. The folding-in tool is gently put down through the mass, across the bottom, and up on the other side. It is shifted when necessary to make one complete revolution. The process is repeated until all the egg is incorporated and distributed evenly throughout the mixture.

Muffin Method. The mixing method most frequently used in the preparation of hot breads is known as the *muffin method*.

The muffin method of combining a flour mixture is used for quick breads—mainly griddle cakes, waffles, muffins and their variations, popovers, fritters, and dumplings. It consists of mixing together the dry ingredients and sifting them into a bowl. The eggs are beaten, and to these the liquid and melted fat are added. The liquid and dry ingredients are mixed together until all particles of flour are moistened. This method may be slightly modified by adding the liquid ingredients and leaving out the fat until the very last.

BATTERS

Popovers. Popovers are crisp, crusty hot breads with a hollow center and are made from the thinnest of all batters (see Table 32-1). In this batter, the proportion of liquid is so great that the particles of gluten tend to separate and float on the liquid rather than to form the strands necessary for elasticity in the product. Therefore, all popover recipes include eggs to provide extensible proteins that supplement the gluten of the flour. Fat is an optional ingredient; salt is used for flavoring. Popover ingredients are combined by the muffin method but are beaten together until the batter is smooth. (The beating helps to develop the gluten.) Popovers may be baked in glass, iron, or aluminum pans. The pans are well oiled and heated before the batter is poured into them. These products are baked at 450°F (232°C) for 20–30 minutes, then at 350°F (177°C) until the crust is quite firm. (Removing popovers from the oven too soon will cause them to soften and collapse.) The high initial temperature is essential because the force of steam causes the popover to pop. When taken from the oven, they should be crisp, brown, thin-walled, and large.

Yorkshire Pudding, Timbale Cases, and Cover Batters. Mixtures whose basic proportions are very similar to those of popovers are Yorkshire pudding, timbale cases, and cover batters. These also are classified as thin batters. The proportions for Yorkshire pudding are identical to those for popovers but the batter is poured into a roasting pan containing hot roast beef drippings. No additional fat is used. The batter is baked at a high temperature (450°F)

(232°C) for 30 minutes. Timbale cases and rosette cases are made of the same batter and are used as the base for creamed dishes. These products are not baked; they are cooked on special irons in deep fat at a temperature of 375°F (190°C). When rosettes are used for a dessert, 1–2 tbsp sugar is added to the mixture. The batter is mixed much as is that of a popover batter, but it is left to stand about ½ hour before frying. At this time, it should be free of bubbles. If bubbles are left in the batter, they form a rough surface on the iron and cause the case to break.

The timbale iron must be just the right temperature before it is dipped into the batter. Batter will not cling to irons that are too cool and will drop from irons that are overheated.

The batter for timbale cases or rosettes should be placed in a bowl with nearly vertical sides so that it will not completely cover the iron. Too much batter on the iron will be difficult to remove once it is cooled.

Cover batters (fritters) are often used when frying pieces of fruit, vegetable, fish, and poultry. The proportions of ingredients and the method of mixing are the same as for popovers.

Griddle Cakes. The flour mixture for griddle cakes is similar to that for pancakes and hot cakes. A very thin batter with a high proportion of eggs makes what is called a *French pancake* or *crepe;* and a very light, fluffy batter with a small proportion of eggs makes what is called a *hot cake.* A griddle cake batter falls somewhere between the two, using 1 cup liquid for 1–1½ cups flour, eggs, baking powder, and salt. The leavening is supplied to some extent by the steam. The muffin method is used to combine the ingredients. Overmixing is to be avoided, for it develops the gluten and produces a soggy griddle cake with holes. When the ingredients are mixed only enough to moisten all the flour particles, the griddle cakes are more tender. The griddle should be brushed with enough fat to keep the mixture from sticking. For excellent results in making griddle cakes, the heat should be so regulated that each side browns evenly and fairly quickly. The griddle cake is turned the moment the top side has lost its sheen and is set. Griddle cakes should be turned only once. Turning more than once makes a flat, poorly colored cake. Overcooking will turn the griddle cake into a dry crust pitted by gas holes. Good griddle cakes are light, tender, and free of "tunnels"; they should have a golden-brown color and a pleasant taste.

Waffles. A waffle is basically a griddle cake baked in a special iron. The batter has more egg and fat than the griddle cake mixture has. Usually, the basic proportions are 1½ cups flour to 1 cup liquid, with 2 eggs and no less than 2 tbsp fat. Baking powder and salt are also used, and sugar may or may not be added. For extra crispness and lightness, the egg whites may be separated, stiffly beaten, and folded into the mixture. A waffle iron should be hot before the batter is poured onto it—a short baking time will produce tender waffles. The thinner the batter, the more cooking time will be required. The finished waffle has an attractive brown surface and loosens easily from the iron. Difficulties that arise in the preparation of waffles are usually related to the heating and cooling of the waffle iron. Batter may stick to an iron that is either too hot or too cold. When the manufacturer of an electric waffle iron supplies instructions for its use, they should be followed. Indicators on a waffle iron are the best guides for knowing when the temperature is right for baking the waffle. Good waffles are crisp and tender and have a golden-brown color and a pleasing taste.

Muffins. Muffins belong to the category of drop batters. The basic proportions of the muffin mixture are 2 cups to 1 cup liquid. Eggs, fat, sugar, leavening, and salt are also added. To produce a good muffin, the batter must not be beaten beyond the stage of slight lumpiness. An overmixed muffin batter is shiny and flows in a long, smooth stream from the spoon. Halliday and Noble state, "The difference between success and failure is a matter of only a few strokes of the stirring spoon."[3] It has been suggested by these same authors that the beginner who wishes to develop skill in making muffins should time the stirring operation and try to correlate stirring time with the appearance of the batter and the standard product. The muffin method of com-

bining ingredients may be used to mix the muffin batter, or a modified method may be used whereby a solid fat is cut into the dry ingredients before the liquid ingredients are added. This modified method is very popular because it makes possible a more even distribution of fat particles. Increasing the minimum amount of fat in a muffin recipe from 1 tbsp to 3 tbsp increases the tenderness and flavor of the finished product.[4] A melted fat may coat some particles of flour with large globules of oils while barely touching other flour particles. Muffins prepared by the standard muffin method are best eaten soon after preparation, for they dry out when stored for any length of time.

An overmixed batter produces muffins that are flat, smooth, tough, and soggy—usually with peaked tops and "tunnels" (formed by the expansion of gas along pathways in the muffin made by elongated strands of gluten). A baking pan with very shallow cups and an excessively hot oven will also cause tunnel development in muffins. In the case of an overhot oven, the crust sets before the muffins are completely risen, so that the batter must push itself up through the crust, falls into an off-center peak, and forms tunnels.

A good muffin is very light, with a somewhat coarse but even texture (Figs. 32-2 and 32-3).

[4] R. H. Matthews, M. E. Kirkpatrick, and E. H. Dawson, "Performance of Fats in Muffins," *J. Amer. Dietet. Assoc.* **47**:201, 1965.

32-2 *A well-baked muffin has a coarse, even grain; the air cells are approximately the same size and evenly distributed. (Courtesy of Betty Crocker of General Mills)*

[3] E. Halliday and I. Noble, *Hows and Whys of Cooking,* rev. ed. (Chicago: University of Chicago Press, 1946), p. 66.

32-3 *Hot muffins are popular quick breads. (Courtesy of Betty Crocker of General Mills)*

The crust is golden brown and has a "pebbly" surface. A plain muffin has a slightly sweet, pleasant flavor.

Not only do muffins require quick mixing, they also require quick baking. Recommended temperatures are 400–450°F (205–232°C). Experiments of short duration undertaken in the author's laboratory showed that 425°F (218°C) produced excellent muffins. Baking time at this temperature varies from 20 to 25 minutes, depending on the size of the muffin cups and on the ingredients used. Muffins should be mixed and put into the oven just before they are to be served. If this is inconvenient, it is desirable to place the muffin batter, after filling the pans, in the refrigerator until it is time to bake them.

Muffin Variations. Some muffin recipes vary from the standard and include considerably more sugar and fat. These muffins are almost like cakes in appearance and taste. Muffin variations are limitless. Other cereal flours—whole-wheat, cornmeal, rolled oats, or bran—may be substituted for part of the white flour. To plain muffin mixtures, a number of fruits—fresh, canned, or dried—nuts, jams, or jellies may be added. Brown sugar, honey, or molasses may be used instead of white granulated sugar. (Additional ingredients are usually stirred into the dry ingredients before the liquid is added.)

Quick loaf breads—such as nut, orange nut, cranberry, and blueberry—are variations of muffins. They are made in a manner similar to that used for muffins and baked in loaf pans. Because of the amount of batter that must be baked, the oven temperature for these products is lowered to between 325 and 350°F (163 and 176°C), depending on the ingredients and on the pan used.

Dumpling batter is a variation of muffin batter. To make dumplings, muffin batter (minus sugar) is dropped by spoonfuls on top of stews and fricassees and steamed for 10–15 minutes. Good dumplings are light and spongy. They will turn out this way only if they are steamed above the liquid.

BASIC DOUGHS

Doughs have less liquid in proportion to flour than batters do. The basic doughs include those for biscuits, pastry, and yeast-leavened bread—and each of these has many variations.

Biscuits. Biscuits (Figs. 32-4 and 32-5) are quick to make, and a little practice will lead to the development of a high degree of skill. Precise measurements and the proper proportion (1 part liquid to 3 parts flour) of ingredients are essential. The other ingredients are baking powder, fat, and salt. The biscuit method of combining ingredients is used for most doughs. The dry ingredients are mixed and sifted together, and a solid fat is chopped or cut into the flour mixture.

32-4 *A rolled biscuit should have a level top, straight sides, and golden brown color. The crumb should be tender, moist, and of a medium fine grain. (Courtesy of Betty Crocker of General Mills)*

395

32-5 *Drop biscuits are an excellent example of an easy-to-prepare quick bread. (Courtesy of Clabber Girl Baking Powder)*

Vegetable oils used in place of a solid fat also produce satisfactory biscuits.[5] The liquid is then added, and the mixture is stirred until the mass adheres firmly together. The dough is formed into a ball, turned out on a floured board or pastry canvas, and kneaded for about half a minute (or 10–20 times). The biscuit dough should be light and soft, but not sticky. Kneading tends to distribute the ingredients in the mixture far more efficiently than stirring does. Kneading also develops a gluten structure capable of retaining the carbon dioxide, thereby giving elasticity to the dough and producing large biscuits with a tender, flaky crumb. Overkneading, however, results in a loss of gas from the dough and a consequent packing down of the structure of the biscuit (see Fig. 32-6).

After slight kneading, the dough is rolled lightly to the desired thickness and is cut with a floured biscuit cutter. The biscuits (½ in. or slightly thicker) are placed on an ungreased baking sheet. As many biscuits as possible are cut from the first rolling, because rerolling the dough for a second cutting usually results in overkneading.

Temperatures of about 425°F (218°C) are the most desirable for baking biscuits, and 13–15 minutes is sufficient time in which to produce a well-baked product of good color. A well-baked biscuit is shapely and symmetrical, with a golden-brown, tender crust.

Scones are a very popular variation of biscuits. The usual ingredients of a rich biscuit dough are used, and eggs—1 or 2 to 2 cups flour—are added. Sometimes currants are also added to the scone mixture.

A shortcake is another variation of biscuit dough. It is considerably richer than the dough used for plain biscuits. The batter for a dessert shortcake may also have added sugar. Shortcake dough is often used instead of pastry dough for such products as fruit turnovers, deep-dish pies, and fruit cobblers.

Pastry. Plain pastry or pie dough has less liquid to flour than any of the other doughs, and is considered a very stiff dough (see Chapter 29).

Yeast-leavened breads are usually made from doughs that are just slightly stiffer than biscuit dough (for a detailed description of yeast-bread doughs, see Chapter 34).

Creampuffs. Creampuffs are made from a batter but are somewhat distinct in ingredients and method of mixing. The batter contains the same proportion of liquid to flour as popover dough has, but a rather larger proportion of eggs and fat is necessary to give a more tender structure than that found in popovers. The fat tenderizes the gluten, and the eggs emulsify the fat. The fat content is so great that heat must be used in combining the fat and water to keep the fat from separating out of the mixture. Liquid is added in large amounts in order to produce steam for the expansion of the creampuff and the formation of its hollow center. (Eclairs are made from the same type of batter.) Cream puffs are baked in a hot oven (425°F) (218°C) for the first few minutes, after which the temperature is lowered to give the pastry or shell time to dry out.

PHYSICAL AND CHEMICAL CHANGES DURING BAKING

The major changes that take place during baking of flour mixtures are the production and expansion of gas (air, steam, and carbon dioxide), the coagulation of proteins (eggs and glu-

[5] R. H. Matthews and E. H. Dawson, "Performance of Fats and Oils in Pastry and Biscuits," *Cereal Chem.* **40:**291, 1963.

(a) (b) (c) (d)

32-6 *Variation in volume of baked biscuits as a result of manipulation: (a) drop biscuit from dough dropped on baking sheet (b) low volume, rough top from undermanipulated dough (c) good volume, straight sides from optimum manipulation (d) low volume, smooth, rounded top from overmanipulated dough. (Courtesy U.S. Department of Agriculture)*

ten), the gelatinization of starch, the evaporation of water, and the coloration of the crust.

The expansion of the leavening is responsible for the increased volume of baked product, and the degree of increase depends on the factors that facilitate the gas-retention powers of the batter or dough structure (see Fig. 32-7).

Proteins coagulate at a rather low temperature. Therefore, baking temperatures should be low enough that the optimum volume of the product is reached before the proteins in the outer layer begin to coagulate. The starch in the mixture is hydrated by the liquid, and when heat is applied, gelatinization takes place. Gelatinization is more complete in batters than in doughs because of the larger liquid content of batters. The liquid must evaporate during baking in order for the product to develop any degree of crispness. Internal temperatures of cakes,

muffins, and biscuits have been found to reach the boiling point at low altitude. Their crusts have been found to reach temperatures higher than boiling. What happens, of course, is that the greatest loss of water from the product occurs on the surface and tends to make that crisp. The browning reaction occurs through the reaction of sugar and protein. Some caramelization of sugar may also contribute to the color change. However, it is doubtful that the temperature will reach levels high enough for this reaction to occur.

FREEZING

Batters and doughs may be frozen baked or unbaked. In either case, studies have shown the freshly baked product to be slightly superior to

32-7 *Three stages of dough. (a) barely mixed (b) partially mix developed (c) fully developed. (Courtesy of Wheat Flour Institute)*

(a) (b) (c)

the frozen baked product. However, in one study, Paul and others reported that baked muffins that had been stored frozen for up to 6 months were similar to those prepared from fresh batter.[6] For frozen muffins stored for longer periods, however, palatability scores decreased.

SUMMARY

Based on the amount of liquid used, flour mixtures can be classified as batters or doughs. Batters contain more liquid than doughs and can be subdivided as pour batters and drop batters. Batters produce such products as popovers, Yorkshire pudding, griddle cakes, waffles, muffins, and cakes. Basic doughs produce biscuits, pastry, yeast-leavened bread, and variations for each type.

A flour with medium to strong protein content is desirable for quick breads; for this purpose, all-purpose flour and cake flour are commonly used. Instant flour may also be used, but finished products will be somewhat different from those made with either all-purpose or cake flour.

The amount of liquid, usually milk, that is in flour mixtures is dependent on flour strength and desired consistency of the mixture.

A wide range of fats and oils are used in flour mixtures. Fat tenderizes the mixture and helps to leaven it. Eggs contribute leavening, color, shortening action, flavor, and nutritive value. Sugar sweetens the mixture, tenderizes it, and develops color and crispness. Most quick breads require a chemical leavening agent; thin batters usually need more of such an agent than do stiffer ones.

Commonly used techniques in combining batters and doughs include stirring, beating, kneading, creaming, cutting in, and folding in. Success depends not only on a proper proportion of ingredients but also on a suitable method of combination. The muffin and biscuit methods of combining ingredients are most frequently used. The method of mixing creampuffs and the proportion of their ingredients are somewhat different from those of a standard batter.

[6] P. Paul, O. Batcher, and K. Gaffner, "Dry Mix and Frozen Muffins," *J. Home Econ.* **46**:253, 1954.

Principal changes occurring in flour mixtures during baking are production and expansion of gases (air, steam, and carbon dioxide), coagulation of proteins, gelatinization of starch, evaporation of water, and crust coloration.

Although batters and doughs may be frozen baked or unbaked, the freshly baked product is thought to be superior to the frozen baked products.

QUESTIONS AND TOPICS FOR DISCUSSION AND STUDY

1. What effect does the amount of stirring have on the quality of a muffin?
2. Explain what happens when "tunnels" form in a muffin.
3. Why does a little-mixed muffin batter drop differently from a spoon than a much-mixed batter?
4. What is the effect of undermixing and overmixing on biscuit dough?
5. How does the amount of fat in the dough influence the quality of a biscuit?
6. What is the role of gluten in flour mixtures?
7. Why is it possible to stir a muffin mixture with a large proportion of fat and sugar longer than one with smaller proportion of these ingredients?
8. What happens when too few eggs are used in popover batter?
9. What makes the difference between a thick griddle cake and a thin, crisp one?

SUGGESTED ACTIVITIES

1. Prepare as many of the following as possible: griddle cakes, waffles, popovers, muffins, biscuits, and coffee cakes. Evaluate products.
2. Watch a baking demonstration of the products you do not have time to make.
3. Compare muffins baked in a conventional oven with those baked in a microwave oven.
4. Compare homemade flour mixtures for muffins, biscuits, and so on with a commercial mix. Compare each pair of products from the standpoint of time required for preparation, cost, appearance, texture, and flavor.
5. Add 2, 4, 6 tbsp nonfat dried milk solids to a basic muffin recipe. Compare with the stand-

ard product as to time required for preparation, cost, appearance, texture, flavor, and nutritive value.

REFERENCES

BOOKS

Halliday, Evelyn, and Isabel Noble. *Hows and Whys of Cooking,* rev. ed. Chicago: University of Chicago Press, 1946, Chaps. 2, 3.

Lowe, Belle. *Experimental Cookery,* 4th ed. New York: Wiley, 1955, Chap. 13.

Paul, Pauline, and Helen Palmer. *Food Theory and Applications.* New York: Wiley, 1972, Chap. 12.

BULLETINS

Mackey, A., and J. Stockman. "Soft Wheat Flour Pancakes." *Circular 584.* Corvallis, Ore.: Oregon State College, n.d.

Mackey, A., M. Strauss, and J. Stockman. "Soft Wheat Flour Muffins." *Circular 547.* Corvallis, Ore.: Oregon State College, n.d.

Flour Mixtures: Cakes and Cookies

Cake batters are classified as drop batters. The ingredients—flour, eggs, milk, salt, and sugar—are similar to those used in other flour mixtures; there are, however, some special requisites of cake ingredients that require different treatment.

Cakes are of one of two types: those made with fat, called *butter* or *shortened cakes,* and those made without fat, called *sponge cakes*. Cakes made with fat include plain yellow, white, chocolate, spice, and pound cakes. A great many recipes are available for each of these cakes, but a careful study will show that the recipes for a given type call for the same basic ingredients. Sponge cakes include angel cakes, yellow sponge cakes, and "mock" sponge cakes. Chiffon cakes contain oil, but resemble sponge cakes.

CAKE INGREDIENTS

Generally, cake flours are used in making cakes, although many cakes of excellent quality can be made from all-purpose flours. Cake flours are normally milled from soft winter wheat, which is characterized by its relatively low protein content. Only the best grades of flour, averaging usually between 7 and 8.5% protein, are used for cake flour.

The granulation of cake flour also appears to affect its overall behavior. According to Pyler,[1] the finer and more uniform the granules, the better the results obtained with the flour, because such a flour forms a soft, yielding gluten that does not grow tough when it is mixed.

The bleaching or maturing treatment to which a cake flour is subjected has some tenderizing effect on the gluten. Flour is the chief ingredient in cakes and it must have some gluten-forming properties to give the cake its characteristic structure.

To produce a cake of good quality, the essential ingredients must be present in the proper quantities and proportions. The main principle involved in a cake formula is to provide the proper proportions of the various ingredients so that the tenderizing agents—sugar, shortening, egg yolks, and chocolate—conteract the toughening or binding ingredients—flour, egg whites, and milk solids.

Liquid. The liquid used in cake is mainly whole milk, but evaporated milk, skim milk, or nonfat dry milk solids with water may also be used. On

---

[1] E. J. Pyler, *Baking Science and Technology,* Vol. 2 (Chicago: Siebel, 1952), p. 564.

occasion, soured milk or buttermilk, fruit juice, or fruit pulp (such as bananas and applesauce) may serve as the liquid ingredient. When these are used, some adjustment in the leavening agent is necessary.

Liquid is needed in the cake batter to bring about the hydration of the proteins and the starch, and also to serve as a solvent for the chemical leavening agent, the sugar, and the salt. The liquid proportion in a cake recipe must be worked out with care; too little liquid will cause a cake to grow dry and stale quickly, and too much liquid will produce a cake of small volume and very moist texture.

Shortening. The fat in a cake batter serves to tenderize the gluten and starch particles, rendering the crumb tender. The fat serves another very important function: it entraps air during the creaming process, thereby contributing to the leavening of the batter and increasing the volume of the baked cake.

Many types of shortenings are used for cakes. Butter is still one of the most popular for use in shortened cake, its chief attributes being its food value, flavor, and color. The disadvantage of using butter as a shortening for cake is its relatively high cost and low creaming quality compared to the hydrogenated fats.

Actually, any fat with a pleasing or bland flavor may be used for cakes. There are on the market, however, hydrogenated vegetable fats that are especially suitable. These are the super-glycerinated shortenings, which make it possible to increase the sugar and liquid content of cake batters. The glycerides act as emulsifiers, facilitating a good distribution of fat in the batter. Some studies indicate that cakes made with superglycerinated shortening have a larger volume than those prepared with a nonglycerinated shortening.[2] This may be attributable to the fact that more air bubbles are dispersed in the batter made with superglycerinated shortenings.

Sugar. Sugar has a tenderizing effect on the gluten and egg proteins of the batter—and the greater the amount of sugar, the more pronounced is this effect. Yet a batter with too much sugar will produce a cake of small volume

with a sugary crust. A finely granulated sugar has the advantage of blending completely with the other ingredients. An equal weight of well-sifted brown sugar may be substituted for white, except in white shortened cakes (cakes made with egg whites instead of whole egg) and in sponge cakes. If this substitution is made, however, the texture of the cake will be different. The grain will be coarser and the volume may not be as great. Syrups of various kinds are used in cake batters, but these too produce a difference in the appearance and palatability of the baked product. For example, cakes made with honey keep moist for a longer period of time, but they are heavier and more compact than cakes made with cane or beet sugar, because the sharp edges of the sugar crystals help to incorporate air into the mixture during the creaming stage. Not only the texture of a cake but also much of its flavor depends on the sugar, and even the color of the crumb is altered with increases and decreases in the sugar content. A substitution that is recommended is one cup of honey for 1¼ cups of sugar minus ¼ cup of liquid. For cakes, substitution of honey for one-half of the sugar ingredients is acceptable.

Leavening Agents. Although the major portion of the leavening in a cake batter is supplied through the evolution of carbon dioxide from the reaction of baking powder or baking soda and an acid, some air is incorporated into the flour mixture through the creaming of fat and sugar, the blending of ingredients, and the folding of beaten egg whites into the batter. Lowe[3] suggests that baking powder has a second function: the salts of the baking powder or their residual products may have an effect on the hydration capacity of the flour proteins, modifying the viscosity of the cake batter.

Eggs. Eggs have a number of important functions in cake batter. Because they contain a considerable amount of protein that is extensible and coagulable by heat, they form a portion of the network of the cake structure. And when egg white or whole egg foam is added, it will impart some leavening action to the batter. The lecithin in egg yolk is thought to act as an emul-

[2] M. E. Jooste and A. D. Mackey, "Cake Structure and Palatability," *Food Res.* **17**:185, 1952.

[3] Belle Lowe, *Experimental Cookery*, 4th ed. (New York: Wiley, 1955), p. 484.

sifier of the fat in the batter. Not the least important of the functions attributed to eggs is the addition of color and flavor to the baked product.

SHORTENED CAKES

A shortened cake should have a delicate sweet flavor and a soft velvety crumb. The top should be slightly rounded—not peaked—and the air cells thin-walled, small, and evenly spaced (Fig. 33-1). If butter is used, its pleasing taste should be discernible in the cake.

Formulas. The old pound cake formula (1 lb each of butter, flour, eggs, and sugar) has served as the starting point for many variations. This formula has been modified; shortened cake batter now has a structure very different from that of the old-fashioned pound cake. Pyler[4] notes that a cake recipe will be well balanced if the following proportions are used:

1. The weight of the shortening should equal the weight of whole eggs.
2. The weight of the sugar should equal the weight of the flour.
3. The combined weight of eggs and milk should equal the weight of the flour or sugar.

[4] Pyler, op. cit., p. 605.

33-1 *The fineness and lightness of the cake grain are shown in this cross-section. (Courtesy of Betty Crocker of General Mills)*

The more recently developed and more frequently used cake recipes have a high sugar content for use with the superglycerinated shortenings. Rules for these recipes have been generalized as follows[5]:

1. The weight of the sugar should exceed that of the flour.
2. The weight of the eggs should exceed that of the fat.
3. The weight of the liquid in the eggs and milk should equal or slighlty exceed the weight of the sugar.

From these rules, it can be seen that the permissible level of sugar varies widely. For yellow or white cakes, the sugar/flour ratio generally does not exceed 3:2 or fall much below 1:1. Batters that have appreciable amounts of cocoa and chocolate may have a sugar/flour ratio higher than 3:2.

Because eggs have a toughening effect on batter structure, an equal or almost equal weight of fat must be used to provide a tenderizing effect. The term *liquid* in the rules refers to the total weight of the liquid ingredient and the eggs. In a high-sugar-ratio cake made with superglycerinated shortening, the amount of milk may be higher than in other recipes, and the combined weight of milk and eggs may exceed the equal-weight rule, going as high as 165% of the flour weight.

The most common proportion of baking powder is 1½ tsp to 1 cup flour, but the high-sugar-ratio cake may require more baking powder.

Stanley and Cline[6] recommend, as a means of predicting the outcome before baking, that three batter proportions be checked:

1. Sugar should not exceed ⅔ of the measure of the flour (in most cases ½ is safer).
2. There should be at least 1 egg per ¼ cup fat.
3. The liquid should be approximately ½ the measure of the soft wheat flour; when less than 2 eggs and ½ cup fat are used, the liquid content is increased.

Just as there are numerous variations of shortened cakes based on several basic formulas, so are

[5] Ibid., p. 606.
[6] A. Stanley and J. Cline, *Foods: Their Selection and Preparation* (Boston: Ginn, 1950), p. 298.

there a great number of modifications of basic mixing methods.

The primary purpose of mixing is to bring about a complete blending of all the cake ingredients and to incorporate into the batter a maximum amount of air. The three basic mixing methods are the *muffin method* (discussed in Chapter 32), the *conventional method,* and the *quick* or *speed method.* Other methods not described here are completely reviewed in Paul.[7]

Physical Characteristics of Cake Batters. The structure of a plain shortened cake is that of an air-in-fat foam distributed in a flour-in-liquid mixture (Fig. 33-2). It is apparent from many reports[8] that the foam structure—that is, the incorporation and retention of air in the fat—is of crucial importance in the production of a high-quality cake. During baking, carbon dioxide combines with the air bubbles in the fat and expands through the batter, causing it to lighten; the starch gelatinizes; and the proteins of the eggs and flour coagulate to give strength to the structure of the cake.

Temperature of Ingredients. If the cake ingredients are brought to room temperature before mixing, the creaming of the fat will be greatly facilitated and the sugar will dissolve relatively quickly. Numerous laboratory experiments have indicated that considerable time is saved in attaining a proper blend when the ingredients are left at room temperature for approximately 28–30 minutes before they are combined.

Variations. Variations of shortened cakes may be made by adding such flavoring materials as chocolate, cocoa, spices, and fruits. A second method of varying these cakes is by using only the whites or the yolks of the eggs, as is done in a gold cake or a white cake.

Chocolate cakes, a popular variation, can be made with either cocoa or chocolate. These cakes range in color from light brown to dark mahogany-red. When chocolate is used, it should be melted in a double boiler and added with the fat ingredient, but cocoa should be sifted with the dry ingredients.

The color of the chocolate cake varies with the kind and amount of chocolate or cocoa and the type and amount of baking powder used. If high-alkaline-treatment cocoa is used, baking soda should be reduced. The acidity or alkalinity of the batter is also a factor.

A deep reddish color is characteristic of a chocolate cake if soda is used in excessive amounts. Studies showed that when soda was used in combination with phosphate or tartrate baking powder the color was reddish but when soda was combined with sodium–aluminum–sulfate–phosphate baking powder the color of the cake was a deep brown.[9]

It has also been noted by researchers[10] that in chocolate cake recipes where relatively small amounts of soda replaced part of the baking powder, the finished cakes had a more velvety crumb, higher compressibility, and greater volume than chocolate cakes made without soda.

Spice cake is made by the addition of such spices as cinnamon, nutmeg, and cloves to the batter. These spices are combined with the dry ingredients.

A fruit cake is a shortened cake to which spices and chopped fruits and nuts have been added—usually at the end of the mixing stage.

White cakes require the substitution of egg whites for whole eggs on a 1:1 basis. Gold cakes, on the other hand, require the substitution of yolks for whole eggs on a 2:1 basis, and sometimes a slight increase in the amount of leavening and liquid.

Gingerbread has a high molasses content, which accounts for the fact that many gingerbread recipes call for baking soda to be com-

[7] Pauline Paul, and Helen Palmer, *Food Theory and Application* (New York: Wiley, 1972), Chap. 12.

[8] G. T. Carlin, "A Microscopic Study of the Behavior of Fat in Cake Batters," *Cereal Chem.* **21:**189, 1944; H. G. Ohlrogge and G. Sunderlin, "Factors Affecting the Quality of Cakes Made with Oil," *J. Amer. Dietet. Assoc.* **24:**213, 1948.

M. Hood and Belle Lowe, "Air, Water Vapor, and Carbon Dioxide Gas as Leavening Gases in Cakes Made with Different Types of Fats," *Cereal Chem.* **25:**244, 1948.

[9] A. M. Briant, L. L. Weaver, and H. E. Skodvin, "Quality and Thiamine Retention in Plain and Chocolate Cakes and in Gingerbread," *Cornell Extension Experiment Station Memorandum 332* (Ithaca, N.Y.: 1954).

[10] Ibid.

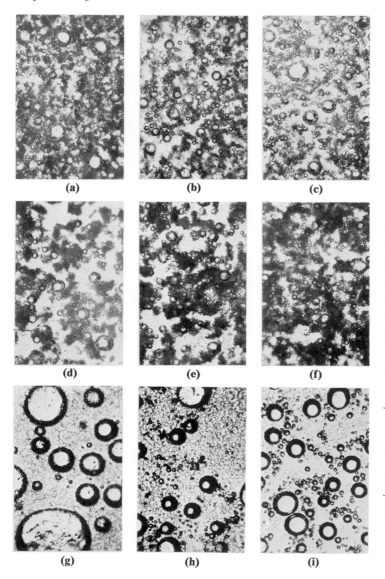

(a) (b) (c)

(d) (e) (f)

(g) (h) (i)

33-2 *Photomicrographs of cake batters prepared from a medium-sugar formula. Top row: Dispersion of hydrogenated shortening at 8°C (a), 22°C (b), and 30°C (c). The fat flakes appear to be uniformly distributed. Middle row: Dispersion of margarine at 8°C (d), 22°C (e), and 30°C (f). Aggregation of fat with clustering of air cells. Bottom row: Dispersion of lard at 8°C (g), 22°C (h), and 30°C (i). The lard for the most part is distributed as a continuous film. (Courtesy of Cornell University Agricultural Experiment Station)*

bined with the acid in the molasses for the leavening. When soda is used, the alkali serves to tenderize the gluten in the gingerbread and impart a dark color. Gingerbread leavened with baking powder, on the other hand, has a lighter and a different flavor.

Preliminary Considerations in Mixing. The pan in which the batter is to be baked should be prepared before the ingredients are combined. The bottom of the pan should be greased with the same fat used in the mixture. Or it may be

lined with a piece of wax paper that has been cut to the size of the pan bottom and greased. The latter method is more effective in preventing the cake from sticking to the bottom of the pan. Cake pans must be clean, or even the fat will not keep the cake from sticking.

Ingredients must be accurately measured or weighed if results are to be good. Basic measuring techniques should be reviewed before the actual cake making begins.

Whether the ingredients are mixed by hand or with an electric mixer, the time required to combine them will be shortened if the ingredients are brought to room temperature first. Also, it is important that the oven be heated before the ingredients are mixed so that it will have reached the proper baking temperature by the time the cake is put in.

Conventional Mixing Method. The conventional method, sometimes called the *cake method,* consistently produces a good cake, if the ingredients are properly balanced and the procedure correctly followed. Hunter and others found that good-quality cakes were prepared using a lean sugar formula by the conventional method of mixing, but cakes mixed with this formula and mixed with the pastry-blend and dump methods were less desirable. In the same study it was shown that when there was an increase in the ratio of sugar–fat to flour in the cake formula, the cell structure of the cakes was finer and more uniform and the crumb increased in tenderness and velvetiness.[11]

In the conventional method of mixing, the fat is creamed until it is light and fluffy, the sugar is added gradually, and the creaming is continued. During this creaming, the sugar crystals and the fat are blended into a smooth fluffy mass in which few if any sugar crystals are left. A well-creamed mixture forms the basis for a fine-grained cake. After creaming, egg yolks or whole eggs are added and the mixing is continued until all ingredients are blended into a homogeneous mass. The sifted flour is measured and sifted again with the baking powder and salt. The milk and flavoring are combined and small quantities of this mixture are added alternately with small quantities of the flour mixture to the creamed fat–sugar–egg base. The addition of the dry and liquid ingredients starts and ends with the flour mixture. If the egg whites have been separated from the yolks, they are beaten until stiff and folded into the batter at the very last. This is a time-consuming method of mixing a cake, yet it is a very popular household method because it produces a fine-grain cake with a velvety crumb.

A modification of this method is called *meringue method.* It differs from the conventional method in that the separated egg whites and part of the sugar may be made into a meringue and folded into the batter at the very last.

Quick Mixing Method. Cakes made by the quick method are formulated to be made with the superglycerinated shortenings. These are the high-sugar-ratio cakes. All the dry ingredients are sifted together in a bowl and then the fat, milk, and flavoring are added. After the mixture has been beaten vigorously for 2 minutes (150 strokes) by hand or by electric mixer, the eggs are added and the mixture is beaten for another 2 minutes. The batter is likely to be thinner than those mixed by the conventional method.

Closely related to the quick method is the *single-stage* or *dump method.* This method consists of placing all the ingredients into a bowel and mixing them until they are well combined.

In the pastry-blend method the fat and flour are creamed together to produce a foam. To this a mixture of the sugar, salt, baking powder, and one-half of the milk is blended, and finally the egg and the remainder of the milk are mixed in.

Many studies have been conducted to show the effect of the mixing method on the quality of the cake. It would appear from the reports of these studies that each method used for combining ingredients produces a cake with a characteristic texture, volume, flavor, and color. The evidence seems to slightly favor the quick, or speed, method.

Baking. The batter should be placed in the cake pans and baked as quickly as possible after being mixed. Cake batters that are not to be baked immediately should be refrigerated in the baking pans until it is time to put them in the oven. Once the baking powder has entered into solution, some carbon dioxide is evolved. If the mixture is left standing for prolonged periods, some of the carbon dioxide will escape and the baked product will have a characteristically coarse cell structure.

Cake batters can be frozen immediately after mixing if they are to be baked at a later time. Lowering the temperature of the batter tends to reduce the loss of leavening power.

TEMPERATURE. Baking temperatures for shortened cakes vary with the ingredients in the batter. Temperatures for fruit cakes and pound cakes, which are baked in heavy pans, are low,

[11] M. B. Hunter, "Cake Quality and Batter Structure," *Cornell University Agriculture Experiment Station Bulletin 860* (Ithaca, N.Y.: 1950).

for such cakes require longer baking periods than shortened layer cakes do.

Cakes with a high sugar content require temperatures lower than those used for cakes of standard proportions. Also, cakes made with molasses and honey, brown at lower temperatures than do cakes made with granulated sugar.

The size or thickness of the cake affects baking temperature. Loaf cakes, for instance, require temperatures lower than those used for cupcakes or cakes baked in sheet pans.

The shape and thickness of the cake also helps to determine the time required to bake it. Generally, layer cakes take 25–30 minutes, standard-size loaf cakes 45–55 minutes. Usually, each recipe gives specific directions for baking time and oven temperature, but some generalizations on baking time, shown in Table 33-1, may prove helpful.

PANS. There is ample evidence that both the shape and size of the pan and the material of which it is made exert an influence on the quality of the cake. Peet and Thye[12] report that cakes baked in pans with sharp corners tend to be browner at the corners and that the texture of cakes baked in shallow pans is coarser than that of cakes baked in deep ones. They also observe that cakes baked in tinned steel, aluminum, or glass all have good shape and a tender light-brown crust, but that cakes baked in aluminum pans require a few more minutes of baking time.

Generally, aluminum baking pans are used in laboratory work—mainly because they provide excellent heat distribution, but also because they are comparatively easy to clean and store.

It is recommended that oven temperatures for cakes baked in glass pans be set 25°F lower than those used for cakes baked in aluminum or tin pans. The reason for this is that glass transmits radiant heat readily, which causes the outer crusts of products baked in the glass to brown too rapidly.

Tin pans tend to darken with use. The darker the pan, the more quickly will the bottom and side crusts of the cake brown.[13]

TABLE 33-1
Baking Times and Oven Temperatures for Cakes

Cake Size	Temperature		Time (min)
	°F	°C	
Cupcake	375	191	20
Layer cake	375	191	25–30
Sheet cake	375	191	30
Loaf cake	350	199	45–50

Lowe suggests that there is a relationship between the height of the shortened cake and the slope of the sides of the pan.[14] The most suitable pans for baking are those with straight rather than sloping sides. Studying the effect of pan size on cake volume, Charley[15] concluded that cakes baked in shallow pans were larger and more tender and had more delicately browned crusts and flatter tops than did cakes baked in pans of equal volume but with 2½- to 3-in. sides.

The practical value of the studies cited has been to point up the importance of using a baking pan of the correct size and shape. Usually, the capacity of the pan is exactly right when the baked cake just fills the pan, without hanging over the sides or bulging at the top.

Cakes should be allowed to stand for 15–20 minutes before they are removed from the pan. This cooling-off period permits the interior of the cake to become firm. Once the cake is removed from the pan, it should be placed on a cooling rack. If the pan bottom has been lined, the wax paper should be peeled off at once.

TESTING. The cake is done if the top springs back when lightly touched with a finger or when a cake tester (or wooden toothpick) inserted into the center of the cake comes out clean. The cake should not be tested until after the minimum baking period is over. There is no advantage to periodic testing of the cake: repeatedly opening the door will only lower the temperature of the oven and prolong baking time.

---

[12] L. Peet and L. Thye, *Household Equipment* (New York: Wiley, 1961).

[13] F. Ehrenkranz and L. Inman, *Equipment in the Home* (New York: Harper & Row, 1967), p. 63.

[14] Lowe, op.cit., p. 460.

[15] H. Charley, "Effects of Size and Shape of the Baking Pan on the Quality of Shortened Cakes," *J. Home Econ.* **44**:115, 1952.

ARRANGEMENT OF CAKES IN OVEN. Oven racks should be placed as close to the center of the oven as possible so that the sides of the cake pan do not touch the sides of the oven. When two pans are put in the oven at the same time, they should be placed so that the heated air can circulate freely around each. The pans should touch neither one another nor the sides of the oven, nor should one pan be placed directly above the other.

ELECTRONIC BAKING. Shortened cakes can be baked in a microwave oven. The texture of cakes so baked compares favorably with that of cakes baked in conventional ovens. But the poor coloration of electronically baked cakes places them at a marked disadvantage when they are judged according to standards set for conventionally baked cakes. The browning of the crusts (caused by the conventional electric unit in the microwave oven) was not as even as that of the crusts on the cakes baked in conventional ovens. A recent study of the effect of electronic cooking on the appearance and palatability of a yellow cake revealed that an increase (1½–3 tbsp) in the liquid content of the batter produced a cake that compared well in cell distribution, moisture content, and volume to a cake baked in a conventional oven.[16]

BAKING FAILURES. Baking failures can be minimized by carefully checking the proportions of the ingredients, by choosing a suitable method of combining the ingredients, and by carefully controlling the baking environment. From time to time, failures do occur. A review of the reasons for cake failure is given in Table 33-2.

Recipe Adjustments for High Altitudes. Experience has shown that cake recipes designed for use at normal altitudes require adjustment if they are to produce satisfactory results at high altitudes (see Fig. 33-3). The ingredient most affected is the leavening agent: the volume of gas obtained from steam, air, baking powder, or soda increases with increases in altitude. Hence, the indicated proportion of baking powder or other leavening materials must be reduced when cakes are baked at high altitudes. (Flour can be

[16] M. Street and H. K. Surratt, "The Effect of Electronic Cookery upon the Appearance and Palatability of a Yellow Cake," *J. Home Econ.* **53**:285, 1961.

added to give batter strength: 1 tbsp per cup flour).

Because the boiling point of water is lower at, say, 10,000 feet than it is at sea level, the internal temperature of cakes during baking at such an altitude is lower. Thus, cakes baked at high altitudes are weaker in structure. Ingredients that make a cake tender (fat and sugar) and those that give it strength (flour and eggs) are affected by changes in altitude. For instance, for baking at 5000 feet, the fat and sugar content should be reduced 10%, at 7500 feet 15%, and at 10,000 feet 30%. At high altitudes, baking pans must be more thoroughly and heavily greased to prevent cakes from sticking to the sides and bottom.

SPONGE CAKES (UNSHORTENED CAKES)

The group of cakes known as *sponge cakes* includes angel cake, ladyfingers. and several others. True sponge cakes depend on air and steam for leavening; hot-water sponge cakes and jelly-roll sponge mixtures use a little baking powder to lighten the batter. A sponge cake does not contain fat as a basic ingredient.

Angel Cake. Angel cake contains only three basic ingredients: egg white (42% based on total batter weight), sugar (42%), and flour (15%). The remainder is made up of salt, flavoring, and cream of tartar. The high sugar content is necessary because no other tenderizer is used. It produces a crust that is crisp and more sugary than that of a shortened cake. Cream of tartar is used in angel cakes to tenderize the egg proteins and to whiten the cake batter. If too much acid is used, the cake tends to shrink during baking and the finished product is excessively moist.

An angel cake should be very light—almost fluffy. The crumb is fine, with thin-walled elongated air cells evenly distributed throughout. It is tender, white, and has a delicate, moist flavor.

The lightness and volume of an angel cake depend to a large extent on the method of combining ingredients. The goal in mixing is to completely blend the ingredients with the beaten egg whites—without losing the air held by the egg foam. A number of procedures may be used for mixing an angel cake. All produce acceptable cakes, but one method appears to be the most

TABLE 33-2
Major Causes of
Baking Failures

Failures	Possible Causes
Coarseness, dryness	Not enough liquid Too much baking powder Too much flour
Poor volume	Not enough baking powder Not enough mixing Too much liquid Too much fat
Heavy layer on bottom	Not enough mixing Too much liquid Too many eggs
Coarseness, thickness, hump in middle	Too hot an oven
Peaked, cracked top	Too much flour Not enough milk Too hot an oven Pan placed too high in oven
Grayish color	Low-grade flour Use of aluminum mixing bowl
Large holes and "tunnels"	Overbeating Too much baking powder
Bitter flavor	Too much baking powder
Sticking to pan	Insufficient greasing of pan Too short a baking period
Tough crust or crumb	Too little fat Too little sugar
Hanging over sides of pan	Too much baking powder Too small a pan

consistent in producing an excellent product. With this method, the egg whites are beaten until foamy, and then the salt, flavoring, and cream of tartar are added. The beating is continued until the egg whites form peaks with slightly bending tips. Then the sugar is folded in carefully, usually 2–3 tbsp at a time. The flour is then added in the same way.

Another satisfactory way of adding the sugar and flour to the beaten eggs is to mix a fourth of the sugar with the flour. This facilitates the smooth blending of the flour into the mixture.

If an electric mixer is used, the sugar may be whipped into the egg whites after they have formed a fairly stiff foam. If the sugar is added to the egg whites before this point, more beating time will be required.

Frozen egg whites have long been used in commercially produced angel cakes. They may also be used satisfactorily in small, household–size recipes. Miller and Vail[17] reported favorable results when using frozen egg whites and noted that frozen thick whites and frozen thin whites are whipped best at a temperature of 70°F (21°C) (that is, at about room temperature). When fresh eggs are used, they must be carefully separated: bits of egg yolk will markedly reduce the volume of the whipped whites. Any traces of fat adhering to the bowl or egg beater coming in contact with the egg whites during whipping

[17] E. L. Miller and G. E. Vail, "Angel Food Cakes Made from Fresh and Frozen Egg Whites," *Cereal Chem.* **20**:528, 1943.

33-3 *Angel food cakes baked at 5000 ft. The cake on the left was baked from a recipe that was adjusted for altitude. The cake on the right was baked from an unadjusted recipe. (Courtesy U.S. Department of Agriculture)*

will have the same effect. Some practical points suggested by Pyler[18] for the commercial production of angel cakes may be equally useful when making small recipes:

1. Use medium speed when beating egg whites.
2. Check to see that the whip reaches the bottom of the bowl so no deposit of unbeaten egg whites is left.
3. Finish the operation by hand when mixing is done by machine, so as to mix completely any materials deposited on the bottom of the bowl.

Yellow Sponge Cake. The yellow sponge cake does not differ much from the angel cake except the yolks as well as the whites are used and lemon juice is generally the acid ingredient. In some sponge cakes, a small amount of water may also be used. In making a sponge cake, the goal is to reduce the toughening effect of the whole eggs by including a sufficient amount of sugar. The rules[19] used in a sponge cake formula are the following:

1. The amount of sugar should equal or slightly exceed that of the whole eggs.

[18] Pyler, op. cit., p. 615.
[19] Ibid., p. 607.

2. The combined weights of the whole eggs and the milk or water should exceed the weight of the sugar.
3. The weight of the sugar or of the whole eggs should exceed that of the flour.
4. The combined weights of the eggs and the flour should exceed the combined weights of the sugar and the liquids (other than whole eggs).

A sponge cake should be golden yellow, very light, with a delicate, velvety crumb. The flavor is delicately sweet, with slight overtones of lemon. There should be no thickened layer at the bottom of the cake.

The methods of mixing a sponge cake are similar to those used for angel cakes. In a true sponge cake, the egg yolks, the sugar, and the liquid are beaten together until they are very light and fluffy. (Insufficient beating of these ingredients will result in a poor-textured cake with marked layering.) The egg yolks are beaten until they are thick and fluffy and the sugar is added gradually (about 2 tbsp at a time). The lemon juice and lemon rind may be added at this point. Then the flour and the salt are gently folded into the egg yolk mixture. The egg whites, beaten stiff but not dry, are folded into the mixture at the very last.

409

Another method for mixing the ingredients in a sponge cake is known as the *syrup method,* which produces a fine-textured cake. In this method, the sugar and half as much water are boiled together to 238°F (124°C). The mixture is slowly poured over the egg whites (which have been beaten until they form stiff peaks). The beaten egg yolks, the salt, and the lemon juice are then folded in; the flour is folded in last.

The Cornell experiments on whole-egg sponge cake are significant from the standpoint of work simplification. As a result of these experiments, a recipe for a 10-in. tube pan was developed.[20] It was concluded that sponge cakes made with whole eggs compared favorably with cake prepared by conventional methods, but that the salt must be added to the dry ingredients and the lemon juice to the eggs before beating. This method does not reduce the total time required, but it does save steps and one bowl.

Mock Sponge Cakes. When it is not feasible to use as many eggs as are called for in a true sponge cake, a "mock" sponge cake can be made. Liquid and baking powder may be substituted for half the total egg ingredient (2 tbsp milk and ½ tsp baking powder for every egg omitted). Although not a true sponge cake, the mock sponge cake has no fat added and in appearance and flavor is very much like true yellow sponge.

Baking. Both angel cakes and yellow sponge cakes are usually baked in ungreased tube pans. The ungreased pan helps to maintain the light structure of the rising cake. The tube in the center of the pan permits circulation of heat during baking and also helps to support the delicate structure of the cake. Temperatures of 325–350°F (163–176°C) have proved to produce cakes of excellent quality. Generally, the lower temperature is used for yellow sponge cakes, the higher for angel cakes. Because these mixtures contain so large a proportion of egg, too high a temperature would cause the top of the cake to coagulate before the heat had penetrated the mixture and before the air mixed into the cake had been heated sufficiently to expand. In a tube pan, sponge cakes require 40–60 min-

utes for baking. The cake is done when it is a delicate brown and the surface springs back when lightly touched with a fingertip. When removed from the oven, the pan is inverted over a cake rack and left while the cake cools. When the cake is thoroughly cooled, it is loosened with a spatula and removed from the pan.

Rinsing the tube pan with cold water before baking leaves the baked cake with light, slightly moist sides.

Chiffon Cakes. Chiffon cakes have some of the characteristics of cakes made without fat, yet oil is one of the ingredients used. The large quantity of eggs used in the basic recipe imparts to this cake the lightness characteristic of sponge cakes. The method of combining ingredients in a chiffon cake is a combination of several methods. The dry ingredients are sifted together in a mixing bowl and a "well" is made in the center. To this mixture, the oil, egg yolks, liquid, and flavoring are added and the whole is combined until the mixture is very well blended. The egg whites and cream of tartar are beaten together until the whites are stiff and then are gently folded into the mixture. The chiffon cake may be baked in an ungreased tube pan, a square pan, or a rectangular pan.

COOKIES

All cookie batters and doughs bear some similarities to cake batters. The main difference is the decreased amount of liquid in the cookie dough. Other differences that distinguish a cookie batter or dough may be increased amounts of fat and egg (in which case the liquid may be entirely omitted) and the smaller amounts of leavening—all of which give cookies a crisp, rather than light, texture. There are hundreds of variations of basic cookie recipes (see Fig. 33-4). Many of these do not fit into any classification; they can be only set down as modified cake products. Generally, however, cookies can be classed as sheet or drop cookies, rolled cookies, refrigerator cookies, and meringue or sponge cookies.

Meringue cookies are made with egg whites, sugar, salt and vanilla. Other materials such as nuts, dates, coconut and cocoa can be added. The eggs are beaten until stiff and the sugar is

---

[20] A. L. Briant and A. R. Willinon, "Whole-Egg Sponge Cake," *J. Home Econ.* **48**:420, 1956.

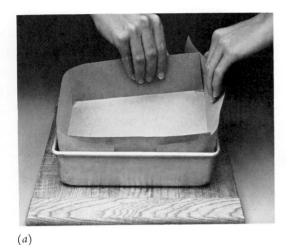

(a)

(b)

(c)

33-4 *Pan preparation for baking bar cookies.*
(a) *brown paper lining* (b) *grease lining* (c) *remove lining carefully to avoid breaking corners. (Courtesy of Diamond Walnut Growers, Inc.)*

added very slowly. Other ingredients are folded in and the batter dropped on a lightly greased tin or waxed paper. They are baked in a very slow oven 225°F (107°C) until dry. In sponge cookies the whole egg or egg yolks are beaten until thick and lemon colored. The sugar is added slowly. Different flavorings may be used. Cookies are dropped on a greased tin and baked in a slow oven. 325°F (163°C)

Sheet or Drop Cookies. A drop batter is used for *sheet cookies*. It is spread out in a thin layer on a greased sheet or pan, and cut into squares, bars, triangles, or other desired shapes after baking. Brownies are an example of the sheet cookie. These are sometimes classified as *bar cookies*. For *dropped cookies,* the mixture is dropped by spoonfuls onto a greased baking sheet. Although the two kinds of batter may be handled similarly, some sheet cookie batters are too thin to be dropped. A good drop cookie batter must contain sufficient flour so as not to spread much upon baking. Sheet and drop cookies are made more interesting by the addition of nuts, raisins, coconut, and dried fruits.

Rolled and Refrigerator Cookies. *Rolled* and *refrigerator cookies* are made from doughs that are stiff enough to be rolled out thin and cut into various shapes. The same type of dough may be used for both varieties. The refrigerator cookie dough is molded and chilled in the coldest compartment of the refrigerator. Then it is sliced into thin cookies (not more than ⅛ in. thick) for baking. Some refrigerator cookies have more fat in them than is found in rolled cookie recipes, so that the chilled dough will be firm enough to slice easily.

Rolled cookie dough, too, must be chilled before rolling. Cookie dough that is to be rolled is handled much as pastry dough is. When the dough is rolled, a minimum of flour should be used; too much flour at this point will modify the flavor and make a hard cookie. Rolling small amounts of dough at a time will cut down on handling and rerolling. Cookies made from rerolled dough are less crisp and tasty than those cut from the first rolling. Cookie dough might well be left in the refrigerator until ready for handling. Rolled cookies are baked on greased baking sheets (unless recipe directions are for ungreased sheets). Because they do not spread very much, only a small amount of space need be left between them.

Refrigerator cookies are usually baked on ungreased baking sheets. These cookies are very convenient to make, because the dough can be sliced quickly and may be stored in the refrigerator for at least a week without deteriorating. *Pressed cookies* are made from rich rolled dough that has been packed into a cookie press. The dough is forced out through cookie dies (cutters). These cookies are usually baked on ungreased baking sheets.

Basic Ingredients. The ingredients used in making different kinds of cookies are similar to those used in making cakes. Traditionally, however, the butter cookie is made with either butter or margarine because of the flavor these impart to the product. In the author's experience, most cookie recipes that list butter as a major ingredient can be made very satisfactorily with margarine. If a hydrogenated vegetable shortening is used, the flavor of the cookies is more acceptable when at least half the shortening ingredient is either butter or margarine.

All-purpose flour may be used for cookies, unless cake flour is specified in the recipe. Shortenings that are not of a pleasant, bland flavor should never be used in cookies; any off-flavor is highly pronounced in the baked cookie.

Mixing Method. Generally, the conventional method of mixing cakes is used in mixing cookie ingredients. Meringues and kisses are mixed much as angel food cake is.

Baking. Cookies are baked at temperatures slightly higher than those used for cakes. Lower temperatures may be necessary for cookies with a very high sugar content or with condensed milk. Excellent results are obtained when cookies are baked only on the middle or top rack in the oven, although this procedure wastes oven space and is not entirely feasible in most household situations. All cookies are baked only until done. Overbaking results in dried-out or overly brown

cookies that are unpalatable and store poorly.

After cookies have been removed from the oven, they should be taken from the baking sheet and placed on a cake rack. Delay in executing this step may reduce the number of removable whole cookies.

Storage. Cookies should be stored in a box with a tight-fitting cover. Soft cookies are kept moist by storing a slice of fresh bread or an apple with them. Crisp cookies have a low moisture content and should be stored separately so as not to pick up moisture and become less crisp.

PREPARED MIXES

The prepared mixes on the market today number in the hundreds, and because most of them are dry flour mixtures, this discussion will give particular attention to the dry ingredients used in these mixes.

Although the popularity of prepared mixes has had its growth spurt only within the last decade and a half, the first prepared mix was introduced as early as 1849, when a self-rising flour (consisting of an aged flour and tartaric acid blended with sodium bicarbonate) appeared on the market. Not long after, a pancake mix was made available. Since that time, increasing numbers of prepared mixes have been introduced. It is estimated that some 90 different types of mixes cover approximately 24 feet of shelf space in the average supermarket. The mixes available include those for casserole dishes, puddings, gelatins, soups, salad dressings, cakes, breads, and cookies.

Cost. The marked increase in consumer demand for the prepared mix has motivated the producers to find ways of reducing cost without altering the palatability and nutritive qualities of the products.

It is rather difficult to compare the costs of home-prepared foods and commercial mixes, for similar products may contain different proportions of ingredients. For example, the cost of a very rich home-baked chocolate cake, may be high compared to the cost of a plain chocolate cake mix. It is essential, therefore, to compare only items that are alike. It is also important to consider the number of servings from a packaged mix and the additional ingredients—such as eggs, milk, nuts, and the like—that it may call for.

For some prepared mixes, packaging costs may be just as high or higher than the cost of the ingredients themselves.

Nutritive Value. A similar problem exists in comparing the nutritive values of the two types of food. Because the ingredients in prepared mixes are not the same in kind and proportion as those in homemade products, there is a difference in nutrient content. For example, flour in the mix may not be enriched, and minimum amounts of egg, milk, and fat may have been used in an effort to reduce cost. Also, baked products made at home frequently have margarine or butter—both of which are good sources of vitamin A—as the fat ingredient. The commercial mix makes use of the highly stabilized fats, which do not have vitamin A.

Bake mixes are classified according to the leavening agent employed. Bake mixes include products leavened by chemicals, leavened by aeration with or without the addition of chemicals, leavened with chemicals and flavored with fermentation products from yeast, or not leavened at all. The mixes leavened by chemicals are doughnuts, cakes, muffins, biscuits, and related products. The foam-type mixes, such as angel food and sponge cake, are packaged with or without the addition of a chemical leavening agent. A third group of mixes, leavened by yeast, includes bread, rolls, buns, and yeast-raised doughnuts. The last group is made up of non-leavened products, such as pie crust.

A few years ago, there was still some hesitancy on the part of the consumer to use a mix. Today, it is recognized that the quality of the home-made product is not necessarily superior to that of the mix, for the skill of the cook plays an important part in determining quality. Institutions have long held that prepared mixes, properly used, provide uniformity as well as speed. Similarly, the household-sized bake mix eliminates the measuring or weighing of individual ingredients, and it assures a good product—if directions are followed.

Before a mix is substituted for a home-prepared product, however, it should be evaluated in terms of nutritive value, cost, convenience, and palatability. To help consumers make good choices, the U.S. Department of Agriculture conducted a study on relative preparation time, yield, cost, and quality of homemade and commercial forms of baked goods.[21] The study showed that commercial forms of baked products saved "active" time (i.e., the period requiring constant attention) and, except for some frozen products and a few mixes, also saved total time required for food preparation. Mixes saved less active preparation time than did other commercial forms of baked products. There was an indication of greater softness in cakes, corn muffins, and yeast rolls made from mixes than in those of other processed or homemade forms. Cookies baked from some mixes and from commercially prepared chilled dough, as well as pancakes and waffles made from mixes, were more tender than the corresponding homemade products. The frozen forms of waffles or pancakes were consistently less tender than other forms, but frozen baking powder biscuits were equal to the homemade in tenderness. Generally, the commercial products were higher in moisture and ash and lower in fat, protein, and energy value than the corresponding homemade items.

Ingredients. FLOUR. Flours used in cake mixes are treated with chlorine because untreated cake flours may cause cakes to fall or to form concave tops.

For a stable cake mix, a 2–6% moisture content is recommended. Too much moisture can cause a premature reaction of the leavening agent, resulting in an excessively small cake.

LEAVENING AGENTS. Sodium bicarbonate, usually in combination with some acid ingredient, is the source of leavening in prepared mixes. In mixes such as self-rising flour and pancake flour, a powdered soda is used, but for mixes that must stand up to long storage, a granular soda is more suitable. The granulation of the soda slows down its rate of solution. When the larger particles of soda are used, the points of contact of the sodium bicarbonate with ingredi-

[21] R. H. Matthews et al., "Baked Products: Consumer Quality, Composition, Yield, and Preparation Time of Various Market Forms," *Home Economics Research Report 22* (Washington D.C.: U.S. Department of Agriculture, 1963).

413

ents that are likely to neutralize it are lessened; thus, there is a minimum loss of leavening power. Too large a particle, however, may not dissolve completely, causing yellow spots to appear in the baked product.

An acid ingredient used in commercial cake mixes is anhydrous monocalcium phosphate monohydrate. This acid has been improved by the addition of a coating material that lowers its solution rate. Sodium acid pyrophosphate is also used as the acid ingredient in some commercial mixes.

The monocalcium phosphate reacts rapidly with bicarbonate, releasing large amounts of carbon dioxide during the early stages of dough or batter development. The coated anhydrous product, however, goes into solution slowly, saving the carbon dioxide for leavening purposes. Dicalcium phosphate, an acid ingredient that releases carbon dioxide from bicarbonate of soda late in the baking process, is used to some extent in dry mixes in combination with a more active baking acid. Its chief use is in canned, refrigerated batters.

Sodium acid pyrophosphate is rather widely used in the bake mix industry. The level of reaction of a pyrophosphate can be adjusted. A fast reaction may be necessary in drying doughnuts; a slower reaction may be desirable in preparing canned biscuits.

Sodium aluminum phosphate is another acid that reacts late in the baking cycle. It is used in combination with coated anhydrous monocalcium phosphate. When the two are used in a cake mix, softness and moist eating quality are retained longer than when a pyrophosphate is used.

Like bicarbonate of soda, acid leavening agents have less tendency to go into fast solution when the particle size is large. The particle size is adjusted to the mix and to the time required for the reaction of the baking powder.

The residual salts of the baking powders leave a distinctive taste. There has been some objection to the taste of products that contain sodium acid pyrophosphate. (This taste occurs when there is a slight excess in the amount of the baking acid used.)

Air beaten into the cake batter and steam leaven the angel food cakes. Some products use a combination of air, steam and the bicarbonate of soda for leavening.

SHORTENING. Shortening is used in nearly all bake mixes; the amount varies according to the desired physical properties of the baked product. The function of fat is to add tenderness, crispness, and volume to a product. Because bake mixes must be able to withstand long storage periods, the keeping quality of the fat used in the mix is of prime importance. Two properties highly desirable in a fat to be used in a mix are resistance to oxidative changes (rancidity) and good baking performance (aeration).

Paralleling the increase in home consumption of bake mixes is an increase in the use of fats and oils in bake mixes. Lard, soybean oil, cottonseed oil, and peanut oil are the four fat materials used in the production of shortenings. In the past few years, lard has undergone certain processing changes that have been effective in producing a high resistance to rancidity. The lard now available to mix manufacturers also has higher creaming properties than that used in the past.

Deodorized lard and lard with natural flavor are used extensively in biscuit and piecrust mixes.

Soybean oil is also widely used in the shortening industry. When it is hydrogenated alone or in blends with other fats, the shortenings produced have high resistance to rancidity, good creaming properties, and desirable texture. Shortenings produced from cottonseed oil and peanut oil have high flavor stability and good baking properties. Blends of these oils with soybean oil and lard are also used in the production of shortenings.

The creaming or emulsification property of a fat is the important factor in determining its usefulness in cake mixes. Fats with high emulsification qualities are capable of dispersing air evenly throughout a cake batter. There is considerable evidence that the emulsion resulting when fats are mixed in a cake batter determines the final character of the baked product. Baked products of coarse grain, poor volume, and low palatability are produced when the fat used has low emulsification properties. According to Harrel,[22] the emulsification requirement is made even more important by the necessity for emulsification of gases in a cake batter. The air creamed into a batter is usually held in suspended

[22] C. G. Harrel, "Manufacture of Prepared Mixes," in *Chemistry and Technology of Cereals,* S. Matz, ed. (Westport, Conn.: Avi, 1959), p. 349.

state by the fats used in the mix. When the chemical leavening agent goes into solution and generates gas, the gas particles are collected in the air spaces.

Although nearly all fats have emulsification properties, and therefore some ability to suspend air or gas within the body of the fat globule, no one fat appears to be perfect for cake mixes. Hence, most fats used in cake mixes have emulsifying agents added. The function of the emulsifying agent here is to improve the aeration quality of the fat. Monoglycerides and diglycerides are the most widely used.

EGG. The use of dried egg products is extensive in bake mixes. Whole-egg solids are used in cookies and layer cakes, dried yolks in doughnuts and sweet doughs, and dried albumen in angel food cakes and macaroons. Both standard egg yolk solids and stabilized egg yolk solids are used in layer cakes, doughnuts, sweet doughs, and cookies. Stabilized egg yolk solids are used in the case of grocery products for which long shelf life is required. In stabilized egg products, the glucose that occurs naturally in eggs has been removed.

A great deal of progress has been made in the fermentation and drying of albumen in the last few years. For angel food cakes, the albumen must have whipping properties that will produce not only a cake of standard volume, but also one that maintains its texture and volume after baking. Whip boosters are used in angel cake mixes to insure good cake volume. However, whipping acids are not effective when used with low-quality albumen.

MILK SOLIDS. Dried milk solids are used in bake mixes. The uniformity of the dry milk is very important in a mix. Of foremost importance is the low moisture level of the milk product. Also, spray-processed nonfat dry milk solids rather than a roller-dried product are desirable for best results in the cake mix. The reason for this is that the spray-dried milk solids have a higher rate of solubility than the roller-dried. Either can be used in cookie and yeast-raised products.

SUGAR AND SWEETENERS. The most important sugar in the bake mix industry is sucrose. Granulated sugar is generally used in the body of the cake mix. Powdered sugar is frequently used for the icings that are packaged and sold to use with the cake mix. Brown sugars are used in mixes for the color and flavor they impart to the finished product, although they are difficult to incorporate as an ingredient because of their tendency to cake. Dextrose or corn sugar is frequently used in pancake mixes because it browns more quickly than cane sugar. Molasses is used in mixes, chiefly for gingerbread. Although dried molasses has been successfully used in gingerbread mixes for some time, honey is too hygroscopic to be used in its dried form.

Dried whey, which is 72 to 73 per cent lactose, may be used in the production of cakes and cookies because of its potential browning and tenderizing properties. The greater browning effect of this sugar material (as compared with that of cane sugar) is thought to be the result of the (Maillard) browning reaction.

FLAVORING INGREDIENTS. Vanilla, lemon, orange, and similar flavors may be added to a bake mix. These are added dry and in very small amounts—and have little effect on baking. But the addition of such flavors as chocolate, cocoa, caramel, or brown sugar, and fruits and nuts, requires that certain changes in the formula be made. For instance, when fruits or nuts are added, it is frequently necessary to use more flour or a strong type of flour.

ANTIOXIDANTS. Antioxidants are incorporated in bake mixes to reduce the rate of oxidative rancidity. The first edible antioxidant approved by the U.S. Food and Drug Administration for use in lard was gum guaiac. During the past few years, propyl gallate, nondihydroguaiaretic acid, butylated hydroxyanisole and citric acid have been used singly and in combination to improve the stability of fat. Some prepared mixes have natural antioxidants. For example, unbleached flour will extend the shelf life of the shortening used in the mix. Ginger and other spices generally used in spice cakes are effective antioxidants. Sugar, acid phosphates and lecithin possess some antioxidant properties.

Bake Mixes. Satisfactory use of prepared mixes requires some understanding of how these mixes are manufactured. Bake mixes are built on good bakery or household recipes. The ingredients, as far as possible are converted to a dry mix.

BISCUIT MIXES. The basic ingredients used in a biscuit mix are flour, salt, soda, phosphate, dried nonfat milk solids, and shortening. The dry ingredients are mixed together first and then the shortening is added. The shortening may be added to the dry mix in the form of a dry shortening, or as a plastic shortening, or by spraying, or by cutting in with high-speed cutters. Dry shortening is usually a mixture composed mainly of shortening and nonfat milk solids. The milk solids coat the fat so as to impart a free-flowing quality to the fat particles. Plastic shortening is incorporated into the mixture by using high-speed cutters that cut the shortening into the mixed ingredients as they come from a conveyor at a controlled rate. This is considered a very simple way of adding the shortening to the mix. Biscuits made from a mix with dried shortening are somewhat moister than biscuits made from a mix in which the plastic fat has been incorporated, and they have a slight tendency to hold more water.

PANCAKE MIXES. One of the earliest mixes, the pancake mix, enjoys wide popularity. A wheat pancake mix differs from the formula for a biscuit mix in that very coarse flour middlings (farina) are added. A small amount of sodium acid pyrophosphate is also used. The farina makes the baked pancake more tender; the sodium acid pyrophosphate is used to slow down the rate at which the carbon dioxide is evolved and allows a delay in baking pancakes after the batter has been mixed.

The most commonly used pancake mix is one in which shortening has been eliminated and corn flour used to obtain tenderness. Cornstarch and rice flour may also be used in pancake mixes to obtain dryness in the baked product. Dried buttermilk and buckwheat flour may be added for flavor. When buckwheat flour is used, the percentages of white flour and yellow corn flour are decreased and plastic fats are added. There is little need in the pancake mix for the creaming properties of the monoglyceride content in fats. In fact, use of these fats may cause the pancake batter to stick.

CORNMEAL MIXES. Cornmeal mixes require a fat that has a high resistance to rancidity. This is because the cornmeal is high in lipase activity and is itself inclined toward rancidity. High-level hydrogenated shortenings are used for these mixes.

MUFFIN MIXES. Muffin mixes, too, are popular in household-sized recipes. The range of muffin mixes is wide. There are muffin mixes that are similar to the baking powder biscuit mix and others that resemble the cake mix. Shortenings for the biscuit-type mix are of the plastic type, whereas the cake-type muffin mix contains a fat with high monoglyceride content.

CAKE MIXES. The cake mix has the largest range in quality of any of the mixes on the market. The basic ingredients in a cake mix are flour, sugar, shortening, egg solids or egg albumen, nonfat milk solids, soda, sodium acid pyrophosphate, monocalcium monohydrate, salt, and powdered vanilla. The flour used is one with a low moisture content (usually 6%). The shortening is one with high resistance to rancidity and containing a high proportion of monoglycerides and diglycerides.

It is a common practice to eliminate the egg product in the shortened cake mixes, requiring the homemaker to supply this ingredient in the fresh form. Although doughnuts mixes have used dried whole-egg solids for some time, there has not yet been developed a dried egg product that performs as well in cake mixes as fresh eggs do.

Angel food or foam-type cakes use dried albumen. The angel food cake is usually a two-package mix. The albumen, some sugar, and some anhydrous monocalcium phosphate are thoroughly mixed. Powdered vanilla may be added to the first part or the second part of the mix. The whipping aid is added to the first packet used. The second part of the two-package mix contains flour, sugar, salt and cream of tartar.

PIE CRUST MIXES. Pie crust mixes are unleavened. Either soft wheat or a mixture of hard and soft wheat flours may be used. The shortening may be sprayed on the flour mixture or added in powdered form. Either form of shortening will produce a mealy crust. A plastic shortening may also be used; if it is, it is added in flakes, which impart flakiness to the pie crust.

PACKAGING OF MIXES. The containers in which the bake mixes are packaged are designed to protect their contents from contamination by dirt; infestation by insects, rodents, and microorganisms; loss or gain of moisture; and deterioration resulting from contact with air, light, or heat. Not only must the packaging material perform these functions, but it must not itself contaminate the contents.

DIRECTIONS FOR USING MIXES. Usually, mix

directions are based on the pans, utensils, and practices that are standard in the home. Hence, some knowledge of how the homemaker equips her kitchen and interprets directions is a requisite for developing useful directions for the package mix. Home economists are employed at this stage of cake mix development, for exactitude and thoroughness are of utmost importance to the successful sale of the mix. Directions on a mix package include step-by-step procedures, pan size, oven temperature, and preparation of pan and oven. Directions are given for mixing by hand and with electric mixers. Baking directions for high altitudes are also given.

EVALUATION OF FINISHED CAKE MIXES. Because of the increased home use of commercially manufactured cake mixes, the Finished Foods Committee, a committee of the Home Economists in Business Section of the American Home Economic Association, has set up guides to be used in evaluating finished (cooked) foods. To date, two reports are available on cakes, one on pie crusts, and three on quick breads. (See the references at the end of this chapter.)

Storage and Deterioration. The most serious problem with bake mixes is deterioration. Although considerable progress has been made in identifying materials that add to the stability of the bake mixes, deterioration occurs with prolonged storage. High temperatures and humidity accelerate the rate of deterioration. It has been suggested that the moisture and lipase content of the flour and the type of baking powder, shortening, and egg ingredients used all contribute to the deterioration of the mix.[23] Various factors can be controlled in the manufacture of the bake mixes to lengthen the shelf life of the product.

The fat ingredient in the mix is the dominant factor in maintaining stability, if the moisture content of the mix is reasonably low and the baking powder has been properly selected. It has been suggested that the final mix should be able to hold up under prolonged storage at temperatures as high as $100\,°F$ ($38\,°C$) without serious alteration in volume, texture, or baking qualities.

It is apparent that the keeping qualities of cakes baked from shortened cake mixes vary from brand to brand, but some work in the author's laboratory showed that maximum storage time at room temperature for any of the cake mixes tested was 24 hours.[24] One class project on chocolate cake mixes showed that for short storage periods, the commercial cake mix reacted favorably to freezing storage at $0\,°F$ ($-18\,°C$). However, the mixes responded less favorably to such storage than the conventionally prepared cakes did.

As for the continued use of mixes by the American homemaker, it seems safe to predict that as long as the mixes provide the consumer with a convenience food and reasonable assurance of palatable finished product, there will be a steady increase in consumer use.

Homemade Mixes. Basic mixes can be prepared in the home for family use. The major advantage of the commercial mix—saving time and energy—is also present in the use of a homemade mix. It is entirely possible, through judicious planning, to keep the cost of the home mix below that of the commercial product. This would appear to be borne out by the study of Gothard,[25] who investigated the practicability of a homemade refrigerated dry corn muffin mix. She concluded that muffins equal or superior to conventionally prepared muffins can be made from the refrigerated home mix with a definite saving of time and energy.

Buying Mixes. Although no federal standards have yet been set for mixes, such mixes must meet general requirements of the U.S. Food and Drug Administration for all foods shipped across state lines, as must all other packaged foods so shipped. Accordingly, mixes must be prepared from wholesome food and be fit to eat, and their labels must list the name of the product, the net contents of the package, the ingredients used (in order of predominance), the name of the manufacturer or distributor, and the place of manufacture.

---

[24] A variety of different brands of yellow, white, chocolate, and spice cake mixes were used in these studies.

[25] M. Gothard, "The Quality and Practicability of a Refrigerated Prepared Dry Cornmeal Muffin Mix," *J. Home Econ.* **43**:713, 1951.

[23] Ibid., p. 349.

SUMMARY

Cake ingredients are similar to those in other flour mixtures, but cakes are classified into two general types: (1) butter or shortened cakes and (2) those made without fat—sponge cakes and angel cakes. Both types are drop batters. In cake making, it is important to have the proper proportions of ingredients so that tenderizing agents counteract the toughening or binding ingredients.

In cake baking, cake flour is generally used, although all-purpose flour can also be used successfully. Milk is the most frequently used liquid, but fruit juice is occasionally used. Many types of fat are used in cake, with butter popular for its food value, flavor, and color. The superglycerinated shortenings are especially suitable for cakes because they facilitate fat distribution in the batter.

Although sugar tenderizes the proteins of the batter, too much of it produces a small cake with a sugary crust. The chief leavening action in cake batters is supplied by a chemical agent, but some aeration is achieved through mixing procedures. Eggs add color and flavor to cake as well as forming a portion of the network of the cake structure.

Basic mixing methods for cakes include the muffin method, the conventional method, and the quick, or speed, method.

Basic ingredients in sponge cakes are flour, sugar, and eggs. Fat is not included. Leavening is by air and steam. The way in which ingredients are combined is a critical factor is success, even though several different methods may be used. Frozen egg whites may be used successfully in angel cakes.

Although oil is included in the chiffon cake formula, these cakes have some of the characteristics of the sponge group.

Increased amounts of fat and egg, decreased liquid, and lessened leavening are characteristic of cookie batters and doughs compared to cake batters. General classifications of cookies are sheet or drop cookies, rolled cookies, refrigerator cookies, and meringue or sponge cookies. Rolled and refrigerator cookies are made from a stiff dough. Cookies are usually mixed by the conventional method for mixing cakes. The angel cake procedure is used for meringues and kisses.

A slightly higher temperature is used to bake cookies than is used to bake cakes. Storage in a box with a tight-fitting cover is recommended for cookies. Soft cookies should be stored separately from crisp cookies.

Although true-cost or nutritive comparisons between homemade and commercial mixes are difficult, because ingredients may differ, prepared mixes generally cost more and are lower in fat, protein, and energy value than are homemade products of the same type. Costs of items added to the mix must of course be included in any cost comparison. The convenience and, to a degree, the palatability of mixes result in a high demand, however.

Deterioration, accelerated by high temperature and humidity, is the most serious problem with bake mixes, so ingredients are carefully chosen or modified to prevent premature reaction within the mix and to retard rancidity. Antioxidants are also used.

Bake mixes are classified according to the leavening agent employed—chemicals, aeration with or without chemicals, chemicals combined with yeast, or no leavening agent.

Chemically leavened products include doughnuts, cakes, muffins, and biscuits. Angel and sponge cakes are leavened by aeration, and a chemical leavener may be added. Yeast-leavened products include bread, rolls, buns, and yeast-raised doughnuts. Pie crusts are included in the nonleavened group.

Mixes are packaged to protect them from contamination. Instructions for use are printed on the package.

Mixes must meet general requirements of the U.S. Food and Drug Administration for all food shipped across state lines. The label must list ingredients in order of predominance.

QUESTIONS AND TOPICS FOR DISCUSSION AND STUDY

1. Why is a fat that contains an emulsifying agent of special value in making a cake?
2. Why are cake batters beaten for a much longer time than muffin batters?
3. How does butter rank with hydrogenated fat for creaming quality?
4. What is the relationship between fat, air, and carbon dioxide in a cake batter during mixing?

5. What happens in the structure of a cake when the fat and sugar ingredients are increased?

6. How does the production of a red chocolate or devil's food cake affect the texture of the cake?

7. How are cake batters aerated?

8. What is the function of the acid ingredients (cream of tartar and lemon juice) in the sponge cake?

9. What are the effects of underbeating egg whites in angel cakes or egg whites and egg yolks in sponge cakes?

10. Why are sponge cakes baked in an ungreased tube pan?

11. How do the ingredients for cookies differ from those for cakes?

12. Why do refrigerator cookies have a large proportion of fat?

13. Why do cookies made with honey and molasses retain their moisture for a fairly long period of time?

14. Why are soft cookies stored separately from crisp ones?

15. Why is it important to control the amount of flour used for rolling cookies?

16. Why is it unlikely that the nutritive value of a mix would be comparable to that of a similar home-prepared product?

17. Why do most muffin and cake mixes require the use of fresh eggs?

18. What are the advantages and disadvantages of using a mix?

SUGGESTED ACTIVITIES

1. Make basic shortened cakes, using conventional and quick mixing methods. Compare the two for the time required for preparation, appearance, texture, and flavor.

2. Prepare a basic shortened cake, using butter or some other fat in place of hydrogenated shortening. Compare with cake made with hydrogenated shortening for cost, time required for preparation, appearance, texture, and flavor.

3. Select a packaged mix for a shortened cake. Compare for cost, time required for preparation, appearance, texture, and flavor with a conventionally prepared cake.

4. Bake an angel food or sponge cake, or both. Evaluate them.

5. Prepare one or more kinds of cookie: rolled, refrigerated, drop, or bar.

6. Suggest ways for cutting down on time spent in making certain kinds of cookies.

7. Make a list of the types of mixes found on the market.

8. Select several mixes, go over the directions, and prepare the products. What improvements in the directions would you suggest?

REFERENCES

BOOKS

Food: The Yearbook of Agriculture. Washington, D.C.: U.S. Department of Agriculture, 1959, pp. 418–434.

Matz, Samuel, ed. *Chemistry and Technology of Cereals as Food and Feed.* Westport, Conn.: Avi, 1959, Chap. 12.

Paul, Pauline, and Helen Palmer. *Food Theory and Applications.* New York: Wiley, 1972, Chap. 12.

ARTICLES AND BULLETINS

Arlin, M. L., and M. M. Nielson. "The Effect of Different Methods of Flour Measurements on the Quality of Plain Two-Egg Cakes." *J. Home Econ.* **56**:399, 1964.

Baker, H. J., and J. B. Mickle. "Milk–Fat Shortenings for Cakes." *J. Home Econ.* **60**:189, 1968.

Baker, H. J., J. B. Mickle, M. E. Leidigh, and R. D. Morrison. "Milk–Fat Shortenings for Cakes." *J. Home Econ.* **58**:468, 1966.

"Baking for People with Food Allergies." *Home and Garden Bulletin No. 147.* Washington, D.C.: U.S. Department of Agriculture, 1968.

Briant, A. L., and A. R. Willinon. "Whole-Egg Sponge Cakes." *J. Home Econ.* **48**:420, 1956.

Elgidialy, D. A., et al. "Baking of Angel Cakes." *J. Amer. Dietet. Assoc.* **54**:401, 1969.

Finished Foods Committee, American Home Economics Association. "Finished Foods, A First Report: Cake-Mix Cakes—Shortening Type." *J. Home Econ.* **53**:281, 1961.

——. "Finished Foods, A Second Report: Cake-Mix Cakes—Foam Type." *J. Home Econ.* **53**:759, 1961.

——. "Finished Foods, A Third Report: Pie Crusts—From Recipe and Mix." *J. Home Econ.* **54**:767, 1962.

——. "Finished Foods, A Fourth Report:

Refrigerated Biscuits, Sweet Rolls and Dinner Rolls." *J. Home Econ.* **56**:737, 1964.

————. "Finished Foods, A Fifth Report: Pancakes and Quick Breads from Mixes." *J. Home Econ.* **57**:118, 1965.

————. "Finished Foods, A Sixth Report: Coffee Cake and Gingerbread for Mixes." *J. Home Econ.* **57**:358, 1965.

Matthews, R. H., et al. "Baked Products: Consumer Quality, Composition, Yield, and Preparation Time of Various Forms." *Home Economics Research Report 22.* Washington, D.C.: U.S. Department of Agriculture, 1963.

Morrison, M. "Ready Mixes for Chocolate Cake." *J. Home Econ.* **49**:283, 1957.

Ostwald, Rosemary. "Fat Content and Fatty Acids in Some Commercial Mixes for Baked Products." *J. Amer. Dietet. Assoc.* **45**:32, 1963.

Paul, Pauline, et al. "Dry-Mix and Frozen Baked Products," *J. Home Econ.* **46**:249, 1954.

Schlosser, Georgia, and Elsie Dawson. "Cottonseed Flour, Peanut Flour, and Soy Flour: Formulas and Procedures for Family and Institutional Use in Developing Countries." *Agricultural Research Service Bulletin 617.* Washington, D.C.: U.S. Department of Agriculture, 1969.

Street, M. "The Effect of Electronic Cookery Upon the Appearance and Palatability of a Yellow Cake." *J. Home Econ.* **52**:285, 1961.

Flour Mixtures: Yeast-Leavened Bread, Rolls, and Cake

CHAPTER 34

Yeast-leavened products—bread, rolls, and cakes—are flour mixtures made light by the fermentation of the carbohydrate in the dough. The fermentation process is brought about by yeast—and, occasionally, by bacteria. Yeast in a flour mixture produces the enzyme zymase, which acts on sugar and produces the carbon dioxide responsible for lightening the dough. A yeast dough falls into the classification of stiff doughs and its basic ingredients—flour, liquid, and yeast—are not very different from those of the quick-bread doughs. Other ingredients, added for flavor and coloration, are salt, sugar, fat, and eggs. (Eggs may or may not be added, depending on the richness desired.)

INGREDIENTS IN YEAST-LEAVENED BREAD

The basic ingredient in bread dough is flour—and the kind of flour used determines the nature of the bread. Bread flours and all-purpose flours are very suitable, for they contain comparatively large amounts of protein. A strong flour with a high protein content gives a high-volume bread. In yeast breads, the development of gluten is very important: it gives the mixture the elasticity required to produce breads of large volume and open grain. The gluten is developed by thorough mixing and kneading.

Flour. Homemade bread is usually made with all-purpose flour, the protein content of which is high enough to yield a loaf of good volume. Enriched all-purpose flours do not differ in palatability, appearance, or baking characteristics from other all-purpose flours.

Liquids. The liquid ingredient of bread dough consists of water, water in which potatoes have been cooked, or milk. Milk increases the food value of the bread. Fluid milk is scalded first to kill bacteria that might interfere with the formation of yeast and to inactivate enzymes. If it is not scalded, the bread will have a coarse texture and poor volume. Care must be taken to cool the milk before the heat-sensitive yeast is added. Pasteurized and evaporated milk need only to be warmed, not scalded. If dry milk solids are used,

421

they may be added to the dry ingredients and a corresponding amount of water may be used as the liquid. The water in which potatoes have been cooked is used because it encourages the growth of yeast. The amylases present in the flour readily degrade the potato starch. When such water contains small amounts of the mashed potato (too much potato interferes with the gluten formation), the bread has a moist crumb. The amount of liquid used varies with the absorptive capacity of the flour.

Yeast. Yeast is the leavening agent used in many flour mixtures (Fig. 34–1). In the commercial production of yeast breads, compressed yeast is the preferred type. For household use, the dry, granular yeast is more easily available and keeps better. The fast-rising granular yeast is quick and simple to use. Directions are on the back of the package, together with the last date on which its use is recommended.

Salt. Salt adds flavor to yeast doughs, as it does to other flour mixtures. Also, there is evidence to indicate that salt has a "tightening" effect on the proteins in the bread flour, permitting them to stretch without breaking. When bread doughs are lacking in salt, the fermentation takes place very rapidly and the dough is too sticky to knead properly. This results in a coarse texture

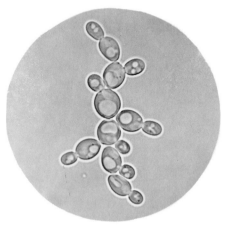

34–1 *Bread yeasts* (Saccaromyces cerevisiae, *magnified*) *reproduce by budding.* (*Courtesy of Fleischmann Laboratories, Standard Brands, Incorporated*)

of the baked bread. Too much salt, on the other hand, may retard the rising process by slowing down fermentation.[1]

Sugar. Sugar is not an essential ingredient in bread dough, but it does contribute to the fermentation process. If sugar is used, only enough is added to start the action of the yeast and to give some color to the crust. Sweet breads have a higher sugar content than plain breads. But because sugar acts as a solvent and competes with wheat protein for water, too large an amount (over 10%) may result in an excessively small loaf.

Any pleasant-tasting or bland fat may be used. Its function is to increase the tenderness of the crust and crumb of the baked product. It has been suggested that fat also helps to increase volume by making the gluten framework more tender. Experience has proved that bread made with fat does not grow stale as quickly as does that made without fat.

Eggs are used in some—but not all—breads, rolls, and yeast-leavened cakes. When whole eggs or egg yolks are used, the baked product has a richer and shinier crust and crumb. Dried and frozen whole eggs and egg yolks may be used in place of fresh eggs in yeast products.

Proportions of Ingredients. Although it is most difficult to give even an approximate flour/water ratio for bread dough, most authorities agree that it falls close to 4:1. But the ratio varies with the strength of the flour. If a given amount of flour produces a sticky dough, more flour must be added until the dough is of a consistency to be kneaded.

The amount of yeast used depends on the flour content of the mixture and on the length of time set aside for fermentation. Usually, the yeast weight should be 2–3% of the flour weight. This will work out as 1 or 2 packages of fast-rising granular yeast to 4 cups flour. Two packages is the maximum—and even this much may impart a slightly yeasty flavor to the baked product. When there is time for long fermentation, the minimum amount of yeast should be used. To these proportions of yeast and flour

[1] E. J. Pyler, *Baking Science and Technology,* Vol. 1 (Chicago: Siebel, 1952), p. 371.

may be added 1½ tsp salt, 2 tbsp sugar, 2 tbsp fat, and (when eggs are used) 1 whole egg or 2 egg yolks. Sweet doughs have a larger proportion of sugar, fat, and eggs—how much larger depends on the kind of sweet bread desired. Some sweet bread doughs may have 25–30% more fat than bread doughs.

PRINCIPLES FOR PREPARING YEAST BREADS

The soluble ingredients—such as salt, sugar, and yeast—are brought into solution and dispersed throughout the liquid. The finer granulation of dry yeast available makes a rapid mix possible. The undissolved yeast can be mixed with the dry ingredients. As the dough is mixed, the gluten develops and the liquid is distributed evenly throughout the mass, resulting in a more uniform development of elasticity. (Too much liquid weakens the gluten strands so that the dough lacks the strength necessary for stretching.) The mixing must be continued until all the ingredients are thoroughly combined. Kneading will further distribute the ingredients so that

the dough becomes smooth, dry, and elastic. Undermixed or overmixed doughs produce coarse, compact breads. When bread or roll dough is mixed by hand, there is probably more danger of undermixing than of overmixing (Table 34-1).

Rising. For dough to be lightened by yeast, it must be allowed to ferment. (For a full discussion of fermentation, see Chapter 31.) As the yeast cells transform the available sugars into carbon dioxide and alcohol, the volume of the dough increases. During the rising that accompanies fermentation, the gluten becomes more elastic and springy and forms thin gas-retaining walls around the individual gas cells. A dough that has attained a maximum gas-retaining capacity and elasticity is said to be *mature*.

ACTION OF YEAST. Yeast cells, like any other living organisms, require food and a favorable environment in order to function. Hence, an adequate amount of moisture, a congenial temperature, the proper degree of acidity, and an adequate supply of fermentable carbohydrates are necessary for the proper action of the yeast. In addition to supplying enzymes that act on the

Failures	Possible Causes
Heaviness	Low-grade flour Insufficient rising period Over-risen dough Too much fat
Thick, tough, pale crust	Too much salt Under-risen dough Overhandling of over-risen dough Too little sugar
Dark crumb	Stale yeast Low-grade flour Too cool an oven
Streaked crumb	Poor mixing of dough Drying out of dough before shaping
Crumbliness	Weak flour (lacking in gluten strength) Over-risen dough
Coarse texture	Low-grade flour Inferior yeast Too cool an oven
Sour flavor	Over-risen dough Incomplete baking

TABLE 34-1
Causes of Baking Failures in Yeast-Leavened Breads, Rolls, and Cakes

carbohydrates in the dough, yeast undergoes considerable growth.

The yeast used for making bread and roll doughs must be in good condition. To obtain maximum efficiency from the yeast, from the time it is added until the bread or rolls are baked the mixture should not be exposed to excessively warm or cold temperatures. Heat kills yeast and makes the dough sticky; cold retards its growth. Yeast will grow well in a temperature range of between 74 and 90°F (23 and 32°C) but for home production of yeast-leavened products, a temperature between 80 and 85°F (27 and 30°C) is recommended.

The alcohol produced during fermentation becomes part of the liquid ingredient in the dough, but during baking it is volatilized and driven off. The carbon dioxide remains, but some of it combines with water to form carbonic acid (a weak acid). The following equation (carbon dioxide plus water yields carbonic acid) explains in part what happens:

$$CO_2 + H_2O \longrightarrow H_2CO_3$$

Starch and protein enzymes are also active at this time; their overall action is to soften the dough and to weaken the gluten.

During the fermenting period, lactic acid is produced by the bacteria that are always present in flour. Lactic acid is a fairly strong acid and may increase the acidity of the dough. Acetic acids are also formed during fermentation and add slightly to the acidity of the dough. It is thought that the increase in acid during fermentation increases the capacity of gluten to imbibe water, thus bringing about a more complete hydration of the dough.

CONTROL OF RISING. As fermentation progresses and the dough continues to rise, the strands of gluten become thinner and weaker. It is essential, therefore, to know at just what point the dough is ready for baking. The dough is ready to bake just before the rate of loss of carbon dioxide from the dough equals its rate of production within. By this time, the gluten is strong enough to give elasticity and springiness to the baked product. If the dough is baked before this stage, the bread will be coarse, compact, and small. Overfermented bread also has a poor volume, a coarse grain, and—frequently—a sour odor (caused by the overproduction of lactic acid). In the household pro-

duction of bread, the readiness of the dough for baking may be determined by inserting two fingers into the dough. If the dough springs back quickly, it is not ready for baking; but if the indentation made by the fingers remains, the dough has reached its optimum gas-retention capacity and is ready for baking. Dough rises satisfactorily when it is kept at a temperature of 80°F (26°C) and protected from currents of cold air.

Kneading. Making bread involves considerable kneading and handling of the dough (Fig. 34-2). The dough is kneaded before it is allowed to ferment and again before it is molded into the desired shapes. (Some authorities suggest that several rising periods and, accordingly, several kneading periods be used.) The purpose of kneading is to remove some of the excessive carbon dioxide in order to prevent overstretching of the gluten strands and to distribute the yeast cells throughout the dough. Kneading also tends to keep the dough at a uniform temperature. Although electric mixers may be used, for home-sized recipes kneading is easily accomplished by hand. It is important to use small amounts of flour on the board during kneading; overflouring will produce a bread that is dry and streaked. Care must be taken not to tear the dough because this will injure the gluten and reduce the elasticity of the dough. The dough is kneaded enough when it has a smooth satiny surface and small bubbles, appear under the surface.

METHODS OF MIXING

The methods of mixing bread dough are the straight-dough, sponge-dough, no-knead, and cool-rise.

Straight-Dough Method. In the *straight-dough method,* all the ingredients are mixed together. The mixture is then kneaded until the dough is satiny in appearance and elastic. After kneading, the dough is set aside in a warm place (80–85°F; 26–30°C) to rise. When the dough has risen to double its original bulk, it is kneaded and divided into loaf-sized pieces. Each piece is made into a ball, covered (to prevent drying), and allowed to stand for about 15 minutes. Then

(a) Add the flour to the liquid and stir until the dough is stiff enough to knead.

(b) Knead the dough until it is satiny.

(c) Allow the dough to rise until it is soft to the touch.

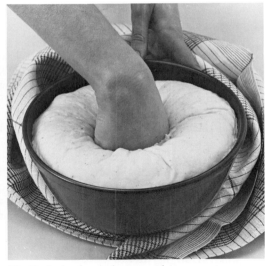

(d) Push the dough down to release excess gas.

(e) Divide the dough into equal portions for loaves or rolls. (Courtesy of Standard Brands Inc.)

34-2 Steps in bread making.

425

each piece is formed into a loaf of bread. The dough is flattened until it is about 1 in. thick and oblong, folded lengthwise, and flattened again. It is stretched to about 3 times the length of the pan and folded in thirds, then stretched to about 3 times the width of the pan and again folded in thirds. Finally, it is folded lengthwise and rolled into the desired shape. The edges are sealed and the loaf is placed, seamside down, in the center of the pan, only the bottom of which has been greased. The molded loaves should be about half as high as the sides of the pan. The tops of the loaves may be brushed with oil or melted fat, and the loaves are then left to rise. When they have again doubled in size, they are put into the oven.

Sponge-Dough Method. The *sponge-dough method* produces a bread with a slightly different flavor than that of bread made by the straight-dough method. It is an older method and not used too much today in the home. Old-type yeast products were uncertain in strength, but the longer fermentation time for the sponge method made up in part for this lack. Improved commercial yeast products have eliminated the use of this method to a considerable extent. The sponge method is not recommended for use with soft wheat flour because of the long fermentation period and the resultant weakening of the gluten part of the dough.

The sponge-dough method consists of two steps: the sponge stage and the dough stage. In the sponge stage, the yeast and liquid are combined and just enough flour (usually between 50 and 75% of the total amount) is added to make a thick batter. The batter is set to rise in a warm place (slightly less warm than that used for the straight method) until it is light or very bubbly. The sugar, salt, fat, and remaining flour are added to the light batter, which has doubled in size, to make a dough that can be kneaded. Thereafter, the method does not differ from the straight-dough method.

No-Knead Method. One method of making yeast-leavened products in the home does not require kneading. The finished product, however, is very different from that made in the traditional manner. The *no-knead method* is designed to produce rolls or bread similar in texture and flavor to those prepared by conven-

tional methods—but in a shorter period of time. The basic proportions for this type of yeast bread are slightly different: less flour and more fat are used in no-knead mixtures. The straight method of mixing the dough is used, and the gluten is developed by beating. Once the ingredients are well blended, the dough is shaped into loaves or rolls, and permitted to rise. When the dough has doubled in size, they are baked. The breads, although of a good volume, have a slightly yeasty flavor and a coarser grain than those made from kneaded dough.

Cool-Rise Method. The *cool-rise method* of making bread was designed to cut down on time and steps used in bread making. The main differences in this and the straight-dough method are (1) not scalding the milk (pasteurized milk need only be warmed), (2) vigorously beating during the first two additions of flour to stimulate formation of gluten, and (3) placing the shaped dough in the refrigerator for one rising period. A fourth difference is that part of shaping the dough is to roll it down with a rolling pin—the intent of this step is to give greater uniformity of shape to the loaf.

Changes During Mixing. When the ingredients of the yeast dough are combined, the liquid is quickly imbibed by the proteins of the flour (and eggs, if present) and a gluten structure is formed. The starch is also thoroughly wetted and hydrated.

BAKING

There is considerable increase in the volume of bread or rolls during the first 10 minutes of baking. This rising is called *oven spring*. If the bread or rolls form a brown crust during this period, it is likely that the oven temperature is too high.

Loaf-sized breads are baked at 400°F (205°C) for 10 minutes, then at 375°F (191°C) until done. This usually takes 35–40 minutes. Rolls are usually baked at a temperature between 375 and 425°F (191 and 220°C). The lower the temperature, the drier will be the rolls. When loaves of bread or rolls are done, they shrink from the sides of the pan, sound hollow when tapped, and have a golden-brown crust (Figs. 34-3 and 34-4).

34-3 *The completed loaf of baked bread has great appeal. (Courtesy of Betty Crocker of General Mills)*

Changes During Baking. Important changes take place in the yeast-dough mixture during baking. The gas in the dough expands, the starch gelatinizes, gluten strands develop to form the framework of the bread product, and the growth of yeast is stopped. Baking also brings about the full development of flavor, which is believed to be caused by a number of factors: the cooking of the starch in the flour, the forming of volatile and nonvolatile compounds as by-products of the action of yeast on sugar, and the dextrinizing of starch to sugar.

Crust formation occurs in baked bread when its surface dries. The crust attains a darker color than the interior crumb because of the conversion of starch to sugar in the crust. This crust coloration is also caused, in part, by the (Maillard) browning reaction that takes place between the sugar and the protein materials of flour and milk.

During baking, there is also some loss of heat-labile thiamine. Studies show that there is greater loss of thiamine from the crust than from the crumb. Thus, rolls with a high proportion of crust to crumb tend to lose relatively greater amounts of thiamine.[2]

[2] A. S. Schultz et al., "The Stability of Vitamin B in the Manufacture of Bread," *Cereal Chem.* **19:**532, 1942.

M. V. Zaehringer et al., "Thiamine Retention in Bread and Rolls Baked to Different Degrees of Brownness," *Cereal Chem.* **26:**384, 1949.

FREEZING

Frozen doughs may lose their gas-forming ability and fail to rise sufficiently when thawed. Another effect of freezing can be a weakening of the yeast dough because of the necessity to increase the proofing time of the frozen dough.

Bread that is frozen may show white areas beneath the crumb surface. These white areas

34-4 *Grain of bread. (Courtesy of Betty Crocker of General Mills)*

may be due to drying out of the bread before freezing.[3]

VARIATIONS

Flour. Like other flour mixtures, the dough for plain breads and rolls can be modified by substituting for all or part of the flour content other cereal flours or meals such as whole-wheat flour, rye flour, cornmeal, bran, rolled oats, and buckwheat. The volume and texture of products made with these substitutes will differ from those of products made with white flour, mainly because of difference in the gluten content of the various flours and meals. In most recipes, some all-purpose flour is combined with the alternate flour.

Some bread recipes include raisins, currants, caraway seeds, cheese, or cinnamon to add flavor to the basic dough. Special breads are made by adding a rather high proportion of eggs to the dough to produce a crusty texture.

Rolls. Rolls are much like bread, both in basic proportions of ingredients and in finished appearance. They are light, golden-brown, and

[3] Pauline Paul, *Food Theory and Applications* (New York: Wiley, 1972), p. 664.

have a thin crust and a fine, satiny, elastic crumb. They are usually made from a yeast-bread mixture that has a slightly larger proportion of fat and sugar. Eggs are frequently added to the basic dough recipe. There is an endless variety of roll styles—from the simple pan rolls to the more complicated butterfly rolls.

With a slight adjustment in the basic recipe for rolls, refrigerator rolls may be prepared. For these, the dough may be mixed and kneaded and kept in the refrigerator (2–3 days) until used. The dough must be covered to prevent crust formation, which makes streaks in the baked product.

Sweet Doughs. Such yeast-leavened products as coffee cakes, sweet rolls, and raised doughnuts are made from a sweet, rich dough (Fig. 34-5). This dough has approximately the same proportion of flour to liquid (usually milk) as bread dough has, but the proportions of fat, sugar, and eggs are increased. There are many interesting ways to use sweet dough. Cinnamon rolls, stollens and Swedish tea rings are additional typical sweetdough products (see Figs. 34-6 and 34-7). These rich doughs are baked at temperatures between 350 and 375°F (177–191°C). An excessively high temperature causes the crust to harden and brown before the rest of the product is thoroughly baked.

34-5 *Many tempting sweet rolls can be prepared from a basic sweet dough. (Courtesy of Betty Crocker of General Mills)*

34-6 *Yeast cake. Stollen (a traditional German Christmas bread)*

BUYING BREADS

Partially Baked Rolls. Partially baked, or brown-and-serve, rolls have grown very popular in the past few years. These rolls have been baked at a temperature of approximately 285°F (114°C) for about 25 minutes—just enough to reach the final volume and produce a firm structure, but not enough to complete the browning of the crust. The rolls are then packaged and distributed to retail stores. The purchaser completes the baking just before serving the rolls. The second baking takes only a few minutes. Brown-and-serve rolls should be stored in the refrigerator until used. Such rolls may also be made at home, frozen, and heated before serving.

If rolls and bread are not to be served at once (rolls are at their best when hot), they should be removed from the pans as soon as they are done and placed uncovered on wire racks to cool. Only when they are thoroughly cooled should they be stored in breadboxes. Yeast breads may be frozen after they are baked. They may then be thawed and heated in the oven before serving.

Baker's Bread. A large portion of the baker's bread on the market is wrapped. The wrapping protects the bread from dirt and helps to prevent it from drying out. All packaged bread is labeled.

The label shows the weight of the loaf, the name of the manufacturer, and whether or not the bread has been enriched. If it is labeled *enriched,* it must meet the minimum federal standards for enrichment. Most states have enrichment laws; those that do not leave enrichment to the discretion of the baker and the miller. According to the Cereal Enrichment Report of 1958,[4] nearly all bread and flour are enriched—even in states that have no pertinent legislation—and nearly all large manufacturers of bread and all-purpose flour who engage in interstate commerce produce only enriched products.

Most bread is sliced before it is wrapped—a practice generally popular with the consumer, for it provides uniform slices. The thickness of the slice is not always adaptable to family needs, however, despite the fact that there are several thicknesses to be had.

Baker's bread, as well as homemade bread, is a perishable product that starts to stale shortly after it has been removed from the oven.

It is thought that the staling of bread is caused by the retrogradation of starch. As the bread ages, the amylose fraction of the starch slowly aggregates, resulting in a hardening of the crumb

[4] Committee on Cereals, Food and Nutrition Board, *Cereal Enrichment in Perspective, 1958* (Washington, D.C.: National Research Council–National Academy of Sciences, 1958).

429

(a)

(c)

(b)

34-7 *Cinnamon twist coffee cake using basic sweet dough recipe. (a) When kneading use the heels of your hands to push the dough away from you using pressure. Turn the dough a quarter of a turn each time you push down. (b) Roll the dough into a 12-inch square and brush with margarine. Sprinkle the center third with a cinnamon-sugar mixture. (c) Fold dough in three layers, cut the dough into 1-inch strips. Twist each strip in opposite directions. (Courtesy of J. Walter Thompson)*

(staling). Retrogradation is faster at low temperatures but above freezing; freezing almost completely prevents staling and retrogradation. Bread stales more slowly at room temperature than at refrigerator temperatures, and factors such as the protein content of the bread mixture may also contribute to the staling of bread.[5] For

[5] Ira Garard, *Introductory Food Chemistry* (Westport, Conn.: Avi, 1976), p. 225.

the commercial loaf, staling can be retarded by the use of proper packaging materials. Most bread on the market is fresh on the day of sale, but several-days-old loaves are also sold.

"Pullman" loaves are specially baked in covered pans so that they have the square shape so popular for sandwiches.

Many types of special breads are sold to meet consumer demand. Usually, the requests for these breads are regional. Some of the more popular breads are French and Italian bread, German and Jewish rye bread, oatmeal bread, and black pumpernickel. These are generally higher in price than the loaf made from milled white flour, and usually they are not enriched. Baker's bread can be frozen to retard staling—but when it thaws, staling resumes and seems to progress at an even faster rate.

SPOILAGE

The main kinds of microbial spoilage are caused by mold and rope. Molds are by far the more common cause of the spoilage of bread. These penetrate the loaf after baking, for the mold spores in the dough are destroyed by the high baking temperatures. They occur on the surface of bread through contact with air, through handling during the wrapping process, or from the wrappers themselves.

Bread molds may be white, black, green, or yellow dots. Experience has shown that certain conditions are favorable to the growth of molds—too long a cooling time in air heavily laden with bacteria and the wrapping of bread while it is still warm are probably the most important.

To prevent moldiness in commercial bread, considerable attention is paid to the surroundings in which the bread is sliced and wrapped. The bacteria level of the air around the bread is kept low by the elimination of potential breeding places, such as cracks, corners, stale loaves, crumbs, and the like.

Sodium or calcium propionate at the rate of 0.1–0.3% of the weight of flour has been used to prevent mold growth. Breads containing these mycostatic (mold–inhibiting) chemicals must be so labeled.

Ropiness occurs in commercial bread, but it occurs more frequently in the homemade variety. It has also been known to occur in such products as doughnuts and cakes. Hot weather promotes its development. Unlike molding, ropiness is not caused by mold but by a special variety of boullus bacteria. The spores of this bacterium resist the high baking temperatures to which the bread is subjected. Hence, they survive in the dough to grow and multiply when conditions are favorable. Ropy bread has a yellow color and a sticky, soft texture. When

drawn out and pulled apart, it forms long strings. Sometimes large holes are formed in the ropy loaf.

Methods used to control ropiness in bread are similar to those used to inhibit the growth of molds. In addition to calcium or sodium propionate, sorbic acid may be used as a rope inhibitor. Freezing bread also may prevent ropiness.[6]

SUMMARY

Yeast dough is a stiff dough that yields bread, rolls, or cakes and is leavened by the fermentation of the carbohydrate in the dough; this fermentation is caused by the action of yeast. Basic ingredients of yeast doughs are flour, liquid, and yeast; salt, sugar, fat, and eggs may be added for flavor and color. All-purpose flour is generally used, although other cereal flours or meals may also be used in whole or part. When fluid milk is used for the liquid, it is scalded to kill bacteria that might hinder yeast formation. Sugar, when used, contributes to the fermentation process. The yeast must be in good condition; a temperature range of between 80 and 85°F (26 and 30°C) is recommended for home preparation of yeast-leavened doughs.

For a successful product, it is important to know when a yeast-leavened dough is ready for baking. In a simple home test, two fingers are inserted in the dough. If the dough springs back, it is not ready; if it does not spring back, it has risen enough.

Kneading removes excessive carbon dioxide, thus preventing stretching of gluten strands, and distributes yeast cells throughout the dough. Yeast doughs may be made by the straight-dough, sponge-dough, no-knead, or cool-rise method. The no-knead and cool-rise finished products have a slightly yeasty flavor and a coarse grain compared to the products made by the straight-dough or sponge-dough method.

Baking halts the growth of yeast, expands the gas in the dough, gelatinizes the starch, and stiffens the gluten strands into the framework of the bread product.

Rolls and sweet doughs are variations of the

[6] D. Melnick et al., "Sorbic Acid as Fungistatic Agent for Foods," *Food Res.* **21**:133–146, 1956.

basic bread dough, with greater amounts of sugar, fat, and eggs.

Partially baked rolls are available commercially or may be made in the home and frozen until needed. Only a brief second baking period is required just before serving.

Nearly all commercial bread marketed today is wrapped, a practice that protects it against dirt and retards staling. If bread is labeled enriched, it must meet minimum federal standards for enrichment. Bread is perishable, and chemical preservatives may be added to inhibit both mold and rope, the two main causes of microbial spoilage.

QUESTIONS AND TOPICS FOR DISCUSSION AND STUDY

1. What is the purpose of kneading yeast-bread dough?
2. What happens when salt is left out of a yeast-dough recipe?
3. What is the function of sugar in a yeast-dough recipe?
4. What is the effect of freezing and very hot temperatures on a yeast dough?
5. What happens if yeast doughs are over- or underkneaded?

SUGGESTED ACTIVITIES

1. Prepare one or more of the following yeast doughs: bread, rolls, and coffee cake.

2. Select a commercial yeast-bread mix. Prepare both the mix and a conventional yeast product. Compare time required for preparation, cost, appearance, texture, and flavor.

REFERENCES

BOOKS

Consumers All: The Yearbook of Agriculture. Washington, D.C.: U.S. Department of Agriculture, 1966.

deMan, John. *Principles of Food Chemistry.* Westport, Conn.: Avi, 1976, Chap. 4.

Food for Us All: The Yearbook of Agriculture. Washington, D.C.: U.S. Department of Agriculture, 1969, pp. 213–225.

Griswold, Ruth. *The Experimental Study of Foods.* Boston: Houghton Mifflin, 1962, Chap. 11.

Paul, Pauline, and Helen Palmer. *Food Theory and Applications.* New York: Wiley, 1972, Chap. 12.

BULLETINS

"Bread, Cakes and Pies in Family Meals." *Bulletin 142.* Washington, D.C.: U.S. Department of Agriculture, 1970.

Dudgeon, L., and M. Dunn. "Yeast Bread and Rolls." *Cornell Extension Bulletin 888.* Ithaca, N.Y.: Cornell University, 1966.

Sugar and Sugar Cookery

Sugars, the simplest of organic foods, are the building blocks of the highly complex starches and celluloses. They are formed in plant tissue by photosynthesis, the process by which green plants convert carbon dioxide from the air and water from the soil into carbohydrates. This highly complex process, which requires the assistance of light is summarized in the following equation:

$$6CO_2 + 6H_2O + Energy \rightarrow C_6H_{12}O_6 + 6O_2$$

It can be seen that six molecules of carbon dioxide combine with six molecules of water to yield one molecule of glucose. The energy is supplied by sunlight, and the six molecules of oxygen are given off as a by-product.

MONOSACCHARIDES

The monosaccharides, simple sugars, include glucose (dextrose), fructose (levulose), and galactose. The first two are very abundant in fruits and syrups; the third is a part of the sugar found in milk (lactose).

Glucose, a monosaccharide, is the basic unit on which the higher carbohydrates are built. Glucose is less soluble in water and is more readily crystallized than fructose is. Glucose in the form of syrup or crystallized sugar is obtainable by the reverse action of the formation of starch from the glucose molecule. This is accomplished by a commercial process that involves the hydrolysis of starch (generally cornstarch or potato starch) with an acid. The breakdown of the starch to simple sugars, however, is incomplete; the products formed are not pure glucose, but mixtures of glucose, dextrin, and maltose (higher forms of carbohydrates). These syrups are referred to as *corn syrups*. Refined glucose is a crystalline white product that is less sweet than sucrose, the sugar most frequently used in cookery.

Fructose is the sugar that gives flavor to many fruits; because it occurs most abundantly in these foods, it is named after them. It is also found in quantity in honey. Fructose is not as easily crystallized as glucose because it is more soluble. It is not produced from starch but from certain tubers that contain inulin, a starchlike carbohydrate.

Galactose, the third monosaccharide found in foods, is not found in quantity in any food but milk.

Monosaccharides cannot be broken down into less simple sugars, but they can be built up into disaccharides.

DISACCHARIDES

The most important disaccharide by far is sucrose. Other names used for this sugar are *cane sugar, beet sugar,* and *granulated sugar.* Chemically, it is made up of one molecule of glucose and one molecule of fructose, with one molecule of water removed. The following equation illustrates this reaction, which is reversible.

$$C_6H_{12}O_6 + C_6H_{12}O_6 \longleftrightarrow C_{12}H_{22}O_{11} + H_2O$$

Sucrose occurs naturally in many plants and is found in concentrated form in sugar cane and sugar beets, both of which are used for the production of sugar. The sap of the maple tree is also a rich source of sucrose. Because this disaccharide crystallizes easily, it can be separated by this process from the plant juices or tree sap. Only sugar cane and sugar beets are used for the manufacture of granulated sugar.

Maltose, also a disaccharide, is made up of two molecules of glucose with one molecule of water eliminated. This sugar is found mainly in malt extract and is present in small amounts in commercial glucose. Malt syrup is used in baking to provide nutritive substances that promote the growth of yeast in the dough.

Lactose, referred to as *milk sugar,* is the third disaccharide and is composed of one molecule of glucose and one of galactose. This sugar is not crystallized or used commercially. The action of lactic bacteria on lactose results in the production of lactic acid. This action is important in making buttermilk and other cultured milks and cheeses.

FORMS OF SUGAR

Sugar and sugar syrups are available in a variety of forms, some of which have commercial importance. A description of their properties will help to make clear why they are used in the production of certain foods.

Granulated Sugar. By far the most important sugar product on the market is granulated sugar.

Sugar cane was for some time the principal source of this sugar, but now sugar beets are also used in its manufacture. Beet sugar and cane sugar are identical in chemical composition. The manufacture of granulated sugar from sugar cane is an industry of great economic importance in the areas of the world where sugar cane grows. (These include the Southern states in this country and the West Indies.) The plant is rather woody and fibrous and contains 16–20% sucrose. Sugar cane stalks are crushed and their juice is extracted. This juice is clarified, evaporated, and crystallized. The raw sugar is then refined until it is 99.9% pure.

To extract sugar from beets, the washed beets are sliced into thin strips and their soluble substances are extracted with hot water. The liquor is strained from the beets and treated with chemicals. The clear syrup that is obtained gives up white crystals that are handled in much the same manner as those obtained from sugar cane. Granulated sugar is retailed as "fine," the type most commonly sold or as "ultra fine," for use in cake making and instant beverages.

Powdered Sugars. Powdered (confectionary) sugar is obtained from granulated sugar by pulverization. An anticaking agent, usually tricalcium phosphate, may be added. Powdered sugar is available in several degrees of fineness, designated by the number of X's following the name. They are Ultra Fine (10X), Very Fine (6X), Fine (4X), medium, and coarse. Confectioners' XXXX is the powdered sugar most commonly used for uncooked icings and for dusting on baked products.

Raw Sugar. The raw product that comes from the sugar mill before refining is raw sugar. It is approximately 96% pure. The Food and Drug Administration has banned its sale to consumers because of contaminants such as fibers, yeast, soil, molds, lints, and waxes.

Turbinado Sugar. Turbinado sugar is the type sold in most health food stores. It is raw sugar that has been separated in a centrifuge and washed with steam. It loses part of its molasses to become 99% pure. Measuring this sugar is difficult because of the variation of the moisture content.

Brown Sugar. Brown sugar is composed of crystals of sugar which are suspended in a flavored and colored molasses syrup. The molasses syrup may be added to white refined sugar or it

TABLE 35-1
Equivalent Weights of Brown Sugars

Brown Sugar	Brownulated® Brown Sugar
1 cup	1⅓ cups
¾ cup	1 cup and 2 tbsp
⅔ cup	¾ cup and 1 tbsp
½ cup	⅔ cup and 2 tbsp
⅓ cup	⅓ cup and 2 tbsp
¼ cup	⅓ cup and 1 tbsp
1 tbsp	Scant 1½ tbsp

may be boiled under a vacuum with the syrup and centrifuged. It is sold as four grades, Numbers 6, 8, 10, and 13. The more it is refined, the lighter is the color and the lower the grade. The higher, darker grades are more flavorful and suitable for cooking strong flavored foods such as gingerbread, mincemeat, baked beans, and plum pudding. Number 13 is usually retailed as dark brown sugar for household use. A lighter brown (Number 8) has less flavor and is used primarily for baking and making butterscotch and ham glazes.

When brown sugar is allowed to dry out, it will harden and form lumps. The hardened sugar can be softened if it is put in an airtight rustproof container and a damp paper towel is placed on a piece of plastic wrap or foil that fits loosely over the sugar. In 8–12 hours the sugar will soften. A quicker method is to heat it briefly in a 250–300°F (121–149°C) oven. However, it will harden again as soon as it cools. A free-flowing brown sugar is now on the market. It is in the form of small granules made up of small sugar crystals. Recipe adjustments must be made because free-flowing brown sugar weighs less, cup for cup, than conventional brown sugar (Table 35-1).

Invert Sugar. This sugar is formed when sugar is heated in the presence of an acid or the enzyme *invertase*. The sugar molecule loses a molecule of water and forms dextrose (D-glucose) and levulose (D-fructose). This mixture of dextrose and levulose in equal amounts is called an *invert sugar*.

$$\text{sucrose} + \text{water} \xrightarrow[\text{invertase}]{\text{acid}} \text{dextrose} + \text{fructose}$$
$$\text{Invert Sugar}$$

Invert sugars are desirable in baked goods and in candies since they resist crystallization and retain their moisture. The confection inside a chocolate-covered cherry turns to liquid as the sugar (to which invertase was added) slowly turns to invert sugar.

SYRUPS

Like sugars, syrups are used as sweeteners in some food products. Actually, they are liquids containing large amounts of sugar, but they are more expensive than sugars because of their bulk and the cost of their distribution. Syrups have unusual flavors that make them useful additions to other foods. Generally, a syrup contains a mixture of sugars. The frequently used syrups are molasses, maple syrup, corn syrup, and honey.

Molasses. Molasses is a by-product of the manufacture of sugar from sugar cane. As the sugar goes through the steps of crystallization and refinement, different qualities of molasses are obtained. The molasses obtained from the first crystallization has a high sucrose content. Those obtained from the second and third crystallizations have less sucrose and larger amounts of invert sugar and minerals. The final sugar purification process produces blackstrap molasses. Some blending of the different grades is necessary to produce commercial molasses uniform in color, flavor, and body.

Cane sugar syrup is similar to molasses, but is not a by-product. It has a high sugar concentration and a light brown color (produced by sulfur fumes).

Maple Syrup. Maple syrup is obtained from the sap of certain varieties of maple trees. Sucrose is the sugar found in the sap, and the commercial maple syrup has a sugar content of 64–68%. Maple sugar is concentrated to 93% solids. The characteristic flavor of maple syrup is derived from the volatile oils in the sap. It must be boiled to achieve its outstanding flavor.

Corn Syrup. Corn syrup is used mainly to flavor other food products. It is prepared by heating starch in a dilute acid to bring about its conversion to such products as dextrose, maltose, and glucose, depending on the length of time the starch is exposed to the acid. Corn syrup is used extensively in baking for its sweetening properties and for its high moisture-retaining capacity. When used in such products as sugar icings or confections, corn syrup prevents the crystallization of other sugars (chiefly sucrose).

Honey. Honey is used as a sweetener for other food products. Its liquid state is due to the presence of invert sugars. It is made by bees from the nectar of flowers and is stored for their future use in a cell-like structure known as a *honeycomb*. For commercial purposes, honey is classified according to its flower source. Hence, there are products known as *orange blossom* and *clover blossom* honeys; these are rated for their mild, pleasing flavor. Buckwheat honey, which originates from the buckwheat flower, is dark, with a strong flavor.

Before honeys can be placed on the market, they must be freed of all foreign material and dirt. To accomplish this, the honey is usually heated to about 140°F (60°C) and held at that temperature for about 30 minutes to destroy microorganisms that may cause spoilage by fermentation. The heated syrup is then carefully strained. Because honey has a very delicate flavor, any strong flavors will decrease its palatability.

One form of honey is *comb honey*. This form is the most expensive, for it is not easily transported. *Extracted honey* is considered the most economical form. The comb is cut or shaved on one side, releasing the honey from the individual cells. The combs are then placed in an extractor and the remaining honey is drawn out by centrifugal force. *Strained honey,* a third form, is produced by crushing the comb and straining out the honey.

The composition of honey varies. Some varieties contain a high fructose/glucose ratio; these show little tendency to crystallize. When the glucose content is high and the fructose relatively low, the honey tends to form crystals and may even cake. The crystals can be dissolved if the honey is briefly heated.

Generally, fructose is the predominating sugar in honey (38%) with glucose a close second (31%). Sucrose constitutes only about 2% of the total sugar content. Honey is approximately 18% water; it also contains some dextrins, small

amounts of mineral salts, and traces of formic acid. One property of honey with great significance in cookery is its capacity to retain water. Hence, cakes, cookies, icings, and candies made with honey remain moist for a longer time than similar products made with most other sweeteners.

USES IN FOOD PREPARATION

Sugar and other sweeteners have various uses in food preparation: beverages, cooked fruits, candies, jellies, jams, baked goods, frozen desserts, and puddings use sugar or other sweeteners to develop the characteristics of a standard product. Sugar provides flavor, color, and helps in the development of the volume and texture of baked products. It is a factor in producing the thickness of puddings, the firmness of products such as jellies and custards, and the color and texture changes of fruit products.

When other sweeteners are substituted for sugar, the resultant product is somewhat different from the standard product using sugar. Honey and molasses add their own characteristic flavor to food and cakes and cookies using these sweeteners will brown rapidly. Consequently, baked products made with honey or molasses require baking temperature and time adjustment.

The use of artificial or nonnutritive sweeteners requires specially developed recipes. While these products add sweetness to products, they do not have the same effect on tenderness, crust color, and viscosity of the prepared food.

Substitutions for sugar can be made successfully by using the following recommendations. Substitute honey or corn syrup measure for measure in quick breads and yeast breads. The amounts are small and the added moisture makes little difference. In fruit breads, up to half the sugar may be replaced with honey or corn syrup without changing the rest of the ingredients in the recipe.

In puddings or custards, honey can be substituted measure for measure, but corn syrup substitution requires reduction in liquid content of the recipe.

Crisp-type cookies may be made with one-third the sugar replaced with honey or corn syrup, one-half the sugar of chocolate brownies may be replaced with honey or corn syrup, and 40% of the sugar may be replaced with honey or corn syrup in yellow, chiffon, and chocolate cakes. Generally, when using honey and corn syrup substitutions, oven temperatures must be reduced by 25°F (4°C).

In recipes using 1 cup of honey or corn syrup as a sugar substitute, reduce ¼ cup of total liquid in the recipes. Also, ¼ tsp of baking soda should be used to neutralize the acidity of the honey. This adjustment improves the volume of the product but is not necessary in products that have soda as a basic ingredient. In white cakes, honey may impart an undesirable color.

A light corn syrup can be used to can fruit.

PRINCIPLES OF SUGAR COOKERY

Sugar is used extensively in sweetening many types of desserts and in making fruit preserves, jams, and jellies. It is the basic ingredient in candy—and indeed it may be the only ingredient (except water). The principles of crystallization are pertinent to making such candies as fondant and fudge.

Crystallization. The crystallization of solutions is of fundamental importance in sugar cookery. A crystal is composed of closely packed molecules arranged in a pattern. Crystallization occurs only if the solution is supersaturated. The size of the crystals produced, however, will depend on the rate of the formation of nuclei about which the crystals grow and the rate of the growth of crystals around these nuclei. If only one or two nuclei are formed, the size of the crystals produced will be large. But if the rate of formation of nuclei is very rapid, many small crystals will form. Both the rate of crystallization and the rate of nuclei formation are modified by the nature of the crystallizing substances, the concentration of the solution, the temperature, how the solution is stirred, and the impurities that may be found in it.

Some substances, such as glucose, do not have the ability to produce very large crystals.

Rather, they produce nuclei rapidly, thus formation of many small crystals, probably because it causes the breaking off of many nuclei from crystals already formed. Stirring also brings the supersaturated solution in contact with each crystal. Impurities that may be deposited on the crystal impede further growth on that side of the crystal. The presence of glucose, for instance, interferes with the crystallization of sucrose. Another way an impurity may interfere with crystallization is by coating the crystal. The use of fat in a candy mixture is a good illustration: the fat interferes with the crystallization of sucrose by coating the sugar crystals.

Saturation. Fairly large amounts of sugar dissolve easily in water; the higher the temperature of the water, the greater the amount of sugar that will dissolve in it. The amount of sugar dissolved in boiling water is roughly twice the amount that will be dissolved in the same volume of water at room temperature. Maltose and glucose are less soluble than sucrose; hence, when syrups containing a large proportion of these two sugars are used, more water must be used to dissolve them than would be needed to dissolve the same weight of sucrose. This difference in solubility has some effect on cooking when syrups are substituted for part or all of the sugar in a recipe.

When heated alone, granulated sugar will melt and form a clear mass without any crystals. If this clear amorphous mass is permitted to cool, it will form a hard cake. This is known as *barley sugar*. If, however, the heating of the sugar is continued until the sugar turns dark brown, the product formed is known as *caramelized sugar*. Caramelized sugar has a very distinctive flavor and, with water added, may be used for flavoring purposes.

A number of candies and cooked icings are made by dissolving sugar in a liquid and heating the mixture. In the first stage of the process, the sugar dissolves and no crystal formation is evident. But once the solution starts to boil and the water evaporates, the solution becomes more concentrated and its boiling point rises in direct proportion to the amount of sugar dissolved in the liquid.

When a sugar solution has reached a certain degree of saturation and is permitted to cool off, crystals start to form. Generally, the crystals that are wanted in candy are the small crystals that make for a smooth texture. Such candies as fondant and fudge fall into this category and are known as the *cream* or *crystalline candies*.

Size of Crystals. For these candies, small, quickly formed crystals are required. It should be noted that the speed of crystal formation is extremely important in achieving just the right texture.

In a solution made with granulated sugar, the sucrose crystallizes very readily. When crystals start to form too soon in a sugar solution, they form only a few at a time. Those formed, however, are large and they continue to grow, resulting in a grainy candy.

To prevent large crystals from forming and to promote the formation of many tiny crystals, a small amount of a simple sugar (glucose) should be present in the sugar solution. These small sugar molecules interfere with the formation of the large sucrose crystals and retard their development. Simple sugar may be added to a candy solution in carefully measured amounts of corn syrup or honey. Or an acid ingredient (cream of tartar, lemon juice, or vinegar) may be added to hasten the inversion of sucrose to glucose and fructose. Either method of providing a small amount of simple sugar must be carefully controlled, for too much corn syrup or honey, or too much inversion of sucrose, will result in a runny product that will not cream when beaten.[1] Corn syrup might be the better choice on a damp day. It will not pick up as much moisture as invert sugar.

A second consideration in getting just the right conditions for rapid crystallization is to have the syrup at exactly the right temperature or, to put it another way, at just the right concentration. The solution must be sufficiently concentrated so that under appropriate conditions it will become supersaturated. When this point has been reached, the solution is ready to be set aside to cool.

The third factor involves allowing the mixture to cool off until it is likewarm (about 100°F; 38°C) before it is beaten. The concentration of the solution is such that it will become supersaturated when cooled. As the syrup cools, the sugar is held in solution in a supersaturated state. If the syrup is beaten while it is still hot, large crystals will form. When the solution is allowed to cool before it is beaten, the tiny

crystals form all at one time, heat is released (a change of state from liquid to solid is involved), and a creamy mass is formed. Beating must be carried on until the crystallization process is complete.

Candies that do not require crystallization are called *noncrystalline candies*. In making these candies, it is important to prevent the formation of crystals. This is achieved by adding such ingredients as butter, cream, egg white, chocolate, or corn syrup directly to the sugar solution. These materials will supply sufficient simple sugars, fats, or air foam to interfere with the formation of crystals.

It is important to determine exactly when the right temperature has been reached. Special candy thermometers may be used for this purpose, or small amounts of sugar syrup may be dropped in cold water. The reaction of the syrup to the cold water corresponds to a given range of temperatures and characterizes a particular stage.

CANDY

The three groups of candy are: crystalline, noncrystalline, and gummy and spongy.

Crystalline. The various crystalline (or cream) candies are prepared in similar ways.

Fondant is a simple cream candy that is used as the center for chocolate creams and for fondant mixtures. Sugar is dissolved in the fondant syrup and the mixture is placed in a covered saucepan. As the syrup comes to a heavy boil, it washes down the crystals that have formed on the side of the pan. Any crystals that continue to cling to the side of the pan should be removed carefully with a wet cloth wrapped around the prongs of a fork. Care must be taken to prevent any crystals from falling into the solution. Any particle, such as a crystal or a bit of dust, that falls into such a concentrated solution serves as a nucleus to which several crystals coming out of solution may attach themselves, producing one large crystal rather than the many small ones desired.

The fondant syrup is cooked until it reaches the soft-ball stage (about 237°F; 114°C) (Table 35-2). This is close to the saturation point of the solution. At this point, the solution is poured—without stirring or scraping—onto a flat platter or marble slab and is allowed to cool to about

[1] E. Halliday and I. Noble, *Hows and Whys of Cooking,* rev. ed. (Chicago: University of Chicago Press, 1946), p. 20.

TABLE 35-2
Tests for Stages of Sugar Cookery

Test	Description	Temperature	
		°F	°C
Thread syrup	Dropped from a fork or spoon, syrup spins a 2-in. thread	230–234	110–112
Soft ball Fondant Fudge Panocha	Dropped into very cold water, syrup forms a soft ball that does not flatten when removed from the water	234–240	112–116
Firm ball Caramels	Dropped in very cold water, syrup forms a firm ball that does not flatten when removed from the water	244–248	118–120
Hard ball Divinity	Dropped in cold water, syrup forms a hard ball	250–266	121–130
Soft crack Butterscotch Taffy	Dropped in cold water, syrup separates into a thread—hard, but not brittle	270–290	132–143
Hard crack Brittle	Dropped in cold water, syrup separates into a thread—hard and brittle	300–310	149–154
Clear liquid Barley sugar	The sugar liquefies	320–338	160–170
Jelly	Syrup runs off cool metal spoon in drops that form a sheet	220	104–5

Source: Adapted from *Handbook of Food Preparation,* rev. ed. (Washington, D.C.: American Home Economics Association, 1975).

104°F (40°C). The fondant is then beaten continuously until it becomes a creamy, mass. At first, the mixture becomes cloudy from the air beaten into it; then it may very quickly harden. If the fondant is too hard, it should be kneaded, which will soften it, remove small lumps, and impart a smooth texture. Fondant becomes creamy and more uniform in texture if it is left to ripen for at least 24 hours before it is used. When stored, it is placed in a covered container to prevent it from drying out or absorbing moisture.

Commercially, fondant is used for the soft cream centers of chocolate candies. The flavored fondant is dipped into sweet or bitter coating chocolate. Softened fondant is used to make mints or to coat small fruits and nuts.

Like fondant, fudge is a crystalline candy. The basic ingredients for each are somewhat similar. A table fat is added to fudge to give it richness. Also, fudge recipes use milk rather than water as the liquid ingredient. (Evaporated milk is fre-

quently used to avoid the problem of curdling.) Chocolate and vanilla are both used to flavor the candy.

The sugar, milk, chocolate, and corn syrup are cooked together slowly until the sugar has dissolved. Milk and chocolate may stick to the bottom of the pan, thereby making it necessary to stir the mixture until the sugar is completely dissolved. The fudge solution is then handled in a manner similar to that for fondant. One difference is that the fat and vanilla are added to the fudge solution after it has reached the boiling point (237°F; 117°C). Fudge is usually allowed to cool to 104°F (40°C) in the saucepan in which it was cooked. Like fondant, the cooled fudge is beaten until creamy. Then it is put into an oiled pan and cut into bars or squares.

Noncrystalline. In the noncrystalline candies, there are no sugar crystals. Caramels, a noncrystalline candy, have a waxy texture and are made of sugar, corn syrup, fat, and concentrated milk products, such as evaporated milk or sweetened condensed milk. During the cooking of caramels, care must be taken to avoid scorching the mixture. It is believed that the characteristic caramel color is due to the browning reaction that takes place between the milk proteins and the sugars. Large quantities of fat increase the richness of caramels.

Nougats are chewy in consistency and are more spongy than caramels. They are made by pouring a sugar syrup over stiffly beaten egg whites. Honey and nuts are other ingredients used. Taffies are pulled candies. Some taffies include molasses, honey, or corn syrup as well as sugar. The cooked syrup is cooled until it just begins to thicken and can be handled. It is then pulled and twisted into various shapes.

Brittles are made of syrups cooked to a high temperature and then spread out over nuts into a thin layer and allowed to cool. Nuts may be stirred into the syrup before it is poured.

Spongy. Gelatin is the basis of marshmallow and gumdrop candies. Marshmallows are made by pouring a syrup that has been cooked to 240°F (116°C) and has had gelatin added to it over stiffly beaten egg white. Another gummy candy, turkish delight, is made by combining gelatin with sugar, water, and fruit juices or fruit pulp or a combination of the two. This mixture is usually cooked slowly for about 20 minutes and allowed to set overnight before being cut into squares.

Gumdrops are made with very large amounts of gelatin added to corn syrup and fruit juices. Gumdrop mixtures are cooked to 280°F (138°C). When made commercially, gum arabic is used instead of gelatin.

SUMMARY

Formed in plant tissue by photosynthesis, sugars are the simplest of organic foods and are the building blocks for complex starches and celluloses. Sugars may be monosaccharides (simple sugars) or disaccharides. The monosaccharides include glucose (dextrose), fructose (levulose)—both of which are found in fruits and syrups—and galactose, a part of the sugar found in milk (lactose). The disaccharides are maltose, found mainly in malt extract; lactose, referred to as milk sugar; and sucrose, commonly known as cane sugar, beet sugar, or granulated sugar.

Derived either from sugar cane or sugar beets, granulated sugar is the most important sugar on the market. Brown sugar differs from granulated sugar in being less refined, whereas powdered sugar is pulverized granulated sugar. Molasses is a by-product of sugar made from sugar cane. Syrups are liquids containing large amounts of sugar. Chief among them are molasses, maple syrup, corn syrup, and honey, which is classified according to flower source.

In cookery, sugar is used in sweetening desserts; in making preserves, jams, and jellies; and in making candy.

In the making of crystalline, or cream, candies, such as fondant and fudge, the principles of crystallization are of significance. Crystallization will occur only if a solution is supersaturated. To promote formation of many small crystals, the candy mixture should contain a small amount of a simple sugar.

Another type of candy does not require crystallization. Known as noncrystalline candy, it has butter, cream, or other ingredients added that interfere with crystal formation. Included in this group are the brittle candies and the chewy candies, such as butterscotch, caramel, and taffy. Spongy candies include marshmallows, turkish delight, and gumdrops.

QUESTIONS AND TOPICS FOR DISCUSSION AND STUDY

1. Why is it possible to use vinegar, cream of tartar, or corn syrup in making fondant? What is the effect of each on the smoothness of the fondant?
2. Why does the container in which a candy solution has been cooked turn warmer just before the solution changes to a solid?
3. Why is it necessary to control the cooking time of a candy solution when using cream of tartar?
4. Why is the fondant syrup cooled before beating?
5. Why must fudge or fondant be beaten or kneaded until all lumps have disappeared?
6. What probably accounts for the slightly sticky texture of fondant made with corn syrup?

SUGGESTED ACTIVITIES

1. Prepare one or more of the following candies: fondant, fudge, peanut brittle, butterscotch, caramels and divinity. If fondant is made, store it in an airtight container for a day or two. Notice the creamy texture of stored fondant.

REFERENCES

BOOKS

Griswold, Ruth. *The Experimental Study of Foods.* Boston: Houghton Mifflin, 1962, Chap. 13.

Halliday, Evelyn, and Isabel Noble. *Hows and Whys of Cooking,* rev. ed. Chicago: University of Chicago Press, 1946, Chap. 8.

Lowe, Belle. *Experimental Foods,* 4th ed. New York: Wiley, 1955, Chap. 3.

BULLETINS AND PAMPHLETS

"Baking Molasses." New York: American Molasses Co., 1956.

"Honey and Some of Its Uses." *Home and Garden Bulletin 37.* Washington, D.C.: U.S. Department of Agriculture, 1962.

"Sweeteners." Hyattsville, Md.: Agriculture Research Service, Consumer and Food Economic Institute, 1976.

Worstall, J., A. William, and I. Searls. "Molasses: A Nutritious Sweet." *Cornell University Extension Bulletin 830.* Ithaca, N.Y., 1951.

Gelatin and Gelatin Dishes

Gelatin is a food product that has little palatability or food value when used alone. But it takes on new and interesting qualities when combined with other foods. Gelatin is prepared commercially in much the same manner as glue. However, gelatin—by federal regulation—must be free of impurities. Gelatin is produced by heating the bone and skin tissue of animals in water. The bones of mature cattle are preferred to those of young animals because they have a lower water content. The process involved in the manufacture of gelatin can be seen in the home when the water in which poultry, fish, or meat has been cooked forms a gelled broth (from the collagen of the connective tissue).

The characteristics of gelatin important in food preparation are its neutral color, its ability to disperse in a hot liquid and to stay dispersed when cooled, and its ability to thicken into a semisolid mass when used in sufficient concentration.

COMPOSITION AND PREPARATION

Gelatin is an incomplete protein and must be mixed or served with foods containing other proteins in order to make a valuable contribu-

tion to the total protein content of the diet. It is quite effective, however, in bringing nutritious foods into very attractive combinations and thereby serving as the basis for palatable dishes.

Gelatin is widely used in the commercial manufacture of such food products as gums, marshmallows, ice creams, and gelatin desserts. In home cookery, it is used mainly in the preparation of jellied desserts, salads (Fig. 36-1), and meats, fish or poultry mousses; and jellied soups.

A gelatin product, properly prepared, will hold its shape at room temperature. The product is firm but not tough; it cuts with little resistance. The change from a liquid form to a gel depends on the concentration of the gelatin and the type and temperature of liquid in which the gelatin is dispersed.

Ratio of Gelatin to Liquid. The structure or stiffness of a gel is related to the concentration of gelatin. Gelation will occur only if the concentration of gelatin is 2% or higher. The amount required depends not only on the amount of liquid but also on the kind and amount of acid used. The general proportion is ½ tbsp gelatin to 1 cup liquid. Acids such as lemon juice, vinegar, and tomato juice increase the gelatin requirement. Products that have high acid content may

442

36-1 *A gelatin salad makes an excellent menu combination with meat or poultry. (Courtesy of Knox Gelatin Company)*

require as much as ¾–1 tbsp gelatin to 1 cup liquid. When milk is used as the solvent, the gelatin concentration need not be so high as when water or an acid juice is used.

Large amounts of sugar appear to interfere with gel formation, but the amounts required in a gelatin dessert are never large enough to warrant a change in the gelatin/liquid ratio.

Methods of Combining Gelatin. It is generally agreed that softening gelatin in cold water prepares the gelatin granules (which take up water and swell) for dispersion in the liquid ingredient (Fig. 36-2). The gelatin is then dispersed in a small portion of the heated liquid, or in the hot liquid ingredients. If only a small portion of the liquid is used, the remainder is added after the gelatin is thoroughly distributed throughout the liquid.

For gelatin dishes to solidify, certain temperatures must be maintained. When sufficient gelatin is present the mixture will gel at room temperature (unless the weather is unusually hot). At this temperature level, however, considerable time must be allowed for gelation. Usually, gelatin mixtures are placed in the refrigerator, where they soon reach the low temperatures that bring about quick gelation.

Rapid gelation can also be brought about by placing the mixture over a bowl of ice. But this method has several disadvantages. The first is the possibility of excessively rapid solidification, which causes the gel to form tough clumps. Second, a quickly formed gel is more likely to lose its structure when removed to higher temperatures than one solidified at higher temperatures.

A gelatin mixture is a colloidal dispersion. It forms a sol in water, but forms a gel when cooled. The action of the gel formation is reversible: if a gelatin mixture is warmed to a certain point, it liquifies; if it is cooled, it forms a gel once again. Lowe[1] states that a gelatin that has liquefied will form successive gels more quickly. Also, if some solid gelatin is added to a fresh gelatin mixture, solidification takes place more rapidly.

Stirring or mechanical agitation of any kind will lessen the rigidity of the gel. When the agitation is discontinued, the gel resumes its rigidity.

Ability to Form Foams. A liquid in which gelatin has been dispersed may be beaten when it has thickened but before it has set. Such beating increases the volume of the gel by two or three times, and gives it a light and spongy texture. If the mixture is beaten when it is too thin, the structure does not hold the air and the foam

[1] Belle Lowe, *Experimental Cookery,* 4th ed. (New York: Wiley, 1955), p. 186.

443

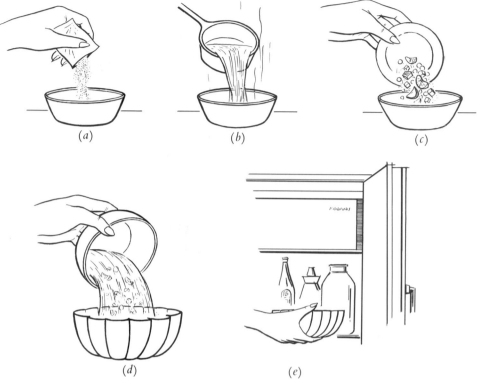

36-2 *Steps in preparing gelatin dishes.* (*a*) *Soften the gelatin in cold water.* (*b*) *Dissolve the gelatin in hot water.* (*c*) *Add other ingredients when the gelatin is slightly thickened.* (*d*) *Pour the gelatin into a mold or dish.* (*e*) *Chill the gelatin in the refrigerator until firm.*

settles on the top, leaving a layer of gel on the bottom. But if the gelatin is too rigid when the beating starts, the gel is only broken and little air is incorporated.

Whipped cream and egg whites are added to some gelatin mixtures—such as Bavarian creams, chiffon pies, and charlotte russes—to give them a spongy texture. These must be added at just the proper time if they are to combine smoothly. Gelatin bases that are intended for beaten mixtures generally have a higher concentration of flavor than those that are used for setting solid foods.

Addition of Other Food Materials. Fresh or frozen pineapple cannot be combined with gelatin to form a solid because its enzyme, bromelin, breaks down the gelatin and destroys its ability to form gels. If fresh or frozen pineapple is boiled for 2 minutes, the enzyme will be inactivated.

Canned pineapple may be used because it has already been heated and the enzyme has been rendered inactive.

Such material as fruits, vegetables, pieces of meat, fish, and the like should be drained thoroughly before being added to gelatin mixtures. Excess moisture would unbalance the gelatin-to-liquid ratio. When the mixture is diluted in this manner, gelation time may be greatly increased and a very tender, watery solid formed.

GELATIN DESSERTS

Gelatin desserts are very palatable and attractive and enjoy a high degree of popularity in American cookery.

Plain fruit jellies and *whips* are made of fruit juice, water, sugar, and gelatin. Whole pieces of fresh, canned, or frozen fruit may be added to

444

the jelly. A gelatin whip may be prepared by chilling a fruit gelatin until it is light and fluffy.

Sponges and *snows* are plain jellies that have been beaten. (Egg whites are added after the mixture has been partially whipped.) Snows are usually served with fruit or custard sauces to improve their flavor.

Spanish creams and *Bavarian creams* are delicate in texture, very palatable, and nutritious as well. Spanish creams are made by setting a soft custard with gelatin and folding stiffly beaten egg whites into the partially gelled mixture. Barvarian creams differ from Spanish creams only in that the custard base is made with fruit juice and whipped cream is folded in along with the beaten egg whites. Crushed fruit and some sugar may also be added to a Bavarian cream.

Charlottes and *mousses* are made by adding cream thickened with gelatin to whipped cream. Charlottes are usually molded with sponge cake or ladyfingers.

Fillings for chiffon pies are usually made from a custard base thickened with gelatin. Beaten egg whites or whipped cream is added to the partially set gelatin; the mixture is poured into a pie shell and chilled. There are numerous varieties of chiffon pie fillings but the method of mixing and the basic ingredients are the same for all.

BUYING GELATIN

The gelatin used for household-sized recipes comes in powdered form, but granulated and sheet gelatins are also available for commercial use. Unflavored gelatin is packaged in uniform amounts (usually 1 tbsp per package). Directions for use are on each package. Gelatin is used in prepared mixes along with sugar, acid, fruit flavors (usually artifical), and coloring. These mixes are very easy to handle, for they require only the addition of water to make a dessert jelly or a gelatin base for various dishes.

Both unflavored and flavored gelatin may be kept for fairly long periods of time. Storage in a dry, cool place will maintain its gelation power.

MOLDING

One of the interesting properties of gelatin is that it can be molded into all sorts of shapes.

Dishes, pans, cups, and molds of every variety can be used to shape gelatin products. Molds used should have an opening larger than their inside circumference. Removing a gelatin dish from its mold requires a certain amount of skill. The mold should be dipped in warm (not hot) water up to the upper edge of the gelatin mixture. This edge is then loosened with a sharp knife. When the mold is inverted on top of a serving platter that has been rinsed with cold water, the gelatin slips out onto the dish.

SUMMARY

Gelatin is an incomplete protein and must be mixed or served with other protein foods to make a contribution to the nutritionally adequate protein content of the diet. Its neutral color, its ability to disperse in a hot liquid and remain dispersed when cooled, its ability to thicken and hold a shape and to enhance other foods give it importance and interest in food preparation.

Factors affecting gelatin and the ratio of gelatin to liquid include the amount of acid used, the amount of sugar used, and the environmental temperature. Gelatin is usually refrigerated for gel formation.

A thickened (but not yet set) gelatin mixture can be beaten into a spongy foam of double or triple the original volume. Foods added to gelatin should first be drained so that the gelatin/liquid ratio is maintained.

Gelatin desserts include plain fruit jellies and whips, sponges, snows, Spanish creams, Bavarian creams, charlottes, mousses, and fillings for chiffon pies.

Many types of salads have a gelatin base. Virtually all foods may be combined with gelatin with the exception of fresh or frozen pineapple. The enzyme bromelin in pineapple breaks down the gelatin and destroys its ability to form a gel.

QUESTIONS AND TOPICS FOR DISCUSSION AND STUDY

1. What kind of colloidal system does gelatin form when it is in solution? When it is coagulated?

2. Why is it possible to incorporate air into gelatin?
3. What will happen to the gel structure of a gelatin mixture if fresh pineapple is added?
4. What factors affect gelation time?
5. Why is the gelatin base chilled before fruits or vegetables are added?

SUGGESTED ACTIVITIES

1. Prepare one or more of the following gelatin dishes: lemon gelatin, Bavarian cream, Spanish cream, and molded fruit salad. Evaluate the products.

2. Prepare a basic lemon jelly and several different brands of prepared lemon gelatins. Compare them for time required for preparation, cost, flavor, and texture.

REFERENCES

BOOK

Vail, Gladys, Jean A. Phillips, Lucile Rust, Ruth M. Griswold, and Margaret M. Justin. *Foods.* Boston: Houghton Mifflin, 1978, Chap. 19.

Frozen Desserts

Frozen desserts are among the most popular desserts eaten in or out of the home. These include ice creams, ices, sherbets, and mousses. Ice cream leads in popularity, probably because of its pleasing flavor and texture. Along with other milk products, ice cream is also valued for its nutritive value. Although some ice cream is still prepared at home, the commercial product is good—and, in many cases, less expensive than the homemade variety. There is value, however, in knowing something about the basic ingredients used in frozen desserts and in recognizing standards of quality.

ICE CREAM

Ice cream is made from a combination of milk products with one or more of the following ingredients added: eggs, water, gelatin, and vegetable coloring. The milk products used may be cream, butter, butterfat, or milk in one of its various forms: whole fluid milk, evaporated milk, skim milk, condensed milk, sweetened dried milk, or dried skim milk.

Standards. Almost every state has set a minimum for the fat content of ice cream, but it varies among states. An average of 10% fat is required in vanilla ice cream—although some states set the minimum as low as 8% and others as high as 14%. For ice creams to which nuts or fruits have been added, the fat requirement is slightly lower. Some states allow a 2% butterfat differential for such ice creams. (It was probably supposed that the food value of the added ingredients made up for the lowered fat content, but this is not necessarily true, for it may only be a flavoring that is added to the vanilla base.) Most states also require 18% total milk solids and up to 33% total solids. During the manufacture of ice cream, large amounts of air are incorporated into the mixture. This increase in volume is known as *overrun* and must be controlled to ensure a uniform product. To check overrun, some states set a standard of 1.6 lb total food solids per gallon of ice cream (or a weight of 4.5 lb to 1 gal).

Kinds of Ice Cream. Ice cream is often designated by special names, such as *Philadelphia, French,* or *American.* Philadelphia ice cream is an uncooked mixture of thick cream, sugar, and flavoring; French ice cream is a cooked mixture of milk, eggs, sugar, and flavoring; American ice cream (or plain ice cream) is similar to French ice cream but may contain cornstarch, flour, or gelatin instead of eggs for thickening.

Preparation and Composition. Whether ice cream is commercially made or homemade, the flavor, body, and texture are the important factors in evaluating its quality.

Ice cream should be delicate in flavor and well blended. It should be free of any unpleasant or overly strong flavors, and it should not be too acid. A good fat content will add to the flavor, for an ice cream with no body has little flavor. The materials in the ice cream mixture—such as eggs, milk, and flavorings—must be selected with care to be sure they are free of off-flavors. The addition of some salt will help to blend the various flavors and point up the one that is to be emphasized.

SUGAR. Ice creams and other frozen desserts have a rather high proportion of sugar and flavoring because low temperatures blunt the tastebuds. The flavor of a frozen dessert is, therefore, not as pronounced as that of similar mixtures served at room temperature. A good proportion of sugar is up to about 16% (by weight) of the total ingredients used. Not only is sugar an important flavoring agent, it is also important in imparting a smooth texture. Granulated sugar is used in most household recipes. Commercial ice cream may use glucose and corn syrup to replace some of the sucrose. The syrups tend to give added smoothness.

FLAVORINGS. Flavorings are added to ice cream in the form of extracts, fruits, nuts, spices, chocolate, or coffee—and only in amounts that will impart a mild, pleasant flavor. In ice cream, it is important that the natural flavor of the cream or butterfat be discernible. Of all the flavorings used in ice cream, vanilla is by far the most popular. Chocolate ice cream, second in popularity, may be made by the addition of cocoa or chocolate to the ice cream mix. Current practices in the production of ice cream have made possible the creation of many more flavor variations. Once the basic proportions for the ice cream mix are established, many different combinations can be evolved.

Body. The term *body,* used with relation to ice cream, refers to the consistency or richness of the product. An ice cream with good body does not melt quickly. This quality is affected by the amount of fat and by the fillers that are used in the mix.

Most manufacturers of ice cream use such materials as milk solids, eggs, dextrins, and starch as stabilizers or fillers. These increase the total amount of materials held in suspension in the cream, thus giving the mixture body before it is frozen. Nonfat milk solids are generally not used in excess of 12% (by weight) of the mix; more would give rise to a sandy texture in the finished ice cream. Most fillers are effective in increasing the amount of air a frozen mixture can incorporate, but gelatin and vegetable gums are especially good for this purpose.

Texture. Ice cream, as well as other frozen desserts, must have a pleasing smooth texture if it is to be considered palatable. Actually, all the ingredients used have some effect on the texture. Texture also depends on the size, shape, and arrangement of the ice crystals in the mixture. Large, flaky ice crystals give ice cream an undesirable texture. Sugar contributes to smoothness because it goes into solution, making the mixture viscous and thereby interfering with the ice crystallization. Other ingredients that do not go into solution—such as fat, gelatin, eggs, powdered milk, and cooked starch—help to produce a smooth texture by separating the ice crystals. The most important of these is fat—and the more finely divided the fat globules, the more effective they are in keeping the ice crystals small and separated. Fine division of the other materials also helps to make a smoother mixture.

Commercially made ice creams may have 0.3–0.5% of a stabilizer such as gelatin or gum arabic to keep the materials in dispersion.

ICES AND SHERBETS

Products similar to ice cream—although less popular—are also sold. In some states, products sold as milk sherbet must not contain more than 5% milk solids. The other ingredients may be the same as those used in ice cream. Ices or ice sherbets, however, do not contain any milk solids; their basic ingredients are sugar, water, artificial coloring, flavoring, and a stabilizer. Beaten egg whites may also be added to the sherbet.

Ices are made of fruit juices and sugar, with or

without fruit pulp. Usually, the proportion is kept to approximately ¾ cup sugar to 1 cup water and ¼ cup lemon juice, because it is difficult to freeze an ice that has a higher sugar content. The flavoring material is very important and is usually added in greater amounts than would be used in similar unfrozen mixtures. Lemon juice helps to point up the flavor of an ice or sherbet and is usually added in small amounts whether or not other fruit juices are used. The texture of an ice or sherbet is influenced by the amount of solids in the mixture and by the thickener used. Frequently, egg white or a marshmallow mixture is added to fruit sherbets after the water and fruit have been frozen to mush. When milk is used in place of water, the product has a smoother texture and a more pronounced flavor.

MOUSSES AND PARFAITS

Mousses and parfaits are very rich mixtures that can be frozen successfully without stirring. They contain large amounts of whipped cream, gelatin, or egg whites to help maintain their smooth texture by incorporating air, which will, to some degree, prevent large crystal formation. The cold mixtures are placed in sealed containers packed in ice and salt to harden. These remain packed in ice until served. Freezing requires 4–6 hours, during which time more ice and salt need to be placed around the containers to complete freezing. The water formed is drawn off through holes in the container.

ICE MILK AND IMITATION
ICE CREAM

Ice milk differs from ice cream in that it has a fat content of 2–7%. Other ingredients in the ice milk mix are similar to those in an ice cream mix. *Mellorine* is probably the most widely used term for an imitation ice cream. The imitation ice cream product is made with a vegetable fat or oil and nonfat milk solids and is sold in only a few states. Although ice cream may be sold without declaration of added color on the label, frozen desserts containing less milk fat than ice cream must have the declaration if color is added.

METHODS OF FREEZING

In freezing a cream mixture (Fig. 37-1), the aim is to maintain its smooth texture. A mixture with water in it, when frozen, will form ice crystals, in order for it to change from a liquid to a solid state, it must give off heat. When ice cream is frozen at home, the ice cream mixture is surrounded with melting ice. Under usual conditions, melting ice has a temperature of 32°F (0°C), but by adding some salt to it, the rate of melting can be increased and the temperature reduced. Household freezers are designed so that an ice-and-salt mixture can be packed around a metal container into which the ice cream mixture is poured. The container comes equipped with a dasher connected to a handle. While the mixture is freezing, the handle is turned, stirring air into the ice cream. The air refines the texture of the ice cream and increases its volume. The older household freezer is operated by hand, but electric mixers are more likely to be used now.

The proportions of ice and salt used in freezing the ice cream mix are very important. The temperature of the mix must be brought below the freezing temperature of water. Most ice creams start to freeze at about 28°F (-2°C). Halliday and Noble report good results by using a salt/ice weight ratio of 1:6, which works out to 1 cup salt to 3 qt chopped ice.[1] The ratio of 1 part salt to 8 parts ice cream also works out satisfactorily. The finished creams are smooth and hold their shape for a reasonable amount of time. If the salt in the ice mixture is increased, the rate of freezing will also increase, making it difficult to turn the handle of the freezer fast enough to incorporate sufficient air to make a smooth mixture.

The dasher in the metal container has a number of important functions. One edge of the dasher is sharp; as it revolves, the sharp edge cuts the formed ice crystals off the wall of the container and brings the unfrozen parts of the mixture to the surface. If the agitation is interrupted, large ice crystals will form where the temperature is lowest (around the sides of the container) and the center of the mixture will remain un-

[1] E. Halliday and I. Nobel, *Hows and Whys of Cooking,* rev. ed. (Chicago: University of Chicago Press, 1946), p. 226.

449

(a)

(b)

(c)

(d)

37-1   *Steps in freezing ice cream. (a) Set the dasher in the ice cream can and put the can in place in the freezer. Pour the mixture into the can and allow for expansion in freezing. Place the lid on the can. (b) Pack 8 parts of ice and 1 part of salt tightly around the can. Repeat the process until the ice mixture is about level with the top of the can. (c) When the crank can no longer be turned, remove the dasher, cover the top of the can with waxed paper, and replace the lid firmly. Add ice and salt, in the same proportions as before, to cover the can, and let the frozen mixture stand until you are ready to serve. (d) The ice cream may be spooned directly from the can into the dessert glasses. Leftover ice cream can be packed in freezer containers and stored in the freezer. (Courtesy of Evaporated Milk Association)*

frozen. The container should never be filled to capacity with the unfrozen ice cream mix, because the introduction of air into the mixture increases its volume.

Automatic Refrigerator. The freezing units of an automatic refrigerator can be used to freeze ice cream. Manufacturers' instructions are more accurate than any set of general rules, but methods that decrease the freezing time tend to improve the refrigerator-frozen product. Several techniques are used to achieve this end. One is to use a fairly rich mixture into which air can be stirred before the mixture is frozen. Because there is no way for the mixture to be stirred while it is freezing, the consistency of refrigerator-frozen ice cream is improved if it is removed from the tray when partially frozen and beaten rapidly to break up the ice crystals and whip in air.

It is interesting to note that the cost of the ingredients for homemade ice cream may have been a factor in increasing the popularity of the commercial product.

BUYING COMMERCIAL ICE CREAM

Federal standards for commercially produced ice cream and related products are given in Table 37-1.

Because ice cream is a milk product that develops bacteria as readily as milk does, some states require that the cream and milk used in ice cream mixes be pasteurized and have a minimum bacterial count. Some knowledge of the conditions under which the ice cream is packed, frozen, and stored might prove to be very enlightening to the consumer. The consumer, however, has very little opportunity to obtain these facts. On the other hand, institutions that purchase large quantities of ice cream can set up certain specifications for the dealer to meet. Usually, the specifications set minimum content levels and require assurance that the product is packaged under sanitary conditions.

FREEZING COMMERCIAL ICE CREAM

Commercial ice cream is sold in various quantities—from the 4-oz to the 1-gal package. Specialty items—such as ice cream cakes, ice cream pies, and ice cream sticks—are also available.

The commercial freezing of ice cream is quite different from home-freezing techniques, although it too is based on the principle of heat absorption. Commercial freezing procedures are completely mechanized. There is a flow of brine at controlled temperatures around the freezer. The brines are cooled by the volatilization of the liquid to a gas and, in turn, supply the heat required for the change of state. The dasher is run by electricity and its speed can be varied. Once the ice cream is frozen, it is packed into containers and placed in refrigerated rooms to harden.

SUMMARY

Frozen desserts include ice creams, ices, sherbets, and mousses; of these, ice cream is the most popular. Ice cream is a combination of cream or cream and milk products and ingredients such as eggs, water, sugar, gelatin, vegetable coloring, and flavorings. It should be well blended and free of overly strong flavors. The important factors in judging quality are flavor, body, and texture.

Most states have set minimum standards for the fat content of ice cream. Ice creams may be designated by such special names as Philadelphia, French, or American. The names indicate ingredients and manner of handling them. The term "body" refers to the consistency or richness

TABLE 37-1
Federal Standards for Frozen Desserts

Ingredient	Ice Cream	Bulky Flavors	Ice Milk	Fruit Sherbets	Water Ices
Fat					
(min. %)	10.0	8.0	2.0	1.0	
(max. %)			7.0	2.0	
Total milk solids					
(min. %)	20.0	16.0	11.0	2.0	
(max. %)				5.0	
(min. lb/gal mix)	4.5	4.5	4.5	6.0	6.0
(max. lb/gal mix)	1.6	1.6	1.3		
Stabilizer (max. %)	0.5	0.5	0.5	0.5	0.5
Acidity (min. %)				0.35	0.35

Source: Federal Register, Part 20, Title 21, 1971.

of ice cream. To be palatable, ice cream should have a smooth texture, free of large flaky ice crystals.

Ices or ice sherbets are a mixture of fruit juices and sugar, with or without fruit pulp. The amount of solids and the thickener used influence the texture. In some states, milk sherbet must not contain more than 5% milk solids.

The aim in freezing a cream mixture is to maintain its smooth texture, both in home and in commercial preparation. Methods of freezing homemade and commercial ice creams differ, although both are based on the principle of heat absorption.

Federal standards have been fixed for commercial ice cream and related products.

QUESTIONS AND TOPICS FOR DISCUSSION AND STUDY

1. What causes overrun in frozen desserts?
2. Why is the freezing temperature of ices lower than that of ice cream?
3. Why do frozen desserts require more flavoring than similar mixtures that are not to be frozen?
4. Why is the texture of ice cream finer than that of ice?
5. Why can a mousse be frozen without agitation?

SUGGESTED ACTIVITIES

1. Prepare one or more of the following frozen desserts: vanilla or custard ice cream (or a variation), using a crank freezer and/or a refrigerator; fruit sherbet; and fruit ice. Compare the texture, flavor, and cost of these homemade products with those of some commercial products.

REFERENCES

BOOKS

Frandsen, J. H., and W. S. Arbuckle. *Ice Cream and Related Products.* Westport, Conn.: Avi, 1977.

Lowe, Belle. *Experimental Cookery,* 4th ed. New York: Wiley, 1955, Chap. 4.

Pauline, Paul and Helen Palmer. *Food Theory and Applications,* New York, Wiley, 1972, Chap. 10

ARTICLE

Eopechino, A. A., and J. G. Leeder. "Flavor Modifications Produced in Ice Cream Mix Made with Corn Syrup." *J. Food Sci.* **35**:398, 1970.

Food Preservation

This section outlines the principles of food preservation in the home and presents some information on new methods of preservation that industry is giving serious consideration at present. Chapter 43 is devoted to a complete discussion of additives. New commercial methods of food preservation have extended the possibilities for the transportation and storage of large amounts of food. More foods are now available throughout the year, making possible a more varied and better-balanced diet for all.

Part Five

Principles of Food Preservation

CHAPTER 38

The proper storage of food for future use is an important field for scientific investigation. Of the foods available to mankind, few can be stored for any length of time without special processing and handling. Delay in the use of fresh food alters its freshness, its palatability, and its nutritive value. Food stored without adequate refrigeration will spoil and become unfit for use. The main causes of food spoilage are microbial growth, enzyme action, and insect damage.

FOOD SPOILAGE: CAUSES AND PREVENTION

Bacteria, yeast, and molds may cause putrefaction, fermentation, and molding in food. Most kinds of food are subject to microbial spoilage unless special methods are used for their protection. Microorganisms are usually found on the skins or skin membranes of food; they penetrate the inner tissues only when the outer covering has been broken. Consequently, an intact protective coating will slow down microbial spoilage.

Food may also spoil through decomposition caused by the action of food enzymes. Enzymes are found in all fresh foods, and although their action is important to the ripening of certain foods (such as fruits and vegetables), the continuance of this action after the peak of maturity brings about undesirable changes in the food tissue. These changes include the darkening of cut surfaces, the formation of soft spots, and the development of off-flavors.

Worms, bugs, weevils, fruit flies, and moths may damage food and render it unfit for human consumption. The bruises and cuts caused by these insects serve as pathways by which microorganisms reach the inner tissues.

An effective method of preservation is one that slows down—or prevents altogether—the action of these agents of spoilage without damaging the food or adding injurious substances to it.

The most common methods for the safe storage of food in the home are freezing, canning, and the making of preserves. Some drying of food is still undertaken in the home. In some areas of the country, the home preservation of food is a significant economic factor in providing nutritious and palatable meals.

455

METHODS OF FOOD PRESERVATION

All methods of food preservation have as their purpose the prevention or delay of microbial spoilage, by controlling heat, oxygen, moisture, and sunlight, the slowing down of decomposition, and the prevention of damage by insects and animals.

Microbial spoilage can be slowed down by providing environmental conditions unfavorable for the growth of microorganisms. Warm, unclean containers, surfaces, and utensils are potential sources of microbial contamination and furnish an environment favorable to the growth of these organisms. Lack of food and moisture and low temperatures, on the other hand, impede their growth. Microorganisms can be directly damaged by the application of heat or irradiation.

HEAT

The killing of microorganisms by heat is thought to be due to the coagulation of the proteins, especially the inactivation of enzymes necessary for metabolism.[1] The specific heat treatment varies with the organism—its kind, its state (spore or vegetative), and its environment. The temperature and exposure period depend on the food to be treated and the other means of preservation that may also be used. (Foods such as milk or certain soft vegetables cannot be heated for long periods of time without undergoing an alteration in appearance.) The more intense the heat treatment, the more effective it will be in the destruction of organisms. Thus, in canning food, boiling temperatures or higher are required to kill all the organisms that could spoil the food during storage. In pasteurization, a method that employs temperatures below boiling, some of the spoilage organisms survive, so the processed food must be stored under conditions that are unfavorable to the development of additional microorganisms and must be subjected to supplementary preservative methods. Because

pasteurization involves the use of temperatures below boiling, it is used for foods that are attacked by organisms with low resistance to heat (such as the yeast spores in fruit juices). Preservative methods used to supplement the protection offered by pasteurization include the addition of high concentrations of sugar (as in sweetened milk) and the addition or development of an organic acid, such as lactic acid.

DEHYDRATION

Dehydrated foods are markedly reduced in weight and are therefore more conveniently stored and transported. The drying of food is an ancient method of preservation. Although a few foods (e.g., grains) have so little moisture that they require little drying before storage, most foods have enough moisture to make it necessary to remove some. The presence of even a small amount of moisture will permit enzyme action as well as microbial action, resulting in spoilage.

Drying usually involves the direct removal of water, but it is also involved with any process that reduces the amount of moisture in a food. An example of this is dried fish that is heavily salted. In this case, the moisture is drawn out from the cell tissues. The water is then bound with the solute, making it unavailable to the microorganisms.

Because the pretreatment of foods for drying may involve much handling during their selection, sorting, washing, and peeling, it is important to control the temperature and to prevent the food from coming in contact with equipment surfaces. Sulfuring is used in the drying process to destroy organisms and to preserve color. In drying certain fruits (see Chapters 17 and 43), this is accomplished by exposing the foods to the sulfur dioxide produced by burning sulfur. Vegetables, after blanching, may be dipped into a sulfite solution. Sulfuring maintains a palatable, light color and conserves ascorbic acid. It is believed that some vitamin A is also conserved.

Piled fruits and vegetables may generate heat and permit the growth of spoilage organisms; fish may be contaminated by its own slime; eggs may be soiled by human handling and hen excreta; milk may be contaminated by handlers, utensils, and containers. Thus, the growth of

[1] W. Frazier, *Food Microbiology* (New York: McGraw-Hill, 1958), p. 89.

microorganisms that contaminate food before drying may continue up until the time of drying.

As a result of the heat applied during the drying process, many of the organisms present in the food are destroyed. (It has been reported that bacteria require 18% available moisture, yeast 20% or more, molds 13–16%.[2]) It is therefore essential in the preservation of food by drying to reduce moisture as much as possible without damaging the essential qualities of the food.

Sun-drying is slow, and because time is of great economic importance in the preservation of food, artificial means of dehydrating food have been developed.

Milk and egg are dried to a powder in spray driers, in which the liquid is atomized and sprayed into a hot-air stream for almost instant drying. The rapid dissolving in water of nonfat dry milk crystals is due to a second drying step (instantizing) that gives the particles a spongelike structure. Skim milk, whole milk, whey, and fat-enriched milk are spray-dried in large quantities. Also, recent developments in spray drying have turned to such processes as the drying of caseinate, which is prepared for use in sausage products and luncheon meats, spray-dried cheese, an ingredient used in the soup and biscuit industries, and dried cream powder, used in the ice cream industry. The instantizing process is very popular because the original single particles of the raw product are transformed into porous agglomerates which become wet very quickly. The particles then sink, disperse, and dissolve rapidly. Agglomeration of spray-dried products reduces bulk density and produces a product with high thermostability. High thermostability prevents coagulation when instant milk powder is added to hot, slightly acid liquids containing tannins.[3]

Tunnel and truck dehydrators with hot air delivered by fans are used extensively to dehydrate certain types of vegetables and fruits. Some modern dehydrators are designed so that fresh food is placed on a belt and conveyed through equipment with temperature, humidity, and air flow carefully controlled for drying with minimum adverse change in color, flavor, or other qualities. Some products can be cut into small pieces and then blown through ducts by hot air, which both dries the products and conveys them to the collecting station.

Dehydration under high vacuum is considered a highly desirable method for a food such as fruit juice that is difficult to handle by conventional drying procedures because its high sugar content causes caking and sticking. Moreover, the development of off-flavors is minimized in the absence of air.

Some fruits and vegetables can now be processed by a method known as *explosion puffing*. Superheated steam is exploded through the partly dried pieces, creating a porous structure. This opened structure, plus the fact that the material is exposed to heat for only a short time, provides the basis for high quality. Blueberries, carrots, beets, and apple slices are items that have been puff-dried. As possible ingredients in dry mixes they offer many interesting variations. Reconstitution of puff-dried items can take place more rapidly than when conventional methods of drying are used.

Concentrated liquids can be made into a foam prior to drying. A gas is forced into the liquid and the foam is dried on a perforated tray or continuous belt. This process is known as *foam matting*.[4]

IRRADIATION

At present, the use of ionizing radiations for the preservation of food is under intensive study. Ionizing radiations that have some possibility for use in food preservation include ultraviolet rays, x or gamma rays, and cathode or beta rays. Of these, only ultraviolet rays have yet been used. Ultraviolet rays are germicidal and have been used successfully in the treatment of bread and cake products and in the packaging of bacon, meat, and cheese. Ultraviolet irradiation is used chiefly to treat the air in storage and processing rooms, thus reducing the number of microorganisms (spores and vegetative cells) found on shelves and walls.

[2] Ibid, p. 129.

[3] K. Masters, *Spray Drying* (New York: Wiley, 1976), p. 557.

[4] "Developing and Testing New Foods and Fibers," *Economic Research Service ERS-210* (Washington, D.C.: U.S. Department of Agriculture, Marketing Economics Division, 1964).

Studies have demonstrated that food spoilage microorganisms can be destroyed by irradiation, but that the radiation doses presently required to sterilize the food completely are so large that they cause undesirable changes in many kinds of food. Very little heat is generated by the ionizing radiation process. According to Proctor and Goldblith,[5] all irradiated foods undergo some change in color, odor, and texture. Blanching food prior to radiation is necessary to slow down undesirable changes. Clearances have been granted for treating potatoes with radiation to inhibit sprouting. One type of flexible packaging material has been cleared for use on foods that have been treated by cobalt 60 or cesium 137.[6]

Some important facts are now known about irradiation and its effects on food components.[7]

1. The amount of irradiation necessary to sterilize food effectively is strong enough to be destructive of the color, odor, or taste of the food.
2. Radiation degradation of carbohydrates is indicated by loss of texture (the softening and increased solubility of cellulose and pectin) in foods such as apples, beets, and carrots, and by changes in color. Glucose linkages are broken and typical products of hydrolysis are formed.
3. Protein degradation is thought to be responsible for certain undesirable changes in color and odor, as well as for liquefaction. Irradiation also causes partial denaturization of the protein. Proteins appear to be involved in pigment changes, especially in meats. The myoglobin pigment in meats irradiated in air shows oxidation to the darker metmyoglobin. Evans and Batzer report the presence of small amounts of sulfmyoglobin after irradiation.[8]

There is an increase in expressible fluids (drip) in irradiated foods.

4. The irradiation of fats may result in the development of off-flavors and off-odors. When fats are irradiated, their natural antioxidants are destroyed, allowing an increase in peroxides. Saturated fatty acids are less susceptible to change than unsaturated fats. For instance, coconut—high in saturated fat—does not develop a serious off-flavor on irradiation.

Work underway to develop a safe method of irradiating food involves the application of atomic or nuclear energy. By subjecting foods to a bombardment of gamma rays or electrons, the microorganisms, insects, and parasites found in them can be destroyed. It is believed that the rays striking the organism disrupt its internal equilibrium, making reproduction impossible.[9] The gamma rays from fissionable materials show the greatest promise for penetrating food, water, and other substances to destroy undesirable organisms. When food is exposed to gamma rays or electrons, there is a slight rise in temperature, but the food is still raw. It has been determined that gamma radiation from cobalt 60 or cesium 137 does not induce radioactivity in foods exposed to them. Some irradiated foods have been approved by the Food and Drug Administration. Irradiated wheat and wheat products have been cleared at levels that will assure insect deinfestation.

Radiation Dose Levels. Radiation preservation has been experimentally considered in terms of two dose levels: low dose and high dose. Dose level is measured in terms of *rads*. A rad is the quantity of ionizing radiation that results in the absorption of 100 ergs[10] per gram of irradiated material at the point of interest. A *kilorad* equals 1000 rads, a *megarad* 1,000,000 rads. A high-dose level is defined as greater than 1.0 megarad and is usually in the range 2.0–4.5 megarads. High-dose levels of radiation are considered to sterilize food by killing microorganisms, thus eliminating the necessity for refrigeration.

[5] B. E. Proctor and S. A. Goldblith, "Preservation of Foods by Irradiation," *Amer. J. Pub. Health* **47**:439, 1957.

[6] "Status of Irradiated Food Petitions to U.S. Food and Drug Administration" (Washington, D.C.: U.S. Department of Commerce, Business and Defense Services Administration, 1966).

[7] B. Morgan, "Current Status of Radiation Preservation of Food," *Food Process.,* June–July, 1957.

[8] J. B. Evans and O. F. Batzer, "Irradiation," in *The Science of Meat and Meat Products,* 2nd ed., J. F. Price and B. S. Schweigert, eds. (San Francisco: Freeman, 1971), p. 304.

[9] N. Desrosier and H. Rosenstock, *Radiation Technology in Food, Agriculture, and Biology* (Westport, Conn.: Avi, 1960), p. 171.

[10] A unit of work or energy.

High-dose radiation is known as *radappertization.* A low-dose level (1 megarad or less) is termed *radurization,* because it destroys or inhibits the growth of certain undesirable bacteria in food, in the same way that conventional pasteurization does. However, the dose of radiation applied to the food is strong enough to destroy a great majority of the bacteria and molds in the food, but not all; the reproduction of the rest is retarded through refrigeration.[11]

United States Army's Radiation Preservation of Food Program. The National Food Irradiation Program is administered by two main federal agencies: the Energy Research and Development Administration (ERDA) and the Department of the Army (DA).[12]

ERDA's program promotes low-dose (sub-megarad) application of irradiation processing to fruits, vegetables, finfish, shellfish, poultry, and meats to retard their deterioration and extend

[11] Eugen Wierbicki, "Preservation of Meats by Ionizing—An Update" *Rapporteur's Papers, Paper 14* (Natick, Mass.: United States Army Natick Research and Development Command, n.d.).

[12] *The United States Army's Radiation Preservation of Food Program* (Natick, Mass.: Natick Research and Development Command, 1976).

their distribution and shelf life (see Fig. 38-1). Petitions have been or are being submitted to the Food and Drug Administration (FDA) for clearances on strawberries, irradiated to retard mold formation, and on papayas, irradiated to eliminate infesting insects.

The Army's Food Irradiation Program concentrates on developing the technology for using higher doses (megarad) to radiation-sterilize (radappertize) prepacked, enzyme-inactivated meat, poultry, and marine products. Radappertization results in a commodity that is familiar in appearance yet completely stable while stored at room temperature. This part of the DA effort has been pioneered by the U.S. Army Material Development and Readiness Command (DARCOM) at the Natick Research and Development Command (NARADCOM). The Army's responsibility for establishing the safety and wholesomeness of radappertized foods is assumed by the Surgeon General's Medical Research and Development Command (MRDC).

Currently, the DA effort is directed toward obtaining clearances for radappertized beef, pork, ham, and chicken. This effort involves long-term animal feeding studies and the acquisition of supporting auxiliary data. Design of these studies was coordinated with the NAS/NRC, FDA, USDA, and internationally

38-1 *An example of food irradiation. (Courtesy U.S. Army Photographs: Natick Research and Development Command)*

NON - IRRADIATED -

IRRADIATED - (0.2 M RAD)

STRAWBERRIES -
15 DAYS STORAGE 38°F (4°C)

459

recognized experts on nutrition and toxicology.

Ionizing radiation cannot be used commercially in treating food until the treated food is approved in this country by the FDA. This approval is required because ionizing radiation legally is a "food additive" as defined by statute here (the 1958 Food Additive Amendment to the Food, Drug, and Cosmetic Act).

USE OF LOW TEMPERATURES

It is a common practice to use low temperatures to retard chemical reactions and enzyme action and to retard or to stop the growth of microorganisms in food. There is a direct relationship between decrease in temperature and decrease in microbial growth and enzyme reaction.

Low-temperature methods of preserving foods include the cooling of food in storage cellars and home refrigerators and the freezing and holding of food at below-freezing temperatures.

Low-Temperature Storage. *Low-temperature storage* usually refers to cellar or pantry storage, where temperatures much below 60°F (16°C) are seldom reached. This kind of storage is suitable for such foods as root vegetables, potatoes, cabbage, celery, apples, winter pears, and onions. Although deterioration proceeds in these vegetables and fruits, it does so slowly, making it possible for them to be safely stored in this manner for a limited period. However, fruits and vegetables so stored must be examined periodically. Damaged or spoiled pieces must be removed to prevent the spoilage organisms from spreading to the sound food.

Chilling by Refrigeration. The most common method of preserving foods for short periods is by chilling. Formerly, this involved cooling the food by putting it on ice; now, mechanical refrigeration is the chief method used. With few exceptions, perishable foods may be kept fresh and unspoiled at temperatures of 32 to 45°F (0–7°C). The temperature of the food compartment of an electric refrigerator fluctuates between 32 and 50°F (0–10°C). Like cooling, chilling does not prevent enzymatic action or

microbial growth, but it slows down both processes considerably.

Humidity. Some foods require, in addition to low temperatures, a certain amount of humidity in the atmosphere in order to slow down spoilage. Too low a relative humidity tends to dry out fruit and vegetables; too high a relative humidity favors the growth of spoilage microorganisms.

For the storage of large amounts of fresh foods, the use of ozone or carbon dioxide in the atmosphere allows an increase in the relative humidity.

Ventilation. Inadequate ventilation accelerates the rate of microbial growth. Control of ventilation in all storage areas is essential to remove odors and to maintain the proper relative humidity.

FREEZING

Freezing food to preserve it is not new. Outdoor freezing, when temperatures were sufficiently low, has long been used as a convenient way of slowing down the processes that result in food spoilage. The purpose of freezing is to retard microbial growth and enzyme action. Most food products today are quick-frozen in 30 minutes or less; the slow-freezing method takes 3–72 hours.

Temperatures employed to quick-freeze foods range from 0 to −40°F (18–40°C). The food may be immersed in a refrigerant—as, for example, when fish is frozen in brine. Or it may be frozen by indirect contact with the refrigerant—as when packaged food is placed on the coils through which the refrigerant flows. A third method, air-blast freezing, involves the directing of frigid air (approximately 0°F; −18°C). across the food.

When food is quick-frozen, there appears to be a preponderance of small ice crystal formation; few large crystals form to cause mechanical destruction of cell wall (see the section on cryogenic freezing of meat in Chapter 24). Because the quick-freezing method causes the solids to form quickly, there is little chance for soluble materials to diffuse in the unbound water portion of the food. Microbial growth and enzyme activity are also slowed down.

Although freezing destroys a considerable number of the organisms in food, it does not sterilize it. The death rate of microorganisms depends on the kind of organism, the temperatures maintained during freezing and storage, the length of storage, and the composition of the food.

Freezing foods offers a good way of retaining nutrients and eating quality. There is little loss of vitamin C during the freezing of fruits. There is, however, some loss of ascorbic acid during the blanching of vegetables before they are frozen, as well as a small loss of other water-soluble vitamins and some minerals.

Properly packaged and frozen meat, poultry, and fish compare very well in food value with their fresh forms. Freezer storage above 0°F (−18°C) hastens nutrient loss.[13]

Freezing kills a large percentage of yeast cells, but mold spores are fairly resistant. Freezing is likely to damage tissues, so that juices released on thawing favor microbial growth.[14] Hence, even at freezing temperatures or slightly lower, microbial spoilage will not be slowed down indefinitely unless the moisture content of the food is also frozen. Another reason for the continued growth of microorganisms is that an increased concentration of dissolved substances occurs in the nonfrozen water content of all frozen foods, thus providing a rich food material for microbial growth.

In addition to microorganisms, most raw foods contain a number of plant enzymes that are not inactivated during freezing. For this reason, vegetables are blanched before they are frozen.

Controlling Temperatures. The temperature maintained during the handling of the food to be frozen affects the kind and growth of microorganisms found in it. The higher the temperature, the more rapid will be the chemical and physical changes and the more quickly will deterioration set in. Exposed surface areas also add to these changes.

[13] "Conserving the Nutritive Values in Food," *Home and Garden Bulletin 90* (Washington, D.C.: U.S. Department of Agriculture, 1963).

[14] Frazier, op. cit., p. 227.

Fruits and vegetables respire after they are harvested—that is, they take in oxygen and give off carbon dioxide. Oxidation, both chemical and enzymatic produces deteriorative changes in flavor and color. When cut surfaces are exposed, these changes are accelerated. This is evident in the darkening of the cut surfaces of apples and other fruit. If temperatures are favorable—that is, high—molds or bacteria will grow rapidly, causing rotting, sliminess, off-flavors, and off-colors.

Meats also continue to undergo change after slaughter. The glycogen in the animal tissue changes to lactic acid and the pigments in the flesh change color. The fat content undergoes changes caused by oxidation and hydrolysis. Microorganisms begin to grow on the warm, moist surfaces of meat and fish and produce undesirable flavors and odors. Sometimes these organisms penetrate the cut surfaces and cause deep decay.

Eggs, too, can be contaminated by handling before freezing. Human handlers and unclean containers and work surfaces with which the eggs come in contact during preparation all help to increase the number of microorganisms adhering to the eggs. High temperatures increase the growth of these organisms.

Effects of Freezing. The most important physical change in food when it is frozen is expansion in volume as ice crystals form and grow larger. The crystals formed during the slow-freezing method are larger than those formed during the quick-freezing method, and some are formed between the tissue cells of the food. To form the ice crystals, water is drawn from the cells. As this happens, the remaining unfrozen liquid becomes more concentrated and its freezing point falls. The increased concentration of solutes in the cells results in the denaturation of proteins and causes irreversible changes in the food. Hence, much of the drip fluid found in frozen meats cannot be reabsorbed during the thawing period.

Storage temperatures for frozen food are usually sufficiently low to reduce to a minimum any enzymatic and chemical reactions. Sometimes a concentrated solution (unbound water with dispersed materials) may ooze from the package before it has frozen. There is also the danger of desiccation (see Chapter 24). Desiccation usually takes place at the surface of the food; it is also called *freezer burn*. The desiccation spot develops a spongy, brown appearance. When the food is thawed, this area remains dry and tough. A similar color change, observed in fresh meats, is accounted for by the conversion of myoglobin to metmyoglobin, which is brown.

During storage of frozen food, the growing cells of the microorganisms are unable to take in food and die from lack of it. Hence, a decrease in the number of microorganisms is apparent during the storage period.

Effects of Thawing. During the thawing of frozen foods, there is a possibility of resumed microbial growth. But this resumption depends on the thawing temperature and on the length of time the food is allowed to stand after thawing. Very slow thawing will cause a marked increase in microbial growth.

The loss of drip from meat and the leakage of moisture from vegetables upon thawing are the result of damage incurred during freezing. Some liquid (but not all) may be reabsorbed by the tissue cells during thawing. Some enzymatic action will also occur; to minimize the effects of this action, the food should be cooked and used quickly.

Much precooked food is frozen commercially in home-sized batches. The precooking is usually effective in killing most of the microorganisms present in the raw foods. After precooking, however, care must be taken to prevent the introduction of any new microorganisms, for they would find little resistance to growth. Cooked food provides a more favorable medium for the growth of organisms than the original raw material did. Thus, it is important that precooked food be cooled quickly and frozen as soon as possible. The reheating of precooked frozen food may not be sufficient to destroy the harmful microorganisms or toxins present. For this reason, it is very important to freeze food while it is relatively free of microorganisms.

THE FREEZE-DRYING METHOD

The process of drying foods in the frozen state, known as *freeze drying,* is of commercial importance. Although it is fairly new to the food industry, it has been used for some time in laboratories to preserve such materials as plasma and penicillin. The freeze-dried food product compares favorably with its corresponding fresh food and is easily and quickly reconstituted. Its volume after being freeze-dried is similar to that of the raw food, and its moisture content is so low that the food remains stable even after long storage.

The solids of a food remain evenly dispersed and distributed as the solvent sublimes (i.e., goes directly into vapor without entering the liquid phase). Consequently, the dry residue becomes a highly porous, solid framework having its original total volume. Because of its spongelike structure, it is highly soluble in water and resumes its original condition very rapidly.

In the freeze-drying process, the food is first quick-frozen and then held at below-freezing temperatures under a high vacuum and dried by the application of heat.[15]

The drying occurs in two stages: first, the ice is sublimed from the frozen mass; then moisture is removed from the final dry solid to lower the residual moisture content still further. In the first stage, 98–99% of all water is removed; in the second, the moisture content is reduced to 0.5% (or less) of the final product.

The loss of volatile substances from freeze-dried food is small when compared with losses that occur in the course of ordinary dehydration, because the temperature for dehydration is below that at which many labile substances undergo chemical change. Also, there is little microbial growth or enzymatic change in the food.

Freeze-Dried Foods. Raw as well as cooked food can be freeze-dried. Foods that are being successfully freeze-dried are orange juice, coffee, crabmeat, shrimp, and meat. Other juices that have freeze-drying potential are pineapple, guava, strawberry, and papaya.

Freeze-dried cubes and strips of meats are available and used in dry soup mixtures and dry main-dish mixtures. Freeze-dried pork chops and small beef steaks refresh quickly and cook like fresh meat; however, they appear to be less moist and more stringy than comparable fresh

[15] D. Tressler and C. Evers, *The Freezing Preservation of Foods* (Westport, Conn.: Avi, 1957), p. 619.

cuts. Other successfully freeze-dried foods are poultry, scrambled eggs, peas, mushrooms, and chives. Freeze-dried precooked items such as beef hash, beef stew, chili con carne, and spaghetti with meat sauce are now used by the armed forces. Freeze-dried salads (salmon, tuna, and chicken) were used on Gemini and Apollo space flights.

NITROGEN FREEZING

Sprayed nitrogen or liquid nitrogen is used to freeze fruits and vegetables in present commercial freezing methods. Nitrogen freezing uses temperatures ranging downward to $-320°F$ ($-160°C$). Minimum freezing time is about 6 minutes for a food such as mushrooms. This appears to be a superior method for freezing tomato slices, mushrooms, melons, strawberries, meats, and seafoods.

CANNING

Canning is the preservation of foods in hermetically sealed containers by the application of heat. The fact that some 25 billion cans of food are processed each year in the United States is evidence of the importance of this process.

Discovery of the principle of sterilization by heat and the development of fundamental heat-processing procedures are credited to Nicolas François Appert, a French confectioner and baker who did his major work at the beginning of the nineteenth century. Shortly after Appert had begun to succeed in his search for a method of preserving food by the application of heat, other investigators—inspired by his accomplishments—engaged in work that led to the use of tin containers for sterilized foods. In addition to his identification of fundamental canning principles. Appert is also credited with initiating the use of the autoclave (pressure canner) in canning.

The creation of the canning industry followed Appert's discovery. Canning was introduced in the United States as early as 1819, when Thomas Kensett and Ezra Daggett set up a seafood-packing plant in New York City. Since then, the canning industry in this country has grown in volume and in importance. In 1907, the National Canners' Association was established; in 1913, this Association established a research laboratory in Washington, D.C.

It is difficult to give a precise figure for the number of foods or kinds of food combinations that are canned, for both are constantly changing. The list, however, includes most fruits and vegetables, a wide variety of meats and meat products, seafoods, soups, and many specialty items—such as breads, puddings, stews, and sauces.

Containers. Glass was the first material used as a canning container, but tinplate was soon introduced. For many years, such cans were made by hand. The modern can, which is sealed mechanically without the use of solder, was developed about 1900 and has since come to be used throughout the canning industry. It consists of tin-coated steel. For certain foods, the interior surfaces of the can may be enameled. To prevent color loss in such foods as blackberries and beets, a material known as *fruit enamel* is used. Also an enamel known as *C2* is used for sulfur-bearing low-acid foods (e.g., corn) to prevent discoloration and for pigmented fruits or colored vegetables to prevent color loss.

Not all food is packed in tin cans; a considerable quantity is packed in glass. The main advantages of glass are its transparency and insolubility. And inasmuch as glass is a very versatile material, glass containers are made in many shapes and colors.

Canning Operations. Most of the operations in the commercial canning process are mechanically performed, but considerable hand labor is still required, especially in the preparation of fruits and vegetables.

Although each food or food combination—because of its unique composition and appearance—must be handled differently, a few general procedures are followed in preparing any raw food for canning.

First, the raw product is inspected and all extraneous or undesirable material is removed. For example, peas are removed from the pod and fish are scaled and cleaned. The food may then be blanched to remove surface materials and to reduce volume so that a better fill of container is possible.

After blanching, the food is placed in the

containers—mechanically or by hand, depending on the product. Whenever possible, mechanical filling is used because it is faster and more accurate. But such products as sardines and asparagus must be handled carefully to avoid breakage. A weak brine is added to vegetables and a syrup is added to fruits, either at the time of filling or immediately after. In some cases, only water is added.

When the product is arranged in the can and covered with a liquor, the can is ready for exhausting. The main purpose of exhausting is to expel air and gas from the can so that its internal pressure, after is has been heated and cooled, will be less than atmospheric pressure. Exhausting also prevents discoloration of some products and undesirable oxidative effects.

Exhausting the can results in the creation of a vacuum when the container cools. Gas may be removed by heating the food (as with cream-style corn) or by filling the head space with steam. Exhausting can also be accomplished by sealing the cans in a chamber under high vacuum. After the exhausting process, the filled cans are permanently sealed mechanically. Milk cans are handled differently: they are filled through openings about ¾ in. in diameter, which are then closed by seaming.

The permanently sealed container is subjected to temperatures designed to destroy the most heat-resistant organism likely to be present. Because bacteria more heat-resistant than those that constitute a health hazard to the consumer may be present and may be the cause of later spoilage, the amount of heat required to process any given food is usually much higher than that required by health standards.

After heating and before storing, the processed cans are cooled. Water is the medium most often used for cooling. The cans may be placed in a cooling canal or under a spray and their temperature is reduced to about 100°F (38°C). Residual heat dries the can's surface, thus preventing rust formation.

The final step in the canning procedure is the casing and storing of the cans. The cans are stored in rooms designed to prevent extremes of temperature.

Nutritive Value. Studies have shown that the nutritive value of canned foods compares favorably with that of fresh foods. And, generally, the quality of the foods put into cans is better than that of fresh foods during off-season months.

Foods do lose some nutritive value during the canning process and the subsequent storage period, but newer canning techniques have succeeded in reducing such losses. The newer methods involve a short, high-temperature heating process, followed by rapid cooling. Also, the practice of exhausting air from the can before it is sealed has cut down the oxidative losses of vitamins at high temperatures. The modern practice of agitating cans reduces processing time and prevents overcooking of food coming in contact with the can wall, thus further reducing vitamin losses.

Nutrient loss during storage is still a factor to be reckoned with. Canned meat loses some of its thiamine when the storage temperatures reach 70°F (18°C) or higher. Similarly, losses occur in canned fruits and vegetables stored at 65°F (18°C) or above. When storage temperatures are as high as 80°F (27°C), these losses may amount to 25% of the total in a year's time. Generally, however, nutrient losses in canned foods are kept at a minimum when storage temperatures are kept within a reasonable range of 55–65°F (13–21°C).

In considering the nutritive value of canned foods, one important factor is that one third of the soluble nutrients may be in the liquid. Cooking practices, therefore, must make use of this liquid. Soon after canning, the water-soluble nutrients distribute themselves evenly throughout the solids and the liquid. The solids thus contain about two-thirds of the soluble nutrients, the liquid the remaining one third.[16] Minimum cooking times are recommended for canned foods, for the food is already cooked and requires only to be reheated.

Time and temperature are the factors most important in the retention of high quality during the storage of frozen foods. It is generally thought that it is the mishandling of the frozen foods after they are processed and not the freezing itself that causes loss of vitamin value. Ascorbic acid is the nutrient used as the criteron for poor packaging or other mishandling of the frozen food. However, the B vitamins appear to be retained to a high degree if the frozen vege-

[16] "Conserving the Nutritive Values in Food," op. cit.

tables are stored under conditions acceptable for ascorbic acid. Maintenance of temperatures of 0°F (−18°C) or lower for storage of frozen food products promotes the best retention of nutrients.

The content of the other major nutrients—proteins, fats, carbohydrates and minerals does not change under normal conditions of storage.[17] The important packaging factors which are protective of the nutritive value of frozen food products are high resistance of light transmission and oxygen permeability.

FERMENTATION

Certain foods are fermented to develop a new flavor and physical appearance. Fermentation may also, because of microbial action, act as a preservative. The two chief preservatives formed in this manner are lactic acid and alcohol. The degree of protection offered by this method of preservation is usually limited and is frequently supplemented by one or more other preservative agents. For example, salt, sugar, heat, or low temperatures may be used to strengthen the preservation effect of fermentation.

Salt, used in vegetables in limited amounts, permits an acid fermentation by bacteria to take place—but excessive amounts will inhibit both the growth of bacteria and the production of acid. The salt or brine draws water from the tissue cells of the vegetable, thereby decreasing the concentration of salt in the liquid. Such vegetables as green peas and lima beans (which are relatively high in protein) and onions and cauliflower (which soften easily) are preserved by the addition of enough salt to prevent any fermentation. Vegetables that are crushed, shredded, or cut and then held at room temperatures will ferment because of their sugar content, and undesirable flavors and odors often form as a result of fermentation. When salt is added to these vegetables some fermentation will continue to take place, but the salt will reduce the number of undesirable bacteria and encourage the growth of the lactic-acid-forming varieties. This action imparts a clean, acid flavor to the vegetable. Sauerkraut is produced by the full

[17] American Medical Association, *Nutrients in Processed Foods* (Acton, Mass.: Publishing Sciences Group, Inc., 1974), p. 76.

fermentation of properly prepared and shredded cabbage in the presence of 2–3% salt. When the sauerkraut has been completely fermented, it should contain not less than 1.5% acid (expressed as lactic acid).

Salt pickles and green olives are also fermented. Salt pickles are produced by immersing immature, washed cucumbers in brine barrels or tanks. The cucumbers are held under the brine by weights and fermentation begins. The initial amount of salt used is high and more is added at weekly intervals. The goal is to get a good fermentation of the sugars within 6–9 weeks.

Green (unripe) olives are first treated with a lye solution and then washed several times to remove the lye. They are next placed in barrels and covered with brine. Fermentation takes 6–10 months.

SUMMARY

An effective method of food preservation prevents or slows down spoilage without damaging the food or adding injurious substances to it. Methods of preservation include drying, freezing, canning, fermentation, and the preservation of food by ionizing radiations.

In canning, boiling temperatures or higher are required to kill all organisms that could spoil food during storage. In pasteurization, temperatures below boiling are used. Thus, food so processed must be subjected to supplemental preserving methods and stored to that development of additional microoganisms is minimized.

Drying involves removal or reduction of the moisture in a food. Heat applied during drying destroys many of the spoilage organisms.

Preservation of food by ionizing radiations, including ultraviolet rays, x or gamma rays, and cathode or beta rays is under intensive study and experimental work is underway. It has been established that gamma irradiation from cobalt 60 or cesium 137 does not induce radioactivity in foods exposed to it. A few irradiated foods have FDA clearance: Wheat, wheat products, and sprouting potatoes.

Low temperatures are used to retard chemical reactions and enzyme action and to retard or stop microbial growth in food. Low-temperature methods include cooling food in storage cellars and home refrigerators and freezing food and holding it at below-freezing temperatures. Quick-freezing methods are employed today in freezing foods. Because plant enzymes are not inactivated by freezing, vegetables are first blanched. Freezing does not sterilize food, so microbial growth may resume on thawing. Desiccation or freezer burn may occur on the surface of food, especially meat. Much of the drip fluid of frozen meets cannot be reabsorbed during thawing. In freeze drying, foods are dried in the frozen state by sublimation.

QUESTIONS AND TOPICS FOR DISCUSSION AND STUDY

1. What are the advantages and disadvantages of preserving food by the freezing, irradiation, and freeze-drying methods?
2. Discuss the causes of food spoilage.
3. What important changes take place during the frozen storage of food?

REFERENCES

Books

American Medical Association. *Nutrients in Processed Foods.* Acton, Mass.: Publishing Sciences Group, Inc., 1974.

Desrosier, Norman. *The Technology of Food Preservation.* Westport, Conn.: Avi, 1970.

Farmer's World: The Yearbook of Agriculture. Washington, D.C.: U.S. Department of Agriculture, 1964, pp. 311–313.

Masters, K. *Spray Drying.* New York: Wiley, 1976, Chap. 15.

Preservation of Foods by Low-Dose Radiation. Natick, Mass.: U.S. Army Quartermaster Engineering and Research Center, 1961.

Stewart, George. *Introduction to Food Science and Technology.* New York: Academic Press, 1973, Chap. 5.

Tressler, Donald, and Clifford Evers. *The Freezing Preservation of Foods.* Westport, Conn.: Avi, 1968.

Van Arsdel, Wallace. *Food Dehydration.* Westport, Conn.: Avi, 1973.

Articles, Bulletins, and Pamphlets

Bishov, S. J., et al. "Quality and Stability of Some Freeze-Dried Foods in 'Zero' Oxygen Head Space." *J. Food Sci.* **36:**532, 1971.

Drodge, John. "Economic Feasibility of Radiation Pasteurizing Fresh Strawberries, Peaches, Tomatoes, Grapes, Oranges, and Grapefruit." *Marketing Economics Division Report ERS 131.* Washington, D.C.: U.S. Department of Agriculture, 1963.

Food Irradiation Activities Throughout the World. Washington, D.C.: U.S. Department of Commerce, n.d.

"Freeze-Drying of Foods—A List of Selected References." *National Agricultural Library,* Library List 77. Washington, D.C.: U.S. Department of Agriculture, 1963.

Josephson, E. S., et al. "Low Dose Irradiation at Natick." *Technical Report TR-78-003.* Natick, Mass.: United States Army Natick Research and Development Command, 1977.

Klicka, Mary. "Convenience—Keynote of the Future." *J. Home Econ.* **61:**707, 1969.

Moy, J. H. "Vacuum-Puff Freeze Drying of Tropical Fruit Juices." *J. Food Sci.* **36:**906, 1971.

Status of Irradiated Food Petitions. Business and Defense Services Administration. Washington, D.C.: U.S. Department of Agriculture, 1966.

"The United States Army's Radiation Preservation of Food Program." Natick, Mass.: United States Army Natick Research and Development Command, 1976.

"Wholesomeness of Irradiated Food." *Technical Report Series 604.* Geneva: World Health Organization, 1977.

Freezing Food in the Home

The quickest and simplest way to preserve food in the home is to freeze it. Modern freezing equipment permits the rapid freezing of food so as to preserve its natural flavor, texture, color, and good appearance. Because rapid freezing is necessary for high-quality frozen products, home freezers are designed to operate at temperatures as low as $-20°F$ ($-2°C$). Successful freezing of food depends on the slowing down of microbial growth and enzyme action rather than on the destruction or removal of microorganisms.

SELECTION OF FOOD FOR FREEZING

Some foods freeze better than others. Good quality and optimum maturity are requisite qualities in food to be frozen. Only top-quality food can be frozen successfully, for freezing does not improve quality. Producers of commercially frozen foods were quick to recognize the relationship between the freshness of the food and the quality of the frozen product. Accordingly, they set up their freezing equipment in areas where production of the food to be processed is

high in order to get food from the farm or orchard directly to the freezer. The practice of freezing food before it has lost any of its fresh quality is also excellent for home use and has been highly recommended by experts in agriculture and home economics.

Generally, foods can be frozen by either slow-freezing or quick-freezing methods. When properly handled, food in home freezers is quick-frozen. When food is frozen slowly, most of its water content forms large ice crystals; upon thawing, there is a loss of juices from the food. Rapid freezing, on the other hand, will bring about the formation of ice crystals so small that there is little chance they will puncture the cell walls of the food and cause leaking of juices. Foods undergoing the quick-freezing process are quickly cooled at a temperature below $0°F$ ($-18°C$).

CHANGES IN FOOD CAUSED BY FREEZING

Holding foods at low temperatures causes the formation of ice crystals within the food tissues. The water content of food differs with kind and variety. Some foods have a large amount of water that is not bound up in cellular material. This free water can be separated out of the plant tissues and, according to present theory, is the portion of water that freezes. Water bound in cellular material does not freeze completely. In general, fruits, vegetables, meats, fish, and poultry have less bound water than products such as bread, cakes, and pie crusts. Foods such as tomatoes, celery, lettuce, and cucumbers have so high a water content that their texture is greatly impaired if they are frozen. When these foods freeze, the pressure from the large ice crystals formed ruptures the cell walls and causes severe loss of tissue fluids. Such action leaves the thawed vegetables limp and spongy. Consequently, these vegetables should not be frozen.

When food freezes, a change takes place in its protein structure. Food that is frozen slowly has a fairly large separation of water from solid content. This separation dehydrates the proteins and causes them to become denatured. Denatured proteins lack the ability to reabsorb water when the food thaws. In foods that have a high percentage of bound water, the change in the protein structure is likely to be small; thus, reabsorption of the juice is possible after such foods have thawed.

Changes caused by enzyme action are also observable in food during freezing. The most obvious of these are the color and flavor changes that occur during storage of frozen foods and are caused mainly by oxidative changes within the food. Although enzyme action is slowed down in frozen foods, slow changes over a long period will cause deterioration.

PACKAGING OF FROZEN FOODS

Packaging is an important step in the proper freezing of food. The aim of packaging is to protect the food from further contamination by microorganisms, to exclude as much air as possible, and to prevent the escape of moisture. Hence, it is necessary to use moistureproof, vaporproof containers or wrapping materials and to seal the packages properly. If the packaging materials do not prevent its escape, the water vapor collects—in the form of frost—on the outside of the package, on the walls of the freezer, and on the freezing coils. Also, the loss of water vapor leaves portions of the food dehydrated and these portions then show a loss of color, flavor, and texture. Poor packaging materials are also responsible for the oxidative changes that take place during freezing and storage. Such changes cause rancidity in fats and loss of nutrients.

Other factors that greatly increase the efficiency of freezer containers and wrappers are lack of odor and flavor, ease in handling, and durability. Freezer containers may be of tin, plastic, glass, or aluminum foil or may be laminated and waxed cardboard cartons. The choice of container is controlled by the size of the freezer. Rigid containers of uniform size may be stacked one on top of the other. Specially prepared papers and bags are used to wrap oddly shaped foods. Plastic, glass, and tin containers with removable tops can be used again and again. Other freezer containers, such as paraffined tubs or cups with slip-on lids, are not always completely effective on second use.

Wrapping material for meat, poultry, fish, and cooked dishes should be moistureproof, vaporproof, greaseproof, odorless, tasteless, noncorrosive, and flexible enough to withstand cracking.

Heavy-duty aluminum foil is excellent for wrapping irregularly shaped foods such as poultry and fish, and—if handled carefully—may be reused. Freezer foil has a layer of plastic laminated to it. This construction offers more protection than other foils, because fewer puncture holes from protruding bones or irregular shapes are likely to occur.

Wide-mouthed glass jars specially treated for freezer use are economical and easy to use. These can be reused indefinitely.

ECONOMIC ASPECTS OF FREEZING

Freezing is not always the most economical method of preserving food. Whether or not to freeze foods at home must be decided on an individual family basis. The availability of fresh products, the cost of electricity, and family food preferences and nutritional needs are some of the major factors to be considered. According to

Woodroof and Shelor,[1] a good plan is one that allows one half the freezer space for meats (including chicken, meat dishes, eggs, and broth); one fourth for vegetables; and one fourth for fruits, juices, purées, pies, and desserts. Relatively little space is afforded fruits and vegetables because there is a large turnover in the supply of these foods; it might be more economical to store some fruits and vegetables in a storage bin or cellar.

The amount of prepared food to be frozen also involves careful planning if freezer space is to be used economically. Foods that can be quickly prepared or that show marked deterioration when stored in the freezer are poor choices.

The factors to consider are the initial cost of the freezer, whether the food is purchased or produced at home, and the costs of electricity, packaging materials, and repairs. As the size of the freezer increases, the cost per pound of food goes down. A quick review of these figures indicates that freezing of food is not so much an economy as it is a convenience.

Not all fruits and vegetables can be successfully frozen. However, snapbeans, peas, corn, lima beans, broccoli, cauliflower, eggplant, spinach, kale, beets, peppers, pumpkins, squash, and sweet potatoes do freeze well. Most fruits lend themselves well to freezing, but the quality of the frozen product depends on the maturity and the variety of the fruit. In many localities, special varieties of fruit are grown for freezing purposes.

FREEZING FRUITS

The maturity of the fresh fruits is important to the quality of the frozen product. Underripe fruits do not develop flavor and color; overripe fruits may develop tough skins, become spongy, and lose flavor. Generally, the fruits best suited for freezing have excellent color, are highly flavored, and retain a firm texture after thawing.

Fruits such as berries are frozen whole or as purées or juice. Apples, peaches, nectarines,

plums, and pineapples are generally peeled and sliced before being frozen.

Sugar is added to fruit to increase its firmness and to protect it from oxidation and consequent loss of color and flavor. Sugar also prevents loss of moisture. Dry sugar or a sugar syrup may be used, depending on the variety of fruit. Dry sugar is used chiefly for fruits that readily produce juice, such as strawberries and peaches. When the sugar is thoroughly mixed with the fruit, a juice syrup is formed that partially covers the fruit. Sugar syrups are used to pack the fruits that form juice slowly, such as pineapples and apples.

Fruits packed in sugar or with syrup generally have a better texture and flavor than those packed dry. Moist fruits packed dry or in water will become flabby upon thawing. Cranberries, blueberries, currants, and pineapples can be frozen without sugar.

A 40% syrup is used for many fruits, but heavier or lighter syrups may be used, according to the kind of fruit to be frozen. Syrup concentrations are usually expressed as percentages based on weight. Hence, a 40% syrup is made up of 40 units (oz) of sugar dissolved in 60 units (oz) of water. Syrup recipes are given in Table 39-1.

The syrup allowance for 1 pt fruit is ½ to ⅔ cup. Up to one-fourth the amount of sugar syrup may be replaced with light corn syrup.

Light-colored fruits—such as apples, apricots, figs, nectarines, and peaches—retain their color better if an antioxidant is added. Ascorbic acid is a very effective antidarkening material and also adds nutritive value. Ascorbic acid is available in

TABLE 39-1
Syrups Used for Freezing Fruits

Type of Syrup	Sugar (cups)	Water (cups)	Syrup Yield (cups)
30%	2	4	5
35%	2½	4	5⅓
40%	3	4	5½
50%	4¾	4	6½
60%	7	4	7¾
65%	8¾	4	8⅔

Source: "Home Freezing of Fruits and Vegetables," *Home and Garden Bulletin 10* (Washington, D.C.: U.S. Department of Agriculture, rev. 1970).

[1] J. G. Woodroof and E. Shelor, "Freezing Food at Home," *Bulletin 601* (Athens Ga.: University of Georgia Experiment Station, 1966).

crystal or tablet form. A good proportion of crystalline ascorbic acid is ¼–½ tsp to 1 qt chilled syrup.

General Directions. The following suggestions should be helpful in producing top-quality frozen fruit products (see also Table 39-2 and Fig. 39-1):

1. Use only good–quality, unspoiled fruit; freeze as rapidly as possible after harvesting.
2. Remove skins from such fruits as peaches by blanching in boiling water for 1–3 minutes before skinning.
3. Make syrup in advance and chill.
4. Avoid using metal containers, such as iron, copper, zinc, or tin. These will discolor some fruits.

FREEZING VEGETABLES

The salad vegetables lettuce, celery, tomatoes, cucumbers, and radishes are not frozen because scalding and steaming wilt their crisp texture. In the main, vegetables that have good color, flavor, and tenderness and are free of defects and uniform in the fresh state are most suitable for freezing. They should be frozen when at the optimum stage for eating. Overmature vegetables should never be used, for they will be poor in color and texture when finally eaten.

Blanching. Vegetables that are scalded or steamed before being frozen maintain better quality during storage than those that have not received this treatment.[2] Scalding or blanching inactivates enzymes, cutting down the deteriorative changes that take place during storage. Frozen vegetables that have not been blanched develop poor color, texture, and flavor as a consequence of unlimited enzyme activity in the plant tissues.[3] Heating also decreases the volume of the vegetable and makes it easier and more economical to pack.

It follows, therefore, that scalding or steaming is an essential step in preparing vegetables for

freezing. It is accomplished by exposing the prepared vegetable to boiling water or to live steam just long enough to wilt it and inactivate the enzymes. In scalding, about 1 lb of prepared vegetable is placed in a wire basket and immersed in a gallon of boiling water. (For scalding time, see Table 39-3.) For steaming, some water is brought to a rolling boil in a covered kettle and the vegetable is suspended over it in a basket. (During the steaming of the vegetable, the kettle remains covered.) After heating, the vegetable must be quickly cooled and loosely packed into containers.

FREEZING MEATS, POULTRY AND FISH

Meats, poultry, and fish constitute a large portion of the foods frozen at home (Fig. 39-2). Meats such as beef, lamb, mutton, and veal are allowed to tenderize or age for 7–10 days before freezing (Table 39-4). Pork, on the other hand, is usually frozen fresh or aged for 2–3 days. Poultry is chilled immediately after slaughter and frozen as quickly as possible. According to Lowe, broilers tenderize within a few hours after slaughter; hence, it is unnecessary to age poultry for longer periods.[4]

Unlike meat, fish requires no aging; it is best frozen as soon as possible after it is caught. Because fish is a very perishable product easily contaminated by bacteria from air and water it may begin to spoil within a few hours after it is caught; rapid chilling is therefore essential. Properly frozen and stored at 0°F ($-18°C$), fish will remain edible for 3–6 months. Some frozen fish has retained its high quality even after as long as 18 months of storage.

Changes During Storage. Deteriorative changes occurring in meat and poultry during storage are desiccation and rancidity. Dehydration occurs on the skin of poultry and on the surface of meat. Poultry skin grows bleached and dry-looking; the cut muscle in beef, lamb, pork, and veal grows lighter in color and the texture of the meat becomes porous or spongy.

Frozen foods lose color, texture, and nutritive

[2] W. Woodburn and D. Strong, "Home Frozen Fruits and Vegetables," *J. Home Econ.* **52**:191, 1960.

[3] I. Noble and J. D. Winter, "Is Blanching Necessary When Vegetables Are To Be Kept in Frozen Storage a Month or Less?" *J. Home Econ.* **44**:33, 1952.

[4] Belle Lowe, *Experimental Cookery,* 4th ed. (New York: Wiley, 1955), p. 100.

(a) (b) (c) (d) (e) (f)

39-1 *To home-freeze strawberries in dry sugar. (a) Select fruit that is fresh, without bruises or decay, and of the right degree of ripeness. (b) Wash the fruit in cold water, handling them gently. Lift from the water and drain. Fruit should not be allowed to stand in the water. Remove leaves and stems. (c) Unless freezing whole fruit, slice the strawberries and spread them in a shallow dish. (d) Add the sugar and gently turn the fruit over and over until the sugar dissolves and juice is formed. (e) Put the fruit and the syrup which forms into airtight containers. Shake the container to pack the fruit as closely as possible without crushing. One-half-inch head space should be left because food expands as it freezes. (f) Wipe the tops of the containers with a clean, damp cloth. Cover tightly and label, indicating the type of pack and the date of freezing. Freeze as quickly as possible after packing. (Courtesy U.S. Department of Agriculture)*

471

TABLE 39-2
Freezing Fruits

Fruit	Amount Required to Yield 1 Pt Frozen Product	Preparation and Packing
Apples	1¼–1½ lb	Peel; slice in twelfths; spread not more than ½ in. deep and steam for 1½ min; pack dry
Applesauce	1½–2½ lb	Make sauce according to favorite recipe and chill; pack as sauce
Apricots	⅔–1 lb	Freeze peeled or unpeeled; to peel, follow directions for peaches, or steam halves 4 min; cover with 40% syrup to which ascorbic acid has been added or crush steamed apricots with sugar (2 cups per 5 lb fruit)
Blackberries	1⅓–1½ pt	Wash and discard all green, red, or immature berries; cover with 40% sugar syrup or ¾ lb sugar
Blueberries	1⅓–1½ pt	Wash and sort; cover with 40% syrup
Cantaloupe	1–1¼ lb	Use only fully ripe, firm fruit; wash, halve, and seed; cut into balls or into ½–¾-in. cubes; cover with 30% syrup
Cherries, sour	1¼–1½ lb	Use ripe, bright-red cherries; sort, wash, and pit; cover with 60% syrup or sugar (1 oz to 3–4 oz cherries)
Cherries, sweet	1¼–1½ lb	Red varieties are best for freezing; cover with 40% syrup (ascorbic acid may be added)
Cranberries	½ lb	Wash and stem; pack dry or with 50% syrup
Currants	¾–1 lb	Wash and stem; eliminate poor fruit; crush with sugar; cover with 50% syrup or 1 lb sugar to 3 lb fruit
Gooseberries	½ lb	Stem and wash; eliminate poor fruit; crush with sugar; cover with 50% syrup or 1 lb sugar to 3 lb fruit
Grapefruit	2 (medium size)	Chill, peel; section fruit, removing all white membrane; cover with 40% syrup
Peaches, white	1–1½ lb	Treat as yellow peaches; add ascorbic acid
Peaches, yellow	1–1½ lb	Dip in boiling water for 15–20 sec to loosen skins; peel, halve, pit, and slice rapidly—directly into syrup; cover with 40% syrup or ⅔ cup sugar to 1 qt. sliced fruit; to prevent browning, add pure crystalline ascorbic acid
Pineapple	1 lb	Select fully ripe fruit (tops will pull out), preferably plant-ripened; peel, core, and dice; cover immediately with 30% syrup or pack dry
Plums	1–1½ lb	Wash, sort, halve, and pit; peel if desired; cover with 40% syrup
Raspberries	1 pt or 1 lb	Clean, stem, wash; crush with 1 lb sugar to 4 lb berries, or pack whole with 40% syrup or dry
Rhubarb	⅔–1 lb	Cut off leaves; cut into 1-in lengths; scald (or omit scalding); cover scalded rhubarb with 40% syrup; unscalded rhubarb may be packed dry in 1 part sugar to 4–5 parts rhubarb or in 40–50% syrup
Strawberries	⅔ qt (1½ lb)	Wash in ice water; lift fruit from water; hull; cut in slices ¼ in. thick and pack in 1 lb sugar to 4–5 lb berries; or pack whole in 40–50% syrup

Source: Adapted from "Home Freezing of Fruits and Vegetables," *Home and Garden Bulletin 10* (Washington, D.C.: U.S. Department of Agriculture, rev. 1970), pp. 14–28.

TABLE 39-3
Freezing Vegetables

Vegetables	Amount required to Yield 1 Pt Frozen Product (lb)	Preparation and Packing
Asparagus	1–1½	Wash; cut into lengths suitable for container; scald spears 1½–3 min (depending on size); cool; drain; pack into containers
Beans, lima (in pods)	2–2½	Shell and scald (small beans, 1 min; medium 2 min; large, 3 min); cool; drain; pack
Beans, snap, green, wax	⅔–1	Snip ends and cut into desired lengths; scald 2–3 min; cool; drain; pack
Beets	1¼–1½	Use small beets whole; cut larger beets into sections; scald 3 min; peel; cool; drain; pack
Broccoli	1	Use firm tender stalks with compact heads; remove leaves and woody portions; separate head in suitable sections; scald 3 min; cool; drain; pack
Brussels sprouts	1	Select medium-sized sprouts; remove decayed leaves; scald sprouts 3 min; cool; drain; pack
Carrots	1¼–1½	Freeze whole or in strips, cubes, or cross section
Cauliflower	1⅓ (one small head)	Use compact heads; trim off leaves and cut into 2-in. sections; scald 3 min; cool; drain; pack
Corn	2–3 ears cut whole-grain corn	Use freshly gathered corn in the milk stage; husk, trim off silk; scald whole ears 8 min; cool; drain; wrap tightly in aluminum foil, plastic wrap, or locker paper (3 or 6 ears to package); scald cut corn 5–6 min, depending on the size of the ear; cool; drain; cut from cob as whole grains; pack
Eggplant		Use when uniformly black in color; peel and cut into ⅓- or ½-in. slices; scald 4 min in boiling water to which 4½ tsp citric acid or lemon juice have been added to 1 gal water; cool; drain; pack
Greens: spinach, chard, kale, collards	1–1½	Use young tender green leaves; cut off woody stems; wash thoroughly; scald 2 min in a large quantity of water; cool; drain; pack
Peas	2–2½	Use young tender peas; shell; scald 1–2 min; cool; pack
Pumpkins		Peel, seed, cut into sections; steam until soft; run through sieve; cool; pack
Squash, summer	1–1½	Use young squash with tender skin; wash, slice; scald 3 min; cool; drain; pack
Squash, winter	1–1½	(See Pumpkins)
Sweet potatoes	⅔	Steam until tender; run through sieve; add ¼ tsp citric acid or ½ tsp lemon juice; cool; pack
Turnips	1¼–1½	(See Beets)

Source: Adapted from "Home Freezing of Fruits and Vegetables," *Home and Garden Bulletin 10* (Washington, D.C.: U.S. Department of Agriculture, rev. 1970), pp. 29–41.

TABLE 39-4
Preparing Meats, Poultry, Fish, and Animal Products for Freezing

Meats	Approximate Storage Time at 0°F (−18°C) (months)	Preparation
Beef, lamb	9–12	Use good-quality meat that has been aged for 5–8 days; cut as for cooking, removing as much bone and waste as possible; wrap family-sized servings in aluminum foil, polyethylene, or a good-grade locker paper; enclose packages in stockinette; pack steaks, chops, or ground-meat patties with a double layer of moistureproof material between each piece
Pork	6–9	Cure or freeze as quickly as possible after slaughter; cuts of pork usually frozen are fresh loin, shoulder, hams, bacon (jowls are usually cured); freshly cured pork products lose desirable color and flavor during frozen storage; pack pork in the manner described above
Chicken	6–7	Tie down wings and feet of whole birds; wrap in the same manner as roasts; pack chicken parts in foil, plastic bags, or moistureproof locker paper
Fish (finfish)	4–6	Clean and ready for cooking; wrap family-sized servings in aluminum foil or moistureproof locker paper; to separate easily, wrap each fish in locker paper and then in packages of 1–2 lb
Crabs	3–4	Use fresh live crabs; remove back shell, eviscerate, and steam for 20 min (or cook in boiling water for 15 min); remove meat from shell, pack in moistureproof, vaporproof container, and store at 0°F (−18°C)
Lobsters	3–4	Use fresh live lobsters; steam or boil (*see* Crabs); remove meat from shell, pack in moistureproof, vaporproof containers, and freeze
Oysters	3–4	Choose fresh live oysters; wash shell and shuck oysters, saving the liquor; wash oysters in a brine of 1 tsp salt to 1 qt water, but do not leave in water longer than 8–10 min; drain; pack in moistureproof, vaporproof containers and cover with liquor; freeze quickly at 0°F (−18°C) (use frozen oysters only in cooked dishes)
Shrimp	3–4	Use fresh shrimp; wash and pack in moistureproof, vaporproof container; cover with a brine made from 1 tsp salt to 1 qt water; freeze
Animal products Butter	5–6	Freeze only high-quality butter made from pasteurized sweet cream; wrap in aluminum foil or locker paper or store in freezer jars or paraffined cartons
Cheese Soft Hard or semihard	1–2 weeks 6–12	Pack soft cheese (such as cottage cheese) in freezer jars or heavily paraffined cartons; slice and wrap Cheddar cheese (*see* Beef); freeze commercially processed cheese in the original package
Cream	3–6	Heavy pasteurized cream containing no less than 40% butterfat may be frozen; add about 10% sugar (by weight)
Eggs	6–12	Select fresh eggs; break each into a dish and examine for odor and appearance before adding it to the other eggs; for whole eggs, gently mix together egg yolks and whites, pack in containers, and freeze; for egg whites, gently mix, pack in containers, and freeze; for egg yolks, mix with corn syrup, sugar, or salt to prevent coagulation and lump formation during storage; use 1 tsp salt to 1 cup egg yolks; 1–2 tbsp corn syrup or sugar to 2 cups egg yolks

Source: Adapted from J. G. Woodroof and E. Shelor, "Freezing Foods at Home," *Bulletin 266* (Athens, Ga.: University of Georgia Experiment Station, 1966).

39-2 *For easily removed portions in a family-sized package of cut meats, separate pieces with squares of plastic covering before freezing. (Courtesy of the Dow Chemical Company)*

value when stored at temperatures higher than 0°F (−18°C) and may also develop off-flavors. As storage temperatures rise, deterioration becomes more rapid. A rise of 5–10° between 0 and 30°F increases the rate of quality loss in frozen products to 2–5 times that in foods stored at 0°F (−18°C).

Once deterioration has started in the frozen food, reducing the temperature in the freezer or compartment will not reverse it. Even small fluctuations in temperature will cause some deterioration in the frozen product.

The development of rancidity in the fat of meat and poultry is destructive to the quality of the frozen product. Changes caused by rancidity are low in beef, lamb, and veal but rather high in pork and turkey meat.

It is not uncommon for frozen meat to lose as much as 10% of its original gross weight within a year. To prevent dehydration, meats, fish, and poultry should be packaged in materials that exclude air and moisture (Fig 39-3). The wrapping material should not crack or become brittle at low temperatures, nor should it absorb water, blood, or oil.

FREEZING PREPARED FOODS

Many prepared foods may be frozen. Freezing cooked, ready-to-eat foods is popular as a con-

venient way of preparing food before it is needed. Not all cooked foods are suitable for freezing. Those suitable from a time-management standpoint are foods that take a long time to prepare or to cook, those that use a large variety of ingredients and require skill and care in preparation, and those that hold up well after a storage period of 2–3 months.[5]

To obtain a good ready-to-eat frozen product, a good raw product must be used. Proper packaging, freezing, cooking methods, and cooking times are requisites for good frozen ready-to-eat foods.

Unlike frozen fresh foods, frozen cooked foods lose their distinctive flavor and texture after a relatively short storage period. Hence, it is wise to plan to use frozen cooked foods within 2–3 months (Table 39-5).

Cooked foods to be frozen should be cooked in the same manner as if they were to be served immediately, with one exception: they should not be cooked to well done. Allowance for reheating must be made. Reheating well-done starchy foods, such as potatoes, macaroni, and rice, will probably cause them to become soft

[5] P. R. Snow and A. Briant, "Frozen Fillings for Quick Lemon Pie," *J. Home Econ.* **52:**350, 1960.

A. M. Briant and P. R. Snow, "Freezer Storage of Pie Shells," *J. Amer. Dietet. Assoc.* **33:**796, 1957.

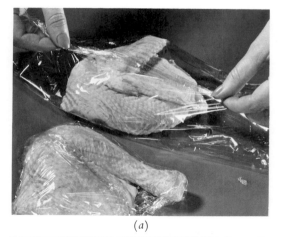

(a)

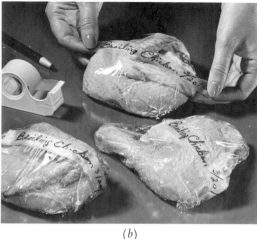

(b)

39-3 *Use of drugstore wrap. (a) Fold wrap down tightly. (b) Fold in ends of wrap and seal with sealer tape. Label with type of poultry and date. (Courtesy of the Dow Chemical Company)*

and to acquire a warmed-over taste and appearance.

Recent research has shown that greater rancidity developed in frozen turkey meat when the birds were roasted than when they were prepared by simmering or in the pressure cooker.[6] Turkey rancidity is especially pronounced when turkey fat is used in the gravy; this suggests the substitution of a more stable fat

[6] H. Hanson et al., "Preparation and Storage of Frozen Cooked Poultry and Vegetables," *Food Technol.* **4**:430, 1950.

in preparing gravies for frozen turkey dishes.

The atmosphere within the food package has a marked effect on the development of off-flavor in the product. Air should be excluded from the package by using a very tight-fitting vaporproof material, by packing food with its gravy or sauce, and by replacing the air in the package with an inert gas (such as nitrogen). The substitution of nitrogen for air within the package is not used in freezing cooked food at home, but this method appears to have great practical significance for commercial freezing of ready-to-eat products.

Texture problems in frozen cooked foods are related mainly to sauces and gravies thickened by eggs, flour, and cornstarch. The chief change is the separation of the liquid out of the gel after the product is thawed. The use of waxy rice flour in such products tends to minimize this reaction. This stabilizer is now used by a number of commercial manufacturers of frozen food products.

Cooked food that is to be frozen must be quickly cooled to stop the cooking process, to maintain palatability, and to prevent the growth of spoilage microorganisms. The food is put in shallow pans and set in a cool place or on a bed of ice. After it is cooled, the food is put into moistureproof, vaporproof freezer containers. The food should be packed in tightly to reduce the amount of air in the package.

Food should be packaged in family-sized containers. Standard containers hold four to six servings, pints two to three. For semiliquid dishes that are to be frozen, rigid containers of glass, plastic, or waxed cardboard may be satisfactorily used. Casserole dishes of ovenproof material are especially good for freezing combination dishes. These can be covered with aluminum foil or freezer paper and sealed with freezer tape. They may be removed from freezer to oven for reheating without danger of breakage.

PREPARATION AND SERVING OF FROZEN FOODS

The goal in preparing and serving frozen products is to keep as much as possible of the natural or fresh flavor, taste, color, structure, and internal juices. To attain this goal, care should be taken to thaw no more food than is

476

TABLE 39-5
Freezing Cooked or Prepared Foods

Dishes	Approximate Storage Time at 0°F (−18°C) (Months)	Preparation
Poultry Creamed dishes and stews packaged with or without gravy; chicken or turkey pie, a la king, and other casserole combinations	½–1	Use standard recipes; replace flour or cornstarch with waxy rice flour, if available; cool quickly and pack in freezer containers; leave ½-in. head space; add hard-cooked eggs when reheating.
Meat Stews, loaves, roasts, and hash prepared from almost any type of meat; vegetable and meat combinations	1–2	Use regular recipe and prepare as for eating (most vegetables freeze well in combinations but may be somewhat softer after reheating); cool rapidly; pack products that contain sauce or gravy in special aluminum foil pie plates or in rigid containers; wrap meats without sauces in aluminum foil or moistureproof, vaporproof material and cover with stockinette
Soups Vegetable, bean, pea, lentil, poultry and meat stock, cream	1–3	Prepare soups according to recipe; to save space, cook meat stock until fairly well concentrated; when reheating the stock add water, vegetables, rice, and noodles
Vegetables	½–1	For boiled vegetables, cook partially to avoid warmed-over flavor and a mushy texture when reheated; for vegetable purée, prepare and cook vegetables, purée, and pack into pint or quart containers; for candied sweet potatoes, prepare according to recipe, cool quickly, and pack in moistureproof cartons or en casserole wrapped in aluminum foil or freezer paper; for french fries, prepare and fry as usual, cool, and pack as candied sweet potatoes
Salads (Freeze only salads that are commonly frozen in the ice trays of the refrigerator)	4–6	Prepare according to recipe; freeze in mold or refrigerator tray wrapped in moistureproof paper
Bread, baked Yeast breads, rolls, quick breads	½	Prepare according to recipe; bake, cool, and pack in aluminum foil, plastic wrap, or other moisture-proof, vaporproof material
Partially baked rolls (Brown-and-serve)	½ or longer	Use plain or sweet roll dough recipe; let rise and bake at 275°F for approximately 30 min; let rolls set in pans 20 min, remove and pack; thaw at room temperature and brown in oven 375°F (191°C) 5–7 min
Baked quick breads		Prepare according to recipe; cool; pack as yeast breads

TABLE 39-5 (Cont.)

Dishes	Approximate Storage Time at 0°F (−18°C) (Months)	Preparation
Cakes	4–6	Prepare according to recipe; cool; place paper between layers to separate them; package layers as baked bread; for frosted cake, place on tray and freeze, pack in a cardboard box, and overwrap with moistureproof paper (powdered sugar frostings freeze satisfactorily)
Cookies	½ or longer	Prepare cookies according to recipe; freeze either baked or unbaked; for cookie dough, pack stiff dough in moistureproof paper, soft dough in rigid containers; for baked cookies, pack in cartons with sheets of paper between the layers and overwrap with moistureproof paper
Pies Fruit, custard, chiffon	1½–4	Most pies are best frozen while still unbaked; thicken ready-to-eat chiffon pies with gelatin and eggs—no starch; reheated prebaked pies may acquire an overbaked flavor; add meringue after pie is removed from the freezer; if pies are to be baked and then frozen, prepare pie in usual fashion and bake; wrap and overwrap with moistureproof paper
Doughnuts	4–6	Prepare doughnuts according to recipe; fry in odorless and flavorless fat; cool and pack in airtight containers or in cardboard carton with overwrap of moistureproof paper
Meringue shells	½	Prepare meringue shells according to recipe; cool and pack as doughnuts; thaw in package
Eclairs or creampuffs	½	Prepare and bake according to recipe; cool quickly; fill with desired filling; freeze on cookie tray until firm; pack as doughnuts; separate layers with sheets of paper.

Source: Adapted from F. Fenton, "Foods from the Freezer: Precooked and Prepared," *Cornell University Extension Bulletin 692* (Ithaca, N.Y.: Cornell University, 1955), and "Freezing Combination Main Dishes," *Home and Garden Bulletin 40* (Washington, D.C.: U.S. Department of Agriculture, rev. 1967).

needed at a particular time. Because thawed foods are very perishable, it is important to use them immediately. Refreezing cooked foods is not recommended because harmful bacteria develop during the first thawing period and may spoil refrozen foods.

Baked Products. Baked frozen products are thawed in the unopened package in order to keep the crust from becoming soggy. If reheating is desired, the product is placed in the oven to thaw and warm. Unbaked yeast breads are thawed and allowed to rise before baking. Unbaked quick breads and cookies, unless rolled out and cut, must be thawed before they are baked. The brown-and-serve rolls need only be thawed and browned. Unbaked frozen pies (Fig. 39-4) are placed in a hot oven 425°F (218°C) and baked for 15 minutes, and then at 350°F (177°C) until done.

39-4 *Fruit, berry, mince, and chiffon pies are good to freeze. (Courtesy of the Dow Chemical Company)*

Fruits. Frozen fruits that are allowed to thaw completely are soft and mushy. For best results, it is desirable to serve frozen fruits when the last traces of ice remain in the fruit tissues. The fruit should be thawed in the sealed container to hold to a minimum losses in aroma, flavor, and color.

Sandwich Fillings. Fillings that freeze well include meat, poultry, egg yolk mixtures, and ground dried fruit and nut pastes. Fillings not suitable for freezing are those with raw vegetables or fruits, hard-cooked egg whites, and fruit jellies.

Only margarine or butter should be used to spread bread, not mayonnaise. Sandwiches are prepared as for eating, and wrapped in moistureproof material. Open-faced sandwiches should be frozen in boxes or on stiff cardboard, then removed and packaged. Sandwiches made with two slices of bread should be thawed in the package. Sandwich fillings can be frozen separately.

Meats. For large cuts of meat and poultry, thawing in the refrigerator is the best method because the thawed part stays cool while the center is defrosting. Large cuts of meat that are to be cooked from the frozen stage must have 15–20 minutes per pound added to their cooking time.

Eggs. Eggs may be thawed in the sealed container in the refrigerator. Thawed eggs can be used in place of fresh eggs in the following proportions: 1 tbsp thawed egg yolk to 1 fresh egg yolk, 2 tbsp thawed egg white to 1 fresh egg white, and 3 tbsp thawed whole egg to 1 fresh whole egg.

SUMMARY

Freezing is the simplest and quickest method of food preservation in the home, although it may not be the most economical. Food selected should be of top quality and optimum maturity. Texture of foods with a high water content such as lettuce, celery, and melons is impaired by freezing, because large ice crystals break the cell walls and cause severe loss of tissue fluids. These foods should not be frozen. Successful freezing is dependent on slowing down microbial growth and enzyme action.

Factors to consider in deciding whether to freeze foods include availability of fresh products, cost of electricity, family food preferences, and nutritional needs.

Freezer containers and wrappers are selected for lack of odor and flavor, ease in handling, and durability. They should be moisture-, vapor-, and greaseproof.

In freezing fruits, those packed in sugar or syrup generally have a better texture and flavor than those packed dry. Use of an antioxidant aids color retention in light-colored fruits. To inactivate enzymes and thus reduce deteriorative changes during storage, blanching or scalding of vegetables is required. Meats to be frozen are allowed to tenderize or age before freezing, but poultry and fish are frozen as quickly as possible.

Changes occurring in meat and poultry during freezer storage are desiccation (dehydration) and rancidity. When frozen foods are stored at temperatures higher than 0°F (−18°C), there is loss of color, texture, and nutritive value. Off-flavors may also develop.

Frozen cooked foods generally should be used within 2–3 months. When prepared for freezing, they should not be cooked to the well-done stage, to allow for reheating. Some baked products may be held for as long as 6 months. A waxy rice flour may be used as a thickener to minimize separation of liquid in sauces or gravies.

Care should be taken in thawing frozen foods, to hold development of bacteria to a minimum.

QUESTIONS AND TOPICS FOR DISCUSSION AND STUDY

1. What changes take place in food when it is frozen?
2. What is the purpose of scalding vegetables before freezing them?
3. What happens to frozen food when it develops freezer burn?
4. What is the function of sugar in the freezing of fruits?
5. What factors are responsible for the oxidative changes that take place during the freezing of food and the storage of frozen foods?
6. What factors influence the decision to freeze a given food?

SUGGESTED ACTIVITIES

1. Observe a demonstration of the freezing of fruits and vegetables; meat, fish, and poultry; and cooked foods.
2. Prepare and freeze fresh foods in season.
3. Freeze prepared foods (as the occasion permits).

REFERENCES

BOOKS

Griswold, Ruth. *The Experimental Study of Foods*. Boston: Houghton Mifflin, 1962, Chap. 7.

Paul, Pauline, and Helen Palmer. *Food Theory and Applications*. New York: Wiley, 1972, Chap. 13.

Tressler, Donald, and Clifford Evers. *The Freezing Preservation of Foods*. Westport, Conn.: Avi, 1968, Vol. 1, Chap. 6.

ARTICLES AND BULLETINS

Doremus, M., and R. Klippstein. "Handbook for Freezing Foods." *Cornell Extension Bulletin 1179*. Ithaca, N.Y.: Cornell University, 1967.

"Freezing Meat and Fish in the Home." *Home and Garden Bulletin 93*. Washington, D.C.: U.S. Department of Agriculture, 1973.

"Home Freezing of Fruits and Vegetables." *Home and Garden Bulletin 10*. Washington, D.C.: U.S. Department of Agriculture, rev. 1971.

"Home Freezing of Poultry." *Home and Garden Bulletin 70*. Washington, D.C.: U.S. Department of Agriculture, 1970.

"How to Choose Meats for Your Freezer." *Home and Garden Bulletin 166*. Washington, D.C.: U.S. Department of Agriculture, 1974.

Kaess, G., and J. F. Weidmann. "On the Formation of Freezer Burn in Liver Tissue Protected with Plastic Film." *J. Food Sci.* **36**:1135, 1971.

McCracken, D. "Home Freezers: Their Selection and Use." *Home and Garden Bulletin 48*. Washington, D.C.: U.S. Department of Agriculture, rev. 1964.

Shelor, E., and J. Woodroof. "Frozen Food Containers." *Food Technol.* **8**:490, 1954.

Simpson, J., and I. C. Chang. "Effect of Low Freezer Storage Temperature and Wrapping Material on the Quality of Frozen Meats." *Food Technol.* **8**:246, 1954.

Canning Food in the Home

Canning is an economical way of preserving food, and families who grow and raise their own food and have surpluses or who can buy food suitable for economical preservation may well find it a desirable use of time and energy. Canning employs heat to destroy enzyme action and spoilage microorganisms. This method, however, depends not only on killing microorganisms but also on sealing the food in sterile, airtight containers to prevent it from coming in contact with new sources of contamination.

Air left in the container is driven out during heating and kept out by the airtight seal. Air that remains in canned food causes the food to darken through oxidation and decreases its palatability. Because the heat required to kill the organisms found in different foods varies, different methods of canning and of applying heat are used for given groups of food. Fruits and tomatoes, for instance, contain acids, sugars, and starches. The yeasts and molds that grow on these foods usually have low resistance to heat and are destroyed at water-boiling temperature. Hence, these foods can be safely processed in a boiling-water-bath canner. On the other hand, low-acid foods—such as meats, poultry, fish, and most vegetables—are hard to sterilize. Bacteria thrive on low-acid foods; water-boiling temperatures will not completely destroy these bacteria or the heat-resistant spores they form. Consequently, low-acid foods must be processed at temperatures higher than 212°F (100°C)—which means using a pressure canner instead of a boiling-water-bath canner. The pressure canner is the only satisfactory device for obtaining temperatures high enough to destroy anaerobic bacteria.

BOILING-WATER-BATH CANNER

The boiling-water-bath canner is used for processing acid foods. Any metal container with a cover can be used. The bottom of the container should be fitted with a wire or wooden rack on which the jars or cans may rest while the water circulates around and under them. (A rack with separate partitions for each jar is most suitable.) The container should be deep enough to allow the jars to be covered with at least an inch of water.

Pressure Canner. The pressure canner makes possible the safe processing of low-acid foods.

The lid is equipped with a steam-pressure gauge, a safety valve, and a petcock. In the bottom of the pressure canner is a rack on which to rest the cans or jars. The dial gauge on a pressure canner should be checked before the canning season begins. (The U.S. Department of Agriculture recommends that Cooperative Extension personnel or the dealer or manufacturer be asked for full information on the checking of the dial gauge.) To prepare the pressure canner for use, sufficient water must be placed in it to furnish steam throughout the processing. The pressure must be kept constant; when processing is finished, the pressure should be permitted to return to zero before the petcock is gradually opened. If the pressure is not released slowly, the liquid tends to be drawn out of the jars. The lid of the pressure canner is not removed until all the steam has escaped.

It is not safe to can nonacid foods in any utensil but a pressure canner, nor is it safe to risk lowering the pressure or altering the amount of time used to process the food. Processing times have been carefully worked out by U.S. Department of Agriculture laboratories; the safe canning of food depends on following recommended procedures. It is also important to follow the manufacturer's directions. If a pressure saucepan is used in place of the pressure canner, 20 minutes must be added to the recommended processing time for each food product.

The use of the pressure canner is the only method recommended for the canning of vegetables (other than tomatoes and pickled vegetables) and meat and poultry (Fig. 40-1). The reason for this is that certain spoilage organisms, as well as the spores of *Clostridium botulinum,* are destroyed only by the high temperature developed in a correctly used pressure canner. If botulinum spores occasionally found in the soil are present in nonacid foods and are not destroyed, they may grow and produce a fatal poison. Reliable up-to-date bulletins on canning are available from County Extension Service offices.

METHODS OF PREPARING FRUITS AND VEGETABLES FOR CANNING

Fruits and vegetables are processed either by the raw-pack method or the hot-pack method. No pretreatment is given the food in the raw-pack method. In the hot-pack method, the food undergoes a short precooking period. The food should be as near boiling temperature as possible when it is packed. In both methods, syrup, water, or juice should be used to fill in the spaces around the pieces of food in the container and to cover the food completely. However, there should be some space left between the liquid and the jar lid. The food is then heat-processed according to recommendations in Table 40-1.

Only fruits and vegetables that are fresh, firm, young, and tender are suitable for canning. They are canned as quickly as possible after gathering to retain their freshness. If they cannot be processed all at once, they should be stored in a cool place. When ready for canning, they are sorted for size, ripeness, and quality. Imperfect pieces are set aside for use in preserves.

All inedible portions, such as tough stems and husks, are removed. The edible portions are carefully washed in small lots, to ensure thorough removal of dirt. Soaking fruits and vegetables is avoided, for it causes them to lose flavor and food value. To avoid unnecessary loss of quality, the food is handled gently to avoid bruising.

Sugar is used in canned fruit to help it keep its shape, color, and flavor. A thin, medium, or thick syrup may be used, depending on the intended use of the fruit (Fig. 40-2). Dessert fruit is often packed in a medium or thick syrup; whole fruit that is to be made into pie fillings may be packed in a thin syrup, in water, in its own juice, or in the juice of other fruits (Table 40-2).

Both corn syrup and light-flavored honey may be used in place of up to one-half the required amount of sugar. A strong flavor, however, results from the use of such sweeteners as brown sugar, molasses, or sorghum; consequently, these are not recommended as substitutes for sugar.

CANNING MEAT, POULTRY, AND RABBIT

The different meats—beef, veal, mutton, lamb, pork, and rabbit—are safely canned at home. Various kinds of poultry may also be canned. For safe canning, only meat from healthy animals that have been slaughtered and handled in a sanitary way should be used. After

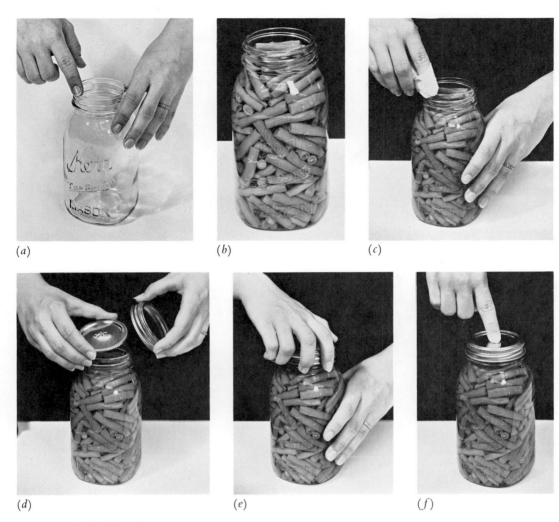

(a) (b) (c)

(d) (e) (f)

(g) **40-1** *Steps in canning string beans.*
(a) Examine the jars to see that there are no nicks, cracks, or sharp edges. (b) Pack the food to not more than ½ inch from the top of the jar. (c) Wipe the jar free of any extraneous matter. (d) Place the scalded lid on the jar with a sealing composition next to the glass. (e) Screw the bond firmly tight. (f) To check the seal, tap the jar when it is cold. A clear ringing sound means a good seal. (g) A pressure cooker or pressure canner must be equipped with an accurate pressure gauge, a lid that locks, a safety valve, and a rack. A timer eliminates over- or underprocessing canned food. (Courtesy of Kerr Glass Manufacturing Corporation)

483

(a)

(b)

(c)

(d)

(e)

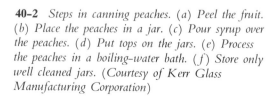

40-2 *Steps in canning peaches. (a) Peel the fruit. (b) Place the peaches in a jar. (c) Pour syrup over the peaches. (d) Put tops on the jars. (e) Process the peaches in a boiling–water bath. (f) Store only well cleaned jars. (Courtesy of Kerr Glass Manufacturing Corporation)*

(f)

TABLE 40-1
Directions for Canning Vegetables

Vegetables and Amounts Required for 1 Pt	Preparation and Packing	Method and Processing Time
Asparagus (1¼–2¼ lb)	Wash asparagus, trim off scales and tough ends; cut into pieces of desired size; cover with boiling liquid and boil 2 or 3 min; add ½ tsp salt and adjust jar lids.	Pressure canner— 10 lb pressure (240°F; 116°C) Hot pack Pt. jars: 25 min Qt. jars: 30 min
Beans, fresh lima (½–2½ lb)	Shell the beans, cover with boiling water and bring to boil; pack hot beans loosely to within ½ in. of top; add ½ tsp salt to pint; cover with boiling water; adjust jar lids	Pressure canner— 10 lb pressure (240°F; 116°C) Hot pack Pt. jars: 40 min Qt. jars: 50 min Cold pack Pt. jars: 40 min Qt. jars: 50 min
Beets (without tops)	Trim and wash; cover with boiling water, boil till skins slip easily—15–25 min; remove skins, slice, pack hot beets in jar, cover with boiling liquid to ½ in. of top; add ½ tsp salt and adjust jar lids	Pressure canner— 10 lb pressure (240°F; 116°C) Hot pack Pt. jars: 30 min Qt. jars: 35 min
Carrots (without tops, 1–1½ lb)	Wash and scrape carrots; cut into pieces of desired size; cover with boiling water and bring to a boil; pack hot carrots, cover with boiling water to within ½ in. of top; add ½ tsp salt and adjust jar tops	Pressure canner— 10 lb pressure (240°F; 116°C) Hot pack Pt. jars: 25 min Qt. jars: 30 min Cold pack Pt. jars: 25 min Qt. jars: 30 min
Corn (cream style, in husks, 3–6 ears)	Husk corn and remove silk; wash, cut corn from cob, and scrape cob; add 1 pt boiling water to each pt. corn; heat to boiling; pack hot corn to 1 in. of top; add ½ tsp salt and adjust jar lids	Pressure canner— 10 lb pressure (240°F; 116°C) Hot pack Pt. jars: 85 min.
Corn (whole kernel, in husks, 3–6 ears)	Husk corn and remove silk; wash corn; cut corn from cob and pack corn in jar to ½ in. from top of jar; fill to top with boiling water; add ½ tsp salt and adjust jar lids	Pressure canner— 10 lb pressure (240°F; 116°C) Hot pack Pt. jars: 55 min Qt. jars: 85 min
Peas, fresh blackeye	Shell, wash, and cover blackeye peas with boiling water; bring to a rolling boil; pack hot peas in jar, cover with boiling water, leaving ½ in. space at top of jar; adjust jar lids	Pressure canner— 10 lb pressure (240°F; 116°C) Hot pack Pt. jars: 35 min Qt. jars: 40 min Cold pack Pt. jars: 35 min Qt. jars: 40 min

TABLE 40-1 (Cont.)

Vegetables and Amounts Required for 1 Pt.	Preparation and Packing	Method and Processing Time
Peas, fresh green	(*See* Peas, fresh blackeye)	Pressure canner—10 lb pressure (240°F; 116°C) Hot pack Pt. jars: 40 min Qt. jars: 40 min
Pumpkins, cubed	Wash pumpkin, remove seeds, and pare; cut into 1-in. cubes; add boiling water to cover and bring to a boil; pack hot cubes to ½ in. of top; cover with boiling liquid, leaving ½-in. space at top of jar; adjust jar lids	Pressure canner—10 lb pressure (240°F; 116°C) Hot pack Pt. jars: 55 min Qt. jars: 90 min
Pumpkins, strained	Wash pumpkin, remove seeds, and pare; cut into cubes and steam until tender; put through strainer or food mill; simmer until heated through; pack hot to within ½ in. from top of jar; add no liquid or salt; adjust jar lids.	Pressure canner—10 lb pressure (240°F; 116°C) Hot pack Pt. jars: 65 min Qt. jars: 80 min
Spinach and other greens	Pick over and wash thoroughly; cut out tough stems and midribs; steam about 10 min until wilted; pack hot spinach loosely to within ½ in. of top; cover with boiling water; adjust jar lids	Pressure canner—10 lb pressure (240°F; 116°C) Hot pack Pt. jars: 70 min Qt. jars: 90 min
Squash, summer (1–2 lb.)	Wash squash and trim ends, do not pare; cut squash into pieces of desired size; add water to cover and bring to boil; pack hot squash loosely, cover with boiling liquid, leaving ½ in. at top of jar; adjust jar lids	Pressure canner—10 lb pressure (240°F; 116°C) Hot pack Pt. jars: 30 min Qt. jars: 40 min Cold pack Pt. jars: 25 min Qt. jars: 30 min
Squash, winter (1–1½ lb.)	(*See* Pumpkins)	(*See* Pumpkins)
Sweet potatoes (dry pack)	Wash sweet potatoes; boil or steam until partially soft (20–30 min) and skin; cut in pieces of large size; pack hot sweet potatoes tightly in jar to 1 in. of top, pressing to fill spaces; add no salt and no liquid; adjust jar lids	Pressure canner—10 lb pressure (240°F; 116°C) Hot pack Pt. jars: 65 min Qt. jars: 95 min

Source: Adapted from "Home Canning of Fruits and Vegetables," *Home and Garden Bulletin 8* (Washington, D.C.: U.S. Department of Agriculture, rev. 1976).

TABLE 40-2
Directions for Canning Fruits, Tomatoes, and Fruit Juices

Amounts Required for 1 Pt	Preparation and Packing	Method and Processing Time
Apples (1¼–1½ lb)	Pare, core, and boil 5 min in syrup or water; pack hot fruit and cover with hot syrup or water; adjust jar lids	Hot pack, boiling-water bath Pt. jars 15 min Qt. jars: 20 min
Applesauce (1¼–1½ lb)	Prepare applesauce sweetened or unsweetened; heat to simmering; pack hot applesauce to ½ in. of top; adjust jar lids	Hot pack, boiling-water bath Pt. jars: 10 min Qt. jars: 10 min
Apricots	(*See* Peaches; peeling may be omitted)	Hot pack, boiling-water bath Pt. jars: 25 min Qt. jars: 30 min Cold pack, boiling-water bath Pt. jars: 25 min Qt. jars: 35 min
Berries (except strawberries, ¾–1½ lb)	Wash berries, drain, and cook with ½ cup sugar to each quart fruit; pack hot berries to ½ in. of top; adjust jar lids	Hot pack, boiling-water bath Pt. jars: 10 min Qt. jars: 15 min
Cherries (¾–1½ lb)	(*See* Berries)	Hot pack, boiling-water bath Pt. jars: 10 min Qt. jars: 15 min
Peaches (1–1½ lb)	Wash peaches, remove skins, and heat through in hot syrup; if fruit is very juicy, heat with sugar; add no liquid; pack hot to within ½ in. of top; cover with boiling liquid, leaving ½ in. space; adjust jar lids	Hot pack, boiling-water bath Pt. jars: 20 min Qt. jars: 25 min Cold pack, boiling-water bath Pt. jars: 25 min Qt. jars: 35 min
Pears (1–1½ lb)	(*See* Peaches)	Hot pack, boiling-water bath Pt. jars: 20 min Qt. jars: 25 min Cold pack, boiling-water bath Pt. jars: 25 min Qt. jars: 35 min
Plums (¾–1¼ lb)	Wash plums, halve and pit freestone varieties; to can whole plums, prick skins; heat to boiling in syrup or juice; if fruit is juicy, heat with sugar; add no liquid, fill to within ½ in of top; adjust jar lids	Hot pack, boiling-water bath Pt. jars: 20 min Qt. jars: 25 min
Rhubarb	Wash rhubarb and cut into ¼-in. pieces, add ½ cup sugar to each quart fruit; bring to boiling; pack hot to ½ in. of the top of the jar; adjust jar lids	Hot pack, boiling-water bath Pt. jars: 10 min Qt. jars: 10 min
Tomatoes (1¼–1¾ lb)	Remove skins from tomatoes by dipping into boiling water for about ½ min; cut out stem ends and peel tomatoes; bring tomatoes quickly to a boil and pack boiling hot to ½ in. of top; add ½ tsp salt to pt; adjust jar lids	Hot pack, boiling-water bath Pt. jars: 10 min Qt. jars: 10 min Cold pack, boiling-water bath Pt. jars: 35 min Qt. jars: 45 min

TABLE 40-2 (Cont.)

Amounts Required for 1 Pt	Preparation and Packing	Method and Processing Time
Fruit juice	Wash, remove pits, and crush fruit; heat to simmering; strain and add sugar if desired—about 1 cup to 1 gal juice; reheat to simmering; fill jars to top with hot juice; adjust jar lids	Hot pack, boiling-water bath Pt. jars: 5 min Qt. jars: 5 min
Tomato juice	Fill jars with boiling juice to ¼ in. from top; adjust jar lids	Hot pack, boiling-water bath Pt. jars: 10 min Qt. jars: 10 min
Fruit purée	Use sound, ripe fruit; wash, remove pits, cut large fruit in pieces; simmer until soft; add a little water, if needed; put fruit through a strainer or food mill; add sugar to taste and heat to simmering; pack hot to within ¼ in. of top; adjust jar lids	Hot pack, boiling-water bath Pt. jars: 10 min Qt. jars: 10 min

Source: Adapted from "Home Canning of Fruits and Vegetables," *Home and Garden Bulletin 8* (Washington, D.C.: U.S. Department of Agriculture, rev. 1976).

slaughtering, the meat should be chilled and kept chilled until it is canned. Chilling requires storage in a refrigerator at 40°F (4°C) or less. The chilled meat should be canned within a few days. Meat that must be held for longer periods of time should be frozen until it is canned. It is then desirable to cut or saw the frozen meat into 1- to 2-in.-thick strips and to avoid defrosting if possible. Thawed meat is highly perishable; if it is necessary to defrost the meat, it must be kept as cool as possible until it is canned.

Like fruits and vegetables, meat and poultry are packed by either the hot-pack or the raw-pack method (Table 40-3). The raw pack method includes heating the meat in open containers before processing. Meat must be processed at temperatures high enough to kill any bacteria that cause spoilage. Thus, a pressure canner is necessary. If meat is not properly processed, it is not safe to eat. The most convenient and economical way to can meat is to precook it. This shrinks the meat and insures thorough processing. Although salt does not preserve canned meat, it may be added to enhance its flavor.

CONTAINERS

Both glass jars and tin cans are used for home canning, but glass jars are generally used in homes where family-sized quantities of food are processed. Tin cans are good for large-quantity canning.

There are a number of excellent glass jars on the market. The most suitable are made of colorless glass and have a wide mouth for ease in packing and a tight-fitting cover that can be adjusted to form an airtight seal. Only completely sound jars should be used; jars with nicks, cracks, rough sealing edges, or any other defects should be discarded.

Glass Jars. Four types of lids are used for the airtight closure on glass jars: porcelain-lined zinc caps, glass lids with rubber rings, glass lids with top-seal rubber rings and metal screw-on bands, and flat metal lids with sealing compound and metal screw-on bands. Properly used, these lids provide a perfect seal. Rubber rings and flat metal lids with sealing compound should be discarded after the jar is opened. Directions for the use of lids are given in Table 40-4.

INSPECTION FOR SPOILAGE

All processed cans of food should be examined for leaks, bulging lids, or gas bubbles around the rubber rings. These signs indicate spoilage. When the jar is opened, no air or liquid should spurt out. The odor of the canned food should be that

TABLE 40-3
Directions for Canning Meat, Poultry, and Rabbit

Amounts Required for 1 Pt	Preparation and Packing	Method and Processing Time
Poultry (3½–4 lb, to be canned without bone)	Cut up chicken and remove bone[a]; trim off large lumps of fat; set aside giblets to can separately; use bony pieces for broth; drain broth and skim off fat, pour hot broth over raw pieces and cook until meat is medium done; pack pieces of poultry and cover meat with hot broth, leaving head space of 1 in.; work out air bubbles with knife; adjust lids on jars	Pressure canner— 10 lb pressure (240°F; 116°C) Hot pack Pt. jars: 75 min Qt. jars: 90 min
Giblets	Can livers alone; gizzards and hearts may be canned together; precook giblets in broth or hot water; pack giblets hot; cover with hot broth, leave 1-in. head space, and work out bubbles; adjust lids on glass jars	Pressure canner— 10 lb pressure (240°F; 116°C) Pt. jars: 75 min
Rabbit (3½–4 lb to be canned without bone)	(*See* Poultry)	(*See* Poultry)
Beef, veal, pork, lamb (2½–3¾ lb, untrimmed)	Cut meat from bone and use bone to make broth or soup; trim away fat; cut into pieces that slip easily into the glass jar; precook meat in water until medium-done; pack meat hot, cover with hot broth, leaving 1 in. at top of glass jar for head space; adjust jar lids	Pressure canner— 10 lb pressure (240°F; 116°C) Hot pack Pt. jars: 75 min Qt. jars: 90 min

Source: "Home Canning of Meats," *Home and Garden Bulletin 6* (Washington, D.C.: U.S. Department of Agriculture, 1970).
[a]Chicken can be canned without bone being removed.

TABLE 40-4
Main Types of Closures and How to Use Them

Porcelain-lined zinc cap with shoulder rubber ring (to fit standard mason jar)	*During canning.* Fit wet rubber ring on jar shoulder, but do not stretch more than necessary; fill jar; wipe rubber ring and jar rim; screw cap down firmly and turn it back ¼ in.
	After canning. Take jar from canner, screw cap down tight to complete seal
Wire-bail jar with glass lid and rubber ring	*During canning.* Fill jar; wipe rim clean; fit wet rubber ring on jar rim; snap the upper bail into position over the glass top but leave the lower bail loose
	After canning. Take jar from canner, snap lower bail down tight to complete seal
Flat metal lid with sealing compound and metal screw-on band (to fit standard mason jar)	*During canning.* Fill jar; wipe rim clean; put lid on, with sealing compound next to glass; screw metal band down tight (this lid has enough "give" to let air escape during processing)
	After canning. Do not tighten screw band further after taking jar from canner

Source: Adapted from "Home Canning of Fruits and Vegetables," *Home and Garden Bulletin 8* (Washington, D.C.: U.S. Department of Agriculture, rev. 1976).

TABLE 40-5
Defects and Spoilage in Home-Canned Products

Defect	Possible Causes
Darkening of food at top of can *Heat food for 20 min before tasting*	Oxidation caused by air left in jars Not enough heating or processing to destroy enzymes
Loss of liquid	Overpacked jar Uneven pressure during processing Sudden lowering of pressure at the end of the processing period
Cloudy or turbid liquid *Boil vegetable for 20 min before tasting*	Bacteria Minerals in hard water Starches in food
Floating fruit	Too heavy a sirup Underpacked jar
Gas bubbles, bulging caps *Discard food without tasting*	Action of gas-forming bacteria
Acids *Discard food without tasting*	Action of acid-forming bacteria
Bad odor, softening and darkening of food *Discard food without tasting*	Action of putrefactive bacteria
Toxins *Discard food without tasting*	Action of *Clostridium botulinum*

of the fresh product; any off-odor is a sign of possible spoilage.

Only sight and smell should be used to determine spoilage. *Questionable canned food should never be tasted. Nonacid foods may be spoiled, yet show no signs of spoilage; even to taste such a food may bring on a dangerous illness–botulism. All spoiled foods should be destroyed; they may be treated with lye and buried, or simply burned.*

The safe canning of food requires precision and a thorough understanding of the causes of spoilage in home-canned products. Table 40-5 gives information about common defects in home-canned foods and the possible causes for each type of spoilage.

SUMMARY

Canning is an economical way of preserving surpluses of homegrown fresh, firm, young and tender fruits and vegetables, or advantageously purchased foods. This process utilizes heat to destroy enzyme action and spoilage microorga-

nisms and includes sealing the food in sterile, airtight containers.

High-acid foods such as fruits and tomatoes can be safely processed in a boiling-water-bath canner. Low-acid foods such as meats, poultry, fish, and most vegetables must be processed at higher than boiling temperatures in the pressure canner to destroy bacteria and assure safety. Strict adherence to processing times and pressures is necessary.

Fruits and vegetables and meat and poultry may be processed by either the raw-pack or the hot-pack method. In the raw-pack method, no precooking of fruits or vegetables is done, but meat is heated before packing. In the hot-pack method, food is precooked briefly and then packed while as close to boiling temperature as possible. The food is then processed for the required time. With fruits, sugar is used to help preserve shape, color, and flavor. Precooking meat shrinks it, permits an advantageous fill of container, and insures thorough processing.

Various types of glass jars and lids are used in home canning, as well as tin cans. All canned foods should be inspected for spoilage. No questionable canned food should be tasted.

QUESTIONS AND TOPICS FOR DISCUSSION AND STUDY

1. Why is it possible to process fruits and tomatoes in a water–bath canner? Why must non-acid vegetables, meat, fish and poultry be processed in a pressure canner?
2. What is botulism? Under what conditions does it develop in canned foods?
3. Why should home-canned foods be boiled before they are tasted?

SUGGESTED ACTIVITIES

1. Can fresh fruits, vegetables, meats, poultry, or fish. Follow the directions in government bulletins for procedures and processing times.

Compare the cost of a home-canned product with that of a commercial product.
2. Compare your canned products with those of other students or those made in the past year.

REFERENCES

BOOKS
Griswold, Ruth. *The Experimental Study of Foods.* Boston: Houghton Mifflin, 1962, Chap. 7.

BULLETINS
"Home Canning of Fruits and Vegetables." *Home and Garden Bulletin 8*. Washington, D.C.: U.S. Department of Agriculture, rev. 1976.
"Home Canning of Meats and Poultry." *Home and Garden Bulletin 6*. Washington, D.C.: U.S. Department of Agriculture, rev. 1972.
Paul, Pauline and Helen Palmer, *Food Theory and Applications,* New York: Wiley, 1972, Chap. 13.

Jams, Jellies, and Conserves and Preserves

CHAPTER 41

The preservation of fruit in jellies, jams, conserves, and marmalades is an older method than canning or freezing. Many fruits contain enough pectin to make a gel product. When sugar and acids in the right proportion are added to these fruits and heat is applied, they can be preserved without the sterilization necessary in canning. It is necessary, however, to cover the surface of the jellied product so that air cannot penetrate to promote growth of molds or fermentation.

A number of fruits are perfectly adapted to the making of jellies and jams. Outstanding among these are crab apples, Concord grapes, blackberries, plums, currants, gooseberries, quinces, cranberries, and citrus fruits. These fruits contain pectin and acid in such proportions that all that is necessary to make the fruit gel is the proper amount of sugar and heat. When these fruits are overripe, however, the pectin changes to pectic acid, a substance that does not aid in gel formation. But it is possible to use any fruit juice or fruit solids to make a jam or jelly by adding commercially prepared pectin and adjusting the sugar and acid proportions accordingly. Cooking time is reduced when prepared pectin is used.

PECTINS AND ACIDS

The significant pectic substances found in fruit are protopectin, pectin, and pectic acid. Protopectin, which inhibits gel formation, is found only in underripe fruit. But protopectin is changed to pectin by the enzyme protopectinase in the ripened fruit, and pectin does form a sol with water. In overripe fruit, the pectin is changed to pectic acid—which, like protopectin, inhibits gel formation.

Although the presence of pectin in the proper proportions is very important in obtaining a gelled product, heat must be applied to extract the pectin. Uncooked fruit juice will fail to gel properly because some of the pectic substances in the fruit remain in the solid portion. The usual way to extract the pectin from fruit is to heat the fruit in a small amount of water. When large amounts of water are used, the pectin strength is diluted and its ability to form a gel is reduced. Hard fruits, such as crab apples and quinces, may be cut into very small pieces or ground—with skin or core left intact—and cooked in a small amount of water so as to extract the maximum amount of pectin.

The principal acids in fruit are citric, malic, and tartaric. Some fruits contain enough acid to furnish the required amount for gel formation. Other fruits, rich in pectin, may contain very little of the necessary acids. To these fruits lemon juice or citric acid is added to make up for the deficiency. It has been found that gel formation cannot take place unless the mixture is fairly acid. In general, increases in sugar accelerate the gel strength and the setting of the jelly, but rate of setting is modified by other factors, particularly the hydrogen ion concentration.[1]

Commercial Pectin. Commercial pectin products are made from apple pomace or citrus products. Fruit pectins come in liquid or powdered form, and special recipes have been constructed on the basis of the jellying capacity of a given form.[2] Powdered pectins are less likely to deteriorate than liquid pectins are.

Effect of Cooking on Pectin. In making jelly, the sugar acts as a precipitating agent. If the concentration of sugar is sufficiently great, it brings about dehydration of the pectin particles, causing them to precipitate and form a network of insoluble fibers. In this meshlike structure, large amounts of water can be held. The gel structure formed by the pectins of a given fruit has special characteristics. For example, a gel formed by citrus pectin breaks readily, whereas the structure resulting from the use of an apple pectin is smooth and elastic.

Kertesz[3] suggests that the formation of a jelly might be regarded as "unsuccessful precipitation." When the jelly is in the sol state, it is stabilized by water layers held to it by electrical attraction. When sugar is introduced, a dehydrating effect is produced that decreases the stability of the pectin by disturbing the water balance. When the acid is added, the destabilization is complete and a jelly forms as the result of an unsuccessful attempt on the part of the pectin particles to precipitate. When added pectin is used and the first batch from a particular fruit is too soft or too firm, adjust the amount of fruit or the cooking time for the next batch. For a softer product use ¼–½ cup more fruit or juice, but for a firmer product use ¼–½ cup less fruit or juice. When pectin is not added, a softer product is formed by shortening the cooking time, and a firmer product can be obtained by lengthening the cooking time.

Tests for Pectin. Because some knowledge of the amount of pectin in a fruit is necessary in order to determine the fruit's suitability for jelly, certain household tests are employed. One simple test involves cooking a small portion of the juice with sugar to see if it will form a jelly. The second method involves mixing 1 tbsp fruit juice with 1 tbsp denatured alcohol. (*Denatured alcohol is poisonous, and the mixture should not be tasted.*) If the pectin precipitates in a solid mass, it is present in sufficient amounts to form a jelly. Insufficient pectin is indicated by the presence of small coagulated clumps and the lack of precipitation. A third method involves use of the *jelmeter*—a device that measures the viscosity of fruit juice and indicates the amount of sugar to be added to it. This instrument operates by comparing the rate of flow of juice with that of water.

JELLY

In selecting fruit for jelly, a mixture of slightly underripe and ripe fruit should be used. The fruit should be washed and spoiled portions removed. Boiling is necessary to extract the pectin. Large fruits should be cut in small pieces or ground; berries are capped and stemmed. A minimum of water and cooking is used to extract the juice and to preserve the characteristic flavor of the fruit.

Yield. Lamb[4] and her associates concluded, after examining the data obtained from preparing 10 kinds of fruit juice, that a yield of 1–1.3 cups fruit juice per pound of fruit (as purchased) was average for the fruits tested. Fruits included

[1] Belle Lowe, *Experimental Cookery* (New York: Wiley, 1955), p. 166.

[2] G. L. Gilpin et al., "Development of Jelly Formulas with Fully Ripe Fruit and Added Pectins," *Food Technol.* **11**:1957.

[3] Z. I. Kertesz, *The Pectin Substances* (New York: Interscience, 1951), p. 194.

[4] J. Lamb, M. Brown, and G. Gilpin, "Yield of Prepared Fruit and Juice for Jam and Jelly Making," *J. Home Econ.* **49**:433, 1957.

TABLE 41-1
Proportion and Time Chart for Making Jelly

Kind of Fruit	Cups of Water to 1 Qt of Prepared Fruit (cups)	Boiling Time for Fruits (min)	Amount of Sugar to 1 Cup of Fruit Juice (cups)
Apples	1	20	1
Crab apples	1	20	1
Blackberries (firm, soft)	¼	10	¾
Currants	¼	10	1
Gooseberries	¼	10	¾
Grapes, Concord	¼	15	¾
Quinces	2	25	¾
Raspberries, black or red	—	10	¾

Source: A. M. Briant and L. Dudgeon, "Fruit Spreads and Preserves," *Cornell University Extension Bulletin 1060* (Ithaca, N.Y.: Cornell University, 1963).

in the study were apples, crab apples, blackberries, cherries, currants, grapes, peaches, plums, quinces, and strawberries.

Water. A minimum of water and cooking to extract the juice is desirable. Because of differences in fruit composition, the amount of water and sugar and the cooking time will vary, depending mainly on the texture and juiciness of a given fruit. Table 41-1 is useful for determining amounts of water, sugar, and fruit juice to use in making jelly. In a study reported,[5] the quantity of tannins increased in drained fruit juice of currants and raspberries and a trend toward increased bitterness and astringency was noted, when cooking temperatures and cooking times were increased.

A broad, flat-bottomed pan deep enough to prevent boiling over is best for boiling the fruit so as to shorten cooking time and prevent scorching. Soft fruits, such as grapes, are crushed before cooking to start the juice flowing. Fruits should not be overcooked: soft fruits need only 10–15 minutes, hard fruits 20–25 minutes.

When fruit is tender and sufficient juice is extracted, it is strained through a cheesecloth bag (see Fig. 41-1). When all the juice is extracted, a second extraction may be made by returning the

[5] Watson, Ellen, "Tannins in Fruit Extracts as Affected by Heat Treatments," *Home Econ. Res, J.* **2:**112, 1973.

mash to the kettles, covering it with water, and allowing it to simmer for 20 minutes. The juice is then extracted a second time.

Sugar. Beet sugar or cane sugar may be used. It appears to be desirable to add the sugar at the beginning of the cooking period, thus increasing the cooking time if a very dilute juice in pectin is used. It is thought that too little sugar is better than too much: too much sugar will result in a gummy product that will not gel; on the other hand, too little sugar gives a tough rubbery product (Table 41-2). (Amounts given in Table 41-1 are reliable unless fruit is overripe.)

General Procedure. It is best to make only six to eight glasses of jelly at a time. If made in larger lots, the jelly will not be of as good a quality. For best results in cooking, the measured juice and sugar should be placed in a large flat-bottomed pan, heated to the boiling point, then cooked to the jelly stage. This is determined by allowing some of the hot mixture to run off the side of a metal spoon. When the jelly separates into two separate lines of drip that "sheet" together, the jelly is done (Fig. 41-2).

The mixture is then skimmed and poured into sterilized jelly glasses. The jelly is sealed with a thin layer of paraffin while still hot. This is accomplished by pouring over its top a layer (less than ⅛ in. thick) of hot, melted paraffin. The paraffin layer protects the jelly from contamination by mold spores. When the jelly has cooled,

(a)

(b)

41-1 *Making fruit jam.* (a) *Strain fruit through a cheese cloth bag.* (b) *For a second extraction, use pressure to obtain all possible juice.* (*Courtesy U.S. Department of Agriculture*)

another layer of paraffin may be added if necessary.

Fruits that are low in pectin but well-flavored may be used for jelly and similar products by adding commercial pectin. Both the liquid and the powdered form can be satisfactorily used, if the directions that accompany them are followed.

Standard for Jelly. A good jelly has an excellent color; it is transparent and palatable and retains its shape when removed from the mold. The texture is tender—easily cut with a spoon

but sufficiently firm so that angles produced retain their shape.

JAM

Making jam is another way of preserving the delicate flavor of some fruits. Jam is a spread made from small fruits or small pieces of fruit. The fruit is mashed, chopped, or diced— depending on the type of jam. Like jelly, jams will retain the delicate flavor of the fruit if made in small batches. Fruit that has little or no juice of its own requires added water to keep from burning. The proportion of sugar used in making jam is ¾ lb, to 1 lb fruit. Once the sugar is added, the mixture must be cooked rapidly and stirred almost constantly to prevent sticking. The jam is done when it breaks off in sheets from the spoon. It is then put into sterilized glasses and treated in the same manner as jelly.

MARMALADES

Marmalades are jellylike products that contain small pieces or thin slices of fruit. They may be made from one fruit or from a mixture of several. Marmalades are usually made from oranges, grapefruit, lemons, but excellent results

41-2 *The jelly is ready when two drops of syrup run together when tested.* (*Courtesy of Kerr Glass Manufacturing Corporation*)

495

TABLE 41-2
Jelly Failures and Their Possible Causes

Failures	Possible Causes
Sugar crystallization (found mainly in grape jelly)	Too much sugar Not enough acid Overcooking Delay in sealing (may be prevented by permitting juice to stand overnight in cold place before making it into jelly)
"Weeping (may be exhibited in jellies made from currants or cranberries high in acid)	Cause not really known
Cloudiness	Squeezing juice out of bag Starch from apples used to make jelly (avoid pressure on jelly bag when straining)
Failure to gel	Lack of proper balance between pectin, sugar, and acid Lack of pectin or acid in fruit Overcooking
Fermented jelly or mold formation	Jelly glasses not well sterilized Jelly stored in warm, damp place Jelly not completely sealed

can be produced by substituting cranberries, limes, pineapples, or peaches for all or part of a citrus ingredient. The preparation of marmalades differs from that of jams and jellies in that water is added to the sliced citrus fruit and the mixture is cooked for a while before the sugar is added. (Some recipes recommend the peel be soaked overnight in the water in which it is to be cooked.) Marmalade is cooked until it reaches the gelled stage. It is then poured into hot sterilized jars and treated much as jellies and jams are.

CONSERVES AND BUTTERS

A conserve is much like a jam; however, it is generally made of a mixture of fruits to which nuts and raisins have been added. The fruit may be diced or pulped. From ½ to ¾ lb of sugar to 1 lb of fruit is used. The fruit–nut mixture is quickly cooked (with sugar) to the proper consistency. Only small batches are cooked at one time. The hot conserve is then poured into sterile jars and paraffin is poured over the top.

Butters made from the pulp of fruit have a texture similar to that of butter made from cream. When cooked, a fruit butter spreads

easily but does not run. Butters can be made from most fruits and from mixtures of several different ones.

PRESERVES

Preserves are made from whole fruit or from fairly large pieces. These are cooked with sugar until they are tender but still retain their shape. Generally, the fruit is cooked until the syrup thickens. The fruits used for preserves are cherries, peaches, pears, quinces, strawberries, and tomatoes.

Fruits are preserved in glass containers with tight-fitting covers. (Those used for canning are suitable for preserves.) The jars must be sterilized before they are filled with the hot preserves.

When the preserves are cooked, they are poured into the hot sterile jars and sealed at once. Processing of jams, conserves, marmalades and preserves is recommended in warm or humid climates. Any large metal container that is deep enough to allow for 1 to 2 in. of water above the tops of the jars, plus a little extra space for boiling can be used. The container should also have a tight-fitting cover and a wire or wood rack with partitions to keep jars from touching each other or the bottom or sides of the container.

The jars are filled to within ¼ in. of the top with the fruit mixture, then the jars are prepared as for canning. (See Chapter 40 for directions.) Process for 5 min.

SPOILAGE OF JAMS AND JELLIES

Jams, jellies, and similar products can be spoiled by fermentation and mold formation. Fermentative yeasts will grow on the surface of the jelly and cause gasiness. Molds are probably the most common cause of spoilage in jams, jellies, marmalades, and fruit butters. Mold formation may also appear on the surface of preserved products that have not been sealed properly.

SUMMARY

Fruit may be preserved by making it into jellies, jams, conserves, butters, marmalades, and preserves. Although recommended in hot or humid climates, the sterilization necessary for canning is not required, the surface of these foods must be covered to prevent growth of molds or fermentation.

Some fruits contain the right proportions of pectin and acid to gel when sugar is added and heat is applied. By using commercial pectin made from apple pomace or citrus products, any fruit may be used in jam or jelly making. Sugar and acid are adjusted accordingly.

In jelly making, a mixture of ripe and slightly underripe fruit should be used. Boiling is necessary to extract the pectin, but a minimum of water and cooking is recommended. Either beet or cane sugar may be used with the extracted juice. Sugar, in proper concentration, dehydrates the pectin particles, causing them to precipitate and gel.

Best results are achieved in jelly and jam making when only small amounts are made at one time. In jams, fruits are mashed, chopped, or diced and then cooked quickly with sugar. In marmalades, the prepared citrus fruit is precooked in water before sugar is added. Similar to jam, conserves usually have added nuts and sometimes raisins. Whole fruit or fairly large pieces are used in making preserves. Cooked with sugar until tender, the fruits should retain their shape.

Sterilized jars are used for all products of this type. Preserves should be packed in jars that can be sealed at once; paraffin is generally used as the covering for other products.

QUESTIONS AND TOPICS FOR DISCUSSION AND STUDY

1. What constituents of fruit are necessary for jelly making?
2. How can the pectin content of a fruit be determined?
3. Why is it desirable to make only small batches of jelly at a time?
4. Why are commercial pectins very suitable products for use in making jelly?
5. Why are different amounts of water used to extract juice from different fruits?
6. How do jellies differ from jams? Marmalades? Conserves? Butters?

SUGGESTED ACTIVITIES

1. Prepare jellies and related products. Use government bulletins for procedures and recipes.
2. Compare a batch of jelly made with pectin with one cooked without pectin.
3. Compare the cost of the homemade product with that of a similar commercial product.

REFERENCES

BOOKS

Griswold, Ruth. *The Experimental Study of Foods.* Boston: Houghton Mifflin, 1962, Chap. 7.

Kertesz, Z. I. *The Pectic Substances.* New York: Interscience, 1951, pp. 193–200.

Lowe, Belle. *Experimental Foods* New York: Wiley, 1955, Chap. 4.

Vail, Gladys, Jean A. Phillips, Lucile Osborn Rust, Ruth M. Griswold, Margaret M. Justin. *Foods.* Boston: Houghton Mifflin, 1978, Chaps. 32, 33.

PAMPHLETS AND BULLETINS

Briant, A. M., and L. Dudgeon. "Fruit Spreads and Preserves." *Cornell University Extension Bulletin 1060*. Ithaca, N.Y.: Cornell University, 1963.

"How to Make Jellies, Jams and Preserves at Home," *Home and Garden Bulletin No. 56*. Washington, D.C.: U.S. Department of Agriculture, 1974.

Yeatman, F., and M. Steinbarger. "Homemade Jellies, Jams, and Preserves." *Farmers' Bulletin 1800*. Washington, D.C.: U.S. Department of Agriculture, rev. 1975.

Food Controls

Because much preparation of food now takes place in industrial plants rather than in the home, there is an increased need to inform the consumer of advances made by private industry and government agencies in setting standards for the processing of foods.

In this section, the techniques for the control and regulation of food are summarized to show the serious effort that has been made to make foods acceptable from a health standpoint and to assure to the consumer the quality claimed.

The principles and application of microwave cookery is included in this section.

Part Six

Government Food Controls

The number of processed foods on the market today is so great and their quality so varied that the average consumer has neither the time to inspect nor the ability to evaluate each article of food she wishes to buy. And in the case of packaged foods, little can be learned from visual inspection. Also, the total volume of packaged food produced increases yearly; consequently, there is a great variety of package shapes and sizes available—but not enough useful information is stated on the package to enable the consumer to make a wise selection. In order to buy food that is wholesome and satisfies their needs, consumers require protective measures. Good laws have been passed to protect consumers against food products that are inferior or misbranded and to protect manufacturers and dealers against unfair competition. But present laws cannot completely insure the public against poor-quality food or fraudulent practices relating to its distribution and sale. The manufacturers and dealers in food products must also help in setting standards of quality and sanitation so the public can buy safely and with full confidence.

The best protective measures for the consumer must come from the government, and considerable effort has been made by the federal government to safeguard the nation's food. The agencies discussed in this chapter give considerable attention to food problems of consumers.

FOOD AND DRUG ADMINISTRATION

The Food and Drug Administration is part of the U.S. Department of Health, Education, and Welfare; its main function is to enforce the Food, Drug, and Cosmetic Act of 1938, and thereby assure that foods are safe, pure, and wholesome (Fig. 42-1).

PURE FOOD LAWS

Through the efforts of dedicated workers for clean, safe foods, the first "pure food" law was passed in 1906. This was the Pure Food and Drugs Act, which went into effect in 1907. Credit for passage of this law, belongs to Dr. Harvey Wiley, who was at that time Chief Chemist of the U.S. Department of Agriculture. Although the Pure Food and Drugs Act of 1906 was the first law to provide protection of this

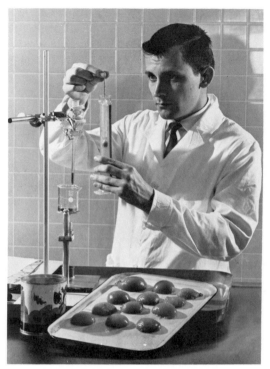

42-1 *A Food and Drug Administration chemist checks canned half peaches to see if they meet the legal standard for hardness and for quality of packing syrup.* (*Courtesy of Food and Drug Administration*)

type and the strongest law of its kind in the world, it soom became inadequate. As food processing became more industrialized and distribution of food became an increasing part of the food industry, stronger controls were needed to protect the food from contamination or adulteration before it reached the consumer. Consequently, strong pressure from consumer groups in the early and mid-1930s resulted in the passage of the Food, Drug, and Cosmetic Act of 1938. This law retained the best features of the 1906 law, but it was sufficiently broad in scope to cover new conditions that had developed in the food field and to strengthen the enforcement provisions of the old law that had proved ineffective. It has been amended several times to cover such new developments as the use of food additives and chemical pesticides. Chiefly, the law provides health safeguards and

sanitary controls (Fig. 42-2), prohibits deceptions, and requires label statements.

Health Safeguards. A food that is unsafe or injurious to health is considered illegal and therefore is prohibited in interstate commerce. The amount of deleterious substances that can be used as a part of the necessary manufacture of a given food is strictly limited.

A raw agricultural product containing residues of pesticides that are in excess of an established tolerance is prohibited from sale.

Food containers must be free from any poisonous or deleterious substance that may cause the contents to be harmful.

Colors used in foods must be established as safe in the amounts used; coal-tar colors must be tested and certified by the U.S. Food and Drug Administration.

Confectionery, including candy, must be free of nonnutritive substances (except harmless colors or flavorings) and must not contain alcohol in excess of 0.5%, which is to be derived from the use of flavoring extracts.

Sanitary Safeguards. Any food that is filthy, putrid, decomposed, or packed or held under unsanitary conditions in which it may have become contaminated is banned from sale. The sale of the flesh of a diseased animal or of an animal that has died other than by slaughter is also prohibited.

Prohibited Deceptions. A food must not be sold under the name of another food. By the same token, no part of substance that is an important constituent of a food may be removed in whole or in part, nor may any other substance be substituted for it. For example, whole milk may not be labeled *milk* if part of the butterfat is removed.

Food containers must not be so made or filled as to mislead the consumer concerning the amount of food in them.

Label Statements. Food labels that are false or misleading in any particular are prohibited. (Failure of the label to reveal material facts may be also considered misleading.) They must be conspicuous. The information must be in English and stated clearly so that the consumer can read

42-2 *A Food and Drug Administration inspector. (Courtesy of Food and Drug Administration)*

and understand the conditions of purchase and use.

The labels must show the name and address of the manufacturer, the packer, or the distributor, and must accurately indicate the weight of the contents. They must also contain the common, usual name of the food and of each ingredient (except for foods for which identity standards have been promulgated), and list the ingredients in order of their predominance in the food.

Special dietary foods must be so labeled to inform consumers about their vitamin, mineral, and other dietary properties.

Foods (except butter, cheese, and ice cream) that are artificially flavored or colored must be so labeled. Any chemical preservatives used must be indicated on the label.

Color Additives. An amendment to the federal Food, Drug, and Cosmetic Act requires that all colors added to the food be within the limits established by the Food and Drug Administration. Before this amendment was enacted in July, 1960, only coal-tar colors were subject to certification and no color was eligible for certification unless it was established as harmless— even if the amounts to be used were much smaller than that shown to be injurious.

Standards of Identity. The Food, Drug, and Cosmetic Act also provides for the issuance of reasonable definitions and standards of identity for certain foods and food products. These standards of identity are concerned with what a given food is, whether its quality is above or below standard, and how full a given package must be.[1] A minimum standard of quality is established for each of these foods. A food that falls below the minimum standard must bear a special label reading *Below-Standard in Quality. Good Food—Not High-Grade.*

Foods for which definitions and standards of identity, quality, and fill of container have been promulgated[2] are the following:

1. Chocolate and cocoa products.
2. Wheat and corn flour and related products.
3. Macaroni and noodle products.
4. Bakery products.
5. Milk and cream.
6. Cheese and cheese products.
7. Frozen desserts.
8. Food flavoring.

[1] These standards assume that the food is properly prepared from clean, sound materials; they should not be confused with the standards for grades that are established by the U.S. Department of Agriculture.

[2] *Definitions and Standards of Identity for Food: Code of Federal Regulations, Title 21* (Washington, D.C.: U.S. Department of Health, Education, and Welfare, Food and Drug Administration, rev. 1971).

9. Dressings for foods (mayonnaise, French dressing, salad dressing).
10. Canned fruit and fruit juices.
11. Fruit butters, jellies, preserves.
12. Shellfish.
13. Fish.
14. Eggs and egg products.
15. Oleomargarine, margarine.
16. Nut products.
17. Canned vegetables.
18. Canned tomato products.

Complete standards of identity currently exists for three meat products. These standards require specific ingredients to be present as follows:

Corned beef hash—Must contain at least 35% beef (cooked basis). Also must contain potatoes (either fresh, dehydrated, cooked dehydrated, or a mixture of these types), curing agents, and seasonings. May be made with certain optional ingredients such as onions, garlic, beef broth, or beef fat. May not contain more than 15% fat or more than 72% moisture.

Chopped ham—Must contain fresh, cured, or smoked ham, along with certain specified kinds of curing agents and seasonings. May also contain certain optional ingredients in specified amounts, including finely chopped ham shank meat, dehydrated onions, dehydrated garlic, corn syrup, other chemical substances as permitted in the federal standard, and not more than 3% water to dissolve the curing agents.

Oleomargarine or margarine—Must contain either the rendered fat, oil, or stearin derived from cattle, sheep, swine, or goats; or a vegetable food fat, oil, or stearin; or a combination of these two classes of ingredients in a specified proportion. Must contain—individually or in combination—pasteurized cream, cow's milk, skim milk, a combination of nonfat dry milk and water or finely ground soybeans and water. May contain optional ingredients specified in the standard, including butter, salt, artificial coloring, vitamins A and D, and permitted chemical substances. Fat in finished product may not exceed 80%. Label must indicate whether product is from animal or vegetable origin or both.

Standards for Meat and Poultry Products. To be labeled with a particular name—such as "All Beef Franks" or "Chicken Soup"—a federally inspected meat or poultry product must be approved by the U.S. Department of Agriculture as meeting specific product requirements. Specific product requirements for meat, poultry, and other ingredients are given in appendix.

Standards of identity are established for additional foods whenever, in the judgment of the Secretary of Health, Education, and Welfare, such action will promote honesty and fair dealing and benefit the consumer.

When a standard of identity is set for a food, the label need not list the ingredients (except specified optional ingredients) because they are specified in the standard. Hence, a product labeled *Mayonnaise* must contain 65% (by weight) vegetable oil, vinegar or lemon juice, and egg yolks. These ingredients need not appear on the label, but if the mayonnaise dressing contains citric acid the label must say so.

The standard for fill of container is designed to prevent the misrepresentation of a product by the use of a can or package larger than is necessary or by the use of excessive amounts of water.

FOOD ADDITIVES AMENDMENT

The Food Additives Amendment to the Food, Drug, and Cosmetic Act was passed in 1958. Its purpose is to assure that the safety of chemicals used in the processing of food is proven before use. Before this amendment was enacted, it was the responsibility of the Food and Drug Administration to prove a given food additive unsafe. This amendment put the burden of the proof on the sponsor of the additive: he must demonstrate the harmlessness of a substance before it can be approved for use.

The law covers not only substances intentionally added to food but also substances that, from their intended use, may reasonably be expected to become a component part of a food or to affect its characteristics. Thus, any substance used in the processing of food that combines with the food in some way is treated as a food additive. Other substances that may affect the characteristics of a food include those intended for use in food production, manufacture, packing, preparation, treatment, packaging, transportation, or storage. This amendment and its regulations are discussed more thoroughly in Chapter 43.

PESTICIDE CHEMICALS AMENDMENT

The Food, Drug, and Cosmetic Act was amended in 1954 in an effort to provide effective control over the use of pesticide chemicals and to minimize potential hazards arising from their misuse. (The term *pesticide chemical* covers insecticides and other chemicals used to control a wide variety of pests.) The 1954 amendment provides a means for establishing safe tolerances for residues of pesticide chemicals in or on raw agricultural commodities. Under this amendment, a food may not be marketed if it bears the residue of a pesticide chemical considered unsafe, or if the amount of residue exceeds the level established as safe.

Before a safe tolerance for a pesticide can be established, the users must submit to the government the name, chemical identity, and composition of the pesticide; the amount, frequency, and time of application; full reports of investigations of the safety of the pesticide; the results of tests of the safety of the amounts of residue remaining, including a description of the analytical methods and practical methods used. The users should also indicate a proposed safe tolerance, if any, and reasonable grounds for support of their request for its approval for use.

Since 1954, more than 2450 tolerances have been established at different levels and for various crops for over 125 pesticide chemicals. Continuous checks for residues on raw agricultural commodities are conducted. For the most part, the residues found are well below the safe tolerance level, but on rare occasions the detection of excessive residues makes it necessary to remove a shipload of food from interstate commerce.

CHEMICALS IN FOOD

The 1954 amendment was an outgrowth of the need to find safe ways to control infestation of crops and to ensure a large supply of agricultural products that meet established standards of food quality. It is not the goal of agriculturists to resort to chemical pesticides to do the entire job of controlling pests. Insofar as possible, farmers try to breed crops for resistance to disease and insects. They also depend on natural forces that tend to keep plant and animal populations in a state of near equilibrium. There are, however, species for which no natural controls are available, and the use of pesticides is the only established means for economically combating the majority of these. This being the case, it is likely that the use of pesticides will continue, attended by the necessary controls.

It has been reported that if the use of pesticidal chemicals were to be banned, the yield of many crops would be reduced 10–90% and the price of most items would increase greatly.[3]

However, consumers continue to be concerned about chemical residues in food. They have read that industrial wastes and agricultural runoffs have contaminated marine crops and industrial pollutants have affected agricultural crops. It is true that metals such as mercury and lead can accumulate in the bone marrow and organs and may be a potential hazard to health. The FDA made a massive study of tunafish and swordfish when high levels of mercury were reported; as a result of this study, swordfish was not recommended to the public for consumption and tunafish exceeding safety tolerance limits was removed from the market. Present FDA–industry monitoring has been set up to prevent the problem from recurring.

Recently, lower tolerances for residues of DDT and its metabolities in many raw agricultural food commodities were published in the *Federal Register*.[4]

NEED TO STRENGTHEN THE PURE FOOD LAWS

Today consumers must depend on labels in order to evaluate the contents of a packaged food or a processed food. And although definitions and standards of identity have been established for many of the chief foods used in this country, there are still many products for which no official standards have yet been set. For example, there are no federal standards to specify

[3] Food Protection Committee, Food and Nutrition Board, "The Use of Chemicals in Food Production, Processing, Storage, and Distribution," *Publication 887* (Washington, D.C.: National Research Council–National Academy of Sciences, 1961).

[4] *Federal Register* (December 1970).

the proportions of ingredients in products such as packaged mixes and heat-and-serve items.

Another area in which the Food, Drug, and Cosmetic Act needs to be strengthened is that of inspection and enforcement. Although all personnel employed by the Food and Drug Administration are highly trained for their responsible positions, there are not enough workers to administer the law. Hence, enforcement is limited, and only a small portion of the total food supply of the country can receive attention in any one period.

As part of its job of policing the purity, quality, and labeling of foods, the Food and Drug Administration functions in the following ways:

1. It makes periodic visits to food establishments for the purpose of inspecting samples from interstate shipments of their products.
2. It checks the safety of all batches of coal-tar dyes for use in foods.

3. It issues and enforces regulations specifying the kinds and quantities of new additives that may be used in or on food products.
4. It establishes the amount of pesticidal residues that may safely remain on food crops and checks interstate shipments to see that residues are in fact within safe limits.
5. It sets standards that guarantee the composition and real value of food products in line with the congressional mandate to "promote honesty and fair dealing in the interest of the consumers."
6. It checks food imports to make sure they comply with federal law.
7. It cooperates with state and local inspectors to inspect and remove contaminated items from the market.

It would be impossible to provide government inspection for every shipment of food that crosses state boundaries; to do so would require a

42-3 *Stacks of commodities can be fumigated more economically and effectively under a gasproof plastic film. Leaving the covers in place helps keep food clean and resists reinfection by insects. (Courtesy of U.S. Department of Agriculture)*

huge army of inspectors and investigators. Reasonable measures, however, are taken. The Food and Drug Administration has about 770 inspectors throughout the United States who visit factories and food and drug plants to test and identify samples of food to make certain they meet minimum standards set by law. Eighteen district offices, located throughout the country, are equipped with laboratories in which specialists in chemistry, biochemistry, bacteriology, and other sciences analyze samples of the products under investigation.

If products are found to be adulterated or misbranded, they may be removed from the market by federal court seizures and the persons or firms responsible for the violations may be subject to criminal prosecution.

The U.S. Department of Agriculture provides grading services for the food industry and passes on sanitary facilities in food-processing plants whose products bear the *Approved* label. It also conducts research on finding new food products as well as new methods of processing and storing food. The National Bureau of Standards provides technical assistance in establishing commodity measurements and performance standards. The Bureau of Commercial Fisheries promotes consumer use of fish products and makes available an official inspection service for all fishery products.

A proposal for voluntary nutritional labeling of all food has been recommended by the FDA. Efforts to enforce the Fair Packaging and Labeling Act have been of economic advantage to the consumer.

CONSUMER AND MARKETING SERVICE

The Consumer and Marketing Service agency of the U.S. Department of Agriculture works with farm, industry, and research groups to establish grade standards to measure quality level of foods, provides a grading service to producers or distributors at their cost, and has the right to withdraw grading services if a plant does not conform to requirements set by the agency. Through its inspectors, this agency can prevent the sale in interstate commerce of meat and poultry products that do not meet federal standards. It requires that all facilities and sanitary practices in egg-processing plants be approved and operations be supervised by a licensed inspector.

The grades that have been established are Grade A, or Fancy, and Grade B, or Choice. The Food, Drug, and Cosmetic Act does not require that these grades be stated on the labels, but if they are stated the product must comply with the specifications for the given grade.

Government grading service is available to any manufacturer who requests it and who pays the cost of the inspector's services.

Quality Grades. At present, quality grades have been established for meats, poultry, eggs, some dairy products, canned fruits and vegetables, and some fresh fruits and vegetables. Grades have also been established for grains but not for related food products such as flour or cereals. (For a complete explanation of the quality grades pertaining to each group, see Chapters 17, 18, 21, 24, and 26).

AGRICULTURAL RESEARCH SERVICE

The Agricultural Research Service is a division of the U.S. Department of Agriculture that develops ways of producing food and fiber and improves methods of marketing and processing food products. Research is conducted to find new methods of processing and storing food. Through the work of this department, such food products as frozen concentrated fruit juices, frozen dinners, dehydrated potatoes, and other vegetable products have been made available to the consumer. Patterns for these processes are made available to industry on a royalty-free basis. This department is also responsible for inspection of products at ports of entry in order to prevent the spread of foreign animal and plant diseases.

FOOD AND NUTRITION SERVICE

The Food and Nutrition Service is another agency of the U.S. Department of Agriculture. Its function is to eliminate hunger and malnutrition in the United States through the administration of the federal food programs. This agency provides money to help schools and other child-care institutions buy foods for breakfasts and lunches served to children. It also supplies foods to states for needy adults and children and provides food stamps to increase the food-buying power of low-income families.

EXTENSION SERVICE

The Extension Service is a division of the U.S. Department of Agriculture. State and county governments share with the federal government the financing, planning, and administration of this service. The Extension Service provides out-of-school programs for youth and adults in agriculture, home economics, and related subjects. Extension Service personnel reach the public through meetings, classes, publications, and newsletters. Much up-to-date information about food and nutrition is brought to large numbers of people through this service.

NATIONAL MARINE FISHERIES SERVICE

This branch of the U.S. Department of Commerce regulates grading standards for fish and fish products. Unlike the U.S. Department of Agriculture, these grades are not required by law to be displayed on the label. Fifteen grades have been established for frozen processed fishery products. These include such products as raw and headless shrimp; raw and fried scallops; cut fish sticks, steaks, and fillets; breaded and raw fish portions and sticks; and semiprocessed raw fish.

THE MEAT INSPECTION ACT

The Meat Inspection Act is enforced by the Meat Inspection Branch of the Bureau of Animal Industry, U.S. Department of Agriculture. It requires that all meat and meat products shipped over state lines or imported from abroad be packed under government license and after inspection as specified by the regulations.

THE POULTRY PRODUCTS INSPECTION ACT

The Poultry Products Inspection Act, also administered by the U.S. Department of Agriculture, requires inspection of all poultry moving in interstate commerce. The Poultry Products Act was amended in 1968 to become the Wholesome Poultry Products Act. It requires inspection of poultry products at least as good as federal inspection of all poultry whether or not it moves in interstate commerce. It provides assistance to states to improve the poultry inspection procedures.

As part of the enforcement of the Wholesome Poultry Products Act, inspectors insist on high standards of cleanliness and efficient equipment. Labels for poultry and poultry parts must be approved by inspectors, and adulterated products are removed from the market. Official tests are run on poultry products to guard against contamination.

EGG PRODUCTS INSPECTION ACT

The Egg Products Inspection Act of 1970, administered by the U.S. Department of Agriculture, provides mandatory continuous inspection of plants processing egg products whether shipping in interstate, intrastate, or foreign commerce.

GOVERNMENT PRINTING OFFICE

The Government Printing Office is set up to print materials for the Congress and other governmental departments. It furnishes government publications at minimum cost. About 27,000 titles are currently for sale. Many of these publications have to do with the production, distribution, and preparation of food.

FEDERAL TRADE COMMISSION

The Federal Trade Commission is an independent agency. The President appoints its five commissioners for a 7-year term. This agency fosters effective consumer protection at state and local levels, encourages a fair and competitive market by preventing price fixing and other unfair practices that are unfair to consumers or business, and prevents deceptive advertising, packaging, and selling. It investigates complaints of false advertising, oral misrepresentation, and misbranding. Of utmost importance in this respect is the fact that the Commission regards misleading advertising, misbranding, and the representing of secondhand or madeover products as new as false and unfair.

False or misleading advertising is sometimes encountered in the food industry. Exaggerated claims for a product may persuade a consumer to pay a high price for a relatively inexpensive food that has a minimum of the attributes claimed for it by the advertiser. If a complaint of this kind is made against a company and is proven valid after investigation, the Commission issues an order to the company to "cease and desist." If the company does not, the Commission appeals to the federal courts.

The Commission's jurisdiction is generally limited to companies that advertise and sell goods in interstate commerce; however, it works closely with state and local organizations.

THE U.S. PUBLIC HEALTH SERVICE

The U.S. Public Health Service is not an enforcement agency; its function is to make recommendations for the establishment of food ordinances by states and municipalities.

The principal function of the U.S. Public Health Service is to offer guidance and help to agencies directly concerned with protecting the health of the public. State and local agencies, private organizations, medical schools, and research institutions work with this agency to improve the health status of the nation. For example, all states now have milk and food sanitation programs that are based on the recommendations of the U.S. Public Health Service.

An important program carried on by this agency is the certification of interstate milk shippers, which enables milk-short areas to obtain milk of high sanitary quality from distant places. A similar program is in operation for the certification of interstate shippers of shellfish.

This program includes all the coastal states and Canada (by international agreement).

In addition to recommending sanitation codes and ordinances, the U.S. Public Health Service cooperates with local authorities to pinpoint the causes of foodborne diseases. The agency's Communicable Disease Center is prepared to investigate the circumstances surrounding the outbreak of food poisonings. Bacteriologists at the Center may identify the organisms in food that cause the illness and recommend ways of reducing or eliminating the source or sources of contamination.

The U.S. Public Health Service conducts research on toxic agents in foods and on chemical and radiological contaminants. One of the most recent investigations along these lines was a nationwide pilot study undertaken to determine the amount of radioactivity in milk.

The U.S. Public Health Service is also concerned with the effect of diet on health and to this end, conducts an extensive program of nutrition research.

NATIONAL BUREAU OF STANDARDS

The National Bureau of Standards, a unit in the Department of Commerce, provides technical assistance in establishing commodity measurement and performance standards. It also provides federal product safety standards provided by law and disseminates technical, scientific, and engineering information to the public and governmental agencies. The Bureau of Standards administers the Fair Packaging and Label Act. It promotes development of uniform laws regarding weights and measurements and cooperates with industry to eliminate unnecessary package sizes and shapes.

U.S. DEPARTMENT OF COMMERCE

This agency promulgates voluntary grades and standards for fish and shellfish as provided for in the Fish and Wildlife Act of 1956. Its criteria stress attributes relating to consumer acceptance, such as appearance and color, odor, presence of defects, and uniformity.

OFFICE OF TECHNICAL SERVICES

This agency, through its voluntary "Simplified Practices Recommendations" as one of its functions, attempts to avoid overdiversification by industry. They try to limit the types and sizes of packages used as milk containers, of cans for processed food, and of butter and margarine cartons. The Office of Technical Services has no regulatory function relating to food.

ENVIRONMENTAL PROTECTION AGENCY

The Environmental Protective Agency issues permits for the deliberate use of pesticides and other chemicals in the environment, including agriculture. It also establishes tolerances for pesticides in food. This agency may provide technical assistance to states.

INTERNAL REVENUE SERVICE

This agency coordinates with the FDA in the enforcement of federal laws pertaining to alcoholic beverages. It also establishes minimum and maximum alcohol content for whiskey, wine, and malt beverages.

CONSUMER PRODUCT SAFETY COMMISSION

This agency has the responsibility for the reduction of injuries associated with consumer products in or around the home, to assist consumers in evaluating the comparative safety of consumer products, and to promote research into the causes and prevention of product-related deaths, illnesses, and injury. The Consumer Product Safety Commission issues a series of fact sheets offering suggestions for the safe use and maintenance of kitchen appliances.

THE CONSUMER PRODUCT SAFETY ACT OF 1972

This act provided for the establishment of the Consumer Product Safety Commission.

STATE AND MUNICIPAL FOOD LAWS

States and cities have food laws that are modeled on federal laws or recommendations. Mainly, attention is given to the drawing up of ordinances for milk and milk products and providing inspection for fish, meat, and poultry (Figs. 42-4 and 42-5). State and community laws may be stricter than federal laws, but they are never more lenient. They usually make provision for inspection of food-handling operations and for the examination of foods, and they may include some recommendations for the examination of food handlers. State and municipal laboratories may be set up for the analysis of products under investigation.

State ordinances are also set up to ensure the wholesomeness of foods produced or manufactured and sold within the state, because federal agencies do not have jurisdiction over such foods. Because each state's problems of food production and consumption are unique, these laws are not uniform for all states. For example,

42-4 *Milk testing in a New York State Laboratory. (Courtesy of New York State Department of Agriculture and Markets)*

42-5 *Analyzing food in a New York State laboratory. (Courtesy of New York State Department of Agriculture and Markets)*

some states have special laws concerning the passage of food from one state to another. Mainly, these have to do with fruits and vegetables that are capable of harboring disease-carrying pests.

SUMMARY

To assure consumers wholesome food, protective laws have been enacted. Manufacturers and dealers are also protected against unfair competition. Initial "pure food" legislation was enacted in 1906. A second, stronger act—the Food, Drug, and Cosmetic Act—was passed in 1938 and amended in 1954 and 1958 to meet new conditions, such as food additives and pesticide residues.

The law prohibits deceptions; requires label statements; assures the safety of food containers, colors, and other additives; establishes the allowable residue of pesticides; limits the amount of deleterious matter that can be used in the manufacture of foodstuffs; prohibits in interstate commerce any food that is unsafe or injurious to health; and bans the sale of any contaminated or decomposed food as well as the flesh of a diseased

animal or an animal that died by other means than slaughter. False or misleading food labels and misleading food containers are also prohibited.

Standards of identity—including a minimum standard of quality, a definition as to what the food is or what the constituent parts must be, and a regulation on how full a given package must be—have been devised for certain foods and food products under the act. Establishment of additional standards of identity would be helpful to consumers.

Enforcement of the law is the main function of the Food and Drug Administration, but other governmental agencies also have a role in food wholesomeness and consumer protection. The U.S. Public Health Service makes recommendations for the establishment of food ordinances by states and municipalities. The Consumer and Marketing Service administers the Poultry Products Inspection Act and the Meat Inspection Act. The Federal Trade Commission prevents unfair competition and "policies" advertising and branding in the food industry.

State and city food laws are primarily concerned with milk and milk products, but they may also be drawn up to insure the safety of food manufactured and sold within the state.

QUESTIONS AND TOPICS FOR DISCUSSION AND STUDY

1. Do you believe that the protection offered by the present Food, Drug, and Cosmetic Act is adequate to assure the consumer safe, unadulterated food?
2. Discuss the advisability of setting up mandatory grades for all fresh and processed foodstuffs.
3. How do grades help consumers get the quality they want?
4. Could the additive amendment to the Pure Food, Drug, and Cosmetic Act be improved?

SUGGESTED ACTIVITIES

1. Make a collection of labels from processed foods: canned, frozen, and packaged. Analyze these labels and summarize the information found on them.

2. Sort out from the collection the labels that bear a seal of approval from various organizations. Do you believe that these seals are entirely reliable?

REFERENCES

Books

Consumers All: The Yearbook of Agriculture. Washington, D.C.: U.S. Department of Agriculture, 1964, pp. 429–431.

Food: The Yearbook of Agriculture. Washington, D.C.: U.S. Department of Agriculture, 1959, pp. 344–352.

Guide to Federal Consumer Services. Washington, D.C.: Office of Consumer Affairs, Government Printing Office, 1971.

Handbook for the Home: The Yearbook of Agriculture. Washington, D.C.: U.S. Department of Agriculture, 1973.

Shopper's Guide: The Yearbook of Agriculture. Washington, D.C.: U.S. Department of Agriculture, 1974.

Stewart, George, and Maynard Amerine. *Introduction to Food Science and Technology.* New York: Academic Press, 1973, Chap. 8.

Articles and Pamphlets

Code of Federal Regulations. Title 21—Foods and Drugs. Washington, D.C.: U.S. Department of Health, Education, and Welfare, Food and Drug Administration, rev. 1971, Parts 1–119.

Day, Paul. "Evaluating Food Products." *J. Amer. Dietet. Assoc.* **41:**97, 1962.

Federal Food, Drug, and Cosmetic Act. Washington, D.C.: U.S. Department of Health, Education, and Welfare, rev. 1970.

"How to Use USDA Grades in Buying Food." *Pa-708.* Washington. D.C.: U.S. Department of Agriculture, rev. 1967.

Food Additives

Man has added spices, preservatives, and flavoring agents to his food for thousands of years. The great exploration voyages of the past, including those of Magellan and Marco Polo, were often in pursuit of food additives. Food grown in the summer had to be stored and preserved in edible form for the winter. To preserve food or to improve its quality it was necessary to add substances, such as salt, sugar, and vinegar, to process the foods by salting, pickling, and drying.

Even today it is necessary to keep food fresh and edible until it is consumed. Without food additives bread would quickly stale and mold, salad dressings would separate, fruit juices would lose their vitamin potencies, fats and oils would turn rancid, and canned fruits and vegetables would lose their texture. The variety of foods presently available to consumers would markedly decrease and convenience foods would be nonexistent. It appears that heavy reliance on food additives will continue in the future.

A food additive is defined[1] as "a substance or mixture of substances, other than a basic foodstuff, which is present in food as a result of any aspect of production, processing, storage or packaging." This definition does not include any chemicals that are contaminants, pesticides, color additives, or new animal drugs.

The widespread use of food additives led to the 1958 Food Additives Amendment and the 1960 Color Additives Amendment, which are discussed in Chapter 42. These laws state that no food or color additive may be used in food unless the Food and Drug Administration has determined by scientific evaluation that they are safe at their intended level of use.

DELANEY CLAUSE

A controversial amendment known as the Delaney Clause was added to the 1958 Food Additives Amendment. It states that no food substance can be considered safe if it is found to produce cancer when fed to man or animals, or can be shown to induce cancer by any appropriate tests.

The purpose of the clause was good, in that it meant to protect consumers from eating carcinogenic agents. However, even common food additives such as sugar and salt have been shown

[1] Food Protection Committee, Food and Nutrition Board, "The Use of Chemicals in Food Production, Processing, Storage and Distribution," *Publication 887* (Washington, D.C.: National Research Council–National Academy of Sciences, 1961).

513

to induce cancer under special conditions. Cancer has also been induced from materials isolated from charred fats and meats. Should these substances therefore be banned from use as food additives?

Moreover, what exactly is an appropriate test? This is confusing, since we are still unclear about the causes of cancer. The Delaney Clause assumes that there is no threshold level for cancer and there must be a zero tolerance level for all known carcinogens. This is contrary to scientific evidence, which indicates that there are certain tolerance levels for producing cancer for particular substances. Should we ban a food ingredient completely if the potential toxicity of that substance is dependent on its level of use?

GRAS SUBSTANCES

An exemption to the legal requirement for proving safety of food additives are substances generally recognized as safe by qualified experts for their intended use. This group of substances comprise the GRAS (generally recognized as safe) list. This classification from the 1958 Food Additive Amendment was based on data derived from scientific evidence or from long-time common usage in foods prior to that time. There are approximately 560 substances that can be used in foods for humans, 108 compounds that can be used for food processing, and another 46 substances used in animal foods.

Typical GRAS substances include raw agricultural products; household spices, seasonings, and flavorings; baking powders; fruit and beverage acids such as citric and malic; and emulsifiers such as lecithin.

It may seem odd that a raw agricultural product would be classified as a food additive. If a potato is eaten as a vegetable, it is considered a food. However, if it is added to a soup or stew it becomes a component of another food and meets the definition of a food additive. Similarly, in eggs, the principal emulsifier, lecithin, is considered to be a food. If the emulsifier is isolated in its chemical form for ingredient addition purposes, it becomes a food additive.

The assumption that a food ingredient is safe because it has been used without harm for a long period of time does not have adequate scientific basis. Therefore, the Food and Drug Adminis-

tration is reviewing the safety of each of the GRAS substances. The safety of each substance will be determined from information based on past scientific studies, present consumer levels of use, and laboratory testing of toxicological effects on different species of animals.

If qualified experts conclude that the substance is still eligible for the GRAS list, it will be reclassified into one of three new GRAS categories[2]:

1. GRAS with no limitations as long as conditions of use are similar to those in which its original status was determined.
2. GRAS with specific limitations, such as food category, function, and use level.
3. GRAS for a specific purpose only.

In the case that the GRAS status of a food ingredient is not continued, its use must be curtailed or dependent on food additive regulation or subject to further study.

FOOD ADDITIVES AND THEIR USE

There is general agreement among scientists[3] that additives should not be used indiscriminately in foods. It has been suggested that the following guidelines be considered when an additive is to be used in a food product:

1. Additives should be used only to maintain the nutritional quality of food, to improve the keeping quality of food, to improve the appearance of food, or to provide aid in processing, packaging, or transporting the food product.
2. An additive is not justified if it reduces the nutritive value of a food, if it disguises faulty quality or processing and handling that is not allowed, if it deceives the customer, or if the desired effect can be got by other manufacturing processes that are economically and technologically satisfactory.
3. The smallest amount of additive should be used that will get the desired effect under good manufacturing practices. The additive used must conform to a standard of purity.

---

[2] Federal Register **41**:53600, 1976.
[3] Codex Alimentarius Commission of the Food and Agriculture Organization.

4. Additives should be subjected to adequate toxicological evaluation and should be kept under observation for possible deleterious effects.
5. The approval of an additive should be limited to specific foods for specific purposes under specific conditions.

As Added Nutrients. The number of foods that have nutrients added to them is steadily increasing. Ingredients added for nutritive value can be classified into four categories:

1. *Restoration.* The ingredients added are intended to restore the original nutritive value of the product which was lost through processing. For example, canned citrus fruits may have vitamin C added (Table 43-1).
2. *Enrichment.* The amounts added are designed to meet specific legal standards of minimum and maximum level of nutrients. It is recognized that in the processing of cereal products that the removal of the bran and germ causes a large portion of the vitamins and minerals naturally found in the product to be lost. During World War II, an effort was made to correct this deficiency by government endorsement of the enrichment of bread, flour, and cornmeal. Wheat flour, cornmeal, corn grits, bread, ready-to-eat and uncooked cereals, and macaroni products have been enriched with thiamin, riboflavin, niacin, iron, and in some cases, calcium and vitamin D.
3. *Fortification.* Ingredients not normally found in a food are added to achieve a particular dietary purpose. Lysine may be added to corn products to increase the biological value of the protein. Salt may be iodized to prevent the occurrence of goiter. Breakfast cereals may be fortified with an array of vitamins and minerals to ensure a completely balanced nutritional meal.
4. *Nutrification.* This is a new term describing foods manufactured by the food industry which may completely substitute for a common food or a complete meal. Doughnuts, cupcakes, potato chips, and other snack foods regarded to have a low nutrient density/calorie ratio may be nutrified to take the place of a nutritionally adequate meal. Critics of nutrification claim that although this does provide a source of nutrients for those who

live on these foods, it does not promote sound nutritional habits.

As Bleaching and Maturing Agents. Bleaching and maturing agents are extremely important to the flour-milling and bread-baking industries. Freshly milled flour, which is golden yellow in color, lacks the capacity to form an elastic, stable dough. For yeast breads this results in a "heavy" product. If the flour is allowed to age, it will oxidize, lose its color, and improve its baking performance. But natural aging takes time, and this creates higher prices, owing to storage costs and losses from insect and rodent damage. Chemicals such as chlorine dioxide, nitrosyl chloride, and chlorine speed up the natural aging and bleaching process. Bromates and iodates are used as dough conditioners since they oxidize the dough and improve its baking qualities.

Bleaching agents are also used in the manufacture of certain cheeses, such as blue and Gorgonzola cheese, to impart a white color. These cheeses have a yellow color because they are now made from cow's milk instead of the goat's milk that was originally used. The bleaching agent used may be benzoyl peroxide.

Tripe, a variety meat, is bleached with a solution of hydrogen peroxide.

As Acids, Alkalies, and Buffers. Additives used to control the acid–alkaline balance of food also add flavor and texture and improve its cooking properties. The right balance of acid is crucial in the manufacture of several dairy products. Excessive acidity that may have developed in cream is neutralized by the addition of an alkaline substance to control the flavor and keeping quality of butter. Citric acid, potassium citrate, and phosphoric acid are used in sherbets, carbonated beverages, and fruit drinks to intensify the flavor and tart taste. These same organic acids may be added to cheese spreads to impart a suggestion of tartness and to improve texture. Other acids commonly used are adipic, lactic, tartaric, and malic. Buffering agents used include sodium bicarbonate, calcium carbonate, hydrogen chloride, sodium citrate, sodium hydroxide, and calcium oxide.

Adding fumaric acid to egg whites will shorten the beating time for foam formation and

TABLE 43-1
Function and Food Uses of Some Common Food Additives

Food Additive	Function	Food-Use Example
Acetic acid	Buffer	Beverages, cereals
Adipic acid	Buffer	Candies
Agar-agar	Thickener	Ice cream, confections
Alginates	Thickener	Pie filling
Alphaionone	Color	Yellow colors
Amylopectin	Thickener	Dessert mixes
Amylose	Filming agent	Sausages
Benzaldehyde	Flavor	Cherry flavors
Butylated hydroxyanisole (BHA)	Antioxidant	Bakery products
Butylated hydroxytoluene (BHT)	Antioxidant	Breakfast cereals
Calcium chloride	Firming agent	Canned fruits
Calcium phosphate	Anticaking	Instant breakfast mixes
Calcium propionate	Preservative	Breads
Calcium silicate	Anticaking	Baking powder
Calcium stearate	Anticaking	Table salt
Capsaicin	Flavor	Hot sauces
Caramel	Color	Brown colors
Carboxymethylcelluose	Stabilizer	Salad dressings
Carotene	Color	Orange colors
Carrageenin	Thickener	Ice cream
Chlorine dioxide	Bleaching	Wheat flour
Citric acid	Acid	Butter
	Antioxidant	Prepared mixes
	Flavor	Beverages
Diglycerides	Emulsifier	Salad dressings
Disodium inosinate	Flavor	Chicken and beef flavors
Disodium phosphate	Emulsifier	Processed cheese
Ethyl butyrate	Flavor	Pineapple flavors
Ethylenediamine tetracetic acid (EDTA)	Sequesterant	Fats and oils
Fumaric acid	Leavening	Doughnuts
Furfuryl mercaptan	Flavor	Coffee flavors
Glyceryl lactopalmitate	Emulsifier	Cake mixes
Glyceryl monostearate	Humectant	Canned coconut
Glycerine	Humectant	Moist pet food
Glucanolactone	Leavening	Pizza dough
Hydrogen peroxide	Bleaching	White cheeses
Lactic acid	Acid	Cookies, beverages
Lecithin	Emulsifier	Chocolate, fats
Maltol	Flavor enhancer	Preserves, desserts
Methyl anthranilate	Flavor	Grape flavors
Methyl salicylate	Flavor	Wintergreen flavors
Monocalcium phosphate	Leavening	Baking powder
Monoglycerides	Emulsifier	Mayonnaise
Monosodium glutamate	Flavor enhancer	Frozen foods
Nitrate, nitrite	Preservative	Cured meats
	Color	Pink colors in luncheon meats
Parafilm	Surface finishing	Fruits
Pectin	Thickener	Preserves

TABLE 43-1 (Cont.)

Food Additive	Function	Food-Use Example
Phosphoric acid	Acid	Carbonated beverages
Polyoxylene sorbitan fatty acids (TWEENS)	Emulsifier	Cake mixes
Propylene glycol	Humectant	Toaster tarts
Silicon	Defoaming	Orange juice
Sodium aluminum sulfate	Leavening	Baking powder
Sodium benzoate	Preservative	Pancake syrup
Sodium bicarbonate	Leavening	Baking powder
Sodium caseinate	Foaming	Whipped cream
Sodium erythrobate	Color	Bacon
Sodium stearate	Anticaking	Garlic powder
Sorbic acid	Preservative	Cheese, pickles
Sorbitan fatty esters (SPANS)	Emulsifier	Cake
Tragacanth	Thickener	Salad dressings
Vitamin A	Nutritive	Margarine
Vitamin C	Antioxidant	Cereals
(ascorbic acid)	Nutritive	Fruit juices
Vitamin D	Nutritive	Milk
Vitamin E	Antioxidant	Oils
(α-tocopherol acetate)	Nutritive	Breads

increase the volume and stability. It will also reduce the curdling effect from overbeating.

As Preservatives. The purpose of using a chemical agent as a preservative is to retard food spoilage caused by microorganisms. The World Health Organization has estimated that approximately 20% of the world's food is lost by this type of spoilage. Partial prevention of this spoilage can be acheived through use of refrigeration, drying, freezing, fermenting, and curing. The use of chemical additives will prolong the life of the food even further.

Chemical preservatives interfere with the cell membranes of microorganisms, their enzyme activity, or their genetic mechanism.[4] Preservatives may also serve as antioxidants, as stabilizers, as firming agents, and as moisture retainers. Chemicals whose function is to preserve food are generally added after the food has been processed and before it is packaged.

The most frequently used inhibitors of microbial growth are table sugar (sucrose) and table salt (sodium chloride). Sugar is used in

[4] W. Frazier, *Food Microbiology* (New York: McGraw-Hill, 1967), p. 131.

making jellies, preserves, and cured hams. Salt is used in brines and in curing solutions, or is directly applied to the food. Their effect is to increase osmotic pressure, thereby causing the cells of microorganisms to dry up. Thus, the cell growth of the microorganism is inhibited or the organism itself may be completely destroyed. Salt also causes food dehydration by drawing out and tying up water from the tissue cells. Salt added to food also ionizes, yielding the chlorine ion, which is harmful to microorganisms, and interferes with the action of proteolytic enzymes. The more salt used, the greater the protection afforded the food.

Sulfur dioxide and sulfites may be added to such foods as dried fruits, fruit pulp and juices, and molasses. They conserve color, act as antioxidants, and control microbial growth and insect damage. Without sulfur, dried apricots would turn an unappetizing black color. When dried fruit is reconstituted by boiling in water, almost all the sulfur is vaporized.

Other fumigants used on dried fruits are ethyl formate, ethylene dioxide, and methyl bromide. These are sprayed on nuts and spices.

Sulfur dioxide is also used in the fermenting of wine since it is more toxic to molds and bacteria than to yeast. The concentration of sulfur dioxide in wine can be as high as 200 milligrams/0.5 liter.[5] The acceptable daily intake (the daily amount of a chemical additive that can be used without appreciable risk to man) is 1.5 milligrams/kg of body weight. This limiting amount is based on studies which have shown that sulfite limits the growth rate of rats, probably by destroying vitamin B_1. The relationship that this may have to man is still questionable.

Carbon dioxide under pressure has been used for preservative purposes. It is commonly found in carbonated soft drinks. Refrigerated biscuits that have carbon dioxide incorporated in the packaging process have a shelf life of several months.

Benzoic acid, found naturally in cranberries, and its salt, sodium benzoate, are used as effective agents against yeasts and molds. These chemicals are used in carbonated beverages, fruit juices and concentrates, margarine, and other acid foods, such as pickled vegetables. The use of benzoic acid has stimulated discussion, since large quantities have been shown to be poisonous. However, concentrations of 0.1% or less used over long periods of time has not been shown to produce ill effects. Therefore, its safety is dependent on the level of use. Ordinary table salt is another chemical that can be poisonous in large concentrations but innocuous in small quantities.

Mold inhibitors are important in the baking industry to control ropiness in bread. Calcium and sodium propionate, monocalcium phosphate, sodium diacetate, and acetic acid will keep baked goods free of mold for a period of time. Sorbic acid, a polyunsaturated acid, is effective in controlling molds in cheese, margarine, pickles, and pancake and waffle syrup. It is also added to beverages and semimoist pet foods.

Nitrate and nitrite (saltpeter) have been used as preservatives for meats for centuries. They are found in ham, bacon, bologna, hot dogs, and sausages. Their use at levels of 150–200 parts per million produces a cured meat flavor and helps stabilize the pink color (see Chapter 24). Without these curing agents, bacon becomes salt pork and ham is a heavily salted roast pork.

Nitrates prevent the growth of *Clostridium*

botulinum, microorganisms that secrete a deadly toxin. These microorganisms grow in anaerobic conditions, readily found in the interior of a ham or in meat that has been vacuum-packaged. However, it has been found that nitrite has the ability to react with amino acids (found in the proteins of meat) to form nitrosamines. These compounds have been reported to induce liver cancer in animals. Under certain high temperatures (as in frying) or acid conditions (in the stomach), nitrosamine formation may occur. Small amounts of nitrosamines, ranging from 0 to 20 parts per billion have been reported to form in cooked bacon and cured hams, depending on the method of cooking and the degree of doneness.[6,7]

Eliminating cured meats from the diet would not, however, completely eradicate the consumption of nitrates. This is because 60–65% of the nitrates consumed are produced in the mouth from residues in vegetables. Thus, we would have to completely ban all vegetables to eliminate nitrate consumption.

The United States Department of Agriculture recently ordered the use of smaller quantities of sodium or potassium nitrates as preservatives in bacon, and the inclusion of larger portions of sodium ascorbate to retain the botulism-fighting qualities of the nitrates. According to this regulation their use would be reduced to 120 parts per million by June 15, 1978, and to 40 parts per million by mid-May 1979.[8]

Antioxidants. Antioxidants are beneficial in preventing rancidity in fats and foods containing fats. Fats exposed to air, light, moisture, heat, or heavy metal ions become activated and oxidize (react with available oxygen) to peroxides. The energy from this transformation is transferred to other fat molecules, setting up a chain reaction. Antioxidants break this chain by taking up the energy. They are not effective if a substantial amount of peroxides have already formed. An-

---

[5] G. O. Kermode, "Food Additives," *Sci. Amer.* **266**:18, 1972.

[6] Committee on Nitrate Accumulation, National Research Council, *Accumulation of Nitrate* (Washington, D.C.: National Academy of Sciences, 1972), pp. 55, 67.

[7] Wasserman, A. E., J. W. Pensabene and E. G. Piotrowski, "Nitrosamine Formation in Home-Cooked Bacon, J. Food Sci., **43**:276, 1978.

[8] New York Times, May 15, 1978

tioxidants are found in fat-containing foods such as margarine, cooking oils, biscuits, potato chips, cereals, salted nuts, soup mixes, and precooked meals containing fish, poultry, or meat. If antioxidants are not used, the shelf life of breakfast cereals would be only 4 months instead of 1 year. The shelf life of a variety of cake mixes and other fat-containing foods would be much shorter, resulting in waste and higher costs.

The most used antioxidants are butylated hydroxyanisole (BHA), butylated hydroxytoluene (BHT), propyl gallate, and natural or synthetic tocopherols (vitamin E). The frequent use of BHA and BHT has raised concern as to their safety. Studies with primates at levels of up to 500 milligrams/kg of body weight have shown no clinical effects. To equate this amount to the food consumption of man, it would mean a fat intake of 1100 lb/day.

Antioxidants delay enzymatic browning in fruits and vegetables that have been exposed to air by peeling, cutting, or grinding. Ascorbic and isoascorbic acids are used in preventing discoloration of certain fruit juices, soft drinks, canned vegetables, frozen fruits, and cooked cured meats such as ham. Acids such as citric and phosphoric act synergistically with ascorbic acid and thus are used in combination to increase their antioxidant effect.

As Leavening Agents. Chemical leavening agents are used to produce a variety of light cakes, biscuits, muffins, waffles, and doughnuts. The lightness and volume achieved in these products is the result of a chemical reaction in which carbon dioxide is liberated from sodium bicarbonate (baking soda) (see Chapter 31). Hydrochloric acid and lactic acid may be added to generate carbon dioxide, in addition. In preleavened cake mixes in which milk may be added by the consumer, acid salts are added to avoid a soapy taste that would result if insufficient quantities of lactic acid are present in the milk.

In commercial baking, batters must wait their turns for the oven, and the gas would be lost before they were baked if specially formulated baking powders were not used. These double-acting baking powders may include baking soda, sodium aluminum sulfate, sodium acid pyrophosphate, potassium acid tartrate, and monocalcium phosphate.

Glucano-delta-lactone (GDL) is another leavening agent that may be used in conjunction with sodium bicarbonate. It substitutes for the leavening action of yeast in doughnuts and pizza. Using this combination will release the carbon dioxide immediately, reducing the fermentation time as much as 70%. The disadvantage of this process is the lack of the customary flavor of yeast.

Color Additives. The acceptance of a food product is determined largely by its appearance. Consumers become accustomed to standardized colors in familiar foods and base their purchasing habits on past experiences. Green hot dogs or blue bread displayed in a supermarket would not find many buyers. To improve the color of foods, colorants are added to carbonated beverages, frozen desserts, gelatin desserts and puddings, maraschino cherries, meat casings, prepared mixes, and some dairy and baked products.

Food colors can also be used to mask undesirable colors or inferior products. This is illustrated in Florida oranges, which naturally may be a mottled green or brown-streaked color when ready to be picked. California oranges, in contrast, are naturally orange in color when ripe. To be able to compete with California oranges in the market, Florida oranges may be colored orange synthetically and stamped "artificially colored" or "color added." The coloring of the oranges would not be necessary if consumers would eat green oranges, but this is not the case. Therefore, the Food and Drug Administration permits the coloring with the stipulation that only ripe oranges be used. The possibility does exist, however, that unripe or damaged oranges may be included in the coloring process intentionally or accidently.

There are two types of coloring agents used for foods: natural and synthetic (Table 43-2). Natural food colors are extracted from foods, insects, seeds, and flowers. Annatto, a yellow to peach color, is frequently used in butter, buttermilk, and cheese. It is obtained from bixin, found in the pulp surrounding the seeds of the lipstick pod plant. *Bixia orellana.* Another yellow color, carotene, derived from carrots, is used in margarine. However, annatto has much more stability and 5 times its potency. American saffron is another natural yellow color used to color meat products. Turmeric, a herb that gives

TABLE 43-2
Artificial Colors on the Food and Drug Administration Provisional Certified Color List

Color	Restriction	Common Name	Permanent List
Citrus Red No. 2	2 ppm on skin of oranges	—	Yes
FD&C Blue No. 1	—	Brilliant Blue	Yes
FD&C Blue No. 2	—	Indigotene	No
FD&C Green No. 3	—	Fast Green	No
FD&C Red No. 3	—	Erythrosine	Yes
FD&C Red No. 4	150 ppm in maraschino cherries	Ponceau	Yes
FD&C Red No. 40	—	—	Yes
FD&C Yellow No. 5	Must be labeled by name	Tartrazine	Yes
FD&C Yellow No. 6	—	Sweet Yellow	No
Orange B	150 ppm in sausage casing	—	No

curry its characteristic yellow color, is also used in meat products, as well as in salad dressings.

A brown color, caramel, is obtained from burnt sugar. Cochineal is a red color derived from carminic acid, which is extracted from dried insects (*Coccus catti*).

Synthetic or artificial colors have been implicated as being hazardous since many are part of the coal-tar colors. However, most artificial colors can now be synthesized without coal tar as a basis. Synthetic colors are less expensive than natural ones, uniform, extremely potent, and remain stable to high processing temperatures, acids, carbon dioxide, and storage.

Two widely used colors in our food products have been banned by the Food and Drug Administration. In 1973, Violet No. 1, used for stamping grades on meat carcass, was withdrawn from the provisional certified color listing because of Japanese studies reporting that 5% levels in the diet were carcinogenic. However, reevaluation of the studies have shown that the test animals had contracted pneumonia and were taking large doses of antibiotics.

In 1975, the basic red color FD & C Red No. 2, with sales of over $3 million per year, was also withdrawn. This ban was based on Russian studies which fed 3% levels to rats, which had no increase in the number of tumors developed but did have more malignancy in those tumors that did occur. There were three major criticisms of these studies. The first was that the animals from the different groups were mixed up and only 80 of the original 500 animals were used. The second criticism was that the amount of coloring in the diet was equal to drinking 15,000 twelve-ounce cans of a carbonated beverage. The last criticism was the long-term testing of up to 7 years which had been conducted by the Food and Drug Administration and other groups which showed no ill effects. The Canadian government, confronted with the same studies, did not withdraw the colorant.

If the food industry is willing to go through the expense of long-term testing, it is possible that these colors may someday be used again.

Flavor Additives. The flavoring agents commonly used are alcohol, esters, ethers, aldehydes, and ketones. Natural spices, protein hydrolysates, and monosodium glutamate are used chiefly in meat products. Many flavoring agents are volatile and are partially lost during processing. Natural food flavors are rarely used because the methods required to obtain the necessary amounts are expensive. In addition, they are not uniform in flavor, quality, or chemical composition and their availability is dependent on the season.

If the demand for flavoring agents in our food supply is to be met, artificial flavorings become a necessity. Suppose that a manufacturer wanted to produce banana ice cream; it would take 5 tons of bananas just to extract 1 pint of banana oil. It would be much easier, as well as cheaper, to use the synthetic banana flavor, amyl acetate.

The consumption of strawberry-flavored products is double the amount of strawberries produced in the fields. We are able to manufacture so many strawberry-flavored products through the use of alphaione, the principal artificial strawberry flavor. The production of grape-flavored products is equal to 5 times the natural flavor available from the U.S. production of Concord grapes. Manufacturers instead rely on methyl anthranilate, a synthetic Concord grape flavor. Similarly, there are simply not enough vanilla beans grown in the entire world to supply all our vanilla-flavored products.

A few of the other synthetic flavors that substitute for natural ones are anethol for anise (licorice), alphaione for raspberry, cinnamaldehyde for cinnamon, allyl caproate for pineapple, and carvone for mint.

Flavors outnumber any of the other food additives. There are approximately 1400 natural and synthetic flavors available, and their use constitutes a large regulatory problem. Many natural flavorings have been used for centuries, and not too much is known about their safety because custom has established their use in cooking and they are without apparent harmful effects.

It is difficult to establish zero risk levels since a particular flavor may be composed of hundreds of compounds which are present in extremely small quantities. Coffee flavor, for example, has been determined to have over 400 separate components, some in quantities of less than 1 part per million. Many of these chemical components (acetone, ammonia diethyl ketone) would be deadly in larger concentrations. Thus, it is the concentration of flavoring compounds rather than their presence which determines possible hazards.

An important group of flavor additives are the *flavor enhancers* or *flavor potentiators*. Some of the foods to which they are added are canned soups, chili, sauces, stews, meat products, and frozen products.

The most common flavor enhancer is monosodium glutamate (MSG), the salt of the nonessential amino acid glutamate. It is commonly found in vegetables, but 50% may be lost within 24 hours of harvest.[9] This may account for the rapid flavor deterioration of vegetables after they are picked.

Although it has no flavor of its own, MSG is able to intensify flavor in foods to which it has been added. The high MSG content of fresh mushrooms and carrots is probably the reason they are so commonly added to soups and stews for flavor.

Monosodium glutamate has been used for centuries by the Chinese, who extracted it from seaweed and soybeans. It is still used in large quantities in Oriental cooking. Some people are quite sensitive to it and within a half-hour of eating it develop a severe headache and dizziness, known as Chinese Restaurant Syndrome.

A few years ago it was reported that large doses caused damage to the central nervous system of immature mice. This prompted careful review by the National Academy of Sciences, which concluded that this observation was irrelevant since the research was done with injections under the skin rather than oral administration. The review reaffirmed its safety but recommended that MSG be eliminated from baby food since it served no purpose other than to please the mother's taste. Baby food manufacturers have voluntarily complied with this recommendation.

Maltol is another flavor enhancer which can make sweet flavors sweeter. It is naturally found in pine needles, chicory, roasted malt, and wood tars and oils. It is used extensively to intensify or modify the flavor of desserts, fruit juices, soft drinks, and preserves. Other flavor enhancers may be found in substances known as the 5'-nucleotides, including 5'-guanylate and 5'-inosinate.

Flavor enhancers are becoming more important with the increase of synthetic foods. The most widely sold simulated foods are meat substitutes made from spun soybean proteins or proteins from other vegetables. With the addition of flavors, colors, vitamins, emulsifiers, acidifying agents, and preservatives, these proteins are manufactured to sell as "steaks" and "bacon bits." Other simulated foods are substitute dairy products and flavored drinks made to simulate fruit juice. Simulated foods are part of the future and as such will require careful monitoring of labeling of ingredients to protect the consumer's interest.

Emulsifiers. Emulsifiers allow molecules that are mutually antagonistic (water and oil) to mix

---

[9] *The Remarkable Story of Monosodium Glutamate* (Washington, D.C.: International Glutamate Technical Commission, 1974).

together. They also improve the texture, volume, and body of baked goods by maintaining an even distribution of ingredients. Without emulsifiers, puddings and salad dressings would separate, shortening would look like oily lard, and milk substitutes would not exist. The paprika and mustard added to vinegar and oil in creating a French dressing are examples of common emulsifiers. Others include monoglycerides, digycerides, disodium phosphate, and calcium salts of fatty acids.

One of the most widely used emulsifiers, lecithin, is naturally found in milk, eggs, and soybeans. Since the form found in milk is easily rendered ineffective by processing, most commercial lecithin is derived from vegetable sources. In combination with glyceryl monostearate and ascorbic acid, lecithin is synergistic (even more effective). An important use of lecithin is to retard "bloom," the separation of the coca butter, in chocolate candy. It is also used in salad dressings, margarine, ice cream, and fermented bread products.

Synthetic emulsifiers used include polysorbate 80 and polysorbate 60 in combination with sorbitan monopalmitate. These are found in whipped vegetable toppings, pie fillings, milk substitutes, dough conditioners, and frozen desserts.

Stabilizers and Thickeners. Stabilizers and thickeners have the ability in water to swell, gel, and thicken. They create a smooth, uniform consistency with body and texture. They have created the existence of such convenience products as packaged sauces, salad dressings, and pudding mixes. The foam in beer, the body of salad dressings, the clarity of wine, and the stability of whipped toppings can be attributed to these additives.

Many of these substances are naturally derived. Examples are pectin, gelatin, and vegetable gums from trees, including acacia, ghatti, karaya, arabinogalactan, and tragacanth. Other stabilizers of importance are derived from seaweed (agar, algin, carrageenan), seeds (guar, locust bean), starch (dextran), and cellulose (carboxymethylcellulose). Cellulose derivatives when added to food provide bulk without adding calories. This will have important uses for diet foods in the future. Bread is a food item that can have cellulose added for bulk.

Sequesterants. Sequesterants or chelating agents are chemicals added to food to bind metals, such as calcium, iron, and copper. When the metals are bound to the chelator and no longer in an ionized form, oxidative changes, such as staleness, rancidity, and off-flavors, are prevented from developing. This is important in fruit juices, canned seafood, milk, and salad dressings. Sequesterants are frequently used to clarify wine and other beverages of minerals.

The most important sequesterant to the fat and oil industry is the sodium salt of ethylenediaminetetraacetic acid (EDTA). Polyphosphates, phytates, and sorbitol are other sequesterants. Sodium acid pyrophosphate (SAPP) is added to cooked potatoes to retard the darkening caused by iron precipitation with tannins.

Humectants. The additives that prevent food from drying out—such as glycerine, sorbitol, glycerol monostearate, and mannitol—are called *humectants* and are used in such foods as canned coconut and marshmallows to help retain moisture. Starch and calcium silicates are added to baking powder as anticaking materials. Table and seasoned salts and powders are kept free flowing by the addition of aluminum calcium silicate, and calcium, magnesium, or tricalcium silicate. Calcium phosphates are added to instant breakfast drinks and dry fruit mixes for this purpose. Calcium salts are frequently added to fruits and vegetables during processing to impart a firm quality. Pickles, maraschino cherries, and canned peas, tomatoes, potatoes, and apples are the chief foods in which firming agents are used.

Others. Certain organic substances may be used to give luster to foods that are naturally dull. Shellac, waxes (beeswax), and paraffin are used for this purpose.

In foods that are susceptible to excess foaming during processing, such as orange and pineapple juice, a silicone effectively prevents this action. Nitrogen, carbon dioxide, and nitrous oxide may be used in pressure-packed cans of food to act as whipping agents or propellants.

ADDITIVES IN ANIMAL FEEDS

Antibiotics. Eighty percent of the feed used in animal and poultry production in the United

States has antibiotics added to it.[10] A few grams of antibiotics in a ton of feed will cause a remarkable increase in the growth of the animals. The antibiotics function by reducing the slight but debilitating effects of diarrhea and minor infections found in the high-density production of livestock. Use of drugs in small concentrations enables a farmer to produce less expensive meat and poultry. It has been estimated by the U.S. Department of Agriculture that a ban on antibiotics in animal feeds would cost the consumer $2.1 billion annually in higher meat bills.

A number of antibiotics have been extensively tested on raw meats, fish, and poultry, as well as on other foods. Chlortetracycline (aureomycin), streptomycin, and tylosin were among the most effective antibiotics tested.

Medicated feeds must be withdrawn prior to slaughter, but some antibiotic residues may still occur in trace amounts. These residues are normally destroyed by cooking. Any milk, meat, or eggs that have residues over tolerance limits may not be legally shipped interstate.

The use of antibiotics in preserving food has both economy and simplicity to recommend it, however, there is reluctance to approve them widely for use in food. This is because antibiotics are highly valued human medicines that must be used with care; they have the property of killing dangerous pathogenic organisms, but, unfortunately, sometimes mutant strains of pathogens develop that are resistant to the antibiotic used. For this reason the Food and Drug Administration has banned chloramphenicol, semisynthetic penicillin, gentamicin, and kanamycin for use in animal feeds.[11]

It is still unknown whether minute amounts of antibiotics will cause resistant strains to develop. This is questionable, since antibiotics have been used for over 25 years and still retain their growth-promoting qualities in the same species of livestock.

Hormones. DES (diethylstilbesterol) is a synthetic female hormone (estrogen) which is used in animal feed to increase its efficiency. It enables the animal to convert a larger percentage of its feed into protein, thereby reducing the cost of meat production.

Until 1972, DES was used as a drug for animal feed as long as it was withdrawn at a specified time prior to slaughter. If the withdrawal was carried out properly, no detectable residues remained in the meat.

It was discovered in 1971 that some young women with cervical cancer had had mothers whom had been given large doses of DES (125 milligrams/day) to prevent miscarriages. The Food and Drug Administration became interested when a new radioactive tracer method was able to detect DES in concentrations of 0.12 part per billion in the livers of some cattle.[12] To equal the amount given the pregnant women would mean the consumption of over 50 tons of beef liver daily. A ban on DES was instituted in 1972 but later revoked because of protests from farmers. A compromise was reached in which farmers were allowed to implant ear pellets or feed DES as long as it was withdrawn 14 days prior to slaughter. A controversy regarding its benefits in terms of reduced cattle feed versus its potential carcinogenicity still exists.

NONNUTRITIVE SWEETENERS

Currently, artificial sweeteners (Table 43-3) are not listed among the additives approved for use in foods by the U.S. Food and Drug Administration. The three major sweeteners that have been used in this century, Dulcin, cyclamates, and saccharin, have been banned because studies have implicated their possible carcinogenicity. Criticism of the testing of cyclamates and saccharin may pressure the Food and Drug Administration to reevaluate the validity of the studies. It is tentatively proposed that saccharin be available only in drug stores as an over-the-counter (OTC) drug. The future of cyclamates is unknown.

Possible alternative sweeteners in the future may be neohesperidin dihydrochalcone, extracted from Seville orange peel; naragen dihydrochalcone, extracted from grapefruit peel; aspartyl phenylalanine methyl ester, formed

[10] FDA Consumer Memo, "Antibiotics and the Food You Eat," *DHEW Publication (FDA) 74–6011* (Washington, D.C.: U.S. Department of Commerce, 1974).
[11] *The Wall Street Journal,* June 6, 1975, p. 14.

[12] T. H. Jukes, "Estrogens in Beefsteaks," *J. Amer. Med. Assoc.* **229:**1920, 1974.

TABLE 43-3
The Relative Potency of Nonnutritive Sweeteners

Sweetener	Source	Relative Potency
Sucrose	Sugar cane	1
	Sugar beets	
Cyclamates	Sulfamide derivative	30
Aspartyl phenylalanine methyl esters	Amino acids	100
Naragen dihydrochalcone	Grapefruit peel	100
Saccharin	Oxidation of toluene	300–500
Neohesperidin dihydrochalcone	Seville orange peel	1500

from the amino acids phenylalanine and aspartic acid; and a protein derived from the African food Miracle Fruit. Their use will depend on the results of testing for toxicity and cancer–causing potential.

AVERAGE INTAKE

It has been estimated that the annual per capita consumption of food additives is 139 lb.[13] It may sound frightening that we are putting so many chemicals into our bodies. But if the total amount is broken down into specific types of chemicals, it creates less alarm (Fig. 43-1). It is surprising to many people to realize that the food additive that is consumed in greatest abundance is sugar (an average of 102 lb/year). Next in popularity is ordinary table salt, of which we use 15 lb/year. This is followed by consumption of 12 lb of corn sweeteners per year. If these totals are subtracted from 139 pounds there is only 10 pounds left for the other 1830 food additives that are consumed.

Nine pounds of the 1830 remaining additives are composed of 33 common food ingredients, such as yeast, mustard, black pepper, lecithin, modified starch, monosodium glutamate, and citric acid.[14] There is now left only 1 pound to be distributed among 1800 compounds. The average consumption of these chemicals is ½ milligram/year or the approximate weight of one grain of table salt.

[13]*Chemicals and Health,* Report on the Panel on Chemicals and Health of the President's Advisory Committee, September 1973.
[14]R. L. Hall, "Food Additives," *Nutrition Today* **9**:20, 1973.

While it is reassuring to realize that the consumption of so many food additives is so very small, we still must continually be cautious about possible long-term toxic effects.

SAFETY

Public interest in food additives has raised concern over their safety. But there is no way to prove that anything is absolutely safe for all purposes. An additive can only be evaluated for its hazards in its intended use.

Testing For Safety. It is very difficult to test the safety of an additive for human beings. To determine whether an additive is absolutely safe, it would have to be tested by people of all ages in specified amounts over a long period. This is impossible to do, so animals are used to test the effects of an additive. The testing procedures involving animals require at least 4–5 years of research at a cost of $0.5–10 million. This cost and time would be increased even more if testing were conducted on massive numbers of animals. Instead, the minimum number of animals that can determine statistical significance for a population are given doses in much larger quantities than human beings would consume. This procedure allows the toxic effect of a substance, if there is any, to be readily seen at a minimum of expense and time.

The first phase of toxicity testing determines the acute toxicity, the effect a single dose will have on two or more species of animals. Different dose levels are tried until one is found that kills 50% of the animals within 1 week (LD_{50}). The LD_{50} is compared with the amount of additive needed to be effective in food. If it is less

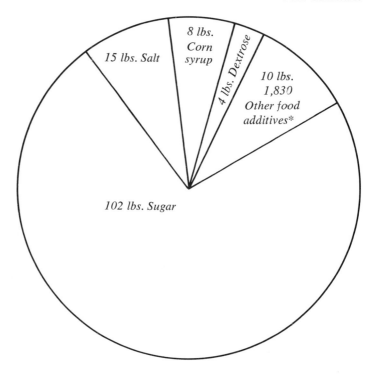

15 lbs. Salt

8 lbs. Corn syrup

4 lbs. Dextrose

10 lbs. 1,830 Other food additives*

102 lbs. Sugar

43-1 *The annual intake of food additives. (* Nine pounds of the 1,830 other food additives are composed of common food ingredients such as yeast, mustard, black pepper, lecithin, modified starch, monosodium glutamate, and citric acid.)*

than the amount needed, the second stage of testing begins.

A short–term toxicity study using two species of animals is conducted. The animals are given three dose levels less than the LD_{50} for 90 days and examined weekly for physiological and biochemical changes. Complete autopsy as well as histological examinations are made on the animals at the termination of the study. The dose level just below any adverse physiological effects that are found is called the *no effect dose* (NED) or *minimum effect dose* (MED). The NED is then divided by 100 to get the acceptable daily intake (ADI), the minimum level allowed for human consumption.

The third phase involves long–term testing of 2 years or more with doses levels between 10 and 50 times the ADI in milligrams per kilogram body weight. The animals are observed for long-term effects on their life span and for changes in fertility, mutations, or birth defects.

If an additive meets the criteria for safety as determined by this testing procedure, the food manufacturer may petition the Food and Drug Administration for acceptance. The petition is published in the *Federal Register* and written opinions are solicited. An average of three new food additives are approved in this manner each year.

Benefits Versus Risk. There does not exist any food additive that is not without some risk, or capable of producing a toxic effect at some level in the diet. Even innocuous table salt in large enough doses can be lethal. The benefits to be obtained from a particular food additive must be weighed against its possible hazards.

How do the benefits of food additives— increased shelf life, quality, and nutritive value—compare with possible harmful effects? The addition of nitrates to cured meats is an excellent example of the uncertainty regarding risk vs. benefits. Nitrates have been used for centuries to cure meats, not only for their flavor but because they prolong the useful life of the product and, even more important, prevent the growth of *Clostridium botulinum*. To prevent the paralysis and death that may result from consumption of these microorganisms is indeed a benefit for mankind. However, there is the possibility that under certain cooking conditions, nitrosamines, which are carcinogenic, may be formed. Is the risk of even one person getting cancer in several hundred years worth the preservative effect of curing meats? This is a difficult, emotional question to answer and indicates why most people, including even scientists, are unable to agree regarding food additives.

FUTURE TRENDS

It may be possible through research in polymer chemistry to create food additives that are indigestible. Scientists are working on attaching large inert polymers to food additives so they will not be absorbed in the intestine. The problem to be solved is to create a permanently bound additive that is not affected by the attached polymer and still retains its properties and functional capabilities.

If the market continues to offer the kind and variety of food products that now exist, it is likely that food additives will also continue to grow as an important part of the food industry. Many food products cannot be offered in their present form without additives. It is true that additives are not always used with beneficial results and are not always essential items in the manufacture of food products. Moreover, chronic ingestion over a life span could have serious health risks, which are still unknown. The Food and Drug Administration is continuously reviewing the safety and status of food additives and imposing increasingly stringent regulations. In the future it is likely that the number of additives allowed in foods will markedly decrease. Hopefully, only those additives that are necessary for the quality and preservation of food and have been found by intensive scientific research to be without risk for human health will be present in our food supply.

SUMMARY

Use of chemicals in the form of additives is a significant continuing development in modern food processing. Additives are used in food to increase nutritive value; to improve storage life and cooking or baking qualities; to enhance color, flavor, and texture; and to delay spoilage.

The Delaney Clause prohibits the use of any food additive if it has been found to produce cancer in man or animals. Substances on the GRAS (generally recognized as safe) list are not subject to food additive regulation.

Initiated several decades ago, enrichment of foods continues to grow, and each year more and more foods have nutrients added to them. Chemicals may be used to bleach foods such as flour, certain cheeses, and tripe; to control acid–alkaline balance, as in dairy products, and thus improve texture and flavor; as preservatives and curing agents for meats; as color conservers in dried fruits; and as leavening agents in flour mixtures.

Additives may be used to improve or maintain desirable color, taste, texture, and odor. Both natural and synthetic colors are subjected to federal testing and must be certified for harmlessness before use.

The food additives used most frequently are artificial flavoring agents. Other additives used include antioxidants, sequestrants, emulsifiers, humectants, and antibiotics.

Federal law requires that the safety of a food additive be established prior to its use. The procedure for testing the safety of food additives includes acute toxicity tests and short-term and long-term tests. The acceptable daily intake is the minimum level allowed for human consumption. Potential risks of a food additive must be weighed against its possible benefits when determining its use.

QUESTIONS AND TOPICS FOR DISCUSSION AND STUDY

1. What kinds of additives are commonly used in foods?
2. How does the use of additives in foods benefit the consumer?
3. How do additives benefit the food industry?
4. Discuss the question: Are additives safe? Give reasons for your answer.
5. Observe the labels on various packaged products. List the additives used and determine their function.

REFERENCES

Books

Bernarde, Melvin. *The Chemicals We Eat.* New York: McGraw-Hill, 1975.

Church, Charles, and Helen Church. *Food Values of Portions Commonly Used*. New York: Lippincott, 1975, pp. 152–178.

Fennema, Owen. *Food Chemistry*. New York: Marcel Dekker, 1976, Chaps. 9, 10, 11.

Frazier, William. *Food Microbiology*. New York: McGraw-Hill, 1967, Chap. 9.

Furia, Thomas. *Handbook of Food Additives*. Columbus, Ohio: Chemical Rubber, 1968.

LaBuza, Theodore, ed. *Food and Your Well-Being*. New York: West, 1977, Chaps. 21, 25, 26.

Packard, Vernal, Jr. *Processed Foods and the Consumer*. Minneapolis, Minn.: University of Minnesota Press, 1976.

PAMPHLETS

"A Primer on Food Additives." *FDA Consumer 74-2002*. Washington, D.C.: U.S. Department of Health, Education, and Welfare, 1973.

Evaluating the Safety of Food Chemicals. Washington, D.C.: National Academy of Sciences, 1970.

"Evaluation of Certain Food Additives," *WHO Technical Report Series No. 599*. Rome: Food and Agriculture Organ. United Nations, 1976.

"Food Additives and Food Safety." *Nutrition Education Resource Series 10*. Berkeley, Calif.: Society for Nutrition Education, 1975.

The Use of Chemicals in Food Production, Processing, Storage, and Distribution. Washington, D.C.: National Academy of Sciences, 1973.

Today's Food and Additives. Minneapolis, Minn.: General Foods, 1976.

Food Packaging

The packaging of food developed as a result of the factory production of specialized foods. With food to be transported from one place to another, a system was evolved whereby the product could be stored for a period of time and be protected from dirt and infestation by insects and rodents in order to meet consumer demands for high standards of sanitation and quality.

The packaging of food protects it from exposure to air, dust, and dirty surfaces; once the food is put into the package in the factory, it is not touched again until it reaches the home. And from the time the package leaves the processing plant until it arrives in the home, it is usually capable of withstanding thermal changes, humidity variations, and all manner of handling.

The long distances that foods must be transported today necessitates that the package not only protect the food from dirt and contamination but also help preserve its freshness and flavor. Considerable research goes into the design of a package which has the ability to retain the moisture, flavor, and aroma of a food product. To ensure adequate protection, packaging materials are frequently subjected to tests of tensile strength, bursting strength, folding endurance,

and resistance to grease, oil, temperature variations, and sunlight.

Of practical importance to both consumer and seller is the convenience that the package affords. The retailer requires a package that is easy to stack and store and will generate impulse buying. More important to the consumer is the availability of a wide range of fruits, vegetables, seafoods, and many other foods at any season of the year. Frozen TV dinners, desserts, orange juice, and appetizers, as well as canned stews and meat products and dried soups and sauces, are convenience foods that exist solely as a result of modern technology and packaging.

TYPES OF RIGID AND SEMIRIGID PACKAGING

The types of containers that were used in food packaging and distribution in the 1800s were limited to a few varieties of wooden boxes, casks, barrels, and burlap bags. These packages were gradually eliminated as paper wrappings, waxed paper, cardboard boxes, and tin cans were introduced. Since 1970 paper packaging has distinctly decreased because of the substitution of foils, laminates, and plastic materials such as high- and low-density polythenes.[1] Tin cans have been replaced by tin-coated steel cans and, more recently, by aluminum drawn and ironed (D & I) cans.

Glass Containers. Glass is widely used for packaging fruits, vegetables, and beverages. It can be produced in a wide variety of shapes which are strong and rigid at a low cost. Since glass is chemically inert, foods do not significantly deteriorate with age. Although its transparency is an advantage to the consumer, ultraviolet light, which passes through clear glass, accelerates biochemical oxidations and color-degradation reactions. These light-catalyzed reactions can be eliminated if the glass is colored amber, as in the case of cooking oils and beer bottles.

The major disadvantages of glass containers is their heavy weight and fragility. Recent advances in glass manufacturing have been made in the area of lightweighting, lower trippage, and encapsulating the containers in plastics or a foam shield.

Increasing concern over the environment has led to some legislation outlawing the nonreturnable bottle. Glass manufacturers have resisted this trend because of problems of breakage, economics, and safety. To be profitable, returnable bottles must make at least eight trips from the store to the home and back again. Safety is another important consideration. What do you do if someone has used the bottle as a storage container for kerosene? Since it is nearly impossible to completely sanitize today's refillable bottle, it has been suggested that it might be better to simply recycle the glass rather than reuse the bottle.[2]

Metal Containers. The most common metal container is the tin-plate (TP) can, which is made of three pieces of electrolytically tin-plated steel. The metal can is chiefly used for fruits, vegetables, and fruit and vegetable juices. Most of the cans used are cylindrical, but they come in a variety of other shapes and sizes. The cylindrical shape is most popular because it best resists internal and external strains. One of the oldest packaging materials used, the metal can is still considered to have many advantages—a chief one being its suitability for hermetic, vacuum, and gas packaging. The inside of the body and the two ends must be coated with a thin layer of polymeric lining to protect against possible rust formation or chemical action after the can has been sealed. An additional coating is placed on the side seam after it has been soldered to prevent the possibility of lead migration. A third very thin acrylic coating may also be applied to the exterior to help protect against scratches, offset, aging, and handling.

Tin-free steel (TFS) cans are appearing on the market as a result of the increasingly high cost of tin.[3] These are made of two pieces of coiled, coated steel. The body of the can is formed by drawing the coated steel into a cuplike shape, then redrawing it through dies to reduce the diameter and increase the length of the sides. After this process, a layer of enamel is sprayed inside the can to protect the future food product from the steel. Lacquer is also applied to the external surface for protection. Easy-open aluminum ends with chromium are used in place of tin ends. The TFS can has the advantage of a lower cost, reduced weight, and better integrity, because of the absence of a side seam.

Aluminum cans, used chiefly for beverages, snack foods, and desserts, are manufactured by a similar process. A blank disk of aluminum is drawn into a tumbler and ironed to the standard size. Coatings are applied both internally and externally. A second piece of aluminum is used to form the top of this lightweight drawn and ironed (D & I) aluminum can.

Furthermore, a variety of closures can be used on metal containers. The ordinary can containing fruits or vegetables has hermetically closed ends, syrup containers have metal friction tops, spice or baking powder containers have slide covers, and some products are packed in metal containers with hinged tops.

Boxes and Cartons. Rigid paper containers can be constructed by winding paper into multiple

---

[1] F. A. Paine, "Trends in Food Packaging, Part 2," *Nutr. Food Sci.* **37**:20, 1974.

[2] "Upheaval in Beverage Packaging," *Pack. Dig.* **14**(11):21, 1977.

[3] "Breakthrough in Tin-free Steel Food Cans," *Pack. Dig.* **15**(2):34, 1978.

layers. The paper containers can be the "set–up" variety or composites. Set-up containers have patterns with reinforced corners and adhesive. Their popularity stems form the fact that they permit a variety of designs. (For example, boxes used for noodles are constructed with a cellophane "window" for visibility.) A special feature of the box or carton is that it can be either coated or impregnated with wax to resist or retain moisture. For frozen foods, which need protection against moisture, an outer paper wrap is pasted all around the box. Boxes used for flour and flour products, which deteriorate if they absorb moisture, may also be prepared with outer paper wrappings.

There are also liquid–tight paper containers used mainly for products that must be kept under refrigeration. These containers are coated with wax to ensure moisture retention and are available in square, oblong, cylindrical, and cone shapes. Rigidity is an important quality in the construction of these containers, for most of them are used for products of liquid or semi-liquid consistency (e.g., milk and cottage cheese).

Composite containers are made of paperboard combined with a paper, metal, foil, or plastic end. These are commonly used to package cocoa, refrigerated biscuits, frozen orange juice, and other fruits. Opening is often facilitated by convolute or spiral winding under a printable exterior wrapping over a protective inner lining.

Ovenable Paperboard. The increasing popularity of the microwave oven has created problems for the frozen food industry which packages TV dinners and other ovenable items in aluminum trays. Since the use of metals in a microwave oven may harm the unit and decrease its life span, aluminum trays cannot be used. Recently, a new ovenable paperboard, capable of withstanding temperatures up to 450°F (232°C) has been marketed.[4] The trays are extrusion-coated with heat-resistant polyester to prevent moisture absorption and allow their use in conventional ovens. A heat-sealed lid of polyester film is attached to the top of the

tray and is peeled off after cooking. The low cost of these trays, their decreased cooking time, their attractive printed designs, and their use in microwave cookery assures their future in packaging.

Plastic Containers. Plastics are widely used in the milk and dariy industry to form packages such as milk bottles, margarine tubs, and cottage cheese and sour cream containers. They are slowly replacing the waxed paperboard containers. Plastic containers used in food packaging are formed by two basic methods: thermoforming and blow molding.

Thermoforming consists of applying pressure to a heated sheet of plastic which subsequently produces a container. Cottage cheese tubs, individual coffee creamers and jellies, clear meat trays and multicavity inserts for candies and cookies are common examples. Polystyrene, a very stiff plastic, is commonly used. Polyvinyl chloride (PVC) was also commonly used, but fear of migration of this carcinogenic chemical into the food has eliminated its use in rigid food packaging.

Blow–molded plastic jars and bottles have substantially increased their share of the market in recent years. Containers are formed by extruding a tube of hot plastic which is sealed at the bottom and blown with compressed air into a shape in a mold. A newer, more precise process, *injection molding,* is used for smaller bottles.

Common plastics used in blow molding include polystyrene, polyethylene, and polypropylene. Polystyrene is very low in cost and is relatively stiff but flexible. However, this is offset by its low impact and chemical resistance, as well as its high moisture permeability. High- and low-density polyethylene are used more commonly. The strength of the polyethylene increases as the density increases. The advantages of polyethylene are that it is nonbreakable, lightweight, and noncorrosive. However, it is expensive, nontransparent, and permeable to aromas, oxygen, gas, and moisture, and is not always resistant to hot fillings.

Polypropylene gives better resistance to chemicals, gases, and moisture than polyethylene does, but it is still not as good as glass. It also has the capability of being filled with hot foods. Orientation of polypropylene will improve its properties even further.

[4] W. H. Lemaire, "Paperboard Packages for Ovens," *Food Eng.* **50**:62, 1978.

FLEXIBLE PACKAGING

Flexible packaging includes covers that conform to the shape of the product (see Fig. 44-1). They are categorized as either partial or total enclosures. Partial enclosures, such as wrappings, are designed to supplement or to aid in the enclosing of the product. Total enclosures (bags, pouches) are what their name implies.

Wrappings. Wrappings for food products are made of a variety of materials. Aluminum foil, glassine, waxed paper, vegetable parchment, polyvinyl chloride, and cellophane are some of the common wrapping materials used today. Butter, cheese and cheese products, baked products, meat, and poultry are generally sold in protective wrappings.

The variety of wrappings available to the consumer has led to confusion over their relative cost and function. A study that compared aluminum foil, plastic wrap, and waxed paper for these qualities found no significant differences between competing brands.[5] The only major difference was that between the types of wrap.

Aluminum foil was found to work best for short- and long-term storage and freezing foods. (It should be noted that in a subsequent study, freezer wrap was found to be superior and cheaper for long-term freezing.) The study also noted that foil should not be reused, since creas-

[5] "Food Wraps," *Consumer Rep.* **41**:522, 1976.

44-1 *Vacuum-packaging meats in polyethylene extends their refrigerator life from a few days to as long as 30 days. The only disadvantage is that the myoglobin remains purple until it is exposed to air. (Courtesy of American Can Company)*

ing the foil creates pinholes and decreases its strength by 40%. Foil should not be used with salted or acid foods, such as berries, pickles, relishes, and tomato sauces, because of corrosion and pinhole development.

Plastic wrap was found to be best for its low cost, storing properties, and transparency. The clingability of the wrap was found to increase when the wrap was pulled out and torn quickly, thereby increasing its static electricity. The recent publicity over migration of vinyl gas from polyvinyl chloride has raised concern among consumers. However, it has been found that this migration occurs only in rigid and semirigid plastics and is not applicable to plastic wrap.

Waxed paper was rated as the least expensive but was not found to be reliable for a tight seal. Rather, its use should be limited to microwave cookery, lining cake pans, providing a waxed sheet for sticky materials, and layering between foods, such as cooked crepes or hamburger patties.

The Retort Pouch. The retort pouch (see Fig. 44-2) is the most innovative idea in food retailing since the development of frozen food. Although it has been successfully marketed in Europe, Japan, and Canada, the retort pouch has only recently been introduced to the United States supermarket.

The retort pouch is a flexible, laminated pouch which combines the advantages of the metal can with the plastic boilable bag.[6] It consists of three layers: (1) an outer layer of polyester (strength); (2) a middle layer of foil (light, gas, and moisture barrier); and (3) an inner layer of either polypropylene or polyethylene (see Fig. 44-3). The product is shelf-stable, requiring no refrigeration or freezing. All that is required for preparation is to boil the bag in water for 5 minutes and serve. Eliminated is the need for a can opener, the discarding of excess liquid, and, most important, a messy pan to wash.

Processing of the food product is done at high temperatures similar to that reached in canning, but the time is reduced as much as 50% because of the thinner profile of the package. This results in food with a fresher taste, better color, and a

[6] N. H. Mermelstein, "An Overview of the Retort Pouch in the U.S.," *Food Technol.* **30**(2):28, 1976.

44-2 *The illustration shows the convenience of heating a ready-to-eat food product packaged in a well-constructed laminated pouch.* (*Courtesy of Reynolds Metals Company*)

firmer texture. The light weight and reduced storage requirements are other advantages. Perhaps one day metal cans for solid food products will be as outdated as wooden barrels are today.

Bags, Pouches, Sacks. These forms of flexible packaging are used for packaging potatoes, carrots, flour, sugar, potato chips (see Fig. 44-4), and other snack foods. For many food products, paper sacks are being replaced with polyethylene bags. Cellophane is also losing its share of the market to polypropylene and metallized polyester.

PACKAGE LABELING

Regardless of type, all food packages have one thing in common: each must bear a label stating what the contents are and giving their weight or number and the name of the producer or distributor. It has been proposed by the Food and Drug Administration that either the drained weight (weight after processing) or the solids weight (weight before processing) be included on the label. The advances made in food packaging gave impetus to the establishment of grades, because consumers could no longer visually inspect the food. It should be noted that any advertising material packaged with a product or displayed in close proximity to it also constitutes labeling.

Nutrient Labeling. Nutrition information of food labels provides consumers with information to help evaluate the nutritional quality of the foods they buy (Fig. 44-5). Labels on different types of foods can be compared to determine

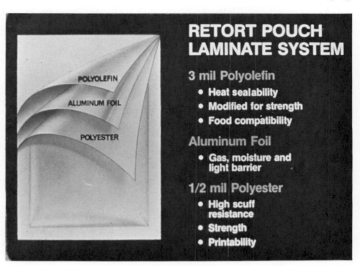

44-3 *The retort pouch consists of three layers: (1) An outer layer of polyester for strength. (2) A middle layer of aluminum foil for protection. (3) An inner layer that is in contact with the food. (Courtesy of Continental Diversified Industries, Flexible Packaging Division)*

which are the best sources of certain nutrients. Consumers can also determine if new and unusual foods are good nutritional buys.

U.S. RDA. The amount of protein, vitamins, and minerals in the food product that is labeled are listed as percentages of the U.S. Recommended Daily Allowances (U.S. RDA). The U.S. RDA's are the amount of nutrients that are needed every day by healthy adults, with an extra 30–50% added for individual variations. Thus, most adults need only two-thirds to three-fourths of the U.S. RDA's and children need only half.

There are actually three U.S. RDA's. The most popular one used on nutrition labels is that for adults and children over the age of 4. The second U.S. RDA was developed for baby foods and vitamin mineral supplements for infants and small children. A third is for pregnant and lactating women.

NUTRITION INFORMATION. The information listed on a typical nutrition label is illustrated in Table 44-1. All the information on the label is based on the serving size. The label shows the number of servings and the average serving size in grams, cups, tablespoons, ounces, slices, and so on. Then calories are listed, followed by the amounts of protein, carbohydrate, and fat, in grams. If desired, information such as percent of calories from fat, grams of polyunsaturated fatty acids, grams of saturated fatty acids, and milligrams of cholesterol may be added. The lower

part of the label gives the amounts of vitamins and minerals found in one serving as percentages of the U.S. RDA. If the quantity that is present is below 2%, a zero or an * followed by a footnote saying "*Less than 2% of the U.S. RDA" is used. If the quantity is 2% or more, up to 10%

44-4 *Flexible glassine polypropylene laminated pouches are often used to package potato chips. The 73 cents package is made of metallized polyester, a more moisture-resistant material. (Courtesy of St. Regis Paper Company)*

533

44-5 *The nutritional information panel lists calories, fat, protein, and available carbohydrate and the percentage of a Standard Recommended Daily Allowance of protein, vitamins, and minerals contained in a normal serving. This was one of the first nutritional labels to appear on the market. (Courtesy of Del Monte Corporation)*

of the U.S. RDA's, the label will list the amount on quantities of 2%, such as 4%, 6%, 8%. From 10 to 50%, the increments are muliples of 5%. Above 50%, up to 150%, the increments are multiples of 10%. If the food contains 100% or greater for any nutrient, it is considered to be a special dietary food with different U.S. RDA's.

Use of nutrition lables allows the consumer to plan more nutritious meals for the food dollar. It is also helpful in selecting foods for special diets, such as weight-control, low-cholesterol, or low-sodium diets.

BRANDS

Brands have been set up by packers and retailers as an effective selling device. An examination of brand names will reveal that, in general, they are short and easy to remember. Some

TABLE 44-1
U.S. Recommended Daily Allowances of Protein, Vitamins, and Minerals Listed on Nutrition Labels

Nutrients That *Must* Appear		Nutrients That *May* Appear	
Protein		Vitamin D	400 I.U.
Protein quality equal to or greater than casein	45 g	Vitamin E	30 I.U.
		Vitamin B_6	2.0 mg
Protein quality less than casein	65 g	Folic acid (folacin)	0.4 mg
		Vitamin B_{12}	6 μg
Vitamin A	5000 I.U.	Phosphorus	1.0 g
Vitamin C (ascorbic acid)	60 mg	Iodine	150 μg
Thiamine (vitamin B_1)	1.5 mg	Magnesium	400 mg
Riboflavin (vitamin B_2)	1.7 mg	Zinc	15 mg
Niacin	20 mg	Copper	2 mg
Calcium	1.0 g	Biotin	0.3 mg
Iron	18 mg	Pantothenic acid	10 mg

534

brands have a symbol or design (known as a *trademark*) that is registered with the government, thus blocking its use by any other manufacturer or packer. The same packer may use several brand names, using each one to identify one level of quality. But because the true function of the brand name is to build prestige for a product, it is unlikely that it will be of much real help in identifying quality for the food buyer. The multiplicity of brands for the same product often makes buying difficult unless the brand is accompanied by a letter grade. However, the consumer who reads the labels on canned foods to secure as much information about the quality of the contents as possible will eliminate some of the risks of haphazard shopping.

PACKAGING REGULATION

Packaged foods usually cost more than similar foods purchased in bulk, and an unusually elaborate package may raise the cost considerably more. It is generally agreed that the costs of packaging are eventually borne by the consumer; nonetheless, it appears that in most instances the public is favorably inclined toward more and better packaging because of the sanitation and convenience it offers.

A consumer problem does arise, however, when the cost of a package is more than 50% of the total cost of the product. It has been suggested that these excessive costs for mere wrapping constitute an element of fraud on the part of the packer—particularly if the package cannot be reused. The practice is self-defeating, however, for it is entirely likely that consumer demand will quickly diminish after one such experience.

It has been noted that packages described with such words as *Regular, Super, Giant,* and *King-Size* are confusing and deceptive. Also, some packages indicate the weight of the contents in tiny, inconspicuous type.

The large size of some packages, in relation to their contents, has also been open to criticism—mainly because such packages make price comparisons difficult. Furthermore, the size and shape of the package may be misleading. Through the use of color, elongation, or inden-

tations, packages may be made to look larger than they actually are.

The Food, Drug, and Cosmetic act has detailed the following as packaging factors that might cause deception.[7]

1. Glass bottles or jars having excessively thick glass panels, long necks, indented bottoms, or irregular shapes.
2. Containers with (a) fake bottoms, such as candy boxes with an empty lower section; (b) indented bottoms, such as cardboard and wooden baskets with excessive recesses in the bottom; and (c) raised covers, such as metal containers with the covers too high above the body of the can, thus causing excessive space above the food.
3. Oversized cardboard cartons that are too large for the inside container. The inner containers should fit the outside cartons closely.
4. Misleading or nonuniform packing of contents, such as the conspicuous placing of chicken against the sides of a glass jar of chicken and noodles.
5. Deceptive color of wrappings. These should not mislead as to the identity of quality of the contents. For example, lightly smoked fish fillets should not be wrapped in a semitransparent brown wrapper through which the fish appear to be more heavily smoked than is the case.
6. Excessive wrappings, such as an unduly heavy corrugated liner around a bottle in a carton.
7. Various devices to increase the apparent fill, such as a confectionery box with 20 pieces of candy in the top layer and 6 pieces in the botom layer.
8. Deceptive face dimensions, where the width and length of the package are too large in relation to the depth, such as an exceptionally thin chocolate bar.

Remedies for these practices may come through legislation, but the consumer's responsibility to read the label and to make comparisons before making a final selection is not lessened.

---

[7] From U.S. Department of Health, Education, and Welfare, "Food and Drug Administration Requirements of the U.S. Food, Drug and Cosmetic Act," *Bulletin 2* (Washington, D.C.: U.S. Food and Drug Administration, 1961), p. 44.

FAIR PACKAGING AND LABELING ACT

The Fair Packaging and Labeling Act requires clear and accurate statements on package labels to identify the product and the manufacturer. If the number of servings is shown, the net quantity that constitutes a serving must be disclosed. Enforcement officials have discretionary authority to regulate the use of such package terms as *Family Size, Jumbo Size,* and *Cents Off.* They may also require disclosure of the ingredients, and they may prohibit slack-filling practices, unless the packages are not full because of a certain type of machine used, or to protect contents.

Efforts have been made to enforce the Fair Packaging and Labeling Act by regulations in *Cents-Off* and other price representations on labels of foods, drugs, and cosmetics. Sponsors of a *Cents-Off* promotion are required to print the number of cents off on the label. The retailer must then stamp on the package the single price to be paid by the consumer and must post a placard or shelf marker listing the product's regular price.

Commodities labeled as *Economy Size, Bargain Size,* and *Budget Pack* must be priced at least 5% less than the lowest price per unit of weight, volume, or measure of all other sizes of the same product offered simultaneously.

Introductory-offer items must bear on their label the anticipated after-introductory-offer price; the introductory offer can last only 6 months and may only be used for new products, substantially changed products, or products being introduced for the first time in the marketing area.

Sponsors of coupon promotions not redeemable at the retail store are required to reimburse the consumers for cost of redeeming their coupon by mail. The *Cents-Off* regulation limits to no more than three the number of promotions for any single size of commodity in the same trade

TABLE 44-2
Grades of Canned Fruits and Vegetables

Fruit Grades	Description
U.S. Grade A (or Fancy)	Excellent quality: highly colored, ripe, firm, free of blemishes, uniform in size, and very symmetrical; a 40–70 per cent syrup may be used
U.S. Grade B (or Choice or Extra Standard)	Fine quality: highly colored, ripe, firm, free of serious blemishes, reasonably uniform in size and in degree of ripeness, reasonably symmetrical; a medium syrup is used (usually about 40 per cent)
U.S. Grade C (or Standard)	Good quality: reasonably well colored, reasonably free of blemishes, reasonably uniform in size and in degree of ripeness, reasonably symmetrical; a 25 per cent syrup may be used
Substandard	Lower than the minimum grade for standard; often packed in water; syrup, if used, is not over 10 per cent
Vegetable Grades	
U.S. Grade A (or Fancy)	Best-flavored, most tender and succulent; uniform in size, shape, color, and tenderness; liquid free of vegetable fragments or foreign material
U.S. Grade B (or Extra Standard)	Well-flavored, tender, and succulent; may be slightly more mature, more firm in texture, and sometimes less uniform than Fancy
U.S. Grade C (or Standard)	Less delicately flavored, more firm in texture; often less uniform in size, shape, and color; more mature than Extra Standard

area within a 12-month period and requires a lapse of 30 days between promotions for any package size.

CANNED FOODS

Purchasing. The almost daily use of canned foods makes their selection of particular importance to the consumer. Wide price variations among the same kinds of canned foods make it important for the consumer to have some basis of comparison before making a purchase. The U.S. Department of Agriculture has made available to the canning industry inspection and grading services that have fostered the development and wise use of official grade standards. All products labeled A, B, or C must meet the standards for the grade, but U.S. Grade A, and so on, may be used only when the processing has been done under continuous inspection and when the grading is done by an approved gov-

ernment agent. Food processed under the supervision of an agent may display a shield-shaped stamp on the label. See Table 44-2.

Sizes. Fruits and vegetables are available in many can sizes, but only a few of these are commonly used. The usual capacities and yields of the common can sizes are given in Fig. 44-6 and Table 44-3. It is important to keep in mind that the net contents and weights vary with the density of the commodity and solidness of the pack.

Storage. Any information about the storage life of a canned food must take into account the fact that storage temperatures have a great deal to do with keeping the canned food in a good wholesome condition. Generally, the higher the storage temperature, the more rapid the deterioration in the canned food.

Changes in canned food are brought about mainly by the reaction of acid in the food with

44-6 *Buying guide for cans. Knowing common container sizes helps the consumer plan servings. (Courtesy of National Canners Association)*

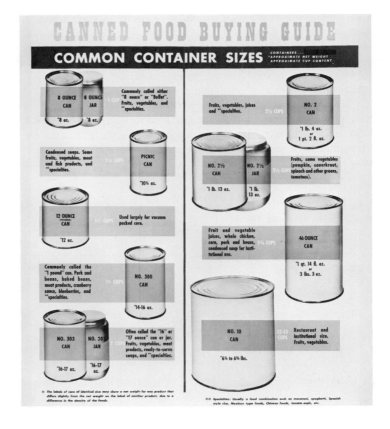

TABLE 44-3
Can Sizes and Yields

Size of Can	Net Weight	Cups	Use
8 oz.	8 oz	1	Fruits, vegetables
Picnic	10½–12 oz	1¼	Condensed soups, fruits, vegetables
12 oz. (vacuum)	12 oz	1½	Vacuum-packed corn
No. 300	14–16 oz	1¾	Pork and beans, cranberries
No. 303	16–17 oz	2	Principal size for fruits and vegetables
No. 2	1 lb 4 oz or 1 pt 2 fl oz	2½	Juices, ready-to-serve soups
No. 2½	1 lb 13 oz	3½	Fruits, some vegetables
No. 3 cylinder	46 fl oz	5¾	Fruit and vegetable juices
No. 10	6½ lb to 7 lb 5 oz	12–13	Institutional-sized fruit and vegetables

some of the tin or iron in solution. This change may be accompanied by the liberation of hydrogen gas, which eventually increases the internal pressure of the can. These changes, however, are extremely slow and, except in rare cases, do not constitute a health hazard.

Once opened, canned foods may be stored in the open can itself. Indeed, the can is the best container for the unused portion of most foods because it was sterile (or nearly so) at the time it was opened, whereas a glass container or dish is likely to serve as a new source of bacteria. The important factor in the storage of opened canned foods is not the container but the temperature at which the can is held during storage and its general treatment as a perishable product.

Canned cured meats that have received a mild heat-processing after canning are intended to be kept under refrigeration after processing and throughout the marketing channels, up to the time they are consumed. The canned hams packed in pear shaped cans and various luncheon meats packed in rectangular cans are examples. These canned products bear prominent labels reading, "Perishable, Keep under Refrigeration". As the label indicates these canned products should be held at all times below 50°F (10°C) preferably below 40°F (5°C).

Spoilage. Spoilage in canned food rarely occurs, and when it does, it is usually the result of under processing. In such cases, bacteria spores with high resistance to heat have survived the processing and have subsequently resumed growth. All spoiled canned food must be destroyed (see Table 44-4).

SUMMARY

With the advent of factory production of specialized foods, the packaging of food has be-

TABLE 44-4
Spoilage in Canned Foods

Chief Types of Spoilage	Characteristics
Flat sour spoilage	Characterized by the production of acid without gas; the product is not greatly changed in appearance but may have a faintly disagreeable odor
Thermophilic gaseous spoilage	Characterized by the swelling of the container; the food has a strong odor
Sulfide spoilage	The can remains flat, but the contents have the odor of hydrogen sulfide and may turn black
Putrefactive spoilage	The can swells, and the contents become putrid; occurs in low-acid foods, especially asparagus

come increasingly prevalent. Packaging protects food from dirt and contamination, retards loss of moisture and aroma, and helps to preserve freshness and flavor. Packaging of foods is a convenience for both the buyer and the seller, as it makes food easier to transport and easier to store, but it also adds to the cost of food.

Packaging includes glass, metal, and plastic containers, as well as various cartons, boxes, and paperboard. Flexible packaging such as plastic wrap, aluminum foil, pouches, bags, and sacks conform to the shape of the product.

Through packaging the availability of many foods has been extended to all seasons of the year. Informative package labels, giving data on nutrient content (see Fig. 44-7) and net weight or volume, are required. Brands have been devised to promote sales, and some packers use several brand names to identify product quality or grade. A letter grade is more informative, however.

The Fair Packaging and Labeling Act sets guidelines for packaging, banning adjectives tending to exaggerate quantity of contents.

Storage temperatures influence the length of time canned foods will remain wholesome. The higher the storage temperature, the more rapid the deteriorative changes. Any spoiled canned food must be discarded.

QUESTIONS AND TOPICS FOR DISCUSSION AND STUDY

1. What are the functions of packaging materials?
2. Because packaged foods cost more than similar foods purchased in bulk, is there any great consumer advantage in promoting packaging?
3. What packaging practices may be misleading to a consumer?

SUGGESTED ACTIVITIES

1. Which foods are commonly packaged in containers of three or more different sizes? Compare the cost of the different sizes on a

44-7 Nutrition labels help the consumer determine the nutritional value of food products. (Courtesy U.S. Department of Agriculture)

NUTRITION INFORMATION

Serving Size. . . . . ⅓ Cup (22.7 grams) Amount required to make an 8 fluid oz. serving.

Servings Per Box. . . . . Forty ⅓ cup servings (10 quarts reconstituted)

RECONSTITUTED
Per 8 oz. cup

Calories 80		Fat . . . . .0 Grams	
Protein . . . . .8 Grams		Cholesterol . . . . .0 Grams	
Carbohydrate . .12 Grams		Sodium . . .126 Milligrams	

Percentage of U.S. Recommended Daily Allowance (U.S. RDA)

Protein . . . . .15% **	Niacin . . . .*	
Vitamin A 10%	Calcium 25%	
Vitamin C 0	Iron 0	
Thiamine 4%	Vitamin D 25%	
Riboflavin 20%	Phosphorus 20%	

**Based on U.S. RDA of 45 Grams.
*Contains less than 2% of U.S. RDA for this nutrient.

Information on cholesterol content is provided for individuals, who on the advice of a physician, are modifying their total dietary intake of cholesterol.

Ingredients: Nonfat Dry Milk, Vitamin A & Vitamin D

per ounce basis. What generalization regarding the economy of package sizes for these foods can you set down?

2. Study the labels on various canned foods. In what way do you think the label influences the consumer's choice of product?

3. Select three grades—A, B, and C—of a canned food. Open the cans and compare the contents for appearance, flavor, and net weight of solids. Examine the different can sizes available. Which sizes are most confusing to distinguish among? What is the capacity of each size in cups?

REFERENCES

Books

Consumers All: The Yearbook of Agriculture. Washington, D.C.: U.S. Department of Agriculture, 1964, pp. 429–431.

Griffin, Roger C., and Stanley Sacharow. *Principles of Package Development.* Westport, Conn.: Avi, 1972.

Protecting Our Food: The Yearbook of Agriculture. Washington, D.C.: U.S. Department of Agriculture, 1966, pp. 102–118, 290–297.

Wright, Carleton. *Food Buying.* New York: Macmillan, 1962, Chaps. 10, 11.

Articles, Bulletins, and Pamphlets

"A Consumer's Guide to USDA Services." Washington, D.C.: U.S. Department of Agriculture, 1964.

Federal Food, Drug, and Cosmetic Act. Washington, D.C.: U.S. Department of Health, Education, and Welfare, rev. 1970.

Greenwald, S., and W. I. Greenwald. "Importance of Price as an Index of Quality." *J. Home Econ.* **58**:144, 1966.

"Nutrition Labeling. Tools for Its Use." *Agriculture Information Bulletin 382.* Washington, D.C.: U.S. Department of Agriculture, 1975.

"Processed Fruit and Vegetable Inspection." *Bulletin PA 803.* Washington, D.C.: U.S. Department of Agriculture, rev. 1967.

Microwave Cookery

Microwave cookery is an exciting, novel form of food preparation. The speed of cooking and the ease of preparation that it offers fits well into today's convenience-oriented life-style. In 1977, 9% of all U.S. homes had a microwave oven, and this figure is expected to reach 50% by 1985.[1] The booming increase in this relatively new method of cooking makes it essential for the student of foods to thoroughly understand its principles and applications.

THE MICROWAVE

Microwaves are short, high-frequency waves of energy, similar to TV, radar, and radio waves. They are created by a magnetron, a vacuum electron tube, which converts household electricity into electromagnetic energy. These waves of energy are "nonionizing" and do not cause dangerous chemical changes as do the "ionizing" rays of nuclear radiation. Rather, they produce a thermal change (or heating) of objects if they are absorbed.

[1] R. F. Schiffmann, "Wanted: New Products for Microwave Ovens," *Food Eng.* **49**(9):117, 1977.

Different substances react differently to electronic energy. Depending on the composition of the substance, the microwaves are either absorbed, transferred, or reflected. Foods and other forms of biological tissue with a high moisture and fat content readily absorb electromagnetic waves. Placed in a microwave oven, these will quickly heat up. Inanimate objects such as paper, glass, and some plastic, however, will transfer the waves without absorbing them. This is the reason that foods can be cooked in a microwave oven on a paper or glass plate without becoming heated. Metals respond to microwaves by reflecting them. Thus, metal coverings and utensils do not allow the waves to penetrate.

THE MICROWAVE OVEN

The microwave oven is a cavity with the floor, ceiling, and walls lined with metal (see Fig. 45-1). When the oven is turned on, the magnetron generates microwaves which strike the food and the inside walls of the oven. The microwaves that strike the food are absorbed and create heat. Those that strike the metal walls are reflected and bounce back into the cavity or the

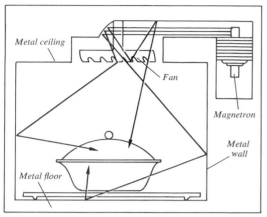

45-1 *The microwave oven. Electromagnetic rays generated from the magnetron are reflected from the metal walls, transferred through the baking dish, and absorbed by the food.*

food. To more evenly distribute the waves coming into the oven and those being reflected from the metal walls, a metal stirrer slowly revolves. This breaks up any continuous wave patterns that might develop.

Excess Moisture. When the oven is turned on, only the moisture- and fat-containing foods absorb the energy to become hot. The cavity of the oven and the utensils used (if not metal) remain cool. The evaporating moisture from the food condenses when it comes in contact with the cool air. This excess moisture is deposited on the food surface and results in an increased vapor pressure of the surrounding air. (Normally, the surface of a cooking food becomes drier with evaporation.) Part of the excess moisture is eliminated by a fan that turns on automatically. However, not all the moisture is eliminated by the fan, and it increases the vapor pressure to the point where the boiling point of water is increased. For this reason, a food that has 50% moisture will heat up to a high temperature faster than a food with 75% moisture.[2] Another example of this principle is shown when several cups of water are heated at the same time. It will

take them longer to reach the boiling point than a single cup, owing partially to the extra vapor pressure that has been formed.

Variability. The type of magnetron that is used in the microwave oven has differing power outputs. They may range as follows: 300–400 watts; 400–500 watts, 600–700 watts; and in commercial use, 700–1000 watts and 1200–1300 watts. Most of the ovens sold for home use fall in the 600–700-watt range. More microwaves can be generated at the same time with an increase in the power of the magnetron. This variability in power outputs means that some ovens will cook more quickly than others. The cooking times in recipe books may not be accurate unless they were written by the manufacturer of the microwave oven.

It is assumed that most recipes are written for the 600–700-watt range. Thus. if an oven has a lower wattage, such as 400–500, cooking times must be increased up to 35%.[3] Likewise, a 500–600-watt oven increases the cooking time approximately 15%. If the microwave oven is higher in wattage than 700, cooking times are decreased. It is important to regard published cooking times for microwave oven recipes as approximate rather than absolute values.

HOW THE MICROWAVE OVEN WORKS

The principle of how microwaves heat food can be understood if the magnetron is compared to a large magnet which has the capacity to create an electrical field. Dipolar molecules such as water (with positive and negative poles) will try to align themselves in an electrical field. If the electrical field is alternated, the dipolar molecules will also alternate, or change their position, in an attempt to keep their alignment. If the frequency of alternation of the electrical field is increased to either 915 or 2450 million times per second, the rapid movement of the dipolar molecules moving back and forth to keep their alignment creates heat as a result of internal

[2] "ABC of Microwave Cooking," *Micro. Appl. Newsl.,* Amherst, N.H., 1970.

[3] M. L. Scott and J. D. Scott, *Mastering Microwave Cooking* (New York: Bantam, 1976), p. 27.

friction.[4] Thus, any substance that contains polar molecules, such as water, will heat up rapidly when exposed to electromagnetic energy.

The frequency set by the Federal Communications Commission for microwaves for food use are in the 915-megahertz (MHz; million cycles/second) and 2450-MHz bands. Microwaves in the 915-MHz frequency can penetrate deeply. This deep penetration allows slow cooking of large quantities and is ideally suited for commercial uses. Ovens for home use operate at the 2450-MHz band, which allows penetration of approximately 2½–3 in. Any reduction in the depth of penetration of the food increases the cooking time.

Penetration of the Waves. The major difference between heating by conventional methods and by microwaves is that food electronically cooked is heated throughout at the same time up to the limit of the depth of penetration of the microwaves. In conventional heating, the food is surrounded by hot air or water. This heats up only the surface of the food. The food is cooked throughout by the slow process of conduction. In microwave cooking, all the food that is penetrated will heat up at the same time. Thus, a small roll will heat up completely, inside and out, at the same time. When a larger, denser, type of food is heated such as a roast, the microwaves again heat up the roast throughout at the same time to the depth of their penetration. The inside of the roast (if very large) is too far from the outside to be easily penetrated and will heat more slowly by conduction. Slower cooking times and rest periods are needed to allow adequate conduction of the heat before the outer, easily penetrated portions are overcooked.

ADVANTAGES

The chief advantage of a microwave oven is the saving of time. Foods can be cooked 2–10 times faster than by the conventional method. A potato, for example, cooks 4–6 minutes instead

[4]J. T. Weizeorick, "How Microwave Ovens Work," in *Consumer Microwave Oven Systems Conference* (Chicago: Association of Home Appliance Manufacturers, 1971), p. 10.

of the normal 45–60 minutes. A cake cooks in only 5 minutes. Frozen foods can be defrosted in minutes rather than hours. A steak solidly frozen can be ready in minutes for cooking. Time is also saved by not having to preheat the oven or to clean baked-on food.

The ability of the microwave to reconstitute leftovers with their flavor and texture intact is another major advantage of the oven. Leftover vegetables (even potatoes), stale baked goods, and meats warmed in a microwave retain their original fresh-cooked taste. Small portions can be saved and warmed directly on the plate.

Another advantage of the microwave oven is the absence of heat in the surrounding air and utensils. Kitchens do not become excessively warm while cooking. The possibility of burns from hot pots and utensils is also reduced. Being able to cook and serve in the same device is another real convenience.

Extensive use of the microwave oven will result in less electricity used. Savings of energy of up to two-thirds have been reported.

DISADVANTAGES

The lack of browning in foods cooked for a short period of time is the major disadvantage. Foods must be cooked for a minimum of 20 minutes for browning to develop. This would severely overcook everything except large roasts. Baked goods such as cakes and breads do not develop a browned crust and lack eye appeal.

Simmering or stewing to tenderize foods is impossible because of the lack of adequate temperature sensitivity. Flavors do not have a chance to blend and develop in a very short cooking time period. Deep-fat frying is also eliminated, because of the mess that would be created by fat splattering.

The speed of cooking decreases in proportion to the quantity of food in the cavity. Thus, it is impractical to use the oven for large quantities. Microwave cookery is limited to small portions.

FACTORS AFFECTING MICROWAVE COOKING

In conventional cooking, temperature is the most important factor. However it is *time,* not temperature, that is more important in micro-wave cookery. Factors that influence the amount of time needed to cook a food include starting temperature, volume, density, and composition.

Starting Temperature. The colder a food, the longer it takes to cook. This is illustrated when pie and ice cream are briefly heated in the microwave oven. The pie will become warm while the ice cream stays firm.

The depth of penetration of the microwaves is also related to the starting temperature. Microwaves were found to penetrate 6 times as far into frozen beef at 0°F (−18°C) than chilled beef at 40°F (4°C).[5] This is the reason that ½ gal of frozen ice cream (a rather large quantity for the microwave) can be softened throughout.

Volume. The greater the volume of a food item, the longer the cooking time. If a small portion of food is in the oven, all the energy that is being generated is available to that food. If a larger quantity of food is placed in the oven, the same number of microwaves are available and must be shared. For example, one potato cooks in approximately 4 minutes, two potatoes in 7 minutes, and six potatoes in 16 minutes (with a standing time of 5 minutes added). Notice that the increase in cooking time is not proportional. Rather, it is usually from one-half to three-fourths of the quantity of food added.

Density. The denser the food, the longer the cooking, heating, and defrosting time. A porous object allows easy penetration of electromagnetic energy. Dense foods limit the depth of penetration, and cooking of the interior must be partially done by conduction. For example, a porous item such as a 1-lb loaf of bread requires much less time to defrost or heat than does a relatively dense 1-lb piece of meat.

Composition. The relative proportions of water, fat, and sugar in the food determine the rapidity of heating. Fats and sugar, because of their low specific heat, absorb heat much faster

than water. Brushing foods with fats will cause the surface to heat more quickly. Salt has the opposite effect. It increases the cooking time. Thus, foods cooked in a microwave should not be salted until after cooking is completed.

COOKING TECHNIQUES

The short period of time that food is cooked in the microwave oven necessitates more careful use and planning of the time. Unlike conventional cooking, food cannot be carelessly placed in the oven and ignored. Precise arrangement, rotating and stirring, covering, and standing time are necessary to achieve a satisfactory product.

Arrangement. The arrangement of the food is a critical factor for the even penetration of microwaves. Since microwaves penetrate to a limited depth, the food should be arranged separately in such a pattern so that the waves can strike it from all sides.

If there are a number of pieces to cook at one time, the pieces should be arranged in a circle to create more outside pieces. Grouping the pieces in a pile would make the center too dense. Longer cooking times would be necessary for conduction to occur. This would probably overcook the outer portions of the food.

A food that is thicker in one part than another, such as asparagus and broccoli, should be arranged in a circle so that the thinnest part forms a dense center.

Stirring and Rotating. The uneven and continuously changing distribution of microwaves striking the food results in some part being cooked faster than others. The distribution of heat in a microwave oven can be determined by placing marshmallows in an equidistant pattern on a plate. The oven is turned on until some of the marshmallows begin to melt; the plate is then removed. Observation of the location of which marshmallows are still cold, soft, and melted will show the heating pattern.

Stirring is necessary at specified time intervals to avoid overcooking of certain parts of the food. The outer, warmer portion of the food should be stirred into the colder, inner portion; and the inner portion toward the outer part.

[5] R. V. Decareau, "Container: Material Shape and Size," *Report of Consumer Microwave Systems Conference* (Chicago: Association of Home Appliance Manufacturers, 1971), p. 51.

45-2 *Foods with varying density such as broccoli must be arranged so that the thicker parts face toward the outside. (Courtesy of Jeanne Freeland-Graves)*

Foods that are not stirred may be separated, rotated one-quarter turn, or rearranged from the center to the outside every few minutes.

Covering. A covering on the food while cooking is often necessary to retain moisture and heat and to prevent fat spattering. Waxed paper is an ideal covering for microwave cookery. It can be placed loosely over the food to prevent moisture and heat loss but allows excess moisture to escape. Plastic wrap may be used for short periods of time if it does not touch the food. The warmth of the steam escaping is hot enough to melt the plastic.

Tight-fitting covers such as glass casserole lids and inverted plates are often used with vegetable dishes to completely retain the moisture. Baked goods are best heated when surrounded with a paper towel or napkin to help absorb some of the excess moisture. Paper goods are also used to absorb fat and prevent spattering of fat-containing foods, such as bacon.

Small pieces of aluminum foil may be used with caution to prevent overcooking of thin and projecting parts of the food. The quantity of aluminum foil used must be small in relation to the amount of food present and must not touch the walls of the oven. The tips of the wings and drumsticks of poultry are often shielded from overcooking by this method.

Standing Time. The molecular agitation of the dipolar molecules continues for a period of time after the magnetron is turned off and the food removed from the oven. The food continues to cook until the molecules decrease their activity. The time between removal of the food from the oven until it finishes cooking and is served is called the *standing time.*

During this process the heat is conducted from the outer, hotter portions to the cooler inside. The denser the food, the longer the standing period required. Large roasts, for example, may increase as much as 40°F during the standing time. Allowances must be made for this continued cooking or the food will be severely overcooked when served.

COOKING UTENSILS

Cooking utensils for the microwave oven must be able to transfer microwaves rather than absorb or reflect them. Since metals reflect heat, standard pots and pans cannot be used. Instead, unconventional utensils, such as paper plates, plastic cups, measuring cups, china, and paper towels may be appropiate. The selection of the type of utensil used should depend on the length of time that the food will be in the oven. A paper plate or napkin is adequate if the food is only to be warmed. If the food is to be cooked for a short period of time, plates, bowls, cups, and some plastics may be used. Food that will be cooked for longer periods of time needs to be contained in heat-resistant glass or ceramic.

Glass, Ovenware, China, and Pottery. Glass and china products may be used as long as they contain no metal trim, such as gold or silver. The bottom of the dish should be checked for a possible trademark. Certain types of dinnerware and pottery have glazes containing metallic substances. If doubt exists concerning its suitability for the microwave oven, the following test can be preformed.

Pour ½ cup cold water in the dish. Cook 1 minute on the highest setting. If the water is warm and the dish is cool, the dish can be safely used. If the dish is slightly warm around the edges, it should be used only for short periods of time. If the water is cool, and the dish is warm, it must not be used for microwave cookery.

Foods that are cooked in conjunction with conventional methods or for extended periods of time should be contained in heat-resistant dishes and ceramics.

Paper Goods. Paper goods, such as plates, towels, cups, napkins, frozen food cartons, and freezer wraps are excellent for defrosting, warming, or cooking foods short periods of time. Paper readily absorbs moisture, preventing sogginess in baked goods that are warmed. Cloth can be substituted for this purpose. Paper is also an excellent absorber of fat drippings from fat-containing foods.

Plastics. Dishwasher-safe plastics may be used for warming and cooking for short periods of time. Prolonged heating is to be avoided because the steam may cause the container to soften. Tight covers with plastic containers are not used since they increase the pressure of the steam.

The suitability of the plastic for even short periods of cooking can be determined by a 15–20-second test in the oven. Plastic and china foam cups and dishes, baby bottles, and spatulas and spoons designed for Teflon pans may be heated for short periods of time.

Frozen foods in plastic boilable bags can be reconstituted in the microwave oven if slits are cut to allow steam to escape. Slits must also be cut in plastic wrap when used as a covering.

Straw and Wood. Straw baskets for rolls can be placed in the microwave oven for only very short periods of time. Wooden utensils, steak platters, and cutting boards should not be used in the microwave oven because of the slight amount of moisture that they contain. This may cause the wood to warm and crack. Wooden-handled spoons will become warm if left in the oven for very short periods of time, but damage to them is usually slight.

Metals. Metal utensils should not be used in the oven because they reflect the microwaves away from the food in the container. This slows the cooking process. In addition, metals can cause "arcing," a static discharge of electricity. The sparks that are formed may set fire to paper or plastic utensils.

Arcing occurs when the metal of the object is separated or has gaps. The metal walls in the oven are smooth and continuous in comparison. When the magnetron is turned on, an electrical field may result and damage the magnetron. Anything containing metal, including paper-coated twist ties, china with gold or silver trim, and ceramics with metallic glazes, must not be used in the microwave oven.

Small amounts of foods in combination with metal produce arcing. When large amounts of food are used in conjunction with a small quantity of metal, the chances of arcing are decreased. For this reason, there are several conditions in which metals may be used in the microwave:

1. Small pieces of aluminum foil with a large quantity of food may be used to shield projecting or thin parts of a food item. The tips of the wings and drumsticks of poultry are frequently protected by this method.
2. A large quantity of dense food may surround a relatively thin skewer, as in shish kabobs. Metal lids on jars with large quantities of foods present may be left in place.
3. Aluminum TV dinner trays may be used only if they are less than ½ in. deep and do *not* touch the walls or floor. New packaging of TV dinners in ovenable paperboard trays will eliminate this problem in the future.

DEFROSTING

Foods can be defrosted with success in a short period of time. Alternating periods of heating and resting are necessary to allow even distribution of heat. The icy side of the food should always be facing up.

New model microwave ovens have an automatic defrosting setting. Defrosting can be performed manually by heating 1 minute for each 8 oz of food and letting it stand for 1 minute. This process is continuously repeated until only a few ice crystals are present. The thawed food is cooked approximately 1½ minutes per cup of food.

BROWNING

Browning increases the number of food products that can be cooked in the microwave oven. Steaks, hamburger, and chicken can be fried in a browning skillet or broiled conventionally to develop the color and flavor. Meats that are browned separately should be cooked first, since browning afterward will be quicker and reduce the excess moisture. The opposite is true when the center of the object is to be heated, as in a sandwich. The bread is toasted first, then assembled, and heated.

Browning skillets (see Fig. 45-3) have a tin oxide base undercoating which interacts with microwave energy to produce heat. The skillet is raised from the floor of the oven by notches to prevent breakage. The time for preheating the skillet depends on the manufacturer's instructions. When heated, food is placed on top and fried. Covering may be used to prevent fat spattering but reduces the browning. Fat does not have to be added. Excess water should be removed between repeated brownings.

Many consumers feel that conventional cooking is no more time consuming than the extra time spent in using a browning skillet or separate broiling.

Clever use of sauces, spices, and dark-coloring foods can disguise the absence of browning. Barbecue, chili, and tomato sauce, Kitchen Bouquet, and gravies cover the unbrowned product. Food may be sprinkled with paprika, grated cheese, dry gravy mix, or covered with melted cheese. Cakes can be frosted with icing. Dark-colored cookies such as date-nut and brownies can be prepared.

THERMOMETERS

Standard meat and candy thermometers may not be used in the microwave oven. They are inaccurate and may be damaged. Special thermometers (see Fig. 45-4), such as silicon in glass and a dial type, have been specially designed for microwave use (but may not be used in conventional ovens).

The newer, elaborate models of microwave ovens have an automatic temperature control sensor which is placed in the cavity of the food item. The oven is automatically turned off and switched to warm when the desired temperature is reached.

Desirable temperatures for reconstituted foods (frozen and warmed) ranges from 140 to 160°F (66 to 77°C). Baked goods should be warmed to 90 to 110°F (38 to 43°C).

FOOD PREPARATION

The preparation of foods for cooking in the microwave oven is the same as for conventional methods. Only the arrangement on the cooking dish is more precise. Consideration must be given in preparation to the lack of browning, the absence of flavor blending, the excess moisture that is produced, and the standing time. Foods should be wrapped in foil or covered while

45-3 *Loin chops or hashbrowns are easily seared in this browning skillet specially designed for the microwave oven. (Courtesy of Litton)*

45-4 *An automatic temperature sensor placed in the food automatically shuts off the microwave oven when the desired temperature is reached. (Courtesy of Litton)*

standing to prevent moisture and heat loss.

Caution must be exercised to prevent spatter. The combined presence of pockets of steam and hot fat results in messy explosions. Deep-fat frying is best left to conventional methods.

Vegetables. Fresh and frozen vegetables retain their flavor, texture, and color if properly cooked in the microwave oven. Care must be taken not to overcook, since chlorophyll readily changes to the olive-green pheophytin when overheated.

Vegetables are best quickly cooked covered in a very small amount of water to prevent moisture loss. High-fiber vegetables such as asparagus require slightly more water, less energy, and more time. Fresh corn may be cooked without being removed from the husk. Canned vegetables should be heated in one-half their liquid.

Baked potatoes must be pricked several times with a fork to avoid explosions caused by the buildup of steam. Potatoes may be wrapped in plastic wrap or placed on absorbent paper towels. A standing time of 5 minutes (wrapped in foil) in necessary for gelatinization of the starch. Microwave-cooked potatoes do not have a crisp skin, because of excess moisture produced during cooking. Sweet potatoes have a tendency to become gummy if not carefully watched.

Meats. The speed of microwave energy does not allow enough time for the collagen of less-tender cuts of meats to solubilize and tenderize. Only tender cuts of meats should be attempted. Hamburgers, meat loaf, hot dogs, and small, boned, uniform-shaped roasts produce the best products (see Fig. 45-5).

Roasts need to be rotated so that hot spots do not develop. Bones interfere with even heat distribution and should be removed. Excess moisture must also be removed. The roast should not be salted until cooking is completed since it toughens the meat.

The high density of a roast requires a long standing time (20–30 minutes). Allowances must be made for this in meal preparation. It is best to undercook and test.

Heating denatures the red oxymoglobin to a brown globin hemichrome. Unfortunately, this change occurs more readily in the interior or in certain hot spots than on the surface. A minimum of 15–20 minutes is needed for surface

45-5 *Newer models of microwave ovens have the ability to cook a three-course meal at the same time. (Courtesy of Litton)*

browning. Steaks and chops need to be browned by skillet or broiling for best flavor.

Poultry. Young, tender poultry (not stewing hens) is ideally suited for microwave cookery. Projecting wingtips and drumsticks may be shielded with aluminum foil to prevent overheating (see Fig. 45-6). Thorough trussing of the bird will minimize projections.

Birds should be cooked on an inverted saucer or nonmetal trivet to be separated from the juices. Rotation and removal of excess fluid is necessary. A waxed paper covering will prevent spatter. Pieces of poultry should be uniformly cut and rearranged during cooking to prevent overheating.

Eggs. Omelets, hardcooked, and fried eggs are not successfully cooked in the microwave oven. Expanding heated air causes eggs cooked in a shell to explode. Whole yolks also explode, because of their high fat content. Yolks of poached or baked eggs must be carefully punctured prior to cooking.

Scrambled eggs are very light and fluffy when stirred occasionally during cooking. The heat-sensitive nature of the egg requires that special attention be given to standing time to avoid a rubbery product. The low specific heat of fat will cause the yolk to cook more quickly than the white.

Cakes. Cakes are cooked in the microwave in

45-6 *Aluminum foil is used to protect the projecting parts of poultry from overheating. (Courtesy of Jeanne Freeland-Graves)*

only 5 minutes, but the crust does not brown. This is not important if the cake is to be frosted. A higher volume is achieved than is found in conventional baking. A knife is stirred through the batter prior to baking to eliminate large air bubbles. Doughy centers can be minimized by baking on an inverted saucer.

The doneness is determined with a clean toothpick. The crust may appear too moist, but this should disappear during the standing time.

Cupcakes are filled only one-third full and must be rotated. Angel food cake is particularly heat-sensitive and must be carefully monitored.

Pies. Pie crusts become very flaky but do not brown. Crumbs crusts are more appealing. Sogginess is avoided by precooking the crust before the filling is added and cooking on an inverted plate. Stirring of the filling and rotating of the pie is essential.

Breads. Recipes for microwave cookery of yeast products have not been developed. It appears that a combination of conventional and microwave cooking is necessary. Doughnuts have been commercially proofed with microwaves. Cornbread is excellent but lacks a browned crust.

Starch Products. Since large quantities of water are heated faster conventionally, it is probably easier to cook pasta in this manner. Starch-thickened sauces are successful if they are stirred

only once during cooking. Overheating causes an explosion of the starch grain, which results in thinning of the sauce. Waxy cornstarch substituted for flour as a thickening agent has less of a tendency toward reversion, particularly after thawing.

Sugar. Sugary mixtures are easy to cook in the microwave oven. Sugar melts and carmelizes to a brown color very quickly because of the loss of moisture. Candy making is easier in the microwave because less stirring is required and scorching does not occur at the bottom of the pan.

ODD USES

The microwave oven can be conveniently used for many odd uses in the kitchen. Cold butter, solid-frozen ice cream, and hard brown sugar are easily softened by microwave energy. Stale baked goods and leftover coffee (which has been refrigerated) taste freshly made when reheated. Croutons and fresh herbs can be quickly dried.

Chocolate can be melted right in the bowl. Fudge toppings for ice cream, pancake syrup, and molasses can be heated without being removed from the jar. Frozen waffles are cooked in 35 seconds. A truly novel idea is the microwave opening of clams and oysters.

NUTRITIONAL ASPECTS

Studies have been conducted on the nutrient composition of microwave-cooked foods. Most have concluded that electronically cooked foods are as nutritious, if not more so, than foods cooked by conventional methods. The rapid, extremely efficient heating of microwaves produces less destruction of some heat-sensitive vitamins. In addition, water-soluble vitamins are not leached in discarded cooking water. Greater retention of vitamin B_6 in chicken,[6] thiamine in

[6]R. W. Wing and J. C. Alexander, "Effect of Microwave Heating on Vitamin B_6 Retention in Chicken," *J. Amer. Dietet. Assoc.* **61**:661, 1972.

pork,[7] and ascorbic acid in vegetables[8] have been reported in foods cooked electronically.

SAFETY OF THE MICROWAVE OVEN

The "nonionizing" radiation of microwaves does not create cellular damage as does the "ionizing" radiation of x rays. The dangerous gamma and x rays are 1 million times more powerful than microwaves. The effect microwaves create is thermal (i.e., limited to heating only). Any harm that could occur would be due strictly to the effect of heat on the food or tissue. For this reason, microwave-cooked foods are not radioactive and are no more harmful than conventionally cooked foods.

Tissue Damage. Microwaves can be harmful to biological tissue if the heat cannot be quickly dissipated. A few areas of the human body are particularly heat-sensitive: the lens of the eye, the testes, and some other tissues.[9] Skin burns have been reported from direct exposure to microwaves. The lens of the eye is vulnerable because it lacks an adequate blood supply to dissipate the heat. Cataract formation may result.

Concern has also been raised as to the possible effect of low-level radiation on unborn fetuses,[10] although no cases of harmful effects in human beings have been reported. Older, unshielded models of pacemakers may be affected by microwaves (as well as portable lawnmowers and transmission towers). Wearers of such pacemakers have been cautioned of their limitations.

Government Leakage Standards. Government standards for leakage of new microwave

ovens have been set at 1.0 mW/cm^2 at 5 cm (2 in.) from the oven door.[11] This leakage may not increase to more than 5.0 mW/cm^2 over the life of the oven. 1.0 mW/cm^2 is one-ten thousandth of the level that will cause harm to biological tissue.

Door Leakage. The most likely place for leakage to occur is around the door. Leakage may result if the door seals are burned, pitted, or ripped; the door is loose on its hinges; part of the screen is missing or cracked; or an object is caught in the door. The most important factor in microwave oven safety is the maintenance of the oven.

Leakage can be crudely determined by slowly running a finger around the door seal while the oven is cooking. If any heat is felt, the oven should not be used again until a serviceman has inspected it.

Safety Features. Three safety features are installed in microwave ovens to prevent leakage. All microwave ovens since 1971 are required to have two interlock switches, which automatically turn off the magnetron when the door is opened. If the safety interlocks fail, a monitoring system is designed to turn off the magnetron.

Most new model microwave ovens have a safety starter. When the microwave cooking is interruped (for stirring or rearranging), the oven will not start again unless it is restarted. This decreases the danger of operating an empty oven.

Operation of an empty oven may cause overheating and damage the magnetron. To prevent this from occurring by accident, it is wise to keep a glass of water in the empty oven when it is not being operated. Extremely small quantities of food may also cause overheating if a glass of water is not present in the oven to absorb the excess energy.

Safety Rules. For safety, the following rules should be followed:

1. Always check a new oven for shipping

---

[7] A. M. Kylen, B. H. McGrath, E. L. Hallmark, and F. O. Van Duyne, "Microwave and Conventional Cooking of Meat," *J. Amer. Dietet. Assoc.* **39**:321, 1961.

[8] J. Gordon and I. Noble, "Comparison of Electronic Versus Conventional Cooking of Vegetables," *J. Amer. Dietet. Assoc.* **35**:241, 1959.

[9] "Facts About Microwave Radiation," *FDA 72-8017* (Washington, D.C.: U.S. Department of Health, Education, and Welfare, Public Health Service, 1971).

[10] "Microwave Ovens. 2. Is Microwave Leakage Hazardous?" *Consumer Rep.* **41**:319, 1976.

[11] "Control of Hazards to Health from Microwave Radiation," *Department of Army Technical Bulletin, Department of the Air Force Manual* (Washington, D.C.: U.S. Departments of Army and the Air Force, 1965).

damage and read the manufacturer's instructions.

2. Never operate the oven with an object caught in the door or with a door that does not close properly.
3. Do not tamper with the safety locks or operate an empty oven.
4. Keep the door seal clean and free from grease without using a cleanser or steel wool. Check periodically for warping, pitting, or tearing.
5. Maintain the oven properly by having it regularly serviced by a qualified person.

Remember, no harm has ever been reported when microwave ovens have been used according to the manufacturer's instructions.

MICROBIOLOGICAL SAFETY OF COOKED FOOD

Destruction of microorganisms by thermal means is dependent not only on the temperature but also on the length of time the food is heated. A greater bacterial survival in meat cooked electronically has been reported.[12] The quick rise in lethal temperature and maintenance of that temperature for only short periods of time allows more bacteria to survive. The implication is that meat cooked by microwaves must be carefully handled and refrigerated to prevent subsequent bacterial growth.

Conversely, microwaves can be used to retard bacterial growth. Fresh meat and poultry that have been subjected to 10 seconds of microwaves have been reported to last a day or two longer in the refrigerator.[13] The bacteria counts are reduced by quick increase in temperature. Longer heat treatment is unadvisable because of moisture loss and heat changes.

SUMMARY

Microwaves are nonionizing waves of energy that create thermal changes. They are absorbed, transferred, or reflected, depending on the composition of the substance they strike. Dipolar molecules, in an attempt to align themselves with the electrical field generated by the magnetron, create heat by internal friction.

Advantages of microwave cooking are speed of cooking, flavor retention in leftovers, absence of kitchen heat, and energy savings. Limitations are lack of browning, lack of slow cooking, and impracticality for large quantities.

Factors affecting microwave cooking are starting temperature, volume, density, and composition. Arrangement, stirring and rotating, covering, and standing time are cooking techniques.

Cooking utensils must be able to transfer microwaves. Glass, paper goods, and some plastics are best. Metals reflect microwaves and should not be used, except for shielding.

Satisfactory cooking of vegetables, tender cuts of meats and poultry, scrambled eggs, cakes, pies, and starch and sugar products is possible. Microwave-cooked food is as nutritious as conventionally cooked food.

Microwaves can cause damage to biological tissue. However, limits for leakage set by government standards are strict. Leakage can be avoided by proper maintenance of the oven. No harm has been reported with proper use of microwave ovens.

QUESTIONS AND TOPICS FOR DISCUSSION AND STUDY

1. What are the advantages of microwave cooking? The disadvantages?
2. How does a microwave oven work?
3. What is the most important factor in microwave cookery? How is it influenced by starting temperature, volume, density, and composition?
4. What new cooking techniques must be used in microwave cookery?
5. Is the microwave oven safe to use? Why or why not? How can you check for leakage?

SUGGESTED ACTIVITIES

1. Place 1 cup of tap water in the oven. Record the time it takes to come to a boil. Repeat

---

[12] F. L. Crespo and H. W. Ockerman, "Thermal Destruction of Microorganisms in Meat by Microwave and Conventional Cooking," *J. Food Protect.* **40:**442, 1977.

[13] "Newsnotes," *Chem. Eng. News,* March 6, 1978.

using 2 and 4 cups. What is the percent increase in time required to boil for each doubling of the volume?

2. Break open five eggs, or enough for 9 tbsp of egg white. Seperate the yolks and reserve for future use. Arrange nine custard cups equi-distant from each other in the oven. Place 1 tbsp of egg white in each custard cup. Turn the microwave oven on until the egg white just begins to turn white, then turn off. De-termine the heat-distribution pattern of the oven by the degree of coagulation of the egg white at the various locations of the custard cups.

3. Freeze two ½-lb packages of hamburger until solid. Defrost one by placing in the micro-wave oven and heating until the ice crystals almost disappear. Defrost the other by heating for 1 minute and resting for 1 minute. Repeat the process until the ice crystals are almost gone. What is the difference between the two pieces of meat? Why is one method better?

REFERENCES

BOOKS

Better Homes and Gardens. *Microwave Cook Book*. Des Moines, Iowa: Meredith, 1976.

Litton Systems. *An Exciting New World of Micro-wave Cooking*. Minneapolis, Minn.: Pillsbury, 1971.

Medved, Eva. *Food—Theory and Practice*. Fuller-ton, Calif.: Plycon, 1978, Chap. 15.

Scott, Maria, and Jack Scott. *Mastering Microwave Cooking*. New York: Bantam, 1976.

Van Zante, Helen. *The Microwave Oven*. Boston: Houghton Mifflin, 1973.

ARTICLES AND PAMPHLETS

Consumer Microwave Oven Systems Conference. Chicago: Association of Home Appliance Manufacturers, 1970.

Korschgen, Bernice, Ruth Baldwin, and Sue Snider. "Quality Factors in Beef, Pork and Lamb Cooked by Microwave." *J. Amer. Dietet. Assoc.* **12**(1):1, 1977.

Lorenz, K., E. Charman, and W. Dilsaver. "Baking with Microwave Energy." *Food Technol.* **27**(12):28, 1973.

Roberts, Robert. "Effect of Microwave Treat-ment of Pre-soaked Paddy, Brown, and White Rice." *J. Food Sci.* **42**(3):804, 1977.

Rosen, Carl-Gustaf. "Effects of Microwaves on Food and Related Materials." *Food Technol.* **26**(7):36, 1972.

Appendix

Glossary of Food Terms

Every subject–matter area includes terms with specific meanings, and knowledge of these is essential to a full understanding of the concepts presented. The following list presents terms commonly met in this book or in supplementary texts. It includes the chemical, bacteriological, biochemical, and technological terms generally employed in the area of food preparation.[1] Detailed information on many of the terms is given in the text.

GLOSSARY OF TERMS RELATED TO FOOD

Acid foods and basic foods Sodium, potassium, magnesium, and calcium are base-forming; phosphorus, sulfur, and chlorine are acid-forming. A food in which basic minerals predominate will when oxidized leave an alkaline residue; a food in which acid-forming minerals predominate will leave an acid residue. An alkaline residue is left by milk, vegetables, some fruits; an acid residue is left by meat, fish, poultry, eggs, cheese, prunes, and cereals; fats and sugars are neutral.

Acid number Used with reference to a measure of hydrolytic rancidity in fats; defined as milligrams of caustic potash required to neutralize the free fatty acids in 1 gram of fat.

Acrolein Compound formed when glycerol is heated to a high temperature; responsible for the acrid odor and vapor produced when fats are heated.

Actomyosin Contractile protein of muscle.

Additives Materials added to food to help manufacture and preserve it and to improve nutritive value, palatability, and eye appeal. May be classified as emulsifiers, flavors, thickeners, curing agents, humectants, colors, nutrients, or mold, yeast, or bacterial inhibitors. Amounts used in food are regulated by law.

Aerobes Microorganisms that need oxygen for growth.

Agar Dried, purified stems of seaweed; partly soluble; swells with water to form a gel. Used

[1] *Sources:* Arnold Bender, *Dictionary of Nutrition and Food Technology* (New York: Academic Press, 1961); Benjamin Harrow, *Textbook of Biochemistry* (Philadelphia: Saunders, 1950); C. Dull, H. Metcalf, and J. Williams, *Modern Chemistry* (New York: Holt, 1958); W. Frazier, *Food Microbiology* (New York: McGraw-Hill, 1958).

in soups, jellies, ice cream, and meat and fish pastes. Also called *agar-agar* or *gum*.

Aging Term applied to treatment of flour with oxidizing agents. Also refers to changes in tenderness that take place in meats after slaughter.

Albedo White pith of the inner peel of citrus fruits, also known as the *mesocarp*. Consists of sugars, cellulose, and pectins. May be used as the source of pectin for commercial manufacture.

Albumen Often used to refer to the white of an egg.

Albumin Often used as a nonspecific name for protein; also used to designate a simple protein (one free from other substances) soluble in water and coagulable by heat.

Aldehyde One of a large class of organic substances derived from a primary alcohol by oxidation; contains the characteristic group CHO.

Aleurone layer The single layer of large cells under the bran coat and outside the endosperm of cereal grains. Rich in protein. Although part of the endosperm, remains attached to the inner layer of bran during milling.

Alginates Salts of alginic acid found free and as calcium salt in many seaweeds; used as thickeners and to stabilize emulsions in ice cream and synthetic cream.

Alimentary pastes Shaped, dried doughs prepared from semolina, a hard durum wheat flour, with water, egg, and (sometimes) milk. Dough is partly dried in hot air for about 20 minutes and then dried more slowly over a period of hours.

Alkanet (or alkannet) Red coloring obtained from root of borage plant; used for coloring fats, cheeses, and essences.

Amino acids Organic compounds of carbon, hydrogen, oxygen, and nitrogen. Each amino acid contains one amino group (—NH) and at least one (—COOH) carboxyl group. In addition, some amino acids contain sulfur. Many amino acids linked together in some definite pattern form a protein.

Amphoteric Describes proteins and amino acids, which carry both negative and positive charges in the molecules. At a certain degree of acidity, depending on the particular protein or amino acid, the substance becomes electri-

cally neutral and soluble. At this point, the substance usually precipitates from solution.

Amylases Enzymes that hydrolize starch and glycogen to maltose.

Amylograph Used to measure the viscosity of flour paste as it is heated from 25 to 90°C, a range comparable to the temperature rise in baking.

Amylolytic General adjective applied to enzymes that can split starch into soluble products.

Amylopectin The principal (75–80%) component of starch; the remainder is amylose.

Anaerobes Microorganisms that grow in the absence of oxygen.

Angstrom unit $1/10,000,000$ mm, or $1/10,000$ micrometer; used to measure wavelength of light. Symbol: Å.

Annatto Yellow coloring matter.

Anthocyanins Coloring matter of many fruits, flowers, and leaves: violet, red, and blue.

Antibiotics Substances produced by living organisms that inhibit the growth of other organisms; used in some countries as food preservatives.

Antifoaming agents Substances that reduce foaming caused by the presence of dissolved proteins.

Antioxidants Substances that retard the oxidative rancidity of fats. Natural fats, particularly vegetable oils, contain naturally occurring antioxidants that protect the oils from rancidity for a limited period.

Antispattering agents Added to fats used for frying; prevent the coalescence of water droplets. Example: lecithin.

Arrowroot Starchy substance obtained from the root of the arrowroot plant; almost pure starch.

Autoclave Vessel in which high temperatures can be reached by using high pressure. Example: the domestic pressure cooker.

Autolysis Process of self-digestion effected by the enzymes naturally present in the tissue. Tenderizing of meat while hanging is example of autolytic breakdown of connective tissue.

Babcock test Test for fat in milk.

Benzoic acid Free acid, or as sodium or potassium benzoate, is a permitted preservative in such foods as pickles, sauces, and soft drinks; has antimicrobial activity.

Botulism Rare form of food poisoning caused

by the toxin produced by *Clostridium botulinum,* an anaerobic organism whose toxin is so powerful that only a small amount is needed to cause death.

Bromelin Proteolytic enzyme in fresh pineapple juice; used for tenderizing meat and sausage casings.

Brix Scale of densities often used for sugar solutions and fruit juices.

Buffers Substances that resist change in acidity or alkalinity. Examples: salts of weak acids and weak bases, also proteins and amino acids, by virtue of their content of both acidic and basic groups.

Catalase Enzyme in plants and animals; splits hydrogen peroxide into water and gaseous oxygen.

Centrifuge Machine that exerts a pull many times stronger than gravity by spinning; used to clarify liquids, by settling the heavier solid (which might take several days under gravity) in a few minutes. Also used to separate two liquids of different densities, such as cream from milk.

Chlorophyll Green coloring matter of all plant materials; used by plants to manufacture foodstuffs from simple salts and carbon dioxide with energy derived from sunlight.

Coliform bacteria Group of aerobic lactose fermenters. Many are not harmful, but as they are found in feces, they are useful as a test of fecal contamination, particularly as a test for water pollution.

Collagen Insoluble proteins in bones, tendons, skin, and connective tissues of animals and fish; can be converted to soluble gelatin by moist heat.

Colloid Fine particles suspended in a second medium, which can be solid, liquid, or gas.

Conalbumin Protein found in egg white; has the property of binding iron in an iron–protein complex that turns pink in the presence of oxygen.

Cryptoxanthin Yellow coloring matter in such vegetables as yellow corn.

Degumming agents Used in refining fats to remove mucilaginous matter consisting of gum, resin, proteins, and phosphatides.

Denaturation A change in protein, usually resulting in its having a very different solubility than the native protein. May be reversible if conditions causing change are very mild.

Frequently irreversible. Can be brought about by changes in pH, heat, ultraviolet irradiation, and violent agitation.

Deodorization Term generally applied to the removal of flavor or odor from fats during refining.

Dextrins Mixture of soluble compounds formed by partial breakdown of starch by heat, acid, or enzymes.

Dextrose Alternative name for glucose, a monosaccharide.

Disaccharides Sugars composed of two monosaccharides combined, with the elimination of a molecule of water.

Elastin Insoluble protein uniting muscle fibers in meat; is not changed on heating.

Emulsifying agents Substances such as gums, soaps, agar, lecithin, glycerol monostearate, alginates, and Irish moss that aid the uniform dispersion of oil in water. Examples of emulsions formed: margarine, salad dressing, and ice cream.

Emulsifying salts Sodium citrate, sodium phosphates, and sodium tartrate; used in the manufacture of milk powder, evaporated milk, sterilized cream, and processed cheese.

Enzymes Catalysts produced by living cells; responsible for most of the reactions carried out in plants and animals; composed of proteins and destroyed by heat and by chemicals that coagulate proteins.

Ester Chemical name of the compound of an acid and alcohol. Example: ethylacetate, a compound of ethyl alcohol and acetic acid. Fats are esters of glycerol (an alcohol) and an acid such as stearic or oleic acid.

Fats, high-ratio Shortenings with a greater proportion of monoglycerides and diglycerides; disperse more readily into doughs and allow the use of a higher ratio of sugar to flour than ordinary shortening does.

Fatty acids Organic acids consisting of carbon chains with a carboxyl group at the end. Example: acetic acid.

Fermentation Transformation or metabolism of compounds without the use of oxygen. Example: the breakdown of sugar by yeast enzymes to carbon dioxide and alcohol.

Firming agents Calcium salts, such as calcium chloride or carbonate, that may be added to fruit or vegetables to keep them firm. The addition of the calcium salt forms a calcium pectate gel, which protects the tissue against softening.

Flavedo Colored outer peel layer of citrus fruits. Also called the *epicarp*. Contains oil sacs and pigments (chlorophyll, carotene, and xanthophyll).

Flour, high-ratio Flour with very fine particles and treated with chlorine; used in cakes mainly, as it is possible to use up to 140 parts of sugar to 100 parts of this flour. (This is twice as much sugar as can be used with ordinary flour.)

Free fatty acids (FFA) Fats are esters of glycerol with three molecules of fatty acids. Under certain adverse conditions, there is some degree of hydrolysis with the liberation of free fatty acids; therefore, the determination of FFA is an index of fat quality.

Freeze drying A method of drying in which the material is frozen and a high vacuum applied. The cooling effect of the evaporation keeps the material frozen while the water distills off as a vapor. Freeze-dried material is very porous and occupies the same volume as the original. The process is applied to foods with advantage as they reconstitute rapidly, with a minimum loss of flavor and texture.

Fructose Levulose or fruit sugar; when combined with glucose, forms sucrose.

Gallates Salts and esters of gallic acid, found in many plants. Propyl, octyl, and dodecyl gallates are legally permitted antioxidants.

Gel Technically, a sol or colloidal suspension that has set to a jelly.

Gelatin A water-soluble protein prepared from collagen by boiling with water.

Glucose Also known as dextrose, grape sugar, and blood sugar.

Glucosides Complexes of substances with glucose.

Glutamate, sodium (monosodium glutamate) Sodium salt of the amino acid, glutamic acid. Enhances the flavor of some foods, especially meat and vegetables. (It is believed that it accomplishes this by stimulating the taste buds.) Commercially manufactured from sugar beet pulp and wheat gluten.

Gluten Name given to protein fraction of wheat; identified as the part of the flour that gives it the elastic properties essential for making bread.

Glycerol Trihydric alcohol manufactured by the hydrolysis of fats and therefore produced during the manufacture of soap.

Glycerol monostearate (GMS) An emulsifier that helps to distribute fat evenly through a product and helps to stabilize an emulsion.

Glycogen Storage form of carbohydrate in the animal body; found in liver and muscles.

Homogenization Process that reduces fat globules to a smaller and approximately equal size.

Hulophilic bacteria Bacteria capable of growing in high concentration of salt.

Humectant Substance that absorbs moisture; used to maintain strength of materials such as baking powder.

Hydrogenated oils Oil hardened by treatment with hydrogen in the presence of nickel. Cottonseed, maize, and wheat oils are commonly hardened and used in cooking fats.

Hydrogen-ion concentration Measure of the acidity or alkalinity of a solution by the concentration of hydrogen ions present.

Hydrolyze The splitting of a compound into smaller units by the addition of water.

Hygroscopic Readily absorbing water.

Iodine value Sometimes referred to as *iodine number,* the measure of the degree of unsaturation of a fat by the extent of the uptake of iodine (the number of grams of iodine absorbed per 100 g fat) by the unsaturated double bonds in the fatty acid chain. Hence, butter with an iodine value of 22–38 is more highly saturated than cottonseed oil with an iodine value of 104–114.

Iodized salt Table salt to which potassium or sodium iodide and a small amount of magnesium carbonate have been added.

Ionizations When a salt such as sodium chloride is dissolved in water, it splits into positively charged sodium ions and negatively charged chloride ions. Some organic acids also ionize. If an acid does not ionize readily, it is considered a weak acid.

Irradiation (ionizing) Pertains to ionizing radiation that destroys various microorganisms. Complete sterilization of food requires high dosages that cause marked changes in odor, color, and flavor. Term may also be used for the treatment of milk with ultraviolet rays so as to enrich it with vitamin D.

Isoelectric point Because proteins and amino acids carry both negative and positive charges in the molecule, they are known as *amphoteric*. Each protein or amino acid has a point at which the tendency to become acid or alkaline in reaction is equally strong. This is its neutral (isoelectric) point, the point at which it is least soluble. At this point, it precipitates out of solution.

Lacquer Layer of gum compound applied to the tin plate of a can and hardened with heat. The layer of lacquer is protective. Acid fruit juices darken the tin lining of a can.

Lactalbumin One of the proteins of milk.

Lactose Milk sugar; a disaccharide.

Lecithin One of a group of lipids known as *phospholipids*. Abundant in brain tissue and egg yolk. Obtained from peanuts, corn, and soybeans for commercial use (as an emulsifier in such products as chocolate).

Livetin A water-soluble protein found in egg yolk.

Lycopene Red pigment in tomato; sometimes used as a coloring material.

Maillard reaction Reaction between proteins or amino acids and sugars that brings about a brown color. Takes place on heating or on prolonged storage, and is one of the deteriorative processes that occur in stored foods. Also known as the *browning reaction* and as *nonenzymatic browning.*

Malic acid Organic acid widely found in many fruits; abundant in apples.

Maltase Enzyme that splits maltose into two molecules of glucose.

Maltose A disaccharide composed of two molecules of glucose.

Melting point Generally characteristic of a particular chemical and used as a means of identification; particularly useful as a measure of purity (impurities lower the melting point).

Microaerophiles Microorganisms that can grow in extremely low concentrations of oxygen; therefore, effective in destroying foodstuffs intended to be stored in the absence of air, if there are any traces left.

Mineral salts Inorganic salts, including sodium, potassium, calcium, chloride, phosphate, and sulfate.

NDGA Abbreviation for *nordihydroguaiaretic acid;* used as an antioxidant for fats.

Nitrates Occur naturally in many foods; added to meat in curing. When added to meat pickle, they are reduced to nitrites. Mixtures of the two are often used. Nitrite combines with the meat pigment, myoglobin, to form the red nitromyoglobin of pickled meat.

Organic Terms used to identify chemicals with carbon in the molecule (except carbonates and cyanides). Substances of animal and vegetable origin are organic; minerals are inorganic.

Organoleptic Technical term for taste and smell.

Osmosis The transfer of materials that takes place through a semipermeable membrane separating two solutions, or between a solvent and a solution, that tends to equalize their concentrations. The walls of living cells are semipermeable membranes, and much of the activity of cells depends on osmosis.

Osmotic pressure Pull exerted by a solution on water molecules. If a concentrated solution of salt is separated from pure water by a semipermeable membrane, the water passes through the membrane to dilute the salt solution until the osmotic pressure on both sides of the membrane is equalized.

Ovalbumin Albumin of egg white.

Ovomucin A carbohydrate–protein complex in egg white.

Ovomucoid A protein of egg white.

Oxalic acid Found in spinach, rhubarb leaves, and chocolate; toxic when ingested in large doses but safe in small amounts.

Oxidases Enzymes that oxidize compounds by removing hydrogen and passing it directly to oxygen to form water.

Oxidation Gain in oxygen or loss of hydrogen or, in general terms, loss of electrons.

Ozone Chemically composed of three atoms of oxygen, O_3; used as a germicide.

Papain Proteolytic enzyme from the juice of the papaya; used in tenderizing meat.

Parts per million (ppm) Method of describing small concentrations; usually used with regard to traces of metallic impurities and food additives.

Pasteurization Mild heat treatment that destroys many vegetative forms of bacteria.

Peroxide number Measure of the oxidative rancidity of fats by the determination of the peroxides present.

pH Abbreviation of hydrogen ion concentration. The hydrogen ion concentration of a neutral solution of any substance in water is $1:10,000,000$ or 10^{-7} gram ion per liter. A hydrogen ion exponent is the exponent, with the sign reversed, of the concentration of hydrogen ions, in grams of ions per liter. Alkalinity of a solution is indicated by a pH higher than 7.0; an acid solution by a pH below 7.0.

Polyoxyethylene An ester of fatty acids of edible oils used as an emulsifying agent in baking.

Polyphosphates Phosphates added to food, particularly meat products; effective in preventing discoloration.

Polysaccharides Complex carbohydrates formed by the condensation of large numbers of monosaccharide units.

Propionates Salts of propionic acid; used as mold inhibitors.

Reduction Loss of oxygen or gain in hydrogen; in general terms, gain in electrons.

Rennet Extract of calf stomach; contains enzyme rennin.

Rennin Digestive enzyme that clots milk.

Rope Form of bacteria that can survive baking of bread; under conditions of warmth and moisture, may convert mass of the bread into starchy patches.

Salinometer Hydrometer used to measure concentration of salt solutions.

Salmonella Genus of bacteria; common cause of food poisoning; destroyed by adequate heating.

Smoke point Temperature at which the decomposition products of fat become visible.

Smoking Process that imparts flavor to meats and fish after pickling. Hardwoods such as oak, elm, and ash are used. Helps preservation by inducing surface dehydration.

Spectrophotometer Optical instrument that measures the amount of light absorbed at any particular wavelength.

Spores Some bacteria form spores. These are in a resting state; they are thick-walled and highly resistant to damage by heat. Certain spores can remain undamaged in the processing of food and the material is consequently not sterile.

Stabilizers Substances that keep emulsions of fat and water in equilibrium. Examples: agar, egg albumen.

Substrate Term used to refer to the substance on which the enzyme acts or the medium in which the microorganisms grow.

Superglycerinated fats Fats are triglycerides; that is, they have three molecules of fatty acid to one molecule of glycerol. Hence, monoglycerides (one fatty acid molecule to one molecule of glycerol) and diglycerides are known as superglycerinated fats.

Tragacanth Gum obtained from a shrub; used as an emulsifying agent or as a thickener.

GLOSSARY OF TERMS USED IN FOOD PREPARATION[2]

The following cooking terms found in recipes should be mastered fully:

Bake To cook by dry heat in an oven or oven-type appliance. Covered or uncovered containers may be used. When applied to meats in uncovered containers, it is generally called *roasting*.

Barbecue To roast slowly on a gridiron, on a spit, over coals, or under a free flame or oven electric unit. While cooking, the food is usually basted with a highly seasoned sauce. Term is popularly applied to foods cooked in or served with barbecue sauce.

Baste To moisten meat or other foods during cooking to add flavor and to prevent drying of the surfaces, usually with melted fat, meat drippings, fruit juice, sauce, or water.

Beat To smooth a mixture or to introduce air into it by using a brisk, regular motion that lifts the mixture over and over.

Blanch (precook) To preheat in boiling water or steam. Done to inactivate enzymes and to shrink food for canning, freezing, or drying, also to aid in removal of skins from nuts, fruits, and some vegetables. (Vegetables are blanched in boiling water or steam, fruits in boiling fruit juice, syrup, water, or steam.)

Blend To mix two or more ingredients thoroughly.

Boil To cook in water, or in a liquid that is mostly water, until bubbles rise continually and break on the surface. [The boiling temperature of water at sea level is $212°F$ ($0°C$).]

Braise To cook slowly in a covered utensil in a small amount of liquid (meat stock or added

---

[2] *Handbook of Food Preparation* (Washington, D.C.: American Home Economics Association, rev. 1975).

water) or in steam. (Meat may or may not be browned in a small amount of fat before braising.)

Bread To coat with bread crumbs; also, to coat with bread crumbs, then with diluted slightly beaten egg or evaporated milk, and again with crumbs. Done before cooking.

Broil To cook by direct heat.

Brown To give a brown surface to a food (such as meat or flour) by applying high heat; also, to make brown by baking or roasting.

Candy Applied to fruit, fruit peel, or ginger: to cook in a heavy syrup until plump and transparent, then to drain and dry. (Product is also known as crystallized fruit, or fruit peel, or ginger.) Applied to parboiled sweet potatoes and carrots: to cook a second time in sugar or syrup.

Caramelize To heat sugar, or foods containing sugar, until a brown color and characteristic flavor develop.

Chop To cut into pieces with a sharp tool.

Coat a spoon To cover a spoon with a layer of thickened food (such as a custard sauce).

Congeal To change a liquid to a solid by lowering the temperature of the food sufficiently to bring about gelation.

Core To remove the core from a fruit.

Cream To work one or more foods until they are soft and creamy, using a spoon, wooden paddle, or other implement. (Applied to fat and sugar in place of *blend*.)

Crumb To cover with crumbs. To break bread, crackers, or cookies into small particles.

Crystallize To cause to form crystals (as in making a crystalline candy, such as fudge).

Cure To preserve by drying or salting.

Cut To divide with knife or scissors.

Cut-in To distribute solid fat in dry ingredients by chopping fat into small pieces with knives or a pastry blender until it is finely divided.

Dice To cut into small cubes.

Dilute To diminish the strength or flavor of a mixture (usually with water).

Dredge To sprinkle or coat with flour or other fine substance.

Fold To combine by cutting vertically through the mixture and turning it over and over by sliding the implement across the bottom of the mixing bowl with each turn.

Fricassee To cook by braising (usually applied to fowl, rabbit, or veal cut into pieces).

Frizzle To cook in pan until food curls up or crimps.

Fry To cook in fat; to cook in a small amount of fat (also called *sauté* or *pan-fry*); to cook in a deep layer of fat (also called *deep-fat frying*).

Garnish To decorate a food so as to make it look attractive.

Glacé To coat with a thin sugar syrup cooked to the crack stage. (When used for pies and certain types of bread, mixture may contain thickening but is uncooked or not cooked to such a concentrated form.)

Grill See *Broil*.

Grind To reduce to particles by cutting, crushing, or grinding.

Knead To manipulate with a pressing, folding, and stretching motion.

Lard To insert strips of fat, called *lardoons,* into (or to place slices of fat on top of) uncooked lean meat or fish to give flavor and prevent surface drying.

Marinate To let food stand in a marinade (usually an oil–acid mixture, such as French dressing).

Mask To cover completely. Usually applied to the use of mayonnaise or other thick sauce, but may also refer to forcemeat or jelly.

Melt To liquefy by heat.

Mince To cut or chop into very small pieces.

Mix To combine ingredients in any way that effects a distribution.

Mold To mix or knead into a required consistency or shape.

Pan-broil To cook uncovered on a hot surface (usually a fry pan). Fat is poured off as it accumulates.

Pan-fry To cook in a small amount of fat. (See *Fry* and *Sauté.*)

Panning To cook a vegetable in tightly covered skillet, using a small amount of fat. No water is added.

Parboil To boil until partially cooked, usually in preparation for further cooking or processing.

Parch To brown by means of dry heat. (Applied to grains, such as corn.)

Pare To cut off the outside covering.

Pasteurize To preserve food by heating sufficiently to destroy certain microorganisms and arrest fermentation. Applied to liquids, such as milk and fruit juices. The temperature used varies with the food but commonly ranges from 140 to 180°F (60–80°C).

Peel To strip off the outside covering.

Pickle To preserve foods by means of brine or syrup and vinegar.

Pit To remove stone (pit) from fruits.

Plank To cook or serve on a plank made especially for the purpose.

Poach To cook in a hot liquid, using precautions to retain shape. (Temperature used varies with the food.)

Pot-roast Term applied to cooking larger cuts of meat by braising. (See *Braise.*)

Reconstitute To restore concentrated foods to their normal state, usually by adding water. Applied to such foods as dry milk or frozen fruit juices.

Rehydration To soak, cook, or use other procedures with dehydrated foods or to restore water lost during drying.

Render To free fat from connective tissue at low heat.

Roast To cook food, uncovered, by dry heat. Usually done in an oven but occasionally in ashes, under coals, or on heated stones or metals. Term is usually applied to meats but may also refer to other foods, such as potatoes, corn, and chestnuts.

Sauté To brown or cook in a small amount of fat. (See *Fry.*)

Scald To heat milk to just below the boiling point: also, to dip certain foods in boiling water. (See *Blanch.*)

Scallop To bake food, usually cut in pieces, with a sauce or other liquid. The top may be covered with crumbs. Food and sauce may be mixed together or arranged in alternate layers in a baking dish, with or without crumbs.

Sear To brown the surface of meat by a brief application of intense heat.

Sift To separate, with a sieve, the fine part of a substance from the coarse. To mix flour with air.

Simmer To cook in a liquid maintained at just below the boiling point (185–210°F; 84–99°C) so that bubbles form slowly and collapse below the surface.

Steam To cook in steam, with or without pressure. Steam may be applied directly to the food, as in a steamer or pressure cooker.

Steep To allow a substance to stand in liquid at a temperature below the boiling point for the purpose of extracting flavor, color, or other qualities.

Sterilize To destroy microorganisms. (For culinary purposes, most often done at a high temperature with steam or dry heat, or by boiling in a liquid.)

Stew To simmer food in a small quantity of liquid.

Stir To mix food materials with a circular motion for the purpose of blending or securing a uniform consistency.

Toast To brown food by means of dry heat.

Truss To skewer or tie a chicken's, duck's, turkey's, or any other fowl's wings and legs to its body.

Whip To beat rapidly to introduce air and thus to produce expansion. (Applied to cream, eggs, and gelatin dishes.)

MEAT AND POULTRY PRODUCTS SPECIFIC PRODUCT REQUIREMENTS

RED MEAT PRODUCTS. (All percentages of meat are on the basis of fresh uncooked weight unless otherwise indicated.)

Barbecue Sauce with Meat—At least 35% meat (cooked basis).

Barbecued Meats—Weight of meat when barbecued cannot exceed 70% of the weight of the fresh uncooked meat. Must have barbecued (crusted) appearance and be prepared over burning or smoldering hardwood or its sawdust.

Beans with Bacon in Sauce—At least 12% bacon.

Beans with Frankfurters in Sauce—At least 20% franks.

Beans with Ham in Sauce—At least 12% ham (cooked basis).

Beef with Barbecue Sauce—At least 50% beef (cooked basis).

Beef with Gravy—At least 50% beef (cooked basis). *Gravy with Beef*—At least 35% beef (cooked basis).

Beef Sausage—No more than 30% fat.

Beef Stroganoff—At least 45% fresh uncooked beef or 30% cooked beef, and at least 10% sour cream or a "gourmet" combination of at least 7.5% sour cream and 5% wine.

Breaded Steaks, Chops, etc.—Breading cannot exceed 30% of finished product weight.

Breakfast Sausage—No more than 50% fat.

Burritos—At least 15% meat.

Chili con Carne—At least 40% meat.

Chili con Carne with Beans—At least 25% meat.

Chili Sauce with Meat—At least 6% meat.

Chop Suey (American Style) with Macaroni and Meat—At least 25% meat.

Chop Suey Vegetables with Meat—At least 12% meat.

Chow Mein Vegetables with Meat—At least 12% meat.

Condensed, Creamed Dried Beef or Chipped Beef—At least 18% dried or chipped beef (figured on reconstituted total content).

Corn Dog—Must meet standards for frankfurters and batter cannot exceed the weight of the frank.

Corned Beef and Cabbage—At least 25% corned beef.

Deviled Ham—No more than 35% fat.

Egg Foo Yung with Meat—At least 12% meat.

Egg Rolls with Meat—At least 10% meat.

Enchilada with Meat—At least 15% meat.

Frankfurters, Bologna, Sausage—May contain meat and meat by-products; no more than 30% fat; no more than 15% poultry unless its presence is reflected in product name; no more than 3.5% cereals and nonfat dry milk, with product name showing that they are added. *"All Meat"*—Only muscle tissue with natural amounts of fat; no by-products, cereal, or binders. *"All Beef"*—Only meat of beef animals.

Fritters—At least 35% meat.

Frozen Breakfasts—At least 15% meat (cooked basis).

Frozen Dinners—At least 25% meat or meat food product (cooked basis, figured on total meal minus appetizer, bread, and dessert).

Ham—Not permitted to weigh more after processing than the fresh ham weighs before curing and smoking. Hams containing up to 10% added water must be labeled as *"Ham—Water Added."* If added water exceeds 10% must be labeled *"Imitation Ham."*

Ham and Cheese Spread—At least 25% ham (cooked basis).

Ham Chowder—At least 10% ham (cooked basis).

Ham Croquettes—At least 35% ham (cooked basis).

Ham Spread—At least 50% ham.

Hamburger or Ground Beef—No more than 30% fat.

Hash—At least 35% meat (cooked basis).

Lasagna with Meat and Sauce—At least 12% meat.

Lima Beans with Ham or Bacon in Sauce—At least 12% ham or cooked bacon.

Liver Sausage, Liver Loaf, Liver Paste, Liver Cheese, Liver Pudding, Liver Spread, and similar liver products—At least 30% liver.

Macaroni and Beef in Tomato Sauce—At least 12% beef.

Macaroni and Cheese with Ham—At least 12% ham (cooked basis).

Meat Casseroles—At least 25% fresh uncooked meat or 18% cooked meat.

Meat Pies—At least 25% meat.

Meat Ravioli—At least 10% meat in ravioli, minus the sauce.

Meat Salads—At least 35% meat (cooked basis).

Meat Tacos—At least 15% meat.

Meat Turnovers—At least 25% meat.

Omelet with Bacon—At least 12% bacon (cooked basis).

Omelet with Ham—At least 18% ham (cooked basis).

Pepper Steaks—At least 30% beef (cooked basis).

Pizza with Meat—At least 15% meat.

Pizza with Sausage—At least 12% sausage (cooked basis) or 10% dry sausage, such as pepperoni.

Pork with Barbecue Sauce—At least 50% pork (cooked basis).

Pork Sausage—Not more than 50% fat.

Sauerkraut with Wieners and Juice—At least 20% wieners.

Scalloped Potatoes and Ham—At least 20% ham (cooked basis).

Scallopine—At least 35% meat (cooked basis).

Scrapple—At least 40% meat and/or meat by-products.

Spaghetti with Meat and Sauce—At least 12% meat.

Spaghetti with Meat Balls and Sauce—At least 12% meat.

Spaghetti Sauce and Meat Balls—At least 35% meat balls (cooked basis).

Spaghetti Sauce with Meat—At least 6% meat.

Spanish Rice with Beef or Ham—At least 20% beef or ham (cooked basis).

Stews (Beef, Lamb, and the like)—At least 25% meat.

Sukiyaki—At least 30% meat.

Sweet and Sour Pork or Beef—At least 25% fresh uncooked meat or 16% cooked meat, and at least 16% fruit.

Swiss Steak with Gravy—At least 50% meat (cooked basis). *Gravy and Swiss Steak*—At least 35% meat (cooked basis).

Tamales—At least 25% meat.

Tamales with Sauce (or with Gravy)—At least 20% meat.

Tongue Spread—At least 50% tongue.

Veal Birds—At least 60% meat and not more than 40% stuffing.

Veal Cordon Bleu—At least 60% veal, 5% ham, and containing Swiss, Gruyere, or Mozzarella cheese.

Veal Fricassee—At least 40% meat.

Veal Parmigiana—At least 40% breaded meat product in sauce. Breaded meat portion, at least 28% meat (cooked basis).

Veal Steaks—Can be chopped, shaped, cubed, frozen. Beef can be added with product name shown as *"Veal Steaks, Beef Added, Chopped, Shaped, and Cubed."* No more than 20% beef or must be labeled *"Veal and Beef Steak, Chopped, Shaped, and Cubed."* No more than 30% fat.

POULTRY PRODUCTS. (All percentages of poultry—chicken, turkey, or other kinds of poultry—are on cooked deboned basis unless otherwise indicated.)

Breaded Poultry—No more than 30% breading.

Canned Boned Poultry:

　Boned (kind), *Solid Pack*—At least 95% poultry meat, skin, and fat.

　Boned (kind)—At least 90% poultry meat, skin, and fat.

　Boned (kind), *with Broth*—At least 80% poultry meat, skin, and fat.

　Boned (kind), *with* (specified percentage of)

　Broth—At least 50% poultry meat, skin, and fat.

Chicken Cacciatore—At least 20% chicken meat, or 40% with bone.

Chicken Croquettes—At least 25% chicken meat.

Chopped Poultry with Broth (Baby Food)—At least 43% poultry meat, with skin, fat, and seasoning.

Creamed Poultry—At least 20% poultry meat.

Poultry a la King—At least 20% poultry meat.

Poultry Barbecue—At least 40% poultry meat.

Poultry Burgers—100% poultry meat, with skin and fat.

Poultry Chop Suey—At least 4% poultry meat. *Chop Suey with Poultry*—At least 2% poultry meat.

Poultry Chow Mein, Without Noodles—At least 4% poultry meat.

Poultry Dinners—At least 18% poultry meat.

Poultry Fricassee—At least 20% poultry meat.

Poultry Fricassee of Wings—At least 40% poultry meat (cooked basis, with bone).

Poultry with Gravy—At least 35% poultry meat. *Gravy with Poultry*—At least 15% poultry meat.

Poultry Hash—At least 30% poultry meat.

Poultry Noodles or Dumplings—At least 15% poultry meat, or 30% with bone. *Noodles or Dumplings with Poultry*—At least 6% poultry meat.

Poultry Pies—At least 14% poultry meat.

Poultry Ravioli—At least 2% poultry meat.

Poultry Rolls—Binding agents limited to 3% in cooked roll.

Poultry Salad—At least 25% poultry meat.

Poultry Soup—At least 2% poultry meat.

Poultry Stew—At least 12% poultry meat.

Poultry Stroganoff—At least 30% poultry meat.

Poultry Tamales—At least 6% poultry meat.

Poultry Tetrazzini—At least 15% poultry meat.

Sliced Poultry with Gravy—At least 35% poultry.

Reference Tables of Weights and Measurements for Food

TABLE A-1
Abbreviations for Weights and Measurements Used in Food Preparation

Abbreviations			
f.g.	few grains	gr.	grain
tsp	teaspoon	g	gram
tbsp	tablespoon	oz	ounce
T.	tablespoon	lb	pound
c.	cup	ml	milliliter
sq	square	gal	gallon
pt	pint	bu.	bushel
qt	quart		

Equivalents			
1 teaspoon	5 milliliters	1 ounce	28.35 grams
1 tablespoon	3 teaspoons or 15 milliliters	16 ounces	1 pound
1 cup	16 tablespoons or 236.6 milliliters	1 pound	453.59 grams
		20 drops	1 milliliter

TABLE A-2
Weight and Volume Measurements

Food	One Ounce (approx. tbsp)	One Cup (approx. oz)	Approx. Grams	One Pound (approx. cups)
Almonds, shelled	3	5½	127	3
Apricots, dried (A.P.)[a]	3	5⅓	127	3–3½
Baking powder	2½		181–217	2¼–2½
Baking soda	2½			2⅓
Beans, dried				
Kidney		6½	186	2½ (uncooked)
				7 (cooked)
Lima		6½	192	2½ (uncooked)
				6 (cooked)
Navy		6¾	207	2⅓ (uncooked)
				6 (cooked)
Bran, all-bran		8	61	2
Branflakes		1⅓	34	12
Bread crumbs, dry		4	182	4
Butter	2	8	204	2
Cheese				
Cheddar, shredded		4	111	4
Cottage		8	233	2–2½
Cream	2	8	230	2
Chocolate				
Melted		9		1¾
Grated	1 square	4 squares grated		4 grated
Citron		6½		2½
Cocoa		4	86	4
Coconut				
Long-thread		2¼	92	7
Moist		3	94	5⅓
Coffee, instant	8	2		8
Cornflakes		1	29	16
Cornmeal		5		3
Cornstarch	3	4½		3½
Crackers				
Graham	4	10–12 crackers		40–60 crackers
Soda		21 crackers		70–90 crackers
Cream				
18% butterfat		8½		2
40% butterfat		8⅓		2
Cream of wheat	3	5		2½–3
Currants, dried		5		3¼
Dates, pitted		6⅓		2½
Eggs, dried				
Whole-egg solids		3		5¼
Whites		3		5
Eggs, fresh				
Whites		8–9	255	2
Whole		8.8	251	2
Yolks		12	240	2
Farina		5⅓		3
Figs, dried		5⅓		3
Flour				
All-purpose, unsifted		4	143	4
Cake, unsifted		3⅓	119	4¾
Whole-wheat		4¼	137	3¾
Gelatin	3	5⅓		3
Gelatin mix, prepared		4½	187	3½
Grapenuts		5⅓	109	3

Food	One Ounce (approx. tbsp)	One Cup (approx. oz)	Approx. Grams	One Pound (approx. cups)
Hominy				
Grits		5½	156	3
Whole		6½		2½
Honey		12	326	1⅓
Macaroni, uncooked		4	136	4–4½
Margarine		8	226	2
Milk				
Crystals		2¼		6½
Dried, nonfat, instant		2.6	75	6
Dried, whole		3¾		3½
Evaporated	¾	9		1¾
Sweetened, condensed	¾	10¾		1½
Molasses				
Dark		12	309	1⅓
Light		12		1⅓
Noodles, uncooked		2⅔		6
Oatmeal, quick		3		5⅔–6
Oil		8	210	2
Olives				
Green		20 olives		
Ripe		44 olives		
Peaches, dried		5⅓		3
Peanut butter		8	251	2
Peanuts, shelled		5⅓–6	138	3–3½
Peas, dried, split		7	203	2¼
Pecans, shelled		3½	105	4
Potato chips		1⅓		20
Prunes, dried		6–8		2–3
Puffed rice		¾	2	16
Rice				
Brown		6.5		2½
Precooked		6.5		2½
White	2	6.8	198	2½ (uncooked)
				8 (cooked)
Wild		5⅓		3
Salt	4	8	292	2
Shredded wheat				13–16
Spices				
Sugar				
Brown		7	212	2¼
Cube				80–200 cubes
Granulated	3	7	195	2¼
Powdered		4.3	123	3–4
Syrup		11½		1⅓
Tapioca				
Granular		5⅓		3
Pearl		6¾		2½
Tea		2⅓		6–8
Wafers, vanilla		5 (crushed)		
Walnuts, chopped		4¼		3⅔

[a] As purchased.

Source: Adapted from *Handbook of Food Preparation* (Washington, D.C.: American Home Economics Association, rev. 1975), pp. 58–109; and "Average Weight of a Measured Cup of Various Foods," *Agriculture Research Series 61–6* (Washington, D.C.: U.S. Department of Agriculture, 1969).

TABLE A-3
Terms Commonly Used to Describe Oven Temperatures

Temperature			Temperature		
°F	°C	Term	°F	°C	Term
250–275	121–135	Very slow	400–425	204–218	Hot
300–325	149–163	Slow	450–475	232–246	Very hot
350–375	177–191	Moderate	500–525	260–274	Extremely hot

TABLE A-4
Conversion Tables

A. Comparison of Avoirdupois and Metric Units of Weight

Ounces to Pounds to Grams			Pounds to Kilograms		Grams to Ounces		Kilograms to Pounds	
1	0.06	28.35	1	0.454	1	0.035	1	2.205
2	0.12	56.70	2	0.91	2	0.07	2	4.41
3	0.19	85.05	3	1.36	3	0.11	3	6.61
4	0.25	113.40	4	1.81	4	0.14	4	8.82
5	0.31	141.75	5	2.27	5	0.18	5	11.02
6	0.38	170.10	6	2.72	6	0.21	6	13.23
7	0.44	198.45	7	3.18	7	0.25	7	15.43
8	0.50	226.80	8	3.63	8	0.28	8	17.64
9	0.56	255.15	9	4.08	9	0.32	9	19.84
10	0.62	283.50	10	4.54	10	0.35	10	22.05
11	0.69	311.85	11	4.99	11	0.39	11	24.26
12	0.75	340.20	12	5.44	12	0.42	12	26.46
13	0.81	368.55	13	5.90	13	0.46	13	28.67
14	0.88	396.90	14	6.35	14	0.49	14	30.87
15	0.94	425.25	15	6.81	15	0.53	15	33.08
16	1.00	453.59	16	7.26	16	0.56	16	35.28

B. Comparison of U.S. and Metric Units of Liquid Measure

Ounces (Fluid) to Milliliters		Quarts to Liters		Gallons to Liters		Milliliters to Ounces (Fluid)		Liters to Quarts		Liters to Gallons	
1	29.573	1	0.946	1	3.785	1	0.034	1	1.057	1	0.264
2	59.15	2	1.89	2	7.57	2	0.07	2	2.11	2	0.53
3	88.72	3	2.84	3	11.36	3	0.10	3	3.17	3	0.79
4	118.30	4	3.79	4	15.14	4	0.14	4	4.23	4	1.06
5	147.87	5	4.73	5	18.93	5	0.17	5	5.28	5	1.32
6	177.44	6	5.68	6	22.71	6	0.20	6	6.34	6	1.59
7	207.02	7	6.62	7	26.50	7	0.24	7	7.40	7	1.85
8	236.59	8	7.57	8	30.28	8	0.27	8	8.45	8	2.11
9	266.16	9	8.52	9	34.07	9	0.30	9	9.51	9	2.38
10	295.73	10	9.46	10	37.85	10	0.34	10	10.57	10	2.64

C. Approximate Boiling Temperatures of Water at Various Altitudes

Altitude (ft)	Boiling Point of Water	
	°F	°C
Sea level	212.0	100.0
2,000	208.4	98.4
5,000	203.0	95.0
7,500	198.4	92.4
10,000	194.0	90.0
15,000	185.0	85.0
30,000	158.0	70.0

D. Steam Pressures at Various Altitudes

Temperature		Steam Pressure (lb) at an Altitude of			
°F	°C	Sea Level	4000 ft	5000 ft	7500 ft
228	109	5	7	8	9
240	115	10	12	13	14
250	121	15	17	18	19
259	126	20	22	23	24

TABLE A-5
Basic Proportions for Mixtures

Product[a]	Flour (cups)	Liquid (cups)	Fat (tbsp)	Eggs	Sugar	Salt (tsp)	Baking Powder[b] (tsp)	Other Ingredients
Beverages								
Cocoa and chocolate		1			2–3 tsp	Few grains		2–3 tsp cocoa or ½ oz chocolate
Coffee, instant		3/8						1 rounded tsp
Coffee, regular		¾						2 level or 1 well-rounded tbsp coffee
Tea		¾						½– tsp tea
Breads								
Biscuits	1	⅓–½	2–4			½	1¼–2	
Griddle cakes	1	¾–⅞	1	½	0–1 tbsp	½	1½–2	
Muffins	1	½	1–3	½	1–2 tbsp	½	1½–2	
Popovers	1	1	1–2	2–3			¼–¾	
Waffles	1	¾–1	1–3	1–2		½	1¼–2	
Yeast bread	1	⅓	0–1		1 tsp–1 tbsp	¼		¼ compressed yeast cake or ¼ small pkg. active dry yeast
Cakes								
Angel food	1 (cake)			1–1½ cups (whites)	1¼–1½ cups	½		Flavoring, ¾–1½ tsp cream of tartar
Chiffon	1 (cake)	⅓	4 (salad oil)	3	⅔ cup	½	1¼–1½	Flavoring; ¼ tsp cream of tartar
With fat	1 (cake or all-purpose)	¼–½	2–4	½–1	½–¾ cup	⅛–¼	1–2	Flavoring
Sponge	1 (cake)	0–3 tbsp		5–6	1 cup	½	0–½	Flavoring; 0–¾ tsp cream of tartar
Cereals								
Flaked (rolled oats)		2–3				1		1 cup cereal
Granular (farina, cornmeal)		4–6				1		1 cup cereal
Whole (rice, oatmeal, hominy)		3–4				1		1 cup cereal

Food	Flour[a]	Liquid	Eggs	Sugar	Salt	Baking powder[b]	Other ingredients
Creampuffs	1	8	4	¼ cup	¼		Flavoring
Doughnuts	¼	1½ tsp	½	1½–3 tbsp	¼	1–2	Flavoring
Egg dishes							
Custards	1		1–⅔		⅛		Flavoring
Omelets	1 tbsp		1		⅛		Seasonings
Soufflés	3–4 tbsp	3–4	3		¼–½		Seasonings or flavoring
Timbales	1	1–2	2		⅛–¼		Seasonings or flavoring
Meringues							
Hard (kisses)			4 (whites)	1 cup			¼ tsp cream of tartar; ½ tsp vanilla
Pastry			2 (whites)	4 tbsp			¼ tsp vanilla
Pastry	2 tbsp	4–5			½		
Puddings							
Cornstarch	1		0–1	2 tbsp	⅛		Flavoring; 1–1½ tbsp cornstarch
Tapioca	1		½–1	2 tbsp	⅛		Flavoring; 1¼ tbsp quick-cooking tapioca
Rice	1			1–2 tbsp	⅛		Flavoring; 2–3 tbsp raw rice
Salads							
Gelatin, creams	2						2 tbsp or 2 envelopes
Gelatin, plain	2						1 tbsp or 1 envelope
Sauces							
Fruit sauce	1			2–4 tbsp	Few grains		¾–1 tbsp cornstarch; fruit (if desired)
White sauce							
Thin	1 tbsp				¼		Pepper (if desired)
Medium	2 tbsp				¼		Pepper (if desired)
Thick	3–4 tbsp				¼		Pepper (if desired)

[a] All-purpose flour, except where cake flour is specified.

[b] In general, the smaller amount is used if using an SAS-phosphate baking powder, an intermediate amount if using a phosphate powder, and the larger amount if using a tartrate powder.

Source: Adapted from *Handbook of Food Preparation* (Washington, D.C.: American Home Economics Association, rev. 1975), p. 16.

TABLE A-6
Cake Recipe Adjustment Guides for High Altitudes

Adjustment	3000 ft	5000 ft	7000 ft
Reduce baking powder			
For each teaspoon, decrease	⅛ tsp	⅛–¼ tsp	¼ tsp
Reduce sugar			
For each cup, decrease	0–1 tbsp	0–2 tbsp	1–3 tbsp
Increase liquid			
For each cup, add	1–2 tbsp	2–4 tbsp	3–4 tbsp

TABLE A-7
Approximate Equivalents of Some Food Materials

Common Material	Equivalent
1 tbsp flour	½ tbsp cornstarch, or potato starch, rice starch, arrowroot starch, or 1 tbsp instant tapioca
1 cup cake flour	⅞ cup sifted hard wheat or all-purpose flour
1 cup corn sirup	1 cup sugar plus ¼ cup same liquid used in recipe
1 cup honey	1¼ cups sugar plus ¼ cup liquid
1 oz chocolate (square)	3 tbsp cocoa plus 1 tbsp fat
1 cup butter	1 cup margarine; ⅞ cup lard plus ½ tsp salt; ⅞ cup rendered fat plus ½ tsp salt; or ⅞ cup oil plus ½ tsp salt
1 cup coffee cream (18–20% butterfat)	3 tbsp fat plus about ⅞ cup milk
1 cup heavy cream (40% butterfat)	⅓ cup fat plus about ¾ cup milk
1 cup whole milk	1 cup reconstituted nonfat dried milk plus 2½ tsp table fat; or ½ cup evaporated milk plus ½ cup water
1 cup buttermilk or sour milk	1 tbsp vinegar or lemon juice plus sweet milk to make 1 cup (let stand 5 min)
1 tsp baking powder	¼ tsp baking soda plus ½ cup fully soured milk or soured buttermilk; or ¼ tsp baking soda, ½ tbsp vinegar or lemon juice plus sweet milk to make ½ cup; or ¼ tsp baking soda, ¼–½ cup molasses
1 tbsp active dry yeast	1 package active dry yeast; 1 compressed yeast cake
1 whole egg	3 tbsp slightly beaten fresh egg; 2 yolks; 3 tbsp thawed frozen egg; or 2½ tbsp dried whole egg sifted, 2½ tbsp lukewarm water[a]
1 egg white	2 tsp dried egg white plus 2 tbsp lukewarm water; 2 tbsp frozen egg white
1 egg yolk	2 tbsp dried egg yolk, 2 tsp lukewarm water; 1⅓ tbsp frozen egg

[a]Reconstitute only as much dried egg as you will use for the recipe you are preparing. To reconstitute dried whole egg and dried egg yolks; sift, place lightly in a measuring spoon or cup, and level off with straight edge of a knife. Sprinkle over lukewarm water in a bowl and stir to moisten. Beat until smooth with rotary beater, wire whip. or electric mixer. To reconstitute egg white: sift, place lightly in a measuring spoon or cup, level off with straight edge of a knife. Sprinkle over lukewarm water in a bowl and stir to moisten. Beat until egg white is very stiff and stands in peaks.

Source: Adapted from *Handbook of Food Preparation* (Washington, D.C.: American Home Economics Association, rev. 1975), p. 12.

Recipes

BEVERAGES
Cocoa

Cocoa should be creamy brown in color; slightly thicker in consistency than milk; free from sediment or film on surface; and have a moderately strong flavor of chocolate.

4 SERVINGS
- 3 tbsp sugar
- ¼ cup cocoa
- ⅛ tsp salt
- 1 cup water
- 3 cups milk

Put sugar, cocoa, and salt in saucepan, and mix thoroughly.

Stir in water gradually.

Cook over low heat, stirring occasionally, for about 5 minutes, or until mixture is thick and syrupy.

Stir in milk and heat, stirring occasionally, until cocoa begins to simmer.

Remove from heat.

Beat with rotary beater until frothy to prevent skin from forming on surface.

Serve in cups, with marshmallow or whipped cream, if desired.

Hot Chocolate

Follow recipe for Cocoa except use 1½ to 2 squares unsweetened chocolate, cut into several pieces, instead of ¼ cup cocoa.

Tea

Tea should be sparkling clear without any sediment. Color depends on kind of tea used in making beverage—black tea; light to medium amber in color, green tea: yellow-green in color. The flavor is distinctive of kind of tea used.

4 SERVINGS
- 4 tsp tea, or 4 teabags
- 4 cups freshly boiling water

Pour boiling water into teapot, cover, let stand for several minutes to heat pot, and then drain.

Put tea or teabags in hot teapot.

Pour freshly boiling water over tea, and cover teapot.

Let stand for 3–5 minutes, depending on strength desired, and then stir.

Strain tea into another hot teapot or remove tea bags before serving.

Serve with sugar and milk or lemon, as desired.

FRUIT SAUCE

A cooked fruit sauce should be thick, not runny, be slightly glossy in appearance, and have a bright color. It should have a slightly tart, pleasant taste characteristic of the fruit.

Applesauce

4 SERVINGS
   6 cooking apples
   ½ cup water (about)
   ⅓–½ cup sugar
   ¼ tsp salt
   few grains nutmeg, cinnamon, or cloves (optional)

Wash apples, pare, quarter, and core.[1]
Add water and cook in a covered saucepan until apples are soft.
Press apples through strainer or sieve. If small pieces of the apple are to be left in the sauce, mash with potato masher.
Add sugar, salt, and spices.

Cranberry Sauce

4 CUPS
   1½ cups sugar
   2 cups water
   4 cups washed and drained cranberries (1 lb)

Combine sugar and water. Cover and boil for 5 minutes.
Add cranberries, cover, and cook until the skins burst.
Pour into serving dish and cool.

[1] If apples have red skins and a red sauce is desired, do not pare, remove cores only. Proceed as above, but strain apples before adding sugar.

BAKED FRUIT

Baked fruit should be tender; it should retain its original form and have a clear syrup that is free from small pieces of fruit. It has a slightly translucent appearance.

Baked Apples

4 SERVINGS
   4 cooking apples[2]
   4 tbsp sugar
   few grains cinnamon
   4 tsp butter or margarine
   ½ cup water

Wash and core apples.
Cut a narrow ring of skin around the top as an outlet for steam.
Place in shallow pan and put the sugar and seasonings into the core holes. Dot apples with butter.
Add water. Bake in medium oven (375°F; 190°C) for 20–45 minutes or until done.
Baste occasionally with liquid in pan, adding more water if necessary.

STEWED DRIED FRUIT

Stewed dried fruits should be plump, rounded, and unbroken. They should have a shiny, bright appearance and the texture should be tender. The taste should be slightly sweet or tart, depending on the characteristic of the fruit. (See Table A-8 for amounts.)

[2] The Rome Beauty is an excellent baking apple.

TABLE A-8
Dried Fruit Cooking Timetable

Amount of Fruit	Amount of Water (cup)	Amount of Sugar (tbsp)	Cooking Time (min)
1 cup apples	2	0–4	20–30
1 cup apricots	1½	0–4	15–25
1 cup prunes	3	0–2	30–40
1 cup peaches	1½	2–4	30–40
1 cup pears	1½	0–4	35

TABLE A-9
Guide for Cooking Fresh Vegetables

These times are approximate. Cook vegetables only until tender. For most vegetables, unless otherwise indicated, use 1 to 2 in. of boiling water, using $\frac{1}{4}$ tsp salt per cup of water.

Vegetable[a]	Boiling Time (min)	Steaming Time (min)	Baking Time (min)	Servings per Pound
Asparagus	15–20	12–18		4
Beans				
Lima	20–30	25–35		6 (shelled)
Snap	15–30	20–35		4
Beets[b]				
Small to large	35–60	40–65	40–60	4
Broccoli	15–25	15–18		3
Brussels sprouts	5–6	10–12		4
Cabbage (shredded)				
Green	3–9	8–14		4
Red	8–15	10–15		4
Carrots	5–20	20–30	30–35	4
Cauliflower (pieces)	8–15	10–18		3
Celeriac	8–10			4
Celery	10–20	30–35		4
Chard	8–20	15–25		4
Collards	16–20			4
Corn on cob[b]	3–10			4 (ears)
Eggplant	5–15	—	Stuffed, 25–30	4
Kale	15–20			4
Kohlrabi	25–30			2–3
Leeks	15–20			4
Mushrooms	5–10			6
Okra	15–20	—	Casserole, 30	4
Onions, whole[b]	15–40	30–40	30	4
Parsnips	10–20	—	30–35	4
Peas in pod	10–20	10–20		2
Potatoes, sweet[b]	20–35	30–35	40–60	3
Potatoes, white (whole)[b]	20–40	30–45	40–60	3
Rutabagas[b]	20–40			4
Spinach[c]	5–10	8–11		4
Squash				
Summer	10–15	15–20	Stuffed, 25–30	3
Winter[b]	35–45	25–30	45–55	2
Tomatoes	3–5	—	Stuffed, 30–35	3
Turnip greens	10–40			4
Turnips	20–30	—	Casserole, 35–45	4

[a] Follow manufacturer's directions for steaming in pressure cooker.
[b] Cook in boiling, salted water to cover.
[c] Cook only in water that clings to leaves from washing.

Wash fruit; add water and soak fruit if necessary.[3]

Simmer, covered, in soaking water until plump and tender or according to timetable.

Remove from heat and add sugar.

FRESH VEGETABLES

A cooked vegetable should retain the natural color of the vegetable; the flavor should be pleasing and characteristic of the vegetable and the texture tender but not soft. (See Table A-9 for cooking vegetables.)

CEREALS, THICKENED PUDDINGS, AND CREAM SOUPS

A well-cooked cereal should be just thick enough to hold its shape when taken up by a spoon. Cereal should be soft and chewy, not pasty, and should have a pleasing, nutty flavor. (See Table A-10 for amounts.)

Add salt to the water and bring to a boil in top of double boiler over direct heat.

Sprinkle cereal slowly over boiling water so as not to stop the boiling.

Stir cereal until it starts to boil; boil 2 or 3 minutes.

Reduce heat to low, cover saucepan, place over bottom of double boiler, and cook for the amount of time given in Table A-10.

---

[3] Packaged dried fruits may be cooked without soaking; follow directions on the package. Those sold in bulk are dry and hard and should be soaked in warm water until plump. Always cook the fruit in the same water in which it was soaked.

Cream of Vegetable Soup

A good cream of vegetable soup has the consistency of thick cream; it is shiny and smooth and has a pleasant, cooked flavor.

4 SERVINGS
  3 tbsp butter or margarine
  3 tbsp flour
  ¾ tsp salt
  ⅛ tsp pepper
  3 cups milk
  vegetable pulp (about 2 cups)

Melt fat over low heat.

Add flour, salt, and pepper; stir until well blended.

Remove from heat.

Gradually stir in milk and return to heat.

Stir constantly, until thick, shiny, and smooth.

Add vegetable pulp. Serve hot.

Blancmange (Cornstarch Pudding)

A well-cooked cornstarch pudding is glossy and creamy, has a delicate texture, and is free of lumps. It has a pleasing flavor and no raw taste.

4 SERVINGS
  3 tbsp cornstarch[4]
  ½ cup sugar
  ½ tsp salt
  2 cups milk
  1 tsp vanilla

Mix cornstarch, sugar, and salt in top of double boiler.

Slowly stir in milk.

Place over boiling water and stir constantly until thick and smooth.

---

[4] 6 tbsp of flour may be substituted for the cornstarch.

TABLE A-10
General Proportions for Cooking Cereals

Type of Cereal	Amount of Water (cups)	Amount of Cereal (cups)	Salt (tsp)	Cooking Time (min)
Granular	2	⅓–½	1	5–10
Rolled	2	1	1	2[a]–15
Whole	2	½	1	12–15

[a] Quick-cooking oats.

Cover and cook for 15 minutes longer, stirring
occasionally.
Chill and add vanilla.

Variations
Chocolate Melt 1 square (1 oz) baking chocolate in scalded milk. Beat with rotary beater to
blend before adding sugar–cornstarch mixture.
Butterscotch Brown sugar may be substituted
for granulated sugar. (Be sure to pack brown
sugar in cornstarch pudding recipe.)
Cream pudding Add 1 tbsp cornstarch to
recipe; cool slightly and fold in two stiffly
beaten egg whites.

EGGS

Fried Eggs
A well-prepared fried egg has a soft luster, is
uniformly coagulated, has a rounded outline, has
an intact yolk that is coated with a thin film of
cooked white, and has a tender texture.

2 tbsp butter or bacon fat
3 or 4 eggs at room temperature

Melt enough butter or bacon fat in a heavy
skillet to cover the bottom.
Break eggs into a saucer and slip them carefully
into the pan.
Cook over low heat, basting eggs with hot fat till
whites are set.
If eggs are to be cooked on both sides, turn with
a pancake turner.

Poached Eggs
A good poached egg has luster, has an evenly
coagulated, uniform coating over its entire surface (veil), and is tender.

1 qt water
1 tsp salt
4 eggs at room temperature

Bring water to a rolling boil and add salt.
Reduce heat immediately so that water simmers.
Break eggs one at a time into a saucer, then slip
them gently into the water. Let eggs steep
until white is firm.
Using a slotted spoon or pancake turner, remove
eggs and drain on absorbent paper.
Trim with a knife or cookie cutter. Serve on
toast.

Plain Omelet
A well-prepared omelet is slightly moist but
well cooked throughout. It has a delicate brown
exterior surface and is tender.

3–4 Servings
3 eggs
1 tbsp cold water
salt
1 tbsp butter or margarine

Break eggs into a small bowl; add water and salt
and beat till light and foamy.
Place omelet pan over moderate heat. Flick a
drop of water into pan; if it skitters about and
disappears almost at once, the pan is ready.
Swirl butter around in pan and pour eggs into
pan.
Shake pan with left hand, with right hand stir in
a circular motion with a fork until omelet is
set. Change left-hand position, to hold handle
with palm turned upward.
Raise skillet to 45° angle. Using a fork, roll
omelet from the top down; turn onto a warm
plate. Garnish as desired.

Baked Custard
A good baked custard has a firm shape, a
smooth, tender texture, and a rich and creamy
consistency. It has a delicate pleasing flavor.

4–6 Servings
2½ cups milk (scalded)
4 eggs
6 tbsp sugar
½ tsp salt
1 tsp vanilla
½ tsp nutmeg

In a bowl, place the eggs and beat with a fork. It
is only necessary to beat them slightly.
Stir into the bowl containing the eggs, the sugar,
salt, and vanilla. Add the scalded milk slowly,
stirring constantly.
Strain custard to remove any possible particles
that might keep it from having a smooth
texture.
Place custard cups in a pan, fill with the custard
mixture, sprinkle lightly with nutmeg. Pour
boiling water up to ⅓ in of the top of the
cups.
Place in preheated oven and bake for 40–45
minutes (350°F; 176°C) or until done. Test

to see if a silver knife tip comes out clean when inserted into the custard.

Soft Custard

A good soft custard has a velvety smooth texture, a rich flavor, and the pouring consistency of heavy cream.

4 SERVINGS
   3 eggs, slightly beaten (or 6 yolks)
   ¼ tsp salt
   3 tbsp sugar
   2 cups milk, scalded
   1 tsp vanilla.

Combine the eggs, salt, and sugar; gradually stir in the milk and cook for 5 minutes in the top of the double boiler. Keep water just below simmering. Stir constantly until mixture thickens.

If done, the spoon is well coated with the custard.[5] Remove top of double boiler immediately from heat. Cool and add vanilla.

Serve well chilled in a glass dish or tall glass. Top with whipped cream, if desired.

CHEESE

Cheese Soufflé

A good soufflé is puffed, has a slightly rounded top, is well blended, and has a golden brown exterior. The interior is slightly moist but coagulated throughout. It has a light, tender texture.

4–6 SERVINGS
   2 tbsp butter or margarine
   2 tbsp flour
   ½ cup milk
   ½ tsp salt
   ⅛ tsp cayenne
   ½ cup grated American cheese
   3 separated eggs

Prepare white sauce with first five ingredients. (See first five steps for Cream Soup, p. 576.)
Remove white sauce from heat and cool slightly.
Add grated cheese. Then add yolks of eggs that have been beaten until thick.

---

[5] If by accident you overcook custard and it curdles, set the pan in cold water and beat smooth with an egg beater.

Beat egg whites until stiff and fold into blended mixture.

Pour into buttered baking dish and bake in moderate oven (375°F; 190°C) 45–50 minutes, placing the baking dish in a pan of hot water. When soufflé is done, an inserted knife comes out clean.

Welsh Rarebit

A good Welsh rarebit is smooth, medium thick, without lumps and stringiness. It has a distinct flavor of cheese.

4 SERVINGS
   2 tbsp butter or margarine
   2 tbsp flour
   ½ tsp salt
   ½ tsp dry mustard
   1 cup milk
   1 cup grated Cheddar or processed cheese
   1 egg, slightly beaten

Prepare white sauce with first five ingredients. (See first five steps for Cream Soup, p. 576.)
Remove from heat, add grated cheese, and stir until melted.
Cool slightly.
Stir in slightly beaten egg.
Place over hot water in bottom of double boiler and cook, stirring constantly, until egg is cooked and mixture is smooth.
To serve, pour over thin slices of toast or crisp crackers.

MEAT, POULTRY, FISH

Meat Loaf

A good meat loaf is plump and juicy, it is well browned and holds together but is easily cut with a fork. It is well seasoned and has a well-developed flavor but is not greasy.

4–6 SERVINGS
   1 lb ground beef or veal
   ¼ lb sausage or ground pork
   3 tbsp chopped onion
   2 tbsp chopped celery (optional)
   ¼ cup chopped parsley
   ½ cup soft bread crumbs
   ½ cup milk or canned or cooked tomatoes
   1 egg, beaten
   1 tsp salt
   pepper

Mix all ingredients together thoroughly.

Mold mixture into a loaf. Place in greased baking pan. Bake at 350°F (176°C) for about 1 hour.

Braised Liver

Braised liver should look plump, not shriveled. It should be tender, juicy, and well flavored.

4 SERVINGS

   1 lb sliced liver (calf, beef, or lamb)
   ¼ cup flour
   ¾ tsp salt
   ¼ tsp pepper
   2½ tbsp shortening, oil, or bacon drippings

Wipe liver with damp cloth, remove any tubes, and cut edge in several places to prevent curling.

Mix flour, salt, and pepper on wax paper, and coat liver on both sides.

Heat shortening or bacon drippings in skillet, and brown liver on both sides.

Reduce heat and cover.

Cook for 15–20 minutes, or until liver is tender when tested with a fork.

Serve on hot platter.

Broiled Chicken

A well-broiled chicken is golden brown, juicy, tender, and uniformly cooked; it has a pleasant flavor.

4 SERVINGS

   plump young chicken (broiler or fryer), about 1½–2 lb
   ¼ cup melted fat or salad oil
   salt and pepper

TABLE A-11
Timetable for Roasting, Broiling, Braising, and Cooking Meats in Liquid

Roasting Meats

Kind and Cut	Approximate Weight (lb)	Internal Temperature		Approximate Total[a] Cooking Time at 325°F (163°C) (hr)
		°F	°C	
Beef				
Standing ribs (8-in. ribs)	6	140 (rare)	60	2–2½
		160 (medium)	71	2–3½
		170 (well done)	77	3⅔–4
Rolled ribs	6	140 (rare)	60	3
		160 (medium)	71	3¾
		170 (well done)	77	4
Lamb Roasts	3–5	180 (well done)	82	2¼–3¼
Pork, cured and smoked (cook before eating)[a] Ham, whole	12	160 (well done)	71	3½
Pork Loin Roasts	4–6	170 (well done)	77	2¼–3½
Veal Roasts	3–5	170 (well done)	77	2½–3
Cook-before-eating smoked half ham (bone in)	5–7	160	71	2–2½
Fully cooked smoked[a] half ham (bone in)		140	60	1–2
Smoked pork arm picnic shoulder	6	170	77	3½

[a]Cooking time is based on meat taken directly from the refrigerator.

TABLE A-11 (Cont.)

Broiling Meats

Kind and Cut	Approximate Thickness (in.)	Approximate Total Cooking Time (min)		
		Rare	Medium	Well done
Beef steaks				
Rib, club, tenderloin, porterhouse, T–bone, sirloin	¾–1	10	14	18
	1½	16	20	26
Ground beef patties	¾	8	12	14
Lamb chops				
Rib, loin, shoulder	¾		12	18
	1½		18	22

Braising Meats

Kind and Cut	Approximate Weight or Thickness	Approximate Total Cooking Time
Beef		
Pot roast (rump, chuck, heel of round)	3–5 lb	3½–4 hr
Round or chuck steak (Swiss)	1–1½-in.	2–2½ hr
Lamb		
Cubed lamb for stew	1½-in. cubes	1½–2 hr
Pork		
Rib and loin chops	¾–1 in.	50–60 min
Shoulder steaks	¾ in.	45 min
Veal		
Loin or rib chops	¾ in.	45 min
Cubed veal for stew	1-in. cubes	1½–2 hr

Cooking Meats in Liquid

Kind and Cut	Approximate Weight (lb)	Approximate Total Cooking Time (hr)
Beef		
Beef tongue, fresh or smoked	3–4	3–3½
Corned beef brisket (whole)	8	4–5
Fresh beef brisket or plate	8	4–5

Source: Adapted from *Handbook of Food Preparation* (Washington, D.C.: American Home Economics Association, rev. 1975).

Wash and dry chicken.

Split the bird down the back and, if desired, cut into halves through the breastbone.

Brush chicken on both sides with melted fat.

Preheat the broiler at 325°F (163°C) and oil broiler rack lightly. Place chicken on the rack, skin side down, with highest part 4–5 in from the heat.

Turn the bird as it browns so that it will cook evenly. Baste often with the pan drippings or

other melted fat. Cook until well done—
40–50 minutes.
Season with salt and pepper.

Baked Stuffed Fish

Good baked fish has a golden-brown exterior,
a juicy, tender, and firm texture, a full, rich,
natural flavor, and an appetizing aroma.

4 SERVINGS
   3 lb whole fish (head and tail may be left on)
   salt
   stuffing (any bread or rice stuffing may be
      used)
   melted fat or oil or 2 strips bacon or salt
   pork, if lean fish
   parsley
   lemon
   sauce, if desired

Select a whole, cleaned fish. Wash and dry care-
   fully.
Sprinkle both inside and outside with salt.
Stuff the fish loosely and sew the opening or
   secure it with skewers or toothpicks and cord.
Place the fish on a greased baking dish.
Cut 3 or 4 gashes through the sides of the fish to
   keep the skin from cracking.
If a lean fish, brush with melted fat or place bacon
   or strips of salt pork on the sides.
Set the oven at 350°F (176°C).
When the oven is hot, place the fish in and bake
   40–60 minutes until the fish flakes when it is
   touched with a fork.
Baste with melted fat if the fish appears to be
   drying.
Garnish with lemon and parsley and serve with
   sauce, if desired.

PASTRIES

Pastry

A well-baked pastry is tender and flaky, has a
blistered appearance and a lightly browned
color—a good pastry cuts evenly with a fork.

TWO 9-INCH CRUSTS
   2¼ cups sifted flour
   1 tsp salt
   ¾ cup vegetable shortening
   ¼ cup water (4 tbsp)

Sift the flour and salt into a mixing bowl.

Take out ⅓ cup flour and mix with ¼ cup water
   in second mixing bowl. Use a fork to form a
   paste.
Cut shortening into the flour left in the first
   bowl, using a pastry blender or knives. Cut
   only until the shortening is the size of peas. Do
   not cut any finer than the size of small peas.
Add the flour paste to the fat-flour mixture.
   Scrape all the flour paste out carefully, for all
   of it is needed.
Mix these two with a fork until well blended.
Place in wax paper and chill for 20 minutes.
Divide the chilled dough in half, place half on
   the board for rolling. The board should be
   lightly floured.
Roll out the dough with short, light strokes,
   always from the center to the edge.
Roll lightly to ⅛ in. thickness to a circular form
   to fit the pie pan.
For the 9-in. pie, roll to about 13 in. in diameter
   to allow for sides and edge.
Loosen pastry with a spatula, if necessary, and
   fold the circle in half for easy handling. Lift
   carefully and place in the pan.
Unfold and fit into the pan without stretching.
   Press firmly around the edges and bottom.
Add the filling to the pie.
Roll the other half of the dough. Make a few
   cuts so that there will be steam vents.
Fold it double, for easy handling. Place on the
   top of the filling and cut ½ in. beyond the
   bottom crust.
Fold the top edge over the lower, seal with
   water, and flute with fingers or with a fork.
Place the pie in a preheated oven at about 400°F
   (205°C). The temperature depends on the kind
   of filling.
For single baked pie shell: Fit pastry into pan.
Flute edges or mark with back of fork tines.
Prick bottom and sides of unbaked shell. Bake at
425°F (218°C) until golden brown.

Lemon Meringue Pie

A good lemon meringue pie has a smooth
texture, a well-flavored filling, a firm consistency for cutting, and a crisp undercrust.

ONE 9-INCH PIE
   1 baked pastry shell
   1½ cups sugar (divided)
   7 tbsp cornstarch
   ¼ tsp salt

2 cups water
3 eggs, separated
2 tbsp butter
2 tsp grated lemon rind
7 tbsp lemon juice (about 2 lemons)

Reserve 6 tbsp of the sugar for the meringue.

Combine remaining sugar, cornstarch, and salt in the top of double boiler. Stir in water. Cook over boiling water until thickened, stirring constantly. (This can be cooked over direct heat but careful attention is necessary to prevent scorching.)

Cover and cook 5 minutes longer.

Stir a little of the hot mixture into slightly beaten egg yolks; add to the remaining hot mixture. Cook over simmering water for about 3 minutes, stirring constantly. Add butter; cool; add lemon rind and juice.

When mixture is slightly cool, turn into baked pastry shell, and cover with meringue. Bake in moderate oven (325°F; 163°C) 15 minutes.

Meringue

A good meringue is ¾–1 in. thick and has a tender texture that cuts easily, a light golden appearance, a crisp exterior, and a soft interior.

3 egg whites
6 tbsp sugar
⅛ tsp salt

Beat the whites of eggs with a dash of salt until stiff but not dry.

Gradually beat in the sugar, sprinkling a little at a time over the surface of the egg whites.

Continue beating until very smooth and glossy.

Apple Pie (two-crust)

A good fresh fruit or berry pie has a pleasing tart flavor, a slightly thickened juice, a colorful filling, and a crisp, tender crust.

4 cups apples (about 6 apples)
pastry for a two-crust pie
¾ cup sugar
2 tbsp flour
pinch salt
1 tbsp lemon juice
½ tsp cinnamon or nutmeg
2 tbsp butter or margarine

Wash, core, peel, and slice the apples.
Line the pie pan with pastry.

Place the apples carefully in the lined pie pan.

Sprinkle with sugar, flour, salt, lemon juice. Sprinkle lightly with cinnamon or nutmeg.

Dot with bits of butter.

Place the top crust on the pie after cutting a few dashes in it or putting in some fork pricks to allow the steam to escape.

Seal and flute the edges.

Bake in a 425°F (218°C) oven for 15 minutes. Lower oven temperature to 350°F (176°C) and bake another 30 minutes or until apples are done. Test with a toothpick to see if the toothpick pierces the apple easily. When the pie is done, the crust is a light-brown color.

Variations

For fresh berry pies (blueberry, huckleberry, blackberry, cherry and raspberry), substitute 4 cups washed berries for apples in the Apple Pie recipe. Increase flour to 3–4 tbsp, depending on juiciness of fruit.

QUICK BREADS

Rolled Biscuits

A good biscuit has a fairly smooth, level top. The crust is golden brown, crisp, and tender. The interior crumb is creamy white, slightly moist, and flaky; the bottom is an even brown

TWELVE MEDIUM-SIZED BISCUITS
2 cups sifted all-purpose flour
3 tsp baking powder
¾ tsp salt
5 tbsp shortening
⅔–¾ cup milk

Sift together flour, baking powder, and salt into mixing bowl.

Cut in shortening with fork, pastry blender, or two knives until it is the consistency of cornmeal.

Make a well in center and add milk; stir quickly with a fork until all the flour is dampened.

Roll onto a lightly floured board and knead for 30 seconds in order to mix ingredients more thoroughly. Roll to a thickness half of that desired in the baked biscuit, because it will rise to twice the rolled thickness.

Cut with floured cutter and place on an ungreased baking pan. Bake in hot oven (425°F; 218°C) for 13–15 minutes.

Variations

Drop biscuits Follow recipe for baking powder biscuits, increasing milk to 1 cup; omit kneading and rolling.

Shortcake Add 2 tbsp of sugar to dry ingredients. Increase shortening to 6 tablespoons. Beat 1 egg and add enough liquid to make ⅔ cup liquid. Mix and bake as for baking powder biscuits, 15–18 minutes. Split biscuits and place sweetened fruit between and on top. Serve warm with cream.

Buttermilk biscuits Substitute sour milk for sweet milk. Reduce baking powder to 1½ teaspoons, add ½ teaspoon baking soda.

Muffins

A good muffin has a pebbly top surface and is symmetrical. It possesses a fine grain, a golden-brown color, and an extreme lightness of weight.

TWELVE MEDIUM-SIZED MUFFINS

    2 cups sifted all-purpose flour
    3 tsp baking powder
    ½ tsp salt
    2 tbsp sugar
    3 tbsp shortening (melted shortening or salad oil can be used; mix liquid fat with egg and milk and proceed according to directions)
    1 egg, well beaten
    1 cup milk

Sift flour, baking powder, salt, and sugar into mixing bowl.

Cut in shortening until mixture has a corn-meal-like texture. Make a well in mixture.

Mix egg and milk and pour into well in dry ingredients.

Stir only until dry ingredients are all dampened. Batter is rough looking.

Bake for 20–25 minutes at 400°F (205°C) in greased muffin pans, filling each muffin well half full.

Variations

Bran Muffins Follow recipe for Muffins except for these differences:

1. Use 1 cup sifted all-purpose flour, and sift with sugar, baking powder, and salt into mixing bowl (step 1).
2. Use 1 cup bran.
3. Add bran to mixture of milk, well-beaten egg, and melted shortening (step 2).

4. Let stand for 10 minutes, and then continue with the remaining steps in basic recipe.

WHOLE-WHEAT MUFFINS:

1. Substitute 1 cup unsifted whole-wheat flour for 1 cup of the sifted all-purpose flour.
2. Stir this into the sifted dry ingredients (step 1).

Date Muffins Follow recipe for Muffins except stir in quickly ½ cup cut-up dates at end of step 3.

Blueberry Muffins Follow recipe for Muffins except for these differences:

1. Use amounts of ingredients as in Muffins but increase sugar to 3 tbsp.
2. Wash, drain, and pat dry 1 cup fresh blueberries, defrosted frozen blueberries, or use ¾ cup well-drained canned blueberries.
3. Stir blueberries in quickly at end of step 3.

CAKES AND COOKIES

Plain Cake

A good shortened cake is delicate and tender, is slightly moist, and has a fine, even grain and a slightly rounded, golden-brown exterior.

    2 cups sifted cake flour
    3 tsp baking powder
    ½ tsp salt
    ½ cup shortening
    1 tsp vanilla
    1 cup sugar
    2 eggs, unbeaten
    ¾ cup milk

Sift flour, baking powder, and salt together.

Cream shortening thoroughly; add vanilla and continue to cream shortening.

Add sugar gradually; continue creaming until mixture is light and fluffy and sugar crystals are completely dissolved.

Add eggs, beating well after each addition, until mixture is light and fluffy.

Add sifted dry ingredients alternately with the milk; begin and end with dry ingredients.

Pour batter into two 8-in. layer pans, greased and floured or lined with waxed paper.

Bake in moderate oven (375°F; 190°C) 25–30 minutes, or until cake springs back when touched lightly with fingers. Place pans on cake rack for 10 minutes before removing cakes from pans to cool.

Quick-Method Cake

  2¼ cups sifted cake flour
  3 tsp baking powder
  1 tsp salt
  1½ cups sugar
  ½ cup shortening, at room temperature
  1 cup milk
  2 eggs, unbeaten
  1½ tsp vanilla

Sift together first four ingredients into bowl of electric mixer.
Add shortening and about ⅔ cup of the milk.
Beat at medium speed for 2½ minutes.
Add the rest of the milk, unbeaten eggs, and vanilla.
Beat at medium speed for 3 minutes.
Pour batter evenly into two 9-in. greased layer-cake pans that have been lined with wax paper that has also been greased.
Bake at 375°F (190°C) for 25–30 minutes, or until cake springs back when touched lightly with finger.
Place pans on wire rack for 5–10 minutes.
Remove cake from pans, and place on wire rack to cool.
Frost when cold.

Angel Food Cake

A good angel food cake has a light-brown, almost macaroon crust. It has a symmetrical top and tender crust. The interior of the cake is tender and has a fine, velvety white crumb.

  1 cup sifted cake flour
  1¼ cups sifted sugar
  1¼ cups egg whites (about 10 whites)
  1 tsp cream of tartar
  ¼ tsp salt
  1 tsp vanilla

Sift the flour and sugar together twice.
Beat[6] egg whites until frothy.
Add cream of tartar and salt and beat until stiff, but not dry.
Sift flour-sugar mixture, a little at a time, onto stiffly beaten egg whites, cutting and folding

[6] Either electric mixer or rotary beater may be used.

gently after each addition, until well blended. Fold in vanilla.
Pour into an ungreased 9- or 10-in. tube pan.
Bake in slow oven (325°F; 163°C) for about 1 hour or until cake springs back when touched lightly with finger. Allow cake to become cool before removing from pan.

Sponge Cake

A well-baked sponge cake has a delicately browned surface. It is golden yellow and has an even-textured crumb that is moderately moist.

  1 cup sugar
  1 cup sifted cake flour
  ¼ tsp salt
  6 eggs
  1 tbsp lemon juice
  2 tsp lemon rind, grated

Sift the sugar, measure, and sift again.
Sift the flour, measure, and add the salt.
Separate the yolks and whites of the eggs. Beat the egg yolks at least 5 minutes until they are yellow and thick.
Add the lemon juice and lemon rind and gradually beat in ½ cup sugar.
Wash the egg beater carefully to remove all the egg yolk. Beat the whites until they stand in stiff peaks. Gradually add the remaining sugar.
Fold the beaten yolk mixture into the egg whites.
Sift about 2 tablespoons flour on the top of the mixture and gently fold it in. Continue until the flour is all added.
Pour into an ungreased 10-in. tube pan and bake for 1 hour at 325°F (163°C).
Test with a toothpick; when it comes out clean from the center the cake is done.
Invert the tube pan for a cooling period of 1 hour. Then loosen the cake with a spatula and invert again. The cake will come out when thoroughly cool.

Chiffon Cake

A well-baked chiffon cake has a delicately browned surface. The interior crumb is soft and moist; air cells are evenly spaced. Flavor is pleasantly sweet.

  1⅛ cups sifted cake flour
  ¾ cup sugar
  1½ tsp baking powder

½ tsp salt
¼ cup oil
2 egg yolks, unbeaten
¼ cup water
1 tsp vanilla
½ cup (about 4) egg whites
¼ tsp cream of tartar

Sift together flour, ½ cup of the sugar, baking powder, and salt into mixing bowl.

Make a depression in center of ingredients and add oil, unbeaten egg yolks, water, and vanilla, but do not beat.

Beat egg whites until foamy, sprinkle cream of tartar over them, and add the rest of the sugar, beating it in gradually with rotary beater or electric mixer at high speed to make a stiff meringue.

Beat flour–oil–egg yolk mixture until smooth.

Pour over meringue, and cut and fold gently until color is uniform.

Pour batter into 9-in. ungreased tube pan.

Bake at 350°F (176°C) for 35–40 minutes, or until cake springs back when touched lightly with finger.

Invert cake in pan on cake rack to become cold before removing (about 1 hour).

Brownies

A well-baked brownie has a shiny surface with a moist interior. It has a sweet, chocolate flavor.

2 Dozen
    ¾ cup sifted all-purpose flour
    ½ tsp baking powder
    ¼ tsp salt
    ⅓ cup butter or other shortening
    2 squares unsweetened chocolate
    1 cup sugar
    2 eggs, well beaten
    ½ cup broken walnut meats
    1 tsp vanilla

Sift flour, baking powder, and salt together.

Melt shortening and chocolate over hot water.

Add sugar gradually to eggs, beating thoroughly.

Add chocolate mixture and blend.

Add flour mixture and mix well; then mix in nuts and vanilla.

Spread in greased 8-in. square pan lined with greased brown paper cut to fit the pan or wax paper. Bake in moderate oven at 350°F (176°C) for 25 minutes, or until done.

Cool in pan, then cut into squares or rectangles.

Refrigerator Cookies

A good refrigerator cookie is light brown, is crisp but tender, and has a pleasant, sweet flavor.

5–6 Dozen
    1½ cups shortening (half butter)
    1 cup brown sugar
    ⅔ cup white sugar
    2 eggs
    ½ tsp vanilla
    ½ tsp soda
    2 tsp baking powder
    1 tsp cinnamon
    4½ cups sifted flour

Cream shortening, add sugar, and continue to beat until light and fluffy.

Add eggs, one at a time, and beat until mixture is light.

Add vanilla.

Sift together dry ingredients and add to first mixture. Blend thoroughly.

Flour hands and shape the dough into rolls about 3 in in diameter and wrap in wax paper and store in refrigerator overnight or until firm.

Slice thin with sharp knife and bake on an ungreased baking sheet at 400°F (205°C) for 5–8 minutes.

Remove cookies immediately from baking sheet and place on wire rack to cool.

Vanilla Cookies

A good rolled cookie is delicately brown around the edges, has a uniform shape, is crisp but tender, and has a pleasant, sweet flavor.

4–5 Dozen Cookies
    3½ cups sifted all-purpose flour
    1 tsp baking powder
    ½ tsp salt
    1 cup shortening
    1½ cups sugar
    2 well-beaten eggs
    1½ tsp vanilla

Sift flour, baking powder, and salt together.

Cream shortening; add sugar gradually and continue to beat until light.

Add well-beaten eggs and blend thoroughly; add vanilla.

Combine the dry ingredients and the creamed

mixture; mix thoroughly and chill (overnight, if possible).

Roll as thin as possible on a lightly floured board with floured rolling pin and cut out with cookie cutter. (Any shape may be used.)

Bake on a greased cookie pan at 400°F (205°C) for 6–10 minutes.

YEAST BREADS

Yeast Bread: Straight Dough Method

A good homemade loaf of bread is symmetrical in shape, with a rounded top (no bulges) and a smooth golden-brown crust. The crust is thin and tender and the crumb is elastic, moist, of even texture, and with no large holes, streaks, or spots.

2 Loaves
    1 package active dry yeast
    1¼ cups lukewarm water
    1 cup scalded milk
    ⅓ cup shortening
    2 tsp salt
    3 tbsp sugar
    6 cups (about) all-purpose flour

Soften yeast in water for about 5 minutes; stir until dissolved.

To scalded milk add shortening, salt, and sugar. Stir well. Cool the mixture until it is lukewarm.

Add milk mixture to yeast.

Add half the flour and blend. Add remainder of flour to make a soft but not sticky dough.

Turn dough onto a well-floured board and knead until dough is elastic.

Wash, dry, and grease bowl. Place dough in bowl, cover with a clean, damp cloth, and place in a warm place (80–85°F; 26–30°C).

Allow dough to rise until it has doubled its bulk (about 1½ hours).

When dough will hold the impression of a finger, remove it from bowl and knead for about 2 minutes; then divide into two equal pieces.

To shape loaves, flatten each piece of dough by slapping and pressing with hands. Stretch dough to an 18- × 10-in rectangle.

Fold one side to center, pressing out air pockets; fold second side to overlap. Then fold over both ends of dough about ⅓ of length and overlap at center. Press edges together.

Place each shaped loaf seam side down in a 9- × 5- × 3-in greased bread pan. Cover with a clean, damp towel and allow to rise until double in bulk and until the center is well above the pan.

Bake at 400°F (205°C) for 40–50 minutes. Remove from pans and cool on rack.

Refrigerator Rolls

Good homemade rolls have a smooth golden-brown crust. The crust is thin and tender and the interior crumb is elastic, moist, and of even texture, with no large holes or streaks or spots.

    2 packages active dry yeast
    ½ cup warm water
    1 cup milk, scalded
    ⅓ cup soft shortening
    ½ cup sugar
    2 tsp salt
    2 eggs, beaten
    about 6–6½ cups sifted all-purpose flour

Soften yeast in water for 5 minutes. Stir.

Pour milk over shortening, sugar, and salt. Stir until shortening is melted.

When mixture is lukewarm, add yeast, eggs, and about half the flour. Beat thoroughly.

Add remaining flour or enough to make dough that can be handled. Turn dough out on lightly floured board.

Knead the dough, working in additional flour only if necessary to keep dough from sticking to board. Knead until light and elastic.

Turn the dough into a smooth ball; place in a greased bowl and turn dough over once to bring the greased side up. Cover with a damp towel and let dough rise in a warm place (80–85°F; 26–30°C) until it is double in bulk.

Punch down dough, cover tightly, and place in refrigerator until needed. Dough can be kept for 24–48 hours. If dough rises in refrigerator before it is needed, punch it down. Keep towel over dough damp.

When desired, remove dough from refrigerator, punch down, and shape into rolls.

Roll Variations
PARKER HOUSE ROLLS
Roll the dough ½ in. thick and cut in 2-in. rounds.

Brush lightly with melted butter or margarine, crease through center, fold over and press down.

Brush tops with fat for a soft crust.

Place rolls on greased baking sheet about ½ in. apart. Let rise until double in bulk and bake at 400°F (205°C) for 12–15 minutes.

CLOVERLEAF ROLLS

Squeeze or cut dough into about 24 uniform pieces; shape them into balls.

Place three balls in each section of a greased muffin pan.

Brush surfaces with melted fat. Let rise until double in bulk.

CRESCENTS

Stretch one quarter of the dough to make a 6-in square. Cut into triangles.

Roll each triangle from broad side to point; curve ends of dough inward. Brush surfaces with melted fat.

BUN-SHAPED ROLLS

Squeeze or cut dough into 18–24 pieces.

Shape each piece into a ball, with half the surface very smooth.

Place each ball smooth side up in a section of the muffin pan or place dough balls, smooth side up, close to one another in a bread pan.

Brush surfaces with melted fat.

GELATIN

Molded Fruit Jelly

A well-prepared molded salad has a smooth and glossy surface. The solid materials are evenly distributed throughout the mass. It quivers but retains its shape.

4–6 SERVINGS

1 envelope unflavored gelatin
½ cup cold water
1 cup boiling water
¼ cup sugar
⅛ tsp salt
⅓ cup lemon or lime juice (about 2 lemons)
2 cups mixed cut up fresh, drained canned, or frozen fruit (do not use fresh pineapple)

Put cold water in mixing bowl, sprinkle gelatin over water, and let stand to soften.

Add boiling water, and stir until gelatin is thoroughly dissolved. Add sugar, salt, and stir until disolved.

Stir in lemon juice.

Chill until mixture is the consistency of unbeaten egg white. Fold in fruit.

Turn into a 3-cup mold or individual molds. Chill until firm.

Unmold and serve plain or with whipped cream.

Variations

LEMON WHIP

Proceed as for Molded Fruit Jelly, but omit fruit.

Pour the mixture into a bowl in which it can be beaten. When it becomes the consistency of raw egg white, beat with a chilled beater until it forms a stiff white foam.

Place in molds and chill. Unmold to serve.

LEMON SNOW

Fold 2 beaten egg whites, stiff but not dry, into lemon whip just before putting into molds.

CANDY

Plain Fondant

Good fondant is creamy white and smooth with no large sugar crystals. It can be molded into small forms and has a sweet flavor.

2 cups sugar
1 cup water
2 tbsp corn syrup or
⅛ tsp cream of tartar

Put the ingredients into a pan and heat; stir until the sugar is dissolved.

When the syrup begins to boil, reduce the heat, cover the pan, and keep covered until the sugar crystals are washed down from the sides.

Remove the cover; boil and concentrate the syrup. During the process, wash down any sugar crystals that form on the sides of the pan with a cheesecloth-covered fork that has been dipped into hot water.

Cook syrup until it gives the cold-water test of soft-ball stage or thermometer reading of 236°F (113°C). Pour at once onto a cold platter that has been rinsed with cold water. Do not try to scrape out the last remaining syrup, as this may cause large crystals to form.

Cool to 110°F (44°C). Beat with a wooden spoon until the glossiness changes to dullness.

Butter hands and knead candy until no lumps remain. Store in covered crock or glass jar and allow to ripen for 2 or 3 days.

FROZEN DESSERTS

Vanilla Ice Cream

A good ice cream has a rich, smooth texture and a delicate taste. It has a natural color and a firm, good body.

4–6 SERVINGS
½ cup sugar
1 tbsp cornstarch
1½ cups light cream
2 eggs, separated
pinch salt
2 tsp vanilla
1 cup heavy cream

Combine the sugar and cornstarch in the top of the double boiler.

Gradually add the cream, mix well, and place over boiling water; stir until it thickens.

Cover and cook for 10 minutes.

Beat the egg yolks in a small mixing bowl.

Stir a little of the hot mixture into the beaten egg yolks. Then stir them into the remaining hot mixture. Cook over hot, not boiling, water, stirring constantly, for 3 minutes. Remove from hot water and cool.

Beat egg whites until stiff; add salt; fold into cooled custard; add vanilla.

Pour into refrigerator tray to freeze until firm throughout.

Remove the frozen mixture from the tray to a bowl and beat with an electric mixer. Add the cream, whip, and return to freezer tray. Freeze until hard and then lower control to normal operation speed or to where mixture is held frozen.

Serving Food

To be appreciated, food must be served attractively. Some dishes require last-minute preparation to be at their best. For example, fresh fish, omelets, soufflés, liver, steaks, and chops must be eaten shortly after they are removed from the oven or range, or pleasure in eating them will be diminished. Similarly, dishes that are intended to be eaten cold should be well chilled and served on cold plates; they are removed from the refrigerator just before serving.

In order to look its very best, food should be served in a manner consistent with the customs of the times. The simple suggestions that follow can serve only as a guide for serving food in laboratory situations. For more detail, books on table service and meal planning may be consulted.

PRINCIPLES OF TABLE SETTING

Because the table is set for the convenience and enjoyment of the persons eating, the table appointments should be placed so that they are in harmony with each other and so that they are easy for the diners to use.

Silver, glassware, china, and decorations are arranged precisely, equally spaced and not crowded (Fig. A-1). To give an orderly appearance to the table, it is best to place all tableware in lengthwise or crosswise lines on the table.

For meals, table coverings, napkins, tableware, and food should harmonize, if possible. If a full meal is not intended, but food is to be placed on a table for evaluation, some effort should be made to have an attractive background.

The Table Cover

The table cover may be a tablecloth of a suitable color or tablemats of cork, straw, linen, cotton, or plastic oilcloth. These are easily cleaned and quite acceptable. Napkins may be matched to the cloth or mats, or paper napkins may be used. Usually, when a tablecloth is used a silence cloth of heavy felt or quilted padding is placed on the table first, to serve as a protective covering for the table and to improve the appearance of the cloth.

Decorations

In setting the table for meals, the addition of a simple, tastefully chosen centerpiece may add its beauty. A small bowl of garden or wild flowers, a bowl of fruit, or a healthy green plant may be

589

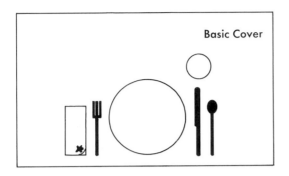

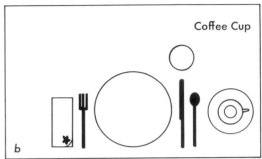

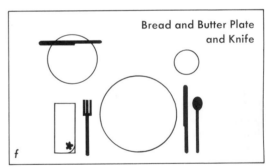

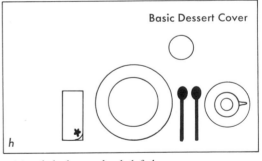

A-1 *Basic table setting. (a) Basic cover (b) second glass (c) salad plate and salad fork (d) salad plate and bread and butter plate (e) coffee cup (f) soup dish and soup spoon (g) bread and butter plate and knife (h) basic dessert cover.*

all that is necessary to give the table a gracious appearance.

Silver

Flatware is placed in the best position for the user. The knife and spoons are placed to the right of the plate with the handles about ½ inch from the edge of the table. The blade of the knife is turned toward the plate, and the bowls of the spoons are turned up. The knife is placed to the right because most people are right-handed. The butter spreader may be placed parallel to—or at right angles with—the lines of the table. But it is also the exception to the crosswise and lengthwise lines rule, and it may be placed slanting across the butter plate, if preferred. If one plate is used for both the salad and bread and butter, the butter spreader may be placed on the table above the dinner plate. For a very simple meal, it is not necessary to use a bread and butter plate, for the dinner plate usually has extra space for this purpose.

To balance the knife, the forks are placed at the left with the tines turned upward. If a knife is not needed at the meal, the forks may be placed at the right of the plate with the spoons; if a salad is served with the meat course, a special salad fork is not required.

Glasses

The water glass is placed about ½ in. above the tip of the knife or a little to the right of it. When another beverage such as milk, iced tea, or lemonade is served, the glass for it is placed to the right of the water glass.

Napkin

The napkin is folded in an oblong or square and put at the left of the forks with the open corner nearest to the plate. Sometimes the open corner of the napkin is turned away from the plate. Either position is correct, but it should be the same at all place settings.

Serving Dishes

For most meals, the food is brought to and placed on the table in serving dishes. These are either placed before members of the family, who proceed to serve from them, or they are passed around the table for each person to serve himself. Regardless of how the food is served serving spoons and forks must be at hand. When the

table is set, these serving pieces are laid on the table rather than put in the dish.

Accessories

Some arrangements at the table must be made for accessory dishes and utensils. Salt and pepper shakers should be placed so that they are in a convenient position for all to use. If one set is to be shared by two persons, it should be placed between the two settings. A usual procedure is to place the salt to the right of the pepper.

Pickle, cheese, and jelly plates are placed parallel to the edge of the table so that they are within easy reach for passing them around the table.

A water pitcher may be placed on a plate or pad on the table if there is room, and a teapot or coffeepot may be placed on a hot pad, tray, or tile at the right of the server's plate. Cups and saucers are placed at the right beside the coffeepot, with cups piled in twos and handles turned at an easy angle for the server to grasp. The creamer and sugar bowl may be either placed in front of the server or placed close to the edge of the table in a convenient spot for easy serving.

PREFERRED WAYS OF HANDLING UTENSILS

The rules for setting the table were devised so that people eating together might use their tools in much the same way. If everyone is familiar with the rules, they are easy to follow. There are techniques for handling eating utensils that everyone should be familiar with and should practice regardless of the simplicity of the meal or the nature of the food partaken. Learning to eat in the accepted manner with the proper tools shows thoughtfulness.

Knife and Fork

When food is cut, the knife is held in the right hand with the handle in the palm and the forefinger against the back of the lower handle to steady it. The fork is held in the left hand in a similar manner. The tines are pointed down, and the forefinger is on the back of the fork, to hold it steady. After the food is cut, the fork may be transferred to the right hand. The knife is placed with its cutting edge toward the center of the plate. Some people prefer not to change the fork to the right hand, but to eat immediately after cutting the meat with the fork, tines down, in the left hand. This is known as the *European custom* of eating and appears a little more efficient to some persons. In either case, when the knife is not in use it is laid across the rim of the plate, making sure that the handle is not allowed to rest on the table. When one is through using both knife and fork, or when the plate is passed, both tools are placed parallel to each other and close together on the plate, with the handles pointing toward the right. The knife is on the right side of the fork, with the sharp edge toward it.

Spoon

The function of the spoon is to handle foods that are too soft to be handled with a fork. A good rule to keep in mind is not to use a spoon if a fork will do the job. Spoons cause trouble if they are left standing in a teacup or in a sherbet glass. They should always be placed on the saucer under the cup or on the plate on which the sherbet glass rests. A spoon is used for stirring, and for testing the temperature and flavor of hot beverages and cold drinks such as iced tea or coffee. The spoon is then placed on the underlying dish and is not used again, unless to stir.

TABLE A-12
Nutrients in Household Quantities of Foods

Food and Approximate Measure or Common Weight	Water (%)	Food Energy (cal)	Protein (g)	Fat (g)	Total Carbohydrate (g)	Calcium (mg)	Iron (mg)	Vitamin A (I.U.)	Thiamine (mg)	Riboflavin (mg)	Niacin (mg)	Ascorbic Acid (mg)	Zinc[a] (mg)	Copper[a] (mg)
Milk and Milk Products														
Milk, cow's														
Fluid, whole (1 cup)	87	165	9	10	12	288	0.2	390	0.09	0.42	0.3	3	0.93	0.10
Fluid, nonfat skim (1 cup)	90	85	9	Tr.	13	303	0.2	10	0.09	0.44	0.3	3	1.0	0.05
Evaporated undiluted (1 cup)	74	345	18	20	25	612	0.4	1010	0.12	0.91	0.5	3	1.94	0.33
Cheese (1 oz)														
Cheddar (1-in. cube)	37	115	7	9	0.6	206	0.3	400	0.01	0.12	Tr.		0.88	0.03
Cream	51	105	3	10	1	19	0.1	410	Tr.	0.06	Tr.	0	0.15	0.01
Swiss	39	105	8	8	0.6	262	0.3	410	Tr.	0.11	Tr.	0	1.11	0.11
Cream, light (1 tbsp)	72	30	Tr.	3	0.6	15	0	120	Tr.	0.02	Tr.	Tr.	0.04	0.11
Cocoa (all milk) (1 cup)	79	235	10	12	27	298	1.0	400	0.10	0.46	0.5	3	1.02	0.07
Desserts														
Custard, baked (1 cup)	77	285	13	13	28	283	1.2	840	0.11	0.49	0.2	1	—	—
Ice cream, plain (8 fl oz)	62	295	6	18	29	175	0.1	740	0.06	0.27	0.1	1	1.21	0.07
Fats, Oils, Related Products														
Bacon, medium fat, broiled or fried (2 slices)	13	95	4	9	Tr.	4	0.5	0	0.08	0.05	0.8	0	—	—
Butter (1 tbsp)	16	100	Tr.	11	Tr.	3	0	460	Tr.	Tr.	Tr.	0	0.01	0.05
Fats, cooking, vegetable fats (1 tbsp)	0	110	0	12	0	0	0	0	0	0	0	0	0.00	0.00
Margarine (1 tbsp)	16	100	Tr.	11	Tr.	3	0	460	0	0	0	0	0.03	0.02
Oils, salad or cooking (1 tbsp)	0	125	0	14	0	0	0	0	0	0	0	0	0.03	0.01
Salad dressings (1 tbsp)														
French	40	60	Tr.	5	3	0	0	0	0	0	0	—	0.04	0.08
Mayonnaise	16	90	Tr.	10	Tr.	2	0.1	30	Tr.	Tr.	0	0	0.03	0.03
Eggs														
Eggs, raw, medium														
1 whole	74	75	6	6	Tr.	26	1.3	550	0.05	0.14	Tr.	0	1.0	1.0
1 white	88	15	3	0	Tr.	2	0.1	0	0	0.08	Tr.	0	0.02	0.05
1 yolk	49	60	3	5	Tr.	25	1.2	550	0.05	0.06	Tr.	0	0.58	0.05
Meat, Poultry, Fish														
Beef, without bone, cooked (3 oz)														
Chuck	51	265	22	19	0	9	2.6	0	0.04	0.17	3.5	0	—	0.09
Hamburger	47	315	19	26	0	8	2.4	0	0.07	0.16	4.1	0	2.9	0.05
Sirloin	54	255	20	19	0	9	2.5	0	0.06	0.16	4.1	0	2.6	0.03

Food														
Beef, canned														
Corned beef, medium fat (3 oz)	59	180	22	10	0	17	3.7	0	0.01	0.20	2.9	0	1.65	0.55
Beef and vegetable stew (1 cup)	79	250	13	19	17	31	2.6	2,520	0.12	0.15	3.4	15	1.36	0.09
Clams, raw, meat only (4 oz)	80	90	15	2	4	109	7.9	120	0.11	0.20	1.8	—	1.70	—
Crabmeat, canned or cooked (3 oz)	77	90	14	2	1	38	0.8	—	0.04	0.05	2.1	—	3.40	1.20
Flounder, raw (4 oz)	83	80	17	1	0	69	0.9	—	0.07	0.06	1.9	—	—	0.30
Halibut, broiled, 1 steak (4 × 3 × ½ in.)	64	230	33	10	0	18	1.0	—	0.08	0.09	13.1	—	—	0.15
Lamb, leg roast, cooked (3 oz)	56	230	20	16	0	9	2.6	0	0.12	0.21	4.4	0	—	0.05
Liver, beef, fried (2 oz)	57	120	13	4	5	5	4.4	30,330	0.15	2.25	8.4	18	—	—
Pork loin or chops, cooked (3 oz without bone)	50	285	20	22	0	9	2.6	0	0.71	0.20	4.3	0	3.9	0.08
Pork, cured ham, cooked (3 oz without bone)	39	340	20	28	Tr.	9	2.5	0	0.46	0.18	3.5	0	3.4	0.03
Pork luncheon meat, canned, spiced (2 oz)	55	165	8	14	1	5	1.2	0	0.18	0.12	1.6	0	—	—
Sardines, canned in oil, drained solids (3 oz)	57	180	22	9	1	328	2.3	190	0.01	0.15	4.1	0	2.47	—
Scallops, raw (4 oz)	80	90	17	Tr.	4	29	2.0	0	0.05	0.11	1.6	—	2.75	0.22
Shrimp, canned, meat only (3 oz)	66	110	23	1	—	98	2.6	50	0.01	0.03	1.9	0	1.78	0.15
Tunafish, drained solids (3 oz)	60	170	25	7	0	7	1.2	70	0.04	0.10	10.9	0	1.36	0.09
Mature Beans and Peas; Nuts														
Almonds, shelled, unblanched (1 cup)	5	850	26	77	28	361	6.2	0	0.35	0.95	6.5	Tr.	2.00	1.10
Beans, canned or cooked (1 cup) Red kidney	76	230	15	1	42	102	4.9	0	0.12	0.12	2.0	0	0.20	—
Navy or other varieties with: Pork and tomato sauce	72	295	15	5	48	107	4.7	220	0.13	0.09	1.2	7	2.09	0.78
Brazil nuts, shelled (1 cup)	5	905	20	92	15	260	4.8	Tr.	1.21	—	—	—	—	1.87
Peanuts, roasted, shelled (1 cup)	3	805	39	64	34	107	2.7	0	0.42	0.19	23.3	0	4.30	0.62
Peanut Butter (1 tbsp)	2	95	4	8	3	12	0.3	0	0.02	0.02	2.6	0	0.46	0.91
Pecans (1 cup halves)	3	750	10	79	14	80	2.6	50	0.77	0.12	1.0	2	4.1	1.14
Walnuts, English (1 cup halves)	3	655	15	64	16	83	2.1	30	0.48	0.13	1.2	3	—	—
Vegetables														
Asparagus														
Cooked (1 cup cut spears)	92	35	4	Tr.	6	33	1.8	1,820	0.23	0.30	2.1	40	—	0.18
Beans, lima, immature, cooked (1 cup)	75	150	8	1	29	46	2.7	460	0.22	0.14	1.8	24	1.53	0.27
Beans, snap, green, cooked (1 cup)	92	25	2	Tr.	6	45	0.9	830	0.09	0.12	0.6	18	0.37	0.13
Beets, cooked, diced (1 cup)	88	70	2	Tr.	16	35	1.2	30	0.03	0.07	0.5	11	0.09	0.04
Broccoli, cooked, flower stalks (1 cup)	90	45	5	Tr.	8	195	2.0	5,100	0.10	0.22	1.2	111	2.33	0.16
Brussels sprouts, cooked (1 cup)	85	60	6	1	12	44	1.7	520	0.05	0.16	0.6	61	0.56	1.04
Cabbage, raw, shredded (1 cup)	92	25	1	Tr.	5	46	0.5	80	0.06	0.05	0.3	50	0.28	0.06

TABLE A-12 (Cont.)

Food and Approximate Measure or Common Weight	Water (%)	Food Energy (cal)	Protein (g)	Fat (g)	Total Carbohydrate (g)	Calcium (mg)	Iron (mg)	Vitamin A (I.U.)	Thiamine (mg)	Riboflavin (mg)	Niacin (mg)	Ascorbic Acid (mg)	Zinc[a] (mg)	Copper[a] (mg)
Carrots														
Raw, grated (1 cup)	88	45	1	Tr.	10	43	0.9	13,200	0.06	0.06	0.7	7	0.44	0.11
Cooked, diced (1 cup)	91	45	1	1	9	38	0.9	18,130	0.07	0.07	0.7	6	0.05	0.12
Cauliflower, cooked flower (1 cup)	92	30	3	Tr.	6	26	1.3	110	0.07	0.10	0.6	34	0.34	0.12
Celery raw, diced (1 cup)	94	20	1	Tr.	4	50	0.5	0	0.05	0.04	0.4	7	0.17	0.08
Collards, cooked (1 cup)	87	75	7	1	14	473	3.0	14,500	0.15	0.46	3.2	84	—	—
Corn, sweet														
Canned, solids and liquids (1 cup)	80	170	5	1	41	10	1.3	520[b]	0.07	0.13	2.4	14	0.77	0.15
Cowpeas, immature seed, cooked (1 cup)	75	150	11	1	25	59	4.0	620	0.46	0.13	1.3	32	0.47	0.47
Cucumbers, raw (6 slices ⅛ in. thick, center section)	96	5	Tr.	0	1	5	0.2[c]	0	0.02	0.02	0.1	4	0.32	0.09
Lettuce, headed, raw (2 large or 4 small leaves)	95	5	1	Tr.	1	11	0.2	270	0.02	0.04	0.1	4	0.40	0.22
Mushrooms, canned, solids and liquid (1 cup)	93	30	3	Tr.	9	17	2.0	0	0.04	0.60	4.8	—	—	0.26
Okra, cooked (8 pods, 3 in. long, ⅝ in. diam)	90	30	2	Tr.	6	70	6	630	0.05	0.05	0.7	17	—	0.09
Onions														
Mature (1 onion, 2½ in. diam)	88	50	2	Tr.	11	35	0.6	60	0.04	0.04	0.2	10	0.20	0.10
Peas, green, cooked (1 cup)	82	110	8	1	19	35	3.0	1,150	0.40	0.22	3.7	24	1.12	0.24
Peppers, green, raw (1 medium)	92	15	1	Tr.	4	7	0.3	400	0.02	0.04	0.2	77	0.06	0.13
Potatoes														
Baked (1 medium, 2½ in. diam)	74	95	2	Tr.	22	13	0.8	20	0.11	0.05	1.4	17	—	0.36
Boiled in skin (1 medium, 2½ in. diam)	78	120	3	Tr.	27	16	1.0	30	0.14	0.06	1.6	22	0.30	0.10
Boiled after peeling (1 medium, 2½ in. diam)	78	105	3	Tr.	24	14	0.9	20	0.12	0.04	1.3	17	0.60	0.20
French-fried, 8 pieces (2 × ½ × ½ in.)	20	155	2	8	21	12	0.8	20	0.07	0.04	1.3	11	0.09	0.09
Potato chips (10 medium, 2 in. diam)	3	110	1	7	10	6	0.4	10	0.04	0.02	0.6	2	0.16	0.06
Pumpkin, canned (1 cup)	90	75	2	1	18	46	1.6	7,750	0.04	0.14	1.2	—	—	—
Spinach, cooked (1 cup)	91	45	6	1	6	223[d]	3.6	21,200	0.14	0.36	1.1	54	1.26	0.25
Squash														
Summer, cooked, diced (1 cup)	95	35	1	Tr.	8	32	0.8	550	0.08	0.15	1.3	23	—	—
Winter, baked, mashed (1 cup)	86	95	4	1	23	49	1.6	12,690	0.10	0.31	1.2	14	—	—

TABLE A-12 (Cont.)

Food and Approximate Measure or Common Weight	Water (%)	Food Energy (cal)	Protein (g)	Fat (g)	Total Carbohydrate (g)	Calcium (mg)	Iron (mg)	Vitamin A (I.U.)	Thiamine (mg)	Riboflavin (mg)	Niacin (mg)	Ascorbic Acid (mg)	Zinc[a] (mg)	Copper[a] (mg)
Sweet potatoes, peeled (1 sweet potato)														
Baked (5 × 2 in.)	61	185	3	1	41	44	1.1	11,410[e]	0.12	0.08	0.9	28	0.12	0.26
Tomatoes														
Raw (1 medium, 2 × 2½ in.)	94	30	2	Tr.	6	16	0.9	1,640	0.08	0.06	0.8	35	0.20	0.11
Canned or cooked (1 cup)	94	45	2	Tr.	9	27	1.5	2,540	0.14	0.08	1.7	40	0.25	0.31
Tomato juice, canned (1 cup)	94	50	2	Tr.	10	17	1.0	2,540	0.12	0.07	1.8	38	0.10	0.17
Turnips, cooked, diced (1 cup)	92	40	1	Tr.	9	62	0.8	Tr.	0.06	0.09	0.6	28	0.43	0.12
Turnip greens, cooked (1 cup)	90	45	4	1	8	376	3.5	15,370	0.09	0.59	1.0	87	—	—
Fruits														
Apples, raw (1 medium, 2½ in. diam)	84	75	Tr.	1	20	8	0.4	120	0.05	0.04	0.2	6	0.06	0.10
Apple juice, fresh or canned (1 cup)	86	125	Tr.	0	34	15	1.2	90	0.05	0.07	Tr.	2	0.10	0.05
Apricots, canned in sirup (4 medium halves and 2 tbsp sirup)	77	95	1	Tr.	26	12	0.4	1,650	0.02	0.03	0.4	5	0.02	0.06
Avocados, raw (½ peeled fruit, 3½ × 3¼ in.)	65	280	2	30	6	11	0.7	330	0.07	0.15	1.3	18	0.64	0.50
Bananas, raw (1 medium, 6 × 1½ in.)	75	90	1	Tr.	23	8	0.6	430	0.04	0.05	0.7	10	0.35	0.30
Blackberries, raw (1 cup)	85	80	2	1	18	46	1.3	280	0.05	0.06	0.5	30	—	0.16
Blueberries, raw (1 cup)	83	85	1	1	21	22	1.1	400	0.04	0.03	0.4	23	—	0.22
Cantaloupe, raw (½ melon, 5 in. diam)	94	35	1	Tr.	8	31	0.7	6,190[f]	0.09	0.07	0.9	59	0.09	0.19
Cherries, raw (1 cup pitted)	83	65	1	1	16	19	0.4	710	0.05	0.06	0.4	9	—	0.08
Cranberry sauce, sweetened (1 cup)	48	550	Tr.	1	142	22	0.8	80	0.06	0.06	0.3	5	0.03	0.17
Dates, "fresh" and dried, pitted and cut (1 cup)	20	505	4	1	134	128	3.7	100	0.16	0.17	3.9	0	0.71	0.78
Figs, dried (1 large, 2 × 1 in.)	24	55	1	Tr.	14	39	0.6	20	0.03	0.02	0.4	0	0.38	0.33
Fruit cocktail, canned, solids and liquid (1 cup)	81	180	1	1	48	23	1.0	410	0.03	0.03	0.9	5	—	0.08
Grapefruit, raw (1 cup sections)	89	75	1	Tr.	20	43	0.4	20	0.07	0.04	0.4	78	0.06	0.06
Grapefruit juice														
Frozen concentrate (6-oz can)	58	295	4	1	77	63	2.4	60	0.24	0.13	1.4	272	0.06	0.14
Grapes														
American type (slip skin)	82	85	2	2	18	20	0.7	90	0.07	0.05	0.3	5	0.05	0.06
Grape juice, bottled (1 cup)	81	170	1	0	46	25	0.8	—	0.09	0.12	0.6	Tr.	—	—
Lemon juice, fresh (1 cup)	91	60	1	Tr.	19	34	0.2	0	0.11	0.01	0.3	122	0.02	0.10
Lime juice, fresh (1 cup)	91	60	1	0	20	34	0.2	0	0.11	0.01	0.3	65	—	—

Oranges (1 medium, 3 in. diam)	87	70	1	Tr.	17	51	0.6	290	0.12	0.04	0.4	77	0.05	0.15
Orange juice														
Fresh (1 cup)	88	110	2	Tr.	27	47	0.5	460	0.19	0.06	0.6	122	0.05	0.02
Frozen concentrate (6-oz can)	58	300	5	1	75	69	2.0	670	0.48	0.11	1.5	285	0.04	0.02
Peaches														
Raw (1 medium, 2½ × 2 in. diam)	87	45	1	Tr.	12	8	0.6	880	0.02	0.05	0.9	8	0.23	0.10
Canned in sirup, solids and liquid (1 cup)	81	175	1	Tr.	47	13	1.0	1,160	0.02	0.05	1.8	11	0.24	0.12
Pears														
Raw (1 pear, 3 × 2½ in. diam)	83	95	1	1	24	20	0.5	30	0.03	0.06	0.2	6	—	0.33
Canned in sirup (2 medium-sized halves and 2 tbsp sirup)	81	80	Tr.	Tr.	22	9	0.2	Tr.	0.01	0.02	0.2	2	0.08	0.06
Pineapple														
Raw, diced (1 cup)	85	75	1	Tr.	19	22	0.4	180	0.12	0.04	0.3	33	0.33	0.22
Canned in sirup (2 small or 1 large slice and 2 tbsp juice)	78	95	Tr.	Tr.	26	35	0.7	100	0.09	0.02	0.2	11	0.08	0.15
Plums, raw (1 plum, 2 in. diam)	86	30	Tr.	Tr.	7	10	0.3	200	0.04	0.02	0.3	3	—	0.02
Prunes, cooked, unsweetened (1 cup, 16–18 prunes and ⅓ cup liquid)	65	310	3	1	82	62	4.5	2,210	0.07	0.20	2.0	2	0.80	0.43
Raisins, dried (1 cup)	24	430	4	1	114	125	5.3	80	0.24	0.13	0.8	Tr.	0.30	0.41
Raspberries, red, raw (1 cup)	84	70	1	Tr.	17	49	1.1	160	0.03	0.08	0.4	29	—	0.57
Rhubarb, cooked with sugar (1 cup)	63	385	1	Tr.	98	112g	1.1	70	0.02	—	0.2	17	0.30	0.12
Strawberries, raw (1 cup)	90	55	1	1	12	42	1.2	90	0.04	0.10	0.4	89	0.12	0.10
Tangerines (1 medium, 2½-in. diam)	87	35	1	Tr.	9	27	0.3	340	0.06	0.02	0.2	25	0.20	0.10
Grain Products														
Biscuits, baking powder, enriched flour (1 biscuit, 2½ in. diam)	27	130	3	4	20	83	0.7	0	0.09	0.08	0.7	0	—	0.06
Breads (1 slice)														
Rye	35	55	2	Tr.	12	17	0.4	0	0.04	0.02	0.4	0	0.40	0.06
White, enriched, 4% nonfat milk solidsh	35	65	2	1	12	18	0.4i	0	0.06i	0.04i	0.5i	0	0.16	0.06
Whole wheat	37	55	2	1	11	22	0.5	0	0.07	0.03	0.7	0	0.47	0.06
Cakes														
Angel food (2-in. sector, 1/12 of cake, 8-in. diam.)	32	110	3	Tr.	23	2	0.1	0	Tr.	0.05	0.1	0	0.07	—
Doughnuts, cake-type (1 doughnut)	19	135	2	7	17	23	0.2	40	0.05	0.04	0.4	0	0.30	0.06
Plain cake and cupcakes (1 cupcake 2¾ in. diam.)	27	130	3	3	23	62	0.2	50j	0.01	0.03	0.1	0	0.07	0.03
Sponge (2-in. sector, 1/12 of cake, 8-in. diam.)	32	115	3	2	22	11	0.6	210	0.02	0.06	0.1	0	0.07	0.01
Cookies, plain and assorted (one 3-in. cookie)	5	110	2	3	19	6	0.2	0	0.01	0.01	0.1	0	0.04	—
Corn grits, enriched, cooked (1 cup)	87	120	3	Tr.	27	2	0.7	100k	0.11	0.08	1.0	0	0.98	—

TABLE A-12 (Cont.)

Food and Approximate Measure or Common Weight	Water (%)	Food Energy (cal)	Protein (g)	Fat (g)	Total Carbohydrate (g)	Calcium (mg)	Iron (mg)	Vitamin A (I.U.)	Thiamine (mg)	Riboflavin (mg)	Niacin (mg)	Ascorbic Acid (mg)	Zinc[a] (mg)	Copper[a] (mg)
Crackers														
Graham (4 small or 2 medium)	6	55	1	1	10	3	0.3	0	0.04	0.02	0.2	0	2.86	0.06
Soda, plain (2 crackers 2½-in. diam)	6	45	1	1	8	2	0.1	0	0.01	0.01	0.1	0	0.03	Tr.
Macaroni, cooked (1 cup), enriched	61	210	7	1	42	13	1.5	0	0.24	0.15	2.0	0	1.20	0.05
Muffins, made with enriched flour (1 muffin, 2¾ in. diam)	37	135	4	4	20	99	0.8	50	0.09	0.10	0.7	0	—	—
Noodles, containing egg, unenriched, cooked (1 cup)	84	105	4	1	20	6	0.6	60	0.05	0.03	0.6	0	3.52	0.27
Oatmeal or rolled oats, cooked (1 cup)	85	150	5	3	26	21	1.7	0	0.22	0.05	0.4	0	1.2	0.07
Pies (4-in. sector, 9 in. diam)														
Apple	48	330	3	13	53	9	0.5	220	0.04	0.02	0.3	1	0.12	0.03
Lemon meringue	47	300	4	12	45	24	0.6	210	0.04	0.10	0.2	1	—	—
Pumpkin	59	265	5	12	34	70	1.0	2,480	0.04	0.15	0.4	0	0.16	—
Rice, cooked, white or milled (1 cup)	71	200	4	Tr.	44	13	0.5	0	0.02	0.01	0.7	0	0.82	0.16
Rice, puffed (1 cup)	4	55	1	Tr.	12	3	0.3	0	0.01	0.01	0.1	0	0.21	0.09
Rolls, plain, enriched (1 roll, 12 per lb)	29	120	3	2	21	21	0.7	0	0.09[l]	0.06[l]	0.8[l]	0	0.20	0.08
Spaghetti, unenriched, cooked (1 cup)	61	220	7	1	44	13	0.9	0	0.03	0.02	0.7	0	2.21	0.09
Wheat flours														
Whole (1 cup stirred)	12	400	16	2	85	49	4.0	0	0.66	0.14	5.2	0	2.9	0.60
All-purpose or family flour: enriched (1 cup, sifted)	12	400	12	1	84	18	3.2	0	0.48[m]	0.29[m]	3.8	0	0.88	0.25
Wheat, shredded (1 large biscuit, 1 oz)	6	100	3	1	23	13	1.0	0	0.06	0.03	1.3	0	0.56	0.09
Sugars, Sweets														
Candy (1 oz)														
Chocolate, sweetened, milk	1	145	2	9	16	61	0.6	40	0.03	0.11	0.2	0	0.13	0.29
Fudge, plain	5	115	Tr.	3	23	14[n]	0.1	60	Tr.	0.02	Tr.	Tr.	—	—
Honey, strained or extracted (1 tbsp)	20	60	Tr.	0	17	1	0.2	0	Tr.	0.01	Tr.	1	0.16	0.01
Jams, marmalades, preserves (1 tbsp)	28	55	Tr.	Tr.	14	2	0.1	Tr.	Tr.	Tr.	Tr.	1	Tr.	Tr.
Sirup, table blends (1 tbsp)	25	55	0	0	15	9	0.8	0	0	Tr.	Tr.	0	0.01	0.09
Sugar (1 tbsp)														
Granulated, cane or beet	Tr.	50	0	0	12	—	—	0	0	0	0	0	0.12	0.04
Brown	3	50	0	0	13	10[o]	0.4	0	0	0	0	0	0.05	1.07

598

TABLE A-12 (Cont.)

Food and Approximate Measure or Common Weight	Water (%)	Food Energy (cal)	Protein (g)	Fat (g)	Total Carbohydrate (g)	Calcium (mg)	Iron (mg)	Vitamin A (I.U.)	Thiamine (mg)	Riboflavin (mg)	Niacin (mg)	Ascorbic Acid (mg)	Zinc[a] (mg)	Copper[a] (mg)
Miscellaneous														
Beverages, carbonated, cola type (1 cup)	88	105	—	—	28	—	—	—	—	—	—	—	0.05	—
Gelatin dessert, plain, ready-to-serve (1 cup)	83	155	4	0	36	0	0	0	0	0	0	—	0.05	0.38
Olives, pickled "mammoth" size (10 olives)														
Green	75	70	1	7	2	48	0.9	160	Tr.	—	—	—	0.06	0.17
Ripe, Mission variety	72	105	1	12	1	48	0.9	40	Tr.	Tr.	—	—	0.14	0.48
Pickles														
Dill, cucumber (1 large 4 in. long)	93	15	1	Tr.	3	34	1.6	420	Tr.	0.09	0.1	8	0.37	0.30
Sweet, cucumber or mixed (1 pickle, 2¾ in. long)	70	20	Tr.	Tr.	5	3	0.3	22	0	Tr.	Tr.	1	0.03	0.04
Sherbet[p] (½ cup)	68	120	1	0	29	48	0	0	0.02	0.07	0	0	0.23	0.02

[a]Adapted from the following: (1) J. H. Freeland, M. L. Ebangit, and P. W. Bodzy, "Trace Mineral Content of Vegetarian Foods: Zinc and Copper," *Fed. Proc.* **36**:1124, 1977, abstract; (2) J. H. Freeland, and R. J. Cousins, "Zinc Content of Selected Foods," *J. Amer. Dietet. Assoc.* **68**:745, 1976; (3) J. H. Freeland, 1977, unpublished data; (4) E. W. Murphy, B. W. Willis, and B. K. Watts, "Provisional Tables on the Zinc Content of Foods," *J. Amer. Dietet. Assoc.* **66**:345, 1975; (5) J. T. Pennington, and D. H. Calloway, "Copper Content of Foods," *J. Amer. Dietet. Assoc.* **63**:43, 1973.

[b]Vitamin A based on yellow corn; white corn contains only a trace.

[c]Based on pared cucumber; unpared contains about 0.6 mg iron and 130 I.U. vitamin A.

[d]Calcium may not be usable because of presence of oxalic acid.

[e]If very pale varieties only were used, the vitamin A value would be very much lower.

[f]Vitamin A based on deeply colored yellow varieties.

[g]Calcium may not be usable because of presence of oxalic acid.

[h]When the amount of nonfat milk solids in commercial bread is unknown, use bread with 4% nonfat milk solids.

[i]Iron, thiamine, riboflavin, and niacin are based on the minimum levels of enrichment specified in the standards of identity of breads proposed by the Federal Security Agency and published in the *Federal Register*, August 3, 1943.

[j]If fat used is butter or fortified margarine, the vitamin A value would be 150 I.U. per cupcake.

[k]Vitamin A based on yellow corn grits; white corn grits contain only a trace.

[l]Iron, thiamine, riboflavin, and niacin are based on the minimum levels of enrichment specified in the standards of identity of breads proposed by the Federal Security Agency and published in the *Federal Register*, August 3, 1943.

[m]Iron, thiamine, riboflavin, and niacin are based on the minimum levels of enrichment in the standards of identity promulgated under the Food, Drug, and Cosmetic Act.

[n]The calcium contributed by chocolate may not be usable because of presence of oxalic acid; in that case, the value may be 11 mg/oz.

[o]Calcium is based on dark sugar; value would be lower for light brown sugar.

[p]Based on 6.8 lb to the gallon, factory packed.

Source: Adapted from "Composition of Foods—Raw, Processed, Prepared," *Agricultural Handbook 8* (Washington, D.C.: U.S. Department of Agriculture, 1963).

Index

NOTES

NOTES

NOTES

NOTES

NOTES

NOTES

NOTES

NOTES

NOTES

NOTES

NOTES

NOTES